D1191110

ELECTRONIC DISPLAYS

ELECTRONIC DISPLAYS

Second Edition

SOL SHERR

A Wiley-Interscience Publication

JOHN WILEY & SONS, INC.

New York • Chichester • Brisbane • Toronto • Singapore

Library of Congress Cataloging in Publication Data:
Sherr, Sol.
  Electronic displays / Sol Sherr.—2nd ed.
    p.   cm.
  "A Wiley-Interscience publication."
  Includes bibliographical references and index.
  ISBN 0-471-63616-9 (cloth)
  1. Information display systems.   I. Title.
TK7882.I6S49   1993
621.39'87—dc20   92-16743
                                                              CIP

Printed in the United States of America

10 9 8 7 6 5 4 3 2 1

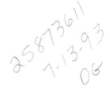

PREFACE

As predicted in the first edition of this book, the growth in the use of electronic displays has far exceeded that anticipated at that time, with a concomitant increase in the number of users of and applications for the devices, equipment, and systems that fall within that rubric. As one result, the number of new products has also increased at an astronomical rate, with many new developments in technology coming to the fore and making the need for up-to-date and expanded information on these technologies of even greater importance than when the first edition was published. Unfortunately, very few new texts in English have been produced since 1979 when the first edition was published, and none by a single author, with the improvements in coherence and continuity that can best be accomplished by a single author. This is not to minimize the accomplishments of those who participated in the various multiauthor volumes that have been produced, several of which have the present writer as editor or co-editor, but rather, to emphasize the unique features of single-author volumes, of which this second edition is the only book known to this writer that deals exclusively with electronic displays.

This edition has been rewritten and expanded extensively to cover the proliferation of new material that has occurred and to update the original material where necessary. As a result, much of Chapters 2, 3, and 5 is new, as is almost all of Chapter 6, which has a new title, "Input and Output Devices and Systems," rather than the original "Applications." This is not because applications are less important but because they have expanded to such an extent that they cannot readily be included in this volume while adding the new technical material necessary to make this revision sufficiently complete and up to date. Indeed, "Applications" warrant a separate book, which may become available in the not-too-distant future.

v

The new and expanded material is almost sufficient to qualify this second edition as a new book. However, since a fair amount of the original material is retained, the title is still appropriate, and the general plan is the same as before, it has been decided to issue it as a second edition, while emphasizing that it is not merely a cursory revision. It is still divided into seven chapters, six of which are the same as before and deal with the same basic material as in the first edition. However, as noted above, Chapter 6 has a new title and consists almost entirely of new material. In addition, to conform with present practice, the title of Chapter 1 has been changed to "Human Factors" from the original "Perceptual Factors," but the material included would have been the same if the earlier title had been retained. Thus, as before, this chapter presents information on the characteristics of human visual perception that affect display requirements and performance. Similarly, Chapters 2 and 3 cover the basic physical principles of the technologies used for cathode-ray and flat-panel display devices, much expanded and rewritten to include the latest information. The same is true for Chapters 4 and 5, where cathode-ray and flat-panel display systems are described, but Chapter 6 contains essentially all new material except for the short sections on keyboards, light pens, data tablets, trackballs, and joysticks from the first edition, which have been re-tained but considerably expanded in both the number of devices covered and the breadth of the examination. The other part of this chapter, dealing with output hard-copy devices, is entirely new to this edition.

Since I have continued to be active in the field during the period of over 10 years since the first edition was published, I have been involved in a number of related activities as Editor of the *Proceedings* of the Society for Information Display and of several volumes in the series "Computer Graphics" published by Academic Press, as well as author of chapters in several handbooks and encyclopedias. This has led to fruitful contacts with many people, all of whom have contributed importantly to my education and support in preparing this book. Unfortunately, there are too many of them for me to name separately, so I should like to limit my acknowledgments to a general expression of thanks and appreciation for all of the SID members and others who have been so generous in providing me with help and encouragement. You know who you are, and I apologize for not being more specific. The same comment holds for the various publications and manufacturers that have so generously pro-vided me with information and permission to use illustrations from their publications and other sources. Here, at least, the credit lines provide rec-ognition. Finally, I should like to stress that reference to any single manu-facturer does not necessarily constitute a special recommendation over other sources that are not mentioned. Every attempt has been made to keep the material in this volume free from both prejudice and bias—so that I can repeat the recommendation found at the end of the preface of the first edition: "Don't leave home without it."

SOL SHERR

Old Chatham, New York
February 1993

CONTENTS

ELECTRONIC
DISPLAYS

1

HUMAN FACTORS

1.1 INTRODUCTION

Human factors are those aspects of the visual appearance of an electronic
display that are concerned with the characteristics of the observer. The term
may also be used to include all the physical attributes of a display station,
and in that respect is equivalent to the term most commonly used in other
English-speaking countries: namely, *ergonomics*. As has been pointed out by
George Bernard Shaw, Great Britain and the United States of America are two
nations separated by a common language, but this condition need not concern
us; we will adhere to the convention used in the United States. A more precise
term might be *perceptual factors*, which is restricted to visual aspects, but this
term has not achieved wide acceptance in the display community and is not
used in this volume for that reason. Therefore, the term *human factors* is
used in this chapter to denote all those characteristics of the human observer
that affect the requirements placed on the visual image: in particular, those
that allow a specific connection to be established between a measurable physical parameter and the resulting physiological and psychological responses.
In general, those parameters are emphasized for which it is possible to assign
a preferred value or range of values leading to the best visual performance
in any given context of applications. However, we first present and define all
the terms used in display evaluation, point out their relevance to different
modes of usage of the display, and finally, indicate the manner whereby both
physical and perceptual measurements may be made to arrive at a reasonable
level of assurance that the display will adequately perform the functions
assigned to it (an operation covered in detail in Chapter 7).

1

1.2   PHOTOMETRY

1.2.1   General Discussion

As a preliminary to dealing directly with those parameters specific to the types of displays found in electronic systems, it is advisable to lay the groundwork by carefully examining a number of terms long used in the field of light measurement, whose applicability to electronically generated displays is not always clearly understood. Another factor contributing to the confusion is the multiplicity of redundant terms and definitions that has grown up over the years. We restrict this review to terms directly relevant and refer the reader to a few of the many texts [1,2] on this subject to obtain a more complete and comprehensive treatment. This is being done in the interest of maintaining clarity and relevance, and not beclouding the question unnecessarily, to use an appropriate visual metaphor. First, as a definition of photometry, we may state that photometry is the quantitative measurement of radiant flux in relation to its ability to evoke the psychological sensation of brightness. Thus it is one branch of radiometry, which is the physical measure of the radiated power and energy producing the luminous flux, and the photometric quantities are obtained from the radiometric ones by superimposing the luminosity functions on the radiometric quantities obtained. The photopic (daylight) and scotopic (nighttime) luminosity functions are shown in Figure 1.1 and were obtained by making comparative recognition measurements on a number of observers. Individuals may differ somewhat in their response characteristics, particularly at the extremes, but the curves are generally relevant and are accepted as the standard for visual recognition.

As can be seen from Figure 1.1, the curves describe the response of the human observer to a constant level of radiated power at different frequencies or colors and are intimately related to the perceptual characteristics of the human visual system. Without going into extensive physiological detail here, suffice it to say that the eye is most sensitive to green, and its sensitivity drops by many orders of magnitude at the extremes of red and blue. The *luminous efficiency* (K) of the visual system is the ratio of the photometric output to the radiometric input and is defined for monochromatic light by

$$K = 680\bar{y}(\lambda) \tag{1.1}$$

where $\bar{y}(\lambda)$ is the photopic function shown in Figure 1.1. Thus at 555 nm, K is equal to 680 lm/W, which is the peak of the photopic response curve and corresponds to the color green. The *lumen* is the unit of luminous flux, defined as the flux through a unit solid angle (steradian) from a point source of 1 cd emitting equally in all directions, and the *candela* (cd) is a basic unit in the international system, defined as the luminous intensity of a blackbody radiator, at the temperature of solidification of platinum, with a projected area of $\frac{1}{60}$ cm. Another important term is *luminance*, which unfortunately is not amenable to a simple definition, but for our purposes it is sufficient to say that

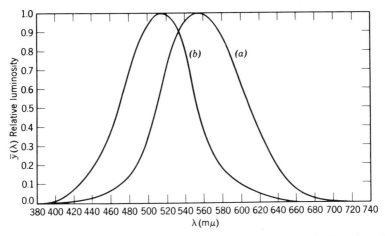

FIGURE 1.1   Photopic luminosity function and scotopic luminosity function. Curve (*a*), standard luminosity function applying to normal vision with good lighting conditions; curve (*b*), luminosity function applying to vision at very low light levels. After Pender and McIlwain [3], by permission.

it is the measure of luminous intensity of a light emitting or reflecting surface in a given direction, per unit of projected area of that surface as viewed from that direction. This is not very clear, but it is accurate, and suffice it to say that luminance is the parameter that determines the brightness of any display. We might make the additional point that *brightness* is a psychological term and most correctly refers to the attribute of perception whereby the observer is aware of differences in luminance. However, it is frequently used as synonymous with luminance, and we may only give the appropriate caveat to the unwary. All these terms are discussed more completely in the paragraphs that follow.

In addition to the three parameters introduced in the preceding paragraphs, there are several others that should be mentioned prior to embarking on a more detailed discussion of each. These are *contrast*, or preferably, *contrast ratio*, which is the ratio of information luminance to background luminance and *illumination*, defined as the density of luminous flux incident on a surface. With the introduction of these terms, we are now prepared to proceed with a more detailed examination, in relation to their significance for different types of display media.

1.2.2   Photometric Parameters

Luminous Intensity (I).   The photometric parameters are best understood by reference to Figure 1.2. Beginning with luminous intensity, it is the solid angle flux density in any given direction, shown in Figure 1.2 as emanating from a point source having the value of 1 cd as defined previously. All other parameters are defined in terms of this basic unit, which is of particular importance

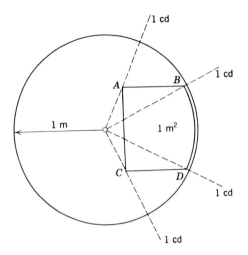

FIGURE 1.2 Relationship among candelas, lumens, and lux. The uniform point source has a luminous intensity of 1 cd at the center of a sphere of 1 m radius. The solid angle subtended by the area $ABCD$ is 1 sr, corresponding to the luminous intensity of 1 cd. The illuminance at any point of the sphere is similarly 1 lux (1 lm/m²). Adapted from Kaufman [4].

in dealing with point sources such as light-emitting diodes (LEDs). Thus LEDs are specified by their luminous intensity, usually in millicandelas. The technology of LEDs is covered in Chapter 3 and is not discussed here beyond pointing out that they are best compared by examining their light output or candle power. Other devices for which luminous intensity is important are gas discharge matrix panels and electroluminescent panels, as well as cathode-ray tubes (CRTs), when the spot intensity is the prime factor. The latter are covered in Chapter 2 and the first two, in Chapter 3.

Luminous Flux (F). Again referring to Figure 1.2, we see that, as defined previously, the luminous flux emitted from the 1-cd point source at the center of the sphere and contained in a unit solid angle in any direction is 1 lm, and many light radiators, such as incandescent light bulbs, have their light output given in lumens. We may see further from Figure 1.2 that 1 lm is the flux on a unit surface with all points at 1 unit distance from the source. Luminous flux is also used to define the light output from certain area radiators such as projection CRTs and other types of television projectors. This is covered in Chapters 2 and 4.

Illuminance (E). Illuminance, or as it is also termed, *illumination*, is defined as the density of luminous flux incident on a surface. Referring again to Figure 1.2, we see that for the 1-m distance the flux is

$$E = 1 \text{ lm/m}^2 \text{ (lux)} \qquad (1.2)$$

and for the 1-ft distance it is

$$E = 1 \text{ lm/ft}^2 \text{ (footcandle)} \qquad (1.3)$$

From these two equations we see that to convert from lm/m^2 to lm/ft^2 we must multiply by 0.0929 and by the reciprocal or 10.76 to do the opposite. The international term is *lux* (lx), but unfortunately, *footcandle* (fc) has shown resistance to desuetude and is included here for that reason. We use the international unit throughout this text. Table 1.1 contains the conversion factors to and from the international units, and is included for reference.

Luminance (L). Luminance is perhaps the most important of the parameters introduced to this point. Cathode-ray tubes are commonly described in terms of their luminance, as are many other light-emitting surfaces. Thus luminance is the first convenient measure of the ability of any light-emitting device, whether CRT or flat panel, to function in a given ambient light environment. It should be stressed here again that luminance is the term to be used when the physical quantity is meant, and not brightness. However, since brightness is still so commonly used as synonymous with luminance, it is frequently encountered, and it is necessary to examine the content to determine whether it is being used correctly or is another example of the lag between definitions and their acceptance by the technical community. We know that human beings are resistant to change, and perhaps this example is a useful warning not to go too far in introducing innovations.

Another source of confusion in the use of luminance is the many terms that are available to express its value. The official international unit is *candelas per square meter*, and Figure 1.2 illustrates the case where the source is 1 cd, so that 1 m^2 on the sphere, at a distance of 1 m from the source, has a flux density falling on it of 1 lm. We assume that the sphere is a uniformly diffusing surface, so that the luminous intensity in any direction, per unit area, varies as the cosine of the angle (θ) between the direction and the normal to the surface, as illustrated in Figure 1.3. The surface appears equally luminous from any viewing direction, and its luminance, as expressed in terms of the flux emitted per unit area, is given by

$$F = \int_0^{\pi/2} I \cos \theta \, d\theta \times 2\pi \sin \theta \qquad (1.4)$$

or

$$F = \pi I \qquad (1.5)$$

Therefore, the flux emitted or reflected per unit area, for I cd, is πI lm (1.5), or π lm for 1 cd. This leads to another of the units used for luminance, still very common in the United States, namely, the *foot-lambert* (fL). The unique feature of this unit is that it is defined as the luminance for a surface emitting or reflecting light at a rate of 1 lm/ft^2. Therefore, since 1 cd leads to π lm,

TABLE 1.1 Multiplication Factors for Unit Conversions

To convert to:	From: Multiply Number of by							
	cd/cm²	cd/in.²	cd/ft²	cd/m²	L	mL	fL (equiv. foot-candle)	m-L
Candela/cm² (stilb)	1	0.1550	0.0010764	10⁴	0.3183	0.0003183	0.0003426	0.00003183
Candela/in.²	6,452	1	0.006944	6.452×10^{-4}	2.054	0.002054	0.00221	0.0002054
Candela/ft²	929	144	1	0.0929	295.7	0.2957	0.3183	0.02957
Candela/m²	10,000	1.550	10.764	1	3.183	3.183	3.426	0.3183
Lambert (cm-L)	3,142	0.4869	3.382×10^{-3}	3.142	1	0.001	0.001076	10^{-4}
Millilambert	3,142	486.9	3.382	0.3142	1,000	1	1.0764	0.1
Foot-lambert (fL)	2,919	452.4	3.142	0.2919	929	0.929	1	0.0929
Meter-lambert (m-L)	31,420	4869	33.282	3.142	10⁴	10	10.76	1

To convert to:	From:			
	Lux	Footcandle	Phot	Milliphot
Lumen/m² lux	1.0	10.76	10,000	10.0
Lumen/ft² foot-candle	0.0929	1.0	929	0.929
Lumen/cm² phot	0.0001	0.001076	1	0.001
Lumen/cm² × 1000 mphot	0.1	1.076	1,000	1.0

Source: After Pender and McIlwain [3], by permission.

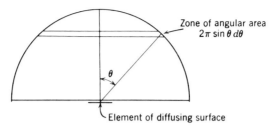

FIGURE 1.3 Relation between luminance and flux emission. Adapted from Walsh [5].

we must divide by π to obtain 1 lm, leading to the equation

$$fL = \frac{1}{\pi} \, cd/ft^2 \qquad (1.6)$$

This has been discussed in some detail because the significance of π in the denominator is frequently misunderstood. As a result, to convert from fL to cd/m^2, it is necessary to multiply by the ratio of m^2 to ft^2, or 10.76, times $1/\pi$, for a total multiplier of 3.426. Conversely, multiply by the reciprocal, or 0.2919, to obtain fL from cd/m^2. The *nit* is also used for cd/m^2 (1 nit). Of course, it is to be hoped that the foot-lambert will be eliminated as a luminance term, but since it has shown considerable resistance to this result, it is well to understand fully the significance of both terms. We use mainly cd/m^2 or nit in the rest of this volume. As to the rest of the terms that have proliferated, they may be found in many older texts, and we leave it to the interested antiquarian to search those texts for further information [3, pp. 14-14 to 14-17; 4, pp. 3–4; 5, pp. 137–138; 6, p. 17]. Table 1.1 may be referred to if necessary.

Contrast Ratio (C_R). As the last parameter in the photometric galaxy, we discuss contrast ratio and its equivalent, contrast. This is not specifically a photometric term, but since it is made up of the ratio of two photometric quantities, it seems appropriate to include it in this section. It is basically a simple term, defined as the ratio of the total luminance $(L_1 + L_2)$ at any information element (L_1) to the background or surround luminance (L_2), or

$$C_R = \frac{L_1 + L_2}{L_2} \qquad (1.7)$$

However, this simple concept is confused both by the existence of the other term, *contrast*, and by the multiplicity of definitions that are used, sometimes interchangeably and incorrectly for the same parameter. As for luminance and illuminance, we try to minimize this confusion by describing only one of the competing terms, and then we return to our definition for the remainder of this volume. The most common other form in which contrast ratio is expressed is as contrast, usually defined as the ratio of the difference between the information and background luminances to the background luminance. Sometimes the terms are interchanged, depending on whether the information or the background luminance is larger, and a fractional or larger than unity result is desired, with the larger-than-unity result called *contrast ratio*, but that is not according to presently preferred practice. It is simple to convert from this form to that in equation 1.7, by multiplying by the ratio

$$\frac{C}{C_R} = \frac{L_1 - L_2}{L_2} \bigg/ \frac{L_1 + L_2}{L_2}$$

$$C_R = C\frac{L_1 + L_2}{L_1 - L_2}$$

(1.8)

We may hope that the need for this conversion will not arise, but we must anticipate the worst. Again, we neglect the various other forms that this parameter may take as being too uncommon or imprecise for our consideration. Contrast ratio is a very important parameter, and it is essential that its form and meaning be well understood to avoid specifying it incorrectly. Too many otherwise well-designed display vessels have foundered on this rock for us to be complacent about its significance and use.

1.3   NONPHOTOMETRIC VISUAL PARAMETERS

1.3.1   Introduction

In addition to the photometric parameters discussed earlier, there are a number of nonphotometric parameters that have a significant impact on the quality of the visual image. They are nonphotometric in that while the characteristics of the light source will influence them, they are affected primarily by other factors associated with the functioning of the perceptual mechanism. We describe this mechanism to a limited extent in the next section, but for a fuller understanding, the reader should consult other texts on physiology and psychology. Too much detail on this subject is probably self-defeating, so we keep the discussion as simple as possible.

1.3.2   Resolution

Resolution is probably the most confused and confusing of this group of parameters, since it has the largest number of competing terms and definitions, frequently used incorrectly and without a full understanding of their meaning and relationship to the characteristics of the visual image. In its simplest form, *resolution* is defined as the smallest discernible or measurable detail in a visual presentation. This seems straightforward enough, but it is amazing how mixed up it has become. It must have taken considerable effort and some small amount of genius to create such a hodgepodge of terms, definitions, and methods of test as exists. We follow our usual practice of selecting one preferred approach, covering it in some detail, and then giving brief descriptions of several other competing techniques so that the reader may recognize them when they occur, in specifications or articles, and will be able to translate them into the preferred approach, or use them if desired.

However, let us first clarify the meaning of the definition given in the preceding paragraph. We may define a human response characteristic known as *visual acuity*, which is the ability to discriminate fine detail in the field of view, in relation to normal acuity at a standard distance D'. Then

$$\text{visual acuity} = \frac{D'}{D} \tag{1.9}$$

where D is the distance at which the minimum discernible test object subtends 1 min of arc. One minute of arc at the eye is the accepted limit of its resolving power, for reasons described later, when we present a brief description of the physiology of the optic system. This leads to another definition for resolution, as the reciprocal of the angular separation between two elements of a test pattern when they are just detected as separable elements. This is the best resolution that can be used by a human observer, and it is generally useless to achieve higher resolution in the display, since it will not be seen by the user. Of course, there are some human beings who can resolve smaller objects, and in some cases a higher resolution may improve the quality of the image, but these cases are unique and should not affect the general rule.

Now that we have a useable definition, the question arises as to how we may specify and measure this parameter. This is where the confusion begins. A common mode of description is to express the resolution in terms of television lines, which appears simple on the surface but rapidly becomes complex as we examine the true significance of the term. *Television lines* in the most common usage means the number appearing alongside the most closely spaced, discernible lines on an EIA (Electronic Industries Association) resolution test chart such as that shown in Figure 1.4. This corresponds well to the definitions given previously, and is a reasonable measure of the ability of the display system to present information that can be recognized by the observer. As such, it is an excellent measure to use when a total television system is involved, such as that described in Chapter 4. However, many of the systems we are interested in have computer-generated imagery, and this type of measurement cannot be made. In this case we must resort to another method, preferred for most cases, termed the *shrinking raster*. Shrinking raster is most applicable to CRT systems, although it may be used for any system in which the visual image is made up of a group of lines or points of light, more or less continuously variable in position. It may not be used for fixed displays, such as matrix panels, and we discuss later the manner in which

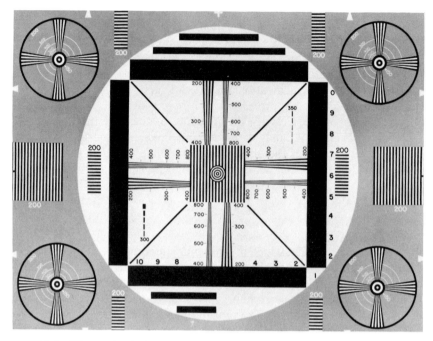

FIGURE 1.4   Electronics Industries Association's resolution chart. By permission of the EIA.

these types of systems may be specified as to resolution. For CRT systems, destined to be with us for a long time, the shrinking raster technique offers a simple, rapid, and reasonably meaningful way to measure and characterize the resolution of the display.

The shrinking raster technique for measuring resolution is illustrated in Figure 1.5. A known number of lines of light is generated by some means and made to appear on the CRT. The spacing between the lines is then reduced until no separation is discernible as illustrated in Figure 1.5. The height of this shrunken raster is then related to the number of lines in the raster, and the resultant number is the resolution in lines/cm when the raster height is standardized at 1 cm, or it may be converted into the resolution of a particular

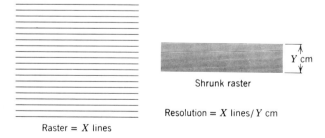

Shrunk raster

Resolution = X lines/ Y cm

Raster = X lines

FIGURE 1.5   Shrinking-raster measurement.

display once the height of the image is known. This method for measuring resolution is quite simple and inexpensive, and it is one of the most popular techniques. However, it measures only the minimum line spacing that can be resolved and tells us nothing about the rest of the system, which is what the television resolution chart method does achieve, since it measures the resolution of the entire system. This aspect of the problem is discussed further in Chapter 4.

The shrinking raster is the preferred method for measuring and specifying resolution in a simple and relatively reproducible fashion. However, since the television chart technique is the official standard of the television industry, it is important to understand the difference between the results obtained by use of either approach. The shrinking raster gives a direct measure of the minimum discernible detail, subject only to the uncertainty due to the characteristics of the observers, both the ones who make the measurement and those who will use the display. However, the numbers obtained by this method will differ significantly from those obtained by using the television chart. The difference is due to the television chart producing essentially a square-wave signal, which is then transmitted through the system, and modulates the lines on the CRT, whereas the shrinking raster looks at the lines directly. It is estimated that the lines will appear to merge, given the usual Gaussian form of the luminance profile, at a spot width equal to 2σ (the standard deviation), as illustrated in Figure 1.6 and occurring at approximately 60% of peak. This is related to the ability of the eye to detect luminance differences of about 3%, and is discussed further in Section 1.4. However, when the square-wave function imposed by the television chart is imposed on the Gaussian spot, the discernible difference occurs at 1.18σ, so that the ratio between the two numbers is 1.7, with the television chart giving the larger number. Naturally, manufacturers prefer to specify their devices in terms of television lines, as measured by the television chart, rather than in lines as measured by the shrinking raster. Strictly speaking, television lines should be used only for the chart measurement, also referred to as *television limiting*, but this proviso is not always adhered to, resulting in much misrepresentation and misunderstanding. Well, to be forewarned is to be forearmed, so look out for this form

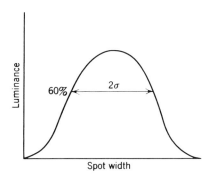

FIGURE 1.6   Significance of 2σ.

of "specmanship." Although these two methods are the most likely ones to be encountered, they both suffer from the same limitation of being influenced by the visual characteristic of the observer. This has not been true of the photometric parameters, all of which may be described without referring to the method of test used. As a result, several other methods are in use when less subjective results are desired. These are termed the slit analyzer and modulation transfer function (MTF) techniques, but since they are considerably more complex and difficult to perform than the two techniques discussed so far, we defer description of them to Chapter 7, where detailed discussions of various techniques of measurement for these and other parameters may be found. Indeed, it was necessary to go into some measurement detail for resolution here, only because the method of measurement has such a profound effect on the result.

1.3.3 Flicker

Flicker is not, strictly speaking, a parameter in itself, in that we do not specify a particular level of flicker but rather insist on the complete absence of flicker in the visual image. The phenomenon of flicker is due to the ability of the observer to detect changes in the luminance level when they occur at a rate below that at which the integrating capability of the eye eliminates the sensation of luminance change. This effect is elaborated on in Section 1.4, and at this point it is only necessary to recognize that it exists and constitutes a serious deficiency if a display is not flicker-free. The majority of CRT displays (with the exception of storage-tube types) and most matrix displays are similarly subject to this phenomenon, with the possible exception of some types of gas-discharge displays that can operate in a storage mode. Therefore, flicker may occur in many displays, and great care must be exercised to ensure that no flicker exists. This is particularly troublesome in that the rate at which changes in luminance are detected is very dependent on the luminance of the image, so that a display that does not flicker at one luminance level may flicker in a noticeable way at a higher level of luminance.

Flicker is a very disturbing phenomenon in that it causes considerable eye strain in the user, even though it may not detract significantly from the information capacity of the image. Flickering images may be permitted for short periods of time, but in general the best practice is not to allow any flicker at all for any condition of operation. Acceptable repetition rates range from 45 Hz up, and the effect of this requirement on the design of a display system is treated in detail in subsequent chapters. We may note here that the phrase commonly used for the minimum repetition rate to avoid flicker is *critical fusion*, or *critical flicker frequency*, usually abbreviated CFF. The simplest expression for the relationship between the luminance and the CFF is given by the Ferry–Porter law,

$$CFF = a \log L_{av} + b \tag{1.10}$$

where a = 12.5 (photopic) or 1.5 (scotopic)
  L_{av} = average luminance of image
    b = 37

This is an empirical expression, and the values for a and b are only approximate. However, it may be used as a first attempt to obtain a value for the CFF and modified as experience with the actual conditions of operation indicates. In addition, whereas luminance in nits (cd/m^2) may be used, it is more accurate when the actual value of the illumination reaching the retina, or the true brightness, is employed. The relation between this illuminance and the luminance is dependent on a number of factors, as demonstrated in Section 1.4, but a simplified version is given by

$$E(\text{trolands}) = LA(\text{nits} \times \text{mm}^2) \qquad (1.11)$$

The *troland* is defined as the retinal illuminance produced by viewing a surface whose luminance is 1 cd/m^2 through an artificial pupil with an area of 1 mm^2 centered on the natural pupil. This leads to curves of the type shown in Figure 1.7, for different sizes of fields. It can be seen that for reasonable levels of brightness, above 100 trolands, the CFF is above 40 Hz. It is also interesting to note that for very low levels of brightness the CFF may be a factor of 10 less than at high levels. This is due to the characteristics of the rods and cones in the retina, with the rods only responding to the low brightness level and having a lower intrinsic CFF than the cones. This is accounted for in the Ferry–Porter law by the two values given for a, with the lower one used for low light levels or scotopic vision. In addition, it should be noted that for illumination levels exceeding about 12 trolands the CFF is independent of

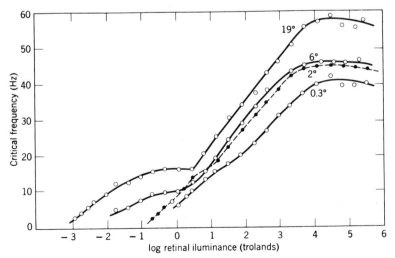

FIGURE 1.7   Critical flicker frequency vs. brightness. After Graham [6], by permission.

color, but that at lower levels the effect of color is quite marked, with blue having the highest, red the lowest, and white an intermediate CFF.

In 1987, a modification of the Ferry–Porter law was proposed that predicts the CFF from the amount of energy in the fundamental refresh frequency. The new law is

$$\text{CFF} = m + n[\ln\{E(f)_o\}] \tag{1.12}$$

where $m = -[\ln(a)/b]$
$\quad\quad n = 1/b$

with m and n dependent on viewing angle, and

$$E(f)_o = ae^{bf} = \text{amplitude of fundamental refresh frequency}$$

where f is the refresh frequency and a and b are constants dependent on display size given by

$$\theta = 2 \arctan \frac{D}{2L_d} \tag{1.13}$$

where θ = viewing angle
$\quad\quad D$ = screen diagonal
$\quad\quad L_d$ = viewing distance

The pupil area may be calculated by means of the equation

$$A = \pi\left(\frac{d}{2}\right)^2 \tag{1.14}$$

where $d = 5 - 3 \tanh (0.4) \log (L_t \times 3.183)$ and L_t is screen luminance. Values for m and n at several different viewing angles are shown in Table 1.2, and flicker thresholds for a number of observers are compared with the values obtained from equation 1.12 in Figure 1.8. Figure 1.9 shows similar

TABLE 1.2   Flicker Parameters for Various Display Sizes

CFF = $m + n\{\ln[E(f)_{obs}]\}$			
Display Size (degrees of visual angle)	Parameter		
	m	n	R^2
10	14.6	7.00	0.998
30	13.85	8.31	0.998
50	8.32	9.73	0.977
70	6.79	10.03	0.991

Source: After Farrell et al. [7], by permission.

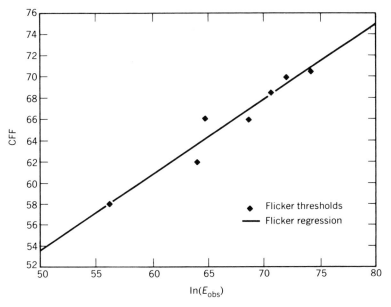

FIGURE 1.8   Critical flicker frequency (CFF) in hertz vs. natural log of absolute amplitude of fundamental frequency, in trolands. Adapted from Farrell et al. [7], by permission.

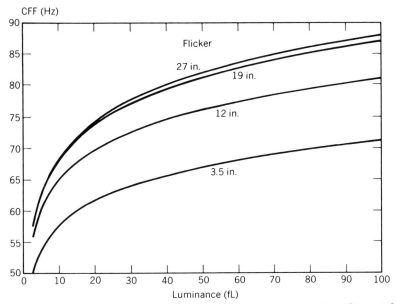

FIGURE 1.9   CFF as predicted by the Farrell equations. After Infante [8, p. 45], by permission.

curves for a number of display sizes, and it should be noted that the predicted CFFs values are higher than those shown in Figure 1.7, especially at the higher luminances and larger display sizes. These results have led to higher refresh frequencies being used, with 70 Hz becoming more common.

There is an important limitation to the application of these data to some display situations, in particular when the CRT is the display device. This arises when most of the data are taken using nonretentive display media, with the brightness going from full on to full off in the designated time period. However, when retentive media, such as CRT phosphors are used, the CFF may be considerably reduced. This is demonstrated by the curves shown in Figure 1.10, where the effect of screen luminance is included. It can be seen that the CFF may be as low as 20 Hz for long decay-time constants, or close to 80 Hz for the shortest decay times. The significance of this lowering of the CFF to the user and display system designer is elaborated on in Chapter 4, and the influence of phosphor characteristics on the CFF is covered further in Sections 1.4.3 and 2.3.3.

As a final observation, the empirical nature of the constants given for the Ferry–Porter law is evident if we substitute numbers for L. For example, if we use 10, the resultant CFF is 60 Hz, whereas the curve in Figure 1.7 shows 35 Hz. Therefore, although the general form of the curve predicted by the Ferry–Porter law is retained, at least over the range 1 to 1000 trolands, the exact value of CFF that it predicts may not be in accordance with these data. For example, the value given for b of 37 applies to color television but not to white light. Therefore, it is best to use data that accord with the application and display type, and treat the law only as a general guide. Also, since flicker

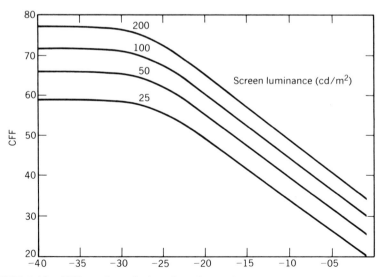

FIGURE 1.10 CFF vs. log of phosphor decay-time constant with luminance as a parameter. After Farrell et al. [7], by permission.

is a highly subjective phenomenon, the true effect becomes fully evident only under actual operating conditions, so that it is best to allow margin by overspecification or the inclusion of an adjustment. Remember that whereas the display may be used even if it flickers, flicker creates fatigue and distraction so that it must not be permitted for any extended period of time.

1.3.4 Symbol Size

The minimum symbol size that will allow reliable identification of the symbol is closely related to resolution and is an extension of the resolution criteria to objects made up of several resolution elements. Thus if we use the resolution limit of 1 min of arc, a seven-element-high symbol should require a size that would subtend 7 min of arc. This is indeed the case, although for reliable recognition it is advisable to at least double this figure. If the symbol is more complex than the standard alphanumeric, the size should be at least twice as large again. Other factors that affect the choice of minimum symbol size are the luminance and contrast ratio to be used. If these are below acceptable values, the symbol size must be increased further. Another aspect of display systems that has impact on required symbol size is the manner in which the symbol is generated. For example, in raster systems such as television, the size is determined by the number of scanning lines, in conjunction with the other parameters mentioned. This is discussed further in Chapter 4. In any event, it is important to specify the minimum symbol size for a given operational situation, or the display will be unusable.

The other characteristics of a symbol set that should be established is the font, which in the case of alphanumerics determines the exact form of the letters and numbers. The characters may be constructed out of combinations of strokes, or, as is very common in matrix systems as well as television, of a group of dots. This is particularly true of the majority of alphanumeric readouts. Various fonts and their features are covered later in this chapter.

1.3.5 Legibility

A final parameter to be considered in the design and specification of a display system is the legibility that is required in its application. By *legibility* we mean the number of correct identifications that a viewer will make in an operational situation. This parameter is affected by all those discussed previously and is the final measure of the effectiveness of the display system. After all, although picture quality is not to be ignored and is of prime importance in naturalistic presentations such as are common in entertainment television, a very large number of systems are used for the purpose of information presentation, and it is essential that this information be identified easily and correctly. So we end up with this criterion, easily stated but very difficult to predict in terms of the other parameters. Thus although we may use the guidelines given later in this chapter, ultimately it is only after the system has been in use that we truly discover whether its performance meets the goals set by the design and specification. Unfortunately, this condition is more prevalent for displays than in other types of systems, although many computer users have discovered that the system does not do what is expected with the concomitant need for extensive changes and redesign. It is to be hoped, however, that careful attention to the principles outlined here and elsewhere in this volume will help to reduce this condition to manageable size.

1.3.6 Color

We cannot leave the subject of human factors as they apply to visual parameters without some discussion of the complex question of how and when to use color. Up to now we have been dealing essentially with monochromatic or white light and have completely ignored the significance of color, other than its possible effect on luminous efficiency, as represented by the luminosity functions shown in Figure 1.1. This has been quite adequate, up to this point, but we must now embark on a consideration of what the situation is when more than one color is present in the display. The choice of the colors is not arbitrary, since we are limited both by those available from the various display devices and also by the physical characteristics of color, as it is perceived by the human visual system. We may begin, as before, with a definition that states that color consists of the characteristics of light, other than luminance or brightness, by which an observer may distinguish between two structure-free patches of light of the same size and shape. This definition tells us merely that color alone may convey information, but it tells nothing about its effectiveness as an information carrier or what colors are needed to produce the best range of color choice. For this we must turn to psychological theory and the experience of artists.

It has long been known that the three primary colors are red, yellow, and blue for pigments and red, green, and blue for electronic displays and that they may be combined in various proportions to produce all other colors. This led to the development of a tristimulus theory of color vision by Helmholtz, which has been substantiated in recent years by the discovery of receptors in the visual system that respond uniquely to these colors. This is covered in more detail in Section 1.4, and at this point it is sufficient to state that the combination may be expressed for electronic displays by

$$C_1 = R_1(R) + G_1(G) + B_1(B) \qquad (1.15)$$

where C_1 = selected color
$\quad R_1(R)$ = proportion of red
$\quad G_1(G)$ = proportion of green
$\quad B_1(B)$ = proportion of blue

The proportions required of each of the three components may be found by varying them until the resultant color matches the desired color, but this is a tedious process. It is made feasible by introducing several other mathematical relationships in terms of *chromaticity coordinates*, x, y, and z, further limited by the relationship

$$x + y + z = 1 \qquad (1.16)$$

We may now plot these coordinates in the form given by Figure 1.11 and further plot the colors on the chromaticity diagram as shown in Figure 1.12, from which it is possible to determine the proportions of x and y and thus of red, green, and blue, necessary to produce any color in the visible spectrum. If the colors available do not fall at the extremes of the plot, then not all colors are available, and this is indeed the case for color television. For example, television red occurs at $x = 0.325$, as shown in Figure 11.11. However, there is a sufficiently large range achieved with less than ideal primaries, as is quite evident from the success of color television both in reproducing naturalistic displays and in information presentations. This situation is discussed further in Chapters 2 and 4.

The original CIE charts were developed in the early 1930s and were found adequate for many years. However, they resulted in unequal color spacings as shown in Figure 1.12, so that new charts were developed using the 1976-CIE-$L^*u^*v^*$ distance as defined by

$$dL^*u^*v^* = (dL^{*2} + du^{*2} + dv^{*2}) \qquad (1.17)$$

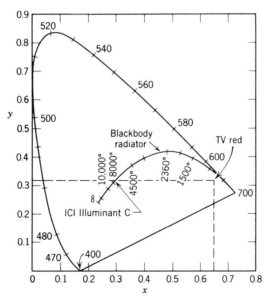

FIGURE 1.11 Commission International de l'Eclairage chromaticity diagram. From Pender and McIlwain [3].

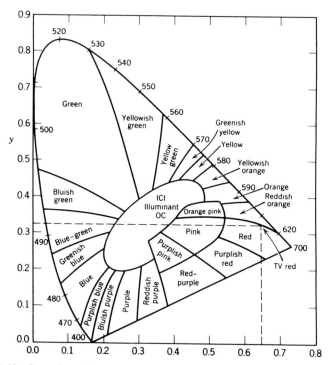

FIGURE 1.12   Location of colors in chromaticity diagram. After Pender and McIlwain [3], by permission.

where $dL^*u^*v^*$ = distance between colors

dL^* = distance between L^* values

du^* = distance between u colors

dv^* = distance between v colors

These charts are shown in Figures 1.13 and 1.14 and are in current use.

1.3.7   Unified Measures of Image Quality

Visual Capacity. The various parameters discussed in the preceding paragraphs may be used to specify a display so as to achieve a desired image quality. However, it is difficult to arrive at an optimum set of values, since there are so many parameters and they all interact in complex and sometimes unpredictable ways. Thus although we do use them in most cases, and with usually acceptable results, it is desirable to have a single figure of merit that can be more simply expressed and for which the relationship between the specific parameters and the actual visual performance can be accurately determined. Several such descriptors have been evolved that seem to show considerable promise. Unfortunately, they tend to be rather complex math-

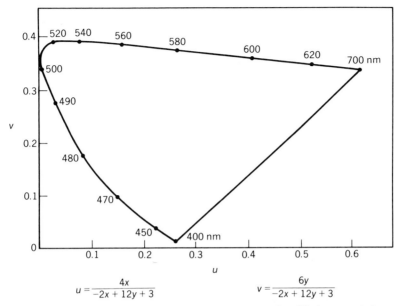

$$u = \frac{4x}{-2x + 12y + 3} \qquad v = \frac{6y}{-2x + 12y + 3}$$

FIGURE 1.13   1960 CIE–UCS diagram. After Keller [9], by permission.

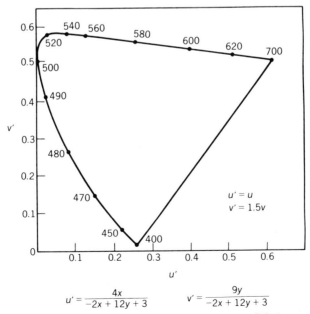

$$u' = \frac{4x}{-2x + 12y + 3} \qquad v' = \frac{9y}{-2x + 12y + 3}$$

FIGURE 1.14   1976 CIE–UCS diagram. After Keller [9], by permission.

ematically and are not easily reducible to the types of measurable quantities delineated in the parameter descriptions, so that we only introduce them conceptually. One such descripter, evolved by Cohen and Gorog [10] and reported on extensively by them, is termed *visual capacity*. It is considered analogous to information capacity, which is very appropriate, since a display system may be treated as the equivalent of an information system, with the appropriate substitutions. This approach to display systems has been treated in considerable detail by the present author in previous publications, but not including the visual system, as has been done by these authors. They describe their term as signifying "the total number of edges that can be perceived by an observer located at a given distance from the display." They state that the calculation requires a single integration of a function that includes the modulation transfer functions (MTF) of the displays and the human visual system. We have mentioned MTF previously, but only in relation to the display system, and it is quite useful to extend this measurement to include the human visual system. However, this is not easily done by the average user of the display system, and we must depend on data obtained by others. This is not necessarily a limitation since many of the data used to establish the preferred parameter values given later in this chapter are also derived from data obtained by many investigators. The difference is that most users can verify these data, if they wish, without undue expenditures of time and money, whereas for the MTF measurement of the human visual system, techniques and skills are required that are beyond most users of display systems. However, despite this limitation we do consider the use of *visual capacity*, because of its potential advantages in accuracy, and ultimate simplicity. In particular, it seems to offer new information as to optimum viewing distances for achieving maximum visual capacity. This is derived from the relationship

$$C_v^T r_{opt} = \frac{\omega_m w}{\pi} O^2 \frac{v_0 r_{opt}}{r_0} \tag{1.18}$$

where r_{opt} = optimum viewing distance
ω_m = angular spatial frequency that characterizes rate of rolloff of MTF of display
w = linear dimension of display
O = MTF of visual system
v_0 = 8 cycles/degree of vision for which $O(v)$ has a maximum
r_0 = 360 v_0/ω_m

Then the numerical solution of equation 1.18 leads to the result

$$r_{opt} = 1.485 r_0 = \frac{4277}{\omega_m} \tag{1.19}$$

and the total visual capacity at this optimum viewing distance is given by

$$C_v^T r_{\text{opt}} = \frac{\omega_m W}{O^2 v_{\text{opt}}}$$
(1.20)

where $v_{\text{opt}} = 1.485v_0 = 11.9$ cycles/degree of vision. Application of these equations to CRTs for which the MTF is known, and using available data for the visual system MTF, leads to the curves shown in Figure 1.15, with the

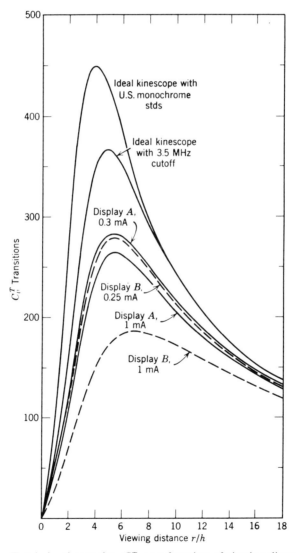

FIGURE 1.15 Total visual capacity, C_v^T, as a function of viewing distance in units of picture height, r/h. After Cohen and Gorog [10], by permission.

interesting result that whereas the optimum viewing distance for the ideal kinescope is about four picture heights, as the usually suggested distance, the optimum viewing distances for actual kinescopes are between five and seven picture heights.

Another aspect of the Carlson–Cohen method is the introduction of a new parameter termed the *just noticeable difference* (JND), which attempts to take into account the nonlinear behavior of the eye. It is assumed that the visual contrast sensitivity function represents the integrated output of seven logarithmically spaced frequency channels with peak sensitivities at 0.5, 1.5, 3.0, 6.0, 12, 24, and 48 cycles/degree, and the levels that can be discriminated are shown by means of discriminable difference diagrams (DDDs). These levels are calculated by means of a model which assumes that an increase in signal must be greater than a constant fraction of interfering noise, and the number of JNDs increases in accordance with Weber's law. An example of such a diagram is shown in Figure 1.16, where A and B represent MTF curves, and the number of tic marks in the total area below these curves is used as a measure of visual resolution quality. Unfortunately, the method is difficult to use because different diagrams are required for each display parameter change, and there may be poor correspondence between calculated and measured values.

Square Root Integral. Another approach, which overcomes some of the difficulties found in the DDD method, is the more recent *square root integral* (SQRI) method devised by Barten. It is similar to the Carlson–Cohen technique, but uses logarithmic integration instead of logarithmic summation. The

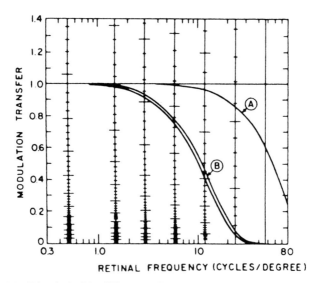

FIGURE 1.16 Discriminable difference diagram for several signal levels. After Carlson and Cohen [11], by permission.

square root integral is given by

$$J = \frac{1}{\ln 2} \int_0^{u_{max}} \sqrt{M(u)/M_t(u)} \, \frac{du}{u} \tag{1.21}$$

where u_{max} is the maximum angular frequency of addressed resolution and, $M(u) = 0$ for $u > u_{max}$.

A fixed mathematical expression is required for the contrast sensitivity of the eye, and this is given by

$$S(u) = \frac{1}{M_t(u)} = au \exp(-bu) \sqrt{1 + c \exp(b\mu)} \tag{1.22}$$

where μ = spatial frequency (cycles/degree)
$a = 440(1 + 0.7/L)^{-0.2}/\{1 + [12/\omega (1 + \omega/3)^2\}$
$b = 0.3(1 + 100/L)^{0.15}$
$c = 0.06$
ω = angular display size (degrees)
L = effective display luminance (cd/m^2)

Equation 1.22 was derived from contrast sensitivity data measured by van Meeteren shown in Figure 1.17, and data measured by Carlson and Cohen shown in Figure 1.18. The effect of various display parameters on the SQRI value may be found in reference 13. Figures 1.17 and 1.18 also show the contrast sensitivity curves as calculated using equation 1.22, and exhibit close correspondence with the measured values.

Modulation Transfer Function Area (MTFA). Another approach to achieving a unified measure that has been adopted in the ANSI/HFS standard is that developed by Snyder [13, p. 97], among others. This technique uses a concept known as the *modulation transfer function area* (MTFA), defined mathematically by

$$\text{MTFA (linear)} = \int_{v_0}^{v_1} R_0(v) - \frac{M_{D,t}(v)}{M_0 \, dv} \tag{1.23}$$

where v_0 = low spatial frequency limit, in lines/mm
v_1 = high spatial frequency crossover of MTF and $M_t(v)$
$R_0(v)$ = MTF value at spatial frequency
$M_{D,t}(v)$ = image target modulation
M_0 = object target modulation

The concept is illustrated by Figure 1.19, where the MTFA is the integral from zero to the crossover frequency of the difference between the modulation

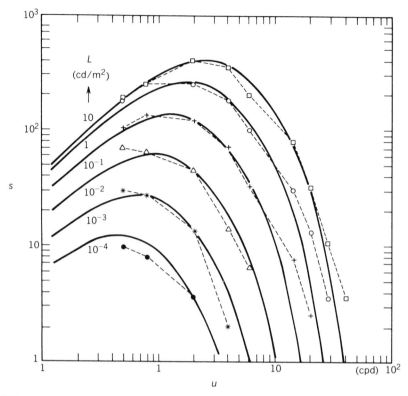

FIGURE 1.17   Contrast sensitivity function of the eye. After Barten [12], by permission.

transfer function (MTF) of the display and the threshold detectability curve of the viewed [13], also known as the *contrast sensitivity function* (CSF). It has been accepted as the standard metric for resolution by ANSI, which requires that the MTFA have a value of at least 5. It may be calculated from the equation provided in the standard, but unfortunately, the procedure is rather cumbersome. Therefore, it may be expedient to use the simpler method for the measurement of lines of resolution such as the resolution chart or shrinking raster methods.

1.4   ELECTROPHYSIOLOGY OF VISUAL SYSTEM

1.4.1   Acuity

It is not our intention here to become involved in an elaborate description of the complexities of the visual system. However, there are certain attributes that may be understood by a limited exposition, and we go only as far as is necessary for that understanding. The main point of interest for our purposes

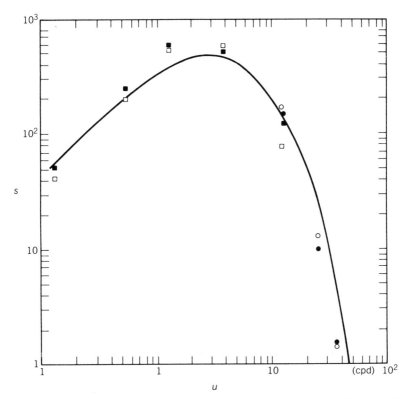

FIGURE 1.18 Comparison of calculated contrast sensitivity with Carlson–Cohen measurements. After Barten [12], by permission.

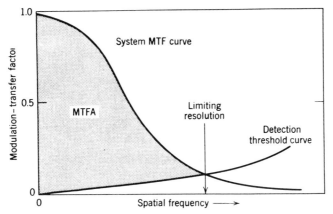

FIGURE 1.19 Modulation-transfer function area concept. From Biberman [2], by permission of the publisher, Plenum Press.

in the structure of the eye is the retina, in which are located the rods and cones that transform the light impinging on them into electrical impulses that transmit information to the brain about light intensity, color, and shape. We need not concern ourselves with the very complex question of how the brain uses this information, not because it isn't important for understanding how the characteristics of light are interpreted by the observer, but rather because we use data on the external manifestations of these operations to arrive at conclusions about parameters and values and thus need not enter into a study of the brain itself. The reader who wishes a more detailed knowledge may consult a number of excellent sources. The retina contains between 75 and 150 million rods and 6 to 7 million cones. The rods are distributed over the total retinal surface, but the cones are most densely packed in the center, termed the *fovea centralis*. This is of significance in determining maximum resolution and gives best resolution when the fovea centralis is used for viewing. Rods vary in thickness from 1 μm near the fovea to 2.5 μm at the periphery, whereas cones are about 1.5 μm thick. This accounts for the 1-min limit on resolution, mentioned previously. Since 1 min of arc covers about 5 μm at the retina, we see that the absolute limit of resolution, assuming that an individual rod or cone sets this limit by its size, is 0.3 to 0.5 min of arc. Tests have established that under optimum conditions, and using the fovea for viewing, it is possible to approach this limit, but for reliable detection at least 1 min is necessary. Indeed, there is also an optical effect due to diffraction, and the actual limit is closer to 2 min of arc. This is achieved when the cones are activated, since they are most densely packed in the fovea centralis. Figure 1.20 shows curves of visual acuity at different levels of illumination, with the lower curve pertaining to rod vision and the upper to cone vision, and since acuity is the reciprocal of resolution, it is clear that

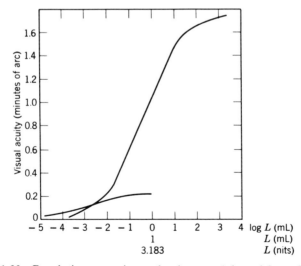

FIGURE 1.20   Resolution or acuity vs. luminance. Adapted from Graham [6].

resolution increases with increasing illumination. This change in acuity is important to remember when specifying resolution and is one example of the interaction among visual parameters.

1.4.2 Brightness

Resolution establishes shape, and we have seen that this is directly affected by the rods and cones found in the retina. The other attributes of the visual image are also affected by the retinal structures. Considering luminance or its retinal equivalent illuminance, which is termed *brightness* as described previously, data are available as to the sensitivities of the rods and cones involved. Rods are about 100 times as sensitive as cones and can respond to as little as 100 quanta of light, where 1 quantum is equal to 3.89×10^{-19} erg. Therefore, the minimum light level to which the visual system will respond is well below any expected level of display luminance. Hence the most significant aspect of the luminance factor is luminance discrimination and, in particular, the minimum amount of luminance change that can be reliably recognized by an observer. This is usually expressed in terms of the ratio of this discriminable amount to the background luminance on which it is superimposed. The curve shown in Figure 1.21 is of this ratio, called the *Weber fraction*, and a small value of this ratio signifies that a small percentage of change in luminance can be recognized. It is clear that brightness discrimination is best at higher levels of luminance, where the cones predominate. The two branches in the curve correspond to the brightness levels at which the rods or cones are active.

Many factors affect the minimum value of the Weber fraction, such as the size, shape, and duration of the varying stimulus, as well as how long the eye

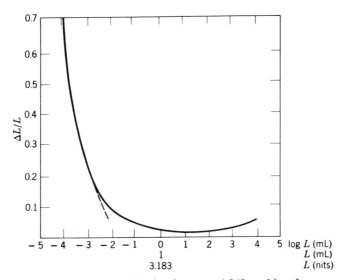

FIGURE 1.21 Relation between $\Delta L/L$ and $\log L$.

has been exposed to the background luminance, or how well adapted it is. This is illustrated in Figure 1.21, which shows that as little as 1% change is discriminable, given the proper conditions for all the variables. From a physiological point of view, the effects of these variables are influenced by the number of cones and rods stimulated and whether the sensitivities have been affected by the amount and duration of the background luminance. For out purposes, if we assume minimum levels of luminance above 7 cd/m^2 (~2 ft-L) and 7 min of arc, the ratio is about 3%, which is the generally accepted minimum value. This is equivalent to a contrast ratio, as defined previously, of 1.03, which is the minimum value possible for this parameter. However, for reliable identification, it is best to use contrast ratios of 8 to 10 or higher, as illustrated in Figure 1.22. Thus the possible range of usable contrast ratios is fairly wide, with the exact minimum value determined by the various factors of image size, luminance, shape, and degree of adaptation. It might also be noted that the physiological basis for brightness discrimination is expressed in terms of the photochemical operation of the retinal elements and the electrophysiology of the visual system. Various models have been developed that give reasonable predictions for minimum detectable levels of luminance and contrast ratio, but the details of these models need not concern us, since we must always turn to data for information about acceptable values of these parameters. However, it is well to understand that when light impinges on the retina it causes a chemical change in the rods and cones, which in turn creates electric impulses that are transmitted to the brain along the optic

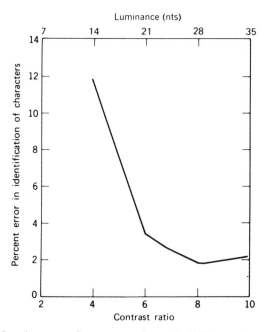

FIGURE 1.22   Luminance and contrast ratio vs. legibility. Adapted from Showman [14].

nerve, where they are transformed by the mysterious processes of the brain into recognition phenomena.

1.4.3 Flicker

Another important aspect of the visual system that is affected by brightness discrimination is flicker. Flicker is evident only when the brightness change is at least large enough to be seen so that higher luminances will generally result in higher CFF values. However, another characteristic of the visual system that must be included is the rate at which the photochemical reactions of the system occur. Several rather complex models and formulations have been derived to explain the various effects of luminance, light–dark duration ratios, and the characteristics of the stimulus wave shape. These theories are useful for conceptual understanding, but we must rely on observational data to arrive at acceptable repetition rates for different sets of conditions. This is because the brain intervenes in such a way as to make the purely physiological formulations inadequate for completely accurate predictions. Some of the predictions from the experimental data are shown in Figures 1.7 to 1.10, and another contributory factor is the response time of the phosphor. These response times as well as the spectral energy distributions for all registered phosphors are given in JEDEC 16, published by EIA [15], and the manufactured phosphors with these numbers are presumed to conform with these curves. There may be considerable variations from these values, but as the curves are the only standard sources available, they must be used.

In addition, the characteristics of the display device have important effects, especially when retentive media such as CRT phosphors are used. This is covered in detail in Chapter 2. However, we may anticipate here by noting that if we assume that a 3% change in luminance is sufficient to produce flicker, an examination of the time it takes a phosphor to decay by 3% should give an important clue as to whether it will flicker when the regeneration rate is slow enough to allow the phosphor to decay by this amount. Figure 1.23 shows one such curve for the P-28 phosphor, and it has a nominal decay time of 600 ms to the 10% level, or about 50 ms to the 90% level. This would correspond to a CFF of approximately 20 Hz, and the effect of the phosphor decay time is quite apparent. At the other extreme is the P-31 phosphor, with a decay time in the microseconds, which has no effect on the CFF, which is strictly a function of the other factors and is dependent on the retentivity of the eye–brain combination.

1.4.4 Color

Color is the last aspect of the physiology of the visual system that we discuss. As stated in Section 1.3.6, it has been established that there are three different types of cones, each sensitive to a different portion of the visible spectrum. It is assumed that each cone type has differing amount of absorption for the different colors, resulting in different electrical impulses when colors are

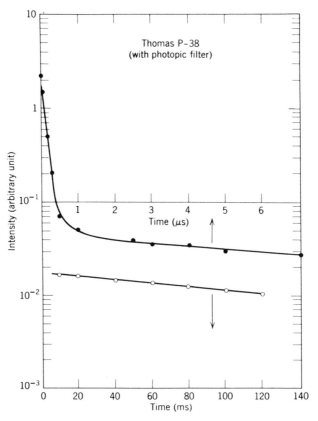

FIGURE 1.23 Phosphor decay characteristics for P-38. After Krupka and Fukui [16], by permission.

viewed. These responses may then be expressed in terms of the tristimulus chromaticity coordinates by

$$R = 661\bar{x} + 1260\bar{y} - 112\bar{z}$$
$$G = -438\bar{x} + 1620\bar{y} + 123\bar{z} \tag{1.24}$$
$$B = 0.708\bar{x} + 417\bar{z}$$

The terms $\bar{x}$, $\bar{y}$, and $\bar{z}$, are related to the chromaticity coordinates x, y, and z by

$$X = \int_0^\alpha S(\lambda)\bar{x} \, d\lambda$$

$$Y = \int_0^\alpha S(\lambda)\bar{y} \, d\lambda \tag{1.25}$$

$$Z = \int_0^\alpha S(\lambda)\bar{z} \, d\lambda$$

and

$$x = \frac{X}{D}$$

$$y = \frac{Y}{D} \qquad (1.26)$$

$$z = \frac{Z}{D}$$

where $(X + Y + Z) = D$, which establ' hes equation 1.16. Equation 1.24 is not the only formulation that has been derived, but it is representative of the forms which these equations take in the attempt to match the data on color vision. In any event, the tristimulus theory seems well grounded in fact, and it is the basis for most attempts to explain the phenomenon of color vision.

A few other points may be made about the usefulness of color as a coding modality. One is that, with the prevalence of color blindness, a significant segment of the population (8%) is limited in the extent to which it can use the information contained in different colors. In addition, studies have indicated that color is not necessarily superior to other means for conveying visual information such as size or shape and thus should not be selected without careful consideration, especially as it may lead to poorer discrimination of these other modalities. In any event, not more than five to seven colors can be reliably recognized when they are used independently, even though many more colors may be identified. Finally, an interesting comment on the common use of red to signify dander is found in studies that have determined that the response to red is more rapid than to other colors.

In summary, color theory and data indicate that it may be used, but in a limited and carefully controlled way for information transfer, other than purely naturalistic presentations and entertainment and esthetic purposes. For the last two, the situation is probably more tendentious and confused than that for straight information, but this is a topic that we leave to others. For our purposes, further discussion of color is found in Chapter 2 in terms of the color CRTs and in Section 4.5. We may note here, in conclusion, that the best colors to use are red, green, yellow, and blue, with white as a possible fifth color, and the absence of any color, or black as the sixth.

1.5   FONTS

The form in which alphanumerics and other symbols are produced is referred to as the *font*. The various techniques for generating characters electronically are covered in Chapters 4 and 5, and we restrict the discussion here to the visual appearance of the characters and the considerations that apply to the various components of the visual image. Electronic displays are rather limited as to the shapes that can readily be generated, and although it is possible to create fonts of typographical quality and to reproduce most of the typefaces used in printing, this requires rather complicated equipment and is used only in very special applications. Therefore, at this point we restrict ourselves to several dot matrix and cursive, or stroke-written fonts and present the relevant information on the best form that these fonts should take.

First let us concern ourselves with the most popular and common format in which alphanumerics are produced, which is the dot matrix format. A basic 5 × 7 matrix is shown in Figure 1.24, and consists of 35 discrete locations in which an illuminated dot may or may not appear. The dots may be large enough to overlap or may appear as discrete elements without seriously affecting the legibility of the display, and both types are used, for example, in CRT or matrix displays. The 35 dots may be used to create a full alphanumeric (A/N) and symbols set, and the character height/dot diameter ratio ranges from 7:1 to 13:1, but to avoid confusion resulting from excessive spacing between dots it is best not to exceed 10:1. Indeed, overlapping or contiguous dots are probably best. This is illustrated in Figure 1.25a for contiguous dots and in Figure 1.25b for approximately 10:1 spacing. In addition, aesthetic considerations, which do affect legibility to some extent, also constrain the ratio to about 7:1 for the 5 × 7 matrix. The height/width ratio of the characters is set for this matrix at 7:5, which is reasonable close to an optimum.

A few other dot matrix formats have been developed that offer some promise in terms of improving the legibility. These are the composite shown in Figure 1.25c, the Lincoln/Mitre shown in Figure 1.25d, and the Huddleston shown in Figure 1.25e, and some improvement in legibility has been achieved by using these fonts. However, the font shown in Figure 1.25a is adequate for the majority of applications. In addition, aesthetic considerations, which do affect legibility to some extent, also constrain the ratio to about 7:1 for 5:7 fonts.

Up to now, only 5:7 fonts have been considered, and they are generally quite adequate for groups of characters presented in a context. However, they do result in some confusion when single characters are shown, and 7 × 9 or 9 × 11 matrices achieve significant improvements. One type of 7 × 9

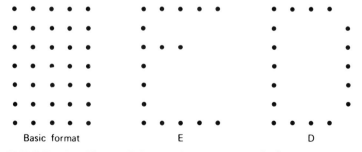

Basic format   E   D

FIGURE 1.24 Five × 7 dot matrix. After Sherr [17], by permission.

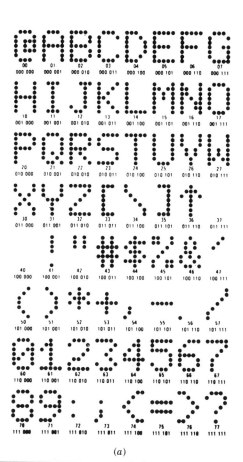

FIGURE 1.25 (*a*) Five × 7 dot matrix font; (*b*) maximum dot font in a 5 × 7 matrix; (*c*) largest readable spacing; (*d*) Lincoln/Mitre 5 × 7 font; (*e*) Huddleston 5 × 7 font. (*a*) From IEE; (*b–e*) from Snyder [18, pp. 200, 69, 210, 195]; by permission.

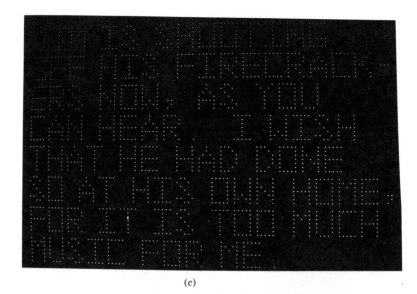

(c)

(d)

FIGURE 1.25 *(Continued)*

(e)

FIGURE 1.25   *(Continued)*

font is shown in Figure 1.26*a*, and Figure 1.26*b* contains the Lincoln/Mitre 7 × 9 font. As an example of the effect of font size, confusion matrices for the 5 × 7 and 7 × 9 Lincoln/Mitre fonts are shown in Tables 1.3 and 1.4, respectively. Some of the most common confusions are shown in Table 1.5, and it should be noted that the 7 × 9 font achieves a considerable reduction, at least for the single-character tests that were used. Other fonts result in different confusion matrices, but as noted previously, the effects on general legibility are small when the characters are viewed in the context of words and sentences. In general, matrices larger than 7 × 9 do not lead to significant improvements, and since these are the most common and least expensive it is reasonable to restrict our choices to these two. This is covered further in Chapters 4 and 5, and Figure 1.27 contains some information as to the relative legibility of the 5 × 7 and 7 × 9 fonts for alphanumerics, with and without overprinting of one symbol on another, and may be used as a basis for selecting matrix size and type of font most suitable for a particular application, always remembering that these data are only as good as the experimental conditions under which they were taken. Thus, if the conditions of luminance and contrast, for example, used in the experiment are not duplicated in the application, the results may be significantly different. Also, if no overprinting is expected, there is little advantage beyond 5 × 7.

Thus far we have considered only dot matrix fonts, but it is also possible to create characters electronically by a proper combination of strokes. The number and type of strokes may vary widely in different character generators. We consider only the most common types, for which the technology is described in Chapters 3 and 5. The simplest one is the "figure 8" or double-hung window, depicted in Figure 1.28, but this structure is limited to numerics and a few alphas (see Figure 1.28) and has as its main, or perhaps only, advantage its extreme simplicity. Its use is generally limited to certain types of numeric displays, such as are in calculators, and is described further in Chapter 5. It operates on the basis of having a fixed set of strokes available and creating only those characters that can be accommodated by those strokes.

(a)

FIGURE 1.26   (a) Seven × 9 dot matrix font; (b) maximum dot 9 × 11 font. (a) From Sherr [19]; (b) from Snyder [18, p. 201]; by permission.

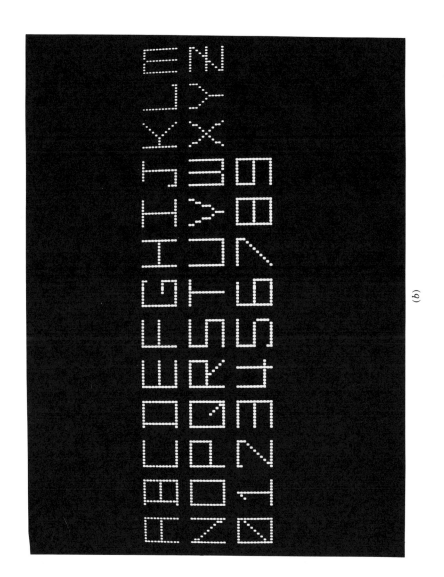

(b)

39

TABLE 1.3 Confusion Matrix for 5 × 7 Lincoln/Mitre Font

S\R	A	B	C	D	E	F	G	H	I	J	K	L	M	N	O	P	Q	R	S	T	U	V	W	X	Y	Z	0	1	2	3	4	5	6	7	8	9	Σ
A																																					10
B																																					11
C																																					3
D																																					1
E																																					6
F																																					2
G																																					3
H																																					4
I																																					38
J																																					3
K																																					0
L																																					6
M																																					4
N																																					15
O																																					6
P																																					10
Q																																			5	30
R																																					—
S																																					23
T																																					4
U																																					1
V																										27												39
W																										25												41
X																																					7
Y																																					6
Z																																					18
0																																				6	30
1																											19											50
2																																					2	29
3																																					7
4																																					6
5																																					6
6																																					3
7																																					7
8																															24							45
9																																						14
Σ	0	5	3	8	3	7	2	3	13	14	7	0	6	5	0	9	7	25	6	29	5	18	16	16	68	46	12	8	30	33	11	10	13	32	6	13	489

TABLE 1.4 Confusion Matrix for 7 × 9 Lincoln/Mitre Font

S\R	A	B	C	D	E	F	G	H	I	J	K	L	M	N	O	P	Q	R	S	T	U	V	W	X	Y	Z	0	1	2	3	4	5	6	7	8	9	Σ
A																								2													3
B																																					0
C						1	6																														8
D																																					1
E																																					0
F					2																																3
G															2		3																				7
H																																					0
I			1					1						2	2		3		3	3				2						1	1	2	3	2			14
J																								1													8
K																																					1
L					2			1																1				1						1			7
M													1																								2
N													1	1												3											2
O																	3	3							3		1										3
P															2																						4
Q																		6																			8
R																										1											2
S																																					0
T																	1	1	1		1				4	1	1	1									6
U																								2													3
V																					1		3	2	18		1					4		2			29
W																																					2
X																																					1
Y																						4			4			5									3
Z																													5								6
0																	1	1	4	4	1	2			7	1		1	1	1	5	1	3	11		2	20
1								3	6	2	2	1						1	4	4			2		7	1							3	11		1	50
2																		1			1		3	2	18	29					5		3	3		2	39
3																									1												0
4																				1	1																3
5																																			1		4
6																																				1	1
7												2				1		1	1	1					2	7		1	1				1	2			11
8																																			1	1	4
9	1																								2	7			1					2		6	2
Σ	1	5	1	3	7	4	8	5	6	2	2	1	2	2	3	3	4	13	8	9	4	4	3	5	36	40	5	3	10	2	7	6	10	26	2	6	257

41

TABLE 1.5   Alphanumeric Confusions

Mutual	One-Way
O and Q	C called G
T and Y	D called E
S and 5	H called M or N
I and L	J, T called I
X and K	K called R
I and 1[a]	2 called Z[a]
	B called R, S, or 8[a]

Source: After Kinney [21], by permission.

[a]These three often comprise 50% or more of the total confusions.

Under the usual conditions of use the font is reasonably legible, although confusion may exist between zero and O, or 8 and B if any attempt is made to include those alphas. However, in the calculator or watch application only numerics are used so that no such confusion exists.

The next stroke font is the 14- or 16-stroke starburst, as shown in Figure 1.29. This font has the same characteristic of fixed strokes as exhibited by the previous one, but considerably expands its capability by increasing the number and positions of the strokes. A full alphanumeric set may be produced using this font, as is shown in Figure 1.30. It can be seen that nothing is gained for an alphanumeric set by using 16 instead of 14 strokes, but the two additional strokes may be advantageous if certain special symbols are required. This font does not bear much resemblance to the printing fonts to which we are accustomed, but although this does detract from its appearance, it does not materially affect its legibility. This font is used in certain types of alphanumeric readouts and in some CRT displays where lower cost makes it preferable to more elaborate stroke-written characters.

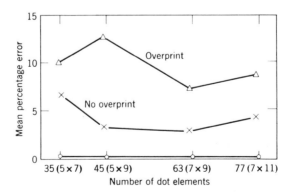

FIGURE 1.27   Accuracy of alphanumeric identification as a function of dot-matrix size. After Shurtleff [22], by permission.

FIGURE 1.28 Seven-segment font.

As a final example of stroke-written fonts, we examine the multistroke characters that provide the closest approximation to print quality, if we except the very elaborate electronic typesetting systems, which go beyond the limits of this discussion. These stroke-written fonts may use from 13 to as many as 30 strokes, with a stroke repertoire of one to five lengths and as many as 40 orientations. One such repertoire is presented in Figure 1.31, with the $\pm x$, $\pm 2x$ and $\pm y$, $\pm 2y$ deflections that are used in combination to create this group. They are customarily used to connect dots in a fixed matrix of perhaps 9×9 and thus bear some resemblance to the dot matrix font. However, instead of the dots being lit, they are connected by a visible stroke and create the characters out of connected lines, thus resembling the fixed stroke characters described previously. However, they differ considerably in appearance from the latter due to the large number of strokes and orientations available and can produce characters that have a pleasing appearance. This is illustrated in Figure 1.32, which is an alphanumeric set made out of a 16-stroke, 24-orientation set and exhibits quite acceptable characteristics of appearance and legibility. The advantage of this type of essentially random stroke format over the fixed stroke formats described previously is clearly demonstrated in Figure 1.33, which shows the large improvements in accuracy attained with the random stroke font. The situation is not quite as clear for dot versus stroke, where the data shown in Figure 1.34 indicate that if similar character fonts are used, either type is equally acceptable. This has particular application to television displays, where stroke characters cannot be generated and where dot matrix equivalents are used, as is discussed further in Chapter 4. There are also several other types of fonts used in special electronic character generators that operate on neither stroke nor dot principle. These generators, termed the *extruded beam types*, are described in detail in Chapter 2. At this point we only state that they are capable of producing very high-quality characters but in general are not applicable to most display systems, or are

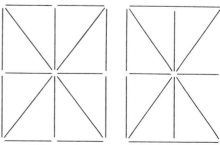

FIGURE 1.29 Starburst patterns.   16 Segments   14 Segments

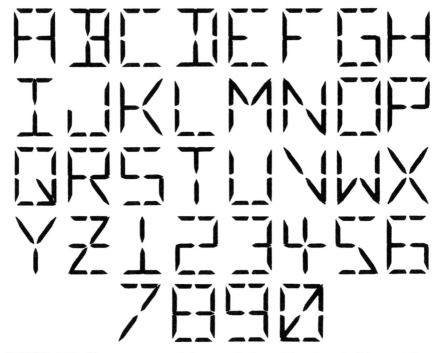

FIGURE 1.30 Sixteen-segment alphanumeric font. After Semple [23, p. 191], by permission.

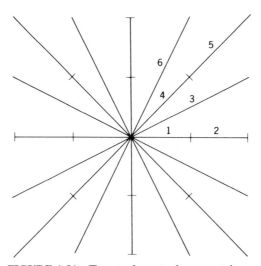

FIGURE 1.31 Twenty-four-stroke repertoire.

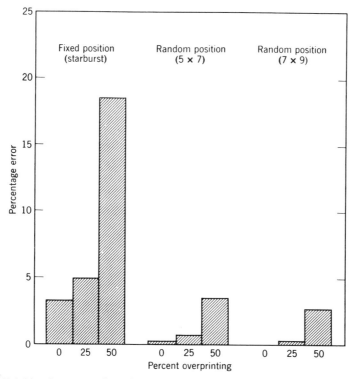

FIGURE 1.32   Twenty-four-stroke alphanumerics.

reduced to the equivalent of dot matrix characters when they are used as character generators for display on a separate CRT. Thus they do not add anything to our discussion of fonts at this point, and we defer further description to Chapter 2.

In summary, various dot matrices and stroke-written formats are used to create fonts acceptable for different types of applications. The simplest dot and stroke formats are usually restricted to numerics, where ambiguity is limited, and the most elaborate stroke formats can produce characters approaching typographical quality. The differences in cost for these various

FIGURE 1.33   Accuracy of symbol identification for fixed vs. random stroke designs. After Shurtleff [20], by permission.

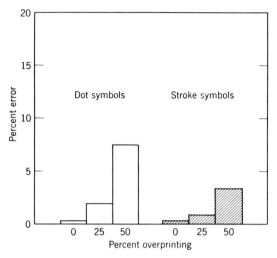

FIGURE 1.34 Accuracy of symbol identification for random stroke vs. dot matrix constructions. After Shurtleff [20], by permission.

formats is one of the determining factors influencing the choice of format, whereas the choice of font is more affected by considerations of legibility, and perhaps aesthetics. Since we all have some response to the quality of the characters, aesthetics should not be completely ignored when selecting a font, but it is of necessity a minor contributor. As to the choice of dot versus stroke, Figure 1.34 demonstrates that for equivalent fonts there is no significant difference in accuracy performance, and the choice hinges on economics and personal prejudice. Since we live in an enlightened age, we must minimize the influence of prejudice, and therefore let us call it taste.

1.6 SPECIFICATIONS

1.6.1 Introduction

Now that we have completed an exhaustive, and no doubt exhausting review of all the major parameters that contribute to the ultimate acceptability of the visual presentation, the question arises as to how we may use this information to ensure obtaining acceptable performance in the actual display system. For this desideratum, it is clearly necessary to prepare a specification that incorporates reasonable values for as many of these parameters as the available data and knowledge of operational conditions will permit. It is the purpose of this section to outline such a procedure and to present examples of representative specifications to get us over the first hurdle in defining the visual characteristics of the display system. Of course, insofar as data are inadequate or ambiguous, it may be desirable to overspecify or to collect the necessary information by actual experiment, and we include some discussion of how such experiments may be performed here and in Chapter 7, as well as how ambiguous data may be adapted so as to be useful. Of course, ultimately the system must be subjected to rigorous testing, once it is obtained, but frequently this may be too late to effect any changes or improvements, so that it is best to be as complete, cautious, and circumspect as circumstances allow. It should always be remembered that the acceptance of a display system is highly dependent on the appearance of the visual presentation, and a bad display will completely dissipate what may be otherwise excellent performance in the total system.

1.6.2 Parameter Set

The parameter set may consist of all of the parameters discussed in this chapter to this point, but in general, for the vast majority of display systems other than the limited numeric types, it is sufficient to limit ourselves to the group listed in Table 1.6. We have not included any of the unified measures of image quality since, as noted previously, they are difficult to use and obtain data on. However, some examples of the use of these is given later, as are a set of parameters and specifications. Most specifically, this parameter set applies to CRT displays and can be extended to include several of the flat panel matrix displays that are currently or may become available in the foreseeable future, as well as the numeric and alphanumeric readouts. Specifications for these are given in Chapters 3 and 5. One major problem that must be considered in arriving at values for these parameters is the interaction among them. This is particularly apparent when we consider resolution and flicker, each of which is greatly affected by the level of contrast ratio and/or luminance used. This interaction is shown in Figures 1.7 and 1.20 for these two parameters, a nd may be combined for legibility as shown in Figure 1.22. It is most convenient to begin with desired resolution using Figure 1.35 and select the other two accordingly. Therefore, first consider those factors affecting resolution, and then proceed to luminance, contrast, and flicker.

1.6.3 Resolution

As noted previously, resolution may be expressed in a variety of ways, but we restrict ourselves to shrinking raster lines, with the other ways and the

TABLE 1.6 Partial List of Visual Parameters

Luminance (photometric brightness)	Size
Brightness	Viewing angle
Resolution	Color
Flicker	Legibility
Contrast/contrast ratio	Jitter (visual)
Luminance levels (shades of gray)	

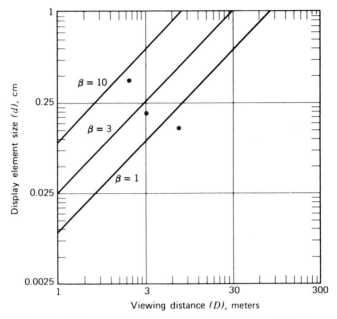

FIGURE 1.35   Resolution vs. viewing distance. After Sherr [17], by permission.

conversion factors for going from one form to any of the others covered in Chapter 7. This applies primarily to CRTs with Gaussian spots, and matrix displays are covered separately next. To arrive at the desired resolution requirement, it is necessary to determine several other factors not yet discussed to any significant extent. One of the most important is the viewing distance for the user. As we can see from Figure 1.35, the image size that will subtend a specified number of minutes of arc (β) at the eye is a direct function of this viewing distance. Therefore, for a given viewing distance of, say, 1 m, and using 2 min of arc as a safe number, the minimum discernible image size is given by

$$S_i = d = \frac{4\pi}{360 \times 60}$$

or

$$S_i = 0.00058 \text{ m}$$

using the general relationship

$$d = \frac{2\pi D\beta}{360 \times 60} \qquad (1.27)$$

where β represents the minutes of arc.

The actual number of shrinking raster lines then depends on the size of the display surface. The manner in which this size is determined is covered later, but if we assume a size of 1 m, the specification becomes 1/0.00058, or 1724 raster lines. Since this number is unreasonably high for most systems, as discussed further in Chapter 4, we must either reduce the display size or accept less than maximum resolution. Thus if we halve the display size and use 3 min of arc, the number of lines becomes 287, which is too low; or for 2 min of arc, it is 862, which may be just right. In any event, by this type of trade-off, which may include the viewing distance as well, we arrive at a resolution number that is reasonable in terms of what available or economically feasible systems allow. Most frequently, other constraints, such as the number of scanning lines in a television system, are the determining factors, and it is necessary to adjust the other elements to conform. The process is the same, except that we begin with the reality rather than the ideal. Since standard television uses 525 television lines, of which 480 are visible, and, to anticipate the discussion in Chapter 7, since shrinking raster gives about half that number, according to Table 7.4, we are faced with a practical limit of about 250 lines, not too far from our discarded low number. Such are the exigencies forced on us by harsh realities. However, this limitation may only be in the vertical direction, and another limit may be set for the horizontal resolution, controlled by amplifier bandwidth and CRT spot size. The conclusion to be drawn from all this is that we may set the resolution requirements to achieve a desired minimum discernible data element, but achieving it in the display system involves consideration of a number of additional factors and constraints.

Once we have established what the desired minimum element size is, we must go beyond the factors discussed previously and determine what the minimum values of luminance/contrast ratio are to permit this resolution to be visually attainable. For this we may use the data in Figure 1.22 and the additional data contained in Figure 1.36. From these data we see that for a resolution of 1 min or arc and a 50% probability of detection we require a minimum luminance of 2 nits at a contrast ratio of 2, which is well below what most displays provide. Therefore, the minimum level of display luminance required is controlled by other considerations, as is shown later. Further, for 100% detectability, Figure 1.37 shows that although 1 min of arc is detectable, we should double it to increase the probability to the higher value.

This becomes more significant if we are concerned with symbol identification, as is shown in Figure 1.22, where luminance levels of 25 nits and contrast ratios of at least 8 are indicated for reliable identification. This is discussed more fully later, but at this point we may conclude that for a resolution of 2 min of arc we may operate at a low level of luminance and contrast when 50% detection of the presence of a data point is involved. However, for the more difficult case of having to accurately identify a character or other object, much higher values are required of these parameters. As a further point, when we are dealing with matrix displays, which consist

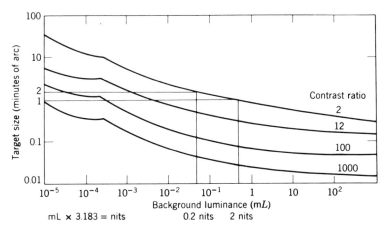

FIGURE 1.36 Relationship among target size, background luminance, and contrast ratio for 50% probability of detection. Adapted from Snyder [24].

of a fixed number of points, the resolution requirement may be used to specify the number of points in the horizontal and vertical directions. If the point size is chosen to provide 2 min of arc at the viewing distance, then the display size may be determined from the total number of points needed for the entire display. Here again, the special requirements imposed by characters must be considered, as are discussed later. Otherwise, the matrix display and the CRT display may be treated similarly, with the realization that for the matrix display the point spacing defines the resolution, unless there is overlap in the luminance profile of the points. If such overlap exists, it is possible that the actual resolution will be less than the point size.

1.6.4 Luminance

We have noted that the minimum luminance required for resolution of 2 min of arc is well below that available from most displays. Therefore, we must

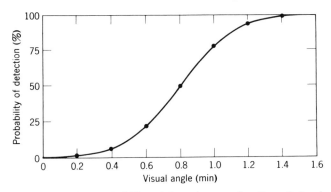

FIGURE 1.37 Cumulative probability of detection as a function of visual angle. After Blackwell [25], by permission.

examine other factors in arriving at a reasonable level of luminance for a given application. In particular, Figure 1.22 shows that at least 28 nits are necessary to get beyond the descending recognition curve. This demonstrates clearly that for any task beyond the limited one of deciding whether a data point is present, we must use considerably higher levels of luminance than previously indicated. In addition, the two factors of surround illumination and contrast ratio are very important. It is generally agreed that the surround luminance should not be more than a factor of 2 larger than the display luminance, so as to expedite eye adaptation. This means that the visual system should not be required to encounter large changes in luminance as it moves from the display to the surrounding environment, both to reduce fatigue and to maintain constant eye adaptation. Since eye adaptation has a major effect on the contrast ratio required for best acuity, as demonstrated in Figure 1.38, it is important to have it controlled primarily by the display luminance so as to have a predictable result. Therefore, if the application is in a location with a high level of illumination, it may be necessary to have a corresponding high level of display luminance or else to reduce the effect of the ambient illumination by means of shades and filters. This is another example of the close interaction among the various factors involved in specifying a display. As a result, in well-lit areas, which may have as high as 500 lux, a display luminance of 300 nits may be necessary.

Ambient illumination also has another effect, in that it may be reflected from the display surface and thus influence the contrast ratio. Although it is possible to reduce this effect by means of filters and hoods, this approach may not always be possible, or else the level of ambient illumination may be so high that it is not possible to reduce it sufficiently to operate with low display luminance. For example, direct sunlight may be as high as 100,000 lux which, if directly reflected from the display surface, creates a condition

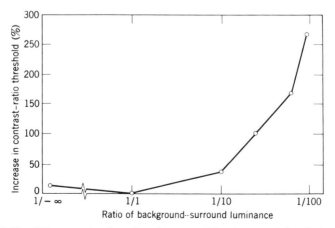

FIGURE 1.38   Effect on visual acuity of surround luminance. After Ireland [26], by permission.

that is impossible to correct by only increasing the display luminance. Even the much lower illumination of a well-lit room may create the equivalent of 50 nits reflected from the display surface, and a minimum contrast ratio of 3 will require 100 nits from the display, which is attainable. However, if we want to increase the contrast ratio to the more acceptable value of 8, then we are up to 350 nits, which is not easy to achieve, particularly from matrix displays. The actual levels of luminance that may reasonably be expected from different types of display devices are covered in Chapters 2 and 3, but, we may state here that luminances higher than 300 nits are not easy to achieve, and neglecting the effect of ambient illumination, may be destructive to the efficacy of the display system.

1.6.5   Contrast Ratio

Contrast ratio has been referred to several times previously in the context of its effect on resolution and luminance requirements. Here we restrict the discussion to contrast ratio alone, assuming that we can meet the luminance and resolution criteria previously presented. A minimum contrast ratio of 2 and a luminance of 2 nits are used in Section 1.6.3. However, if we reexamine Figure 1.36, we see that for 2 min of arc, a contrast ratio of 2 and a luminance of 0.2 nit are sufficient. This further illustrates the interaction among these three parameters. But for most applications the curve shown in Figure 1.22 is more useful, since more than perception of a target point is usually necessary. We are primarily interested in accuracy of identification of characters, and for this we may examine the data shown in Figure 1.39 and Tables 1.7 and 1.8, where we see that for over 95% correct identification we require characters to subtend over 16 min of visual angle at a contrast ratio of over 10 with no blur, where blur is as defined in Figure 1.39. This corresponds to the data given in Figures 1.22 and 1.36 and establishes both the angular resolution and contrast ratio required for accurate identification. Further data on character size are given in Section 1.6.6.

At this point we have arrived at a range of contrast ratios required for both data point identification and character recognition. Armed with these data, we may proceed to an examination of the requirements for reliable character identification and conclude this section with a few comments on the significance of contrast ratio. First, we see that a range of 5 to 1 is involved in going from minimum data point recognition to reliable character identification and that contrast ratios over 10 offer little advantage in system performance. Finally, we should stress that adequate contrast ratios are of great importance in achieving desired performance and should not be reduced merely because higher luminance levels are attained. Thus they are truly minimum values, once the luminance levels are high enough to ensure proper visual images, and cannot be traded away against increased luminance. There is some trade-off against increased visual angle, but this is marginal once the minimum values for point and character identification have been reached.

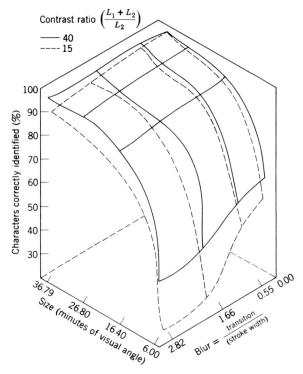

FIGURE 1.39   Percent of characters correctly identified as a function of size, blur, and contrast ratio of letters and numbers. After Howell and Kraft [27], by permission.

Thus, whereas not all data are in complete conformance for marginal performance, once we wish to achieve reliable performance we do not have a great deal of latitude in selecting the proper specification for this parameter.

1.6.6   Character Requirements

We have already established some of the requirements for reliable character identification. In this section we present additional information that allows us to specify fully all the characteristics that effect the quality and legibility of character sets. These include the number of dots in a dot matrix font, the stroke width/character height ratio for stroke-written characters, and some special fonts to minimize some of the confusion that exists in recognition of certain characters. All of these attributes influence accuracy of identification and must be considered when a display is specified from the visual point of view. We also present additional data on comparisons between stroke-written and dot matrix– or raster-written characters. These data should make possible reasonable choices among the various techniques and fonts for particular applications. Finally, we summarize the relevant information on the other visual parameters, as they relate to character identification, and given an

TABLE 1.7   Mean Scores on Oral Reading Task with Capital Letters

Visual Angle (minutes of arc)	Contrast Ratio	Stroke Width (percent of symbol height)	Spacing (percent of symbol height)	Accuracy of Identification (percent correct)	Rate of Identification (symbols per second)
22.0	15	9.8	35.6	99.7	3.2
			63.2	99.6	3.1
		20.1	35.6	99.8	3.2
			63.2	99.6	3.3
		30.0	35.6	98.8	3.1
			63.2	99.0	3.2
	10	9.8	35.6	99.2	2.8
			63.2	99.0	2.7
		20.1	35.6	99.4	3.1
			63.2	99.8	3.1
		30.0	35.6	99.1	3.0
			63.2	98.8	2.9
	5	9.8	35.6	94.7	1.7
			63.2	95.9	1.7
		20.1	35.6	99.1	2.8
			63.2	98.5	2.7
		30.0	35.6	95.8	2.3
			63.2	95.6	2.2
16.0	15	9.8	35.6	98.8	2.7
			63.2	98.9	2.8
		20.1	35.6	99.4	3.1
			63.2	99.7	3.1
		30.0	35.6	97.3	2.7
			63.2	97.9	2.7
	10	9.8	35.6	97.3	2.2
			63.2	97.0	2.3
		20.1	35.6	99.1	2.8
			63.2	98.8	2.7
		30.0	35.6	96.7	2.6
			63.2	96.1	2.4
	5	9.8	35.6	80.6	0.8
			63.2	78.2	0.9
		20.1	35.6	95.3	2.1
			63.2	95.3	2.1
		30.0	35.6	88.8	1.8
			63.2	87.5	1.6
11.0	15	9.8	35.6	94.0	1.7
			63.2	91.8	1.7
		20.1	35.6	96.7	2.3
			63.2	94.9	2.3
		30.0	35.6	89.8	1.9
			63.2	90.2	1.8

TABLE 1.7   *(Continued)*

Visual Angle (minutes of arc)	Contrast Ratio	Stroke Width (percent of symbol height)	Spacing (percent of symbol height)	Accuracy of Identification (percent correct)	Rate of Identification (symbols per second)
11.0	10	9.8	35.6	81.1	0.9
			63.2	78.0	1.1
		20.1	35.6	93.7	1.8
			63.2	89.4	1.7
		30.0	35.6	86.8	1.6
			63.2	84.3	1.4
	5	9.8	35.6	62.7	0.2
			63.2	53.9	0.3
		20.1	35.6	75.9	0.8
			63.2	68.0	0.9
		30.0	35.6	65.8	0.8
			63.2	58.3	0.8

Source: After Semple [23], by permission.

example of a specification which might be used for defining these requirements.

A first consideration is the size of the character, expressed in terms of the visual angle subtended at the eye. We have stated previously that at least 16 min of arc should be used, and we may expand this claim with the curves shown in Figure 1.40, plotted in terms of another parameter—lines per symbol height—which applies specifically to raster displays. However, these curves all demonstrate that the percentage of correct identification begins to level off at 14 to 16 min of arc and, therefore, substantiate the claim that at least 16 min of arc should be used for reliable identification. Figure 1.39 led us to the same conclusion, but Figure 1.40 adds the other factor of lines per symbol height, introducing the question of matrix size. This is illustrated in Figure 1.41 and in Figure 1.18, which show that there is little difference in percent correct identification between a 5 × 7 and a 7 × 11 matrix, and indeed that even 6 min of arc will give a high percentage of correct identifications. However, if we include speed of identification, as is done in Figure 1.42, we see significant differences between 6 and 22 min of arc, and since we do not have unlimited time in most applications, the reason for the choice of the larger angle becomes clear. It is interesting that if we halve the difference between 6 and 22 and add it to 6, get 14. Considerable data have been accumulated on this question, and we may accept these conclusions as well verified. When we couple them with the previously established requirements for contrast ratios of about 10 and luminances of about 30 nits, we have the beginning of a good objective specification for the characters.

The question of scan lines per character height has been introduced without explanation, and it is appropriate at this point to discuss it further. It is

TABLE 1.8   Accuracy and Rate of Symbol Identification for Howell–Kraft Study

Visual Angle (minutes of arc)	Blur	Contrast Ratio	Percentage Correct	Symbols per Second
36.8	2.82	40	95.4	1.26
		15	88.8	1.20
	1.66	40	96.9	1.31
		15	94.7	1.24
	0.55	40	97.3	1.36
		15	96.7	1.29
	0.00	40	98.0	1.34
		15	97.9	1.30
26.8	2.82	40	96.4	1.27
		15	93.6	1.21
	1.66	40	97.7	1.34
		15	96.4	1.22
	0.55	40	97.9	1.36
		15	97.3	1.31
	0.00	40	98.3	1.34
		15	97.3	1.32
16.4	2.82	40	94.2	1.16
		15	87.4	1.03
	1.66	40	96.9	1.30
		15	93.0	1.10
	0.55	40	96.8	1.28
		15	96.3	1.21
	0.00	40	97.6	1.29
		15	96.3	1.26
6.0	2.82	40	47.0	0.70
		15	23.2	0.66
	1.66	40	48.3	0.72
		15	30.0	0.66
	0.55	40	57.7	0.82
		15	48.3	0.66
	0.00	40	65.3	0.78
		15	50.8	0.65

Source: After Semple [23, p. 166], by permission.

basically associated with raster scan or dot-matrix characters, covered in Chapters 4 and 5 from a technological point of view. At this juncture we merely present the appearance of characters made up from scan lines (Figure 1.43) and do not get involved in describing how the characters are produced. We can see from Figure 1.43 that a character made up of a group of scan lines is very similar in appearance to the dot matrix character, and we may expect the same considerations to apply, as indeed they do. Figure 1.44 clearly demonstrates this, with the preferred number of lines per symbol height lying between 7 and 11, and having 10 as the optimum number. Of course, the

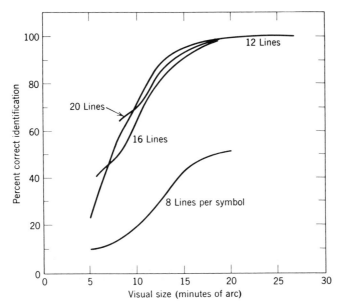

FIGURE 1.40 Accuracy of identification as a function of visual size and symbol resolution. After Shurtleff [28], by permission.

other criterion of 16 min of arc still applies, as do the values for contrast ratio and luminance.

We may now proceed to stroke-written characters. Several of the parameters adduced previously, such as angular subtense, contrast ratio, and luminance still apply, but several new ones must be added. These are: whether a fixed or random position stroke format is used, the number of strokes in

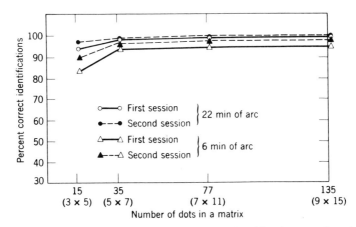

FIGURE 1.41 Accuracy of alphanumeric symbol identification as a function of dot matrix size. After Shurtleff [20], by permission.

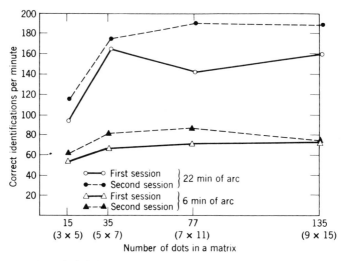

FIGURE 1.42   Speed of alphanumeric symbol identification as a function of dot matrix size. After Shurtleff [20], by permission.

the random position format or the size of the matrix in which the strokes are developed, the height/width ratio, and the height/line-width ratio. As noted previously, the fixed-position stroke formats are limited in the fonts that can be achieved and, especially in the case of the double-hung window, in the characters that can be produced. Thus whereas the double-hung window does provide a numeric font that has found considerable acceptance in numeric readouts, its application is very limited, and it is not considered further here. The case of the 14- or 16-segment fixed stroke is different, in that a full alphanumeric set may be produced, and it is used for certain readouts, such

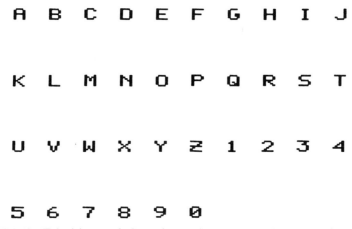

FIGURE 1.43   Television symbols made up of rectangular elements. After Shurtleff [20], by permission.

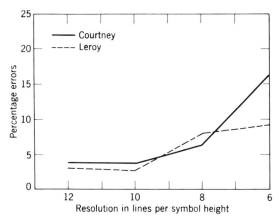

FIGURE 1.44   Relationship of identification accuracy and number of television scan lines. After Shurtleff [20], by permission.

as those made with liquid-crystal cells or LEDs covered further in Chapter 3. At this point we compared the legibility of this type of character generation format with the more flexible random-position stroke-written formats. Figure 1.45 gives an example of the letter B written in the 14- and 16-segment fixed-stroke format, and in a 5 × 7 and a 9 × 9 random-position stroke format, whereas Figure 1.46 shows a full alphanumeric set in three formats; using the high-legibility font known as the *Lincoln/Mitre font*. On the whole, the fixed-stroke format does not appear to be too unacceptable, but when we examine the error data given in Figure 1.33 we see that it is far inferior to the random position formats, although the improvement in going from a 5 × 7 to a 9 × 9 matrix is not too significant. The same situation holds for speed of identification, as shown in Figure 1.47, although here the advantage of the 9 × 9 is more significant. We may therefore conclude that for certain not too demanding applications the fixed stroke format is usable, but that for most purposes one of the random stroke formats is preferable.

The next question is whether there is any important difference in accuracy or speed of identification between dot matrix–written characters and random-

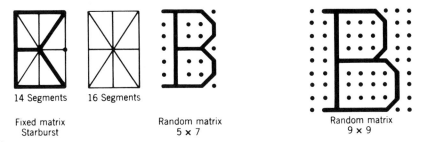

FIGURE 1.45   Illustration of symbol construction by fixed versus random strokes. After Shurtleff [20], by permission.

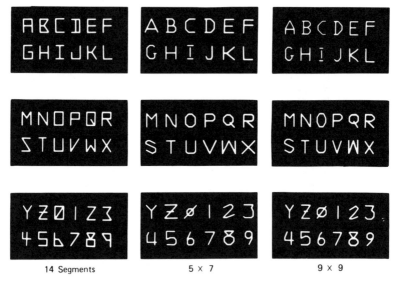

FIGURE 1.46 Lincoln/Mitre font in fixed and random stroke designs. After Shurtleff [20], by permission.

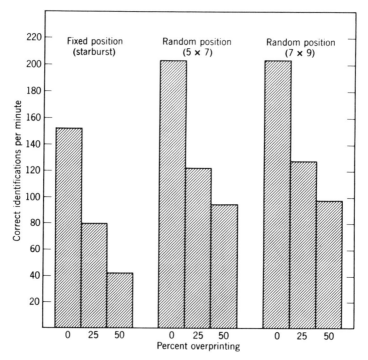

FIGURE 1.47 Speed of symbol identification for fixed vs. random stroke designs. After Shurtleff [20], by permission.

position stroke-written formats. The relevant data are shown in Figures 1.36 and 1.48. It is clear that when a 7 × 11 dot matrix is compared with a 9 × 9 random-position stroke format there is no difference, and the choice is purely a matter of aesthetics and economics. This information is very important, since frequently the choice of one particular format affects the design of the entire system. For example, if a random-position stroke format is chosen, then a raster system is not possible, thus limiting the choice to one of the various random-position vector systems available, usually at some increase in cost. However, the vector systems may have other advantages and capabilities, such as higher resolution, so that these factors must be considered as well when the choice is made. The discussion has been limited to character presentations up to this point, and the data presented are to be used only for this type of display, although they are relevant to symbols other than alphanumerics. The last features of character fonts we must consider are the preferred character height/stroke width ratio and the acceptable range of character height/width. These are generally established once we chose the dot matrix or random stroke matrix, by the format, and in the cases we have considered, lead to height/stroke width ratios of 7:1 to 9:1. Any ratio larger than 10:1 is not satisfactory, and it is generally better to use the thickest possible line. Character height/width ratios are similarly constrained to 7:5 or 9:7. Although the data are not too clear, they indicate that there is little difference in results achieved with ratios ranging from 2:1 to 1:1, and about 3:2 is a satisfactory choice. For stroke width/character height we may use the data given in Table 1.7, which lead to a range of 5:1 to 8:1 for this characteristic. Again, aesthetics and economics establish the major constraints.

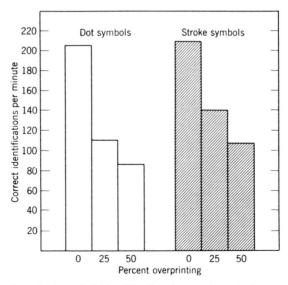

FIGURE 1.48   Speed of symbol identification for random stroke vs. dot matrix construction. After Shurtleff [20], by permission.

1.6.7   Color

We have noted previously that color is only one of several possible means for presenting information, and not, despite subjective opinions, obviously better than the others. Thus the choice of multicolors as one of the attributes of a specific display system may become a matter of economics and aesthetics. Of course, if multicolors are required to obtain realistic presentations, as in television, other criteria apply and the number of colors will be defined by the applicable standards. However, for the majority of information display applications, a fairly small number of colors will suffice. It is usually not necessary to supply more than eight, with 16 a common maximum, as in the EGA standard. Indeed, human factors research has shown that the meanings attributed to more than five colors are difficult for most users to remember, and more than eight colors will require special training. Of course, modern systems supply many more colors, but their primary use is for television, presentation graphics, and slide making.

Once color has been selected as an information modality, the question arises as to which colors are best suited to this application. Here uncertainty arises, as evidenced by the data shown in Figure 1.49 and Table 1.9, although there is general agreement on all colors. In any event, all of the colors may be used in information displays, although red and yellow are best, and blue and green are worst.

We may therefore conclude that the decision on whether to use color in a display system is affected by many factors, not all of them easily quantified, and that considerable care should go into the decision and the choice of both the number and types of hues to be used. However, if the criteria given are adhered to, it appears safe to include color as one of the attributes of the

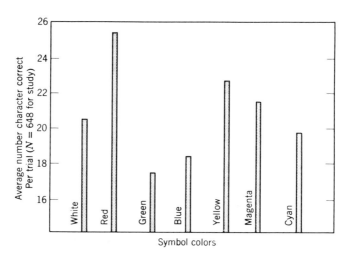

FIGURE 1.49   Subject performance for symbol colors averaged over all conditions. From Semple [23, p. 191], after Rizy [29, p. 120].

TABLE 1.9   Relative Ranking of Different Colors in A/N Recognition Studies[a]

Color	Meister and Sullivan [30]	Rizy [31]
Red	2	1
Yellow	1	2
Magenta	4	3
White	3	4
Cyan	5	5
Blue	7	6
Green	6	7

Source: After Salvedy [22], by permission.

[a]Lower ranking indicates better performance.

display, which at the very least adds visual interest to what is usually a pretty drab and colorless result.

1.6.8   Linearity

We have not had any discussion of linearity up to this point, not because it is not important, but because it does not easily fit into the various visual categories we have used. In addition, there are very few hard data about the effect of nonlinearities on the apparent quality or legibility of a display. A corollary to linearity is pattern distortion, for which again we have few data. Linearity may be defined as the deviation of a straight line from its exact form, expressed as a percentage of the total length of the line, whereas pattern distortion is the deviation of any element of a pattern, such as a grid from its exact location, expressed as a percentage of the dimensions of the total pattern. These are illustrated in Figures 7.25 and 7.26, and the test methods are given in Section 7.3.6. Although we cannot give any firm limits, it appears safe to say that if this type of distortion does not exceed the resolution capability of the visual system, it will not be noticeable, and even larger deviations are frequently acceptable, with entertainment television as a case in point. However, for graphic displays linearity and pattern distortion are very significant and should be kept to a minimum.

1.6.9   Size

There are two aspects of size to be considered in preparing a specification. One is the minimum size of the data point, or the character, and the other is the total size of the display viewing surface. The first is determined by the combination of the required visual angle and the viewing distance, and the second is controlled by the data point or character size and the total amount of information to be presented on the viewing surface. We have already established the minimum visual angles as 2 min of arc for data points and 14 to 16 min of arc for characters.

Starting with the minimum visual angle, we may rewrite equation 1.27 as

$$d_p = 0.00058D \tag{1.28}$$

for a 2 min of arc data point, and

$$d_c = 0.004D \tag{1.29}$$

for a 14 min of arc character and use them to establish the size of the data point or character once we have established the maximum viewing distance. For example, at a viewing distance of 0.5 m, which is common for CRT displays, d_p is 0.00029 m, and d_c, 0.002 m. Such are the wonders of simple arithmetic. If we wish to chose other numbers for the subtended angle, then, of course, other numbers for data point and character size will result, but we leave this difficult exercise to the students among our readers. Armed with these equations and numbers, we may now arrive at another important feature of the display, namely, the size of the usable display surface. First, however, we must establish the number of data points or the characters that we wish to display, or that are capable of being displayed. Therefore, if we wish the data points to appear in a 1000 × 1000 matrix, the display viewing surface size must be 0.29 by 0.29 m for a 0.5-m viewing distance. Characters involve a few more factors, since we must consider the height/width ratio, and the horizontal and vertical spacings between characters and lines of characters. We have not yet discussed this aspect of a character presentation, and we introduce it here by stating (as is demonstrated by Table 1.7) that spacings between about 35 and 65% of character height are acceptable, and that a common number is 25%, since this corresponds to approximately 2 dots in a 5 × 7 dot matrix. Then if we use a 3:2 height/width ratio, the character space is within a $1.25C_h \times 0.91C_h$ rectangle, where C_h is the character height. The number of characters in a selected viewing area is then given by

$$N_c = \frac{A_v}{1.14C_h} \tag{1.30}$$

where N_c is the number of characters and Av is the viewing area.

Similarly, the number of characters on a line is given by

$$L_c = \frac{L_l}{0.91C_h} \tag{1.31}$$

where L_c is the number of characters in a line and L_l is the line length, and the number of character lines is given by

$$C_1 = \frac{H_d}{1.25C_h} \tag{1.32}$$

where C_1 is the number of character lines and H_d is the display viewing surface height.

We may readily determine that for a display to show 24 lines of 80 characters a line, at a viewing distance of 0.5 m, the display viewing surface dimensions must be 0.91 m × 0.002 m × 80 m or 0.1456 m wide, and 1.24 m × 0.002 m × 24 m or 0.05952 m high. This is by no means an optimum viewing dimension, for a number of reasons, having to do with angle of view, as is covered later, and the usual dimensions of viewing surfaces, which tend to follow the 4:3 width/height ratio used in television displays. Therefore, it may be desirable to alter the number of lines or the number of characters in a line to achieve more favorable viewing surface dimensions. However, the dimensions just calculated meet all other requirements for legibility and could be used if desired. Or we may plot a range of viewing distances for different subtended angles, using equation 1.27 and choose any combination we prefer. Again, equations 1.31 and 1.32 will give us the line length and number of lines, thus leading to the selection of the display surface size.

1.6.10   Viewing Angle

The viewing angle has not been discussed thus far since it was necessary to establish the contribution of the various other factors before we could examine this one. Viewing angle is the angular relationship, in degrees, between the normal to the viewing surface on the line between the viewing surface and the observer's visual axis, and the line between the visual axis and the point being viewed. As we may conclude from our knowledge that maximum resolution is obtained when the image is on the fovea, the best resolution is obtained when the observer is viewing data on the line normal to the surface and on the visual axis. Figure 1.50 shows the drop-off in visual acuity at different angles from this direct line, and we may conclude from it that for anything outside of a 10° cone, or 5° in any direction from the center of the foveal region, the drop-off in visual acuity is so large that the region outside of that cone cannot be used. However, Figure 1.51 does show that if the visual angle is greater than 30 min of arc, a 30° viewing angle is acceptable. In addition, head movements of ±15° in the horizontal and ±10° in the vertical are quite reasonable, so that we may assume viewing angles of this size as acceptable. Another factor influencing the angle of view is the fact that there may be a decrease in the illumination from a viewing surface as a function of the angle of view. For a perfect diffuser, this is expressed by

$$E = E_m \cos^4 \theta \qquad (1.33)$$

where E_m is the illuminance at center and θ is the angle between normal and viewer line to center.

If we wish to restrict the variation to less than 10%, the θ is 15°, thus giving the same angle of view arrived at by acuity consideration. However, this angle

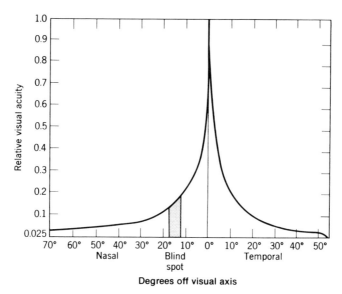

FIGURE 1.50   Relative visual acuity at different angles from the fovea for photopic vision. From Semple [23, p. 191], adapted from Wulfeck [32, p. 294].

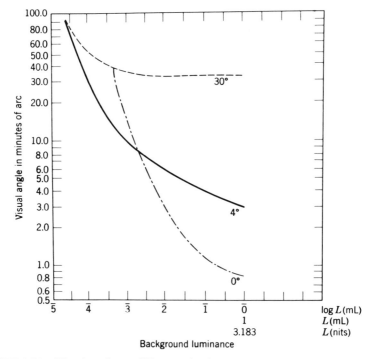

FIGURE 1.51   Visual acuity at different viewing angles away from the visual axis as a function of background luminance. After Wulfeck [32, p. 296], by permission.

applies to a different viewing condition, since here the viewer is located at an angle, whereas in the preceding case the data are at an angle with the viewer line of sight. The latter usually applies to group viewing, where reflective screens are used, and the light falloff at this angle meets the stated conditions. In either case there are definite restrictions in the maximum angle of view that may be used if proper recognition of data is to be achieved.

1.7   SPECIFICATION EXAMPLE

1.7.1   Introduction

We may now put together all of the information that has been presented on the various parameter requirements and produce a specification for those aspects of the display system that are measurable at the display and affect the legibility of the visual image. To do this, we must first establish those operational conditions that have a direct impact on the choice of specific values for the parameters. These conditions are the viewing distance, the ambient or surround illumination, and the illumination that will impinge directly on the display surface. We may also wish to set the angle of view for observers not directly in front of the display surface, but in this specification we assume a single viewer who is placed directly in front of the center line of the display surface. We may now refer to the parameter set shown in Table 1.6, and go through the calculations necessary to arrive at the objective values required to ensure adequate visual performance.

Let us assume a viewing distance of 1 m, an ambient illumination of 500 lux, and an illumination at the viewing surface of 300 lux. These are not uncommon conditions for a reasonably well-lit room, and viewer location, relative to the display surface, so that our specification will be a realistic one. We may further assume that the viewing surface has a reflectivity of 50% usually encountered when CRT phosphors are involved. We will probably find it necessary to introduce contrast enhancement filters to achieve the necessary contrast ratios, but we do not discuss this further when we deal with this parameter. So, armed with a light meter and an educated eye, we begin our task.

1.7.2   Resolution

We chose resolution as the first parameter to be specified, since it is basic to the performance of the display system and has a direct impact on the other parameters. We assume our display to consist of both characters and data points, so that resolution requirements for both types of presentations must be included. To allow for a conservative estimate of the acuity of the expected observers, the minimum subtended angle for a data point is set at 3 min of arc. This results in a data-point size of 0.00087 m, which we may round off to 1 mm. We are similarly conservative in character resolution, and use 30 min of arc, so as to use wide viewing angles without significant loss in legibility. We may find it necessary to change some of these values later to allow reasonable sizes for characters and display surface, but for the moment we use these numbers. We also convert these resolution numbers into shrinking raster lines to be compatible with our chosen method of measurement for a CRT display. However, we cannot do this too readily now, since we prefer to express it in terms of the total number of lines in the display, which cannot be done until we know the display size. We can state at this point that it is 10 lines per centimeter, while the character size is 10 mm.

1.7.3   Contrast Ratio

Contrast ratio comes before luminance, because it will affect the amount of luminance required, depending on the extent of the actual reflected luminance due to the ambient illumination impinging on the display surface. We might manage with a contrast ratio of 3 for the data points, but to ensure high accuracy in character recognition, we use the figure given by the curves in Figures 1.22 and 1.39 and use a contrast ratio of 10. It will be possible to lower this somewhat if the luminance requirement is too large as a result.

1.7.4   Luminance

As we have noted, the required contrast ratio and the reflected ambient illumination will determine the amount of luminance required, to which we must also add the size of the display surface. Since we cannot determine the size of the display surface until we establish the amount and format of the data to be presented, it is perhaps somewhat premature to attempt to see the luminance level at this point. However, we make the attempt, in the interest of maintaining the same sequence of parameters as before, and assume a display size of 0.5 × 0.5 m for this purpose, which is not an unreasonable size to begin with.

Referring back to our expected illumination, we have specified that there will be 300 lux at the viewing surface and a reflectivity of 50%. Since 300 lux is 300 lm/m² and the area of the display surface is 0.25 m², then, with a reflectivity of 50%, the reflected flux density will be 37.5 lm/m². Referring to equation 1.5, we see that the luminance is 37.5 × (1/π) cd/m², or about 12 nits. Therefore, for a contrast ratio of 10 we require a display luminance of 108 nits, which is a very reasonable value of luminance. As a result, we seem to be in good shape, except that there is another factor to be considered, namely, the ratio of display luminance:surround luminance. We have stated that for best acuity this ratio should not exceed 2, and we may substantiate this by referring to Figure 1.29, which demonstrates that a large increase in contrast ratio is required to maintain resolution if we depart from this criterion. Unfortunately, it is difficult to establish the probable surround luminance, without making direct measurements of the operational area, but if we assume that the same conditions apply as for the display surface, then the display luminance requirement becomes only 24 nits. Clearly, we cannot meet both requirements, and we may need to compromise on contrast ratio or increase the surround luminance by some means, without adversely affecting the contrast ratio. No doubt we will have to do both finally, but for now let us reduce the contrast ratio to 8, resulting in a requirement for 84 nits from the display surface, and somehow increase the surround luminance to 30 so that the ratio of surround luminance:display luminance is less than 3. This is not completely satisfactory, but very little is in this difficult world. In any event, we have arrived at a value for display luminance and have not reduced the contrast ratio below an acceptable level. Incidentally, we should point out that we have adjusted the levels so that eye adaptation to all levels of luminance encountered in the various viewing conditions, that is, surround, background, and display, will remain within acceptable limits. Of course, the conditions we have imposed have not been very difficult to meet, and it would be much more of a problem if very high levels of ambient illumination were involved. We leave that as an exercise for the reader.

1.7.5 Character Requirements

We have already established a character size of 10 mm, so that all that remains is to select the format and font. Since dot matrix characters are easier to produce, as is shown in Chapters 4 and 5, we opt for a dot matrix character set, and to ensure high legibility, we use a 9×7 matrix. Other choices are possible, of course, even with the same overall requirements, but the mechanism of making this choice can become so involved that it will do us little good to attempt it here. One can merely consult the various relevant data and then make the choice on economic and aesthetic grounds. In addition, since most character generators have a preset font, we are not free to chose any special font, such as the Lincoln/Mitre font, which might be desirable to achieve maximum legibility. However, we can usually do well enough for most purposes with standard fonts and character generators, so we stay with this simplified approach. As has been pointed out, the 7×9 font does meet most of the criteria for height/width and height/line width, so that this choice will not detract excessively from the performance of the display system.

1.7.6 Color

Here the first reaction is to throw up one's hands and let someone else make the decision. But we will be brave and attack even this controversial topic. Of course, we have established several criteria, once the decision has been made, so that if we assume that it is made based on factors unrelated to the actual display system requirements, then our task is much simplified. Indeed, this is not an uncommon situation, so we need not belabor the question, and assume that it has been decided by some means that color must be included.

We may then proceed with some assurance to establishing the more objective criteria for the use of color.

First, of course, we should attempt to use as few colors as possible, preferably not more than four, and certainly not more than seven. Once we have surmounted that hurdle, we can easily select the colors that will be used, within the technical constraints of the type of display surface available. These will be the ones previously recommended, namely, red, yellow, magenta, and white, or more likely red, yellow, green, and white, as being more readily attained. We should remember, however, before we blithely proceed with these selections, that once we decide on including color we may find our resolution specification changed, since most color CRTs are limited in the maximum resolution they can achieve. However, we defer any further discussion of this factor until we discuss the size considerations, and it is covered fully in Chapter 2. We cannot leave color specification without noting that there appears to be considerable emotional response to this aspect of display system specification, even more than in the question of whether to use group displays, so look out.

1.7.7   Flicker

Although we did not include any further discussion of flicker in our examination of general specification parameters, this was not because it is not important, but rather because enough has been presented in earlier sections. However, no specification is complete without some type of flicker statement. The simple phrase "no observable flicker" rather begs the question. Conversely, a statement of refresh rate, luminance level, type of phosphor, display size, and a firm insistence that absence of flicker be substantiated by tests may be excessive, if much more reliable. However, all of these factors affect the CFF, as is evident from Figures 1.7 to 1.9 and Figure 1.52, and it may be necessary to include them if absolute assurance is desired.

We may now proceed to the rather herculean task involved in deriving the CFF from all of the relevant data. Starting with Figure 1.7, at the chosen level of luminance it is over 45 Hz, so that a lower level has been established. However, Figure 1.53 indicates that the phosphor choice may bring the CFF up to over 75, and the display size (see Figure 1.9) has a similar effect. Thus a CFF above 70 is indicated, and this is definitely the trend in modern displays. This is considerably higher than the 60 Hz commonly used in the United States, let alone the 50 Hz found in Europe, to say nothing of the much lower values arising from interlaced scanning. The answer may be to reduce the luminance or contrast ratio, or to shield the display from ambient illumination in order to arrive at at least 60 Hz, noninterlaced, which is still the prevailing standard. The choice of a long-persistence phosphor is usually unacceptable, as it results in smear, but it may be adequate in simple A/N displays. In any event, we shall chose 60 Hz, so that sychronization with the power line frequency can be achieved and annoying beat frequencies avoided. The 30

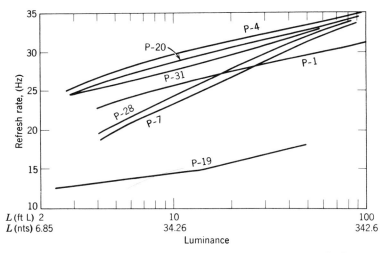

FIGURE 1.52 Flicker threshold of average observer. After Semple [23], by permission.

Hz found when interlace scanning is used is possible, but it reduces the information capacity of the display if flicker is to be minimized, and may cause portions of the display to flicker if higher densities are required.

1.7.8 Size

We have now arrived at the point of firmly specifying the size of the display surface, which we have set previously at 0.5 m × 0.5 m for convenience. The actual size required will depend on the data density to be accepted. Thus if we wish to present data in an array of 500 × 500 points, our previously determined point size of 1 mm means that our display surface must be 0.5 × 0.5 m, which is just the size we have chosen. Further, our character size of 10 mm will allow 50 × 64, or 3200 characters to be shown. Even if we subtract the spacing of 1 dot in horizontal and vertical, we are still left with a capability of presenting up to 45 × 55 characters. In actual practice, we will probably use 10 vertical × 8 horizontal dots per character, or a total of 50 × 62, although this means that our character size will be 9 mm instead of 10 mm. As a result, it is unnecessary to change our previously assumed size. This is not entirely fortuitous, since the choice was made with some knowledge of what the most common sizes are and the realization that these sizes have been determined by need. However, this does not negate the need for going through the process just described, of calculating the size required to accommodate the designated data density. Also, note that if we were to chose a 1000 × 1000-point matrix the resultant size would exceed that available in CRTs, so that it would be necessary to change either the viewing distance or the acceptable angle subtended by a dot at the eye to reduce the display surface size to a reasonable value. Therefore, this exercise in size determination is not without justification.

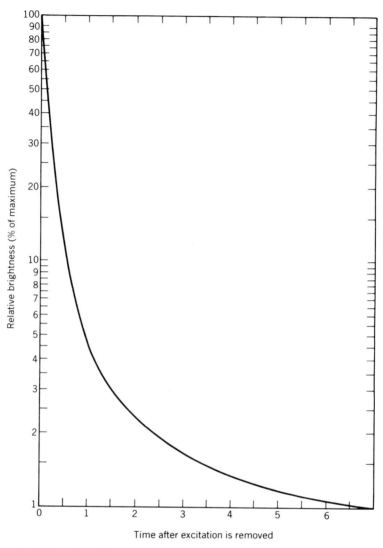

Time after excitation is removed

FIGURE 1.53 SQRI vs. bandwidth. After Infante [8], by permission.

1.7.9 Viewing Angle

We have established previously that for 30 min of arc-subtended angle, a viewing angle of 30° is acceptable. If we calculate the viewing angle for an observer seated 1 m from the display, and directly on a line with the center of the display, we find that it is $\tan^{-1} 0.25$, or $\pm 14°$. Thus we have once more made a fortunate choice, and the observer should have no difficulty in identifying characters at the extreme edges of the display surface. The data points may be similarly identified by means of head movements within the $\pm 10°$ we may allow ourselves in the horizontal and vertical. In addition, it is possible for viewers seated at the extreme edges of the cube outlined by the display surface, and at a 1-m distance, to obtain adequate legibility. Thus our display will be satisfactory for either condition of viewing.

1.7.10 Shades of Gray

Shades of gray is a new term, introduced at this point because it is frequently encountered in specifications and is usually misunderstood. The exact definition of shades of gray is a luminance ratio of 1.4, between two specific levels of luminance. However, it is customarily confused with minimum discriminable levels, which as we have seen may be as little as 3% different, and are certainly not greater than 10%. Thus there is a large difference between the number of shades of gray as defined by the standard definition and as determined by some arbitrary choice of minimum discriminable levels. We adhere to the standard definition, and if smaller ratios are required, they should be otherwise stated.

Shades of gray (the *gray scale*) is a measure of the luminance range available in any display surface, and thus specifying more than are necessary may involve extending the display to its extremes, if not beyond. If we are using luminance levels as a coding dimension, we should remember that more than four levels are not readily identified and should restrict our choice accordingly. Since CRTs are limited to about 10 shades, as is discussed further in Chapter 2, we see that if we allow two shades for each level, we are well within this capability. Additional gradations may be desired for other types of pictorial information, such as naturalistic scenes, or graphic presentations, but we defer these to the television and graphic display discussions in Chapter 4 and 6.

1.7.11 Other Parameters

There are other parameters, not specifically visual in nature, which may affect the quality of the image, such as repeatability, jitter, drift, and accuracy. We do not include them in the specification at this juncture, since they are intimately related to various aspects of equipment performance discussed in Chapters 4 and 5, and specifications are evolved for them at that point. In addition, we have excluded linearity, where, although it may be classified as a visual parameter, along with distortion, as previously noted, the requirements are too closely related to the actual operational situation for us to generalize. Therefore, we defer these as well.

1.7.12 Specification

It is now possible to develop a specification for a display, using the results of the previous sections. This specification may be for any type of display device, but a CRT is assumed as the display device, as it is still the most common type. In addition, for simplicity, an A/N display is assumed, as it involves most of the parameters and does not require as detailed an examination of such aspects as high resolution and large number of colors. Thus the specification shown in Table 1.10 is not too complex for ease of comprehension, yet does demonstrate the most important features of display system requirements. It includes the preferred values for the parameters as given by the ANSI HFS 100-1988 Standard, which has been issued as the American National Standard for Human Factors Engineering of Visual Display Terminal Workstations.

The MTFA may be calculated from equation 1.23 or determined by measurements. However, it is not commonly listed in the manufacturer's specification, so that television lines, or spot width, are easier to determine. The refresh rate is for a noninterlaced display, but the ANSI Standard recommends that the display be tested for flicker by subjecting a number of subjects to the display and determining that at least 90% report no perceptible flicker.

1.7.13   Specifying Unified Measures of Display Quality

Of the three unified measures that are discussed in Section 1.3.7, only the MTFA approach has been given official approval in the ANSI Standard. This standard provides fairly complete descriptions of the techniques to be used and includes other anthropomorphic data as well. This is not true of the other two, but they have provided some results of interest that may be presented here. Specifically, using the Carlson–Cohn method, if the optimum distance is calculated, using equation 1.17 and Figure 1.15, it is found to be about $2\frac{1}{2}$ times the picture height. Similarly, when the Barten SQRI method is used, curves such as those in Figure 1.54 may be generated, which allow the video bandwidth and a fixed number of lines of resolution to be related to each other, and to both the MTFA and the SQRI. This is useful information, but again it is somewhat difficult to calculate, and is rarely shown in manufacturers' specifications. Therefore, all of these approaches, although quite useful, have not reached their full potential for the user in the form of require-

TABLE 1.10   Specification for CRT Video Display Terminal

Parameter	Value	ANSI Recommendation
Ambient illumination (lux)	500	200–500
Screen luminance (nits)	50	35 minimum
Contrast ratio	10:1	3:1 minimum >7:1 preferred
Character height (minutes)	18 of arc	12 minimum 22 preferred
Character height/width	1.4	2 maximum 1.25 preferred
Character font	7 × 9	4 × 5 minimum 7 × 9 preferred
Between-character space (pixel)	1	1 minimum
Between-line space (pixel)	2	2
Viewing distance (cm)	45	30 minimum
Screen size (cm)	20H × 28W	As required
Refresh rate (Hz)	60–70	Flicker test
Resolution	400 × 800	MTFA = 5 min

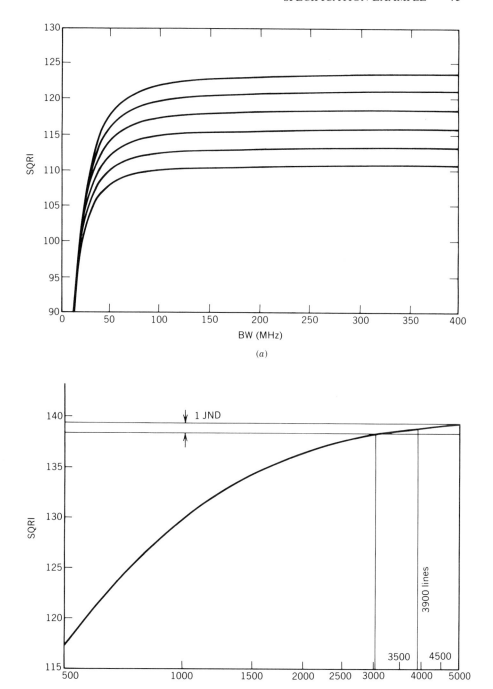

FIGURE 1.54   Ultimate SQRI. After Infante [8, p. 63], by permission.

ments that can readily be obtained and used in a specification. However, it is probable that their use will increase as the need for more precise specifications becomes more widespread, and the inclusion of the MTFA in the ANSI Standard indicates such a trend.

REFERENCES

[1] Cornsweet, T. N., *Visual Perception*, Academic, New York, 1970.

[2] Biberman, L. M., Ed., *Perception of Displayed Information*, Plenum, New York, 1973.

[3] Pender, H., and McIlwain, K., Eds., *Electrical Engineers' Handbook*, Vol. 2, *Communication-Electronics*, 4th ed., Wiley, New York, 1950.

[4] Kaufman, J. E., Ed., *IES Lighting Handbook*, 4th ed., Illuminating Engineering Society, New York, 1966.

[5] Walsh, J. W. T., *Photometry*, Dover, New York, 1958.

[6] Graham, C. H., Ed., *Vision and Visual Perception*, Wiley, New York, 1965.

[7] Farrell, J. E., et al., "Predicting Flicker Thresholds for Video Display Terminals," *SID Proc.*, **28**/4, 1987, 451.

[8] Infante, C., *CRT Lecture Notes*, 1989.

[9] Keller, P., "1976 CIE-UCS Chromaticity Diagram with Color Boundaries," *SID Proc.*, **24**/4, 1983, 320.

[10] Cohen, R. W., and Gorog, I., "An Image Quality Descriptor for Display Evaluation," *SID Proc.*, **15**/2, 1974, 53–62.

[11] Carlson, C. R., and Cohen, R. W., "A Simple Psychophysical Model for Predicting the Visibility of Displayed Information," *SID Proc.*, **21**/3, 1980, 233.

[12] Barten, P. G. J., "The SQRI Method: A New Method for the Evaluation of Visible Resolution on a Display," *SID Proc.*, **28**/3, 1987, 254.

[13] Snyder, H. L., "Image Quality and Observer Performance," in Biberman [2].

[14] Showman, D. J., "The Relative Legibility of Leroy and Lincoln/Mitre Alphanumeric Symbols," *Inform. Display*, **4**/2, Mar./Apr. 1967, 32.

[15] JEDEC *Optical Characteristics of Cathode Ray Tube Screens* Publication No. 16-B, 1977, EIA, Washington, D.C., p. 102.

[16] Krupka, D. C., and Fukui, H., "The Determination of Relative Critical Flicker Frequencies of Raster-Scanned CRT Displays by Analysis of Phosphor Persistance Characteristics," *SID Proc.*, **14**/3, 1973, 89–91.

[17] Sherr, S., *Fundamentals of Display System Design*, Wiley, New York, 1970.

[18] Snyder, H. L., and Maddox, M. E., *Information Transfer from Computer-Generated Dot-Matrix Displays*, HFL-78-3/ARD-78-1, Oct. 1978.

[19] Sherr, S., "Applications of Digital Television Displays to Command and Control," *SID Proc.*, **11**/2, 1970, 65.

[20] Shurtleff, D. A., "Legibility Research," *SID Proc.*, **15**/2, 1974, 41–51.

[21] Kinney, G. C., *Studies in Display Legibility*, MTP-21, The Mitre Corp.

[22] Salvendy, G., Ed., *Handbook of Human Factors*, Wiley, New York, 1987.

[23] Semple, C. A., Jr., *Analysis of Human Factors Data for Electronic Flight Display Systems*, Tech. Rep. AFFDL-TR-70-174, Wright-Patterson Air Force Base, Ohio, 1971.

[24] Snyder, H.S., "Human Factors in Visual Display Systems," notes for lecture at George Washington University, Washington, D.C.

[25] Blackwell, H. R., "Contrast Thresholds of the Human Eye," *JOSA*, **10**/11, 1946, 624–643.

[26] Ireland, F. H., *Experimental Study of the Effects of Surround Brightness and Size on Visual Performance*, AMRL-TR-67-102 (AD 666 045), Wright-Patterson Air Force Base, Ohio, 1967.

[27] Howell, W. C., and Kraft, D. L., *Size, Blur and Contrast as Variable Affecting the Legibility of Alphanumeric Symbols on Radar-Type Displays*, WADC-TR-50-536 (AD 232 889), Wright-Patterson Air Force Base, Ohio, 1959.

[28] Shurtleff, D. A., *Design Problems in Visual Displays, Part II. Factors in the Legibility of Television Displays*, ESD-TR-66-299 (AD 640 571), Mitre Corp., 1966.

[29] Rizy, E. F., *Color Specifications for Additive Color Group Displays*, RADL-TR-65-278 (AD 621 068), Rome Air Development Center, Griffiss Air Force Base, N.Y., 1965, in Semple [23].

[30] Meister, D. and Sullivan, D. J. Guide to Human Engineering Design for Visual Displays (Report No. 14-68-C-0278). Washington, D.C.: Office of Naval Research (AD 693237), 1969.

[31] Rizy, E. F., Dichroic Filter Specifications for Color Additive Displays (Report RADC-TR-67-513) Griffiths Air Force Base, N.Y.: Rome Air Development Center (AD 659346) 1967.

[32] Wulfeck, J. W., *Vision in Military Aviation*, WADC-TR-58-399 (AD 207 780), Wright-Patterson Air Force Base, Ohio, 1958, in Semple [23].

2

CATHODE-RAY DEVICES*

2.1 INTRODUCTION

Cathode-ray devices are of considerable antiquity, going back to the early work of Crookes and Roentgen and the invention by Ferdinand Braun in 1896 of the cathode-ray tube (CRT). However, many of the specific types of devices discussed here are of much more recent origin, including a large number of devices that use the beam of electrons to control or effect a change in some other element of the device, although it is remarkable how closely Braun's CRT resembles modern units. It should also be noted at this point that we are restricting ourselves primarily to those devices that operate to transform or create visual images, thus eliminating various devices such as klystrons and traveling-wave amplifiers from consideration.

With these provisos we propose, as a definition for *cathode-ray devices*, the statement

> Any device that uses the electron beam to cause a change in, or affect some characteristic of, one or more other elements of the device.

This differs somewhat from the IEEE definition of the electron-beam tube, which reads

> An electron tube, the performance of which depends upon the formation and control of one or more electron beams.

*Portions of this chapter appeared in the *Encyclopedia of Computer Science and Technology*, Vol. 4, J. Belzer, Ed. Marcel Dekker, New York, 1976.

However, since this definition includes those devices that have just been precluded, we must use our definition as more appropriate. Similarly, the dictionary definition for the cathode ray is

> A kind of ray caused by the discharge of electricity in a vacuum vessel and generated at the cathode.

Finally, we may add the JEDEC definition for the CRT, which is

> An electron beam tube in which the beam, or beams can be focused to a desired cross section on a surface and varied in position and intensity to produce a visible or otherwise detectable pattern. Unless otherwise stated the term cathode ray tube is reserved for devices in which the screen is cathodoluminescent and in which the output information is presented in the form of a pattern of light.

Armed with these definitions, we may now proceed to a general survey of the various types of cathode-ray devices, as a preliminary to a more detailed description.

2.2   GENERAL SURVEY

2.2.1   Cathode-Ray Tube

The CRT is by far the most common and ubiquitous cathode-ray device to be found in both general- and special-purpose usage. Its predominance is assured for many years to come by its prevalence in television sets, and more recently in the variety of computer-driven terminals that have become such a commonplace of business and data-transmission applications. Thus it is by far the most important of the various devices we cover, and it exists in a wide variety of types and categories, the main purpose of which is to make available for viewing a visual image of some type of information. The visual image may range from the naturalistic scenes of entertainment television to the complex imagery and coded data appearing in computer-generated data displays.

The basic CRT category may be subdivided further into the classes of electrostatic or magnetic deflection with either electrostatic or magnetic focus, monochromatic or multicolor, and single or multiple beam. We defer *further* discussion of the exact meaning of these terms until we reach the detailed descriptions in later sections. Suffice it to say at this point that each type performs the function of converting the data from some form, usually electrical, into the visual image, or into a form compatible with producing the visual image. We may also note that the demise of this class of device, although often predicted, is still far from showing any sign of being consummated.

2.2.2 Nonviewing

The nonviewing cathode-ray devices still in use at present are primarily those used for producing hard copy, either in printed or in slide form. However, for historical reasons at least one other remains of interest, and this is the analog scan converter. Its function is to convert from randomly generated images into some scanning format, or from one scan rate to another, and this function is of increasing interest as high-definition television becomes more common. However, digital scan converters have more or less taken over this function, and the analog versions are of rapidly decreasing interest. However, some discussion of these types is included for completeness. The other types of nonviewing cathode-ray devices are the extruded beam and multiple-beam character generators, and the direct-writing electrostatic CRTs, all of which are used primarily for printing hard copy. These devices have much in common with direct-viewing CRTs, and differ largely in the form of the faceplate and the manner in which the electron beam energy is transferred from the faceplate to the hard copy surface.

2.2.3 Image Converters

Image converters are those devices that convert a visual image into some form of electronic signal that may then be amplified or otherwise altered so that the signal may be used to reproduce the image at some other location. In general, the mode of operation is to focus the visual image on a light-sensitive target that is altered in proportion to the light intensity, and generates an electrical signal when it is scanned or otherwise activated. The light-sensitive target may be resistive or capacitive, with the photosensitive types using a variety of photosensitive materials as the target materials, and the capacitive types using charge-coupled devices (CCDs) as the visible image sensory array. The latter are becoming increasingly popular as advances in silicon VLSI technology have made it feasible to build large solid-state arrays. However, the photosensitive types, which are various versions of the popular *Vidicon*, remain in widespread use, especially in broadcast and cable television. The others have seen extensive use in a number of industrial applications and are beginning to take over more of the entertainment television field.

2.2.4 Special Types

A number of special types of cathode-ray devices have come and gone over the years, and some of them have resurfaced periodically or embody principles of continuing interest. Prime among these are the flat panel types and a few of the unique attempts at large screen projection. These could be included in the direct-view section, but are covered separately because they are not in the mainstream and have never achieved any significant acceptance. In addition, some of the specialized types intended only for large screen projection, such as oil-film light valves, are covered separately in Chapter 4.

2.3 PHYSICAL PRINCIPLES

2.3.1 Introduction

Since the electron beam is basic to the operation of all of the electron devices under examination, it is proper to preface the treatment of the specific devices with a discussion of the general physical principles applying to the electron beam. To this end, we must pay particular attention to the motion of electrons in electrostatic and magnetic fields and in combinations of these fields. Therefore, we begin with the basic laws of motion of the electron in these fields, proceed to the effects of electrostatic and magnetic lenses, and conclude with the beam-deflection characteristics of these two types of fields. The material presented is limited in nature and is intended only to establish a basic understanding of the physical principles involved. More specific examples of focusing and deflection configurations are deferred to the sections dealing with the specific devices, as are some of the equations applying to these devices.

In addition to the electron beam, we must also consider the phenomena of luminescence, photoconductivity, and secondary emission, since each of these is used to varying extents in many of the electron devices described. In particular, cathodoluminescence is an integral part of direct view CRTs, photoconductivity appears in many image converters, and secondary emission is used in storage devices and some character generators. Each of these subjects is, therefore, treated in a general way as introductory to the specific use in the particular devices.

2.3.2 Electron-Beam Formation and Control

Laws of Motion. The basic laws of motion for an electron in a uniform electrostatic field may be obtained from Newton's second law, the solution of which leads to the expression for velocity (v) of the electron,

$$v = \left(\frac{2eV}{m}\right)^{1/2} \tag{2.1}$$

where $V = -Ex$ (the potential through which the electron has fallen). Substituting the values for e and m in practical units [1.6×10^{-19} coulomb (C) and 9.1×10^{-28} g, respectively] gives

$$v = 5.93 \times 10^5 V^{1/2} \qquad \text{m/s} \tag{2.2}$$

If the electron enters a uniform field with its velocity at an angle θ to the potential gradient, the equation describing the motion of the electron is

$$y = -\frac{Ex^2}{4V_0 \sin^2\theta} + \frac{x}{\tan \theta} \qquad (2.3)$$

where V_0 is the potential corresponding to the initial velocity and the other terms are as defined previously. This is the equation of a parabola, as shown in Figure 2.1, with the maximum height (y_m), the x displacement (x_m), and the slope of the curve (α) at any point given by

$$y_m = \frac{V_0 \cos^2\theta}{E} \qquad (2.4)$$

$$x_m = \frac{2V_0 \sin \theta \cos \theta}{E} \qquad (2.5)$$

$$\tan \alpha = -\frac{Ex}{2V_0 \sin^2\theta} + \frac{1}{\tan \theta} \qquad (2.6)$$

Equation 2.6 is used later to develop the equation for electrostatic deflection. If the effect of a uniform magnetic field is considered, we obtain for the radius of an electron path when the electron enters the field at right angles

$$R = \frac{3.38 \times 10^{-6}V^{1/2}}{B_m} \quad \text{meters} \qquad (2.7)$$

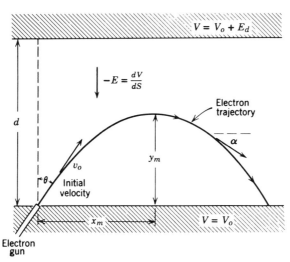

FIGURE 2.1   Electron trajectory in electrostatic field. After Spangenberg [1], by permission of McGraw-Hill Book Company.

where B_m is the magnetic flux density and the same numerical values are used as before. If the electron enters the field at an angle (θ), equation 2.7 becomes

$$R = \frac{3.38 \times 10^{-6}V^{1/2} \sin \theta}{B_m} \quad \text{meters} \qquad (2.8)$$

The electron follows a helical path, and the pitch of the helix is given by

$$P = \frac{21.1 \times 10^{-6}V^{1/2} \cos \theta}{B_m} \quad \text{meters} \qquad (2.9)$$

with the same numerical substitutions as before. Equation 2.9 is used later to develop the equation for magnetic focusing.

When the electrostatic or magnetic fields are not uniform, or when both fields exist, the differential equations for the paths followed by the electron become quite complex and are in general not amenable to direct solution. Solutions for some special cases may be found in the references, and in the simple case where the two fields are parallel, the motion will be unaffected by the magnetic field if the electron starts from a rest condition. However, the equations derived for the uniform field condition are adequate for most purposes.

Electrostatic Lenses. Electrostatic lenses may be understood by analogy with optical lenses. Thus if we examine Figure 2.2, the electron entering the constant V_1 region after being emitted at zero velocity and potential will move in the V_1 region at a straight-line velocity given by equation 2.1. When it crosses the surface it experiences a velocity change in region V_2 to a new velocity, again given by equation 2.1, but with V_2 replacing V_1. The tangential component of velocity (v_t) is the same on both sides, since only the normal component will change for an electron entering at the normal. Therefore,

$$v_t = v_1 \sin I_1 \qquad (2.10)$$

$$v_1 \sin I_1 = v_2 \sin I_2 \qquad (2.11)$$

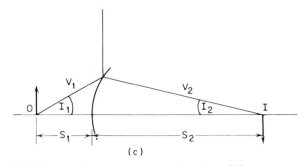

(c)

FIGURE 2.2   Electron optics. After Sherr [2], by permission.

The similarity of equation 2.11 to Snell's law is apparent, and the parallelism is furthered by substituting for the velocity from equation 2.1, leading to

$$V_1 \sin I_1 = V_2 \sin I_2 \qquad (2.12)$$

Therefore,

$$\frac{\sin I_1}{\sin I_2} = \frac{V_2}{V_1} \qquad (2.13)$$

which may be rewritten as

$$\frac{\sin I_1}{\sin I_2} = \frac{N_2}{N_1} \qquad (2.14)$$

thus making the equivalence complete if we define N_1 and N_2 as the corresponding indices of refraction. Then, using equation 2.14 and Figures 2.2 and 2.3, the formula for magnification is

$$m = \frac{(V_1/V_2)^{1/2}S_2}{S_1} \qquad (2.15)$$

or for the thin unipotential lens, where V_1 equals V_2, referring to Figure 2.3,

$$m = \frac{h_2}{h_1} = \frac{f_2}{X_1} = -\frac{X_2}{f_2} \qquad (2.16)$$

Other formulas may be derived from the same figures, but these are sufficient to illustrate the operation of an electrostatic lens.

As a final consideration, two types of distortion should be mentioned, not apparent from first-order, or Gaussian optics. The first is astigmatism, which results from the condition that, in an off-axis object, lines toward the axis have a different focal length than lines perpendicular to these. The resultant effect is shown in Figure 2.4 and illustrates the compromise that must be made for best focusing over the entire image. The second effect is field distortion, commonly known as *pincushion* for positive, and *barrel* for negative distortion. This effect results from variations in linear magnification with

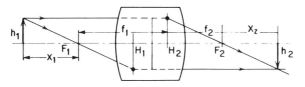

FIGURE 2.3 Thin unipotential lens. After Sherr [2], by permission.

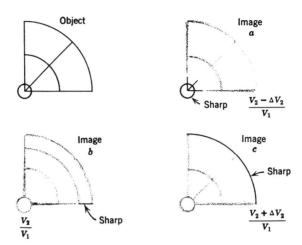

FIGURE 2.4   Astigmatism. After Spangenberg [1], by permission of McGraw-Hill Book Company.

the radial distance, with increase in magnification causing pincushion, and decrease causing barrel distortion. These two types of distortion are illustrated in Figure 2.5, by comparing an object with the images containing these defects.

Magnetostatic Lenses.   Equation 2.9 demonstrates that the pitch of the helical path described by an electron in a magnetic field is insensitive to θ for small angles. As a result, the electrons will return to their original relative positions in a distance P along the magnetic path parallel to the beam, thus avoiding spreading of the beam, but with no reduction in entering beam diameter. The beam may be focused by adjusting the current in the coil used for this purpose, until the proper value of P is achieved for best spot size. The exact manner in which the focus coil is placed to surround the beam is covered later when we discuss magnetic focus CRTs. However, at this point we may present several equations that help define the form of the focusing coil. If the equations for the focal length of a short magnetic lens, and the image rotation by

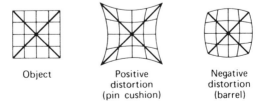

FIGURE 2.5   Pin-cushion and barrel distortion. After Spangenberg [1], by permission of McGraw-Hill Book Company.

that lens are integrated, the resulting equations are

$$\frac{f}{d} = \frac{48.5V}{N^2I^2} \quad \text{meters} \tag{2.17}$$

where f = focal length
 $V = -Ex$ as before
 d = diameter of wire loop
 NI = current in ampere turns

and

$$\theta = \frac{0.19NI}{V^{1/2}} \tag{2.18}$$

with the usual substitutions for e and m to obtain numerical values. Equation 2.17 applies reasonably well for a short coil, whose mean diameter is d, with N turns and current I. When plotted as a nomograph, it may be used approximately for an iron-encased coil with small NI and with d as the diameter of the pole pieces.

Deflection. To complete this section, we derive the deflection equations for the electrostatic and magnetic cases, using equations 2.6 and 2.7. From equation 2.6, and referring to Figure 2.6, the deflection is

$$\tan \alpha = \frac{V_d}{2a} \frac{b}{V_0} \tag{2.19}$$

since the potential gradient (E_d) is (V_d/a) and X is replaced by b. The second term in equation 2.6 goes to zero because the angle θ is 90. Further, since

$$\tan \alpha \cong \frac{y_d}{l} \tag{2.20}$$

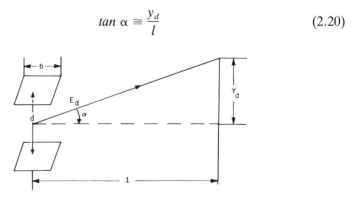

FIGURE 2.6   Electrostatic deflection. After Sherr [3], by permission of Marcel Dekker, Inc.

then

$$y_d = \frac{lb}{2a} \frac{V_d}{V_0} \qquad (2.21)$$

Equation 2.21 holds for parallel plates and neglects fringing at the edges. If the plates are not parallel, but slope apart, the gradient is

$$\frac{dv}{dy} = \frac{V_d}{a_1 + [(a_2 - a_1)/b]X} \qquad (2.22)$$

where a_1 = plate separation at entering end
a_2 = plate separation at leaving end
X = distance in plates

and the other symbols are as before. By integrating the expression for crosswise acceleration to obtain crosswise velocity, and taking the ratio of this velocity to the axial velocity, divided by the distance to the screen, we get

$$y = \frac{lbV_d}{2V_0a_1} \frac{\ln(a_2/a_1)}{(a_2/a_1) - 1} \qquad (2.23)$$

as the expression for deflection, which reduces to equation 2.21 when $a_1 = a_2$.

The magnetic deflection equation may be derived by referring to Figure 2.7 and equation 2.8. The deflection angle (α) is given by

$$\sin \alpha = \frac{2.97 \times 10^5 bB_m}{V^{1/2}} \qquad (2.24)$$

Since the center of deflection is at the center of the field, the deflection is given by

$$y_d = \frac{2.97 \times 10^5 blB_m}{V^{1/2}} \qquad (2.25)$$

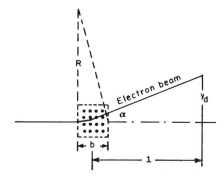

FIGURE 2.7   Magnetic deflection. After Spangenberg [1], by permission of Mc-Graw-Hill Book Company.

since y_d equals $l \tan \alpha$, when the angle (α) is small. If the deflection angle is too large for this assumption to hold, the deflection will not be directly proportional to the current, since $\sin \alpha$, and not $\tan \alpha$, is proportional to current. The correction that must be introduced to compensate for this discrepancy is done by special circuitry and is covered in Chapter 4.

2.3.3 Cathodoluminescence

Luminescence is defined as the emission of light beyond that caused by thermal radiation according to Planck's law. Luminescence may occur in either gases or solids, but the primary material used in display applications is the crystalline solid, commonly termed a *phosphor*. Phosphors usually have bell-shaped emission spectra, at longer wavelengths than their absorption spectra, so that they are transparent to their own radiation. Luminescence may be excited by many energy sources, such as high-velocity electrons, electric fields, x-rays, and ultraviolet (UV) radiation, with electric fields (as in electroluminescence) and high-velocity electrons (as in cathodoluminescence) the two most frequently encountered sources. The former is used in the electroluminescent panels and matrices and light-emitting diodes discussed in Chapter 3, and the latter phenomenon is basic to the CRTs covered in this chapter. The light output from a CRT, or its luminance, comes as a result of these high-velocity electrons striking a phosphor and causing the emission of light of some spectral distribution determined by the composition of the phosphor. Two basic expressions for the emitted light intensity from the phosphor are

$$L = \alpha k N_0 e^{-t} \qquad (2.26a)$$

where α = reciprocal of mean lifetime of excited state
k = photon light content
N_0 = maximum number of excited centers due to electron bombardment
t = time

and

$$L = \frac{kN_0}{(1 + N_0 \beta t)^2} \qquad (2.26b)$$

where β is a proportionality constant. These equations are derived from solid-state theory, in particular the occurrence of impurity atoms at lattice sites, and the activation of electrons by energy transfers, followed by radiation as the electron returns to the ground state. Although we need not concern ourselves unduly at this point with the complexities of the theory, which is covered in Chapter 3, it is well to recognize, from equations 2.26a and 2.26b, that the light output decays with time and is a function of the current. Of more significance to our discussion is the empirical expression

$$L = Af(\rho)V^n \tag{2.27}$$

where $f(\rho)$ = function of current
V = accelerating voltage
A = constant
n = 1.5 < n < 2

There are also secondary-emission effects on the operation of the phosphor screen, but we defer any consideration of them until the next section on secondary emission. However, we state here that these effects determine the maximum potential to which the phosphor luminance will increase, before the secondary emission causes the screen potential and hence the luminance to become independent of the anode potential. But this anticipates the more complete treatment in later sections of this chapter. Further information on commonly used phosphors is shown in Table 2.1, which lists efficiency, spectral peak decay times, and type of luminescence involved for a group of commonly used phosphors, whereas Figure 2.8 has spectral distribution curves for several phosphors. Complete information about all registered phosphors may be found in Publication 16C of the Electronics Industry Association, which is the standard source of this information for all phosphors in use for CRTs.

The three factors to be considered in choosing a phosphor type for any CRT to be used in a display system are the luminous efficiency, the decay time, and the color, to which we may add the anticipated life. The luminous efficiency, as shown in Table 2.1, is a direct indication of the amount of light output to be expected for a specified input power. It is expressed in terms of lumens per watt and is the radiant efficiency as modified by the photopic curve. Thus although a phosphor may have a high radiant efficiency in the red, whereas another has a low radiant efficiency in the green, the second may have the higher of the two luminous efficiencies due to the peak in the photopic curve at the green wavelength. In addition, examination of the relative luminous efficiency gives a measure of the relative visual performance among the various phosphors and is an important criterion in choosing a phosphor, particularly when high light output is required. Table 2.2 is a list of the luminous equivalents of all presently registered phosphors, but it does not tell the whole story since it does not include the radiant or absolute efficiency. Thus P-1 phosphor has the highest number of lumens per radiated watt, but P-20 has the highest luminous efficiency among the phosphors listed in Table 2.1, due to P-1 peaking at very close to the peak of the scotopic luminosity function at 513 nM, and 520 nM for the P-20. As a result, the other factor of color must also be considered when luminous efficiency is the criterion.

The color of each phosphor is listed in terms of its CIE (Commission Internationale d'Eclairage) x and y coordinates and the spectral energy-

TABLE 2.1 **Characteristics of Registered Phosphors**

JEDEC No.	Color[a]		Absolute Efficiency, η (radiated W) Beam W × 100	Luminous Efficiency, k_b (lumens) Beam W	Spectral Peak Decay Time to 10% Point	CFF (Hz)
	Fluorescent	Phosphorescent				
P-1	Y–G	Y–G	6.0	31.1	24.5 ms	42
P-2	Y–G	Y–G	7.0	32.4	35–70 μs	50
P-4(Su)	W	—	15.0	42.0	22–60 μs	42
P-4(Si)	W	—	15.0	36.0	12.5 ms	50
P-7	B–W	Y	9.5	14–26	400 ms	44
P-11	B	B	10–21	14–27	34 μs	—
P-16	B–P	B–P	5.0	0.09	0.12 μs	—
P-19	O	O	—	14.5	3 s	—
P-20	Y–G	—	16.0	62.2	60 μs	50
P-22	G	—	—	50.0	6 ms	50
P-22	B	—	—	5.0	4.8 ms	50
P-22	R	—	—	12.0	1.5 ms	50
P-24	G	G	2.6	9.7	1.5 μs	50–54
P-26	O	O	—	15.5	3–17 s	—
P-28	Y–G	—	—	—	600 ms	—
P-31	G	—	22	49.8	38 μs	50–54
P-38	O	O	—	10.1	1.1 s	21
P-39	G	G	—	15.0	400 ms	31
P-43	G	—	—	41.5	1.5 ms	50
P-44	G	—	—	20.5	1.7 ms	50
P-45	W	—	—	7.7	70 ms	50

Source: After Sherr [2] and Martin [5], by permission.

[a]Y, yellow; G, green; W, white; B, blue; P, purple; R, red; O, orange.

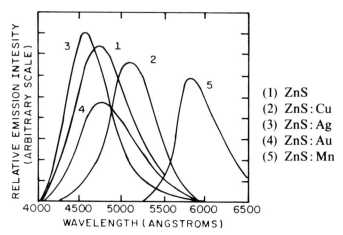

FIGURE 2.8   Spectral distribution curves for phosphors. Used by permission of Marcel Dekker, Inc. Reprinted from Sherr [3, p. 156]. Adapted from Klick and Schulman [4].

distribution characteristics, as well as the CIE coordinates for registered phosphors may be found in EIA Publication 16C previously referred to. A full range of single colors is available, as well as the multicolor combinations found in the different types of color CRTs discussed later. The choice of color for the phosphor is, therefore, dependent on both perceptual considerations, as presented in Chapter 1, and the efficiency characteristics just presented.

The third factor mentioned is the decay time. The effect of decay time on the CFF is covered in Section 1.7.7 and the differs may be quite large between different phosphors. Figure 2.9a shows the decay characteristics of the P-1 phosphor, which may be compared with that for the P-31 phosphor as shown in Figure 2.9b. As is the case for the P-38 phosphor shown in Figure 1.23, the P-1 phosphor has a longer time constant than the P-31 phosphor and may be expected to show a lower CFF. This is demonstrated by the curves shown in Figure 1.52, although these were obtained quite a while ago. However, the curves shown in Figure 2.10 are of somewhat more recent origin, and although not specific as to the exact phosphors involved, do exhibit the effect of phosphor decay time on the CFF as well as the effect of screen luminance. These are predicted CFFs, using the method described by Farrell [8], and have been substantiated by extensive testing.

This technique for predicting relative CFFs for different phosphors proposed and tested by Krupka and Fukui a number of years ago [9]. It has not received much use between then and the present, but is included here because this type of data is rather sparse and is worth having, if only as an example of how the CFF results have moved up in frequency. The approach was to use data on the CFF as a function of modulation index, defined as the ratio of the amplitude of the component at a given frequency to the average illumination. Then the modulation index for the phosphor is computed from the

TABLE 2.2   Luminous Equivalents of Registered Phosphors

Phosphor	Lumens per Radiated Watt	Phosphor	Lumens per Radiated Watt
P-1	520	P-23	330
P-2	465	P-24	365
P-3	380	P-25	330
P-4—Sulfide	285	P-26	420
P-4—Silicate sulfide	295	P-27	165
P-4—Silicate	235	P-28	500
P-5	85	P-29	—
P-6	345	P-30	Cancelled
P-7—High blue	230	P-31—Low current	425
P-7—Average	285	P-31—High current	350
P-7—Low blue	370	P-32	350
P-8	—	P-33	440
P-9	—	P-34—During excitation	310
P-10	—	P-34—Normal and stimulated	510
P-11	140	P-35	365
P-12	410	P-36	465
P-13	150	P-37	180
P-14—High blue	225	P-38	345
P-14—Average	260	P-39	515
P-14—Low blue	300	P-40	285
P-15	255	P-41	445
P-16	2.45	P-41	443
P-17	360	P-43	416
P-18	240	P-44	548
P-19	400	P-45	289
P-20	480	P-46	514
P-21	360	P-47	74
P-22—Sulfide silicate phosphate	230	P-48	378
P-22—All sulfide	225	P-49	—
P-22—Sulfide vandate	245	P-50	—
P-22—Sulfide oxysulfide	280	P-51	—
P-22—Sulfide oxide	240		
P-22—Sulfide oxysulfide (modified)	320		

Source: After JEDEC [6], by permission.

decay characteristic by means of a piecewise approximation of the initial portion of the decay characteristic. The resultant combination of the CFF curves and the phosphor modulation index is shown in Figure 2.10, and the predicted CFF is the intersection of the phosphor curve with the modulation index curve at different levels of luminance. Tables 2.3 and 2.4 list the predicted CFFs for a number of phosphors, and the similarities between these and those determined by means of the Farrell technique can be noted.

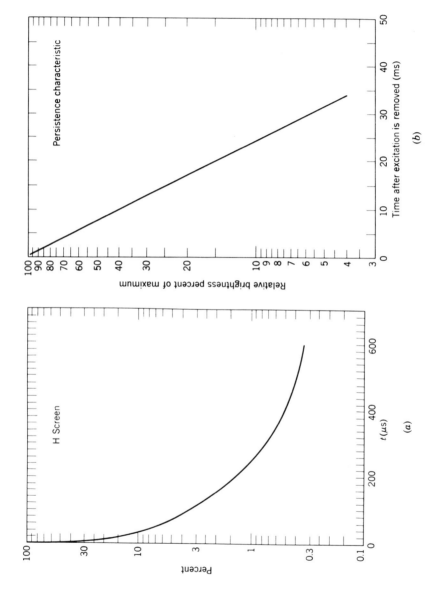

FIGURE 2.9 Persistence characteristics of (*a*) P-1 and (*b*) P-31 phosphor. After JEDEC [6], by permission.

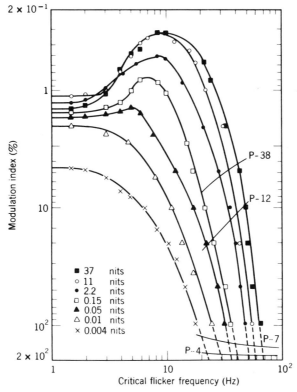

FIGURE 2.10   Plots of modulation index as a function of CFF together with calculated plots of modulation vs. frequency. Results of calculations are curves running transversely. After Krupka and Fukui [7], by permission.

These techniques are useful for determining the probable CFFs without having to conduct extensive tests on the actual phosphor. However, unless the CRT manufacturers make more information available on the expected CFFs for their CRTs, it may still be necessary to go through an elaborate human factors test to be certain that no flicker is apparent under actual operating conditions. Thus it is safest to use the highest refresh rate possible, to ensure that no flicker will be observed. In addition, the use of longer-persistence phosphors is of questionable value, as smear and blur are possible results, both of which reduce legibility.

As a final point in this discussion of phosphors, the aging characteristics, which determine the lifetime of the screen, should be mentioned. A general equation for aging is

$$I_0 = \frac{I}{1 + CN} \tag{2.28}$$

where I_0 = intensity after aging
I = initial intensity
C = burn parameter in cm^2
N = electrons deposited per cm^2

Figure 2.11a is a plot of equation 2.28 for one phosphor, and the slope of this curve is the burn constant (C), related to the rate of decay in the luminescence, whereas $1/C$ is the number of electrons that will reduce the luminescence to 50% of the initial value. Figure 2.11b is the same information in a somewhat different form, where the light output is shown in terms of the accumulated charge. Unfortunately, not many aging data are available on the different phosphors. However, CRT manufacturers minimize the effect of this reduction by aging the phosphor until it has passed the initial rapid drop shown in Figure 2.11b. Table 2.5 shows the drop to 50% for a number of phosphors.

2.3.4 Secondary Emission

It has been known since 1902 that when solids are bombarded by primary electrons, secondary electrons leave the solid and go into free space. This

TABLE 2.3 Phosphor Critical Flicker Frequencies

Phosphor	Luminance (nits)	200% Sine Modulation CFF (Hz) Extrapolated	Pulse Modulation (2% Duty Cycle) CFF (Hz)
P-1	30	34	33
	100	38	38
	300	42	43
P-4	30	32	35
	100	37	41
	300	42	47
P-7 (Y)	30	33	32
	100	38	38
	300	44	43
P-12	30	26	25
	100	29	29
	300	35	32
P-20	30	37	40
	100	42	47
	300	55	54
P-31	30	34	37
	100	46	44
	300	54	51

Source: After Turnage [10], by permission.

TABLE 2.4 Critical Flicker Frequencies at 35 Nits of Some Commercially Available Phosphors

JEDEC Designation	Material	Screen	CFF (Hz)	Comment
P-4	ZnS:Ag,Al ZnCdS:Ag,Al	Picturephone tube	40–45	
P-7	ZnS:Ag ZnCdS:Cu (cascade screen)	Tube supplied in ITT Model KM 708 slow-scan monitor	35–40	Used long-wavelength pass filter with sharp cutoff at 6000 Å
		Laboratory-settled phosphor plaque—using GE P7 phophors	30–35	
P-12	ZnMgF$_3$:Mn	9M36 tube from Thomas Electronics, Wayne, N.J.	25–30	
		Laboratory-settled plaque	25–30 25	
P-38	ZnMgF$_3$:Mn	9M36 tube from Thomas Electronics, Wayne, N.J.	22–28	

Source: After Krupka and Fukui [9], by permission.

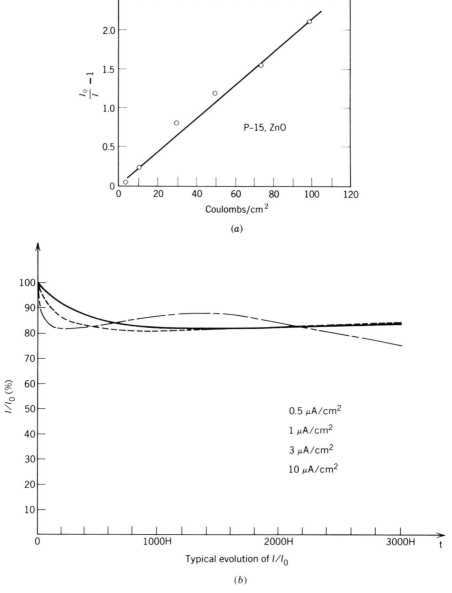

(a)

(b)

FIGURE 2.11   (a) Phosphor aging curve. After Pfahnl [11], by permission. (b) Typical evolution of I/I_0. After Thomson CSF [12], by permission.

TABLE 2.5   Reduction to 50% by a Variety of Phosphors

Phosphor	Phosphor Efficiency, η (l/W)	Life to 50% of Initial Brightness, ρ_s (C/cm²)
P-1	30	>100
P-4	30 (color depend)	35
P-7	20	35
P-12	12	0.2
P-19	12	0.2
P-20	40–70	35
P-22(G)	40–70	35
P-26	10	0.2
P-28	30	35
P-31	40–60	35
P-33	12	0.2
P-38	12	2
P-39	20	>25
P-40	20	35
P-43	40	>100
P-44	35	>50
P-45	20	>100
P-49 P-50 P-51	1–2 (red) 4–8 (green)	50
P-53	30	>200
P-55(P22B)	9	35
P-56(P22R-oxide)	18 (W/W %)	100
P-11	10–15	25
P-16	3	0.2
P-46	5	>100
P-47	5	>100
P-48	5	>100
P-52	2	100

phenomenon is known as *secondary electron emission* and has been made the basis of a number of devices used in display systems. Its significance in the operation of CRTs has been briefly noted in the previous section, and more detailed discussion of the operation of a number of units embodying secondary emission is included in various references. More recently, the theory of secondary emission has advanced to the point where the phenomenon is reasonably well understood and predictions based on the theory may be made. The basic process consists of primary electrons striking and secondary electrons whose emission is caused by three factors: (1) reflections due to elastic collisions at the surface, (2) reflections from within the material, known as *rediffusion*, and (3) true secondary emission resulting from electrons displaced within the crystal structure, primarily from the conduction band if free electrons are available or the valence band if the energy gap is small. The energy distribution of the secondary electrons may be plotted against the primary electron energy, resulting in the general curve shown in Figure 2.12. The peak occurring at the higher primary energy has the energy E_p of the primary beam and is the result of elastic reflections. The electrons between this peak and the second peak are the rediffused electrons, whereas those constituting the second peak are the true secondary electrons emitted by the solid.

The quantity of secondary electrons emitted, divided by the primary electron number causing this emission, is known as the yield of the target, or

$$\delta = \frac{i_s}{i_p} \qquad (2.29)$$

The yield increases with increasing primary energy, passing through a maximum at some value of primary energy, and then decreasing monotonically. The maximum yield (δ_m) is 0.5 to 1.5 for metals and 1 to 20 for semiconductors and insulators.

If the true secondary electrons are considered separately from the reflected and diffused electrons, then equation 2.29 should be changed to

$$\delta_c = \delta + a + b \qquad (2.30)$$

where a and b are the fractions of primary electrons making up the reflected and diffused components. There is also a field-dependent expression for yield given by

$$\delta = B \exp\left(\frac{A}{V_c}\right) \qquad (2.31)$$

where A and B are constants and V_c is the collector voltage, which holds over narrow ranges of V_c. It should also be remembered that yield curves are

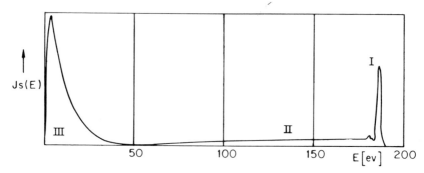

FIGURE 2.12 Energy distribution of secondary electrons (I, II, III are different secondary emission regions). Reprinted from Sherr [3], by permission of Marcel Dekker, Inc. Adapted from Hackenberg and Brauer [13].

temperature dependent, although this factor does not significantly effect the performance of those devices that exhibit secondary emission characteristics, both wanted and unwanted.

A prime example of an unwanted secondary emission effect is the effect on the maximum luminance from a CRT, referred to in the previous section. This maximum luminance is limited by secondary emission because when the voltage V_a is applied to the accelerating electrode of the CRT, the actual voltage accelerating the electrons will become another voltage V_s, usually less than, but sometimes slightly larger than, V_a. This situation is pictured in Figure 2.13. Under these conditions, if we assume a function $S(V_s)$, giving the secondary emission ratio in terms of V_s, and another function $C(V_a - V_s)$, which describes the variation of collector current with collector voltage and is the ratio of the current actually collected to the saturated secondary emission current, the current collected is

$$i_c = i_b S(V_s) C(V_a - V_s) \qquad (2.32)$$

where i_b is the beam current. For equilibrium, the beam current must equal the collector current, and

$$\frac{1}{S(V_s)} = C(V_a - V_s) \qquad (2.33)$$

A plot of $1/S(V_s)$ and the saturation curve are shown in Figure 2.14. Between A and B the secondary emission ratio is larger than 1, and the screen voltage may be higher than the anode voltage, whereas at B the screen voltage drops below the anode voltage and remains there independent of the anode voltage. The breakpoint (B) depends on screen material and processing, and is also called the *sticking potential*, varying between 5000 and 8000 V for the orthosilicate willemite and zinc sulfate. The breakpoint is also affected by screen thickness, age, and residual gas, among other less significant factors. In brief, the thinner the screen, the lower the breakpoint, and the older the CRT, the higher the breakpoint.

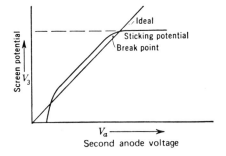

FIGURE 2.13   Effect of secondary emission on accelerating potential. After Zworykin and Morton [14], by permission.

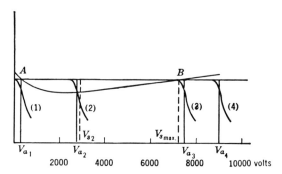

FIGURE 2.14   Equilibrium conditions for secondary emission (A, bombarding volt-age; B, constant screen voltage; parenthetical numbers are different values of V_a). After Zworykin and Morton [14], by permission.

2.3.5   Photosensitive Phenomena

Photoconductivity. A number of materials exhibit the phenomenon of a change in conductivity when they are irradiated in the range from UV to infrared (IR). This characteristic has been used in devices such as the television image tubes described later. The mechanism of photoconductivity is similar to that of luminescence, except that the absorption of a photon creates free carriers, rather than the excited carriers emitting energy. Although not all luminescent materials exhibit photoconductivity and not all photoconductive materials have luminescent capabilities, the two effects frequently appear in the same material, and it may be used for either purpose. Photoconductive phenomena are explained in terms of general solid-state theory and involve the concepts of free carriers known as *holes* and *electrons*, created by light impinging on the photoconductor. Without going into the complexities of solid-state theory, covered in Chapter 3 in detail, a few statements are necessary to arrive at some understanding of what photoconductivity is. So let us bravely plunge in. The change in conductivity due to the absorption of photons is expressed by

$$\Delta\sigma = e(\Delta n\mu_n + \Delta p\mu_p) \tag{2.34}$$

where Δn and Δp are the changes in electron and hole densities, respectively, and μ_n and μ_p are the mobilities. The electron and hole densities are the number of free carriers available to contribute to the conductivity of the material, which may be a conductor, a semiconductor, or an insulator, and the mobilities are related to the transit time of the carrier across the material, on the application of a field across the specimen, by

$$T = \frac{L^2}{\mu V} \tag{2.35}$$

where L is the length of the material between the two contacts and V is the voltage across the two contacts. Another term of significance is the lifetime (τ), which is the amount of time that the carrier remains free to travel in the material before it recombines and becomes inactive. Lifetime may be used to express photosensitivity or the change in conductivity caused by the excitation, divided by the intensity of the excitation. Photosensitivity is also known as the gain of the material, given by

$$G = \frac{\tau_n}{t_n} + \frac{\tau_p}{t_p} \tag{2.36}$$

where t_n is the transit time for holes and t_p is that for electrons.

We may then combine equations 2.35 and 2.36, resulting in

$$G = \frac{(\tau_n\mu_n + \tau_p\mu_p)V}{L^2} \tag{2.37}$$

The rise time of the photoconductor, defined as the time required for the photocurrent to reach some percentage of its final value, is then given by

$$I = I_0(1 - e^{-t/\tau}) \tag{2.38}$$

and the decay time is

$$I = I_0 e^{-t/\tau} \tag{2.39}$$

Photoconductive materials are most commonly found in certain of the television camera pickup tubes, such as the Vidicon, discussed later. Some of the more popular materials used are amorphous selenium, and antimony trisulfide, widely used in Vidicons, as well as lead oxide, which is the material found in the Plumbicon, also discussed later.

There are three possible conditions existing in photoconductors, each leading to its own gain formula. First we have the case where both carriers are mobile and replenished at the electrodes, for which equation 2.37 applies. Next we have the situation where both carriers are mobile but only one is replenished, for which the gain formula is

$$G = \frac{\mu_n + \mu_p}{\mu_p} \tag{2.40}$$

Finally, there is the condition where only one carrier is mobile, and it is replenished at the electrode. Here the gain formula is

$$G = \frac{\mu\tau V}{L^2} \tag{2.41}$$

Up to this point we have been dealing only with homogeneous photoconductors. However, it is also possible to have nonhomogeneous photoconductors, characterized by the existence of some type of barrier to the flow of carriers. An example of this type is the $P-N$ junction, where the height of the barrier is given by

$$V = \frac{kT}{e} \ln \frac{n_p}{n_n} = \frac{kT}{e} \ln \frac{p_n}{p_p} \tag{2.42}$$

Here k is Boltzmann's constant, T is the absolute temperature, e is the electron charge, and the subscripts denote N or P type in which the densities exist. These junctions have a current flow in the dark due to thermal excitation, and when light is absorbed at the junction electron hole pairs are created, separated by the field across the junction, with the holes moving into the P region and the electrons into the N region. This photocurrent density is given by

$$j = qf(L_p + L_n + W) \tag{2.43}$$

where f = number of electron hole pairs generated per unit volume
   L_p = average distance a hole travels in N region before it recombines
   L_n = average distance and electron travels in P region
   W = width of space-charge region

The maximum gain is unity, and the response is linear with light intensity. In addition, since the $P-N$ junction is reverse biased it functions as a capacitance and can be operated in a storage mode. This type of reverse-biased junction is used in the silicon diode array camera tube, discussed later. Further theoretical descriptions of the operation of $P-N$ junction diodes are found in Chapter 3 in the section on light-emitting diodes.

Photoemission. As a corollary to the use of photoconductive materials in imaging tubes, we should also consider photoemissive materials found in many of the non-Vidicon types, in particular the earliest examples of such tubes, such as the iconoscope and image orthicon. Thus photoemissive materials have considerable historical as well as contemporary interest. Such photoemissive materials are used in the form of a cathode, which will emit electrons when it is irradiated with light energy in the spectral range to which it is sensitive. Photocathodes covering the range from the UV to the IR are possible by choosing proper materials, although the majority in use fall in the visible and near IR. The materials making up these cathodes are primarily the bialkali and trialkali photosurfaces, with an older surface, the Ag–O–Cs, still in use when sensitivity in the far IR is required. Figure 2.15 contains response curves of these cathodes in terms of their quantum efficiencies and illustrates the spectral range to be obtained.

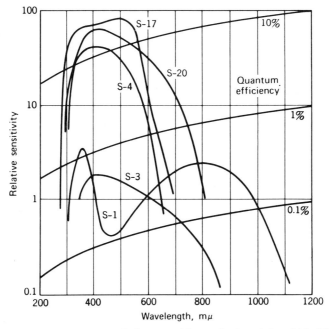

FIGURE 2.15   Response curves of photosensitive cathodes. After Akin [15], by permission.

Two other characteristics of photoemissive cathodes of importance are the dark current and the contrast. The dark current is the current that flows in the absence of illumination, and it may be due to various causes, such as thermionic emission, field emission, and many others. In general, only thermionic emission remains, after proper design precautions are taken, as a significant source of dark current. This current increases with increasing long wavelength response, as is demonstrated by Figure 2.16 in terms of the photoelectric threshold. Radiant response is defined as the response of a photocathode to the total radiation from a lamp operating at a temperature of 2854 K and emphasizes the long-wavelength response, because the lamp has a peak output near 1 μm. An empirical relationship between radiant sensitivity (R) in A/W and thermionic dark current (D) in electrons/cm²/s is

$$\log D = 0.6R - 0.42 \tag{2.44}$$

Temperature also has an effect on thermionic emission, and it is quite large as well as unique for each type. For example, in the case of the bialkali photocathode it will double for each 9°C temperature increase.

We now come to the contrast (c), defined as the signal divided by the sum of the signal and background. It would be more convenient to use the same form of contrast ratio as previously, but since this definition is still current we curb our passion for standardization and adhere to that in use by prac-

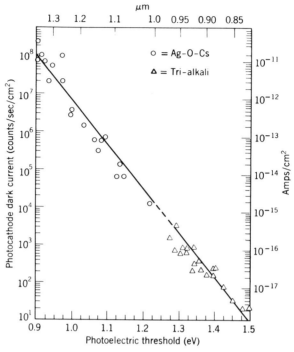

FIGURE 2.16   Dark current as a function of photoelectric threshold at 20°C. After Rome [16], by permission of Plenum Press.

titioners in this specialized field. The background is essentially the dark current, and the contrast is given by

$$c = \frac{\sigma E/k}{\sigma E/k + D} \tag{2.45}$$

where (σE) represents the photocathode response to the irradiance (E) in W/cm². Further detail on photocathodes in specific image tubes is found in that section of this chapter.

2.4   DEVICE CHARACTERISTICS

2.4.1   Introduction

We now proceed from the general discussion of the relevant physical principles to a more detailed examination of various specific types of cathode-ray devices, which embody one or more of these principles, and achieve a wide variety of display-system functions. Although we cannot be complete and exhaustive, within the limits of a reasonably sized volume, we do cover all major types, emphasizing those that have received major usage, but without neglecting several that are of interest because of unique features or because they offer some possibilities of increased usage and improvement in performance. In particular, we pay extensive attention to the new developments in color CRTs and in image tubes, which have greatly extended the performance capabilities of these devices, and we offer the display system user a much wider range of choices, once these capabilities, and, as usual, the associated limitations are appreciated and understood. These have to do in general with such factors as luminance, resolution, sensitivity, and reliability. In addition to the technical descriptions of the various devices, we include separate sections on application considerations relating to each group of devices, expressed primarily in terms of the perceptual factors covered in Chapter 1. Thus it is possible to arrive at some reasonable assessment of the performance potential of these devices in display systems and thus avoid misapplying them in potentially disastrous ways. It is important to bear in mind constantly that the ultimate function of all these devices is to produce some kind of visual image, and hence the visual perceptual factors are the determining elements in assessing performance capabilities and limitations.

2.4.2   Direct-View Monochromatic CRTs (Nonstorage)

Electrostatic Deflection and Focus. The conventional CRT is a well-known device and is widely used. Hence it is the most familiar display device, at least in its external appearance. Its shape is a glass or metal bottle, flaring rapidly or gradually from a narrow neck to a circular or rectangular surface of different dimensions. Internal to this bottle is an electron gun, providing an electron optical system of the type described previously. This gun, in the narrow neck, consists of the elements shown in Figure 2.17, as are the deflection plates and the postacceleration anode, whose functions are discussed later. The CRT illustrated in Figure 2.17 is an electrostatic deflection, electrostatic focus type, and serves as the basis for the following treatment.

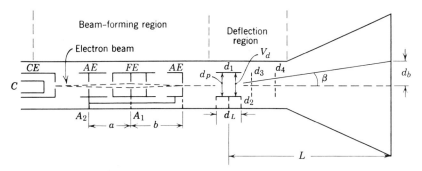

FIGURE 2.17 Electrostatic deflection and focus CRT: C, cathode; CE, control electrode; AE, accelerating electrode; FE, focus electrode; d_1, d_2, horizontal deflection plates. After Sherr [2], by permission.

The electron gun contains a heater, an oxide-coated cathode that emits electrons when heated by the heater, and an assemblage of elements to control beam intensity and focus. The grid, designated as CE in Figure 2.17, acts as the intensity-control grid and results in an amplification factor

$$\mu = -\frac{V_{A2}}{V_{CE}} \qquad (2.46)$$

which determines the current cutoff and is the ratio of the first accelerator voltage to the control-grid electrode voltage at cutoff. The structure also contains a postdeflection accelerator or intensifier that allows the beam to be deflected by the deflection plates (d_1, d_2, d_4, d_4) at a relatively low voltage and then applies the high voltage to the deflected electrons to increase their velocities. Table 2.6 lists some typical voltages used in this type of structure, assuming the intensifier to be at ground and the cathode negative, a common technique to avoid high voltage on the tube shell.

Deflection. The deflection plates are shown schematically in Figure 2.17, with their actual location such that the two pairs are orthogonal to each other and surrounding the electron beam. The action of the deflection plates may be understood by examining the motion of an electron in electrostatic field, which has been done in Section 2.3.2. Therefore, the electron entering the field will follow the trajectory given by equation 2.3 and is shown in Figure 2.1, with the slope of the curve given by equations 2.4–2.6. Similarly, the deflection is expressed by equation 2.21, which may be rewritten as

$$d_b = \frac{L d_L V_d}{2 d_p V_b} \qquad (2.47)$$

where V_b is the acceleration voltage and the other terms are as in the geometry shown in Figure 2.17. We may note from equation 2.47 that the deflection distance (d_b) is directly proportional to the deflection voltage (V_d), so that as beam voltage is increased, deflection voltage must be increased proportionately to maintain deflection distance. Common values for deflection sensitivities have been in the neighborhood of 100 V/cm, so that a 2000-V swing

TABLE 2.6 Cathode-Ray-Tube Potentials

Element	Potential to Cathode	Potential to Ground
Cathode	0	− 15,000
Control grid	− 100 to + 2	− 15,100 to − 14,998
First anode	+ 400	− 14,600
Focus electrode	0 to 400	− 14,600 to − 15,000
Second anode	15,000	0

Source: After Sherr [2], by permission.

would be required for 20-cm deflection. However, more recent designs have reduced this requirement considerably, so that it is possible to get larger deflections at more reasonable voltages while still maintaining the accelerator voltage at a sufficiently high value to achieve good luminance. Hence electrostatic deflection CRTs have become more competitive with magnetic deflection types in those applications calling for both high resolution and good luminance.

These new designs have concentrated on improving the deflection sensitivity by means of incorporating new types of beam accelerators. Although it has been known for many years that deflecting the beam at low potentials, and then accelerating it to the target potential, is one way to achieve better sensitivity, no successful CRT incorporating this principle has been developed until recently, which achieves sizes comparable with those attained by magnetic deflection types. The new designs use the principle of scan magnification, as illustrated in Figure 2.18. Beam acceleration is performed by the gauze or mesh structure shown, and the result is larger scan angles and better deflection sensitivities than those found in electrostatic deflection CRTs using more conventional postdeflection acceleration. The exact technical details of this CRT need not concern us, but it is important from the point of view of applications in that it makes available a reasonable alternative to the magnetic deflection CRT, at luminance levels, resolution and screen sizes that can be used in a variety of applications. Thus screen sizes above 50 cm in diameter, at spot sizes equivalent to 1000 shrinking raster lines and with luminances up to 170 nits, are available and have been incorporated in a number of different display systems, in particular where fast deflection is required. The factors that affect the deflection speed in electrostatic systems are covered in detail in Chapter 4, and at this point it is sufficient to merely note that electrostatic deflection systems are generally faster than magnetic deflection systems for equivalent power consumption, and from a practical point of view are easier to design for high-speed deflection. By high-speed deflection we mean deflection times for a full diameter deflection of less than 10 μs, readily achieved in electrostatic systems using the new CRT designs, at deflection voltages as

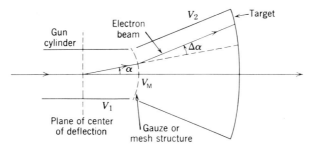

FIGURE 2.18   Scan magnification by means of divergent gauze lens. After Hutter [17], by permission.

much as an order of magnitude less than for the previously available tubes. Another advantage of the new type is that the length of the bottle can be considerably reduced, with lengths comparable to standard television types, and allows the use of electrostatic deflection CRTs in television monitors.

Focus. The beam is focused by means of an electrostatic lens consisting, as shown in Figure 2.17, of A_1 and A_2 with focusing accomplished by changing the voltage on A_1. This is one possible arrangement of elements, with the focusing electrode placed between the two parts of the first accelerating anode, so as to minimize the interaction between the control grid and the focusing electrode. By this means a fixed potential is maintained close to the control grid and the focusing lens is shielded from the control grid, although there is still some interaction and it is necessary to readjust the focus voltage for best spot size whenever the beam current is changed. The basic equation is equation 2.15, and further information about the effect of focus voltage on spot size may be found by rewriting it in terms of Figure 2.17 as

$$\frac{r_s}{r_0} = \frac{b}{a}\left(\frac{V_{a2}}{V_{a1}}\right)^{1/2} \tag{2.48}$$

where r_s = image spot size
r_0 = crossover spot size
b = image distance
V_{a2} = voltage at $A_2(V_1)$
a = object distance
V_{a1} = voltage at $A_1(V_2)$

The significance of equation 2.48 is that the spot size varies as the square root of the voltage ratio and is dependent on the location of the beam crossover point. Since the beam crossover point is affected by the control electrode voltage, this explains the effect of changing the control electrode voltage on the focus voltage required for minimum spot size.

Several other causes of spot size change are independent of the focusing technique employed and apply as well to electromagnetic as to electrostatic focus. They are introduced here for convenience but should be considered as part of the magnetic focus section as well. One such effect may be obtained from the expression

$$dz = K^{1/2}d\left[\frac{r/r_0}{(\ln r/r_0)^{1/2}}\right] \tag{2.49}$$

where r is spot size, z is position on beam, and the value for K has been derived as

$$K^{1/2} = \frac{32.3r_0V_{kV}^{3/4}}{I^{1/2}} \tag{2.50}$$

The solution is

$$\frac{dr}{dz} = \frac{I_{ma}^{1/2}(\ln r/r_0)^{1/2}}{32.3V_{kV}^{3/4}} \tag{2.51}$$

The beam spread may be found by consulting a nomogram such as is shown in Figure 2.19, which gives the change in spot size as a function of the changes in beam voltage and current.

The final effect on spot size to be discussed here is that due to deflection defocusing. Using the approximate proportionality

$$\Delta(r_s) \sim \theta^2 Z\phi \tag{2.52}$$

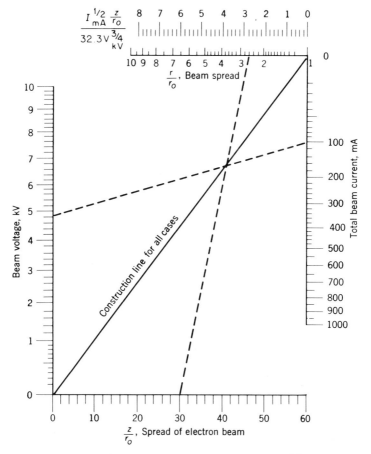

FIGURE 2.19 Beam-spread nomograph. After Spangenberg [1], by permission of McGraw-Hill Book Company.

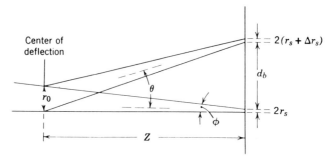

FIGURE 2.20   Deflection defocusing. After Moss [18], by permission.

and the geometry shown in Figure 2.20, we may derive, as the expression for this change,

$$\Delta r_s = C \frac{d_b^2}{Z^2} r_0 \tag{2.53}$$

where C is the constant ($\approx Z$/length of deflection plates), which is the equation for the variation in spot size due to distance from the center. This variation introduces the need for dynamic focus control, proportional to the distance from the center.

Magnetic Deflection.   Another method for deflecting the electron beam is to apply a magnetic field orthogonal to the beam over a short portion of the beam length, as illustrated in Figure 2.21. This assumes the same gun structure as is shown in Figure 2.17, but with the electrostatic plates replaced by the

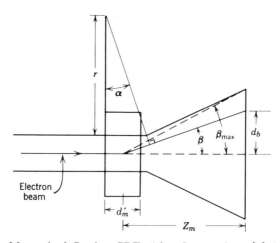

FIGURE 2.21   Magnetic deflection CRT. After Spangenberg [1], by permission of McGraw-Hill Book Company.

magnetic field caused by the current in the deflection yoke. An electron passing through the yoke field will travel in an arc because of the field and will leave the region at some angle relative to the original direction of motion. The radius of the arc may be determined by rewriting equation 2.24 as

$$R = 3.38 \times 10^{-6} \frac{V^{1/2}}{B_m} \tag{2.54}$$

The deflection can be found by noting from Figure 2.21 that the angle α is approximately equal to the angle β and, therefore,

$$\frac{d_m}{R} \approx \frac{d_b}{Z_m} \tag{2.55}$$

Substituting equation 2.55 in equation 2.54 results in

$$d_b = \frac{d_m Z_m B_m}{3.38 \times 10^{-6} V^{1/2}} \tag{2.56}$$

The deflection angle may be expressed in terms of the yoke inductance (L), the CRT anode voltage (V_c), the current through the yoke (I_y), and a yoke sensitivity factor (k) as

$$\sin \alpha = \frac{(k_m L_y)^{1/2} I_y}{(2V_c)^{1/2}} \tag{2.57}$$

which, for small values of α, becomes

$$\sin \alpha = \alpha = d_b \tag{2.58}$$

The change in spot size due to deflection defocusing may be expressed as

$$\Delta r_s = r_0 \left[\frac{(d_b^2 + Z_2)^{1/2}}{Z} - 1 \right] \tag{2.59}$$

and the effect is less than in electrostatic deflection.

Magnetic deflection yokes are located around the tube neck and take the form of a coil with a gap through which the electron beam passes. The center of deflection is determined by the location of the coil, with the amount of deflection controlled by the yoke sensitivity and the allowable angle before the beam goes beyond the neck of the tube, as can be seen from Figure 2.21.

The advantage of magnetic deflection over electrostatic deflection can be deduced by comparing equations 2.47 and 2.56. It can be seen that deflection sensitivity is inversely proportional to $V^{1/2}$ for magnetic and to V for electrostatic deflection, so that higher accelerating potentials may be used with magnetic deflection, allowing better spot size and luminance.

Magnetic Focus. Magnetic focus is illustrated by the arrangement shown in Figure 2.22. In this case, the gun contains the cathode, the control electrode, and the first and second anodes, with the coil outside of the envelope, and around the second anode. Some electrostatic focusing action occurs, but the main effect is due to the focusing coil, and the focusing action is described by equation 2.9. Since, according to equation 2.9 the electrons return to their original relative position in a distance P, along a magnetic path parallel to the beam, beam spreading is avoided, but no reduction in the entering beam diameter is achieved. The beam is focused by adjusting the focus coil current until the proper value of P is reached for best spot size. The combination of magnetic focusing with magnetic deflection is common and has the advantages of high luminance and good resolution.

Luminance. The light output from a CRT, termed luminance, is the result of electrons striking the phosphor and causing the emission of light of some spectral distribution determined by the composition of the phosphor, as described in Section 2.3.3, which discusses the characteristics of interest, such as the luminance under specific conditions of excitation and the decay of this light output with time, once the excitation has been removed. The basic expressions for emitted light intensity are equations 2.26 and 2.27, which may be combined and rewritten in terms of the accelerating voltage (V_b) and current (I_b) as

$$L = \frac{k_b I_b V_b^n}{A} \tag{2.60}$$

where k_b = proportionality factor shown in Table 2.1 in lumens/beam watt
  = $\eta\gamma$
γ = lumens/radiated watt (Table 2.2)
η = phosphor efficiency
A = area of phosphor surface

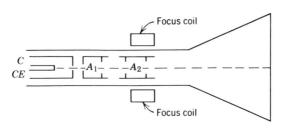

FIGURE 2.22 Magnetic focus CRT. After Sherr [2], by permission.

Values for k_b, γ, and η for various phosphors are given in Tables 2.1 and 2.2. Others may be found in the references, as well as spectral distribution curves for commercially available phosphors.

Equation 2.60 may also be derived from Lenard's equation,

$$L = kI_b(V_b - V_0) \tag{2.61}$$

where I_b and V_b are as before, k is a constant depending on the material, and V_0 is the voltage at which fluorescence begins. Equation 2.61 may be further modified to read

$$L = kI_b(V_s - V_0)^n \tag{2.62}$$

where V_s is the fluorescent screen potential rather than the beam potential and n has a value in the neighborhood of 2. An additional change is introduced by the use of an aluminized backing to improve heat dissipation, and there is a reduction in V_b because of the drop due to the aluminized backing. Finally, the effects of secondary emission on the phosphor screen should be considered. This has been previously described, and is covered by equations 2.32 and 2.33. It is illustrated by Figures 2.13 and 2.14 and is the effect that sets the maximum potential that will increase phosphor luminance, before the secondary emission causes the screen potential and thus the luminance, to become independent of the anode potential. Thus when the voltage V_a is applied to the second anode, the actual voltage accelerating the electrons will be some other voltage V_s, usually less than but sometimes slightly larger than V_a. The equations given are approximately correct over the linear region but do not apply if phosphor saturation occurs. Also, deflection sensitivity, spot size, and luminance are all interrelated, so that usually one is improved at the expense of the others.

Application Considerations. At this point we may pause to ask ourselves what it all means in terms of the actual uses to which these types of CRTs can be put in practical display systems. Detailed discussion of monitors, and display consoles using CRTs is deferred to Chapter 4, but it is appropriate here to look at the CRT as a component and to establish what the pertinent performance parameters and limitations are, independent of the system in which the CRT may be the display device. To this end we evolve a set of CRT specifications, present a range of performance limits in terms of these specification parameters, and compare the relative capabilities of the different types, such as those using electrostatic versus magnetic deflection, the same for the two focus techniques, and at least some of the many phosphor types available. Screen-size limitations, resolution, contrast ratio, and luminance are also considered.

Specification Parameters. Several of the parameters to be considered in determining the application capabilities of a CRT are the same as those developed in Chapter 1. This is not surprising, since they are visual parameters, and the CRT is used as the visual output device. Obviously, the four mentioned in the preceding paragraph are relevant, although in a slightly different form than previously. In addition, as indicated in the preceding paragraph, the type of deflection and focus is important, as well as which phosphor is chosen. We also have deflection sensitivity, tube geometry, and acceleration voltage to examine. Let us look at each one in turn.

ELECTROSTATIC VERSUS MAGNETIC DEFLECTION. The choice of electrostatic or magnetic deflection is influenced by several factors. The two most important are deflection speed and spot size, or resolution. As noted before, for deflection speeds less than 10 μs, electrostatic deflection begins to be superior to magnetic deflection, whereas for deflection speeds less than 5 μs, electrostatic deflection is the only practical way to go. However, as an unavoidable concomitant, for resolution better than about 600 television lines and for luminances above 150 nits it is advisable to choose magnetic deflection, for the reasons described previously. Finally, if tube length is a problem, then magnetic deflection types are up to 30% shorter if wide-angle tubes are used, even when postdeflection magnification is employed in the electrostatic deflection CRT. These comparisons are listed in Table 2.7, which summarizes these factors. It is clear that there is some area for choice where the parameter values overlap, and it may be necessary to include other aspects, such as total power and acceleration voltage, to arrive at a final choice.

ELECTROSTATIC VERSUS MAGNETIC FOCUS. This is a much easier choice to make than electrostatic versus magnetic deflection, since for spot sizes equivalent to more than about 1500 television lines it is generally necessary to select magnetic focus, although there are some special electrostatic types which approach 2000 television lines. However, the need for such high resolution is relatively rare, and in the vast majority of the cases the capabilities

TABLE 2.7   Electromagnetic and Electrostatic CRT Parameters

Parameter	Electromagnetic	Electrostatic
Shape	Round, rectangular	Round, rectangular
Overall length (cm)	36 (55°)	40.5 (50 V/cm)
Useful screen area (cm)	37.5 (nominal)	37.5 (nominal)
Deflection angle (degrees)	55–110	25–50
Deflection factor (V/cm)	—	25–500
Focus voltage (V·s)	0–400	2200
Accelerator voltage (kV)	10–27	10–15
Postaccelerator voltage (kV)	—	18
Line width (cm)	0.005	0.01
Phosphor	Any	Any
Luminance (nits)	>300 (P-31)	>100 (P-31)

of electrostatic focus are adequate. It is also possible to achieve an almost 2:1 improvement in resolution by going to certain special gun designs described later in Section 2.4.6, although only a limited number of types and sizes are available with these guns. Thus magnetic focus is required only for special applications such as printing and flying spot scanners, whereas some of the special CRT types are discussed later in this chapter.

PHOSPHOR TYPE. As we have noted previously, phosphors are characterized by luminous efficiency, color, and decay time. When using monochromatic CRTs, the color is specified by the phosphor coordinates given in the EIA Publication 16C and may be determined by consulting the lists given in the same EIA document. Of course, the actual choice of color is affected by the various perceptual factors given in Chapter 1, as well as the luminous efficiency required. The luminous efficiency values given in Table 2.1 are of some assistance in making this choice, but unfortunately such information is not easy to come by for all phosphors, and it may be necessary to sacrifice some luminous efficiency for the sake of assured values and desired color. As far as the decay characteristic is concerned, if we assume that the system will operate at well above the CFF for the expected luminance level, it is best to choose a phosphor with a decay time fast enough to eliminate any objectionable smear. Thus decay time could be as long as the 36 ms to 1% of P-4, which ensures that no detectable image will remain from a previous frame, and yet not introduce any flicker. The advantage of using the longest decay for avoiding flicker, is that the average light output is maximum due to the phosphor emitting for the longest possible time. The relevant factor is the duty cycle, or what percentage of each frame the light output is above some specified value, such as 10% of maximum. It turns out that the average luminance is given by

$$L_a \cong L_p d_c \qquad (2.63)$$

where L_p is the peak luminance and d_c is the duty cycle, so that the importance of maintaining the light output and, therefore, using the longest possible decay time is evident. The actual average luminance that can be achieved, however, may be better for a fast-decay phosphor, if its peak luminance is high, than for the longer decay time, lower-peak luminance one, so that the choice is not always, if ever, obvious.

RESOLUTION. Resolution is somewhat difficult to define for a CRT because it is so dependent on many factors such as acceleration voltage to be used, beam current, whether focus correction circuits are to be included to compensate for variations over the face of the tube, and in particular what method is to be used to specify the resolution measurement. Manufacturers will frequently give information on line width or spot size at some stated acceleration voltage and beam current, but the exact point at which the width or size is measured is not always given. Thus it may be necessary to obtain more specific information, using nomographs of the type given in Figure 2.19 to convert to spot size at expected voltage and current values, and then converting to shrinking raster for uniformity by means of the conversion factors given in Table 7.4. Several of the measurement techniques have been discussed in the resolution section of Chapter 1, and the others are covered in Chapter 7. At this point it is only necessary to stress the importance of knowing the conditions under which the measurements are made, and the type of measurement used in specifying this parameter. In general, shrinking-raster resolutions of over 500 lines are not difficult to obtain with standard CRTs, and 1000-line capability may also be achieved without undue cost or effort. However, anything over 1000 lines may lead to special types or the need for careful circuit design and adjustment, so that resolution requirements should be set this high only after judicious examination of the visual data presentation. Thus it is not unreasonable to go as high as 2000 lines, if needed, although at some considerable increase in complexity and cost of the total system.

SIZE. The main limiting factor in size determination is the maximum bulb size obtainable. Because of the strong influence of entertainment television on bulb manufacturers, it is extremely difficult to get CRTs in sizes and shapes other than those current in the television market. This puts a definite limitation on the maximum size that can be found, which is about 65 cm, although there have been some CRTs made as large as 75 cm. However, apart from the mechanical difficulties of handling a bulb this large, the realities of the marketplace make it inadvisable to build any display system around a scarce or hard-to-get component. This situation has progressively worsened over the years, as the bulb manufacturers become fewer in number, to say nothing of CRT manufacturers, who are also rapidly leaving the field. As a result, once the basic size requirements are determined by means of the methods described in Chapter 1, it is then most advisable to adapt them to a standard-size bulb and certainly not to ask for sizes beyond that found in catalogs of standard types.

Another aspect of size is bulb length. As noted previously, this is affected by whether electrostatic or magnetic deflection is used, and by the deflection angle in the case of the magnetic deflection types. It is possible to get 90° tubes with a 40 cm × 50 cm viewing area in a total length of under 60 cm. Wider deflection angles result in even shorter bulbs, so that although it is not quite as good as the flat tube described later, it is certainly manageable.

LUMINANCE. Luminance is in many ways as difficult to specify as is resolution. As we can see from equations 2.60 and 2.62, many factors enter into determining the luminance that may be obtained from the CRT. In addition, manufacturers' data are not always as clear and specific as one might wish. The best form for luminance data from the user's point of view is with the acceleration voltage, current, line-deflection time or raster rate, and phosphor

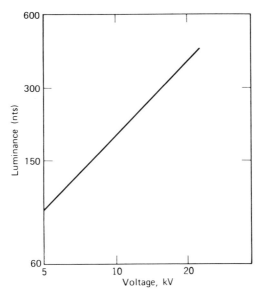

FIGURE 2.23 Luminance vs. beam voltage. After Sherr [2], by permission.

type all specified. If the phosphor type has been chosen and the resolution specified, then the measurement may properly be made or extrapolated from the data supplied by the manufacturer. Extrapolation may be done by means of the curves in Figures 2.23 and 2.24, which relate luminance at any voltage, current, and deflection speed to that at different values of these parameters. As a word of warning, it should be recognized that these curves, while reasonably accurate are not precise, and deviations from predicted values of ±20% are not uncommon. As to the range of luminance values that may be achieved, we may go from the barely visible to as high as 5000 nits, so that this choice is limited primarily by other factors such as resolution and phosphor type.

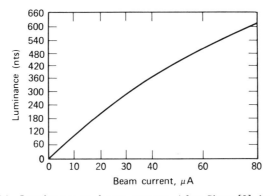

FIGURE 2.24 Luminance vs. beam current. After Sherr [2], by permission.

SPECIFICATION EXAMPLE. We may ask ourselves what the value is to the user of going into such detail about a component that will be part of a monitor or console and may not be readily changed from the one supplied in the complete display unit. In some cases it may be necessary to live with what can be obtained, but in others there is some flexibility in CRT type and other operating parameters that determine CRT performance. In the first case, it is at least possible, by applying these data, to assess the probable performance of the system against the claimed performance, whereas in the other the specification for the CRT can lead to the selection of the most appropriate type with the corresponding advantages in performance. To this end, representative specifications are given in Table 2.7, which may be used as a standard when needed.

2.4.3   Color

Although the color CRT has received considerable development because of its extensive use in home entertainment television, the designs that have been satisfactory for that application are not adequate for all information display systems. However, since the standard television color tube is basic and is used so extensively, several techniques for producing such color CRTs are discussed first, followed by the only approach that has been successful in providing a non-television-oriented color CRT, namely, the penetration type.

Shadow Mask. The most successful color CRT is that adopted by the majority of the television industry and incorporated in the innumerable color television sets that are contributing so effectively to the entertainment if not the edification of the viewing public. This large-scale utilization has led to levels of production that have reduced the cost while achieving the type of performance adequate to meet the requirements of that market. As a result, although the unit may be inadequate for the needs of the designer of complex information display systems, it is a very successful design and should be considered in terms of its capabilities. For this purpose Figure 2.25 may be used, which shows a schematic arrangement of the basic elements making up the shadow-mask color CRT. These elements consist of three electron guns so arranged that the beams will pass through the apertures in the mask and impinge on the phosphor screen in specific locations. The phosphor screen is made up of triplets or triads of dots, each triad containing one dot of each of the three primary colors, red, blue, and green. The arrangement is such that the beam corresponding to the desired color will strike only the phosphor dots producing this color. All three beams are deflected together, with a single yoke, and the electrostatic focus elements for the three guns are connected in parallel so that a single focus control is sufficient.

Even if perfect alignment of the mask and phosphor triads is assumed, the CRT is still subject to certain limitations, chiefly in regard to resolution and luminance. The resolution restriction is due to the necessity for aligning the

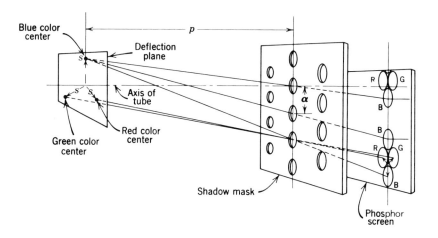

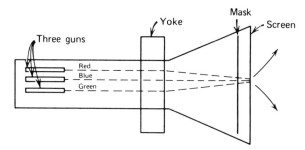

FIGURE 2.25   Shadow-mask color CRT. After Law [19], by permission.

mask apertures and the phosphor dot triads, so that the mask aperture size
controls the resolution that can be attained. This is shown by the equations

$$N = \frac{2A}{\sqrt{3}}\left(\frac{h}{a}\right)^{1/2}$$ (2.64)

where N = number of color triads
     A = w/H = aspect ratio
     h = mask height
     a = distance between mask apertures

and

$$R_h = k_h(N)^{1/2}$$
$$R_v = k_v(N)^{1/2}$$ (2.65)

where R_h = horizontal resolution
     R_v = vertical resolution
     k = proportionality factors

The proportionality factors range within 0.67 to 0.82 for k_h and 0.72 to 0.93 for k_v. Using the standard number of 357,000 dot triads, 0.75 for k_h, and 0.8 for k_v, results in

$$R_h = 440 \text{ television lines}$$

$$R_v = 475 \text{ television lines}$$

as the approximate resolution. Higher-resolution versions have been built, and are available at some increase in cost, but the version just described remains the one in common use.

The luminance is a function of the phosphor-screen current and voltage. The current is given by

$$I_s = I_0\left[1 - \exp\left(\frac{-M^2}{4b^2}\right)\right]\frac{\pi}{18\sqrt{3}}\left(\sqrt{3} - \frac{M^2}{S}\right) \tag{2.66}$$

where I_s = screen current
$I_0 = \pi\rho_0 b^2$
ρ_0 = current density on beam axis
b = beam location values for current density ρ_0/e
M = diameter of beam in deflection plane
S = separation of beam axis from tube axis in deflection plane

The maximum beam efficiency is about 9%, so that with three beams the total efficiency is 27%, as compared with a monochrome tube efficiency of 80%. This leads to a significant reduction in luminance for the shadow-mask CRT from that attained by a standard type.

Misalignment and misregistration of the three beams will lead to loss of purity for colors produced by combinations of the primaries, as well as some reduction in luminance due to a smaller part of the beams passing through the apertures. In addition, there are a number of effects due to the magnetic field of the earth, deflection-angle change in the yoke-deflection center, and asymmetrical spreading (degrouping) of phosphor dot triads due to nonuniform magnification. The first effect is compensated for by means of magnets placed around the tube neck, and the other two are corrected for in the manufacturing process. This process uses a light source with a correction lens to predistort the location of the phosphor dots laid down by means of a photoresist. The light source location can be used in a similar fashion to compensate for the spreadings. The manufacturing processes involved are rather complex and are economically practical only because of the large quantities involved. However, when they are applied to the much smaller quantities required of special designs such as the very high-resolution versions, costs increase considerably, and the resultant device may be an order of magnitude more expensive than the standard version. Most recently, this condition is being alleviated by the growing market for high-resolution monitors to be used in HDTV and computer-generated displays, where the new standards call for resolution in the 1000-television-line range.

Somewhat earlier there have been several improvements in the design of shadow-mask color CRTs, leading to better visual performance, smaller size, simpler registration of the three colors, and freedom from doming, with the last associated with the potential for higher resolution at lower cost, better luminance, and higher contrast ratios. All of these developments are sufficiently important to warrant some further discussion.

The matrix screen is an attempt to overcome the loss in luminance and resultant brightness due to the use of a neutral density filter as the face plate to increase the contrast ratio. This arises as a result of the large amount of area in the viewing surface not covered by any phosphor, as can be seen from Figure 2.25, where the need to align the phosphor dots with the mask holes to improve convergence leads to as much as 50% of the surface merely reflecting ambient light. The matrix screen covers all this area with black, thus reducing back-scattered and reflected light by the same amount as the faceplate. It is thus possible to reduce the loss in the faceplate without affecting contrast, and a brighter picture is the result.

Two other improvements are concerned with the electrical characteristics of the CRT. First, wide angle deflection permits the length of the tube to be decreased by a significant amount from the earlier 45° and 70° tubes, as can be understood by reference to Figure 2.21. It is apparent from the geometry of the deflection process that, in order to cover a given length on the faceplate, the distance from the deflection center to the faceplate is governed by the deflection angle. This is also shown by equation 2.58, where the deflection distance equals the deflection angle. Deflection angles of 120° are common in modern CRTs, and the resultant reduction in overall length is significant.

The next improvement, the in-line gun, has been a feature of the Trinitron (discussed in the next section) from its inception. Indeed, this feature incorporates some of the techniques used in the Trinitron, specifically the use of vertical stripes and horizontal beams, as shown in Figure 2.26. It is claimed that this construction is superior to that used in the Trinitron, but the main advantage for the in-line gun version of the shadow-mask CRT is that the three guns and the yoke are prealigned at the factory and no convergence adjustments are required. This principle is illustrated in Figure 2.27, with the yoke rendered astigmatic, so that a circular object becomes a vertical line and the three beams converge to the center. All yokes are essentially identical and are positioned and fixed on the tube at the factory, thus eliminating the 12 convergence adjustments required by the standard shadow-mask tube (SMT).

The last improvement among the four is the use of the flat tension mask (FTM) technology. The increasing demand for high resolution has led to the need for ultrastable masks so that the bowing of the mask due to heating could be minimized without having to reduce the beam current. The bowing leads to misregistration, and the reduction of beam current results in lower

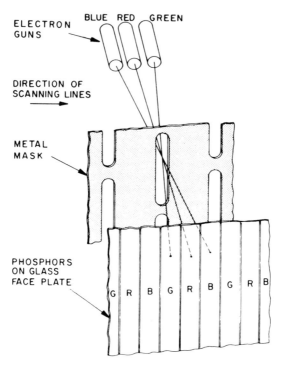

FIGURE 2.26 Vertical stripe shadow-mask color CRT. After Herold [20], by permission.

luminance so that this reduction is an undesirable way to minimize bowing. One solution that has achieved considerable success is the use of the flat tension mask. In this concept a tensed foil mask is used, and high-ultor power is possible since mask deformation occurs only when the temperature rise causes total loss of map tension. Figure 2.28 shows the basic FTM construction, and Figure 2.29 shows the doming reduction achieved through the use of this technique. The higher currents possible before mask tension is lost permit up to eight times greater raster power before the first loss of purity than with a conventional mask. In addition, the flat mask allows inexpensive flat glass to be used as the faceplate, which facilitates improvements in optical features such as the reduction of extraneous reflections by the use of anti-reflective coatings.

Trinitron. The Trinitron is the most successful alternative to the shadow-mask CRT for color television. It is an outgrowth, albeit with considerable modifications, of the Chromatron, which at one time offered promise of achieving a certain success in improving on some aspects of shadow mask performance while still permitting economical manufacturing processes. The Chromatron consisted of parallel stripes of color phosphors in alternating red, green, and blue triplets, with a grid structure in front to focus and deflect the beam so

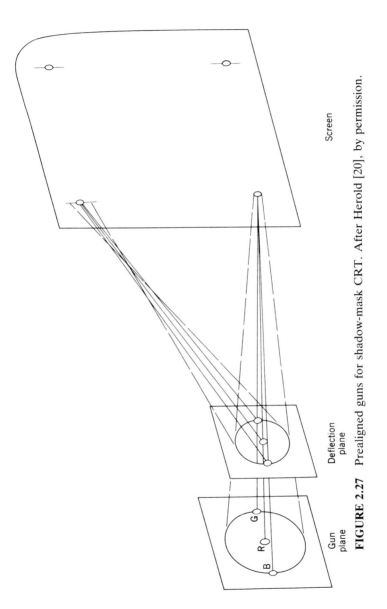

Screen

Deflection
plane

Gun
plane

G

R

B

FIGURE 2.27 Prealigned guns for shadow-mask CRT. After Herold [20], by permission.

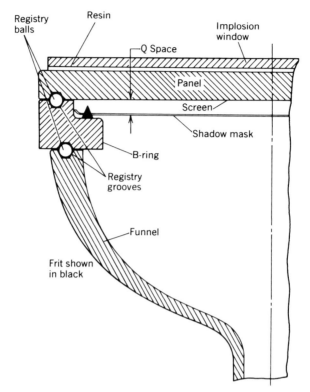

FIGURE 2.28   Basic FTM construction. After Dietch et al. [21], by permission.

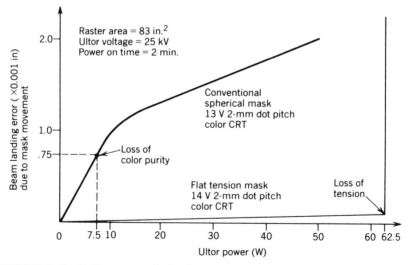

FIGURE 2.29   Full raster mask doming. After Dietch et al. [21], by permission.

as to direct it to the appropriate color stripe. Although a three-gun version was considered, the main concentration had been on the single-gun device, shown in Figure 2.30. For this design the deflection is given by

$$E_d = \frac{2E_i}{\pi} \frac{D}{d} \ln \frac{D}{R}$$ (2.67)

where E_i = voltage between deflection grid and cathode
   D = grid spacing
   d = grid to phosphor-screen distance
   R = grid wire diameter

With characteristic values for the physical parameters and an E_i of 4 kV, E_d is approximately 500 V to deflect the beam across the stripes. Since the grid spacing and stripe width can be made smaller than the shadow-mask apertures and the phosphor dot triplets, higher resolutions may be attained more readily with this structure, although the use of more than 1000 television lines does not appear practical. Also, since the mask transmission loss is eliminated, the potential luminance approaches that of a monochrome CRT and is 50 to 100% better than that of the shadow mask CRT. The Chromatron appeared, therefore, to be a tube with better performance potential, but production problems were never completely solved, so that it has been replaced by the

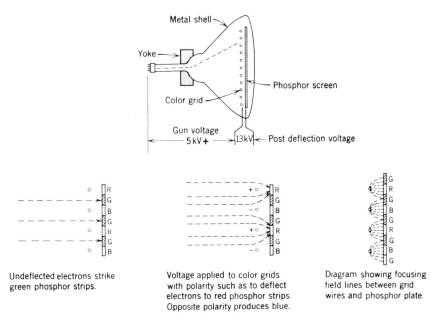

FIGURE 2.30 Chromatron color CRT. After Dressler [22], by permission.

Trinitron as the only successful competitor to the shadow-mask color CRT for mass use.

The structure of the in-line gun Trinitron is shown schematically in Figure 2.31, and its resemblance to the Chromatron, at least superficially, is evident. It began with the stripe structure of the Chromatron but altered the grid so that it consisted of a more rigid structure, closer to the one used for the conventional shadow mask. However, there are no horizontal ties, so that vertical resolution is not affected. In addition, since a single lens with a large diameter is used, in conjunction with a three-aperture plate or three in-line guns to produce the three in-line beams, aberrations are kept small, and small spot sizes may be achieved. The in-line guns also simplify convergence, and as a final advantage the transmission of the apertures is one-third better than the shadow mask, as is evident from the delta-gun structure, also shown in Figure 2.31. However, if we examine the horizontal and vertical resolving power of the two structures, as shown in Figure 2.32, the mask SMT is seen to be better in the horizontal direction. However, the Trinitron is frequently found to be subjectively sharper in appearance. The reason for this has been attributed to the better rise-time characteristics (demonstrated by Figure 2.33) and is said to be due to the greater transmittance of the Trinitron aperture,

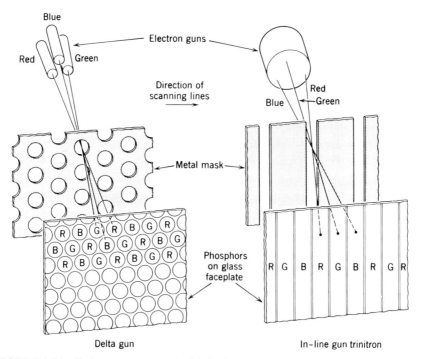

FIGURE 2.31   Delta gun compared with in-line gun Trinitron. After Herold [20], by permission.

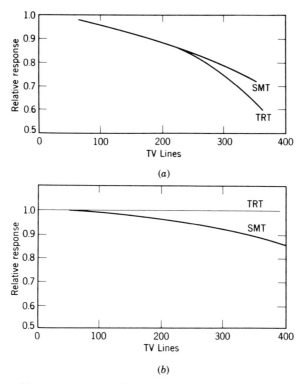

(a)

(b)

FIGURE 2.32 (a) Horizontal and (b) vertical resolving power in television lines for shadow-mask and Trinitron color CRTs. After Machida and Fuse [23], by permission.

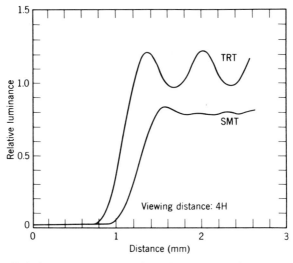

FIGURE 2.33 Relative step response of shadow-mask and Trinitron color CRTs. After Machida and Fuse [23], by permission.

and the single set of aperture rows. This results in a figure of merit advantage of 45%, where the figure of merit is given by

$$F_m = \frac{kT}{R} \tag{2.68}$$

where k = proportionality factor
T = transmittance of aperture
R = step response rise distance

There has been some questioning of the significance of these results, but until some alternative explanation is offered, it may be assumed that they are valid. In addition, further improvements in the gun structure have added focus control and astigmatic correction to the Trinitron gun. This improvement has led to significant reductions in spot size at the edges of the screen. When added to the new self-convergence yoke, it has led to a high-resolution 20-V version of the Trinitron as well as a 1080-mm diagonal flat, square color CRT that achieves state-of-the-art results.

These improvements in Trinitron performance are being matched by shadow-mask systems using in-line guns that are also designed to minimize spot distortion but do not use a self-converging yoke. This is termed the DAF-Q system, and the results in reducing spot size and distortion are comparable to those achieved with the new Trinitron. Thus the battle between the two basic approaches continues and the designer of CRT displays can count on having cathode-ray display devices available that can meet the high-resolution requirements imposed by HDTV and computer graphics applications, among others. The Trinitron is becoming more readily available to designers so that it may play a larger role than its restriction to Sony products has allowed.

Beam Index. Another attempt to improve on the performance of the shadow-mask color CRT is one in which a scanning beam is used to determine the position of the color beams. This is conceptually the simplest approach to color CRTs, since no mask is required, and either one or three beams may be used for the color dots or stripes. It has not achieved much success over the years, although the technique was considered as long ago as 1925 by Zworykin, and the first intensive effort to develop a tube based on the general principle of a scanning pilot beam was by the Philco Corporation in the early 1950s. Thus it is primarily of historical interest, but there have been some renewed efforts to improve the device and find new uses for it that make some discussion of the earlier efforts warranted.

The CRT developed by Philco was called the "apple tube," which has no connection with the "Apple" computer. It turned out to be an unfortunate designation since the effort was abortive and it ended up as the "bad apple" tube. The basic structure of this "beam index" tube, shown in Figure 2.34, incorporates the major features of any such system. The version shown con-

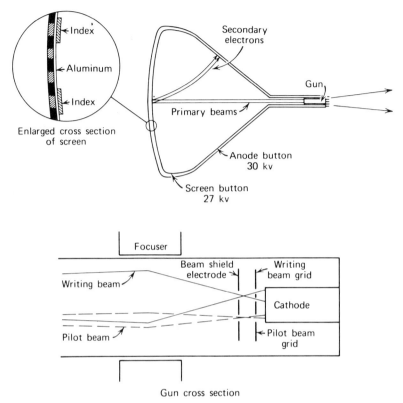

FIGURE 2.34 Beam index color CRT. After Barnett [24], by permission.

tains an electron gun made up of a single cathode and a means for splitting up the electrons into two beams, one of which is termed the *pilot beam*, and is the scanning beam used to determine the position of the color beam or beams. In the case shown in Figure 2.34, a single color beam is used and is made to converge at the deflection center with the pilot beam, so that a single deflection system may be used. Magnetic deflection and focus are used, and the color phosphors are laid down in parallel stripes, somewhat as in the Trinitron. The index stripes are laid down behind the red phosphor stripes, and the pilot beam is separated from the main beam by a vertical distance of 2.5 mm and is modulated at 41.7 MHz. This carrier is then modulated by the color change frequency of 6.4 MHz due to the 350 phosphor line triads, and the sum frequency term of 48.1 MHz is selected by means of a 2-MHz-wide amplifier centered at 48.1 MHz. This signal is then mixed back with the 41.7 MHz signal as shown in Figure 2.35, and the modulated writing beam hitting the phosphor stripes produces a sum-frequency term, which is in turn mixed with the color signal, resulting in a difference term given by

$$A \cos(\omega_c t + \phi_c - \phi_r - \phi_i) \tag{2.69}$$

where $\omega_c/2\pi$ = 6.4 MHz

ϕ_c = color phase

ϕ_r = reference phase

ϕ_i = index beam phase

Then, if the index stripes are behind the red stripes, ϕ_r is set equal to zero and the red color signal will reach its maximum at $\omega_c t$ equal to ϕ_i. We now have a means for determining when the color beam is at the red phosphor stripe, with the other colors coming at fixed periods in relation to this time. Unfortunately, this system, although it has been made to work, imposes too many severe requirements on the structure of the CRT to be practical, and it was abandoned after several years of intensive development. Another version has been developed using UV phosphor index stripes in place of the secondary-emission index stripes found in the "apple" tube. This approach has the advantage that only a single beam is needed, and the index current becomes zero when the beam leaves the index stripe. However, most of the other problems found in the construction of the "apple" tube remain. The operation of the tube is illustrated in Figure 2.36, and it can be seen that the indexing beam is replaced by a photomultiplier that picks up the output from the UV-emitting index strips. Again, this index signal must be mixed with the chrominance signal, in a manner similar to the secondary-emission version, to produce a chrominance component of the video signal applied to the CRT grid, also expressed by equation 2.69. The gun is similar to the signal gun of

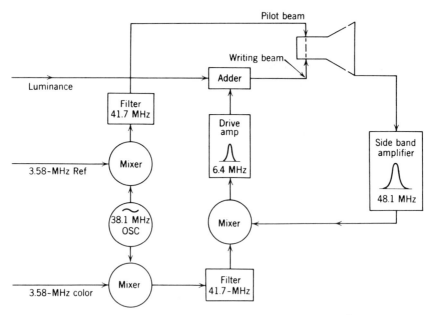

FIGURE 2.35 Block diagram of "Apple" system. After Morell [25], by permission.

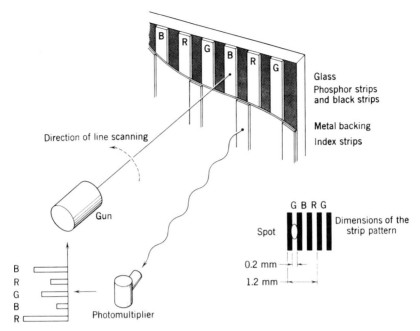

FIGURE 2.36   Principle of the beam-indexing color television display. After Hasker and de Klerk [26], by permission.

the secondary-emission tube, and considerable effort was expended by Philips Eindhoven on the design of this gun.

Most recently, a new design of a 5-in. V-beam index tube has been designed for use in a color monitor intended for automotive applications. The basic configuration of this tube is shown in Figure 2.37, and it is somewhat similar to the Philips design, differing in the location of the index stripe and in the type of material used in the index stripe. The characteristics of this CRT are shown in Table 2.8, and it can be seen from this table that the index stripe is a P-46 green phosphor. The light from the index stripe is converted from 510 nm to 610 nm by means of a dye on the condenser plates to match the PIN diode peak sensitivity point. This index tube has achieved a peak white luminance of 5000 nits, and a contrast ratio of 6 under an ambient of 5000 lx with a 36% transmission filter. The resolution of 264 triplets is not high but may be sufficient for the designated application. In any event, the beam index approach is not completely forgotten and may find other applications for which it is better suited than the shadow-mask and Trinitron types.

Beam Penetration.   The beam penetration CRT is another approach to the production of a color image that does not require multiple beams, masks, stripes, or index strips. As such, it appeared to offer a feasible alternative to the shadow-mask and Trinitron types, in particular when high resolution was required. However, the development of the high-resolution color CRTs using

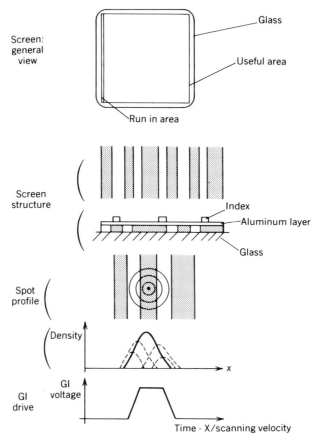

Screen: general view

Glass

Useful area

Run in area

Screen structure

Index

Aluminum layer

Glass

Spot profile

Density

GI drive

GI voltage

Time - X/scanning velocity

FIGURE 2.37 Beam index CRT. After Thomson CSF [27], by permission.

shadow-mask or Trinitron techniques has caused the penetration tube to fall into desuetude, and it is primarily only of historical interest. However, it is an alternative approach and may return at some time in the future. Therefore, some description of this type is included here.

This color CRT is based on the principle that the depth of penetration of an electron beam into a phosphor is expressed by the Thomson–Whiddington

TABLE 2.8 Beam Index CRT

Parameter	Value
Viewing Area (in.)	$4 \times 3.1 - 6.1 \times 6.1$
Number of Triads per Line	330–417
Index: Color Stripe Ratio	1:2–1:3
Luminance (ft L)	650–2200

law

$$V_0^2 - V^2 = bX \qquad (2.70)$$

where V_0 = initial electron energy
   V = energy remaining after penetration to depth X
   b = a constant

Thus a single beam and a multilayer phosphor may be used to generate the different colors, eliminating the need for masks or grids to ensure that the proper beam hits its correct phosphor. On first glance this approach appears to have all the advantages of the index CRT, without any of the attendant disadvantages in complicated tube structure. The resolution is limited primarily by the beam size, as in the monochromatic CRT, and the full beam energy is available at the phosphor. Unfortunately, as in all things in nature, there is never an improvement that does not introduce new problems. In this case it has to do with the associated circuitry required, covered in Chapter 4. At this point we restrict ourselves to a description of the structure of the CRT and the characteristics that lead to the circuit problems. A structure that has been devised for such a tube is shown in Figure 2.38, consisting of an electron gun of the magnetic deflection, electrostatic variety, and a phosphor sandwich made up of two layers of different phosphors. Additional layers are possible, but two are enough to illustrate the principles involved, and the only versions that are commercially available have been limited to two layers.

To understand the operation of the beam-penetration tube, we must add to equation 2.70 Lenard's absorption law for the variation in beam current caused by penetration, which is

$$\frac{i[X + dX]}{i(X)} = \exp(-\alpha/dX) \qquad (2.71)$$

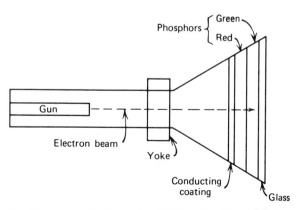

FIGURE 2.38   Beam penetration color CRT. After Sherr [2], by permission.

where $\alpha = b'\rho/V^2$
ρ = density
b' = constant
i = beam current

Combining equations 2.70 and 2.71 leads to an expression for the ratio of the energy $W(X)$, dissipated in the depth (X) to the initial energy W_0,

$$\frac{W(X)}{W_0} = (1 - bX)^{1/2 + ab'} \tag{2.72}$$

or, if we assume the two layers to be red- and green-emitting, as shown in Figure 2.38, then the red-green luminance ratio is given by

$$\frac{R}{G} = \frac{V_0 - V}{V} \tag{2.73}$$

We might note at this point that in the actual CRT, instead of two layers, the phosphor particles are coated with a thin onionskin covering exhibiting different resistance to the penetration of the beam for the different color phosphors. Thus the same result is achieved of differentiating the emission from the two phosphors as a function of beam voltage, as in the two-layer structure, but in a form that is much easier to manufacture. The analysis applies to either structure but is somewhat easier to understand if the two-layer structure is used, which is why we return to it for further explanation.

Since $(V_0 - V)$ is the energy lost in the red layer, substituting for V, the use of equation 2.70 and addition of a correction for the energy scattering of the beam leads to the corrected expression

$$\frac{R}{G} = \frac{V_0^{(2c+1)}}{V_0^2 - bX} - 1 \tag{2.74}$$

where $c \cong 2.5$. The electron beam loses 50% of its energy in the first 22% of its penetration and 80% in half the range. This is illustrated in Figure 2.39, which contains a plot of equation 2.72, although the actual measurements on aluminum have indicated a somewhat lower absorption. In any event, the emission from each phosphor is clearly a function of the accelerating voltage, and we may favor one or the other by the proper selection of this voltage.

We now have a one-gun color CRT, with no mask, that can approach the resolution of the monochromatic tube and will deliver full beam energy to the phosphors. However, as noted previously, there are several circuit complications involved in using this CRT. The most significant one is the need for switching high voltages at rather high rates of speed, if one is to meet the requirements for color television. Normal accelerating voltages range from 6 kV for red to about 12 kV for green in the types that are commercially

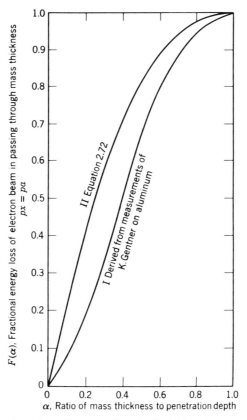

FIGURE 2.39   Fraction of total energy absorbed within a layer containing a fraction α of the penetration mass thickness. After Morell [25], by permission.

available. Thus to enable switching of colors at television rates, it is necessary to be able to change this voltage in about 100 ns, assuming standard sweep rates and horizontal resolution with a single sweep time assumed to be 60 μs and the number of resolution elements in one sweep time to be 480. The exact number is not very important, since switching 6 kV into over 100 pF is a formidable task, requiring high-power radar techniques. In addition, the deflection sensitivity and focus change with changes in accelerating voltage (equations 2.47 and 2.48), so that it is necessary to incorporate dynamic compensation operating at the same rates. The latter two requirements are not insuperable, in reasonable terms, but the 6-kV switching at this speed is impractical; hence this form of the CRT does not lend itself to television use. However, it by no means limits its use in many other applications, where the colors can be grouped so that much longer switching times are available, as is covered further in Chapter 4. It should be noted also that the colors are not as highly saturated as in the other types, except for the red, since there is always some component of the lower-voltage phosphor emission present.

This does not impede generation and recognition of at least four colors, even with the dual phosphor version pictured in Figure 2.38, so that the CRT has its place in the appropriate applications, where the better resolution capabilities compensate for the limited color range and some increase in circuit complexity and cost.

Before leaving the penetration color CRT, one other version should be considered, which proposes to overcome the high-power switching problem by incorporating three guns, one for each color. A possible gun structure for this version is shown in Figure 2.40, and is certainly a conceivable design. The problem in this case is the need to operate the separate cathodes at voltage levels differing by the same amount as the switching voltage, leading to some difficulty in constructing the CRT gun and other difficulties in the circuitry. The circuit difficulties are rather readily surmounted, but the CRT gun construction may not permit easy implementation. In any event, it is an approach that lends itself to standard television use and may receive further development, for the same reasons that were adduced to explain the continuing effort on index tubes. Therefore, when and if the time comes when this type of CRT is available and is incorporated in operating systems, we will not be caught with our cathodes down.

Aiken Tube. As another example of the many efforts to achieve color CRTs, we should mention a rather interesting type, named after its inventor, W. R.

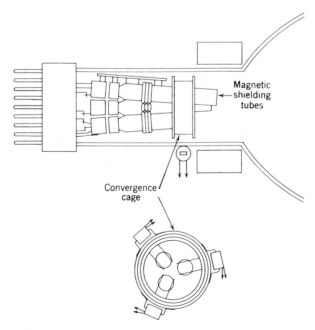

FIGURE 2.40 Gun structure for three-beam penetration color CRT. After Morell [25], by permission.

Aiken [28]. The main initial incentive for this tube was to produce a CRT with a flat structure, as illustrated in Figure 2.41. We include it here because, although it has seen little acceptance even as a monochromatic type, despite its flat structure, with the continuing interest in color tubes, it may be resurrected at some time and is, therefore, of interest. The principle of operation is depicted in Figure 2.41, which shows a set of horizontal plates followed by an essential field-free region and then a set of vertical deflection plates. The gun is electrostatically focused and the beam electrostatically deflected by two sets of deflection plates, so that the basic equations for this type of structure apply. In addition, a unique focusing effect occurs because of the structure of the deflection system, as is illustrated in Figure 2.42. Two electrons separated by Δy_0, converge at F, where V_0 is greater than the deflection-plate potential, V_n. This leads to the expression for the focal length

$$f = \frac{\Delta x}{\Delta \theta} \sin \theta \qquad (2.75)$$

and the coordinates of F are

$$X_f = \tan \theta \, \frac{\Delta x}{\Delta \tan \theta} \qquad (2.76)$$

Another effect is due to the exit slot in the x direction at V_0, and since the deflection in the yz plane is given by

$$\tan \alpha = \frac{V_x}{V_y} \qquad (2.77)$$

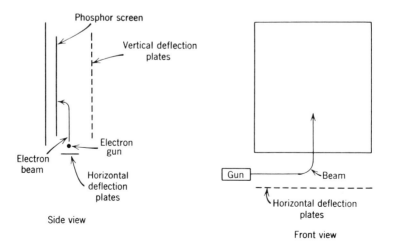

FIGURE 2.41 Structure of Aiken flat CRT. After Aiken [28], by permission.

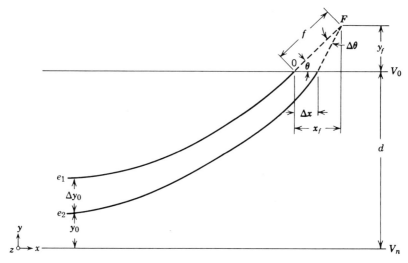

FIGURE 2.42   Aiken flat CRT deflection focusing. After Aiken [28], by permission.

or

$$\tan \alpha = \frac{z}{f_{yz}} \tag{2.78}$$

then

$$f_{yz} = \frac{2E_1(d - y_0)}{E_2 - E_1} \tag{2.79}$$

where E_1 is the electrostatic field on the incident side of the aperture plate and E_2 is the electrostatic field on the exit side of the aperture plate. This effect may cause either divergence or convergence, depending on whether E_1 is greater or less than E_2. The usual number of deflection plates is 10, and in the absence of deflection voltage the beam will pass directly through the deflecting region. By applying voltage to the appropriate plates, either successively for a sweep or independently for random deflection, the beam may be deflected to the desired location. Since the device requires only a thin envelope, it is very attractive for space-limited applications, although rather high deflection voltages (8 kV) are required. The color version that has been designed is shown in Figure 2.43, using a two-sided target structure and two guns. This version is limited to two colors, and somewhat elaborate ridged structures would be required to add a third basic color. However, although the monochromatic type has been built and operated successfully, the color version remains more of a theoretical possibility than a practical approach to the production of useful color CRTs. This should not lead to the conclusion

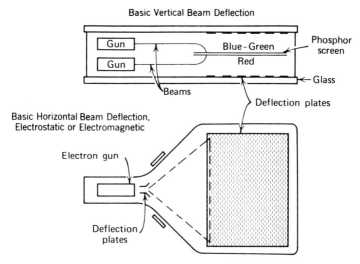

Basic Vertical Beam Deflection

FIGURE 2.43   Two-color Aiken flat tube. Courtesy of Video Color Corporation.

that it cannot be made to work, given enough interest, and of course money, that universal catalyst.

Application Comments. We can hardly dignify this section with the heading "application considerations," because of the limited choice available. Thus we content ourselves with the more modest one of "comments." As has been pointed out in the previous sections, there are only two practical types of color CRTs that meet the requirements of raster systems, and one additional one that may be used in certain special applications. The relevant characteristics of these three types are listed in Table 2.9, which provides as complete a basis for choice as is reasonably needed. It is clear from Table 2.9 that the selection of shadow mask or Trinitron must be less from performance than from economic and other less easily defined considerations, whereas the decision to use the penetration type can be made only on the basis of its one significant advantage, namely, resolution. In almost every case, cost becomes the overwhelming factor, and is not within the province of this book. However, we may note, without abandoning this restriction, that when quantity goes up, cost usually goes down, and we leave the readers to draw their own conclusions.

Liquid-Crystal Shutter. Tektronix has developed a technique for converting a monochromatic CRT into a color unit by adding a color shutter to the CRT in the manner shown in Figure 2.44. This is also a single-beam device, but it eliminated the need for a high-voltage switch, which is one of the weakest points of the beam penetration type. The phosphor used in the CRT has both red and green components, the shutter filters the desired color by means of the neutral polarizer, and the switching Pi cell changes the plane of

TABLE 2.9 Comparison of Shadow Mask, Trinitron, and Penetration-Color CRT Characteristics

	Shadow Mask	Trinitron	Penetration Tube
Basic phosphors	Green, blue, red	Green, blue, red	Green and red or red and white or special phosphors
Type of screen	Dots, stripes	Stripes	Layers
Number of guns	3	3	1
Number of colors displayed when used for a display console	>5	>5	At least 4
Full-screen luminance	100 cd/m^2	200 cd/m^2	200 cd/m^2
Resolution TV lines by raster height	550–1024	650–1024	1000–1500
Type of scanning	TV raster compulsory	TV raster compulsory	TV raster or random scanning
Needs for use	Convergence coils and associated circuitry, special deflection yokes	Convergence coils, as for the shadow mask, and special deflection yokes	High-voltage switching and associated deflection correction, standard deflection yokes
Sensitivity to earth and stray magnetic fields	Important	Important	Very small displacements without any loss of purity
Moiré or interference patterns	Important	Moderate	None
Sensitivity to shock and vibrations	Important	Important	Very small

Source: After Martin [29], by permission.

142

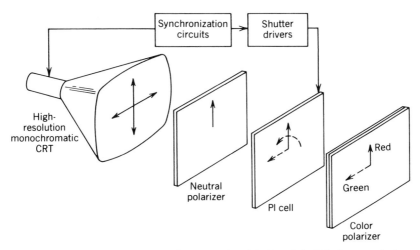

FIGURE 2.44   Liquid-crystal shutter. After McCormick [30], by permission.

polarization so that either the red or the blue light is passed by the color polarizer. The manner in which this is accomplished is discussed further in Section 3.3.6, and the device is included here because it does present a means for achieving color from a single-beam CRT. However, it is quite limited in its color gamut, and although it is a relatively low cost way to achieve high resolution in a color unit it is unlikely that it can compete with the new high-resolution shadow-mask and Trinitron units. However, it is of some historical interest and should not be totally ignored.

Matrix-Driven Flat-Panel CRT.   Another approach to a flat-color CRT is the multipanel one under development by Matsushita. This unit consists of a number of modules assembled as shown in Figure 2.45, and the structure of each panel is shown in Figure 2.46. The cathode emission occurs when the high-voltage pulse of one horizontal scanning interval is sequentially applied to the vertical scanning electrodes by the vertically scanning driver. Thus the electron beams are simultaneously emitted when this high-voltage pulse is applied and the cathodes are negative simultaneously for one line. Each electron beam is then modulated by the first grid and focused by the beam-forming electrodes before it is electrostatically deflected by the horizontal deflection electrodes over a small region. This techniques bears some resemblance to the digitally addressed flat tube discussed later in this section and is introduced here because it includes color capability and differs from the other in that it has scanning electrodes. It may be considered as one prototype for future flat CRTs, although it will probably be made unnecessary because of the improvements in non-CRT types of flat-panel displays.

Channel Multiplier Flat CRT.   Another attempt at achieving a flat CRT with color capabilities is the channel multiplier type developed by Philips. This

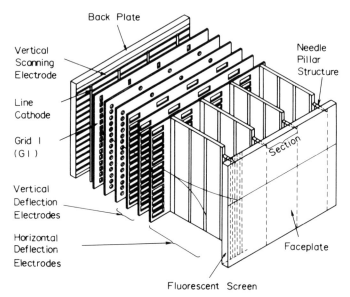

Back Plate

Vertical
Scanning
Electrode

Needle
Pillar
Structure

Line
Cathode

Grid I
(G I)

Section

Vertical
Deflection
Electrodes

Horizontal
Deflection
Electrodes

Faceplate

Fluorescent Screen

FIGURE 2.45   Fundamental structure of the panel. After Nonomura et al. [31], by permission.

was originally a monochromatic unit, but a color version has been developed and is described here. A cutaway view of the basic unit is shown in Figure 2.47. It is a thin tube that consists of two sections, one of which is a low-energy picture-generating section and the other is a high-power section for generating the light output. These two sections are separated by a large-area two-dimensional electron multiplier array that allows the scanning to be accomplished by means of a low-voltage and current beam, whereas the output consists of a high-power beam that is delivered across a short gap to the phosphor screen.

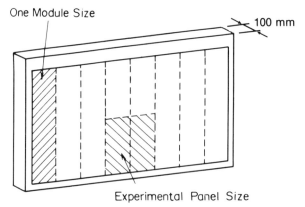

One Module Size

100 mm

Experimental Panel Size

FIGURE 2.46   Concepts of the 40-in. HDTV panel and the experimental panel. After Nonomura et al. [31], by permission.

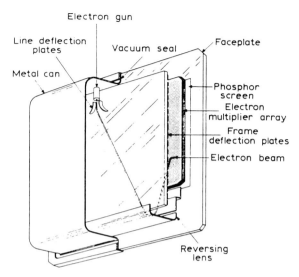

FIGURE 2.47   Channel-multiplier CRT. After Mansell et al. [32], by permission.

This technique allows the deflection scanning to be done at low power while achieving the power necessary to generate high luminance. The multiplier consists of a planar array of minute current amplifiers, each of which operates independently of the others. Either a glass or a metal dynode electron multiplier may be used, with the first limited in size to under 25 mm, and the second able to attain larger sizes. The electron trajectories in the latter are shown in Figure 2.48 and all of the dynodes are lined up to provide continuous channels through the entire assembly. The beams are turned through 90° before entering the channel multiplier so that the entire assembly can remain thin.

The first design was for a monochrome tube, but color has been added to the latest versions. This is achieved by several means, the most successful of being the linear deflected method illustrated in Figure 2.49. Here the output from each channel is focused in the horizontal direction and deflected onto the appropriate phosphor by means of the deflection electrodes. This approach requires the beam from the single gun to be shared, and to avoid the high refresh frequencies that are needed to avoid flicker, a line sequential scheme is used. This has resulted in what appears to be a feasible approach, albeit still not capable of true full color. Progress is continuing and it may become a fully practical system in the future, although again the rapid development of solid-state displays may preclude its being used for other than specialized purposes.

Guided-Beam Display Tube. As a final example, albeit not the only other one, of an at least partially successful attempt to develop a flat-color CRT, there is the guided beam unit developed by the RCA Laboratories before

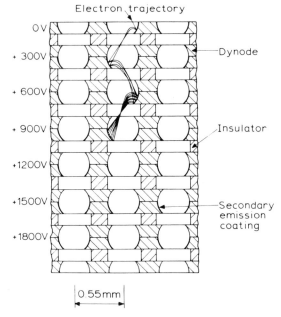

FIGURE 2.48   Metal-dynode channel-electron multiplier. After Mansell et al. [32], by permission.

they became the David Sarnoff Laboratories. This is another attempt to meet the goal set up by David Sarnoff in the days when he controlled the RCA Corp. and constantly encouraged developments of this type of device. Those days are gone with the absorption of RCA into GE, and all work on this development has been terminated. However, the approach was quite interesting and is worthy of some description.

Briefly, the design goals for this unit are given in Table 2.10, and they compare favorably with what has been achieved by some other devices. The

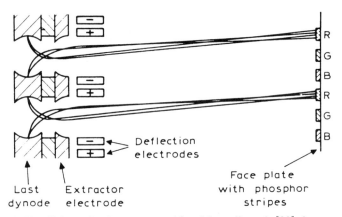

FIGURE 2.49   Color selection system. After Mansell et al. [32], by permission.

TABLE 2.10   Design Goals for a Large-Screen Display

Parameter	Value
Screen size	75 cm $\times$ 100 cm (30 in. $\times$ 40 in.)
Thickness	$\geq$ 10 cm (4 in.)
Pixel size	1.5 mm (0.060 in.)
Brightness	350 cd/m^2 (100 fL) peak, full color
Contrast	50:1
Power	<300 W
Weight	<50 kg (110 lb)

Source: After Credelle [33], by permission.

basic structure is shown in Figure 2.50, consisting of a top and bottom piece of glass and four sidewalls within which are placed the electron source, the beam guide channels, and the electrodes. The electrode patterns are placed on the back wall and the front is coated with the phosphors. The electrons from the sources travel up the guides and are deflected toward the phosphor surface by means of the extraction electrodes. Either element or line at a time addressing are possible, using somewhat different structures, and Figure 2.51 shows a structure for line at a time addressing. This technique uses a line of multiple electron sources, with a discrete modulation point for each vertical beam guide. It has the advantage of reducing the beam currents by a large amount, but at the cost of increased complexity. The beam guide is based on those originally designed for use in traveling-wave-tube amplifiers, and one type used in this guided-beam tube is shown in Figure 2.51. This is known as a ladder beam guide and both focuses and extracts the electron

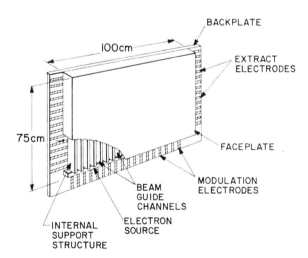

FIGURE 2.50   Schematic view of a 127-cm diagonal guided-beam flat-panel TV. After Credelle [33], by permission.

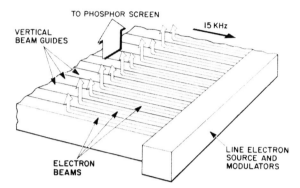

FIGURE 2.51   With line-at-a-time addressing, each beam guide has its own modulated source of current. After Credelle [33], by permission.

beams, depending on what the applied voltage level is. A few experimental tubes were built and incorporated into operating systems with some indication of future success. However, as noted above, the program was not carried much beyond the feasibility stage. However, it did show promise and may be rejuvenated in the future if the demand for flat-color CRTs grows.

Current-Sensitive Color CRT.   As a final example of color CRTs, the current-sensitive type should be mentioned. This type has some resemblance to the penetration tube, in that it has a single gun and does not use color triads in either the dot or stripe configuration. Rather it uses a mixture of superlinear green and sublinear red phosphors and selects the color by varying the current in the beam as shown in Figure 2.52 (34a). Thus a low current beam produces a display that is largely red, and a high current beam results in a predominantly green display, with other colors generated by intermediate currents. A tube of this type was developed many years ago by ITT but did not achieve any acceptance. However, more recently another version was developed by Sony and designated the Currentron. This type of unit was offered by Sony in engineering samples for a while but has essentially been withdrawn. However, despite its essentially limited color gamut, it does offer high resolution at less complexity than the shadow-mask or Trinitron types and may be rejuvenated at some time in the future, although the success of the high-resolution versions of these types makes this rather unlikely. It is included here primarily for historical reasons.

Application Considerations.   There have been a plethora of attempts to develop color CRTs to compete with the shadow-mask and Trinitron types, but only these two have remained as the predominating devices. Thus the user is essentially limited to choosing between these two for the majority of applications. The relevant parameters for these are listed in Table 2.9 for comparison, and there is little difference between them. Therefore, from the

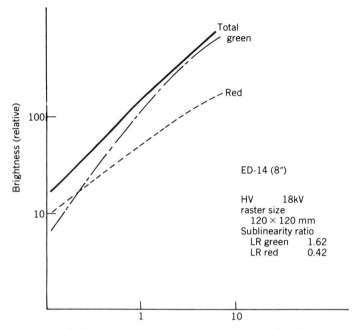

FIGURE 2.52   Brightness versus current. After Takeuchi [34a], by permission.

performance point of view either one is acceptable, and other considerations, such as cost and availability, are the determining factors. These are beyond the province of this volume, and the readers must turn to other sources for the relevant information.

Apart from the question of which color CRT to use, there is the general question of whether to use color at all. This has been covered to a considerable extent in Chapter 1 and will not be elaborated upon here. Assuming that the choice of color has been made on a more or less reasonable basis, the selection of the best type for the application, ignoring cost, will depend on the significance to the application of the various parameters listed in Table 1.6. As noted above, there is little to choose from beyond the two most successful types, but new ones or improvements in the others may change the situation in the future. In addition, the rapid growth in non-CRT color displays presents feasible alternatives that may take over, especially for the large displays that are most suitable for HDTV. However, it should be remembered that the demise of the CRT has frequently been predicted in the past, and it remains the predominant display device for the majority of applications.

2.4.4   Direct-View Storage CRTs

All of the CRTs discussed in previous sections have at least one characteristic in common: namely, that the light output decays at a rate determined by the

decay rate of the phosphor. This has imposed the requirement for refresh
rates exceeding the CFF, with the accompanying trends toward higher rates
imposed by the latest human factors data. Another problem resulting from
the need for high refresh rates is the limitation in maximum luminance that
can be attained due to maximum beam current and duty-cycle considerations.
These problems were much more significant in the past then they are now,
and one successful attempt to overcome them was the direct-view storage
CRT. Although phosphor decay rates cover a wide range, and it is possible
to choose one that has a long enough decay time to begin to approximate a
constant light output, none fully satisfies this requirement, although there is
one type, the bistable storage tube, discussed later, in which the storage in
accomplished by the phosphor in combination with other elements. Another
characteristic of the true direct-view storage CRTs, not true of the bistable
type, is that they are capable of very high levels of light output. These two
factors have led to the extensive use in the past of these types in radar and
other applications requiring long storage times and very high luminances,
although this usage has been considerable diminished with the advent of
nonstorage CRTs with improved capabilities. Indeed, direct-view storage CRTs
have largely fallen into desuetude but are worthy of some discussion, if only
for historical reasons. This is done in the next section.

Halftone Mesh Type. This type is one example of a direct-view storage tube
embodying the principles of a separate element for storage and separate beams
for writing on the storage element and for exciting the phosphor. Although
other CRTs have been produced with these features, this one is sufficiently
representative that we may limit our discussion to the one type. It is illustrated
in Figure 2.53 and consists of a conventional electron gun for writing, depicted

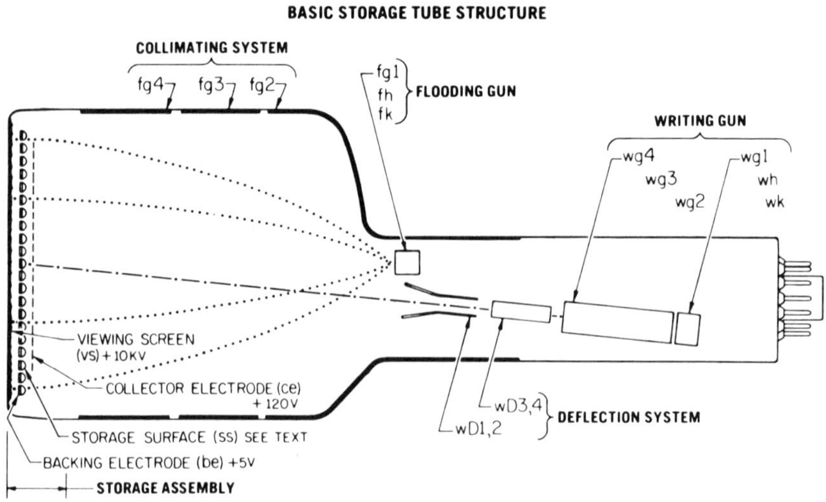

FIGURE 2.53 Halftone mesh-type direct-view storage CRT. Courtesy of Hughes
Aircraft Company.

by the electrodes designated by w and a special flood gun indicated by f. In addition, the phosphor screen has a storage assembly between it and the electron guns, and this assembly is made up of a dielectric plate and a fine-mesh backing electrode.

The writing gun produces a focused high-energy beam that is deflected by the electrostatic deflection plates to the desired position and is the equivalent of the electrostatic deflection and focus CRT described previously. The flood gun provides a flow of low-energy electrons, caused by the collimation system to arrive orthogonally and uniformly over the whole storage surface. These electrons initially charge the storage surface to the flood-gun cathode potential, after which all flood-gun electrons are accelerated into the high-voltage field generated by the viewing screen. These electrons strike the phosphor on the viewing screen, and the resultant luminance level is set by the beam power and phosphor efficiency. The equation for the luminance is obtained from equation 2.60, rewritten as

$$L_s = LT_b \tag{2.80}$$

where L_s = saturation brightness
L = luminance as determined by equation 2.60
T_b = loss factor due to electrons not passing through the mesh

The saturation brightness is the maximum luminance that can be achieved, and once it is achieved the tube is in the fully written condition. The luminance can be removed only by applying a positive potential or pulse to the backing electrode, and the amplitude of this pulse must be equal to the cutoff potential of the storage surface. The positive pulse causes the storage surface to rise in potential, but it is charged down by the flood-gun electrons, and when the positive pulse is removed the backing electrode and the storage surface drop a like amount, so that the cutoff condition exists. This operation is termed *erasure*.

Writing is accomplished by modulating the grid of the writing gun so that the beam is energized and appears at the storage surface at a location set by the deflection-plate voltages. This operation is illustrated by the secondary emission curve shown in Figure 2.54, which applies to the dielectric of the CRT. The electrons are emitted as the result of the electrons striking the storage surface, as has been described previously and illustrated in Figure 2.12. The flood gun operates in the negative charging region, where the secondary emission ratio is less than 1, and the storage surface emits fewer electrons than it receives. As a result, it is charged negatively by the flood gun. However, the writing gun energy is in the positive charging region, so more electrons are emitted than received and the storage surface is charged positively to varying levels, depending on the modulation of the writing beam. The flood-gun electrons are permitted to pass through to the phosphor screen in an amount proportional to the positive charge.

The resultant luminance of the phosphor screen is a function of writing speed, spot size, and the number of times the information is written. Assuming

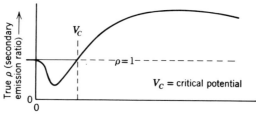

FIGURE 2.54   Secondary-emission curve. Courtesy of Raytheon Company.

no loss between writing cycles, the expression is

$$L_i = L_s\left(1 - \exp\left(-\frac{t}{w}\right)[\ln(1 - K_s)]\right) \tag{2.81}$$

where L_i = integrated luminance
L_s = saturated luminance
t = writing speed
w = line width
K_s = fraction of saturated luminance at writing speed

   Deflection, spot size, and deflection defocusing are all controlled by the same considerations as those that apply to the electrostatic tube described previously. However, resolution is dependent on both the spot size and the pitch of the storage backing mesh (mesh holes per millimeter), with the latter usually the controlling factor. The mesh pitch also affects luminance, as well as erase and storage times. The storage time is theoretically infinite but is actually subject to leakage caused by ionized gas striking the storage surface, although once written, an image may be retained for at least several minutes and in some cases for several hours at usable luminance levels. This storage CRT, although extremely useful in certain applications, is subject to several significant limitations. The first relates to the resolution, determined by the mesh pitch, and the second is concerned with the maximum tube size. Although a mesh pitch of over 40 lines/cm is perfectly feasible, tube sizes of over 12 cm have proved very difficult to build, so that this is the practical limit, resulting in a maximum overall resolution of about 500 lines. This is sufficient for many purposes, if the largest tube can be used. However, frequently the maximum size possible in the application is less with the concomitant reduction in resolution, so that combinations of nonviewing, electrical storage tubes, called *scan converters*, and standard CRTs have proved to be more effective. The scan converters are discussed later in this chapter, and the combinations are described in Chapter 4.
   One interesting version of the direct-view storage tube is the high-contrast display-storage tube. This CRT overcomes one of the deficiencies of the standard type, which is the existence of background luminance caused by

flood-gun electrons striking the phosphor during the erase pulse on time. Erase pulse times range within 3 to 40 ms, and a significant amount of luminance results from the integration of the background luminance over a number of erase cycles. As a result, the inherent contrast ratio of the tube may be limited to as little as 10, independent of the effect of ambient illumination. This has been overcome by the introduction of a suppressor electrode between the backing electrode and the viewing screen in the arrangement pictured in Figure 2.55, where it is compared with the standard arrangement. When a voltage in the order of 75 V is applied to this electrode, the background luminance is eliminated, and the contrast ratio is affected only by the CRT luminance and the reflected luminance from the ambient illumination. Table 2.11 contains a comparison of the two types, in terms of the various parameters involved. On the average, the useful viewing surface is about 10 cm, with a center resolution of 40 shrinking raster lines per centimeter and a minimum display luminance of over 3500 nits. Magnetic deflection is also used, and Table 2.11 applies to these types as well.

Bistable Phosphor Type. The bistable phosphor tube operates on essentially the same principles as the mesh type, but with the important difference that instead of the mesh the phosphor particles are deposited directly on the storage dielectric, thus combining the storage and viewing surfaces. The main advantages of this approach are that the construction is simpler than the mesh type and the resolution is not limited by the pitch of the mesh. Hence relatively low-priced tubes with resolution of better than 800 television lines and in sizes up to 50 cm are available and have been incorporated in low-cost graphic terminals.

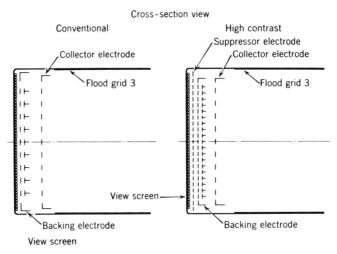

FIGURE 2.55 Comparison of conventional and high-contrast direct-view storage CRTs. Courtesy of Westinghouse Corporation.

TABLE 2.11   Electrical Characteristics of Direct-View Storage Tubes

Parameter	High Contrast		Non-High Contrast	
	WX-5444	WX-4951	WX-5047	WL-7269A
Erase time (s)	0.009	0.009	0.015	0.025
Usable levels	7	7	4	5
Contrast ratio	Very high	Very high	10:1	10:1
Luminance (nits)	7000	3400	4200	7000
Writing speed (cm/s)	10×10^4	38×10^4	100×10^4	200×10^4
Maximum resolution (lp/mm)	2.4	2.6	3.6	2.6
Storage time (s)	30	30	30	30
Screen voltage (V)	10,000	10,000	10,000	10,000
Display diameter (cm)	10	10	10	10

Source: Courtesy of Westinghouse Corporation.

The structure of this tube is shown in simplified schematic form in Figure 2.56 and the screen structure in Figure 2.57. It is basically similar to the mesh type in its operation, with the phosphor acting as part of the storage target as well as the light-emitting surface. In addition, the device operates between two stable points, as shown by the extended secondary emission curve depicted in Figure 2.58. The storage surface is erased by being maintained at the proper potential, between that of the grounded flood-gun cathodes and the first crossover point, by means of the flood beam. The writing beam electrons then cause the target to shift above the first equilibrium point, and the flood gun shifts it farther in the positive direction, thus producing a potential pattern on the phosphor surface. It should be noted that it is also possible to write in a nonstore mode by maintaining the target backplate at ground. In this case the tube operates as a standard CRT, and the trace may be viewed directly.

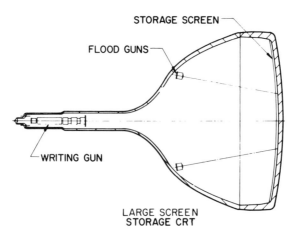

FIGURE 2.56   Bistable phosphor storage direct-view CRT. After Curtin [34b], by permission.

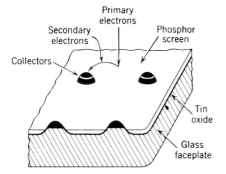

FIGURE 2.57   Flat-screen structure for bistable phosphor storage direct-view CRT. After Curtin [34b], by permission.

Viewing in the stored mode is accomplished by increasing the number of flood-beam electrons reaching the target. These electrons land with more energy on those target areas with stored information, so that a visible output pattern is created. The screen may then be erased by applying the erase pulse shown in Figure 2.59. The initial pulse shifts all areas to the stored potential, whereas the following negative potential allows the flood beam to charge the whole surface. Then, as the pulse rised to zero, the flood beam keeps the surface at the low-voltage equilibrium point, so that the phosphor is in the erase state. It should be noted that bistable tubes are also made with a mesh, but the phosphor versions are simpler and cheaper.

The bistable storage tube was incorporated in a number of graphics terminals of the type described in Chapter 4, because it was so much cheaper than those available at the time it was made available, while still offering good resolution. However, it was subject to several important limitations, prominent among which were the low luminance and contrast ratios that could be achieved and the need to erase the entire screen in order to make any change. In addition, color was not available, although some attempts were made to add a very limited color capability. As a result, it has been completely superseded by the modern refresh types and has become something of a museum piece. It seems unlikely that it will ever be resurrected, but it is still worth knowing about, which is why it is included here.

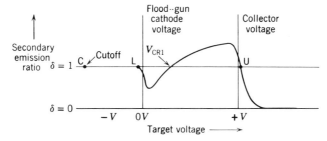

FIGURE 2.58   Extended secondary-emission curve. Courtesy of Tektronix.

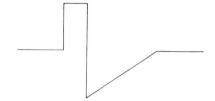

FIGURE 2.59   Erase pulse. After Sherr [2], by permission.

Application Comments. Given the present state of the direct-view storage tube, there appears to be no reason to decide which type is most appropriate for any application. Indeed, even for radar, which remains as a possible application, standard refresh CRTs with very long persistence phosphors such as the P-38 with 1.1 s or the P-57 with 20 s are preferred, leaving the direct-view storage tubes without a source or a rationale for continuing to exist.

2.4.5 Flat CRTs

Flat CRTs are covered to some extent in Section 2.4.3 with the discussion of the Aiken tube and several other color types. In addition to these, a number of other flat tubes have been developed, including several that followed techniques similar to those used for the Aiken tube, but never resulted in color versions. In addition, a number of other approaches have been employed, and this section is devoted to descriptions and discussions of these other types of flat CRTs. The earlier versions, especially the noncolor types, have been superseded by the color LCDs that have become available, but interest in flat-color CRTs has been somewhat rejuvenated by the advent of HDTV, and color versions of these types may still find a place in the market. Therefore, they are worthy of some attention.

Sony. Sony has developed several versions of flat CRTs that were based on the techniques used for the Aiken tube, but differed in some important aspects. The basic structure of the first is shown in Figure 2.60 and it can be seen that it also uses an electron beam parallel to the phosphor screen. This beam is deflected at right angles by the vertical electrode so that it strikes the screen, but this results in considerable distortion, as shown in Figure 2.61. One of the improvements over the Aiken tube introduced in the Sony tube is the addition of new horizontal and vertical deflection circuitry that correct this distortion. Another change is the restriction of the CRT size to diagonals up to about 10 cm.

   This resulted in a fairly usable device, and it was incorporated in the earlier versions of the Watchman TV, although the resolution was only 250 lines. However, it was not found to be fully satisfactory, and it was replaced by another version, which is shown in Figure 2.62. Here the faceplate is not fully parallel to the electron beam, but rather is at a small angle. This arrangement considerably reduces the deflection distortion and also allows as much as 600 lines of horizontal resolution to be achieved. The tube has been used suc-

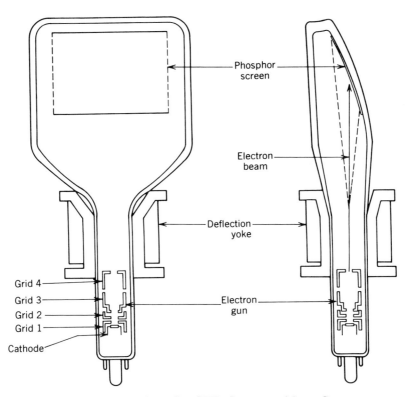

FIGURE 2.60   Sony flat CRT. Courtesy of Sony Corp.

cessfully in Watchman products but has been superseded by the LCD flat panels, which are capable of achieving larger sizes and also have color capabilities. More information on these types may be found in Chapter 3, but it may be noted here that they have essentially made the flat CRT versions obsolete.

Sinclair. Another version of a flat CRT that followed the Aiken technique is the one developed by Sinclair and used in the TV produced by that organization. The structure of that tube is shown in Figure 2.63 and its similarity to the Sony tube is quite apparent. Again the electron beam is parallel to the phosphor screen and is deflected through 90° to strike the screen at the proper angle. It was subject to the same limitations as the first Sony versions, and the television that used it was withdrawn after a short period. It has been withdrawn from the marketplace and is unlikely to reappear unless unexpected improvements occur and the LCD versions are found unsatisfactory for some reason.

Hitachi. Hitachi has developed a flat color CRT that is quite similar in its physical appearance to the Sony version. The electron beam is at an angle

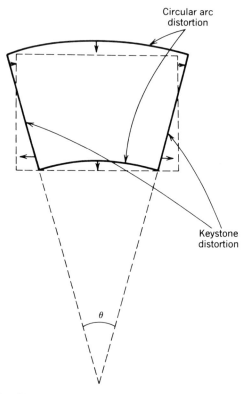

FIGURE 2.61   Flat CRT raster shape. Courtesy of Electronic Packaging and Production [35].

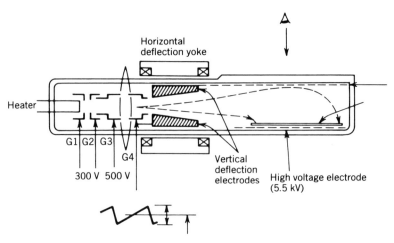

FIGURE 2.62   Sony's FD television picture tube. Courtesy of Electronic Packaging and Production [35].

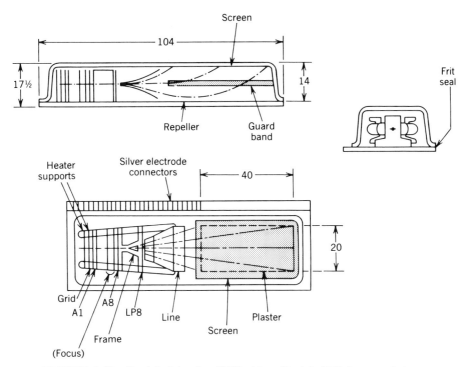

FIGURE 2.63   Sinclair 2-in. flat CRT. After Sinclair [36], by permission.

of about 20° to the phosphor screen, as in the Sony version, and the tube uses a special yoke. This tube is of the beam index type, as shown in Figure 2.64, and the color phosphors are laid down in stripes. The index stripes are between the primary stripes and emit ultraviolet light which passes through the glass and strikes a light collector plate that convert the UV into visible light that is detected by the photodiode. However, apart from the use of stripes and the addition of the light converter and photodiode, the mono-chrome tube is physically the same as the color tube.

Digisplay. An interesting type of flat CRT is the digitally addressed version that was originally developed at Northrup. It was given the designation of Digisplay and went through a long and checkered career of development, having been taken over by Texas Instruments after Northrup relinquished it. It is not presently active in its original form, but as noted previously, the version developed by Matsushita bears some resemblance to the Digisplay. In any event, working versions of the original design were produced, and it is worthy of detailed description.

The digitally addressed flat tube combines the advantages of matrix addressing with the desirable structural features of a thin envelope. The basic arrangement used in this type of CRT is shown in Figure 2.65. It consists of a series of apertured plates, with the apertures lined up so that individual

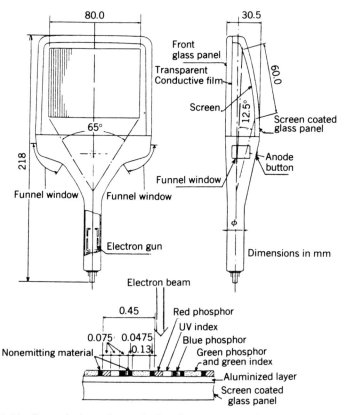

FIGURE 2.64 Beam index tube and phosphor screen. After Inoue et al. [37], by permission.

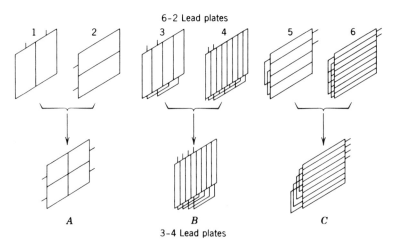

FIGURE 2.65 Alternative decoding techniques for an 8 × 8 Digisplay multileading. After Goede [38], by permission.

electron beams can travel through the sequence. The electron beams are all
created by the large area cathode that covers the entire plate surface, and in
this respect the tube is one form of a multibeam tube, although it acts like a
single-beam tube as illustrated in Figure 2.65. If the plates are connected in
the fashion shown in Figure 2.65, then the beams will be permitted to pass
through only those portions that are energized, and the individual plates act
as control grids. In the example shown, binary coding is used, but other
combinations are also possible. Since the beam deflection process is somewhat
novel, it is described here in some detail, with the general principles applying
to other matrix systems. Referring to Figure 2.65, which is a simplified representation of two possible connection patterns, in the top set it is evident
that plate 1 is divided into two vertical strips, and the electrons will pass
through only the portion that is energized, indicated by the shaded area.
Next, plate 2 is divided into two horizontal strips, and the electrons that have
passed through the energized section of plate 1 will be able to pass through
only the energized section of plate 2 that coincides with the equivalent area
in plate 1. The combination of the two plates will then restrict the electrons
to one of the four quadrants. This is further restricted in the following plates
by division into 4, and 8 as shown, thus ending up with an 8 × 8 array, in
which any one of the 64 points can be individually selected. The selected
beam then strikes the phosphor and acts as an ordinary CRT beam as is
illustrated in Figure 2.66. Since there is no need to deflect the beam in the
conventional sense, the envelope may be made very thin, and tubes less than
5 in. thick, with as many as 160 × 256 addressable points have been constructed.

There are many decoding arrangements possible, but it can be shown that
the most efficient arrangements is that which uses two leads on each plate,
as shown in Figure 2.66. The number of points, in terms of the number of
plates, and the number of leads required to address the plates, is then given
by

$$P = T_x^n \tag{2.82}$$

$$T = nT_x \tag{2.83}$$

where P = number of addressable points,
T_s = number of leads per plate
n = number of plates

If we substitute 2 for T_x and 20 for n, then P is 2^{20} and T is 40, which is the
optimum combination for this number of points. Thus over 1 million points
can be individually selected with only 40 leads. Group selection is also possible
if several leads are simultaneously activated and if larger combinations of
leads are used. The power dissipation may be similarly calculated from

$$P_b = V_c I_c + \sum_{i=1}^{N} V_i I_i + V_p I_p \tag{2.84}$$

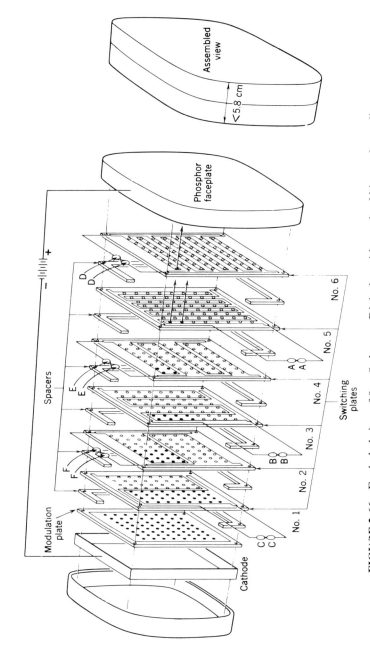

FIGURE 2.66 Exploded view of 8 × 8 element Digisplay with two-lead binary electroding. After Goede [38], by permission.

where P_b = beam power
$\quad\quad\quad V_c$ = collector or cup voltage
$\quad\quad\quad I_c$ = collector current
$\quad\quad\quad N$ = plate number
$\quad\quad V_i, I_i$ = plate voltage and current
$\quad\quad V_p, I_p$ = phosphor voltage and current

which can be simplified to

$$P_b = V_p I_p \tag{2.85}$$

as it has been established empirically that all other currents are negligible. The cathode power has been determined to be about 100 mW/cm², and the total power range is 2 to 30 W, depending on the size and number of elements. The difficulties in obtaining large-area cathodes have led to the demise of this specific tube, but they have been overcome by the multiple-cathode approach used by Matsushita, and the addition of color has made that device quite practical. Again the question of whether any of the flat CRTs can compete with the non-CRT devices remains as a significant factor.

Other Techniques. There are a few other approaches to achieving flat CRTs that should be mentioned for completeness. These are the microtips, hybrid plasma, and VFD types. However, as the last two use somewhat different technologies than do the other CRTs covered in this chapter, they are deferred to Chapter 3. The microtips type is sufficiently similar to be included, although it also somewhat resembles the VFD type. It was originally developed at LETI and taken over by SRI.

The basic structure of the microtips fluorescent display is shown in Figure 2.67. It consists of a vacuum cell, with the back plate supporting a matrix array of field emissive cathodes facing a front plate that is the anode and is covered with a phosphor. The emissive cathodes are arranged in a crossed electrodes network containing cathodes and gates. Next is an insulating layer in which a very large number of microguns are placed, each of which looks like a thin-film field emission cathode, as shown in Figure 2.67. When a voltage is applied between a cathode and a gate, the microtip at the intersection emits electrons that are accelerated toward the anode that is positively biased at a low voltage. The typical field emission characteristics of the microtips are shown in Figure 2.68 for a color version. As a result, each pixel has associated with it an emissive surface that contains a plurality of microguns, leading to a high degree of redundancy. Thus the resultant device also has a high degree of redundancy, leading to good stability and uniformity of the operating characteristics. In addition, it is a matrix addressed unit, without requiring the multiple plates used in the other matrix addressed units described previously in this chapter. The approach is still in the early prototype stages but may be expected to become commercially available in the near future.

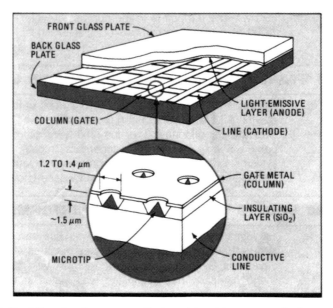

FIGURE 2.67   Microtips fluorescent display. After Meyer et al. [39], by permission.

Color may be achieved by using a proper combination of color phosphors as shown in Figure 2.68 in either a dot or stripe arrangement on the anode.

Application Comments.   The flat CRT has not fulfilled its early potential, due primarily to the development of the flat panel display devices using other technologies. This has led to some of the early programs being dropped, as in the case of the RCA effort, or deferred, as has happened to the Sinclair and Sony units. However, this approach to CRT development is not forgotten, with at least Philips and Sanyo continuing to devote some effort to continued development, and the new microtips and special VFD devices as other examples of CRT-like flat displays. Thus, although other than the Sony unit they can hardly be said to have been in large-scale production or readily available, there is still some possibility that one or more of these approaches will result in devices that can be considered for commercial and industrial products. Therefore, it is advisable to be familiar with the approaches to flat CRTs described previously and be prepared to utilize them when and if they reach full commercial viability.

Multibeam Tubes.   The most common and successful examples of the multibeam CRT are the shadow mask and the other versions designed to meet the needs of color television. These have been covered in detail in previous sections and are not discussed further here. However, in addition to these well-known types, there are several others designed to meet special needs and at least one is of sufficient utility to warrant separate treatment.

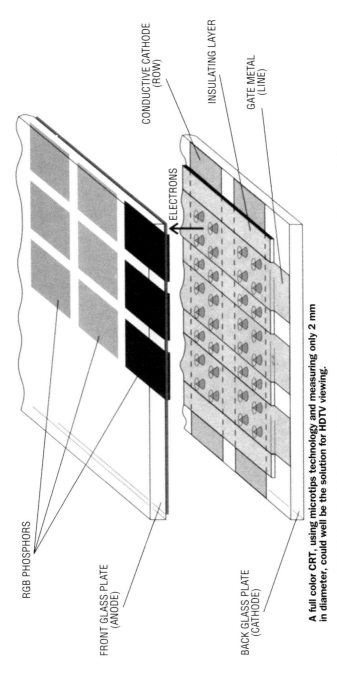

CONDUCTIVE CATHODE (ROW)

INSULATING LAYER

GATE METAL (LINE)

ELECTRONS

RGB PHOSPHORS

FRONT GLASS PLATE (ANODE)

BACK GLASS PLATE (CATHODE)

A full color CRT, using microtips technology and measuring only 2 mm in diameter, could well be the solution for HDTV viewing.

FIGURE 2.68 Full-color CRT using microtips technology. After Mannion [40], by permission.

The earliest among these is a device originally designed with high-speed computer-output printers in mind, that has received more attention as a direct view unit, in which the multiple beams make it possible to produce alphanumeric displays while still operating at relatively low deflection and writing speeds. For example, a seven-beam tube can have its beams arranged so that they create a vertical set of seven spots, which can then be deflected in a group to produce a standard 5 × 7 dot character array. Figure 2.69 is a photograph of a group of characters and dots formed on this tube. Each beam is individually intensified, and they are all deflected and focused by a single magnetic deflection and focus system. Tubes with 30 to 40 beams are considered practical, and 35-beam tubes, arranged in a 7 × 5 matrix are available. Work is continuing on additional types, and larger numbers of beams may become available. Other possible improvements may be the use of electrostatic instead of electromagnetic focusing, which will result in simpler and less expensive structures.

Laminar Flow Guns. One potentially significant improvement in electron-gun design is the laminar flow gun. This gun offers the possibility of improving resolution by a significant amount with corresponding increase in complexity,

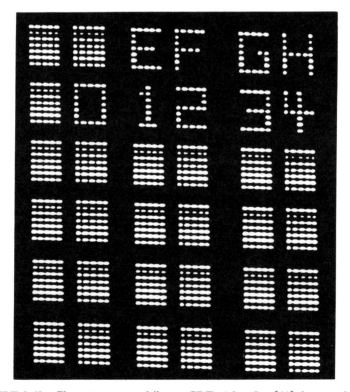

FIGURE 2.69 Characters on multibeam CRT. After Say [41], by permission.

although cost is another matter. The basic structure of the Laminarflo gun is compared with the standard crossover type in Figure 2.70, and it bears some similarity to the collimated gun shown in Figure 2.48*b*. The Laminarflo gun improves resolution without increasing the CRT length by using a longer-focal-length lens, thus reducing space charge effects, as shown in Figure 2.71. The result is the elimination of beam spreading, with the result that the beam striking the phosphor is of the same size as that leaving the focus lens.

Another feature of the Laminarflo gun is that it permits higher currents to be produced from a cathode of the same size as in an equivalent crossover gun. Currents as high as three times that from a conventional gun allow the increase in luminance that results from the increased current, as illustrated in Figure 2.24. This can be extremely important in electrostatic deflection CRTs, where the luminance may be as much as doubled without increasing the acceleration voltage with the resultant increase in deflection voltage as given by equation 2.47.

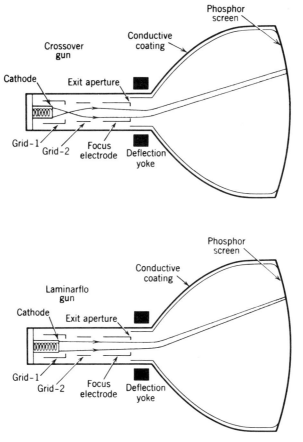

FIGURE 2.70   Electron-beam trajectory for the crossover and Laminarflo gun cathode-ray tubes. Courtesy of Watkins-Johnson Company.

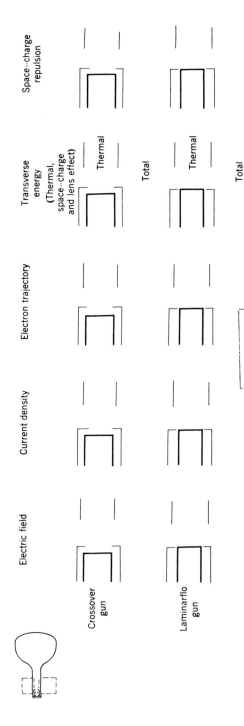

FIGURE 2.71 Comparison of characteristics (ideal) for crossover and Laminarflo gun cathode-ray tubes. Courtesy of Watkins-Johnson Company.

As noted previously, there is a limited number of CRT types available with this gun, but there appears to be no limitation other than economics to introducing it into almost any standard type. Therefore, it may be considered as a serious candidate for those applications that require the improvements in resolution and luminance that it can offer.

2.4.6 Projection CRTs

Although there are numerous types of CRT and pseudo-CRT devices that have been invented, designed, and built for use in large-screen projection systems, some of which actually work, the only one that can be readily described without reference to the system in which it is used is the projection CRT. It is included among the direct-view types because, although the viewer does not look directly at the light-emitting surface, the images created there are made available for viewing without any changes other than magnification. Thus these CRTs retain the essential features of the direct-view CRTs discussed in the previous sections, although they do introduce several new considerations that necessitate separate treatment.

Primary among these special considerations is the need for very high luminous flux output so that the projected image can achieve the necessary levels of light output for viewing on the large screen. We are speaking of screen sizes in the order of 3 m × 3 m, with magnifications from the CRT source of 20 or more. The details of these and other projection systems are covered in Chapter 4, and at this point we restrict ourselves to the requirements imposed on the CRT. These tubes are all of the magnetic deflection type, ranging in size from 7.5 to 15.5 cm in diameter and operating at 40–80 kV of accelerating voltage. The high voltage is necessary to achieve the very high luminous flux output required, since it is proportional to this voltage raised to a power as indicated by equation 2.60. Values as high as 41,000 lm/m^2, or 1000 lm at the faceplate of the CRT have been achieved as highlight values, but at the cost of high input power so that external cooling is needed, usually in the form of forced air. In addition, the high voltages result in potentially dangerous x-radiation, so that special shielding must be used. However, even with these drawbacks, the projection kinescope remains an effective way to create large screen displays for multiple viewing. Color displays use three systems with color filters, since the color phosphors are not of sufficient intensity for direct projection. The P-45 is one phosphor used for projection.

2.5 NONVIEWING CRTs

2.5.1 Storage-Tube Fundamentals

Writing. The purpose of the storage CRT is to convert some type of input information into a stored pattern on the storage surface, which can then be read out at some later time and in some selected scan format. The first step in this process is the writing of the information into the storage surface in a manner similar to that used for the direct-view storage CRT. The storage surface is initially charged to some uniform potential close to the equilibrium potential, and then charges are added or subtracted from the surface by some means, so that the charge pattern remaining corresponds to the input information. The basic structure is similar to that shown in Figure 2.53 without the flood gun, and with variations in the storage surface materials.

The uniform charging may be done either by flooding the target with a single beam of electrons or by scanning it with an unmodulated writing beam. Once the target is thus uniformly charged, the writing may be done by several means, such as equilibrium, bistable, nonequilibrium, electron-bombardment conductivity, and redistribution writing. There is also photoconductive writing in those cases where the target is a photoemissive surface. However, since the majority of storage tubes do not use photoconductive targets, we defer any consideration of photoemisssion to the section on television pickup tubes. The input information may be applied to the writing beam by a variety of methods, such as primary current and cathode, barrier grid, or backplate voltage modulation. Scanning velocity modulation is also possible and accomplishes this function by charging the target elements through control of the number of electrons hitting the target. The same method is used for primary-current modulation, and the phenomena of secondary emission, electron-bombardment conductivity, and secondary-emission conductivity are all used in different types of storage devices. In contrast, the voltage-modulation techniques, with the exception of cathode voltage, control the number of secondary electrons leaving the target, whereas cathode voltage modulation varies the secondary emission ratio.

The writing and modulation techniques employed for any specific device depend on the exact structure of the device, as well as other factors relating to electronic means available. For example, those devices with a barrier grid use equilibrium or nonequilibrium writing, whereas electron-bombardment conductivity is appropriate for those devices with an insulating target. Similarly, barrier grid and backplate voltage modulation apply to the barrier grid types, whereas the other methods can be used for either type.

Reading. Once the charge pattern has been established it is necessary to convert it into some kind of electrical signal so that it may be transmitted to some other location, usually to a viewing device. This conversion may gradually destroy the stored information or leave it relatively unaltered for many reading cycles. The reading process may be carried out sequentially with the writing process, or simultaneously, depending on whether separate reading and writing beams are available. In general, reading is accomplished by scanning the target area with a beam of primary electrons, which converts the stored pattern, through such means as capacity discharge, redistribution, transmission modulation, and various other modulation techniques into a flow of electrons to a target, and creation of the desired electrical signal is accomplished by the resultant flow of current through a load resistor. The writing beam or a separate beam may be used for reading.

In capacity-discharge reading, each target element, which is effectively a small capacitor, is discharged by the unmodulated reading beam to an amount determined by the charge pattern set up by the writing beam. The discharge current flows in the backplate, whereas opposite polarity currents, corresponding to the difference between the scanning current and the backplate current, leave the target and travel to the collector electrode and the barrier grid (when it exists). The resultant currents may be converted into an electrical signal by placing a resistor in any of the current paths, with the amount of current determined by the magnitude of the reading beam current, as is the number of times the target can be scanned before the entire charge pattern is destroyed. It also controls the halftone capability of the device, and a large current ensures that the halftones will be retained since complete discharge will generate signals linearly related to the charge pattern, whereas small reading currents will depend on where on the target yield curve the target potentials lie. Of course, in the case of bistable operation, no halftones are possible since the target elements are at either of two potentials.

In addition to capacitive discharge, there are a number of modulation reading techniques, including transmission, emission, landing and deflection modulation reading. In the first the target is a metal mesh on either side of the insulating material, and the low-velocity reading beam electrons are controlled by the electrostatic fields from the stored charges. As a result, the number of electrons landing on the target is controlled, and the output signal consists of the variations in the current that can pass through the target mesh holes. Emission modulation is similar to transmission grid modulation, except that the signal current is created by secondary emission from the target, whereas in deflection modulation reading electrons are reflected in different trajectories from charged and uncharged areas of the target, and only those from charged areas reach the collector. Finally, the conductivity of the target may be modulated by bombardment with high-velocity electrons, so that target element potentials are shifted as a result of this induced conductivity. A dielectric or semiconducting target is required, and the resultant device is known as the *electron-bombardment, induced-conductivity storage tube*, commonly referred to as the EBIC storage tube.

Erasing and Priming. Any target will spontaneously discharge over some period of time due to leakage and the reading process. However, if it is necessary to change the stored information at some time before complete decay, this is done by means of a process termed *erasing*. Erasing may be accomplished through secondary emission or induced conductivity, and the reading beam may be used as the erasing beam by changing potentials and current levels. In the capacity discharge case, the erasing is done completely by the reading process, as is also the case for equilibrium writing, except that the writing beam performs the function. After erasing, in those situations where the target is not at the proper potential for writing, an additional step, termed *priming*, is taken whereby the entire surface is shifted by some means, such as secondary emission, to the required potential. This completes the operations needed to employ the storage cathode-ray device.

2.5.2   Types of Nonviewing CRTs

Barrier Grid. Barrier-grid devices come in the form of single- and double-gun tubes. Since the same principles are involved in both types, we concern ourselves only with the double-beam unit, which is the more common of the two and has seen considerable use in numerous applications, where the ability to simultaneously read and write is of prime importance. This type of application usually involves scan conversion, and the storage device is referred to as a *scan converter*. The schematic structure of this dual-beam device is shown in Figure 2.72 and bears some resemblance to the storage portion of the direct-view storage tube, so that the curve shown in Figure 2.54 applies to the scan converter. The device consists of two electron guns with a storage screen and collector electrode between them. The writing gun is initially used to prime the storage screen at the cathode potential by operating the screen below the initial potential, at a potential for which the secondary emission ratio is less than 1. This priming operation may be either complete or partial, depending on whether all stored information is to be removed or only some decrease is desired. The storage screen is a dielectric with a metal mesh backing, known as a *transmission grid*.

After priming, the writing beam performs the writing operation, with the storage screen set at a voltage that achieves a high secondary emission ratio. Thus the surface is charged positively to various levels, in response to the modulation. The time to fully write any one element at the storage screen may be determined by treating the screen as a group of discrete capacitors, with the cathode to collector voltage as the charging voltage. This results in the expression for charging

$$e_c = E_k(1 - e^{-kt})C_c \tag{2.86}$$

where e_c = charge in dielectric
E_k = collector to cathode potential
k = charging time constant
C_c = dielectric capacity

Therefore, charging to 99.9% will take approximately seven time constants, and the time to fully write the entire target is Nt_1, where N is the number of elements and t_1 is the time value of seven time constants.

Reading occurs when the "read" side of the target is scanned by the reading beam while the target is negative with respect to the read beam cathode, thus

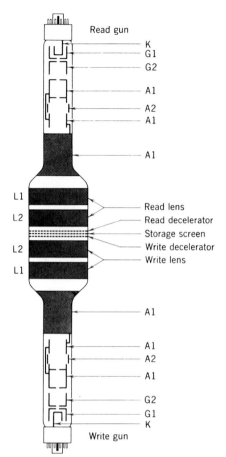

Read gun

K
G1
G2

A1

A2
A1

A1

L1
L2

Read lens
Read decelerator
Storage screen
Write decelerator
Write lens

L2
L1

A1

A1
A2

A1

G2
G1
K

Write gun

FIGURE 2.72 Barrier grid storage CRT. Courtesy of Raytheon Company.

collecting no electrons. The most negative portions, however, do allow some read beam electrons to pass through to the collector, and as the read beam scans over the target, varying amounts of current pass through, depending on the charge in the different areas. Thus the collector current will contain the stored charge information in the form of a varying signal, which is the output signal. The two decelerator electrodes slow down the beams for controlled prime and read operations. Simultaneous read and write is possible because of the two independent guns, but some crosstalk may be caused by both beams impinging on the collector. This crosstalk is reduced by using a radio-frequency (RF) carrier, modulated by the read beam, and the high-frequency output may then be separately amplified, thus minimizing the crosstalk.

The decay time is theoretically infinite, but in actual practice some read electrons generate positive ions, which are captured by the storage screen and tend to discharge it. As a result, the storage time is inversely proportional to the read current, or

$$\Delta t = \frac{\Delta e_i}{K i_r} \text{ (dwell time on element)} \tag{2.87}$$

where i_r is the read current and K is the proportionality factor. This is the major contribution to the reduction of storage time, so that whereas storage time of several hours may be achieved in the absence of a read beam, only several thousand operations may be possible before the charge decays to unusable levels.

Insofar as the other characteristics of the tube are concerned, the deflection and video drive functions are the same as for the standard magnetic deflection and focus CRT. However, resolution is affected by a number of factors in addition to the beam focus, such as variations of scanning speed of beam current and the relative scanning angle between write and read scan. Again, as for the direct view storage tube, the major contributor to resolution limitation is the pitch of the storage mesh. Although resolutions of over 1000 television lines have been achieved with this structure, this limitation has led to the development of types that do not use any mesh. These are discussed in the next sections.

Electron-Bombardment-Induced Conductivity. The EBIC storage tube uses a thin insulating target and a high-velocity writing beam. The high-energy primary electrons penetrate the insulating target and generate free carriers, which in turn cause an increase in conductivity of local target areas. The target resistivity must be large enough to prevent any significant leakage from the unbombarded areas during the frame time. The potentials of the bombarded areas will be changed by the induced conductivity, as the result of leakage, and will move toward the backplate potential. This change occurs during reading, and the variations in output current may be used to create an output signal across a load resistor. This type has the advantage that since the target is a continuous dielectric and a thin metal plate is used, its resolution capability is better than the barrier-grid type. Thus resolutions approaching 2000 television lines have been obtained. In addition, the higher writing energy makes more rapid writing rates possible than with the secondary emission types. As a result of these advantages, this type has seen considerable acceptance in a variety of applications, such as air-traffic control and other scan-conversion operations on radar signals.

Silicon Dioxide Target. An interesting new development is that based on the use of a mosaic of dielectric elements made of silicon dioxide, which functions as a grid to control the current flow to the adjacent conductor surface. The tube is similar to the Vidicon image tube, described in the next section, so it will not be further described here other than to note that the photoconductive target of the Vidicon is replaced by the silicon target that makes up the storage surface. Writing is accomplished by means of secondary emissions, and reading, by lowering the target voltage and scanning it with the same beam, since this is a single-beam device. The current flow at any point depends on the amount of charge removed during writing, and an output video signal may be generated. The target is erased by setting it at the erase voltage and scanning it with the beam for a few cycles. Resolution of the target is over 600,000 elements, and the overall resolution is limited primarily by beam size. This type has the advantages of low operating voltages, in the vicinity of 200 V for writing and under 20 V for reading and erasing.

Application Considerations. In examining the question of which storage tube to use, we must first discuss why storage tubes are used in the first place. One major application has been in scan conversion, that is, the writing of information in one sequence and the reading out of the information in another sequence, for example, as a television raster. Indeed, this type of cathode-ray device is frequently referred to as a *scan converter*, and one early use was in converting from one television-line standard to another. This is covered in more detail in Chapter 4. Another important example is the acceptance of data in some random sequence from sensors or computers and then presenting the data in a raster format on a CRT. Frequently, the data are combined with visual information also converted into raster format by one of the image pickup tubes described in the next section. Attempts to use electrical storage tubes for storage purposes only have been unsuccessful and have been negated by the development of low-cost magnetic and solid-state storage media. Indeed, even the scan-converter function is being taken over by the so-called digital scan converter, or digital television system, as described in Chapter 4. Thus the choice may be between digital and analog scan converters, and the selection of the best analog scan converter is a second stage of the application question. However, assuming that the analog approach is chosen, for reasons discussed in Chapter 4, the three basic types may be compared for the relevant parameters. The barrier grid offers the longest storage time and the widest dynamic range but does not lend itself easily to selective erase, whereas the EBIC has better resolution and short storage time. The silicon dioxide target seems to offer the best overall performance but is not available from as many sources as the other two. It has been incorporated in a graphics terminal and has seen some usage in that application. The transmission-grid type has seen extensive use in air-traffic control as a means for converting raw radar images into raster scan, thus permitting the use of large CRTs with high luminance, but it is being supplanted as the systems become completely digital. The EBIC has been used as an alternative to a direct-view storage tube in radar systems, again with raster scan output and high luminance CRTs, but it is being replaced by digital scan converters. All in all, we may anticipate decreasing use of analog scan converters, but we still find them in many systems, and economic considerations may continue to make them viable.

In closing, it should be noted that there are several other types of scan converters, which use a combination of an image source such as CRT and an image-pickup tube for the scan conversion. Storage may be either in the image

CRT as in the bistable phosphor CRT or in the image-pickup tube. However, these tend to be more systems than components, and some aspects are covered in Chapter 4.

2.5.3   Hard-Copy Devices

There are three basic types of CRT devices that are used to produce hard-copy output. These are the extruded beam, also known as the *Charactron*, those using electrostatic processes, and those with fiber-optic faceplates. They are covered separately below.

Charactron. The extruded or shaped beam tube is a character generator that is used extensively for producing computer output microfilm (COM). In its original form it was also used as a direct-view CRT which combined the character generator and image display functions in a single envelope. The structure of this type is shown in Figure 2.73, and it is a combination of a standard electron gun assembly with electrostatic deflection plates and a special plate placed between the deflection plates and the phosphor screen. The electron beam is extruded through the character matrix, with the deflection plates directing the beam to the selected character. After the beam passes through the selected character, it takes on the shape of the character and is focused by another set of electrodes, which also converge the beam, in conjunction with the convergence coil, so that the center of the matrix is imaged at the center of the second set of plates, known as the *reference plates*. The shaped beam is then accelerated by the helical accelerator and enters the deflection yoke field, where it is magnetically deflected to the desired location on the CRT phosphor viewing surface. Thus we have a combination of electrostatic deflection (equation 2.47) and magnetic deflection (equation 2.57), with the first representing character selection and the second character position on the screen. Focus is electrostatic (equation 2.48), and luminance is the same as for the previously described CRTs (equation 2.60). The other considerations in regard to spot size and deflection defocusing also apply.

Versions of the tube using magnetic deflection and character selection also exist, as shown in Figure 2.74. In addition, a collimated beam gun is used where electrons are kept in an almost parallel beam after leaving the cathode, as illustrated in Figure 2.75, where the collimated beam gun is compared with the typical CRT gun. This achieves a significant increase in luminance. However, its use as a direct-view device has fallen into desuetude, and its main use now is as a character generator for computer output microfilm (COM). In this application, the image on the screen is transferred directly to the microfilm.

Printers. There are two other basic types of CRTs used in printing—that employing electrostatic processes, and the one with a fiber-optic faceplate. The electrostatic one has a matrix of many wires embedded in the faceplate,

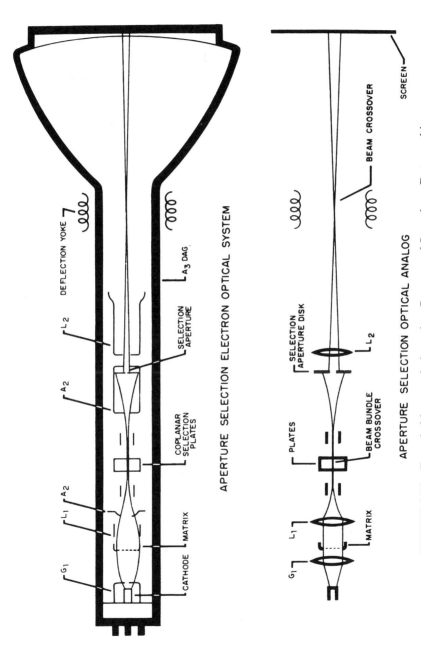

APERTURE SELECTION ELECTRON OPTICAL SYSTEM

APERTURE SELECTION OPTICAL ANALOG

FIGURE 2.73 Extruded-beam printing tube. Courtesy of Stromberg Datagraphix.

177

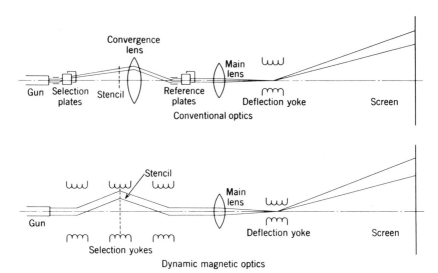

FIGURE 2.74   Schematics of two types of Charactron shaped beam tubes. After Haflinger [42], by permission.

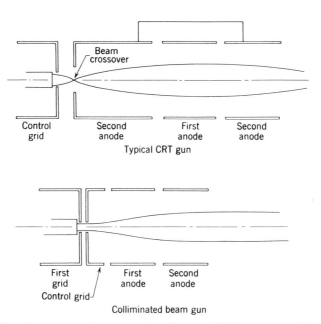

FIGURE 2.75   Comparison of typical and collimated CRT beam guns. After Haflinger [42], by permission.

and these wires conduct the electrostatic charges generated by the scanning electron beam on a surface within the evacuated envelope. Thus the wires make the charge patterns available externally, and these patterns may be transferred to the special paper used in electrostatic printing. Information on these techniques may be found elsewhere [26], and at this point it is sufficient to note that the charge pattern can be converted into a printed image.

The tube may be of the magnetic-deflection and focus type and includes a high-resolution gun. There may be over 100,000 wires embedded in the faceplate, which is usually made with one dimension much smaller than the other. A photograph of such a tube is shown in Figure 2.76. Characteristic dimensions of the faceplate are 20 cm by 5 mm; by this means it is possible to print a line of 20 cm length in one operation.

A second version of the printing CRT has a phosphor surface and a fiber-optic faceplate to convey the images generated by the phosphor to the surface of the CRT, in a manner analogous to the wires in the electrostatic tube. Photographic processes are used in this case to produce the printed result. The extruded-beam version of the optical printing CRT is referred to previously and is shown schematically in Figure 2.73. In this case the total character is produced by directing the beam through the appropriate aperture and is then transferred to the surface by means of the same type of fiber-optic faceplate as that used in the matrix unit. The extruded-beam device has seen considerable use in computer-output microfilm systems.

2.6 IMAGING DEVICES

2.6.1 Introduction

Imaging tubes have seen widest application in the demanding field of entertainment television but have also been used for a wide range of purposes in industrial, educational, and military applications. These devices are the means

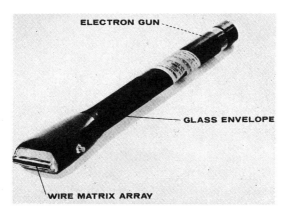

FIGURE 2.76 Electrostatic printing tube. After Stone [43], by permission.

for converting from the visual image to the electrical signals necessary to permit viewing of the image on some other device, such as a CRT. The imaging surfaces have used various phenomena for effecting this conversion, among them photoemission, photoconductivity, secondary emission, and $P-N$ junctions. We examine examples of each type and describe their performance characteristics. We do not include all the many different types that have been developed and used to varying degrees for special purposes, since we are primarily concerned with providing information of commonly used devices or those with potential for future use. The material included in this section should suffice for most purposes and serve as a basis for investigation of special types if these are required. Table 2.12 is a list of a number of these tubes, of which we discuss the image Orthicon, the Vidicon, the secondary electron conduction (SEC) Vidicon, the electron-bombarded silicon diode, and the silicon Vidicon as the most representative types for monochrome use, and the Plumbicon as the one used for most color applications. We might note here that several other devices that do not use electron beams, such as the charge storage and self-scanned mosaic types, are covered in Chapter 3. Finally, a few words about image intensifiers are also included here.

2.6.2 Image Orthicon

Although it is not the first successful example of an imaging device using a photocathode as the image-conversion mechanism, which distinction is held by the Iconoscope, the image Orthicon was the most widely used camera tube before the advent of the Vidicon. As such it is appropriate to use the image Orthicon as our example of a device using photoemission as the physical phenomenon for going from light to electrons. It is also a very versatile tube and may still be useful for certain purposes.

The structure of the image Orthicon is shown in Figure 2.77. It consists of a partially transparent photocathode on which the visual scene is imaged by appropriate optics, and it then emits electrons in the same intensity pattern as contained in the original image. The photoelectrons are focused by means of the focusing coil, which images the photocurrent pattern on the target. The phenomenon of photoemission has been briefly discussed in Section 2.3, and the photoemissive material used in this device is the same Ag–O–Cs referred to there.

TABLE 2.12   Image-Pickup Devices

Iconoscope	Permachon
Orthicon	Plumbicon
Image Iconoscope	SEC Vidicon
Image Orthicon	Return-beam Vidicon
Isocon	Solid-state Vidicon
Vidicon	Silicon charge storage

Source: After Sherr [2], by permission.

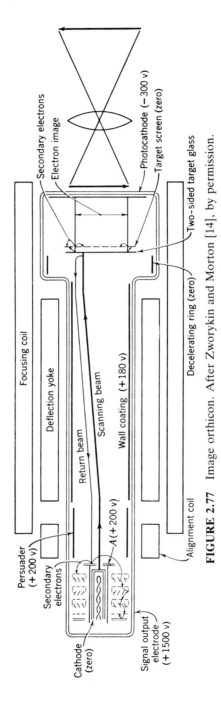

FIGURE 2.77 Image orthicon. After Zworykin and Morton [14], by permission.

The target is two-sided, and is usually made of a thin sheet of glass of sufficient conductivity so that the charges deposited on the side facing the photocathode will leak through to the other side within one television frame time. Since the photocathode is maintained at a negative potential of about 500 V with respect to the target, secondary-emission ratios of more than 1 are maintained at the target for the photoelectrons, and the charge pattern is created as a result of this secondary emission. The process is similar to that described for the other secondary emission devices such as the direct view and electrical storage tubes, but in this case the source material is the visual image.

Reading of the target is accomplished by means of the reading beam, which is scanned over the opposite side of the target by means of magnetic deflection. The reading beam operates at a landing energy sufficiently low that the secondary emission ratio at the target is less than 1, and the reading beam deposits a negative charge at each element of the target surface that is equal to the charge lost due to the photoelectrons. The beam leaving the target is modulated by these variations and returns to strike the anode that surrounds the photocathode. Known as the *return beam*, this causes secondary emission at the anode. These secondary-emission electrons are then multiplied by striking a series of targets, each with a secondary emission ratio greater than 1, so that the signal reaching the output has been multiplied by these cascaded gain stages. This technique of secondary-emission multiplication is used in a number of devices to increase sensitivity, as is the low-velocity scanning-beam energy allowed by the return-beam technique. The latter allows maximum photoelectric saturation without redistribution of the charges and results in best sensitivity and resolution. Characteristics of this type of tube are shown in Figure 2.78, and we can see that it will operate at extremely low levels of illumination, close to 10^{-3} lux.

The signal/noise (S/N) ratio of this as well as the other image-pickup devices discussed later is of prime importance in determining the ultimate sensitivity of these devices. That for the image Orthicon is given by

$$\text{S/N} = K\sqrt{i_p(\delta - 1)} \sqrt{\frac{M}{1 - M}} \tag{2.88}$$

where K = constant dependent on photocathode
i_p = photoelectric current
δ = secondary-emission ratio of target
M = ratio of current into multiplier to electron gun current

Signal/noise ratios of 35 or more are achieved at photocathode currents of 1 picoampere, resulting in resolutions of 400 to 500 television lines. Although the image Orthicon has been largely supplanted by the Vidicon for applications not requiring high sensitivity and by the SEC Vidicon for those requiring high sensitivity, the same factors affect the performance of these devices, and

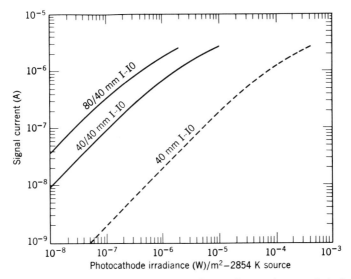

FIGURE 2.78 Signal current vs. photocathode irradiance characteristic for the 7.6-cm thin-film metal-oxide-targeted image orthicon with and without an intensifier. After Rosell [44, p. 554], by permission of Plenum Press.

this rather lengthy examination of the image Orthicon is useful as a means for setting a performance base and for comparison. It deserves some recognition for its important role in the development of image-pickup tubes, if only for historical reasons.

2.6.3 Vidicon Types

Basic Structure. The Image Orthicon, although exhibiting many desirable features, suffered from a lack of ruggedness that made it difficult to use. The solution to this deficiency was found in the Vidicon, the generic name for the family of tubes making use of photoconductivity as the mechanism for conversion of the visual image into an electrical signal. A variety of photoconductors have been used, and Figure 2.79 shows the spectral response of a number of photosensitive materials that have been used. Similarly, Figure 2.80 presents the light transfer characteristics of camera tubes using these materials, compared with several other types. The major characteristics of the tubes are described in the following sections.

The structure of the typical Vidicon is shown in Figure 2.81, with the target material consisting of a photoconductive layer placed on a conducting semitransparent plate facing the source of the illumination. Low-velocity scanning is used, which signifies that the electrons in the scanning beam are moving slowly as they strike the target. A schematic diagram of the structure of a photoconductor is shown in Figure 2.82, and the equivalent circuit is shown in Figure 2.83. The resistance varies in proportion to the amount of light

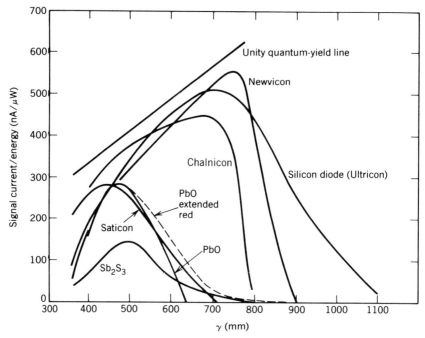

FIGURE 2.79   Absolute spectral response curves of various camera tube photoconductors. After Neuhauser [45], by permission.

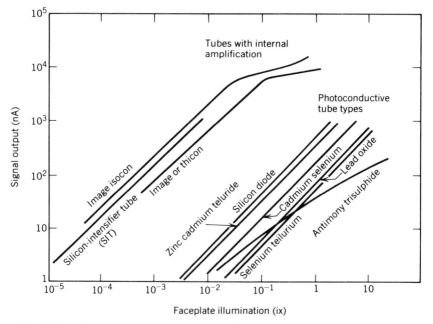

FIGURE 2.80   Light-transfer characteristics of typical camera tubes. After Neuhauser [45], by permission.

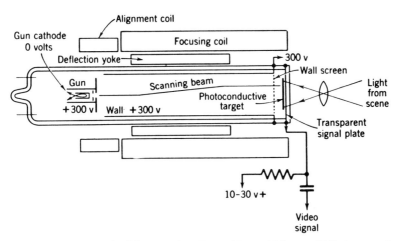

FIGURE 2.81   Standard Vidicon. After Zworykin and Morton [14], by permission.

impinging on the surface, and the photoconductor has a high resistance in the absence of light. When it is illuminated the resistance drops by a large amount. In the absence of illumination the scanning beam drives the target surface to the cathode potential, and a small amount of dark current flows when the beam is removed, leaving the surface slightly charged. The drop in resistance due to illumination results in a greater accumulated charge, and a charge pattern is created that corresponds to the illumination pattern. This image is scanned by the electron beam which charges the surface, creating a current that produces a video signal by flowing through the load resistor. The

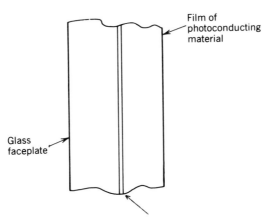

FIGURE 2.82   Camera-tube target cross section. After Neuhauser [45], by permission.

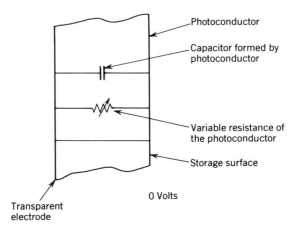

FIGURE 2.83 Photoconductor equivalent circuit. After Neuhauser [45], by permission.

current is proportional to illumination according to

$$I_p = kL^n \tag{2.89}$$

where k = proportionality factor
$\quad L$ = illumination
$\quad n$ = some value between zero and 1, depending on the photoconductor

Typical dark currents of 20 nA and signal currents of 900 nA at resolutions above 1000 television lines, so that many requirements may be met. Representative units may not have the sensitivity of the Image Orthicon, but they are far more rugged and have taken over where extreme sensitivity is not required.

A number of different photoconductors have been used, and they are covered in the following sections. The majority of Vidicons use magnetic deflection and focus for the scanning beam, but electrostatic deflection and focusing may also be used. Of course, since the same considerations hold for resolution as in CRTs, the magnetically focused units give the best resolution, and the magnetically deflected units give the lowest distortion. The devices are used for color television, with either one or three tubes, depending on which type of photoconductor is employed, and the three tube versions requiring associated color filters.

2.6.4 Plumbicon

The Plumbicon is identical in its structure to the Vidicon and in the operation of the gun and target. However, instead of the photoconductor used as the

Vidicon target, the photosensitive layer is lead oxide, which acts as a $P-I-N$ diode rather than a photoconductor. We defer consideration of semiconductor diodes to Chapter 3 since all that we need know here is that when the target is irradiated, charge carriers are generated and swept to the contacts. The contacts act as blocking electrodes and prevent the injection of carriers. This results in very low dark currents, since only thermally generated carriers can exist that are generated at a very low rate. The ratio of signal current to dark current at saturation, which occurs at about 45 V of target potential, may be greater than 1000:1, with the minimum detectable signal determined by noise, and not dark current. This noise is essentially shot noise, and S/N ratios of over 50 dB are attainable in a standard situation. The performance of the Plumbicon may be compared with that of the Vidicon by examining the transfer characteristics of both, as shown in Figure 2.84. It is apparent that the Plumbicon has much better sensitivity at very low dark currents, although it is about the same as a Vidicon with a much higher dark current. The better signal/dark current ratio has been mentioned, and there is also an improvement in lag from about 100 ms for the Vidicon to less than 50 ms for the Plumbicon.

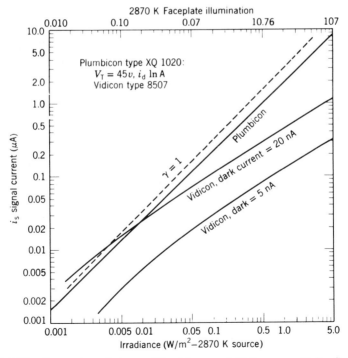

FIGURE 2.84 Comparison between Plumbicon and Vidicon sensitivity (i.e., signal current vs. faceplate illumination). A curve with a slope of unity ($\gamma = 1$) is shown for further comparison. After Redington [46], by permission of Plenum Press.

There are some disadvantages to the Plumbicon, in that since the sensitivity cannot be controlled by changing the target voltage, it cannot handle more than about 200:1 light range, and the resolution is limited by the thick PbO layer to under 1000 lines. However, none of these factors has restricted its use in professional broadcast studios, where the advantages have far outweighed these disadvantages. Thus it is the tube used in practically all color pickups, although three tubes must be used as with the Vidicon. As its cost remains higher than the simpler Vidicons, it is in not much demand for various other industrial type applications, where the Vidicon remains the primary device for image pickup.

2.6.5   Photoconductors

Selenium. Amorphous selenium is used in this photoconductor, and it is used in the Saticon type of Vidicon. It also includes arsenic and telurium, the first to inhibit crystallization of the glassy material, and the second to cause it to have an adequate red response. Thus it covers the visible spectrum, and Saticon tubes are used primarily in three-tube color cameras, as well as single-tube types with adequate filters to separate the colors. The main application is in studio, field production, and telecine cameras.

Cadmium Selenide. Chalnicon is the name given to the tube using this photoconductor. It has a microcrystalline layer of cadmium selenide, and is also made by doping the layer with cadmium telluride to increase the response in the red. It has very high sensitivity, although the dark current is greater than in the selenium type.

Antimony Trisulfide. Although selenium was the first photoconductor used in the early versions of the Vidicon, antimony trisulfide has been used successfully for applications such as closed-circuit surveillance systems. This photoconductor consists of alternating layers of porous and solid material, and the dark current is fairly high, increasing approximately as the cube of the target voltage, whereas the sensitivity varies as the square. It is quite rugged, sensitive throughout the visible spectrum, and has some sensitivity in the infrared, as can be seen from the curve shown in Figure 2.79.

Lead Oxide. Tubes using this material as the photoconductor have a number of names, of which Plumbicon is most common. The photoconductor is a porous vapor-grown crystalline layer of lead monoxide on an n-type signal electrode, and takes on the form shown in Figure 2.85. There is no significant response in the red, so that specially doped versions, termed "extended red," are used to extend the response into the near infrared, as shown in Figure 2.79. A main use of this photoconductor is in three-tube broadcast color cameras.

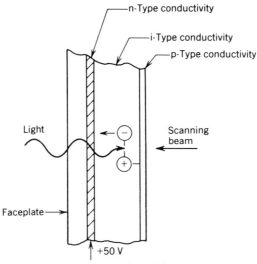

FIGURE 2.85 Lead oxide photoconductor cross-sectional view illustrating output signal generation. After Neuhauser [45], by permission.

Silicon Diode. The last photoconductor considered here is the one that consists of a mosaic of silicon *p-n* diodes, arranged as shown in Figure 2.86. It goes by a number of names, of which Silicon Vidicon is the most common. The structure of the tube is also shown in Figure 2.86, and it contains the usual scanning beam, magnetically deflected, and either magnetically of electrostatically focused. The target has one side facing the image, and the diodes are arranged in a matrix of 600 to 700 diodes on a side, leading to over 400,000 diodes on the target. The target is similar to that shown in Figure 2.89, and in normal operation the substrate is positively biased with respect to the cathode of the electron gun. The electron beam charges the diodes negatively, so that the diodes are reverse biased, and the negligible leakage current ensures that the diodes will remain in this condition throughout the scanning period. In addition, the silicon dioxide film that surrounds the diodes insulates the substrate from the beam, and since the SiO_2 has a very high resistivity, charge accumulates on this surface and it is charged to very close to the cathode potential, remaining there. The reverse bias on the diodes then creates a depletion region in the silicon under the oxide, which is a region having a shortage of free carriers.

The light falling on the target is absorbed by the *N*-type region, and a hole–electron pair is created by each photon that is absorbed. The majority of the carriers are generated near the surface facing the light, and the minority carrier density exceeds the thermal equilibrium value. As a result, holes diffuse toward the diodes, and a large fraction contributes to the junction

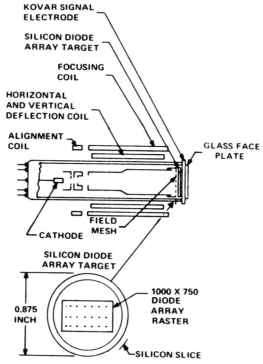

FIGURE 2.86 Silicon Vidicon. Courtesy of Texas Instruments.

current. This light-induced current flows throughout the frame period as long as the diodes remain reversed biased and discharges the junction capacitance. The video output occurs when the scanning beam recharges the diodes to an amount determined by the previous discharge. Thus the video current is proportional to the light intensity in the image. This image tube has a number of excellent features, one of which is the very low dark current, coupled with a sensitivity several times that of the standard Vidicon. In addition, the target is not damaged by being exposed to intense light, such as direct sunlight. The resolution is limited by the number of diodes that can be placed on the substrate, and is presently in the region of 700 television lines. It has good spectral response, with very high efficiency from the near IR to the UV. Its only disadvantage appears to be that its sensitivity cannot be controlled by changing the target voltage, so that optical means must be used to change sensitivity. This problem also exists in the Plumbicon. It can be used as a direct replacement for the standard Vidicon in pickup cameras, if certain minor changes are made in circuitry and voltages, but we do not cover those here, since they are dependent on the type of pickup camera and have nothing to do with the silicon Vidicon as such. It is an extremely effective tube, and apart from economic considerations may replace standard Vidicons in many applications, especially as its lag time is better.

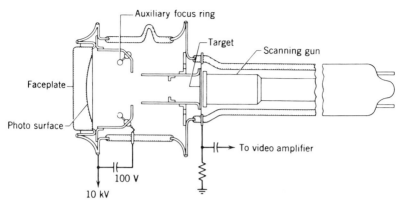

Auxiliary focus ring

Target

Scanning gun

Faceplate

Photo surface

To video amplifier

100 V

10 kV

FIGURE 2.87 Secondary-electron conduction Vidicon structure. After Doughty [47], by permission.

2.6.6 Charge Storage Targets (SEC Vidicon)

The SEC camera tube, sometimes referred to as the SEC Vidicon, has the same readout method as the Vidicon but differs completely in the physical phenomenon used for image sensing. Specifically, the image section contains a photocathode, as in the image Orthicon, and the photoelectrons are focused on a target made up of a supporting layer of aluminum oxide followed by an aluminum signal plate, and then a layer of potassium chloride. This structure is shown schematically in Figure 2.87, and that of the target in the total tube is shown in Figure 2.88. The tube operates by having high-energy electrons from the photocathode penetrate the backplate and create low-energy secondary electrons in the KCl layer. The high-energy photoelectrons are the result of the high voltage of about 7 kV between the photocathode and the target, and the backplate is maintained at about 10 V to ensure that the secondary electrons are transported through the KCl layer as a secondary

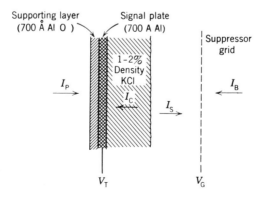

Supporting layer
(700 Å Al O)

Signal plate
(700 A Al)

Suppressor
grid

1-2%
Density
KCl

I_P

I_C

I_S

I_B

V_T

V_G

FIGURE 2.88 Schematic diagram of the SEC target. After Goetze and Laponsky [48], by permission of Plenum Press.

conduction current. The target surface has previously been stabilized at the potential of the reading-gun cathode by means of the reading beam, and a uniform field is produced across the insulating layer. The secondary electrons generated by the photoelectrons cause areas of the target to shift toward the positive backplate potential, in proportion to the number of secondaries in any area, so that a potential pattern is established on the insulating surface that corresponds to the image. Reading is accomplished as in the Vidicon by having the low-energy reading beam scan the target surface, shifting each element to the reading-gun cathode potential. Thus currents flow through the load resistor, producing a video signal that is equivalent to the original image. The gain of the target, defined as the ratio of secondary electrons : primary electrons (equation 2.29), can be controlled by varying both the photo-cathode : target potential and the target : reading-gun cathode potential. However, the latter potential is usually kept constant at about 15 V to avoid increases in dark current and deterioration of the response characteristic. Target gain can be varied over a 5 : 1 ratio by means of the target potential, so that sufficient control is available without changing the second potential. Gains in the range 100 to 150 are achieved, and sensitivities better than 5×10^{-4} lux are possible. This is better than that attained by the image Orthicon, so that the SEC Vidicon is quite effective for low-light-level applications. It is also made with a burn-resistant target incorporating a mesh support instead of the Al_2O_3 layer. This mesh support has a much greater thermal capacity than the Al_2O_3 layer and allows the target to withstand very severe overexposure without burning, which is one of the limitations of the image Orthicon. The SEC tube has a lag time of about 50 ms, the same as the Plumbicon and a resolution capability of well over 1000 television lines in the standard size tube, which is 2.54 cm. Thus it appears to have many advantages over the other types, and it can be used as a direct substitute. However, it has not supplanted the Vidicon in those applications where low cost is more important than high sensitivity, nor has it made any inroads on the Plumbicon in studio color broadcasting, for reasons probably having little to do with technological considerations. In any event, it is a tube with many interesting and unique features, although a number of these features may also be found in the silicon target tubes discussed in the next section. As a final point, the tubes may use either electrostatic or magnetic focusing and magnetic deflection as in the Vidicon.

Electron-Bombarded Silicon Diode Array. This type of imaging tube goes by a variety of names, all of them based on the use of a silicon diode array as the charge-storage target. Without going into the intricacies of solid-state theory, covered in Chapter 3 in relation to light-emitting diodes, and non-CRT image-pickup devices, we may say that the target consists of an array of $P-N$ junction diodes, arranged in the target structure as shown in Figure 2.89. The tube construction is the same as that of the SEC Vidicon, with the

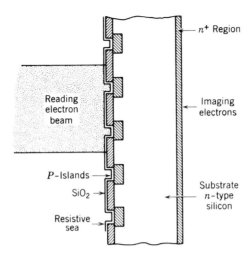

FIGURE 2.89   Schematic of silicon-diode-array target. After Geotze and Laponski [49], by permission of Plenum Press.

exception that the silicon diode array target replaces the SEC target. The N-type substrate is biased to about 5 V with respect to the reading-gun cathode, and the back surface of the target is scanned by the reading gun so that the SiO_2 surface and the P-islands are charged to the reading-gun cathode potential. Thus the $P - N$ junctions are reverse biased and retain this bias because of the low leakage current until hole carriers are generated in the N-type silicon and diffuse to the P-islands. These holes are generated by the photoelectrons, and the amount of discharge is converted by the reading beam, in charging the diodes, to a video signal. As in the SEC tube, the charge gain can be controlled by changing the photocathode to target potential, and the target gain may be as large as 2000. This results in a considerably higher sensitivity than for the SEC tube, as is shown in Figure 2.90, which compare the sensitivity of the two types. It can be seen that the sensitivity of the silicon diode array target is better by a factor of about 20, resulting in a sensitivity of 10^{-5} lux. That makes this the most sensitive of all the image tubes, although the actual sensitivity improvement is closer to a factor of about 30. This brings it close to photon noise limits, if only one stage of image intensification, to be described next, is used. Thus we are approaching the limits of attainable sensitivity.

The tube is extremely rugged and is capable of being exposed to direct sunlight for extended periods of time without damage. Resolution exceeding 500 television lines per picture height are achieved at light levels of 5×10^{-3} lux, and both the lag and dark current are better than any other type. All in all, this is an extremely impressive image-pickup tube and permits applications that were previously impossible.

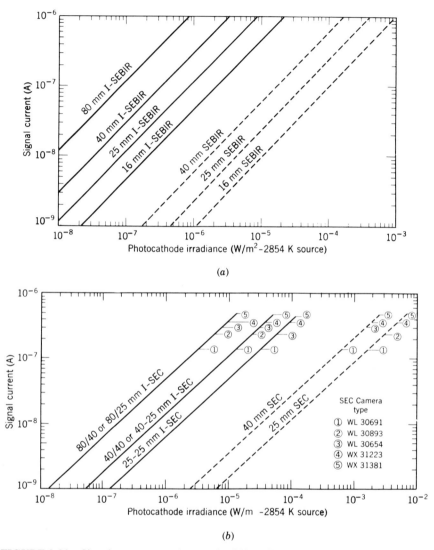

FIGURE 2.90   Signal current vs. photocathode irradiance characteristics. (*a*) For the silicon-EBIR cameral for various input photocathode diameters. After Rosell [44, p. 547], by permission of Plenum Press. (*b*) For the SEC and intensifier SEC cameras as a function of input photocathode diameter. After Rosell [44, p. 569], by permission of Plenum Press.

2.6.7   Image Intensifiers

Reference has been made to image intensifiers without describing what such a device is. An image intensifier is a device in which the light input is increased so that the light intensity falling on the image-tube photocathode is greater than that from the image itself. This image intensifier is placed between the image source and the image-tube photocathode, as shown in Figure 2.91, and consists of a photocathode with a phosphor layer behind it. The photoelectrons are accelerated and focused electrostatically on the phosphor so that the output of the phosphor is equivalent to the image but at a higher intensity level. Gains of up to 300 can be achieved, and it is possible to cascade several stages for higher gains. An intensifier may be used with most of the image tubes previously described but is most effective when used with the high-sensitivity types such as the SEC and silicon target devices. As noted, one stage is enough to reach photon noise limits for the silicon target tube, but two stages are necessary to reach this limit with the SEC tube. There is some degradation in overall resolution, since the intensifier resolution is about 1200 television lines per picture height, so that it is better to use one stage if maximum resolution is required. This combination results in image tubes that approach the ultimate in sensitivity while retaining excellent performance characteristics in other aspects.

2.6.8   Solid-State Imagers

Solid-state imagers are not, strictly speaking, cathode-ray devices, in that no electron beam is employed. Therefore, they might be considered as belonging in Chapter 3, as another type of matrix solid-state device. However, they perform the same function as all of the cathode-ray imaging devices discussed in this chapter, and therefore more logically belong in this chapter. They are covered next as the last example of devices that convert illumination into electrical signals.

The development of solid-state image sensors that could match the performance of a beam-scanned camera tube has been going on for over 25 years, but it is only recently that they have begun to attain this level of performance. The invention of the charge-coupled device (CCD) was instrumental in achieving this result, initially leading to linear scanners, with advances in VLSI technology now making it possible to attain linear arrays with over 5000 elements, and matrix arrays as large as 4096 × 4096, thus bringing standard and even HDTV well within reach.

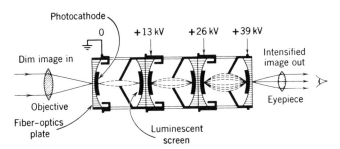

FIGURE 2.91   Schematic diagram of modular-type cascade image intensifier. After Schnitzler and Morton [50], by permission of Plenum Press.

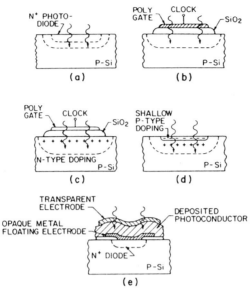

FIGURE 2.92 Cross-sectional views of five types of sensing elements with storage currently used in solid-stage imagers: (*a*) diffused photodiode, (*b*) surface-channel MOS capacitor, (*c*) buried-channel MOS capacitor, (*d*) virtual-phase MOS capacitor, (*e*) hybrid two-level photoconductive element coupled to an underlying silicon scanner. After Weimar and Cope [51], by permission.

A few of the sensing elements in use as the storage medium for solid-state imagers are shown in cross-sectional views in Figure 2.92. The elements shown in Figure 2.92 are all made of silicon and that shown in Figure 2.92 has a photoconductor placed on the silicon storage element. These sensors may be connected as linear or matrix arrays, shown in Figures 2.93 and 2.94, re-

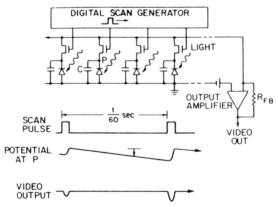

FIGURE 2.93 Multiple scanning of a row of photodiode sensing elements. After Weimar and Cope [51], by permission.

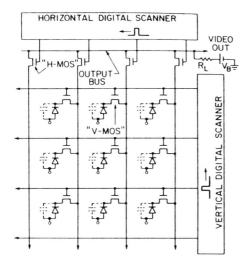

FIGURE 2.94 Multiplexed digital scanning of an $X-Y$-addressed MOS-photodiode array. After Weimar and Cope [51], by permission.

spectively. The charge in each of the elements is then transferred out by means of the scan generator in a manner analogous to that used for solid-state memories. However, the CCD and bucket brigade charge transfer registers, shown in Figure 2.95, have become the preferred way to scan solid-state imagers. The charges are introduced directly into the registers either by

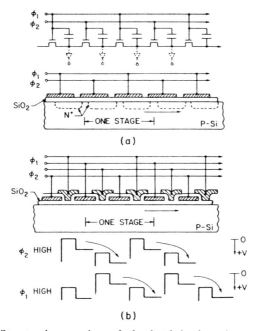

FIGURE 2.95 Structural comparison of a bucket-brigade register and a charge-coupled register; (*a*) BBD cross section; (*b*) four-electrode CCD. After Weimar and Cope [51], by permission.

illumination or through photosensors, and then all of the charges are transferred to the output amplifier, at which point a video signal is created by measuring the size of the charge packets. CCD registers are favored and have charge transfer efficiencies of close to 1 per stage. Cameras using these techniques are available in a range of resolutions and formats, and have many applications, including standard television, where they show a number of advantages.

2.6.9   Application Considerations

The answer to the question of which type of image tube to use must depend on the actual requirements imposed by the application. The most important parameters are sensitivity, resolution, resistance to burn, and last but not least, cost. As noted previously, the advent of CCD imagers has made cameras using these devices as the preferred types. This is not to say that the earlier Vidicon and Plumbicon types, to name a few, have gone completely out of favor, especially as there are so many of them in use, but the tendency appears to be that CCDs will take over, especially as there are so many of these in use. However, the majority of the new cameras will use solid-stage imagers, so that the others may have a short life.

REFERENCES

[1] Spangenberg, K. R., *Vacuum Tubes*, McGraw-Hill, New York, 1948.

[2] Sherr, S., *Fundamentals of Display System Design*, Wiley, New York, 1970.

[3] Sherr, S., "Cathode Ray Devices," in J. Belzer, Ed., *Encyclopedia of Computer Science and Technology*, Marcel Dekker, New York, 1976.

[4] Klick, C. C., and Schulman, J. H., "Luminescence in Solids," in F. Seitz and D. Turnbull, Eds., *Advances in Solid State Physics*, Vol. 5, Academic, New York, 1957.

[5] Martin, A., "The CRT/Observer Interface," *Electro-Opt. Syst. Design*, **9**/6, 1977, 38.

[6] Joint Electron Devices Engineering Council (JEDEC), "Optical Characteristics of Cathode Ray Tube Screens," *JEDEC Publication 16C*, Electronic Industries Association, Washington, D.C., 1975.

[7] Krupka, D. C., and Fukui, H., "The Determination of Relative Critical Flicker Frequencies of Raster-Scanned CRT Displays by Analysis of Phosphor Persistance Characteristics," *SID Proc.*, **14**/3, 1973, 91.

[8] Farrell, J. E., et al., "Predicting Flicker Thresholds for Video Display Terminals," *SID Proc.*, **28**/4, 1987, 449–453.

[9] Krupka, D. C., and Fukui, H., "The Determination of Relative Critical Flicker Frequencies of Raster-Scanned CRT Displays by Analysis of Phosphor Persistance Characteristics," *SID Proc.*, **14**/3, 1973, 89–91.

[10] Turnage, R. E., Jr., "The Perception of Flicker in Cathode Ray Tube Displays," *Inform. Display*. **3**/3, 1966, 49.

[11] Pfahnl, A., "Aging of Electronic Phosphors in Cathode Tay Tubes," *BTL Monograph H-3989.*

[12] Thomson-CSF, *Color Display Beam Index CRTs*, Thomson Electronic Tubes and Devices Corp., Dover, N.J.

[13] Hackenberg, O., and Brauer, W., "Secondary Electrons Emission from Solids," in L. Martin, Ed., *Advances in Electronics and Electronic Physics*, Vol. 11, Academic, New York, 1959.

[14] Zworykin, V. K., and Morton, G., *Television*, 2nd ed., Wiley, New York, 1954.

[15] Akin, R. H., "Photosensor Problems in Display Luminance Measurements," *Inform. Display*, **2**/1, 1965, 26–31.

[16] Rome, M., "Photoemissive Cathodes: I. Photoemissive Surfaces in Imaging Devices," in L. M. Biberman and S. Nudelman, Eds., *Photoelectric Imaging Devices*, Vol. 1, Plenum, New York, 1971.

[17] Hutter, R. G. E., "The Deflection of Electron Beams," in B. Kazan, Ed., *Advances in Image Pickup and Display*, Academic, New York, 1974.

[18] Moss, H., "High Resolution CRT's for Precision Display System," *Electron. Ind.*, April 1964, 64–65.

[19] Law, H. B., "A Three Gun Shadow Mask Color Kinescope," *Proc. IRE*, **39**/10, 1951, 1186–1194.

[20] Herold, E. W., "History and Development of the Color Picture Tube," *SID Proc.*, **14**/4, 1974, 141–149.

[21] Dietch, L., Palac, K., and Chiodi, W., "Performance of High-Resolution Flat Tension Mask Color CRTs," *SID 1986 Dig.*, 322.

[22] Dressler, R., "The PDF Chromatron: a Single or Multi-gun Tri-color Cathode Ray Tube," *Proc. IRE*, **41**/7, 1953, 851–858.

[23] Machida, H., and Fuse, Y., "The Gain in the Definition of Color CRT Image Display by the Aperture-Grille," *IEEE Conference Record of 1972 Conference on Display Devices*, New York, 1972.

[24] Barnett, G. F., "A Beam-Indexing Color Picture Tube—The Apple Tube," *Proc. IRE*, **44**/9, 1956, 1115–1119.

[25] Morell, A. M., "Color Television Picture Tubes," in B. Kazan, Ed., *Advances in Image Pickup and Display*, suppl. 1, Academic, New York, 1974.

[26] Hasker, J., and DeKlerk, J. J. M. J., "Improved Electron Gun for Beam-Indexing Color Television Display," *IEEE Trans. Electron. Devices*, **ED 20**/11, 1973, 1049–1051.

[27] Thomson-CSF, *Color Display Beam Index Tubes*, Thomson Electron Tubes and Devices Corp., Dover, N.J.

[28] Aiken, W. R., "A Thin Cathode Ray Tube," *Proc. IRE*, **45**/12, 1957, 1599–1604.

[29] Martin, A. F., "Penetration Color Tubes Are Enhancing Information Displays," *Electronics*, Jan. 18, 1973, 155–160.

[30] McCormick, J. J., "Liquid-Crystal Shutter Adds Low-Cost Color to Monochrome CRTs," *Electron. Design*, **3**/7, 1985, 180.

[31] Nonomura, K., et al., "A 40-in. Matrix-Driven High-Definition Flat-Panel CRT," *SID Proc.*, **30**/4, 1989, 303–304.

[32] Mansell, J. R., et al., "The Achievement of Color in the 12-in. Channel-Multiplier CRT," *SID Proc.*, **29**/3, 1988, 203–205.

[33] Credelle, T. L., "Large-Screen Flat-Panel Television: A Guided Beam Display," *Electro-Opt. Syst. Design*, Jan. 1982, 34.

[34a] Takeuchi, H., et al., "An Improved Current Sensitive CRT Display," *Japan Display '83*, 1983, 142.

[34b] Curtin, C., "A Large Screen Display for Bistable Storage of Up to 17,000 Characters," *SID 1973 Dig.*, 98–99.

[35] Electronic Packaging and Production, "Sony's Flat Screen TV Marks New Advance in CRT Packaging," *Electron. Pack. Prod.*, Aug. 1982, 15.

[36] Sinclair, C., "Small Flat Cathode Ray Tube," *SID 1981 Dig.*, 139.

[37] Inoue, F., et al., "A 4-V Flat Color TV Receiver," *Proc., Japan Dis. '86*, 1986, 168.

[38] Goede, W. F., "A Digitally-Addressed Flat Panel CRT-Review," *1973 IEEE Intercon*, **5**, **33**/2, 1–8.

[39] Meyer, R., et al., "Microtips Fluorescent Display," *Proc. Japan Display '86*, 1986, 512.

[40] Mannion, P., "Microtips revitalize the CRT," *Electron. Proc.*, Dec. 1991, 17.

[41] Say, D. L., "A Multi-beam CRT," *Inform. Display*, **7**/5, 1970, 29–37.

[42] Haflinger, D. J., "A New CRT for Alphanumeric Computer Terminals," *SID 1976 Dig.*, 126–127.

[43] Stone, J. J., "The VIDEOGRAPH Electrostatic Printing Process," *IEEE Trans. Electron. Devices*, **ED 19**/4, 1972, 563–568.

[44] Rosell, F. A., "Television Camera Tube Performance Data and Calculations," in Biberman and Nudelman [16], Vol. 2.

[45] Neuhauser, R. G., "Photosensitive Camera Tubes and Devices," in K. B. Benson, Ed., *Tel. Engineers' Handbook*, McGraw-Hill, New York, 1985.

[46] Redlington, R. W., "Introduction to the Vidicon Family of Tubes," in Biberman and Nudelman [16], Vol. 2.

[47] Doughty, D. D., "SHC Camera Tubes—Their Physics, Characteristics, and Applications," *Inform. Display*, **7**/9, 1970, 23–30.

[48] Goetze, G. W., and Laponsky, A. B., "Camera Tubes Employing High-Gain Electron-Imaging Charge-Storage Targets," in Biberman and Nudelman [16], Vol. 2.

[49] Goetze, G. W., and Laponsky, A. B., "Silicon-Diode-Array Charge-Storage Target," in Biberman and Nudelman [16], Vol. 2.

[50] Schnitzler, A. D., and Morton, G. A., "Cascade Image Intensifiers," in Biberman and Nudelman [16].

[51] Weimer, P. K., and Cope, A. D., "Image Sensors for Television and Related Applications," in B. Kazan, Ed., *Advances in Image Pickup and Display*, Academic Press, New York, 1983.

3

MATRIX AND ALPHANUMERIC DEVICES

3.1 INTRODUCTION

Will the CRT always be the predominant display device? This question has been asked many times in the past, and until quite recently the answer has always been yes, despite the large amount of effort that has been invested in the development of alternative technologies. However, with the advent and proliferation of hand-held, laptop, and portable computers, flat-panel displays have become of increasing importance in information display systems, and CRTs, even of the flat-panel variety, with the exception of vacuum fluorescent displays (VFDs), have not met the special requirements of these products. Another important application, albeit still in the somewhat preliminary stage, is *high-definition television* (HDTV), and it appears that flat-panel displays will be required for this application as well. Finally, as a result of the growth of the markets for small alphanumeric displays, and the improvements in and reduced cost of non-CRT units, the other technologies have completely taken over these applications, again with VFDs as the only exception.

This is not to say that the CRT will not continue to have a useful life for a number of years to come, as it is still the best display device for a host of important applications, which is quite remarkable as it is over 90 years since its original conception by Braun, but rather that it is being replaced by other types to an increasing extent. These devices and technologies are the subjects of this chapter.

It is convenient to group these devices into two basic families, that is, those that use matrix addressing to generate multiple-line displays, and those that are restricted to numeric and A/N presentations of limited sets of characters. There is some ambiguity in this classification in that the latter two frequently use matrix addressing. However, they are easily differentiated from the first, in that they are restricted to small sets of numerics and/or A/Ns, whereas the matrix-addressed group consists of those displays structured in a large matrix made up of multiple points, each of which is separately addressable. A number of the flat CRTs covered in Chapter 2 do fall into the latter group, but they are covered in that chapter and are not repeated here. Therefore, the division is sufficiently clear for our purposes.

There have been many attempts to produce flat-panel displays, using a variety of technologies, and we do not cover each of them to the same extent, which would take a book in itself. However, we do deal with the major types in considerable detail, in order to provide a firm basis for understanding the possible modes of operation and for evaluating the capabilities and limitations of each type and technology. The large number of approaches attempted, with varying success, are listed in Table 3.1. Out of these, we select first those that have achieved sufficient acceptance to be generally available as display devices, and then those that exhibit sufficient advancements and/or enough advantages to raise expectations for feasible results in a reasonable period of time. The first group consists of various forms of electroluminescent (EL) devices, such as powder, thin film, and light-emitting diodes (LEDs); dc and ac gas discharge (plasma) matrix arrays and A/N displays; vacuum fluorescent displays (VFDs); liquid-crystal displays (LCDs) in their several manifestations, including nematic and ferroelectric; and finally, electromagnetic displays (EMDs), which is an older technology but still has a place in the market.

TABLE 3.1   List of Flat Panel Display Approaches

Group	Technology	Type
1	Electroluminesent (EL)	Light emitting diodes (LEDS)
		Matrix panel (ac, dc)
	Gas discharge (plasma)	Planar readouts, bar graphs
		Matrix panel (ac, dc)
	Vacuum fluorescent (VFD)	Readouts, bar graphs
		Matrix Panel
	Liquid crystal	Twisted nematic (TN), supertwist nematic (STN), ferroelectric (FE)
		Matrix (passive, active)
	Electromagnetic (EM)	Readouts
		Matrix panels
	Incandescent (IN)	Standard bulbs
		Special matrix
2	Electrochemical (EC)	Electrochromic (organic, inorganic)
	Particle	Electrophoretic (EPID)
		Suspended particle (SPD)

Finally, incandescent displays are not completely forgotten, as they are still used, albeit to a very limited extent, in outdoor signs and scoreboards. The solid-state imagers might also be included in this group, but they are covered in Chapter 2, for the reasons noted there.

The second group is much more limited in scope and includes only electrochromics, electrophoretics, and ferroelectric ceramics. Each of these technologies has been investigated to varying extents, and at least the first two have advanced to the point where some products have been offered, although with limited success. However, they have some potential advantages and may become feasible in the future, which warrants their inclusion in this discussion.

3.2 GENERAL SURVEY

3.2.1 Electroluminescent Devices

Electroluminescent (EL) devices are placed first in this introductory discussion because of their long history of unfulfilled promise, partial desertion as an information display technology, and finally, resurrection as the result of new developments and products into one of the recent technologies. This change has been due primarily to the initial work of Sharp on *thin-film EL* (TFEL), followed up by important advances from Finlux and Planar, now combined into one company. In addition, the work of one of the earliest proponents of TFEL—Sigmatron Nova—should be noted. Unfortunately, it was somewhat ahead of its time and failed in its original attempts to achieve successful products. It was resurrected after the new developments made TFEL workable, and did manage to achieve some technical success but failed, at least partially, for financial reasons. However, Planar and Sharp remain active and continue to offer and develop products. Thus TFEL is one of the important flat panel technologies.

Another EL technology that has come to the fore is that based on the use of power rather than thin film. In this respect it bears some similarity to the early types of EL products, which also used powder formulations, and were based on the work of Destriau. However, it differs in one important respect, namely that dc rather than ac voltage is used as the driving force. The work was begun at Phosphor Products in England and has been carried forth by Cherry in the United States to the point where a number of matrix products are available. Thus DCEL must be added to the list of workable technologies.

Finally, the first unqualified success using one form of EL is the *light-emitting diode* (LED), which might be considered as a completely separate technology, as it is based on an entirely different structure than the other two but may legitimately be designated as electroluminescent, as it emits light upon the application of an electric field. It is a solid-state device, embodying a $P-N$ junction, whose operation may be understood by applying solid-state and semiconductor theory, but that discussion is deferred until Section 3.3. Suffice it to note at this point that LEDs have achieved phenomenal success as replacements for incandescent indicators and for small A/N displays. They are also beginning to achieve some acceptance as larger matrix displays, due to the improvements in performance resulting from higher efficiencies. Although included here under the general rubric of EL, the technical differences between LEDs and the other two EL technologies are sufficiently large to warrant their being treated separately from TFEL and DCEL in Section 3.3.3.

3.2.2   Gas-Discharge Displays (Plasma Display Panels)

The use of gas discharges as a means for producing light has a long history, dating back to the early neon indicators and the well-known Nixie numeric displays originally offered by Burroughs, which left the display field a number of years ago and is now part of Unisys. Several other companies are now providing products that match those originally developed by Burroughs and Sperry, both of which are part of Unisys but have left the display products field. Other large companies that have expended a great deal of effort in developing and manufacturing *plasma display panels* (PDPs) are Owens Illinois and IBM, which have also left the field. The former has been replaced by Electro-Plasma and Photonics, and the latter by Plasmaco which has taken over its equipment and is providing devices that have some of the characteristics of the IBM units, with changes and improvements added. Therefore, there are still a number of U.S.-based companies left, but the defections of the others has left the United States without a large organization that concentrates on plasma products.

As is the case for EL devices, both dc and ac excitation are used to energize plasma displays, with significant differences in the structures used and the mode of operation between the two types. However, the basic physical mechanism is the same, consisting of ionizing the gas by the application of a field across the gas, with radiative recombinations of the ions and electrons, resulting in the emission of photons. The gas in its ionized form is referred to as a *plasma*, which is the reason for the use of plasma display as the general designation for this type of display. The term may be used for both types but is more generally applied to ac-driven group. This term is used interchangeably here for both, and they are differentiated only by the excitation means employed. Plasma displays have been used extensively in A/N displays and are among the first examples of true matrix addressed flat panel displays. They have reached the point of being widely available as production units in a variety of forms and sizes. They are being used to a considerable extent as displays for portable, laptop, and hand-held computers, and the advent of HDTF has made them attractive as displays for TV systems. Thus they are among the leading contenders for FPD products and warrant the considerable attention given to them in subsequent sections of this chapter.

3.2.3   Vacuum Fluorescent Displays

Vacuum fluorescent displays (VFDs) are essentially flat CRTs but are covered in this chapter rather than the CRT chapter because they partake of many of the unique physical characteristics of FPDs and are closer to them in characteristics than to CRTs. In addition, they were originally restricted to A/N devices, and it was only with the development by ISE of units with flat structures that they became capable of wider applications. In any event, the modern type of VFD is basically a triode, consisting of a directly heated filamentary cathode, a metal mesh grid, and multiple anodes, each of which is coated with a phosphor. All of these elements are contained within an evacuated envelope, transparent on at least one side, and the front-to-back dimensions are small enough for it to qualify as an FPD. This describes a flat CRT, but it differs from those covered in Chapter 2 in that the anode voltage is much smaller, in the range of 25 V dc. In addition, its construction makes it practical both as a multidigit A/N tube and a multielement matrix panel. It has been used effectively in both forms, and has found an important place in the FPD market.

3.2.4   Liquid-Crystal Displays

Liquid crystal are materials that, although liquid in form, exhibit some of the ordered molecular arrangements found in solid-state crystals. They have been known to chemists for over 100 years, but their first application to display devices is only about 30 years old, dating back to the investigations by Heilmeir and his associates at what was then RCA Laboratories and now is the David Sarnoff Research Center. An enormous amount of effort has been expended in the intervening years, and *liquid-crystal displays* (LCDs) have become the leader in all types of FPDs, albeit the original form using dynamic scattering has more or less disappeared, to be replaced by a variety of other configurations and effects. The first important advance was the invention of the twisted nematic structure by either Fergason or Schadt and Helfrich, or perhaps by all three, leading to much litigation. In any event, the twisted nematic approach resulted in the development of devices with excellent display characteristics, although somewhat on the slow-response side, and they soon became one of the preferred types for A/N displays, especially for battery-operated equipment due to their low current and power requirements. Matrix displays came somewhat later, and the development of the supertwist approach further enhanced the operation of the matrix-driven LCDs. More recently, active matrix drive has advanced to the point where it is possible to build high-resolution color displays with excellent visual characteristics, and these are becoming the FPD of choice for portable and laptop computers.

This wide variety of product types makes it impractical to give an adequate description of the technology in this introductory section. However, it may be noted that it is a nonemitting technology, and image generation is accomplished by controlling whether light is transmitted or reflected at the segments of the A/N or the dot locations in the matrix assembly that are activated by the application of a voltage across the two plates that enclose the liquid-crystal material. The original dynamic scattering technique employed the fact that the liquid-crystal material caused scattering of the light passing through the device at the activated locations so that an image could be formed. The twisted nematic technique differed in that polarized light had its plane of polarization twisted through 90° when the material was activated, so that light could be either blocked or passed by the addition of an analyzer. The basic structure uses a combination of a polarizer and analyzer to achieve the desired effect. The later development of devices that used twists of 180° or 270° considerably enhanced the performance of the devices, and this approach has become a preferred technique for many LCDs. Finally, the active matrix drive technique, where a solid-state switching device is placed at each matrix intersection and switches the material at the selected intersection from one state to another, has become the approach used for the most advanced color matrix displays and may take over that area entirely. The wide availability of all of these product types has made LCDs a leader in the marketplace.

3.2.5   Electromagnetic Displays

One of the earliest forms of nonemissive displays, the *electromagnetic display* (EMD), uses magnetized rotating elements of macroscopic size as the display elements. In this respect it is a blown-up version of the microscopic magnetic display discussed in the preceding section but preceded it by many years. It has achieved considerable acceptance and may be found in the form of A/N assemblies and large matrix displays: the elements are in the form of disks or bars, with different colors on each side. A matrix or other type of electromagnet assembly is placed behind the elements, and they may be rotated by means of a pulse of current applied to the electromagnet. The residual magnetism in the electromagnet then holds the element in the desired position, and an image is formed by the color differences among the elements. The technique is widely used in outdoor displays and indoor signs, and continues to hold its place for these types of applications. Further information on the construction and operation of this type of display is given in subsequent sections.

3.2.6   Incandescent Displays

The use of *incandescent displays* (INDs) as the basic elements for information display devices is probably the oldest example of FPDs. The best known forms are probably the outdoor scoreboards and advertising displays found in many locations that generally use standard light bulbs in various arrangements, but smaller types using special incandescent elements are also found in locations requiring the high luminances they can achieve, such as aircraft cockpits. Both the types of elements may be assembled in either A/N or matrix forms, and are activated by addressing the combinations and driving them with ac voltages.

3.2.7   Electrochemical Displays

Electrochemical displays (ECDs) may use the physical phenomenon of elec-
trochromism, defined as the changing of the light-absorbing or light-reflecting
properties of a material by the application of an electric field that causes
current to flow through the material. Other external stimuli, such as heat,
light, or an electron beam, may also cause this type of change to take place,
but current flow is the only one that has achieved any significant level of
success. In this phenomenon, the light absorption characteristics are controlled by turning the current flow on and off, resulting in a color change.
Initial attempts to find materials that would respond with an adequate contrast
color change over an extended number of reversals were unsuccessful. However, in the early 1970s several materials, both organic and inorganic, were
found, notably tungsten oxide and viologen derivative materials. Displays
were built using these materials that appeared to offer a number of desirable
qualities, among which the lower power requirement and the nonemissive
characteristic are most prominent6. In addition, the construction of the display
is quite simple, consisting merely of a chemical cell with two electrodes.

In these respects, ECDs are similar to LCDs, and it was anticipated that
they would be competitive with LCDs in certain applications such as A/N
displays. However, after ECDs had been on the market for a while it was
determined that they had inadequate lifetime as measured by the number of
switching cycles that could be achieved, poor threshold values, and slow
response times. Therefore, they fell into a state of desuetude, despite their
attractive appearance, and further development work was curtailed. Therefore, it would seem that ECDs are not worthy of further discussion. However,
there has been a small resurgence of interest in the phenomenon, resulting
in the development of new materials, so that it should not be completely
neglected as a potential technology for FPDs. To this end a limited discussion
is included in this chapter.

3.2.8   Electrophoretic Image Display (EPID)

Electrophoresis may be defined as the movement of charged particles suspended in a liquid upon the application of an electric field across the liquid.
The liquid is contained in a cell consisting of two plates with attached electrodes, one of which is transparent. When a properly oriented dc voltage is
applied to the electrodes, the charged particles will be attracted to the transparent plate. Thus if the electrodes are in the form of an $x-y$ matrix or some
other pattern, the charged particles will form the pattern selected, and light
will be reflected in that pattern, with the color corresponding to the form of
the pattern. One arrangement used has black particles in a white liquid, and
by directing the particles to one plate or the other, either a black-on-white
or white-on-black display may be created. When the voltage polarity is reversed, the particles return to the liquid and the *electrophoretic image display*
(EPID) returns to its original condition.

The resulting image is quite attractive, and different color combinations are possible. In addition, the device has inherent memory, is nonemitting, and has an attractive appearance and contrast ratio. The device suffers from slow response time and relatively high voltage requirements when compared with LCDs. In addition, it has poor threshold characteristics in it simplest form, but this has been overcome by the addition of nonlinear elements in the form of an active matrix drive unit, which also improves the response time. However, the number of switching times, and lifetime in general, remain inadequate, so that this technology is still in the developmental stage, although it has not been forgotten and continues to elicit some interest.

3.2.9 Other Particle Displays

There are several other types of particle displays that have been developed but have had very limited acceptance by the market. These are the *suspended particle display* (SPD), developed by Research Frontiers; the *twisting ball display* (TBD), developed by Xerox and Sony; and the *magnetic particle display* (MPD), developed by Magnavox. These have reached different levels of development, ranging from laboratory prototype for the last to limited marketing for the others.

The SPD consists of a suspension of colloidal needle light-absorbing particles held in a transparent liquid between a pair of transparent plates. When no voltage is applied across the plates, Brownian motion keeps the particles oriented in all directions so that incident light is absorbed or scattered and the cell blocks light. When an ac voltage is applied, it polarizes the particles longitudinally, and they are aligned in the field direction, thus allowing light to pass. This is similar in some respects to the operation of an LCD, and images can be formed by patterning the electrodes.

Next, the TBD, also known as the Gyrikon, is constructed with microscopic spherical particles contained in oil-filled cavities in which they can freely rotate. The hemispheres are colored differently and are made of different materials in each half so that the surface charges are also different in each hemisphere. An applied electrical field turns the spheres so that they all face in the same direction, and when the direction of the field is reversed the spheres will also reverse. By this means, and with patterned electrodes, an image may be formed. This display has the advantages of being capable of being made in large sizes, inherent memory, and low power consumption. However, it is difficult to manufacture and appears to be limited to special applications.

Finally, the MPD consists of magnetized spherical particles with different colors on the two hemispheres, as is the case for the SPD. The particles are in the form of microcapsules and are spread out on a transparent sheet. This sheet is laid on an x grid, a y grid, and a memory substrate in succession. Addressing is achieved by driving the x and y grids as in a magnetic memory, and controlling the direction of magnetization of the memory layer at the intersection of the grids. This in turn rotates the magnetic particles so that either of the two colors can be seen. It is an interesting approach but has not attracted much attention in the recent past.

All three of these particle approaches have attractive features and are worth at least some mention in this introductory section. However, they all appear to be too limited in their applications and market acceptance to warrant extensive analysis and discussion. Therefore, they will not be covered in the more detailed sections that follow, and the reader is referred to the references for further information.

3.3 PHYSICAL PRINCIPLES

3.3.1 Introduction

A number of basic physical principles are involved in the operation of the various devices covered in this chapter. Although it is not possible or advisable to attempt any full-scale discussion of each, or for that matter any of these principles, it is essential to an understanding of the characteristics and limitations of them to examine, at least to a limited extent, the basic physics and chemistry involved. This is not intended to provide textbook material, but rather to place the description of the devices in the proper context, with reference to proper source material for additional information, if required. However, it is intended that the material contained in this chapter be sufficient for most purposes.

In the field of physics we are primarily concerned with solid-state and semiconductor physics, in particular as they apply to the generation and emission of photons under proper conditions of excitation. Some discussion of holes and electrons, their place in solid-state theory, and the physics of $P-N$ junctions is necessary for an understanding of the EL devices and also applies to the charge-coupled and charge-injection sensors.

In the field of chemistry we are interested in electrical discharges in gases and in the characteristics of liquid crystals. We restrict the discussion only to those aspects with direct meaning to the display user, and we avoid the complication of elaborate chemical formulations wherever possible.

3.3.2 Semiconductor Physics

To fully understand the principles behind the operation of the various solid-state, image-pickup, and luminescent devices, it is necessary, if only to a limited extent, to begin with some aspects of atomic theory. Modern atomic theory evolved from the need to explain the results of the spectroscopic analysis of atomic radiation and from the experiments of Rutherford, resulting in the discovery of the atomic nucleus. The theoretical work of Planck, Einstein, Bohr, and others led to quantum theory, which is the basis of modern physics, along with relativity. The first steps were taken by Planck when he introduced the concept of quanta and was able to derive a formula for the spectral distribution of blackbody radiation, which corrected the discrepancies from experimental evidence found in previous formulations and conformed to the empirically determined Wien's law.

The next step in developing the theory of atomic structure consisted of the discovery of the electron and the nucleus and the development of Rutherford's model, in which all positive charge and essentially all mass are concentrated in one small region called the *nucleus*. This led to Bohr's theory, which successfully predicted the radiation spectrum of hydrogen and resolved the contradiction between experimental data and the predictions of classical theory. The dilemma of classical theory was that if the radiation from the atom occurred due to a moving charge, then, to satisfy the laws of mechanics and electrostatics, there must be energy loss, and since the frequency of oscillation is given by

$$f = \frac{(2/m)^{1/2}(-E^{3/2})}{\pi e^2} \qquad (3.1)$$

where m = mass of the electron
   E = energy
   e = charge of the electron

then the frequency and the distance of the electron from the nucleus must decrease until the radiation ceases or the electron falls into the nucleus, neither of which occur for the hydrogen atom, to the confusion of tradition. Bohr's theory, which he applied to the hydrogen atom, combined the concept of the quantum number introduced by Planck with that of a nucleus and an electron revolving about it in a manner that conformed brilliantly with experiment, although it was not adequate to explain more complicated atomic structures than the hydrogen atom.

Bohr's theory postulated that the electron could move only in orbits for which its angular momentum is an integral multiple of Planck's constant divided by 2π and that the electron did not radiate while in orbit, maintaining a constant energy. Radiation was emitted if an electron of energy E_0 changed its orbit discretely to an orbit of energy E_n, and the frequency of the emitted radiation is given by

$$F = \frac{E_0 - E_n}{h} \qquad (3.2)$$

where h is Planck's constant, found from

$$\epsilon = nh$$

where $\epsilon\epsilon$ = energy of oscillation

   n = 0, 1, 2, 3, . . . , quantum number

The energy is given by

$$E = \frac{-(mZ^2e^4)}{en^2h/2\pi} \tag{3.3}$$

$$\nu = (mZ^2e^4)\left(\frac{h}{2\pi}\right)^3\left(\frac{1}{n_n^2} - \frac{1}{n_0^2}\right) \tag{3.4}$$

where Ze = charge on the nucleus
ν = frequency of oscillation
n_n = principal quantum number $(1, 2, 3, \ldots, n)$
n_0 = azimuthal quantum number $(1, 2, 3, \ldots, n)$

This formulation was subjected to certain corrections but still fell down for any atoms other than the simple hydrogen, or singly ionized helium, and the quantum numbers could not take on the value zero. Thus although it had attractive simplicity and served to establish the validity of quantum theory, further theoretical development was necessary to arrive at a more complete theory. This is found in the quantum-mechanical wave equation, or the Schrödinger equation.

Einstein had postulated in his theory of the photoelectric effect that energy is emitted in quanta, where the relation of a quantum of energy (ϵ) and its frequency (ν) is given by

$$\epsilon = h\nu \tag{3.5}$$

and de Broglie, in attempting to explain the wave–particle duality, that is, that particles exhibit wavelike properties, further postulated that the wavelength (λ) and the frequency (ν) of the particle are given by

$$\lambda = \frac{h}{p} \tag{3.6}$$

$$\nu = \frac{E}{h} \tag{3.7}$$

where p is the momentum and E is the total relativistic energy.

Schrödinger followed these postulates and developed his famous equation, which is quite similar to the classical wave equation and may be solved by the same procedures as used for that equation. Without getting involved in the form of the equation or its solutions, we may note that a third quantum number is added to the two previously introduced, and the rules for the values the quantum numbers may take become

$$n = 1, 2, 3, 4, \ldots,$$
$$1 = 0, 1, 2, 3, \ldots, n - 1 \tag{3.8}$$
$$m_1 = 1, -1 + 1, \ldots, 0, \ldots, +1 - 1, +1$$

Solving for the allowed energy levels, or eigenvalues, in a one-electron atom results in

$$E_n = \frac{\mu^2 Z^2 e^4}{2(h/2\pi)^2 n^2} \tag{3.9}$$

where $n = 1, 2, 3, \ldots$, which is identical with equation 3.3, if one substitutes a corrected value (μ) for the electron mass (m). Thus the predictions of the Schrödinger equation and the Bohr theory are identical, and the allowable energy levels are dependent only on the principal quantum number (n). However, since several values of l and m_1 are possible for each value of n, a number of electrons will be found with the same eigenvalue and are said to be in the same shell.

To complete the set of quantum numbers, one more number must be added, based on the two possible values for electron spin. This number, designated m_s, takes on the value $\pm\frac{1}{2}$. Therefore, there are four quantum numbers, and all must be considered when calculating the number of available states for electrons. Finally, the definition of the quantum conditions is completed by the Pauli exclusion principle, which states that each state may be occupied by only one electron. It is now possible to list the energy ordering and capacity of the various subshells making up the basic shells, and an energy-level diagram for a hydrogen, atom is shown in Figure 3.1. It should be noted that the energy levels become more closely spaced as they depart from the ground level and are a continuum at the higher values of n for atoms with large numbers of electrons. The significance of this is apparent in the next section on solid-state theory. The frequency of radiation or absorption is still determined by the change in energy level as the electrons move from one level to another, and all the results of spectroscopic analysis may be predicted or explained by this formulation.

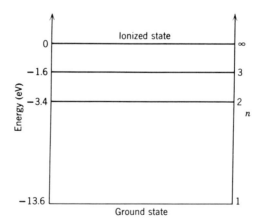

FIGURE 3.1   Energy diagram for a hydrogen atom.

Solid-state theory is concerned primarily with the outermost shells of any atom, since these are most susceptible to the forces that create and maintain the congregation of atoms called *molecules* and *crystals*. When atoms are brought close together, the available energy levels are so near to each other that a splitting occurs that tends to fill the available bands, so that a band is created instead of levels. The allowed energy bands, and the occupancy of energy levels by electrons in a perfect metal, a perfect semiconductor, and an insulator, are shown in Figure 3.2. The conduction band of the perfect insulator is empty, and the energy difference between this band and the valence band is known as the *forbidden band*, since there can be no electrons at those energy levels. The valence band contains the number of electrons required to complete the particular atom and bind it to the other atoms in the crystal. Known as *valence binding*, this creates a stable structure, and the only free electrons are those created by thermal energy. When an electron is freed from the valence band and passes to the conduction band, it leaves behind a vacant energy state, known as a *hole*. In the pure semiconductor the holes and electrons occur in pairs and are relatively few in number. Both the electron and the hole may be considered as free particles, with the hole carrying a positive charge.

Since the numbers of electrons and holes are normally very small in the pure semiconductor crystal, they must be increased by the introduction of impurities to have a sufficient number of charge carriers available for the various uses to which these semiconductors are put. The technique of introducing controlled amounts of impurities is highly refined, and either holes or electrons may be created by the addition of these impurities, leading to *P*- and *N*-type semiconductors, respectively. These carriers are free to move through the crystal lattice, and the conductivity of the material is altered. To calculate the density of free electrons and holes, it is necessary to introduce a statistical model that follows quantum mechanics and takes into account the Pauli exclusion principle. The usual Boltzmann distribution does not hold, and in its place is the Fermi–Dirac function, given by

$$F_F = \frac{1}{1 + \exp(E - E_F)/kT} \tag{3.10}$$

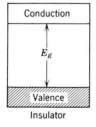
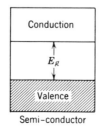
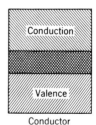

FIGURE 3.2 Energy diagrams for insulator, semiconductor, and conductor.

where E = energy level
$\quad\quad E_F$ = Fermi level
$\quad\quad k$ = Boltzmann constant
$\quad\quad T$ = absolute temperature

The function represents the probability that a specific energy level or state is occupied by an electron, and the Fermi level (E_F) is that at which the probability of being occupied is 50%. The Fermi level, of particular importance in relation to the operation of LEDs, is discussed in greater detail later. At this point we only note the location of the Fermi level for intrinsic, N-type and P-type semiconductors, which moves closer to the conduction or valence bands, depending on whether electrons or holes predominate as free charge carriers. The product of the numbers of electrons and holes in the intrinsic semiconductor is independent of the Fermi–Dirac function and increases exponentially with the increase of the energy gap. The numbers of electrons and holes are equal, and we may extend it to the case where impurity atoms are present by assuming that all donor or acceptor atoms supply carriers. If we further assume that the number of donor or acceptor carriers are much larger then the number of intrinsic carriers, then the number of carriers is given by

$$p = \frac{n_i^2}{N_d} \tag{3.11}$$

$$n = N_d$$

for the donor case and

$$n = \frac{n_i^2}{N_a} \tag{3.12}$$

$$p = N_a$$

for the acceptor case, where N_d represents donors and N_a represents acceptors. The conductivity is then given by

$$\sigma = e(n\mu_n + p\mu_p) \tag{3.13}$$

Equation 3.13 is essentially the same as equation 2.34, and the discussion here applies to photoconductivity as well, insofar as holes and electrons as charge carriers are concerned. The electron and hole mobilities (μ_n, μ_p) are as defined there, which we may restate as being the constants of proportionality between the velocity of the carriers and the applied field. One type of structure of interest is the P–N junction, which, when operated in the forward direction, may be an electroluminescent source, or, in a matrix of diodes, may be the storage surface for the image-pickup devices described later in this chapter and in Chapter 2. Although we do not cover the manner in which the $P-N$ junction operates as an electroluminescent source or as an image storage device at this point, we do examine the characteristics of this structure relevant to those applications. We are interested primarily in two aspects: what happens when minority carriers are injected under forward bias and what the charge-storage capabilities of the junction are under reverse bias.

Minority carriers are charge carriers of the sign opposite to those predominating in the material, that is, P-type for N-type material, and the opposite for P-type material. Minority carriers are injected at a surface making an N contact with a metal, or at a $P-N$ junction, formed when N- and P-type material are made from a single crystal by the introduction of first N- and then P-type impurities. The interface of the N and P types results in a junction where electrons diffuse into the P side and holes into the N side, thus creating minority carriers on both sides of the junction. The diffusion continues until a potential barrier is developed, which stops the flow of charge carriers, with the Fermi level passing through the junction. When a forward bias is applied to the junction, there is minority carrier injection, and the energy states will appear as shown in Figure 3.3. Radiative combinations occur when electrons move from one energy level to a lower energy level, and Figure 3.3 exhibits both intrinsic ($h\nu_i$) and extrinsic ($h\nu_e$) radiation, with the intensity of this radiation a linear function of the applied voltage up to some maximum.

In the reverse-biased junction there is no injected current, but any thermally generated minority carriers are swept across the junction by the high field, and there is a net current, proportional to the sum of the net rates of generation minority carriers on each side of the junction. This reverse current may be increased if additional carriers are generated by photons striking the junction, so that the net current is a measure of the amount of light. The

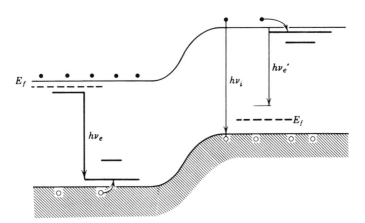

FIGURE 3.3 Electroluminescent forward-biased $P-N$ junction. Piper and Williams [1, p. 103], by permission of Academic Press.

photocurrent is given by equation 2.43, and the process is described in Chapter 2. A reverse-biased step junction has a capacitance given by

$$C = \frac{(e \epsilon N_d N_a)^{1/2}}{2(N_a + N_d)^{1/2}(\psi_n - \psi_p)^{1/2}} \qquad (3.14)$$

where ϵ is a dielectric constant and ψ_n and ψ_p are the internal potentials at the boundaries of the depletion region. Similarly, ψ_N and ψ_P are the same potentials at thermal equilibrium, and the Fermi potentials levels are designated φ_N and φ_P for the N and P sides of the junction. The voltage across the junction is

$$V = (\psi_N - \psi_P) - (\psi_n - \psi_p) = \varphi_P - \varphi_N \qquad (3.15)$$

which demonstrates the meaning of the Fermi levels. The junction may be treated as a capacitor with the plates separated by the width of the diffusion layer and the voltage V across it. Equation 3.14 is obtained from the standard formulas for capacitance and charge by substituting the appropriate equivalents for the junction diode. A somewhat different expression is obtained for a linearly graded junction, but need not concern us, since we are interested in the process and not in all the possible relations of parameters. In either case, the diode capacitance may be charged by a voltage and discharged by photons, which leads to the operation of the solid-state image-pickup devices described later, as well as the cathode-ray types discussed in Chapter 2. Finally, in addition to the $P-N$ junction as an electroluminescent source, there is another type where the electroluminescence is due to the acceleration of charge carriers to optical energies. These charge carriers are conduction electrons, created by introducing activators such as copper or manganese into the crystal structure of the basic EL material, which may be energized by either ac or dc fields and may be in either powder or film form. One example of this type is zinc sulfide (ZnS), for which the energy-level diagram is shown in Figure 3.4. The activator ions in the crystal establish luminescent centers that radiate when excited by the activation energy, E_a, if the sites near the ions are not occupied by another activator ion. Various combinations of basic EL materials and activators used, and different physical arrangements into which the materials are placed for specific device purposes are described later.

   In summary, then, this brief review has established the basis for the emission of radiation from the different solid-state materials and structures used as electroluminescent sources. In addition, the application of the $P-N$ junction to image-pickup devices has been further examined from the point of view of solid-state theory. The existence of energy bands and the transitions of carriers from higher to lower energy levels cause the emission of radiation, with the frequency of the radiation a function of the change in energy, whereas the capacitance of the junction is due to the width of the depletion layer and may be discharged by photon-generated carriers, thus creating a current pro-

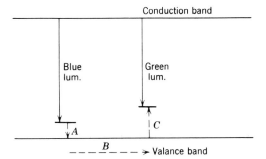

FIGURE 3.4 Energy level diagram for a ZnS phosphor with blue and green luminescent centers. The mechanism for the transport of energy from blue to green centers by hole migration is shown by the arrows A, B, and C. From Ivey, [2, p. 51], by permission of Academic Press.

portional to the light energy that may be used for image-pickup devices. Thus we have covered enough of the basic general theory to understand the more specific discussions to follow.

3.3.3 P–N-Junction Injection Luminescence

Injection luminescence, as exemplified by the $P-N$-junction light-emitting diode, commonly referred to as the LED, is the outstanding example of successful application of electroluminescence to widely used devices. Although it is much newer than field electroluminescence, to be discussed in the next section, it has far surpassed the older type in its achievements and acceptance, and may continue to do so despite the resurgence of interest in new versions of field electroluminescence. The emergence of LEDs as highly effective light sources is another tribute to the phenomenal achievements of solid-state theory and technology, which have led to so many developments in the whole area of electronics. These light-emitting diodes have benefited from this broad-based effort, and the results have placed the various devices using them in a predominant position, although other technologies are beginning to challenge this position because of unique characteristics that they may have. We compare these devices and technologies later, when we examine the actual devices.

The basic mechanism of the LED has been briefly indicated in the preceding section, and we examine it in greater detail at this point. Figure 3.5 is an expanded version of Figure 3.3 and illustrates the different steps in the generation of light from the junction. First we have the potential barrier created in the $P-N$ junction due to diffusion of the charge carriers, and the important feature is that the band gap, or the height of the forbidden band, as well as the doping concentrations in the P and N regions, determine the barrier height. Since the frequency of the radiation is a function of the band gap, as indicated by equation 3.7 and the injection efficiency depends on the doping, these two parameters may be used to control the characteristics of LEDs.

Next in Figure 3.5 are shown the conditions on the application of forward bias large enough to overcome the barrier height. The minority carriers are injected and combine with the majority carriers, which is not sufficient in itself to cause visible radiation, as is evident from the fact that not all *P–N*-junction diodes radiate light under these conditions. However, in LEDs the judicious combination of proper material and doping leads to a sufficiently

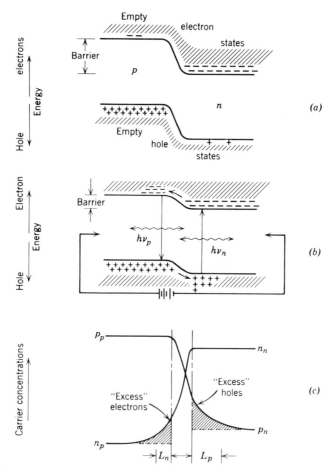

FIGURE 3.5   *P–N* operation. (*a*) Zero bias. The intrinsic potential drop across the *P–N* junction presents a high barrier to the flow of electrons and holes. (*b*) Forward bias. The application of the external voltage reduces the potential barrier height. (*c*) Majority and minority carrier concentrations on the *N* and *P* sides of a forward biased junction. From Goodman [3], by permission.

large number of radiative combinations so that light energy is emitted from the junction. It is also possible to have energy outside the visible spectrum emitted, and many of the earliest LEDs emitted in the near IR. However, it is now possible to obtain LEDs that emit at various points in the visible spectrum, as shown in Table 3.2, which lists a number of specific devices that are commercially available and the basic material used to achieve the particular emission wavelength. It can be seen from Table 3.2 that gallium phosphide and gallium arsenide phosphide (GaP and GaAsP, respectively), in various concentrations and with various levels of doping by zinc, nitrogen, and oxygen, are the only combinations that have been used successfully and that the most efficient units emit in the red region. This is somewhat compensated for by the photopic response curve, so that reasonably good luminous efficiency is possible at the different colors, although blue remains a problem.

The basic structure of a LED is shown in Figure 3.6. The typical device has a substrate of either GaAs or GaP, with the latter allowing better overall efficiency because it can be rendered transparent to the LED radiation if the proper LED material is used. This in combination with other factors such as the type of encapsulation and the use of lenses and reflectors in the total package result in significant improvements in the overall luminous efficiency and are evident from the examination of the actual luminous output at different levels of input power, as detailed in the data sheets for the specific LED. This is covered more fully in Section 3.4.2.

Another important characteristic of the LED is that it is indeed a diode and has the usual current voltage relationship found in diodes. Figure 3.7 shows this relationship for a forward-biased LED, and the nonlinearity of the curve is quite evident. The sharpness of the break at the turn on point of about 1.5 V affects the multiplexing and matrix addressing of this type of display device, whereas the linear range, up to the maximum forward current that can be tolerated without destruction, determines the dynamic range that can be achieved. Since the luminous output is essentially directly proportional to the current over the linear range, it is possible to have a gray scale range with LEDs, although the exact output level for a given input may vary by as much as 50% from one LED to another with the same designation.

A few other points about the relation between band gap and frequency of radiation should be made before leaving this topic. The conditions for direct and indirect band structures are those where the transitions are from the bottom of the conduction band to the top of the valence band and those where the conduction band minimum and the valence band maximum are at different momentum values. In the second case an additional particle is required to conserve momentum, and this is provided by phonons. The equations for the frequencies in the two cases are

$$\nu = \frac{E}{h} \quad \text{(direct)} \tag{3.16}$$

TABLE 3.2 Status of Visible LEDs

LED	Color	Peak Emission Wavelength (Å)	Luminous Output (lm/W)	External Quantum Efficiency		Best Luminous Efficiency (lm/W)	Luminance (L/A-cm^{-2})	Commercially Available
				Best (%)	Commercial (%)			
GaP:Zn,O	Red	6990	20	15	2.0–4.0	3.0	350	Yes
GaP:N	Green	5700	610	0.7	~0.05–0.1	4.2	470	Yes
GaP:NN	Yellow	5900	~450	0.1	~0.05	0.45	—	Yes
GaAs$_{0.6}$P$_{0.4}$	Red	6490	75	0.5	0.2	0.38	—	Yes
GaAs$_{0.35}$P$_{0.65}$:N	Orange	632.0	190	0.5	~0.2	0.95	—	Yes
GaAs$_{0.15}$P$_{0.85}$:N	Yellow	5890	450	~0.2	0.05	0.90	—	Yes
Ga$_{0.7}$Al$_{0.3}$As	Red	6750	~35	1.3	—	0.45	140	No
In$_{0.42}$Ga$_{0.58}$	Amber	6170	284	0.1	—	0.28	470	No
SiC	Yellow	5900	~500	0.003	—	0.01	10	No
GaN	Blue	4400	~20	0.005^a	—	—	—	No
GaN	Green	5150	420	0.1^a	—	—	4000	—
GaAs:Si with YF$_3$YbEr	Green	5500	660	0.1	—	0.6	—	No
GaAs:Si with YF$_3$;Yb:Tr	Blue	4700	60	0.01	—	0.006	—	No
InSe	Yellow	5900	450	0.1	—	—	—	No

Source: After Bhargava [4], by permission.

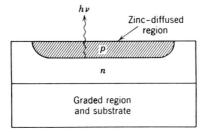

FIGURE 3.6 Cross-sectional view of LED. After Goodman [3], by permission.

and

$$v = \frac{E \pm \epsilon_p}{h} \quad \text{(indirect)} \tag{3.17}$$

where ϵ_p is the phonon energy with a factor k, which is a wave function given in terms of the momentum by the de Broglie relation of equation 3.6, rewritten as

$$k = \frac{\epsilon_p}{\lambda} \tag{3.18}$$

and thus directly proportional to the charge-carrier momentum. Indirect band-gap LEDs tend to be inefficient because of the additional process of phonon interaction involved. This can be overcome if one of the charge carriers is localized at an impurity center and then attracts the oppositely charged carrier.

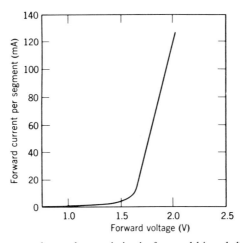

FIGURE 3.7 Current–voltage charcteristics in forward-biased direction for a LED. After Goodman [3], by permission.

Unfortunately, relatively few impurities can be used to achieve this result. However, it has been employed successfully in both green- and red-emitting LEDs and may be extended to other frequencies. The final characteristic of interest in LEDs is the luminance capabilities of the devices. This is given by the expression

$$L = \frac{1150\eta_{ext}A_jJ}{\lambda A_S(L_r)} \qquad (3.19)$$

where η_{ext} = external quantum efficiency
A_j = P–N-junction area
J = junction current density (A/cm²)
λ = emission wavelength (μm)
A_S = observed emitting surface area
L_r = visual photopic curve

The external quantum efficiency in turn is related to the internal quantum efficiency by

$$\eta_{ext} = \frac{\eta_{int}}{1 + (\alpha V/T_{av}A)} \qquad (3.20)$$

where α = average absorption coefficient in the diode
V = diode volume
T_{av} = average transmission coefficient
A = emitting surface volume

and η_{int} is given, in turn, by

$$\eta_{int} = \frac{I_e}{I_f} \qquad (3.21)$$

with I_e as the electron current and I_f the total forward current.

Armed with these expressions for frequency, efficiency, and luminance, we may proceed to an evaluation of the many devices available with an understanding of the basic mechanisms underlying their operation. Of course, the LED designer must take many other factors into consideration in arriving at acceptable values of these three parameters, but these need not concern us since we are interested in what has and can be achieved, and not in the specific manner in which it is done. However, by bearing in mind the basic mechanisms, we can recognize the probable limitations in performance that will exist, such as maximum frequency of operation, highest efficiency, and maximum luminance. Since it is difficult to make LEDs with wide-band-gap materials that can be doped to be sufficient efficiency, it is unlikely that good LEDs will appear in the UV and blue regions of the spectrum, and maximum luminous efficiencies greater than 10 are unlikely. However, luminances above 3000 nits are quite reasonable in spite of these limitations, particularly for red-emitting diodes, so there are many applications in which these limitations will not be restrictive. These characteristics and limitations are discussed further in Section 3.4.2.

3.3.4. Field-Excited Electroluminescence

Field-excited luminescence has been the primary type of luminescence for many years and remains the primary means for inducing luminescence in a number of materials. The process involved is considered to be the acceleration of charge carriers to optical levels, and the materials need not be single crystals, as is the case for all carrier injection devices. High fields are required for the release and acceleration of carriers, in the order of 10^3 to 10^6 V/cm. To achieve these fields, one technique that has been widely used in the past is to imbed particles of phosphors, such as zinc sulfide (ZnS) in a dielectric medium that is placed between two parallel conductors about 50 μm apart. In this type of cell the field strength (E_1) across randomly distributed spheres embedded in a uniform dielectric is given by

$$E_1 = \frac{E_0 \times 3K_2}{2K_2 + K_1 - f_v(K_1 - K_2)} \tag{3.22}$$

where E_1 = average field strength (V/d)
  K_1 = dielectric constant of phosphor
  K_2 = dielectric constant of medium
  f_v = fraction of volume occupied by phosphor spheres

Other phosphors that may be constructed in this form are cadmium sulfide (CdS), zinc selenide (ZnSe), and cadmium selenide (CdSe), with activators such as copper (Cu), manganese (Mn), and the lanthanides. For ZnS phosphors with various concentrations of different activators, radiation occurs when an electron moves from the bottom of the conduction band to the activator band and combines with a hole there, whereas for ZnS:Mn, an electron is raised from the metastable state and then drops to a level near the ground state. Metastable states are those in which carriers are forbidden to have radiative transitions to lower states but may be raised to higher states from which radiative transitions to lower states are allowed. The traps are centers that can capture an excited electron without allowing it to fall into a normally filled level. There may be hole traps as well as electron traps, with the former occurring when the impurity introduces localized filled levels above the highest normally filled level of the host phosphor crystal. Thus there may be radiative transitions by having the holes transferred by thermal action causing an electron to rise up from the topmost filled band and filling the hole, so that the hole is free to move to the topmost filled band and move through the crystal until it is tapped by an electron falling from a local filled impurity level in the forbidden region. The whole process is quite complex, as are the phosphor crystals, and there is still something of the black art in the preparation and use of phosphors, but it is becoming better understood, and various more complicated models exist to explain the operation of field-excited phosphors. However, the relatively simple one we have described is sufficient for a general understanding of the process, and we need not go into it further.

The earlier phosphors used in field-excited devices suffered from many limitations in life and luminance, which resulted in a bad reputation for devices of this type. However, in recent years there have been considerable advances in theoretical understanding, as well as practical manufacturing techniques, so that it is not possible to achieve lifetimes of over 10,000 hours at luminances well above 39 nits. This has been particularly true for the ac-driven thin-film and dc-driven powder (thick-film) types discussed later. As a result, there are a number of products using these two technologies and they have found a place in the FPD market, although the original technique using ac-driven powder is now used primarily for light sources. These devices are described in some detail later in this chapter, and at this point the discussion concentrates on the different way in which excitation may be applied and the basic phosphor structures that are used.

There are five different combinations of excitation of excitation and phosphor-layer structure that have been employed, although only three of them have achieved any significant success. These are listed in Table 3.3, and each of them has its own unique characteristics. All of them use some type of EL formulation, and distribution of the wavelengths of the emitted light from a number of them is shown in Figure 3.8, with curve E coming closest to the eye sensitivity curve. It can be seen that ZnS is the basic luminescent material, with a number of activators added to obtain different emission wavelengths.

The oldest form, first discovered by Destriau, is the ac-driven powder layer (also termed dispersed) mentioned previously, and for which equation 3.22 applies. The basic form in which this type of device is constructed is shown in Figure 3.9, and it consists of a light-emitting layer made up of light-emitting phosphors embedded in a transparent dielectric, with each individual phosphor independent of the others. This layer is then placed between two other transparent conductors that act as the electrodes across which the drive voltage is applied. Electroluminescence is achieved by applying a voltage of 100 to

TABLE 3.3 Electroluminescent Technologies

Ac powder
Dc powder
Ac film
Dc film
Dc and ac composite

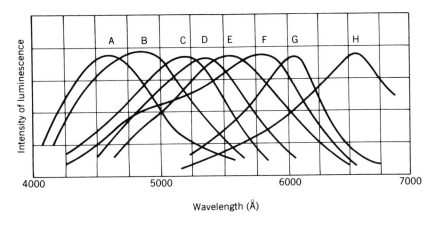

A — ZnS : Cu, Cl   B — ZnS : Pb, Cu (blue)
C — ZnS : Pb, Cu (green)   D — ZnS : Al, Cu
E — ZnS : Mn, Cu (yellow) F — ZnS : Mn, Cu (orange)
G — Zn(S, Se) : Cu   H — ZnS : Cu

FIGURE 3.8   Distribution of luminescence wavelengths. After Matsumoto [5, p. 192], by permission.

200 V across the cell, and a number of empirical formulas have been proposed to relate luminance to the applied voltage, all of which take on the basic form

$$L = K \exp(-aV^n) \tag{3.23}$$

where K and a are constants and n takes on various values from $-\frac{1}{2}$ to -1. Another form of this equation that is used is

$$L = K \exp\left(-\frac{C}{V}\right)^{1/2} \tag{3.24}$$

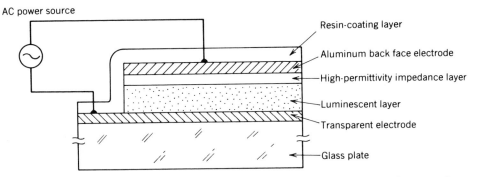

FIGURE 3.9   Structure of typical dispersed ac ELD. After Matsumoto [5, p. 192], by permission.

where L, K, and V are as before, and C is another constant, determined by excitation, structure, and phosphor material.

The next type of EL device in Table 3.3 is the dc powder layer, which substitutes dc voltage drive for ac voltage, and also uses somewhat different techniques in producing the phosphor layer. The powders are, as before, ZnS:Mn phosphors, with copper used as the coactivator. A thin layer of this phosphor, mixed with an organic binder, is spread on an etched tranparent glass plate, and it has a copper-rich surface. A forming process is used that causes a p-type copper sulfide layer to be created on the surface of each copper particle. This occurs when a dc voltage is initially applied across the EL cell, and the junction that is formed, due to the diffusion of Cu away from the front transparent electrode, allows the existence of a high-field region suitable for the injection and acceleration of carriers. Figure 3.10 illustrates the condition of the phosphor before and after the forming process, and Figure 3.11 shows the cross section of a panel after forming. The diode shown in Figure 3.10 is of special interest because it results in a nonlinearity useful for matrix addressing, as described in more detail later in this chapter. The panel operates in the resistive mode, and its structure differs from the ac type, as shown in Figure 3.12, in that the phosphor is scribed in order to achieve isolation between pixels. Pulsed operation is preferable for long life, and because of the nonlinear nature of the relationship between luminance and voltage, is given over a limited range by the expression

$$L = kV^n \tag{3.25}$$

where k is a constant and n is a constant greater than unity.

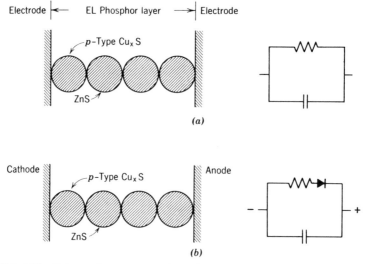

Electrode |← EL Phosphor layer →| Electrode

p-Type $Cu_x S$

ZnS

(a)

Cathode p-Type $Cu_x S$ Anode

ZnS

(b)

FIGURE 3.10 Schematic representation of EL layer and its equivalent circuit (a) before and (b) after "forming process." After Kawarada and Ohshima [6], by permission.

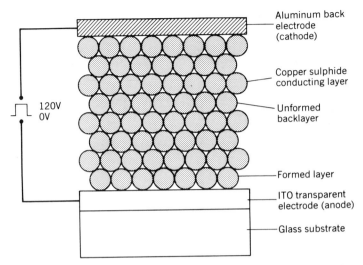

FIGURE 3.11 Cross section of a dc EL powder panel after the forming process. After Vecht [7], by permission.

This approach was pioneered by Vecht in the early 1960s and resulted in a number of products by the 1980s, including color panels using a variety of materials. It was subsequently taken over by the Cherry Electrical Products Corp, which overcame the four main failure mechanisms of previously built thick-film EL displays:

1. Further forming due to moisture, heat, and contaminents, causing an increase in the threshold voltage
2. Load-line flattening due to an increase in the resistance of the copper layer
3. Degradation of the efficiency and the threshold voltage
4. Light rise-time lagging applied current

All of these deficiencies have been overcome to a significant extent, and workable panels are now available from this manufacturer, although no other

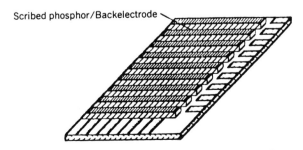

FIGURE 3.12 Scribed dc EL powder panel. After Vecht [7], by permission.

companies are producing dc powder panels now that the original group, led by Vecht, has essentially left the market.

The next EL technology listed in Table 3.3 is the thin-film EL (TFEL), and this is the most successful of the five. The earliest work with this type of structure was done at Sigmatron in the early 1970s and showed some promise. However, it was not until Sharp developed panels with good life and luminance characteristics that the ac-driven TFEL became a success. The basic form of a TFEL device is a multilayered structure, as shown in Figure 3.13, and in some respects it appears to be physically quite similar to the dc-driven thick-film EL device. However, the differences are more important than the similarities. They consist of having a transparent electrode evaporated on a glass substrate with an insulating layer on top. The phosphor is next evaporated on the insulator, and a memory effect may be achieved by increasing the amount of the doping element. Another insulating layer and an aluminum back element are evaporated to complete the cell. The whole cell is then assembled on a glass plate, which seals in silicone oil and improves the life. It exhibits a much steeper response curve than does the ac powder cell, as shown in Figure 3.14, and is therefore much more suitable than the earlier type for matrix addressing. This characteristic and the longer life attained by Sharp initially, and by Planar and others subsequently, have been important factors in making this technology a successful competitor in the FPD market.

The fourth technology shown in Table 3.3 is the dc-driven thin film, which partakes of some of the characteristics of both the dc powder and the ac thin-film types. The structure is shown in Figure 3.15, and like the ac thin film it consists of an evaporated metal electrode followed by the luminescent layer and a transparent electrode, with the entire assembly mounted on a glass plate. Its similarity to the dc powder is in the processing step, when a junction is formed between the ZnS and the CuS regions, thus creating *p-n* diodes, as was the case for the dc powder types. Unfortunately, the panel is subject to thermal runaway and electrical breakdown, and no practical designs have been achieved as yet. It is included here for completeness only.

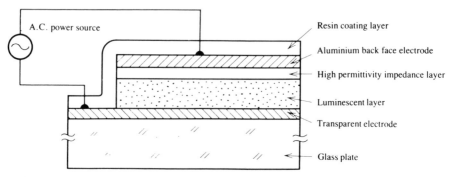

FIGURE 3.13   Structure of three-layer thin-film ELD. After Matsumoto [5, p. 192], by permission.

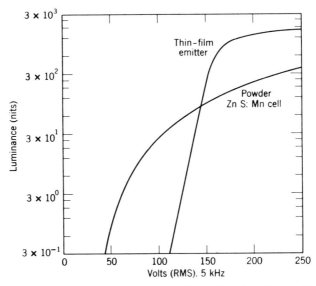

FIGURE 3.14   Luminance vs. voltage for typical powder phosphor and light-emitting film. After Soxman [8, p. 32], by permission.

The final type of EL structure listed in Table 3.3 is the one termed *composite*. It has been mentioned by Vecht in several publications but more or less ignored by other investigators. Vecht describes it as consisting of a light-emitting EL film "backed by a layer of powder, such as MnO_2 or PbO." He claims that "the introduction of such a powder prevents electrical break and runaway." However, it has been neglected by investigators, and no panels have been reported on, either in the literature or at meetings available to the general public.

In summary, the only two structures that have achieved any success in display panels are the dc powder and the ac thin film, with the latter achieving a larger measure of success than the former, although this may change as the

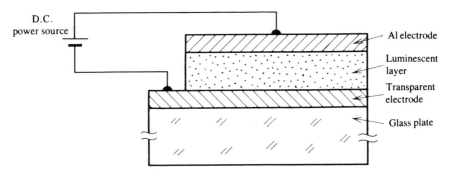

FIGURE 3.15   Structure of thin-film dc ELD. After Matsumoto [5, p. 199], by permission.

TABLE 3.4 Characteristics of ac Thin Film and dc Thick Film

Parameter	AC Film	DC Film
Efficacy (1m/W)	0.3–1.5	0.5–1.0
Luminance (nits)	65–135	70–100
Contrast ratio	10–30	10–30
Response time (ms)	100	100
Voltage drive	175–235 ac	75–100 peak
Current (mA/cm²)	1–10	1–5

new versions using thick film appear to have overcome some of the deficiencies found in the earlier versions. The oldest form, ac powder, is used almost exclusively for light sources, although it still has some potential for A/N displays and possibly for very large panels. Therefore, it is of some interest to compare the characteristics of ac thin film with dc thick film to determine the differences as well as the similarities in performance. This is done in Table 3.4.

This comparison demonstrates that both technologies are capable of being used for FPDs with not easily discernible advantages for either one. Both have produced usable panels, and color has been demonstrated on each type. Figure 3.16 presents response curves of luminance vs. voltage for a number of EL materials and demonstrates the range of colors that may be achieved and have been to some extent with both technologies. Thin-film EL remains somewhat ahead, especially as it has been pursued by more investigators and has a larger group of products. The choice of one over the other may depend more on the factors influencing a market-driven economy, but these considerations are beyond the scope of this volume.

3.3.5 Gas-Discharge Displays

General Principles. Gas-discharge displays have been around for many years, in their early manifestations as neon signs and indicators and, of course, in the form of the well-known Nixie numeric indicator. However, more recently there has been a tremendous growth of activity in this type of display device, sparked by the development of the ac gas-discharge display, as well as several new types of dc gas-discharge numeric and matrix displays. We discuss the difference between the ac and dc types in greater detail later, but we preface that discussion with some general information on the character of the gas discharge and the mechanisms whereby a visual output results that may be used as the display device in a system. This review enables us to properly assess the capabilities and potential of both existing and potential gas-discharge display devices and systems, of which there are at present a significant number, several with application to matrix systems.

Light emission from gases occurs, as in solid-state materials, when an electron moves from one energy level to a lower energy level, with the dif-

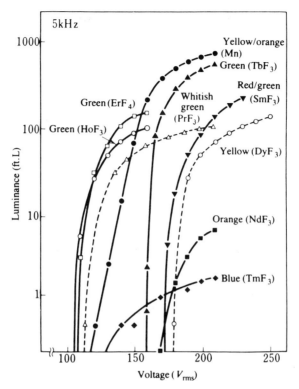

FIGURE 3.16 Luminance vs. voltage of ELs of various colors. After Matsumoto [5, p. 216], by permission.

ference that in the gas the electrons are separated from the atoms, and the gas is said to be in the ionized state when a sufficiently large number of the atoms have lost at least one electron. The limit is when all atoms have lost one or more electrons, but the glow occurs when the concentration of electrons and ions is less than 1%, and the gas is then referred to as a *plasma*. In this condition it is most likely to emit radiation, and all the gas-discharge displays we cover are made to take on this condition, hence the term *plasma display*. Although the term has become primarily associated with one specific form of ac-discharge display, it is more properly employed with reference to the dc types as well, and we use it in this general sense, differentiating the two by the manner in which the gas discharge is initiated and maintained.

To ionize a gas, it is necessary to apply energy high enough to separate electrons from the field of the ion, and this energy, known as the *ionization potential*, is the highest state in an energy-level diagram for an element. Ionization potentials for a number of different gases are given in Table 3.5, along with the first potential for radiative excitation and the color of the discharge. The color of neon is the well-known orange, and this is the characteristic color of the majority of plasma displays, since they are basically

TABLE 3.5   Characteristics of Gas Discharge

Gas or Vapor	Ionizing Potential (eV)	First Radiative Excitation Potential (eV)	Discharge Color
A	15.7	11.6	Blue
Cd	8.96	3.78	Red
He	24.5	20.6	Yellow
Hg	10.4	4.88	Purple
Na	5.12	2.09	Yellow
Ne	21.5	16.7	Orange

made of neon, although with admixtures of other gases for purposes that become apparent when we cover some specific structures. In addition, traces of radioactive material are sometimes added to the gas to provide another ionizing agent, since emitted particles may have sufficient energy to free electrons and thus begin the ionization process without depending completely on the field energy. The collisions of electrons with nonionized atoms may then impart sufficient energy to the atom to free other electrons and thus continue the ionization process. Electrons in metastable states may also be elevated to higher energy states, and due to the longer lifetime of these states there is an increase in the probability of ionization, and ionization may occur at a voltage much lower than the normal ionization potential of the gas. The sum of all these processes results in the ionization of the gas and the maintenance of the plasma, as long as sufficient energy is provided. The volt-ampere characteristic of the glow discharge is shown in Figure 3.17, where the significant points are the ignition voltage at E, and the sustaining voltage at F. The basic structure of a gas-discharge tube and the distribution of light intensity and potential along the tube are shown in Figure 3.18, and we may note that there are two regions that exhibit light output, namely, the negative glow region and the positive column. The negative glow is close to the cathode and is more intense than the positive column-light output. The majority of gas-discharge displays use the negative glow as the light source, but the positive column has been used to excite phosphors in fluorescent lamps, and, its possible application to displays has been investigated, with improvements in overall efficiency indicated by the use of phosphors. The discussion to this point has assumed a dc potential, but the same principles apply to the ac-activated units, although they require certain special characteristics and drive voltages to operate successfully. One problem is to ensure that the cell does not turn off when the ac potential drops below the sustaining voltage. This is accomplished by effectively including a capacitor in the structure so that once the cell is fired the capacitor retains enough charge to ensure firing on each half cycle. This is covered in greater detail later. Various structures have

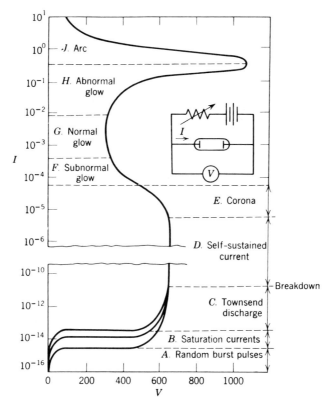

FIGURE 3.17 Volt-ampere characteristics of gaseous discharge. After Nasser [9], by permission.

been used for gas-discharge displays, but the one most common is that shown in Figure 3.19. It consists, in its simplest form, of two glass plates with conductors, one of which is transparent, and a gas mixture enclosed between the two plates. The energizing potential is applied across the gas by connecting it to the conductors, and the gas fires when the potential is of the proper magnitude. The dc type must have the conductors on the side of the glass facing the glass, but the ac type may have the conductors on the outside of the glass. However, although they have been constructed with the electrodes on the outside, this has been changed to the arrangement shown in Figure 3.20, but with the addition of a dielectric layer between the electrodes and the gas to provide the capacitance needed to store the sustaining charge. In the dc panel the cathode is made of a material such as graphite, that can serve as a source of secondary emission electrons to aid in sustaining the discharge. The ac panel has the two plates serving alternatively as the anode and cathode, and the discharge is maintained by the capacitive charge as previously described.

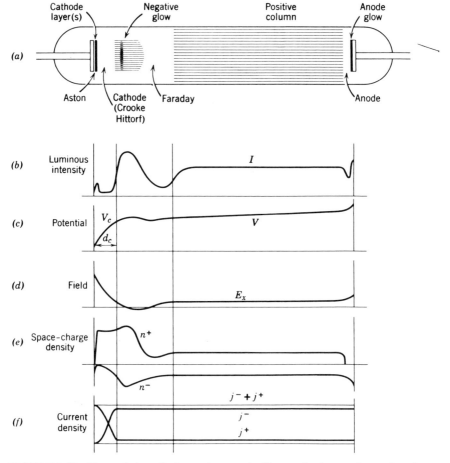

FIGURE 3.18   Normal glow discharge in neon in 50-cm tube at $p = 1$ torr. Luminous regions are shown shaded. After Nasser [9], by permission.

Direct-Current Discharge. The current in a dc gas-discharge display is given by

$$i = i_0 \frac{\exp(V - V_i)}{1 - \gamma \exp[\eta(V - V_i)]} \tag{3.26}$$

where i_0 = current due to primary electrons

V = applied voltage

V_i = gas-ionization voltage

γ = second Townsend coefficient (number of secondary electrons emited from the cathode per bombarding positive ion)

η = first Townsend coefficient (number of electron-ion pairs per volt)

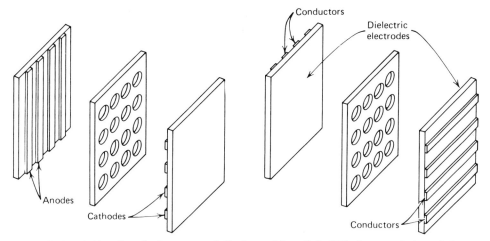

FIGURE 3.19 Gas-discharge panel displays. After Cola [10], by permission of Academic Press.

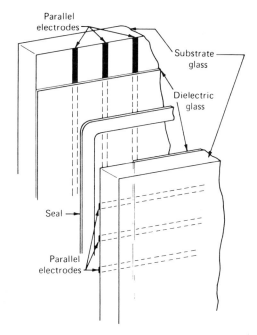

Panel construction

FIGURE 3.20 Owens Illinois "Digivue" geometry, consisting of electrodes insulated from gas by a dielectric film. The film produces memory and bistable operation. After Chodil [11], by permission.

We see from equation 3.26 that an infinite current flows when the denominator goes to zero, and in practice a series resistor is used to limit this current. The value of V to meet the condition that the denominator be zero is known as the *breakdown voltage* (V_B), and solving for this voltage results in the expression

$$V_B = \frac{1}{\eta} \ln\left(\frac{1}{\gamma}\right) + V_i \qquad (3.27)$$

At this voltage the positive ions generated in the gas are just sufficient to free enough secondary electrons at the cathode to balance the ions generated in the gas. As a result, the discharge current is maintained without the need for an external source of electron generation. It has been found that the breakdown voltage is only a function of the pressure (p) and the electrode separation for a given gas, so that different breakdown voltages may be designed into the device. The minimum breakdown voltage is given approximately by

$$V_{B_{min}} = \frac{1}{\eta_{max}} \ln\left(\frac{1}{\gamma}\right) + V_i \qquad (3.28)$$

The breakdown voltage may also be written as

$$V_B = V_{B_{min}} + K(pd) \qquad (3.29)$$

where K = coefficient depending on gas mixture used
p = gas pressure
d = electrode spacing

K, $1/\gamma$, and η have been tabulated, and for the noble gases breakdown voltages in the order of several hundred volts are found when metal is mixed with the gas.

Once the breakdown has begun, a space charge forms near the cathode, and most of the voltage drop occurs at the cathode. In addition, the coefficient (K) increases to some maximum determined by the growth of the space charge. The sustaining voltage (V_s) may then be found by substituting in the equation for V_B the effective value η' for η that applies only to a cell with a uniform field, which is not the actual case, yielding the equation for v_S. In the glow region of such a self-sustaining discharge, η' is kept near its maximum and the voltage at the sustaining level by the stable equilibrium that exists. Then the cell current may be expressed by

$$i = Jp^2 A_K \qquad (3.30)$$

where A_K is the cathode area and J is a constant determined by η and γ. Values for J may be found in tabulations and range from 10^{-6} A/cm²·torr² to 10 times as much.

We have noted previously that other gases may be mixed with the noble gases, which are the major constituents of gas-discharge displays. The purpose of this mixture is to form what is known as a *Penning mixture*, in which the metastable energy level of the noble gas is greater than the ionization energy of the added gas. As a result, metastable atoms of the main gas collide with atoms of the added gas and create additional ions. This leads to lower break-down voltages, as is illustrated in Figure 3.21 for a mixture of neon and argon. It can be seen from Figure 3.21 that very small amounts of added gas lead to considerable reductions in the breakdown voltage, and all plasma panels, whether dc or ac, use mixtures of this type, with the exact mixture frequently a proprietary item.

Up to this point we have been dealing primarily with the general charac-teristics of a gas-discharge display under dc excitation. Before leaving the dc type, we should mention one other characteristic, the memory margin, defined by

$$\text{memory margin} = \frac{V_B - V_S}{V_S} \tag{3.31}$$

where V_S is the sustaining voltage.

The sustaining voltage is normally lower than the breakdown voltage by some amount and is a function of the electrode separation and the various constants associated with the type of gas and the cell construction. A typical

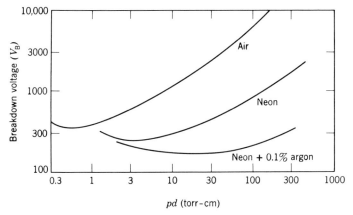

FIGURE 3.21 Paschen curves for air, neon, and neon–argon mixtures relating break-down voltage, V_B, to product of pressure and electrode spacing, pd, for a parallel-plate cell configuration. After Cola [10], by permission of Academic Press.

value of the memory margin is about 0.5, so that for a breakdown voltage of 150 V, V_S is 100 V.

Alternating-Current Discharge. Turning to the ac gas-discharge cell, we have noted previously that it differs in construction from the dc cell in that the electrodes are placed on the outside of the glass plates. It was originally hoped that this arrangement would protect the electrodes from sputtering due to ion bombardment, since the electrodes are protected from the gas by the glass plates. However, when a discharge is initiated, the charge particles flow to the cell walls and build up a charge that quenches the discharge. Therefore, it is necessary to reverse the polarity of the drive voltage to overcome the effect of this charge buildup, and the need for ac drive is apparent. In this type of cell there is no need for current-limiting resistors, since the discharge current is limited by the capacitive reactance in series with the cell, which reactance is a function of the drive frequency and various characteristics of the cell. This is one advantage of the ac cell, to which can be added the ability to operate in a memory mode by using a voltage below the discharge voltage but large enough to sustain the discharge once it has been initiated. This is analogous to the memory margin of the dc cell, but no resister is required.

The lower voltage can maintain the discharge because the wall charge voltage adds to the sustaining voltage on each half cycle, and the firing voltage, which is the same as for a comparable dc cell given by equation 3.28, is exceeded by the sum of the sustaining and wall-charge voltages, thus causing the cell to fire and the wall charge to reverse. The sequence of events is illustrated in Figure 3.22, where V_s, the sustaining voltage, is a sine wave, V_f is the firing voltage, V_w is the wall voltage, and V_c is the voltage across the cell. The situation may be shown schematically as illustrated in Figure 3.23, and the actual voltage across the cell capacitance (V_c') is given by

$$V_c' = \frac{C_0}{C_0 + 2C_c} V_s = V_w'$$ (3.32)

where C_0 is the capacitance due to the glass plates, and C_c is the capacitance of the gas cell itself. The actual firing voltage may be similarly expressed as

$$V_f = \frac{C_0 + 2C_c}{C_0} V_f'$$ (3.33)

where V_f is the external voltage and V_f' is the firing voltage. In practice, C_0 is much greater than C_c, so that V_f and V_f' are essentially equal.

In the ideal case the walls are fully charged, and at the time when the wall charge reverses the wall voltage equals the drive voltage, and the walls are fully charged. Therefore, for all values of V_s between $\frac{1}{2}V_f$ and V_f the cell refires on each half-cycle and has a bistable range equal to $\frac{1}{2}V_f$. However, in the actual case the wall charge does not reverse instantaneously, but rather

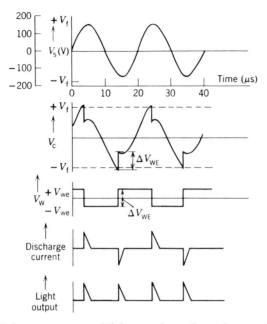

FIGURE 3.22   Voltage, current, and light waveforms for a plasma cell. After Jackson and Johnson [12], by permission of Academic Press.

follows the sustaining voltage with some delay. In addition, the cell walls are usually not fully charged so that the bistable range is less than $\frac{1}{2}V_f$. The difference between V_f and the minimum amplitude of sustaining voltage to maintain discharge is analogous to the extinction voltage of a dc discharge and leads to a figure of merit given by

$$M = \frac{V_f - V_e}{\frac{1}{2}V_f} \tag{3.34}$$

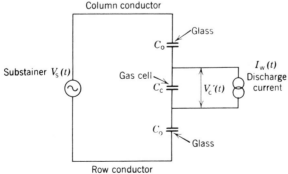

FIGURE 3.23   Simple equivalent circuit of a plasma cell. After Jackson and Johnson [12], by permission of Academic Press.

where V_e is the difference between V_f and minimum sustaining voltage. Further discussion of the characteristics of specific ac cells is given later.

3.3.6   Vacuum Fluorescent Displays

Basic Principles.   *Vacuum fluorescent* (VF) *displays* are essentially flat CRTs, but as they exist only in the FPD and matrix addressed form, they are included in this chapter. They were originally single- and multidigit round tubes and did not become part of the FPD group until 1974 with the development by Ise Corp. and Futaba of flat, multidigit units, and the subsequent development of the matrix addressed VFDs. The basic structure of these units is shown in Figure 3.24a, which is an exploded view of a single numeric. It consists of a cathode filament, a grid, a set of anode segments with their associated wiring, and a front glass plate on a transparent conductive film, with all of these components sealed in a vacuum envelope. The character selection is accomplished by applying a voltage to the appropriate segments, causing the phosphor on those segments to emit light. A multicharacter assembly can be created by combining a number of elements and they can be energized selectively by switching the grid voltage in conjunction with selecting the proper segments on the switched character. This technique, known as multiplexing, is discussed in more detail later in this chapter. A dot matrix assembly is shown in Figure 3.24b, and each dot is selected by driving the proper row and column electrodes, where the row is the anodes and the column is the grid. This is done in the standard matrix addressing manner, also described further later in this chapter.

The equation for luminance is

$$L = 3.2E_p J_p D_u n \qquad (3.35)$$

where E_p = anode voltage in volts
  J_p = anode current density in mA/cm^2
  D_u = duty cycle
  n = luminous efficiency of phosphor in lm/W

Similarly, the equation for luminance versus voltage is

$$\frac{L = nD_u G}{1 + k}(E_p)(n + 1) \qquad (3.36)$$

where G = perveance
  k = distribution rate (grid current/anode current)
  n = constant (≈ 1.7)

Low-voltage phophors are used that operate in the range 10 to 25 V, and Figure 3.25 shows the emission spectra and constituents of phosphors in

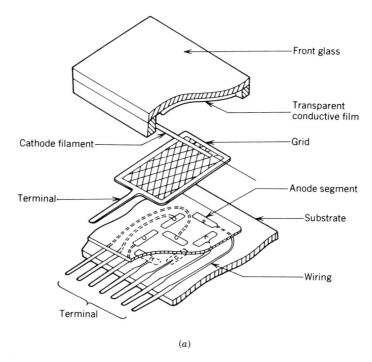

(a)

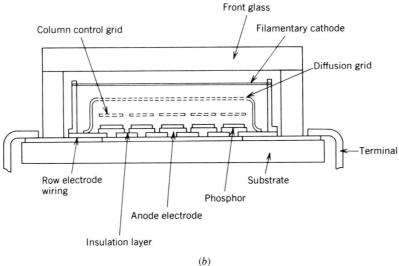

(b)

FIGURE 3.24 (a) Basic structure of flat VFD; (b) Normal-type dot matrix VFD. After Morimoto and Pykosz [13], by permission.

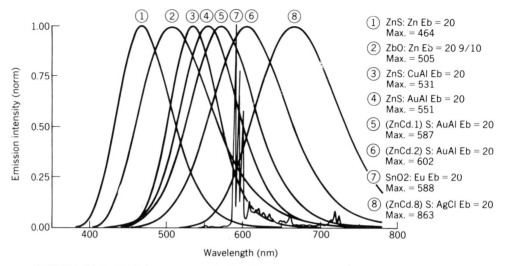

FIGURE 3.25 Emission spectra of phosphors in current use. After Morimoto and Pykosz [13, p. 1.2.28], by permission.

present use. Multicolor displays are made by using different phosphors in different sections of the display and up to four separate colors are possible.

3.3.7 Liquid Crystals

Basic Principles. Although the liquid-crystal phase was discovered as long ago as 1888, it was not until Heilmeier and his associates first discovered ways to use it for display devices that it became a display material. Liquid-crystal technology has advanced very rapidly in the last 10 years, although its initial spurt after the early developments was considerably slowed down as the result of poor life and visual characteristics. However, the invention of the twisted nematic device in the early 1970s, for which several investigators have claimed credit (Fergason, Schadt, Helfrich) but which we leave to the courts to decide, overcame many of these objections, and LCDs returned to favor, albeit primarily for A/N devices used in battery-operated instruments.

Much work was expended on improving materials and applying the various states in which the material can be fabricated, but it was not until the supertwisted nematic was developed, and an active matrix drive was applied that LCDs became the strong contender for the preferred FPD material that it is at present. It differs from the other competitive technologies, such as LEDs, EL, and plasma, in that it is not a light-emitting material, but rather one that requires a separate light source, which may be ambient illumination or a dedicated lamp, and controls the transmission or reflection of that light. The control is achieved by placing the LCD cell in the light path, and altering the optical characteristics of the cell by applying electric fields across the cell. This allows LCDs to have a number of unique characteristics, some of which are extremely useful, and others of which are undesirable to varying degrees. In particular, the very low power required to control the cell, and the low cost of the basic material, make it an effective competitor for use in a wide variety of display devices, ranging from simple A/N displays to complex matrix panels.

To fully understand the modes of operation possible with liquid-crystal materials, it is necessary to examine some of the basic physical and chemical characteristics of the medium. It is not practical to go into these properties in full detail here, which would require a book in itself, but the relevant information is presented in sufficient detail for the reader to achieve a good understanding of the phenomena involved and an appreciation of what may be done with the material.

Liquid crystals look and pour like ordinary liquids over the usable temperature range, which is on the order of -10 to $+70°C$ for some popular composite materials, and can be raised to higher values by the addition of certain special types, but at the cost of increased viscosity. They differ from other liquids in that they have an ordered structure, somewhat like that found in the EL materials and are made up of elongated organic molecules that arrange themselves into three types of ordering: *nematic, cholesteric,* and *smectic.* The three types are illustrated in Figure 3.26, where the nematic has all the molecules parallel to each other, the cholesteric has consecutive layers of molecules parallel to each other, but with the alignment in each layer in a preferred direction that rotates continuously from one layer to the next, thus following a helix in its ordering pattern, and the smectic has a layered structure with a constant preferred direction. Outside the operating temperature range, the material freezes at the low end and becomes an isotropic liquid above the high end. It is not necessarily destroyed by freezing, and may recover from excessive heat, although it is not advisable to leave it in either of these states for any appreciable length of time. The majority of LCDs use the nematic type, but there are examples of devices that use cholesteric, cholesteric–nematic, and smectic mixtures. In particular, certain chiral–smectic forms have been used that exhibit spontaneous polarization, and the LCDs containing this type of material are termed *ferroelectric.*

Liquid crystals are rather complex organic chemicals, as is evident from Table 3.6, which lists a number of types as well as their chemical formulas. Many other types have been developed in the constant search for formulations

Smectic

Nematic

Cholesteric

FIGURE 3.26   Schematic representation of ordering in the three mesomorphic states. Courtesy of Atomergic Chemicals Company.

TABLE 3.6 Representative Liquid Crystals

Chemical Compound	Abbreviation	Chemical Structural Formula	Mesomorphic Temperature Range (°C)	Mesophase
4-Methoxy-4'-n-butylazoxybenzene	MBAB	CH_3O — ⬡ — N=N(→O) — ⬡ — n-C_4H_9	42–77	Nematic
N-(p-Methoxybenzylidene)-p-n-butylaniline	MBBA	CH_3O — ⬡ — CH=N — ⬡ — n-C_4H_9	20–41	Nematic
N-(p-Ethoxybenzylidene)-p-n-butylaniline	EBBA	C_2H_5O — ⬡ — CH=N — ⬡ — n-C_4H_9	35–77	Nematic
Eutectic mixture of methoxy and ethoxy-p-n-butylaniline	50% MMBA, 50% EBBA	Equal parts by weight of preceding two compounds	0–60	Nematic
Cholesteryl erucate	CE	n-$C_8H_{17}CH$=$CH(CH_2)_{11}CO$ (cholesteryl skeleton)	10–62	Cholesteric
Cholesteryl nonanoate	CN	n-$C_8H_{17}CO$ (cholesteryl skeleton)	78–91	Cholesteric

Source: After Soref [14], by permission.

244

that exhibit wide operating temperature ranges and fast response, and a number of them may be found in reference 5. Out of the hundreds of liquid crystals available, relatively few operate over a temperature range large enough to be useful, and even less over a desirable range, but there are enough to meet most requirements, and more are being developed on a continuous basis so that there are sure to be enough to meet most if not all of the present and future requirements. Thus LCDs are an important part of the display repertoire.

Cell Structure. A liquid-crystal cell, in its simplest form, consists of two glass plates separated by spacers and sealed around the periphery, as shown in Figure 3.27. The liquid-crystal material is contained between the plates, and the electrodes are internal to the cell so that a voltage can be applied directly across the material. The molecules are made to align themselves either parallel (homogeneous) or perpendicular (homeotropic) to the plates in manufacture by a variety of means that need not concern us here, and examples of the two arrangements are shown in Figure 3.28, and the dielectric constant ($\epsilon_{\parallel}$) for the parallel direction is greater than that for the perpendicular direction ($\epsilon_{\perp}$) in the homogeneous case, and smaller in the homeotropic case, for nematic materials.

Electrically Controlled Birefringence (ECB). One way to achieve an LCD is to control the birefringence of the cell by the application of an electric field across the cell. Figure 3.28 illustrates the ordering in the absence of an applied field, and if a field of sufficient magnitude is applied by connecting a voltage source to the transparent electrodes, the molecular alignment is changed as shown in Figure 3.29 for the homeotropic ordering. This change in the alignment of the molecules causes a change in the birefringence of the cell. In the homogeneous ordering the birefringence of the cell changes from large to small, whereas the opposite occurs in the homeotropic case. Since this change in the birefringence causes a change in the light transmission of a properly polarized light, it is possible by using a polarizer–analyzer combination, as shown in Figure 3.29, to control the light transmission. The light output from

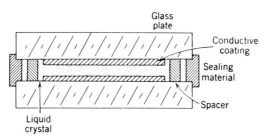

FIGURE 3.27 Schematic cross section of a LCD. After Goodman [15], by permission.

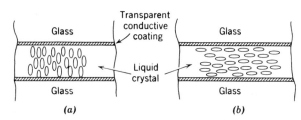

FIGURE 3.28   Side view of (*a*) homeotropic and (*b*) homogeneous orientations. After Goodman [15], by permission.

the cell (I_0) is given by

$$I_0 = I_i \sin^2 2\phi \, \sin^2 \sigma \tag{3.37}$$

where I_i = input light after passing through the two polarizers
ϕ = angle between input light polarization direction and oscillation direction of ordinary light in cell
$\sigma = d\Delta nV/\lambda$
d = cell thickness
ΔnV = voltage-induced change in birefringence
λ = wavelength of light
$n = n(1) - n(2)$
$n(1)$ = refractive index for extraordinary ray
$n(2)$ = refractive index for ordinary ray

It should be noted here that birefringence is the characteristic of an optical transmission medium whereby different indices of refraction exist for vertically and horizontally polarized light waves, so that the polarized light leaves the cell at a different angle and polarization than at entrance, thus changing

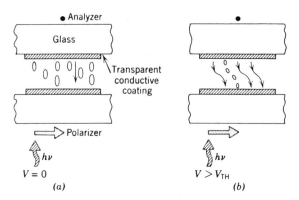

FIGURE 3.29   Schematic illustration of induced birefringence effect with and without an applied voltage. Arrows represent director orientation. After Goodman [12], by permission.

the transmission through the second polarizer or analyzer. This effect in a liquid-crystal cell, termed *distortion of aligned phases* (DAP), is interesting in that it is sensitive to both the applied voltage and the wavelength of the input light, as can be seen from equation 3.37. Thus it is possible to achieve a color change if white light is used and the applied voltage is altered. However, despite this desirable characteristic, it has not been found possible to build displays with reliable control of the color because of temperature sensitivity and the difficulty encountered in controlling the rotation of the molecules so that a specified color always appears at a specified voltage. Despite this deficiency, it has been incorporated in several prototype systems and should still be considered as a possible approach to multicolor displays.

Other LCDs using ECB are the *homogeneous* and *hybrid aligned nematic* (HAN) types. The first does not differ in principle from the DAP type, but the color change with voltage is opposite and the threshold voltage is much lower. The HAN type uses hybrid orientation where the liquid-crystal molecules are aligned perpendicular to one substrate and parallel to the other in the same direction and the orientation curves continuously through 90°. There is no clear threshold voltage for this type, and a very low drive voltage may be used. These effects also suffer from the deficiencies found in the DAP effect.

Twisted Nematic (TN) Structure. The TN LCD was the first to achieve large-scale acceptance after the failure of the dynamic scattering technique and continues to find wide applications both in its original form and in the improved supertwist versions that have superseded the original form. The unique characteristic of this form is that the cell is constructed in such a fashion that the molecular axis of the liquid-crystal material is made to rotate continuously through 90° from one plate to the other. As a result, linearly polarized light incident on one of the plates is rotated in the same way and emerges from the second plate with its plane of polarization at 90° from the incoming light. This is illustrated in Figure 3.30, which shows the molecules aligned homo-

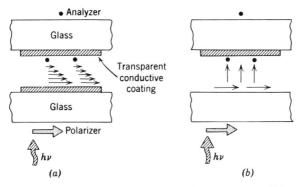

FIGURE 3.30   Side views of twisted nematic for (*a*) $V = 0$ and (*b*) $V > V_{TH}$. Thin arrows represent orientation of nematic molecules. After Goodman [3], by permission.

geneously, but with a twist of 90° from the top to the bottom layer. As a result, if the second polarizer, or analyzer, is parallel to the first, which originally polarized the light, the light will be blocked by the analyzer. We should perhaps mention here, for clarification, that a polarizer is an optical element that passes light of one polarity and blocks light of the opposite polarity, depending on how the polarizer is aligned with the direction of polarization of the light. Thus if the first polarizer is used to pass light of one polarity, that light will be in the proper polarity to pass through a second polarizer, commonly referred to as the *analyzer*, aligned with its axis parallel to that of the first polarizer. Similarly, if the second polarizer is aligned at right angles to the first, the light is blocked. The effect is well known and has been used for many different applications, and its importance in liquid crystal displays lies in the fact that it must be used in the most successful type, the twisted nematic, and it imposes certain important limitations in angle of view and light transmission on the display device as well as temperature range.

To return to the operation of the twisted nematic cell, we have noted that the molecules are rotated through 90° in the absence of a field. When a field is applied, the molecules are untwisted and line up in the direction of the applied field. As a result, the light is not rotated on passing through the liquid crystal cell and is blocked by the right-angle analyzer. This allows light to be blocked in the activated condition and transmitted in the quiescent condition, as is illustrated in Figure 3.30. Of course, the opposite results may be achieved by turning the polarizer so that it is aligned parallel to the analyzer. This provides the option of a light on a dark or a dark on a light display, and is an extremely useful characteristic. The color effect described for the DAP effect is very small for the twisted nematic, since there is very little birefringence, and the major effect is the rotation of the direction of the light polarization. Another important advantage of the twisted nematic structure is that very small voltages are sufficient to align the molecules, and cells have been built that need less than 1 V to operate, although 5 to 10 V is a more common requirement. In addition, the current flowing through the cell is in the microampere range, so that only microwatts of power are needed, which accounts for the popularity of this type of display in watch applications, as is discussed further later. This, then, appears to be an almost ideal display device. However, as always, nature is against us, and there are several important limitations in the performance of this type of display device. The first has to do with the need for a polarizer–analyzer combination to achieve the desired optical effect. Unfortunately, the contrast ratio that can be attained is determined by the extinction ratio of the polarizer–analyzer pair, that is, the ratio of the light transmitted in the parallel condition to that transmitted in the right angle arrangement. Polarizers that have good extinction ratios tend to have rather poor transmission in the nonblocking case, frequently less than 20% of the impinging light, so that we are left with considerable light loss through the combination. This may be overcome by supplying more light, but this is not always possible and limits the areas of application for these devices. A second drawback is the angle dependence of the contrast ratio, which restricts the angle of view to something less than $\pm 45°$ for satisfactory operation. Although it is not completely clear why this occurs, it appears to be due to the lack of perfect alignment in the molecules of the liquid-crystal material, and this limitation may be removed as manufacturing techniques improve, and better alignment is achieved over the entire cell. This may also permit larger cells to be built, although at present cells larger than about 3 cm on a side are difficult to fabricate with good uniformity. A third undesirable feature is the relatively slow response of displays fabricated in this fashion, in the order of 100-ms rise and fall time. Although various techniques have been proposed and tried to improve this characteristic, they remain laboratory achievements, and both multiplexing and matrix addressing are severely limited by the slow response, as is apparent when we discuss these techniques later. Finally, the temperature dependence of the threshold voltage makes it difficult to operate in any mode dependent on good control of threshold, as is the case in some multiplexing approaches. All these disadvantages combine to restrict the areas of application of this otherwise excellent device. However, it has found extensive use in a variety of numeric and A/N displays, especially where low power is important as in battery-operated test equipment, radios, and watches.

Supertwisted Nematic (STN or SBE) Structure. Many of the limitations found in the original versions have been overcome with the advent of the super and double supertwist versions as developed by Scheffer and his associates. These use the same basic structure as the TN types, with the important difference that the twist is increased to 180° or 270°. This type of structure has been variously termed the supertwisted birefringence effect (SBE), supertwisted nematic (STN), and double supertwisted. The high twist angle is combined with a high pretilt angle at the LCD's alignment layer, and the result is a significant improvement in the viewing angle and contrast ratio over that attained with the standard TN type. A schematic view of a cell with a 270° twist is shown in Figure 3.31 and demonstrates the large difference in the orientation of the molecules between the select (V_s) and nonselect (V_{ns}) voltage states. However, although the cell has the same basic form as the standard TN type, it is necessary to align the polarizers in an off-axis polarization in a birefringence mode to achieve improved contrast ratio. An offset of 30° for the front and 60° for the rear results in a display that is yellow in the nonselect condition and black for the select condition. Rotating either polarizer by 90° changes the colors to purplish blue for the nonselect state and colorless in the select state. The transmission spectra of the yellow and blue modes are shown in Figure 3.32. The high twist angle when combined with a high pretilt angle produces a much wider viewing angle and higher contrast ratio than can be achieved with the standard 90° twist TN type.

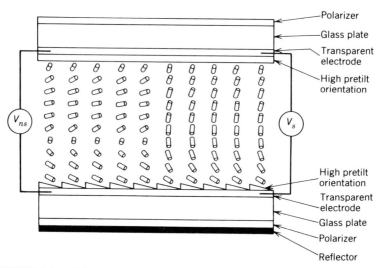

FIGURE 3.31   Schematic view of HyperTwist display. Courtesy of Tektronix.

The majority of SBE displays use the smaller 180° twist because it is easier to build. However, this type has a smaller distortion curve as shown in Figure 3.33, and the transition from off to on is not as sharp and cannot be multiplexed as well besides having smaller viewing angles and contrast ratios.

Finally, if a color-compensating LC plate is added, as shown in Figure 3.34, this is termed the double-supertwist display. The compensator is not electrically driven, and it has its optical axis orthogonal and the direction of twist opposite to the driven cell. The result is that the birefringence colors are canceled, and the display is a pure white on black. In addition, the contrast ratio is almost doubled and the viewing angle increased over that achieved in the STB type. Therefore, this is a preferred structure but has the disadvantages that the increased transmission loss due to the compensator necessitates a higher-power backlight, and it is more expensive than the others because of the more complex assembly. The answer to the increase in cost, while maintaining the white-on-black display, is the monochrome supertwist display. In this arrangement the compensating plate is replaced by an optical retardation layer that is placed between the front polarizer and the front glass plate. The optical retarder is made from a polymer material that is less expensive than the glass plate but has the disadvantage that the thickness of the polymer material must be carefully controlled. However, the lower cost and transmission loss has made this the structure of choice.

It is also possible to turn the supertwist and double-supertwist versions into full-color displays if a filter consisting of a color mosaic is placed over the cell, and white light is used. The mosaic has one color over each intersection and is arranged in groups of RGB combinations similar to those found in the shadow-mask CRT. Color is achieved by switching the cells behind proper combinations of the three colors into the transmissive state and the

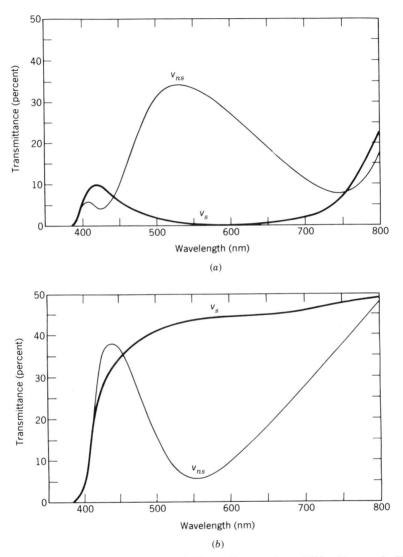

FIGURE 3.32   Transmission spectra of (*a*) a yellow mode and (*b*) a blue mode SBE display measured at operating voltages V_s and V_{ns}. After Scheffer, et al. [17], by permission.

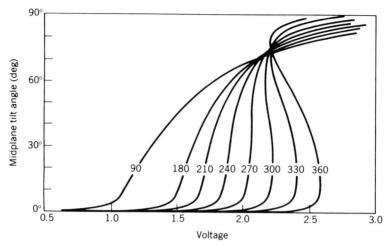

FIGURE 3.33   Distortion curve for various twist angles. Courtesy of Tektronix.

results can be quite acceptable. A few versions of this type of display have been offered, especially for projection systems, but it has largely been superseded for other applications by the active matrix technique for color LCDs, described later in this chapter. Therefore, the major applications for supertwist and double-supertwist displays are as monochromatic display panels for laptop, notebook, and portable computers, and monochromatic displays for various types of numeric and A/N readouts.

Guest–Host (GH) Display. The guest–host version of an LCD is one attempt to add color to a cell that was first proposed by Heilmeier and his associates in 1968. It had some success initially, and products using this technique were available for a time, but it is not in much use at present. The basic principle employed is that of a dichroic dye guest with anisotropy in the absorption of visible light when it is in solution in a liquid-crystal host. The molecules of the dye then align themselves parallel to the liquid-crystal molecules, and will follow the host molecules when they are realigned. This effect is illustrated in Figure 3.35, and the result is that the transmitted light is colored in one orientation and colorless in the other. This occurs when the cell has homogeneous orientation and contains a p-type dye in an N_p-type liquid crystal. With no voltage applied, the dye absorbs light and the transmitted light is the same color as the dye. Then when voltage is applied, the combined guest–host molecules are rotated through 90° and no light is absorbed so that the output light is colorless. The opposite effect can be achieved if the liquid crystal is the N_n type and the dye is n-type, so that either combination is possible. In addition, if a smectic or cholesteric liquid crystal instead of nematic or a two-layer nematic cell is used, the polarizer is not required. Thus a fairly simple construction is possible, and a variety of colors can be achieved if different color dyes are used. As noted, this approach was used for awhile

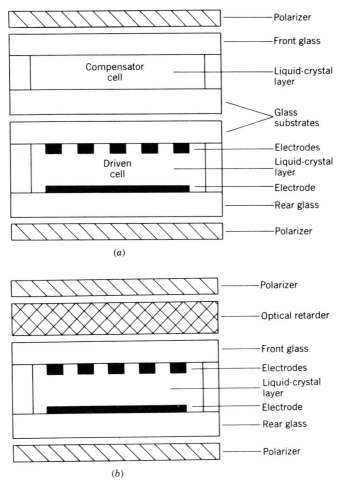

FIGURE 3.34   (a) Double-supertwist and (b) monochrome supertwist construction. After Pyrce [18], by permission.

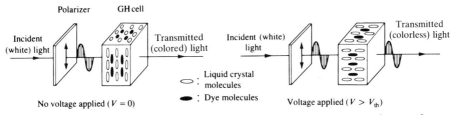

FIGURE 3.35   Principle of guest–host (GH) display. After Matsumoto [5, p. 43], by permission.

and appeared to be a feasible way to construct a display with limited color capabilities. However, it has fallen into disfavor now that other, more satisfactory color displays have been developed, especially those using active matrix addressing and drive.

Phase Change (PC). Another electrooptic effect of interest that is field induced is the cholesteric to nematic phase transition. This occurs in a cholesteric material with positive dielectric anisotropy, that is, $\epsilon\| - \epsilon\perp > 0$. The cell has the cholesteric planes perpendicular to the walls, and the helical axes have a random orientation, so that the liquid crystal scatters light. The effect of the field on the molecules is illustrated in Figure 3.36, and the areas with light scattering cause a change in the appearance of the cell. When a field is applied, the liquid-crystal material changes into an ordered nematic phase, adn the cell appears transparent. Thus it is possible to alter the optical properties of the cell by applying the proper electrical field, in the order of 10^4 V/cm. Since cell thicknesses are just under 1 mm, rather high voltages are required, although these have been reduced to below 400 V for certain combinations of cholesteric and nematic compounds. After the field is removed the material returns to its original state, and the process may be repeated. It may also be used with polarizers, since there is retardation in the cholesteric phase, but not in the nematic phase. Although the material appears to have several interesting characteristics, such as memory and potentially much faster switching times than the twisted nematic, it has seen its main application in various projection systems, described later.

Ferroelectric (Smectic) Display. The latest form of LCD is the one where a thin layer of chiral smectic liquid-crystal molecules is used, with the characteristic that the average molecular orientation can be switched between two states, both in the plane of the liquid-crystal film. It is termed the *surface-stabilized ferroelectric* (SSF), and the parallel states are illustrated in Figure 3.37. The device has a birefringence effect that results in bistability and fast

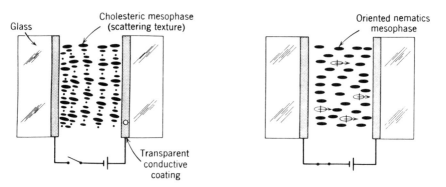

FIGURE 3.36   Side-view representation of the electric-field-induced cholesteric-to-nematic phase change. After Goodman [16], by permission.

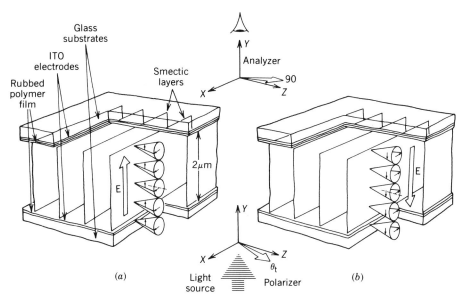

FIGURE 3.37   The two uniform parallel states characteristic of surface-stabilized devices formed by chiral tilted smectic mesaphases; (a) uniform "up" state; (b) uniform "down" state. After Crossland et al. [19, p. 238], by permission.

response, leading to a memory capability and good multiplexibility. The light transmission is

$$I_0 = I_i \sin^2 4\theta_0 \sin^2 \pi \Delta \frac{nd}{\lambda} \tag{3.38}$$

where θ is the cone angle of the chiral smectic and the other terms are the same as in equation 3.37. The preferred cone angle is 22.5°, which leads to the best contrast ratio. The switching speed for smectic C* material is given by

$$\tau = \frac{\mu}{P_s} E \tag{3.39}$$

where τ = response time
   μ = viscosity term
   P_s = spontaneous polarization
   E = electric field

and switching times in the range 10 to 100 μs have been achieved, as shown in Figure 3.38 for various materials. Bias voltages on the order of 50 kHz and pulse drive voltages in the range 20 to 50 V dc have been used to attain this type of performance. A prototype of a 4-in. diagonal panel with 1280 ×

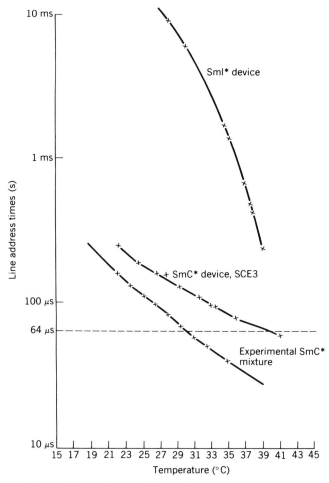

FIGURE 3.38   Line address times of 64 × 64 pixel displays operated under multiplexing conditions. After Crossland et al. [19, p. 243], by permission.

1120 pixels has been demonstrated, and an analog device has been developed by Hartmann et al. using a novel technique termed the *texture method*. A great deal of effort is being expended, and it seems reasonable to assume that ferroelectric LCDs will become an important display technology within the next five years. However, it should be noted that another promising technique using ferroelectric phenomena—ferroelectric ceramics—described later in this chapter, also exhibited great promise but failed to fulfill that promise.

Thermal Effect. Another application for smectic A LCDs is the thermally addressed light valve. The principle involved was first investigated by Sasaki et al. in 1972, and Kahn reported in 1973 on the use of thermoelectric effects for partially or totally erasing a thermally addressed light valve. Several systems using this type of addressing have been developed by a number of companies, and it appears to be a feasible approach. The basic characteristic involved is that if a cell consisting of a thin film of smectic A material is heated into the isotropic state and then cooled, it will become either cloudy or transparent when cooled, depending on whether the cooling is rapid or gradual. The cloudy state corresponds to the focal conic and the clear state to the homeotropic orientation of the liquid-crystal material. Either orientation will be retained until erased, which can be accomplished by heating the cell while a voltage is applied across it. This enables the heat source to act as both a writing and erasing means, and scanning a laser beam has been found capable of performing these functions effectively. The different states are shown in Figure 3.39, and the same effect can be achieved by using another heating source, such as an *X-Y* matrix. Thus an image can be formed and retained until erased. This technique has been incorporated into several projection systems that are discussed in detail in Chapter 4.

Dynamic Scattering. Finally, we come to the progenitor of all liquid crystal display devices, the dynamic scattering nematic liquid crystal. Although it was first in discovery and implementation, it has been largely supplanted by the twisted nematic for the majority of applications, and hence we place it

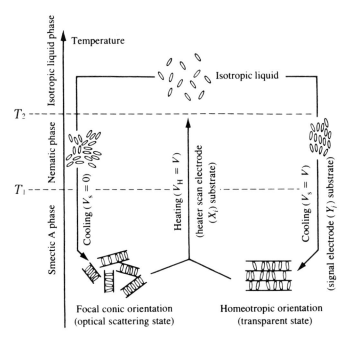

FIGURE 3.39 Principle of thermal addressing drive display. After Matsumoto [5, p. 72], by permission.

last in our discussion. However, this type of liquid crystal display still has certain advantages, and warrants examination not only for historic reasons. The basic alignment of molecules in the nematic cell may be either homogeneous or homeotropic, with the homogeneous more commonly used. The cell is normally transparent, but when a voltage of sufficient magnitude is applied the molecules go out of alignment in what is essentially a random fashion as shown in Figure 3.40. The arrangement of the molecules is such that there are moving birefringent regions in the turbulent liquid, and optical scattering occurs due to the irregular refractive index gradients present in the liquid. The appearance of the cell may be milky white or golden, depending on what type of liquid crystal is used, but the main feature is that the activated regions may be readily differentiated from the inactive regions. It is necessary for the conductivity of the liquid crystal to be greater than about 10^{-11} (Ω-cm)$^{-1}$ for the effect to occur, and this leads to currents several orders of magnitude larger than those found in twisted nematic cells. In addition, the voltage for full activation is several times as great as that required for twisted nematic, so that the total power used is much larger for dynamic scattering than for twisted nematic. This is one important advantage of the latter over the dynamic scattering types and has resulted in the predominance of twisted nematic in those applications requiring very low power, such as watches and battery-operated calculators. However, even the power for the dynamic scattering units is relatively low, in the order of 1 μW/cm^2 of active area, so that we are still dealing with a very low-power device, particularly when we compare it with gas-discharge and LED displays.

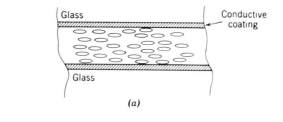

(a)

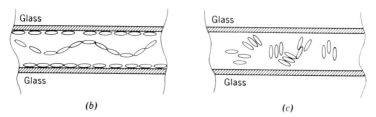

(b)   *(c)*

FIGURE 3.40 Side view of the various steps in formation of dynamic scattering uniform parallel orientation; (a) $V = 0$, (b) $V = V_w$, (c) $V > V_w$. Orientational periodicity is caused by vortical fluid flow that occurs at V_w. After Goodman [3], by permission.

The history of the dynamic scattering mode of LCDs is another example of a development that began with great promise but soon threatened to be a failure because of inherent limitations. However, the liquid-crystal medium was saved by the discovery of other modes of operation, such as the twisted nematic, and whereas dynamic scattering is no longer in use it should be remembered as the progenitor of all of the very successful forms in which it is presently being used. Thus it warrants at least the short discussion that is provided here.

Nematic Curvilinear Aligned Phase (NCAP). One form of nematic LCD that still uses dynamic scattering as the optical phenomenon involved is the NCAP type. This was invented in 1971 by Fergason and has resulted in a group of products. It differs from the standard nematic versions in that very small spheres of the nematic liquid are encapsulated in a polymer matrix and then laminated between large panels of a flexible plastic film. Each capsule acts as a light-switching element, going from parallel to an applied field to alignment along the curved walls of each cell when the field is absent. The light is then scattered in the nonenergized state and passed unchanged in the energized state. This is similar to the standard nematic cell, but differs in that the alignment in the nonenergized condition is created by interactions between the polymer and the liquid crystal. In addition, the structure permits large assemblies to be built, allows switching speeds of about 10 to 50 ms, and can be operated at temperatures as low as $-30°C$. It appears to be a significant improvement over the standard dynamic scattering units, but it has not yet competed successfully against the new supertwist types. However, it does have some interesting features, in particular the ability to build large displays, and it might be considered as a possible form for these types.

Summary. There are eight different types of LCDs covered in this section. They are listed in Table 3.7 with some information on performance for each one included. The most important types are the TN, SBN, and double SBN, with the FE rapidly developing as a potentially significant technology. The PS and thermal have potential, but the others are included more for completeness than for present usefulness.

3.3.8   Electrochromic Displays

Although electrochromic displays (ECDs) have not achieved much acceptance as display devices, they do have a number of interesting characteristics and warrant consideration for certain applications in which their drawbacks are not significant deterrents. The basic phenomenon involved is the change in the light-absorption characteristics of certain materials on application of an electric field. Most of these materials are transparent to visible light in their nonactivated condition but develop an absorption band when the field is applied, and a color becomes visible. This color remains after the field is

TABLE 3.7   Liquid-Crystal Technologies

Type	Principle	Polarizers	V_t	V_o	Power (μW/cm^2)	Optical Phenomenon
ECB	Optical interference	2	1–5	1–10	3–30	Color change
TN	Optical rotation	2	1–3	2–5	2–20	Luminance change
STN	Optical rotation	2	1–5	3–10	2–20	Luminance change
GH	Dichroism	1, 0	1–5	5–10	5–30	Color luminance change
PC	Light scattering	0	3–10	5–20	5–20	Turbid to transparent
FE	Optical interference	2	5–10	5–20	5–10	Luminance change
Thermal	Light scattering	0	10–20	15–40	5–20	Transparent to turbid
DS	Light scattering	0	5–10	7–30	200–300	Transparent to turbid

removed, but the material may be returned to its original transparent state by the application of a field of the opposite polarity to the one that first caused the color change. Another type exhibits one color in the unexcited state and changes color when a field is applied. Again the change is reversible when a field of the opposite polarity is applied, so that we have an electrically controllable optical change. Displays made of these materials are passive since they do not emit light and are thus comparable to liquid crystal displays, as differentiated from light-emitting displays such as electroluminescent and gas-discharge types.

The basic form of the electrochromic display device is shown in Figure 3.41. It consists of the thin film of some electrochromic material, such as tungsten trioxide (WO_3) which is an inorganic solid material and is evaporated on the glass substrate over the conductive surface. This film is about 1 μm thick and is followed by an electrolyte made up of a mixture of water, glycerol, sulfuric acid, and a white reflecting powder. Next is a layer of insulating material, and finally a back electrode made of a solid plate of stainless steel. The cell is normally white, due to the white pigment in the electrolyte and the transparent electrochromic material, but when the transparent electrode on the glass is made about 1.5 V negative with respect to the steel palte the WO_3 will turn blue, and the cell will have this color. Thus it is possible to create blue characters on a white background if the proper shape is imparted to the transparent conductor, as is described in more detail later. This color may remain for days or may be bleached if the opposite polarity voltage is applied. The current is about 5 mA for coloration and 15 mA for bleaching, but flows only during a relatively short portion of the time required for the

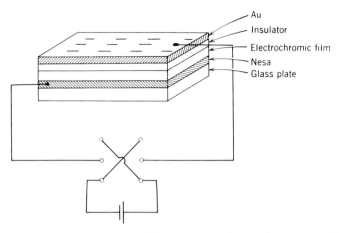

FIGURE 3.41   Typical multilayer solid-state electrochromatic structure. After Deb
[20], by permission of IEEE.

total change to occur. This is illustrated in Figure 3.42, and it can be seen
that the duty factor is small, thus reducing the total amount of power used
to well below what it would be if the peak current flowed continuously.
Therefore, the total power used is well below that for the LED and is comparable with dynamic scattering liquid-crystal displays. Although the device
as described is reflective, it may be rendered transparent if the electrolyte
and the steel plate are replaced by a transparent electrode. Several mechanisms have been proposed to explain the color change, and it is contended
that it is due to the formation of tungsten bronze as the result of two carrier
injection, but the validity of this model need not concern us provided that
the results are predictable and controllable. Of course, a good understanding
of the phenomena involved usually leads to better control of the manufacturing processes and rapid advances in device development, as is demonstrated
by the achievements of solid-state technology, but then again, CRT phosphors
have been made for years with only a limited understanding of the processes
involved, and yet with notable results. The same might be said of beer. In
any event, the present theory attributes the color change to the injection of
electrons from the negative electrode and the injection of hydrogen ions from
the electrolyte. When the electrons and ions return to their starting location
the electrochromic film is bleached with approximately the same charge removed as is injected. The charge-transfer process may be expressed by

$$xA^+ + xe^- + WO_3 \text{ (uncolored)} = A_x^+ WO_3 e_x^- \text{ (colored)} \qquad (3.40)$$

and the current is a function of many factors including the area, the voltage,
the number of electrons involved in the reaction, various parameters of the
material, and the time. For our purposes the applied voltage is the only

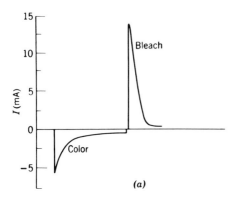

(a)

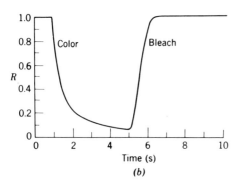

Time (s)

(b)

FIGURE 3.42 Device characteristics of a WO_3 electrochromic cell. Active area is 0.33 cm²; R is the diffuse reflectance of light reflected by the powder in electrolyte. After Goodman [16], by permission.

important parameter, and the diffusion-controlled current is given by

$$i = nKf(W) \int (V)t^{-1/2} \tag{3.41}$$

where n = number of electrons
K = constant
$f(W)$ = material parameters
V = voltage
t = time

Similarly, the optical density resulting from the flow of charge is given by

$$D = a\frac{i\,dt}{2.3nFA} \tag{3.42}$$

where a,F = constants of the material
A = area
D = density

Unlike liquid crystals, electrochromic cells are driven with dc voltages, which simplifies the drive circuitry. In addition, the electrochromic cells do not suffer from the restricted viewing angles of liquid-crystal cells using polarizers, but the response times are slower and the contrast ratio is not as good.

Other materials that have been investigated are a combination of lutetium diphthalocyanine and lead fluoride, another combination of polystyrene sulfonic acid and tungsten trioxide, and tin oxide films to name a few. There has been a rash of recent investigations by various laboratories, which have achieved some interesting results, but successful devices for large-scale use are still in the future, if ever.

Another form of ECD is the one that uses organic materials, in particular viologen derivative types. Some of them and their chemical formulations are shown in Figure 3.43, and they combine the advantages of both a plating and a dye reaction. In addition, a multicolor display can be achieved by combining several of the derivatives in one cell. Good color has been achieved, but switching lifetimes remain inadequate at less than 10^7 times. As an additional example of an ECD, there is the one using an electrically induced chemical

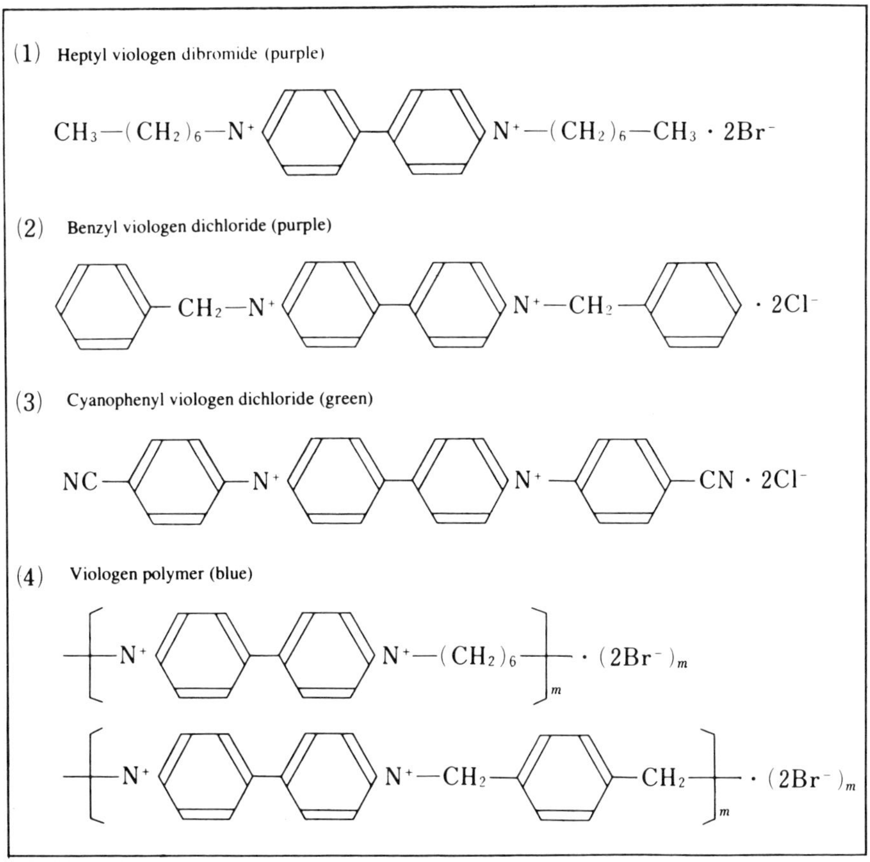

FIGURE 3.43 Various colorations of viologen derivatives. After Matsumoto [5, p. 113], by permission.

reduction, of a colorless liquid, resulting in a colored, insoluble film on the cathode surface. When oxygen is absent the colored film is unchanged if no current flows, and when the voltage is reversed the film dissolves into the liquid, returning the cell to its original condition. The cell structure is much like that used for liquid-crystal displays with the liquid contained between two glass plates having transparent conductive electrodes on the inside surfaces, or both anode and cathode conductors may be placed on the front plate. The liquid that has been most successfully used for this type of display is an aqueous solution of potassium bromide (KBr) and an organic material, and a purple film due to electrochemical reduction is produced when a dc voltage of about 1 V is applied. The cell may be transmissive if both electrodes are transparent or reflective if a white, reflective material is mxied with the electrochromic liquid. The general characteristics of displays using the liquid form are similar to those using a solid material, although better life is claimed for the liquid form.

These displays appear to have their best application in small numeric and alphanumeric arrays, although the slow response has made them somewhat unsuitable for watches that display seconds. Also, the lack of a well-defined voltage threshold makes it difficult to use them in matrix displays, as is described in further detail later.

3.3.9   Ferroelectric Ceramics

Ferroelectric ceramics are both piezoelectric and birefringent and derive their name from the similarity of their response characteristic when an electric field is applied to that of ferromagnetic materials when a magnetic field is used. The material most extensively studied is transparent lead lanthanum zirconate titanate (PLZT), which exhibits three major electrooptic effects: variable birefringence, variable light scattering, and variable surface deformation. The properties depend on the composition and grain size of the ceramic, and the electrooptic effects are due to the electrically induced changes in the orientation of the ferroelectric domains and lattice distortion of these domains. The material is originally made up of randomly oriented ferroelectric domains, and the material is optically isotropic. However, when a dc electric field is applied across the ceramic for a short time the domains favorably oriented with respect to the electric field grow preferentially to those not so oriented, and polar effects occur, causing an anisotropic response to optical inputs. This process is called *poling* and produces a permanent change in the ceramic, so that it can be used as an electrooptic device. The method employed in poling the ceramic plate is illustrated in Figure 3.44, and the remnant polarization is unidirectional in the plane of the plate. This is known as the *L state*, and the plate has uniform birefringence for the polarized light that is normally incident on the plate.

Another method for achieving poling of the ceramic is to apply a mechanical strain to the plate. This strain is achieved by bonding a plexiglass substrate

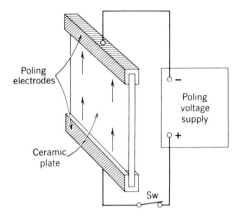

FIGURE 3.44 Poling of ferroelectric PLZT plate. Storage is achieved by switching domains at points corresponding to image's high-intensity regions. Reprinted from Meitzler and Maldonado [21]; copyright © McGraw-Hill Book Company, 1971.

to a thin ceramic plate, and the bonded substrate is bent to produce the strain. The strain produces a distortion of the lattice in the ceramic, which favors switching but constrains the domains to switcch by 180°. This poling effect is shown in Figure 3.45, where the domains are rotated by 90° aligning in the direction of the tension axis. These domains may then be switched by the application of an electric field, and the birefringence of the material is changed

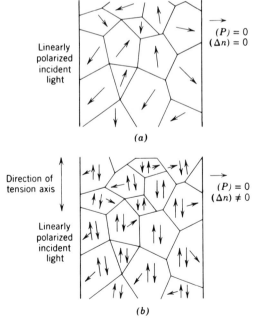

FIGURE 3.45 Straining. Strain-biased ceramic plate achieves 90° domain rotation without a transverse field. Randomly aligned domains (*a*) align in the direction of the tension axis (*b*). Reprinted from Meitzler and Maldonado [21]; copyright © McGraw-Hill Book Company, 1971.

electrically. Then if polarixed light impinges on the plate at right angles to the direction of tensile stress, the output light may be changed by applying the electrical signal across the plate in the direction of the light vector, and the output light is given by

$$I = I_0 + I_1 \sin^2 \frac{\pi \Gamma}{\lambda} \tag{3.43}$$

where I_0 = intensity of light depolarized by scattering in the ceramic
I_1 = intensity of light incident on the ceramic
Γ = optical retardation in ceramic
λ = wavelength of light

This strain-biased ceramic has been combined with a photoconductor into a device known as a *Ferpic* (see Figure 3.46). In this device the light impinging on the photoconductor causes the electric field to be applied across the ceramic in those areas where the light intensity is sufficient to change the resistivity of the photoconductor, and domain switching occurs in the activated areas. The image is retained in the ceramic until a reverse field of about half the amplitude of the writing field is applied, at which time the Ferpic returns to

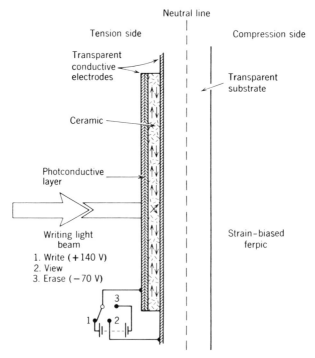

FIGURE 3.46   Cross section of a strain-biased ferpic illustrating the domain alignment in L and T states. After Maldonado and Meitzler [22], by permission.

its original state. This technique may also be applied to an electrically poled unit. In addition, by using a multiple electrode structure, it should be possible to matrix address the Ferpic and write individual picture elements, although this has not been fully demonstrated. Another method for point at a time addressing is to use a scanned laser beam as the light source and electrically address the Ferpic in synchronism with the scanning light beam. This method has been used in a large-screen projection system and is included in the discussion of such systems in Chapter 5.

The discussion to this point has dealt primarily with fine-grained ceramics, which exhibit the phenomena described above. Another type of device may be made using the optical scattering effect found in coarse-grained ceramics. This occurs when the electric field is applied at right angles to the major surface of the ceramic, and incident polarized light is multiply scattered and depolarized as it passes through the plate. If crossed polarizers are used, as in the twisted nematic liquid crystal devices, then the contrast ratio depends on the ratio of polarized:unpolarized light, and ratios as large as 20 dB have been demonstrated. This technique has been used in a seven-segment numeric device, in which a mesh electrode structure was deposited on one side in the appropriate configuration and a solid electrode on the other side, as shown in Figure 3.47. Voltage applied across the ceramic produces a fringing electric field at the edges of the mesh strips, and the longitudinal component of this field causes the depolarization scattering just described. The device is placed between crossed polarizers, and then acts as an electrically controllable numeric display.

Although electrooptic ceramics appear to offer great promise for the solid state, low-power device so desired by all display designers, they are still in a rather early state of development, and we include them among the groups of matrix-addressable and alphanumeric devices only because they have many inherently desirable properties. It certainly appears possible that if certain problems in fabricating usable devices as well as the relatively high voltages ($\sim$100 V) required to operate the devices are overcome, this may be the best of all the materials discussed to this point for a wide range of applications. Thin assemblies are needed for low voltages, in the order of 25 μm, to achieve 10-dB contrast ratios at 20-V levels, but this is certainly not unreasonable, and we may see even thinner plates constructed with correspondingly lower voltages that improve response time beyond the milliseconds presently required to switch. The memory capability minimizes the need for fast switching and is an important advantage of this type of material for displays. In any event, we may conclude that electrooptic ceramics in some form will probably emerge as a viable display device material in the near future, if not sooner.

3.3.10   Electrophoretics

As stated previously, electrophoretic displays use the phenomenon of electrophoresis or the motion of charged particles in a fluid under the influence

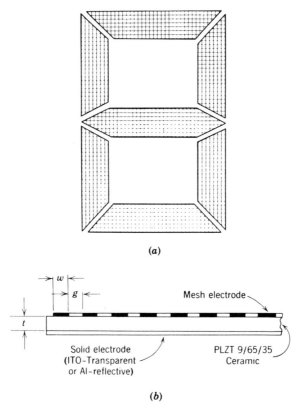

(a)

(b)

FIGURE 3.47   (a) Seven-segment numeric mesh electrode configuration; (b) Electrode configuration for fringe-field type. After Land and Smith [23], by permission.

of an electric field. The structure of one form of display using this principle is illustrated in Figure 3.48. As in the liquid crystal display, there are front and back glass plates to contain the liquid, with conducting surfaces on the glass plates contacting the liquid. The front electrode must be transparent, of course, and the rear electrode may or may not be transparent, since it is obscured by the liquid. The liquid may be any color, as may the charged particles, but black for the first and white for the second is a good choice since it leads to a black-on-white or a white-on-black display. The use of other color combinations allows other color reversals to occur, and conceivably individual elements may be shown in either of the two available colors. This may be achieved in an alphanumeric display by having a separate backplate electrode for each individual alphanumeric and surrounding the patterned electrode with conductive surfaces. Then by connecting the patterned electrode and the surrounding conductive surfaces to separate dc sources, the particles may be made to migrate either to the pattern or to the surrounding surfaces. Of course, the parts of the pattern not used for the particular character must also be at the same potential as the surrounding surface. It is also

Cross section of an
electrophoretic image display cell

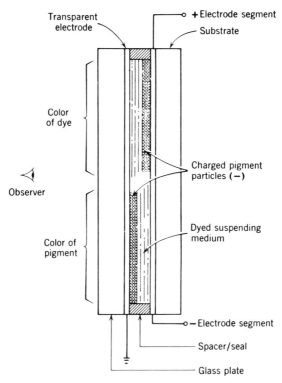

FIGURE 3.48   Schematic of simple EPID cell. After Dalisa [24], by permission.

possible to have two kinds of particles suspended in the liquid, differing in color and charge polarity, so that the choice of color depends solely on the polarity at the patterned surface, and the surrounding conductive surfaces may be eliminated, or if retained, may allow three colors to be achieved. In addition, the colors of the particles and the suspending fluid may be mixed by applying ac voltage to the device. Finally, particles with different mobilities may be combined in one liquid so that different response times result. This makes available one more modality for highlighting selected information and may be useful in certain applications.

The suspension consists of pigment particles, the suspending liquid, dye for coloring the liquid, and control agents. It is prepared by dissolving the dye and then mixing and blending in the pigment particles. The densities of the pigment particles and the suspending liquid must be equal so that the pigment particles do not precipitate out with time. Organic pigments are most easily used, but high-density inorganic pigments must be encapsulated with a resin to prevent precipitation. The control agents are used to improve the dispersion and charge the particles. The thickness of the suspension layer is

TABLE 3.8   Characteristics of EPID Cell

		Suspension	
		BW-05	BY017
Parameter	Particle:	TiO$_2$ + Polyethylene	Hansa Yellow
Average size (μ)		3	0.5
Color of particles		White	Yellow
Charge polarity of particles		Positive	Negative
Densities of particles and liquid (g/mL)		1.98	1.76
Particle volume concentration (%)		2.50	2.50
Dye concentration (wt/vol %)		1.50	1.50
Viscosity of suspending liquid (cP)		1.97	1.90
Viscosity of suspension (cP)		3.50	8.75
Current density (μA/cm^2 at 100 V/100 μm)		2.00	0.16

Source: After Ota [25], by permission.

controlled by spacers, and is 25 to 200 μm in one example. Characteristics of two suspensions that have been used are given in Table 3.8 and demonstrate the color and charge differences that are possible. The contrast ratio is a function of the concentration of the dye and the pigment, as well as the thickness of the suspension layer, and peaks at a specific concentration for a given voltage. This is illustrated in Figure 3.49, which shows a maximum contrast ratio of 7 at 40 V for a dye concentration of 4 mg/ml and a pigment

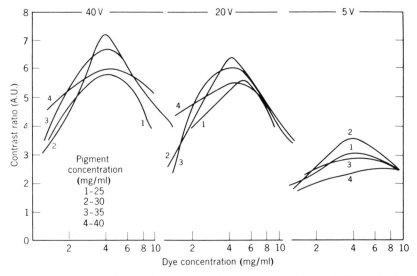

FIGURE 3.49   Dependence of contrast ratio on concentrations of dye and pigment in typical EPID suspension, for three different operating voltages. After Dalisa [24], by permission.

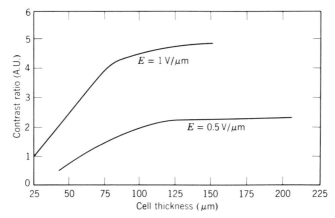

FIGURE 3.50   Contrast ratio versus thickness of EPID cell for a given suspension at applied electric fields of 1 and 0.5 V/μm. After Goodman [16], by permission.

concentration of 30 mg/ml. Figure 3.50 demonstrates the thickness effect reaching a maximum at about 75 μm and a field of 1 V/μm. There is a steady current of 0.3 μA/cm² at this voltage and thickness for the By-17 mixture, and the rise and fall times are 10 to 20 ms, although times in the order of 100 ms are to be expected in practical devices.

3.3.11   Suspended Particle Displays

Of the three particle displays described previously, the *suspended particle display* (SPD) is the one closest to market availability, and therefore warrants more detailed discussion. It is also termed a *colloidal display*, and the operating principle is illustrated in Figure 3.51a. In the absence of an activating voltage, the particles are randomly oriented, and light is uniformly absorbed. However, when an ac field is applied, the particles take on an electric dipole and align themselves parallel to the field. In this condition, the light passes through the cell with very little absorption. A schematic of a display cell is shown in Figure 3.51b, and its operation is similar to the GH LCD in that the dichroism of the particles varies its light absorption characteristics.

3.3.12   Electromagnetic Displays

Electromagnetic displays (EMDs) continue to be used to some extent in a variety of special applications. Most important among these are the large information displays that are found in such locations as airports and other terminals. In addition, they are used extensively as mimic boards in electrical utility control rooms and as outdoor message displays in parking lots and other similar locations. Thus they remain as examples of FPDs that are in wide use, although there is little change in their operating characteristics.

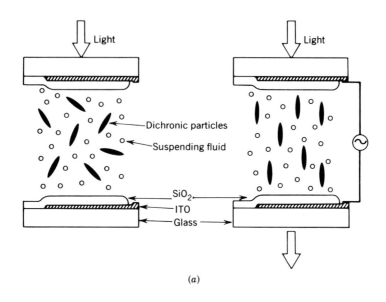

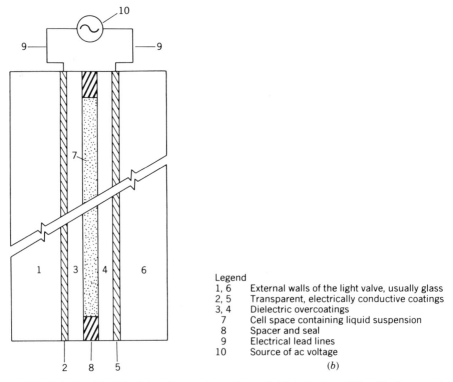

Legend

1, 6	External walls of the light valve, usually glass
2, 5	Transparent, electrically conductive coatings
3, 4	Dielectric overcoatings
7	Cell space containing liquid suspension
8	Spacer and seal
9	Electrical lead lines
10	Source of ac voltage

(b)

FIGURE 3.51 (a) Principle of operation of a colloidal display. After Rachner and Morrissy [26, p. 2], by permission. (b) Diagrammatic cross section of a light valve. After Saxe et al. [27, p. 177], by permission.

However, it is worth including some information about this technology, as it should remain in use for some years.

The basic structure of one form of such a display is shown in Figure 3.52. It consists of a disk located within the field of an electromagnet, with a permanent magnet either attached to the disk or making up the entire disk. Once a current pulse of sufficient magnitude is applied to the electromagnet, the disk rotates to a position determined by the polarity induced in the electromagnet, and is retained in this position by the residual magnetism in the electromagnet. By using different colors or black and white on the two sides of the disk and by properly addressing the elements of the display panel, it is possible to create characters or other iamges that are within the capacity of the panel, and in this respect it is the same as the other dot matrix panels. It is possible to arrange the individual elements so that they can be matrix driven, as is shown in Figure 3.53, with the steering diode required to avoid sneak paths. The basic expression describing the relationship between the magnetic fields and the mass of the disk is given by

$$M_d a_d = B_{em} B_{fm} \sin \theta \qquad (3.44)$$

where M_d = mass of disk
$\quad a_d$ = angular acceleration of disk
$\quad B_{em}$ = electromagnetic field
$\quad B_{fm}$ = fixed-magnet field
$\quad \theta$ = angle between fields

The value B_{em}, in turn, is given by

$$B_{em} = \frac{4\mu NI}{L} \qquad (3.45)$$

where μ = permeability of total magnetic path
$\quad N$ = number of turns of coil
$\quad I$ = current through coil
$\quad L$ = length of magnetic path

It has been found possible to activate the disk with a 1-mW·s or 1-ms·s pulse of 250 mA at 4.2 V. The actual time for the disk to rotate to its new position is several hundred milliseconds, but since it is not necessary to continue addressing any individual element once the current pulse has been applied, it is possible to scan through the board at rates determined by the width of the scanning pulse. Very large arrays have been built, containing

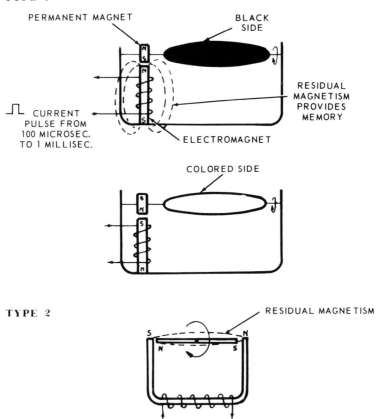

FIGURE 3.52 Basic structure of electromagnetic matrix element. Courtesy of Ferranti-Packard.

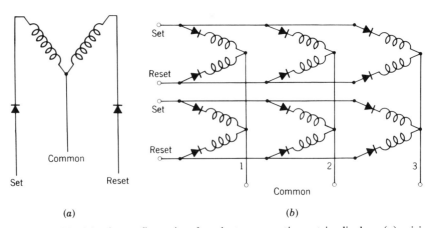

FIGURE 3.53 Matrix configuration for electromagnetic matrix display: (a) wiring schematic of an indicator with steering diodes; (b) 2 × 3 array requires seven control wires; a 16 × 16 array would require 48 control wires. Courtesy of Ferranti-Packard.

TABLE 3.9   Electromagnetic Disk Characteristics

Parameter	Value
Drive requirements	4.2 V at 250 mA ± 10%, 1 ms minimum to 100 ms maximum pulse
With steering diodes	Current averaged over 0.4 s should not exceed 62.5 mA
Without steering diodes	3.1 V at 250 mA
Resistance of coil	12.5 Ω at 25°C
Standard disk size	7.5 mm
Color	Standard disk colors are white, fluorescent orange, or fluorescent green; standard body color is black
Life	Over 20 million operations
Power to hold data	None
Energy to change indication	1 m W · s
Weight	Single indicator—4.5 g; dual indicator—8 g
Dimensions	Single indicator—1 cm × 1 cm × 2 cm deep
	Dual indicator—1 cm × 2 cm × 2.1 cm deep

Source: Courtesy of Ferranti-Packard.

thousands of characters, and the maximum number of dots is only limited by the amounts of pulse power available and the average power requirements. Individual elements as small as 7.6 mm in diameter, and alphanumeric modules of 68 to 457 mm in height in a 5 × 7 matrix are available, and by using different color combinations on different disks, a wide range of colors may be achieved. Graphic symbols may be created, and this type of matrix display has seen wide application. A single-disk specification is given in Table 3.9.

3.3.13   Incandescent Displays

Incandescent displays (INDs) are probably the oldest form of FPDs that have been in common use. They have seen such use as small A/N readouts, and large message displays, especially in those applications that require very high luminances, such as airplane cockpits and outdoor signs. They have largely been replaced by other technologies, such as LEDs for small readouts, but continue to find a market as outdoor signs and scoreboards. In the latter applications they are made up of assemblies of standard light bulbs and have no special characteristics other than those found in these well-known devices. The main advantage of these displays is the very high luminances that can be attained, which is offset by the high powers and currents that are needed for any unit with a large number of elements. However, the advent of lower power and long-life units, especially the fluorescent bulbs designed to emulate standard incandescents in shape and socket type, may make these types of elements attractive.

3.3.14   Comparison of Technologies

Five active and six passive FPD technologies were discussed in previous sections. These, in turn, may be broken down into two EL, two plasma, nine LC, and two EC technologies, which results in too large a number for reasonable comparisons of performance to be contained in a single table. Therefore, the technologies shown in Table 3.10 combine the subgroups except where the drive voltages differ in type, as is the case for the ac and dc EL and plasma.

In general, we may note that LEDs have by far the fastest response times, LCDs provide full-color matrix panels capable of video display, ACEL and AC plasma now offer color matrix panels, VFDs have the highest luminance with LEDs not far behind, and the various nonemitting types have the potential for good visibility in high ambients. In addition, it should be noted that INDs, although not listed, also achieve high luminances and are used in outdoor environments. Unfortunately, no one device type offers the best of all possible worlds, so it remains a matter of examining the application requirements and relating them to the available performance, as is done in detail when the devices are described later in this chapter.

In respect to the question of availability, all of the technologies are used to various extents in matrix assemblies, and only the EL technologies fail to offer A/N displays. Thus there is a wide range of choices and application considerations become of prime importance, although price is frequently the determining factor.

3.3.15   Multiplexing and Matrix Addressing

General Principles.   We have made numerous references to matrix addressing in the previous sections, as is only appropriate in a chapter on matrix and alphanumeric devices. However, we have done no more than hint at what matrix addressing is and how it might be implemented for the various types of devices. Now we are prepared to rectify that neglect and present a full discussion of the basic techniques involved, although the specific circuits are deferred to Chapter 5. We begin with a definition of matrix displays and extend this definition to include multiplexed displays as a subset of the general class. Matrix displays are those displays that consist of an assembly of light-emitting, light-reflecting, or light-transmitting elements, where the optical characteristics of the elements may be individually altered by the application of some type of externally applied signal. This signal is not necessarily electrical in nature, and there are examples of matrix displays that use pneumatic forces, but we restrict the discussion to those types using electrical signals as the source of the optical alteration, since we are dealing only with electronic displays in this book.

The basic structure of a matrix display is illustrated in Figure 3.54, which shows a collection of elements arranged in an *X–Y* array, with connections made to row and column elements by single lines for each row and column.

TABLE 3.10 Technology Comparisons

		Light Emitting				
		EL		Plasma		
Parameter	LED	Ac	Dc	Ac	Dc	VFD
Voltage (V)	2–5 dc	150–250		90–150	180–250	12–40 dc
Current (mA/cm²)	10	1–10	1–10	1–10	1–10	2–5
Contrast ratio	30–40	20–40	15–20	20–30	20–35	35–50
Response Time (μs)	<1	10–40	10–50	10–20	10–20	10–15
Luminance (nits)	30–300	25–250	100	150	150	150–1300
Luminous eff (1 m/W)	0.1	0.3–1.5	1–1.5	0.3	0.1	10
Colors (No.)	4[a]	4	1	3	3	5[a]
Memory	No	No	Yes	Yes	No	No

		Non-light Emitting				
Parameter	LCD	ECD	EPID	SPD	PLZT	EMD
Voltage (V)	2–5 ac	.5–3 dc	~50 dc	5–10 ac	50–100 ac	1–5 dc
Current (μA/cm²)	1–10	>5MC/cm²	~10	1–10	~50	>1A Peak
Contrast ratio	10–20	10–20	15–25	10–30	10–15	10–25
Response time (ms)	25–250	~500	50–150	90–300	1–10	100–500
Colors (no.)	All	3[a]	3[a]	2	2	3[a]
Memory	No	Yes	Yes	No	Yes	Yes

Source: After Matsumoto [5].

[a]One per pixel.

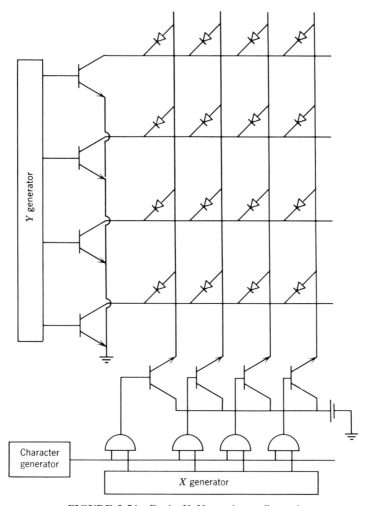

FIGURE 3.54   Basix X–Y matrix configuration.

This arrangement is widely used in electrical memories, and many similar principles apply to both types of assemblies, but there are a number of special considerations involved for matrix displays that require special examination, namely, the particular characteristics of the display elements and the various visual factors such as luminance and contrast ratio. However, in its simplest manifestation a matrix display may be thought of as an array of individually addressable elements equivalent to memory elements, but with the important difference that the readout is optical rather than electrical. It is assumed that each element has at least two terminals, one of which is connected to the row address line and the other to the column address line, and that it is possible to choose the element selection signals so that no element will be selected by either a row or column signal alone but will be fully selected by the combination of a row and a column signal. Unfortunately, this condition is not met unambiguously by several of the devices previously discussed, and many of the techniques evolved for matrix addressing of displays have been attempts to circumvent this lack.

The problem may be understood by reference to Figure 3.55, which presents the optical response of an ideal and a practical display element to an electrical signal. It can be readily seen that if the signal on a row line is below V_{on} while the column line is at zero, the element will remain off. Similarly, if both the row and column lines are driven with a voltage just below V_{on} and are of such polarity that they add so that approximately $2V_{on}$ appears across the element, the element will be driven full on, and the maximum change in the optical characteristics of the display element will occur. The criteria are

$$V_{off} < V_{on} \qquad\qquad (3.46)$$
$$2V_{off} \cong V_{on} \text{ (saturation)}$$

and the ideal element easily meets these criteria. However, in the case of the practical element there are compromises that must be made. Since V_{sat} is usually greater than a safe value of $2V_{off}$ it is not possible to reliably drive the element to saturation using this technique, and this leads to a loss of contrast ratio, which we define here as the ratio of the light reflected, transmitted, or scattered in the on condition to that in the off condition. This is the same as equation 1.7, if we assume that the background luminance is the same as the off luminance at an element. It may be possible to achieve

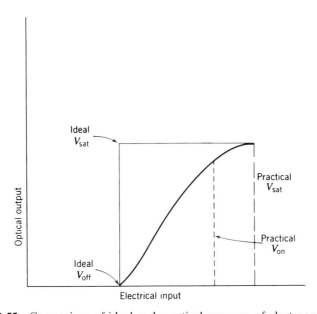

FIGURE 3.55   Comparison of ideal and practical response of electrooptical device.

adequate contrast ratios without driving the element to saturation, but in most cases it is desirable, if not absolutely necessary, to operate at maximum contrast ratio, so that this limitation may be detrimental to the display appearance. Another problem arises from the variability of the transition point between on and off, as a function of temperature, material characteristics, and structural factors. Thus a value of V_{off} that is safe for one element may be inadequate for another, and the second element may be partially turned on by a signal on the row or column line alone. This is the familiar cross talk, in which elements that are not addressed turn on sufficiently to be visible and lead to uncertainty in the data presentation. We discuss various ways to minimize these effects later.

Duty Factor Effect on Contrast Ratio. Assuming that the cross talk can be eliminated and that the element can be driven to saturation, there is still another difficulty arising from the scanning process. Since the elements are addressed sequentially, either one at a time, or a row or column at a time, the addressed element or elements are on for only a fraction of the total time required to write the full frame. If the luminance from the element in the off condition is L_{off} and the additional luminance in the on condition is L_{on}, the peak contrast ratio is

$$C_p = \frac{L_{on} + L_{off}}{L_{off}} \tag{3.47}$$

Then if the duty factor, or the fraction of a frame time that the element is on, is n, the contrast ratio of the scanned element is

$$C_s + \frac{nL_{on} + (1 - n)(L_{on} + L_{off})}{L_{off}} \tag{3.48}$$

Expressing C_s in terms of C_p, we have

$$C_s = n(C_p - 1) + 1 \tag{3.49}$$

If C_p and nC_p are much larger than 1, this reduces to

$$C_s \cong nC_p \tag{3.50}$$

or the scanned contrast ratio is approximately equal to the duty factor times the peak contrast ratio. However, if we substitute a few reasonable numbers for n, L_{on}, and L_{off}, such as 0.01, 100, and 0.01, the pixel contrast ratio becomes 10.99, which is satisfactory, so it is apparent that all three factors are important in determining the pixel contrast ratio.

This situation applies to the case where the element is normally in the off condition and the contrast ratio may be improved by increasing the on luminance or decreasing the off luminance. However, somewhat different conditions exist when the element is normally in the on condition, that is, light emitting, reflecting, scattering, or transmitting. The appropriate expression for the scanned contrast ratio is

$$C_{\text{so}} = \frac{L_{\text{on}}}{nL_{\text{off}} + (1 - n)L_{\text{on}}} \tag{3.51}$$

with the equation inverted to provide a number larger than 1. Using the same numbers as before, the contrast ratio becomes approximately 1 and it is clear that multiplexing is not practical.

Discrimination Ratio. Another aspect of matrix addressing related to the contrast ratio, and of importance, is the discrimination ratio. This is the ratio of the "on" to the "off" luminance, given by

$$\text{DR} = \frac{L_{\text{on}}}{L_{\text{off}}} \tag{3.52}$$

and is a measure of how well an "on" pixel can be discriminated from an "off" pixel when the matrix array is addressed on a row-at-a-time basis. This leads to a duty factor of $1/N$ for a matrix with N rows and M columns, and equation 3.47 may be rewritten for the "on" pixel by substituting $1/N$ for n as

$$C_{\text{s}} = \frac{L_{\text{on}}}{NL_{\text{off}}} + \frac{N - 1}{N} \tag{3.53}$$

Then, if D is substituted into equation 3.53, the result is

$$C_{\text{s}} = \frac{D}{N} + \frac{N - 1}{N} \tag{3.54}$$

and if N is much larger than 1, equation 3.54 may be rewritten as

$$C_{\text{s}} = \frac{D}{N} + 1 \tag{3.55}$$

Equation 3.55 shows that for a scanned element contrast ratio greater than 10, D must be greater than nine times the number of scanned rows. This leads to a rather severe requirement for D when a large number of rows are scanned, and many technologies have difficulty in meeting this requirement.

Advantages. Now that we have examined one of the limitations introduced by matrix displays, which applies also to multiplexed displays, we might ask what the advantage of a matrix display is over a nonmatrix type. This question may be answered by referring to equations 2.82 and 2.83, where it is shown that for a multielement display, the number of connections needed to excite each element individually is reduced from one per element to the nth root of the number of elements, where n is determined by the number of planes in which connections may be made. In terms of the matrix shown in Figure 3.54, there are two planes, and the number of connections is the square root of the number of points times the number of planes. Thus 10^6 points may be addressed with 2000 leads, leading to a great simplification of circuitry and wiring. Indeed, displays with a large number of discrete points would not be practical without matrix addressing, which is why we look for ways to overcome the limitations. We may reduce the number of leads required still further by using the multiple-plane approach described in Chapter 2 for the digitally addressed flat tube, but we defer descriptions of devices employing this approach until later. There are also changes in the contrast-ratio equations that occur when multiple layers of light-transmitting or -reflecting cells are used due to the light losses in the multiple layers.

Light-Emitting Diodes. There is another set of problems occurring when sequentially addressed matrix or multiplexed displays are used, and these have to do with the response time of the electrically altered optical element. Remember that the same flicker requirements exist for matrix displays as for CRTs, so that a full frame of information must be written at a refresh rate that avoids flicker. In the case of LEDs, which have response times in the nanosecond range, the refresh rate must be high enough to meet the criteria established in Chapter 1, but because the individual element has such a rapid capability there is no difficulty in writing a large number of elements. For example, if the frame rate is 60 Hz, or 16.6 ms, 1 million elements could be written at an element time of 16.6 ns, which is within the bounds of possibility, although for practical reasons it is only a dream, as is evident when we examine the peak luminances available from LEDs, both real and imaginary. Table 3.11 lists the peak luminances, and average luminances achieved with several

TABLE 3.11 Average Luminance and Luminous Efficiency of Display Media

Display Medium	Peak Luminance (nits)	Maximum Average Luminance at 1/500 Duty Cycle (nits)	Efficiency (lm/W)
Plasma	25,000	35–50	0.5–1
Ac EL	1,700	3.5–17	5–10
Dc EL	10,000–17,000	85–170	0.5–1
LED	17,000	17–34	0.5
Cathode-luminescent phosphors	300,000	1700	100

Source: After Van Raalte 28, by permission.

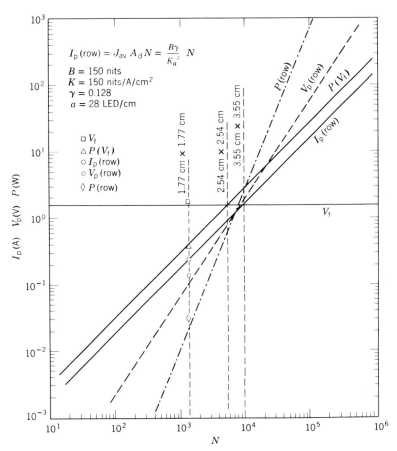

$$I_p \text{ (row)} = J_{av} A_d N = \frac{B\gamma}{K_a^2} N$$

B = 150 nits
K = 150 nits/A/cm^2
γ = 0.128
a = 28 LED/cm

□ V_f
△ $P(V_f)$
○ I_p (row)
○ V_p (row)
◇ P (row)

FIGURE 3.56 Peak current, peak voltage, and power vs. number of LEDs. After Frescura [29], by permission.

of the technologies we have considered, at duty cycles of 0.2, which means only 500 elements, and we see that 10^6 elements are completely impractical. A comparison with CRTs is also shown, and at least 1000 times as many points can be addressed, which is fortunate, since CRTs are restricted to point-by-point addressing, whereas matrix displays can use the expedient of line at a time, or other forms of multielement addressing, which considerably extends the number of points that can be addressed while still retaining acceptable luminances and contrast ratios. Another limitation that should be mentioned regarding LEDs is the resistive drops that occur in the leads at the relatively high currents involved. Figure 3.56 shows representative values of peak current, voltage, and power for different numbers of LEDs. The peak current for a row with all LEDs on, and row-at-a-time addressing is

$$L_p \text{ (row)} = J_{av}A_dN = \frac{L\gamma}{k\alpha^2} N \qquad (3.56)$$

where J_{av} = average current density in LED
  A_d = area of LED
  N = number of LEDs in array
  L = luminance
  γ = fraction of total area emitting light
  k = L/J
  α = linear LED density

For reasonable currents and powers, and keeping the parasitic voltage drops below levels compatible with LED charactgeristics, it is possible to strobe an array 2.5 cm × 2.5 cm with 72 LEDs on a side, given the values of the parameters shown in Figure 3.56. This means that any larger array must be made up of assemblies of these modules, which leads to many problems in construction and interconnection but is still feasible. The parameter values for a 1.3-cm, 2.5-cm, and 3.6-cm array are also shown in Figure 3.56.

At first glance, LEDs appear to be prime candidates for the large assemblies of display elements that we have defined as matrix displays, in contrast to the limited conbinations described in the alphanumeric section. As noted, many of the latter type are in small matrices comprising groups of 5 × 7 or 7 × 9 arrays, and it would seem a simple extrapolation to extend this to larger matrices, setting the lower limit at several thousand elements and going up to a maximum of 10^6. However, this has not proved to be the case, and although there are a few examples of LED arrays of this type, primarily for military applications, we cannot refer to the same multiplicity of examples as exist for the alphanumeric types. The reasons for this lack have to do primarily with cost and power consumption. Power consumptions of 50 to 100 mW per element lead to a total power requirement as high as 100 W for a 10,000-element display, even if only 10% of the elements are on at one time. This means that large arrays of discrete LEDs are impractical for most purposes, although there is one example of a military development using 10^6 diodes that has proved to be viable. However, a more practical approach is one that has resulted in a monolithic assembly of 32 × 64 elements in a 35 mm × 75 mm size, at a power consumption of 340 mW per 650 mm², with 20% of the elements on. The luminous intensity may be as high as 400 microcandelas per LED die, which for a die area of 0.001 cm² leads to a very high die luminance of over 3000 nits. However, when we calculate the luminance on the basis of the total display area, such as 2625 mm², the luminance would be under a nit, a value that is completely unacceptable. Thus larger die areas and the acceptance of unlit areas around each element is necessary, to arrive at the 30 nits that might be needed. This has been done for certain devices, but the screen sizes remain small, with 5 cm × 10 cm as a maximum, although larger screens may be built up by combining a number of the basic modules. The power consumption is under 6 mW per element, which is an order of magnitude improvement over discrete diodes and comparable with the best results in the smallest numeric arrays at much lower luminances. The cost remains high, at 10 to 20 cents a diode for the panel alone, but the results are encouraging, and we may certainly consider LEDs for matrix displays of under 10,000 elements, although larger numbers, whether obtained by assemblying several modules or by using discrete diodes, are still difficult to justify unless some special feature, such as dynamic color or rapid scanning is a requirement. Of course, the addition of color means that two or three times as many diodes will be needed, but why not dream.

Electroluminescence. Electroluminescent panels have long been considered appropriate for matrix addressing. However, the early powder types suffered from short life, low luminance, and excessive crosstalk. These limitations have been overcome in the thin- and thick-film types, and EL panels have become successful contenders for matrix-addressed panels. Active matrix addressing has been used with some success but has largely been abandoned because of the poor yield due to the large number of thin-film layers required by this approach. Fortunately, the TFEL device has a well-defined breakpoint, as shown in Figure 3.57 for a number of aging times. Line-at-a-time addressing is used, but this leads to crosstalk problems because the pixels are capacitively coupled. This is demonstrated in the equivalent circuit for one row shown in Figure 3.58 for a panel containing M columns and N rows. Here there are m driven pixels for the selected row and columns, $(M - m)$ nondriven pixels

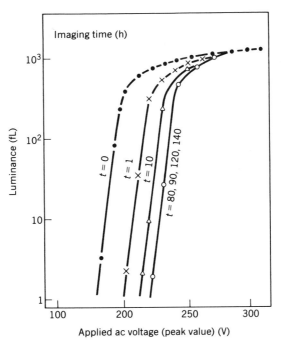

FIGURE 3.57   Typical luminance vs. voltage characteristic of TFEL display. After Matsumoto [5, p. 192], by permission.

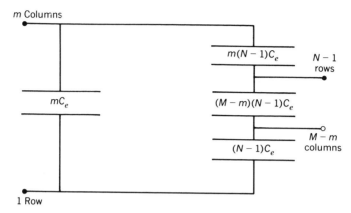

FIGURE 3.58   Equivalent circuit for TFEL panel. After Miller [30], by permission.

in the row, $(N - 1) \times m$ pixels for the nonselected rows and selected columns, and $(N - 1)(M - m)$ pixels for the nonselected columns and rows, all of which add up to $M \times N$ pixels. When multiplied by the element capacitance, C_e, the resulting distribution of the capacitance for a single row is shown in Figure 3.58.

The voltage applied to the pixels in the nonselected rows may then be calculated by multiplying the voltage applied to the selected columns by the capacitance dividers, for the pixels in the selected and nonselected columns. As an example, if $-V_n$ is applied to the selected row and V_c is applied to selected columns, the selected pixels see the sum of the two voltages, while the nonselected columns are grounded and the nonselected rows are floating. The voltage applied to the nonselected pixels in the selected row is now $-V_r$ and the voltages seen by the pixels in the nonselected rows are

$$V_{cs} = \frac{V_c(M - m)}{m}$$

$$V_{cn} = \frac{V_c m}{M} \tag{3.57}$$

where V_{cs} = voltage across pixels in selected columns
V_{cn} = voltage across pixels in nonselected columns
m = number of selected columns

It is clear from this that some of the nonaddressed pixels may turn on if the breakpoint is not clearly defined.

Gas-Discharge (Plasma) Panels

AC. The ac gas panel is another example of a successful matrix display for which resolutions as high as 2048 × 2048 on a 1.5-m diagonal have been achieved, and numerous other resolutions are available in a variety of sizes. It is used only in the matrix panel format, and a column and row addressing system is used for pixel selection and drive, along with row-at-a-time addressing. A panel may be operated in either the refresh or memory mode, but in the memory mode a sustain voltage must be applied. This is shown in Figure 3.22 as a sine wave but is most commonly a square wave, as shown in Figure 3.59.

The write/erase pulses are applied to the X/Y electrodes in the two electrode memory-mode addressing, with the concomitant need for a large number of drivers. This problem has led to the development of various means for reducing the number by the use of on-panel decoding. One such scheme is that used by Fujitsu, where each row line is connected to two drive lines by means of capacitors. This enables an "and" logic to select a line if both drive lines have a write/erase pulse applied, and only half the drive voltage applied if one of the drive lines is selected. The reduction in Y drivers is illustrated

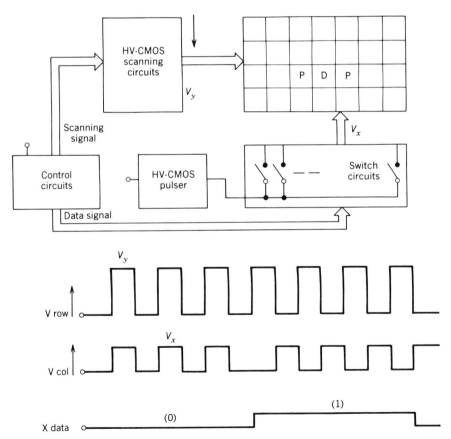

FIGURE 3.59   NEC-type refresh mode ac plasma panel structure. After Dick [31], by permission.

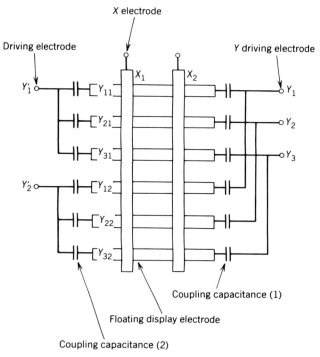

FIGURE 3.60   Linear threshold decoding as used by Fujitsu. After Dick [31], by permission.

in Figure 3.60 for a 2×3 matrix, and a 20×20 matrix can lead to a total of 40 drivers and row connections on a 400-line panel.

Another technique, originally developed at the University of Illinois and incorporated in the panels offered by Plasmaco, is the *independent sustain and address* (ISA) technique illustrated in Figure 3.61. A special electrode pattern is used, where additional write/erase electrodes are placed between the display electrodes of a standard panel, and a sequential addressing procedure reduces the X and Y addressing lines required by a factor of 2.

The ac plasma panel can also be designed to operate in the nonmemory or refreshed mode, with pure neon as the gas rather than a Penning mixture. A somewhat different structure is used as shown in Figure 3.62, and the device has no memory. In this mode, line-at-a-time scanning of the row is used and the columns are synchronously driven with a small sustain signal that either supports or opposes the row signal. A high-magnitude frequency-sustain signal is also used and only a single element current per column is required at a time. This type of panel has been developed by NEC and is offered only by that organization. The matrix addressing is accomplished by means of the type of circuit shown in Figure 3.59, and is essentially the same as may be used for other refresh panels.

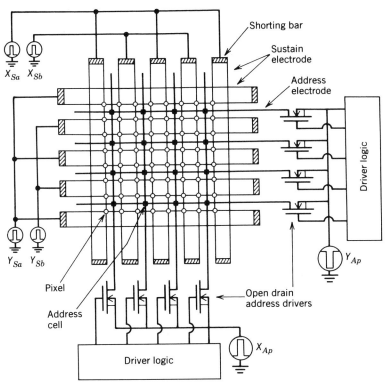

FIGURE 3.61 Electrode geometry and drive circuits for the ISA technique. After Weber [32], by permission.

DC. The dc plasma panel predates the ac type by many years, going back to the neon bulbs that were used as display elements in the past. Modern dc plasma panels have gone far beyond these early versions and are available in both limited A/N units and full matrix panels. One ingenious approach to limiting the number of connections required to address a large number of elements is the *Self-Scan* technique developed by Burroughs and taken over by several other companies after Burroughs left the display field. The most interesting feature of this technique is that it can perform line sequencing or selection internally so that most of the drivers along one axis can be eliminated. The basic principles involved are illustrated in Figure 3.63, which shows a single-line of elements. This represents a two-layer assembly and uses some of the principles of multilayer addressing previously described. The bottom side of the panel consists of the scan anode and the bottom side of the cathodes, whereas the top side contains the display anode and the top of the cathodes. The glow is established at the rear or scan side of the reset cathode and is transferred sequentially from the reset cathode to the adjacent cathode, and then to the subsequent cathodes by the three phase signals. The discharge on the reset cathode lowers the breakdown voltage at the adjacent cathode

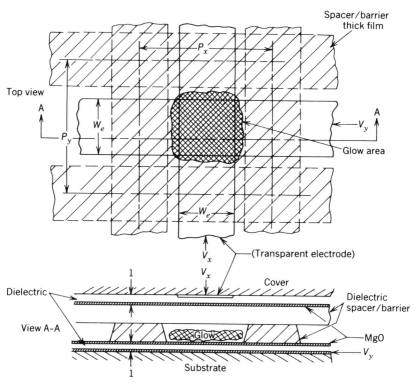

FIGURE 3.62   Refresh mode of operation in an ac plasma panel. After Disk [31], by permission.

by means of the priming mechanisms previously described, so that the discharge is initially transferred only to the adjacent cathode when phase 1 is switched to ground, but the other cathodes connected to phase 1 are not primed, and the sustaining voltage is less than the firing voltage required for an unprimed cell. Thus only one cell will fire, and the next adjacent cell will fire when its phase signal is switched to ground. This permits interconnection of the cathodes, reducing the number of connections from six to three in this case. At the end of the sequence the reset cathode is again switched to ground, thus initiating the next cycle.

Up to now the process is fairly standard, but the unique feature is that the discharges occur on the bottom side and cannot be seen from the viewing side. Further, there are small priming holes in each cathode, which allow some metastables to leak through to the viewing side and thus prime the corresponding section on the viewing side. Then, if the front anode is addressed in accordance with whether that section is to glow, the visible pattern depends on the display anode addressing, whereas the scan will be continuous and controlled by the scanning side. Of course, the usual requirements for maintaining the proper cathode and anode voltages apply to avoid reversing

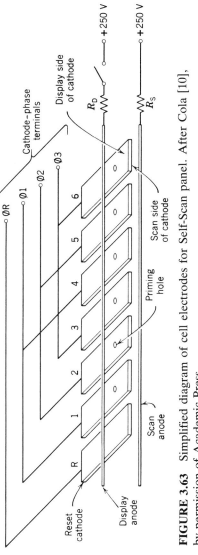

FIGURE 3.63 Simplified diagram of cell electrodes for Self-Scan panel. After Cola [10], by permission of Academic Press.

cathode and anode operation and ensuring that the addressed element is the only one that glows, but the interesting result is that each element can be individually addressed without requiring access to each element independently. This becomes more significant in simplifying the circuitry when a large number of elements is involved, as in the matrix panel discussed later, but it is of value in the single-line alphanumeric panel we consider now.

The actual panel construction differs somewhat from the simplified structure shown in Figure 3.63 in that separate scan anodes and display anodes are used instead of the single ones shown. An exploded view of such a panel is given in Figure 3.64, and the assembled panel is pictured in Figure 5.5. This includes a keep-alive cathode and anode pair in addition to the reset cathode, to ensure reliable operation. A 7×7 array of elements is shown, and it may be extended in a line by adding more cathodes and anodes. Thus 112 columns are needed to permit 18 characters in a 5×7 matrix arrangement with single-element spacing. This is the approximate limit for scanning rates of 60 Hz, since the same on and off time requirements exist as in the other dc gas-discharge panels. The on time can be reduced from the usual 125 to 150 μs at the cost of a loss in luminance, but the off time must be at least 250 μs, which is two clock times, using a three-phase clock and a refresh rate of 60 Hz. The only way to maintain this off time with more than 115 columns is by going to more phases, such as a six-phase clock, which permits twice as many cathodes while retaining the 250-μs time before any phase repeats at any cathode. This technique is used in the larger matrix panels, but, although 2000 character Self-Scan panels are available, the matrix-display application is more common for the larger number of characters. One other aspect of the timing sequence that should be noted is the timing of the display anode signals. Display anodes must be blanked at the beginning of each scan glow transition so as to allow the development of sufficient amounts of prebreakdown ionization and avoid breakdown of the previously scanned display cell, which is still primed. This leads to a duty factor for the display cells less than that for the scan cells, given by

$$ D = \frac{1}{N(1 - (t_B + t_I)/t_S)} \tag{3.58} $$

where N = number of cathodes including the reset cathode
t_B = display blanking time
t_I = display cell-ionization time following t_B
t_S = line select time

Using characteristic values of 15 μs for t_B and 3 μs for t_I, and assuming 112 cathodes and a line time of 105 μs, leads to a duty factor of 0.74%, with the resultant reduction if display luminance. However, peak luminances over 30,000 nits are obtained, leading to average luminances over 200 nits even when this duty factor is combined with the usual duty-factor reduction. The

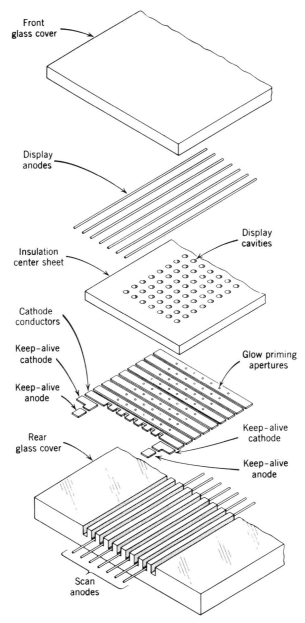

Front
glass cover

Display
anodes

Display
cavities

Insulation
center sheet

Cathode
conductors

Keep-alive
cathode

Glow priming
apertures

Keep-alive
anode

Keep-alive
cathode

Rear
glass cover

Keep-alive
anode

Scan
anodes

FIGURE 3.64   Self-Scan panel exploded view. Courtesy of Burroughs Corporation.

average cell dissipation is about 2.5 mW, so that the same value of 1 mW/ nit holds as for the units described previously. In general, then, we may conclude that this is a feasible approach to alphanumeric displays, particularly when up to 40 characters are desired and the dot matrix format is preferred. The average luminance and power consumption are of the same order as the other dc gas-discharge units, so that the circuit simplification may be the deciding factor. Some circuits are presented in Chapter 5 and may be used to assess the value of this simplification. Larger arrays are similar but may use seven phase clocks.

The Self-Scan was the only dc plasma matrix display available for many years, but the growth of the demand for panels that could be used with computers has led to a number of different refreshed X–Y matrix displays, with the old type essentially restricted to bar graphs and A/N panels. The dot matrix format using electronic scanning rather than Self-Scan is shown in Figure 3.65. As shown in Figure 3.66, the cathodes are scanned sequentially a column at a time, whereas the data switches are connected to the anodes and activate the rows as determined by the input data. Several hundred columns can be scanned at a 60-Hz refresh rate, within the limitations imposed by the intensity requirements and the discharge initiation time required to achieve the desired intensity. Peak luminance levels in the range of 30,000 nits can be achieved in time periods of about 10 μs, allowing average luminances of over 60 nits to be attained in a panel with up to 500 columns. Initial startup is assured by providing several pilot cells with overvoltage drive. Another form of refreshed dc plasma display is the one initially developed by Dixy Corp. and subsequently taken over by Mitsubishi. This design is unique in that it uses ac triggering with a trigger electrode under a dielectric

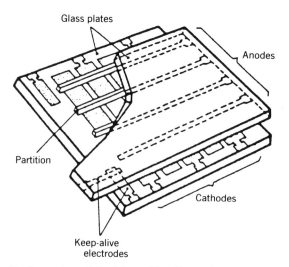

FIGURE 3.65 Early version of the Matsushita Corp. dc refresh-mode plasma panel. After Dick [31], by permission.

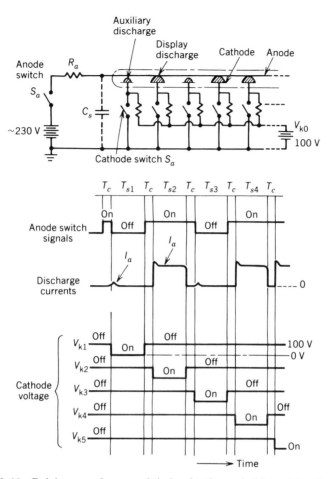

FIGURE 3.66   Driving waveforms and timing for the early Matsushita display. I_a and I_d; auxiliary and display discharge currents, respectively. After Dick [31], by permission.

layer and parallel to a few cathode electrodes, as shown in Figure 3.67. A positive trigger pulse of about 250 V and a negative trigger in the range 30 to 50 V are applied at time t_1, and a discharge is formed in the gas between the dielectric surface and a selected cathode. Electrons then accumulate on the dielectric surface, reducing the voltage across the discharge until it is extinguished. Next, the anode voltage is reduced to about 150 V, which is above the sustaining voltage but below the original firing voltage. Finally, the trigger pulse is reduced to zero, the dielectric surface goes negative, and is neutralized by the discharge ions. This technique reduces the discharge delay to a few microseconds, and lower voltages are used. As a result of the lower discharge control voltage, undesired visible background is eliminated and better contrast ratios can be achieved. This technique is also used in the

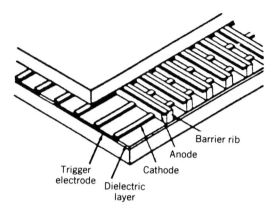

FIGURE 3.67 Isometric view of Dixy display. After Dick [31], by permission.

refreshed dc displays from Matsushita. These types of plasma displays have achieved considerable success as matrix displays, due to their improved contrast ratio and appearance.

Vacuum Fluorescent Displays (VFDs). Vacuum fluorescent displays have achieved their greatest acceptance as multidigit units in both segmented and dot matrix formats. However, a number of dot matrix units capable of graphics presentations have become available, with as many as 400×600 pixels, so that matrix addressing for both these and the multidigit units with a large number of digits has become the preferred approach. The grid arrangements and anode connections are shown in Figure 3.68, and matrix addressing is achieved by applying a positive voltage to a grid–anode pair. However, this arrangement is not satisfactory when high resolution is desired, because re-

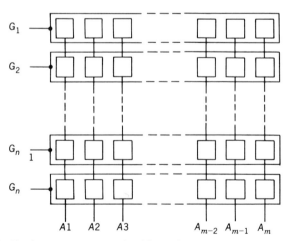

FIGURE 3.68 Basic arrangement of grids and connections of dot anodes. After Matsumoto [5, p. 254], by permission.

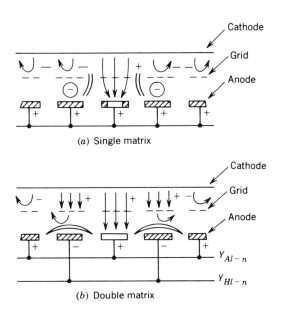

(a) Single matrix

(b) Double matrix

FIGURE 3.69 Electrode connections and voltage application in dot matrix display; (a) single matrix; (b) double matrix. After Matsumoto [5, p. 255], by permission.

ducing the dot pitch of the anode and grid causes the light output at the edges of the selected anode to be affected by the negatively biased adjacent grids, as shown in Figure 3.69a. This is overcome by dividing the dot anodes into two sections separately driven, as shown in Figure 3.69b, with a different voltage distribution, so that the full anode can be activated.

Another way to achieve the same effect is to offset the grids by one half-pitch from the anodes while retaining the same double-matrix arrangement. Finally, there is the scrolling display, where the pattern is shifted from left to right, one element at a time at a constant rate. The single- and double-matrix connections for this type of operation are shown in Figure 3.70. All of these modes of operation make VFDs versatile FPDs for graphics displays, limited primarily by the maximum sizes, which are considerably smaller than those obtained by the other technologies with small probability of any changes occurring.

Liquid-Crystal Displays (LCDs). Liquid-crystal displays are probably the most difficult of all these types to operate in the matrix-addressed mode. This is because they lack all the characteristics necessary for successful matrix addressing, that is, well-defined thresholds, high contrast ratios, and rapid response. In addition, the threshold characteristic varies with temperature and in twisted nematic cells, with viewing angle. This is illustrated in Figure 3.71, which demonstrates the effect of viewing angle on the threshold characteristic of a twisted nematic device. The difference between normal incidence and 30° incidence is significant, and it is estimated that not more than three or

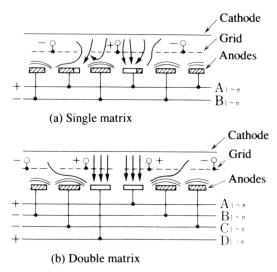

(a) Single matrix

(b) Double matrix

FIGURE 3.70   Electrode connections and voltage application in scrolling display. After Matsumoto [5, p. 261], by permission.

four lines could be scanned in such a display, neglecting the speed of response limitation. Another problem that arises in scanned liquid-crystal matrix displays is due to the fact that the liquid-crystal cell responds to the room-mean-square (rms) value of a driving signal rather than the peak, primarily because of the time-integrating response characteristic of liquid-crystal material. If we assume the driving wave forms shown in Figure 3.72, where the signal amplitudes are correct for driving the display into an acceptable on condition when they are in phase, and for turning the display off when they are out of

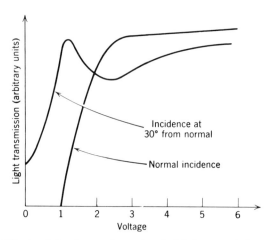

FIGURE 3.71   Effects of viewing angle on threshold characteristics of twisted nematic device. After Goodman and Meyerhofer [33], by permission.

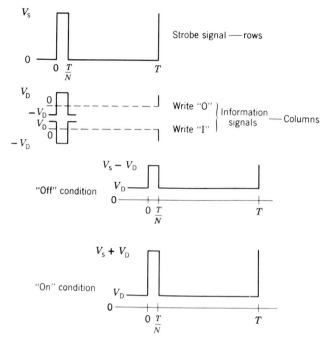

FIGURE 3.72   Liquid-crystal matrix-drive waveforms. After Alt and Pleshko [34], by permission of IEEE.

phase, the rms requirement leads to the expressions

$$V_{rms}^2(\text{off}) = (V_S - V_D)^2 n + V_D^2(1 - n) \qquad (3.59)$$

$$V_{rms}^2(\text{on}) = (V_S + V_D)^2 n + V_D^2(1 - n) \qquad (3.60)$$

where n is the duty factor as in equation 3.48 and the similarity of these equations to equation 3.48 is apparent. The duty factor, in turn, may be written in terms of the number of scanned lines as

$$n = \frac{1}{N} \qquad (3.61)$$

where N is the number of scanned lines. We may then maximize N as a function of V_D and find that V_D for a maximum N is

$$V_D = \tfrac{1}{2}[V_{rms}^2(\text{on}) + V_{rms}^2(\text{off})]^{1/2} \qquad (3.62)$$

and that N_{max} is given by

$$N_{max} = \frac{[V_{rms}^2(\text{on}) + V_{rms}^2(\text{off})]^2}{[V_{rms}^2(\text{on}) - V_{rms}^2(\text{off})]^2} \qquad (3.63)$$

We may further find that for maximum contrast ratio, where the contrast ratio is defined as the ratio of $V_{rms}(on)$ to $V_{rms}(off)$, V_S and V_D are related to N and to each other by

$$V_s = N^{1/2}V_D \qquad (3.64)$$

and if we let V_{off} equal V_{th}, or the threshold voltage for the liquid crystal cell, V_{on} equal $V_{th} + \Delta$, and P equal to Δ/v_{th}, then

$$V_D = \frac{v_{th}}{2[(1 - P)^2 + 1]^{-1/2}} \qquad (3.65)$$

Plots of P versus V_D/V_{th}, N, and V_S/V_{th}, shown in Figure 3.73, demonstrate the limits imposed by this situation. Thus it is not practical to scan much over 100 lines, even if the other limitations of response time and maximum contrast ratio are ignored. This has led to modules of 100 lines on a side, in combination with some type of solid-state switch at each element as one successful approach to matrix-addressing liquid-crystal displays. It should be stressed, however, that this effect is due to the integrating nature of the response of the liquid-crystal cell, just as the contrast ratio equations depend on the integrating effect of the eye. Thus if the scanning rate is low enough that the cell relaxes

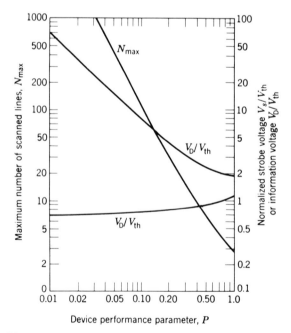

FIGURE 3.73   Liquid-crystal maximum scanning capability and requirements as function of device performance parameter. After Alt and Pleshko [34], by permission of IEEE.

back completely to its unexcited optical state, the cell integration contribution is gone, and the rms response restraints do not hold. Of course, the slow response of most liquid-crystal materials, particularly in the turn-off mode, limits this rate to 1 to 5 Hz, which is certainly not adequate for a flicker-free display but may be useful in some applications where a slow rate is acceptable. Also, the day may come when liquid-crystal materials and devices are available with response times sufficiently rapid to eliminate the rms effect at flicker-free rates. When that occurs, we will have only the contrast ratio and threshold voltage variability to contend with.

One other way to maximize the contrast ratio and eliminate the threshold voltage problem is to operate the matrix display in only the full-on and full-off modes. The selected element is the one that has no voltage across it, whereas all other elements have either full on or twice full on voltage across them. This is illustrated by the waveforms shown in Figure 3.74, and has the advantage over the half select mode described previously in that it uses the well-defined and constant zero and saturation levels as the operating points. Of course, if the rms condition holds, the contrast ratio rapidly approaches

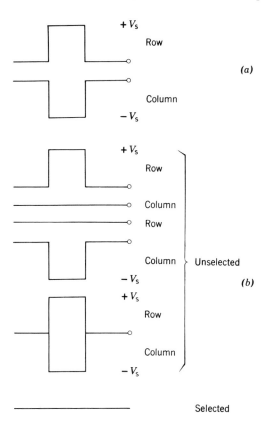

FIGURE 3.74   Saturation drive matrix-selection waveforms: (*a*) waveforms used; (*b*) waveforms applied during selection.

1, so this technique is not usable for matrix addressing of arrays at nonflickering refresh rates. However, for sequential selection at slow rates, as in the second hand of a clock, it works very well. In a static type of matrix display, such as a bar graph meter, it may also be used, as is described later.

Several other approaches to matrix addressing should be mentioned before we leave the subject. One is an attempt to overcome the limitations of half select addressing, where the relationship between the on voltage and the off voltage is given by equation 3.46. In the event that the cell does not go fully into the on condition at twice the off or threshold voltage, there is a loss in contrast ratio. This may be overcome to some extent by going to a 3:1 ratio for the on:off voltage. However, to avoid turning on unwanted elements, it is necessary to go to the arrangement shown in Figure 3.75. The selected element will have 3 V across it, whereas all other elements will have either plus or minus voltage across them. As a result, the unselected elements will be at the threshold, and the selected element will have three times the threshold voltage across it, thus fulfilling the 3:1 ratio requirement and putting the cell well into saturation, if all goes according to plan. It does have the drawback that not as many lines or points can be scanned as when the rms criteria are used. This is demonstrated by the equations for N_{max} for both cases, which are

$$N_{max} = \left[\frac{(1 + P)^2 + 1}{(1 + P)^2 - 1}\right]^2 (rms) \tag{3.66}$$

$$N_{max} \cong \left(\frac{1}{P}\right)^2 (rms) \tag{3.67}$$

$$P \ll 1$$

and

$$N_{max} = \frac{8}{P^2 + 2P} (3:1) \tag{3.68}$$

$$N_{max} \cong \frac{4}{P} \tag{3.69}$$

$$P \ll 1$$

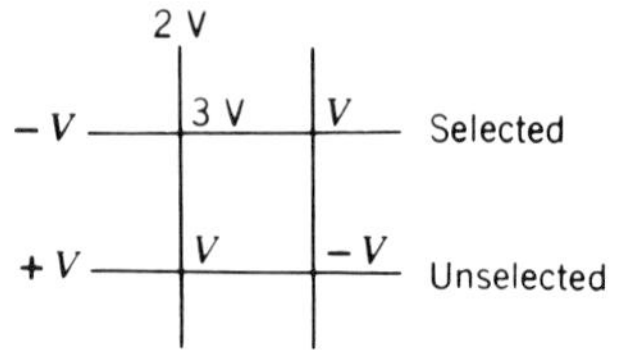

FIGURE 3.75   Voltages used and method of application for 3:1 matrix addressing.

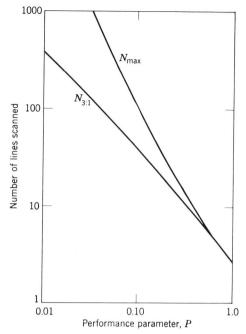

FIGURE 3.76   Comparison of the scanning capability achieved with 3:1 section and rms selection schemes. After Alt and Pleshko [34], by permission of IEEE.

where $P = (\Delta/V_{th})$, Δ representing the transition voltage or the difference between the on voltage and the threshold voltage. The equations for the two cases are shown graphically in Figure 3.76, and the advantage of the rms approach is clear for small values of P, which occur when the transition voltage is small compared to the threshold voltage, as is frequently the case.

Another scheme used for matrix addressing is the two-frequency technique. This technique is based on the characteristic of certain liquid crystal materials that the threshold voltage for the low-frequency drive voltage can be changed by the application of a second signal at a frequency well above the cutoff frequency. This behavior is illustrated in Figure 3.77, which demonstrates that selection of an element can be implemented by setting the on voltage at the threshold level with high-frequency bias. Then when the high-frequency bias is removed the element will be in the on condition. This approach raises the threshold voltage while keeping the transition voltage constant, so that P is smaller and more lines may be scanned. It involves switching both the low-frequency scanning signal and the high-frequency selection signal so that the cutoff frequency of the liquid crystal cell still imposes limitations. An alternative approach is to use a constant low-frequency bias on all elements and scan with the high-frequency signal, which improves the selection capability, since it is not limited by the cutoff frequency, and materials with a lower cutoff frequency, which are less sensitive to temperature variations,

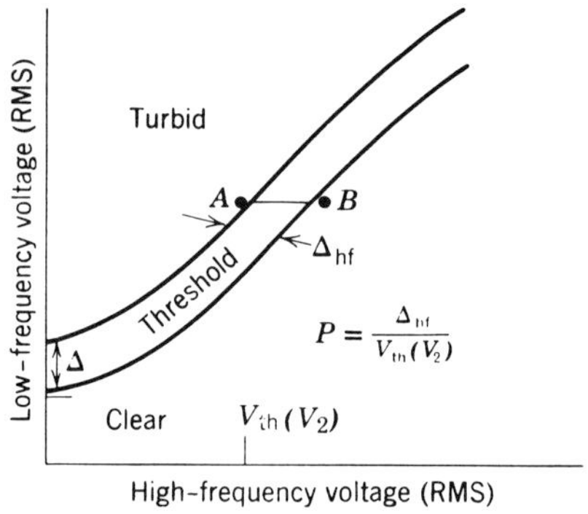

FIGURE 3.77 Operating points for a high-frequency address scheme: unselected element at point A, selected element at point B. After Alt and Pleshko [34], by permission of IEEE.

may be used. However, at best, this technique is limited in its applications by temperature sensitivity and variability in threshold voltage, so that it has achieved only partial success in practical applications.

Multilevel Addressing. Finally, in concluding this discussion of matrix-addressing techniques, further mention should be made of the multilevel addressing schemes that permit a further reduction of the number of drive lines required over that achieved by the two planes that constitute the standard matrix panel. The technique is applicable to most of the technologies described to this point and has been implemented in a two-layer gas-discharge display, a three-layer EL–PC structure, and a three-layer liquid-crystal array. However, since the liquid-crystal device has been the most successful example of the use of multi-axis addressing and demonstrates the principles involved most clearly, we restrict the description at this point to that technology.

The basic approach is a variant of the one used for the digitally addressed flat tube described in Chapter 2, and equations 2.82 and 2.83 apply, except that we may generalize them somewhat by not assuming that each plane has the same number of leads, which assumption is implicit in the equations and descriptions of matrix addressing to this point. However, any combination of leads is possible, and the generalized equations are

$$P_n = P_{xn}P_{xy} \tag{3.70}$$

where P_n = number of points at nth level
$\quad P_{xn}$ = number of x addressable inputs at nth level
$\quad P_{yn}$ = number of y addressable inputs at nth level

and the nth level is assumed to be the one with the largest number of points, although it need not necessarily be the last one of the sequence. Similarly,

$$L_T = \sum_{n=1}^{n} T_{xn} + \sum_{n=1}^{n} T_{yn} \tag{3.71}$$

where L_T = total number of leads
$\quad\quad n$ = panel level (1,2,3, . . . , n)
$\quad\quad T_{xn}$ = number of leads in x at panel level n
$\quad\quad T_{yn}$ = number of leads in y at panel level n

If we then assume a square matrix, these expressions reduce to

$$P_n = T_x^{2n} \tag{3.72}$$

$$L_T = 2nT_x \tag{3.73}$$

which are equivalent to those for the digitally addressed flat tube, except that we are dealing with panels, each of which contains two planes. As a result, the same savings in total number of matrix selection leads and drivers may be achieved as for the CRT. We have also assumed the same number of leads per panel level to complete the equivalence.

The manner in which the multilevel addressing scheme may be applied to a liquid crystal matrix display is illustrated in Figure 3.78, representing a two-level scheme. We begin with the first panel and address it so that only sector P-1 is light transmitting. Then we add panel 2 on top of panel 1, arranged so that each group of 16 elements coincides with the corresponding sector of panel 1; that is, the 16 elements in the upper left-hand corner of panel 2 are on top of sector P-1, and so on. We then interconnect panel 2 in a 4 × 4 array, as shown, and address it so that sectors L_{11}, L_{15}, L_{51}, and L_{55} are the only transparent sectors and L_{11} is the only one that is transparent through both panels. Thus we have selected sector L_{11}, using 12 leads instead of the 16 leads that would be required for an 8 × 8 array. The reduction is trivial in this case, but it improves rapidly as the number of elements increases. For example, a two-level structure with 8 × 8 leads on each level can address 8^4 elements with 32 leads instead of the 128 required for a single-panel matrix display. The drawback is that only eight elements can be addressed at the same time, so that line-at-a-time addressing is not feasible. This makes the response time limitations of the liquid-crystal media more restrictive, and less elements can be addressed in a given frame time unless faster material is used. So the trade-off is between simplification of the matrix-addressing circuitry and connections and total number of elements that can be addressed. It might be mentioned that any of the methods described for applying the voltage across the element may be used, but that the on–off technique is particularly useful here.

Active Matrix (AM) Addressing. The most successful approach to matrix addressing LCDs is the use of some form of active matrix assembly to overcome the inherent difficulties due to poor breakpoints and slow response times. Although these deficiencies have been overcome to some extent by the development of supertwist and ferroelectric types, active matrix addressing re-

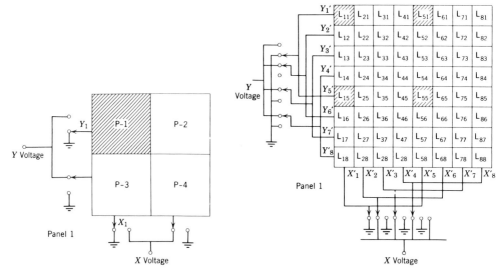

FIGURE 3.78   Example of single-point selection using multilevel matrix addressing.

mains the preferred approach, especially when panels with a fairly large number of rows and columns are involved and multiple color is desired. The basic approach is to have a separate switching element at each of the X–Y intersections of the display matrix, and rely on the excellent switching characteristics of these elements to overcome the limitations of the LCD panel.

Some of the earliest investigations of this principle were in the early 1970s by Lechner, but the first developments that led to actual products were by Brody and were applied initially to EL panels, and subsequently to LCDs. An example of the design of an elemental matrix circuit using thin-film transistors is shown in Figure 3.79a. This assembly consisted of the matrix-addressed logic transistor followed by a power transistor and a storage capacitor to provide enough drive current and a long enough time constant to maintain the drive in the "on" condition. A simpler structure for an LCD panel is shown in Figure 3.79b and the much lower drive current allowed a single transistor to be used.

Although AM drive is applicable to most of the technologies, and examples of such use have been reported on, it has found its greatest use as the matrix select and drive circuitry for LCDs. Therefore, this discussion concentrates on its use for these types of display panels, in particular those that offer multicolor displays. Much effort has been expended on investigating various approaches to achieving workable AM assemblies, and a number of devices using a variety of configurations and materials have been investigated. Of these, the earliest was the thin-film transistor (TFT) developed by Brody using cadmium selenide (CdSe). Successful operating units have been con-

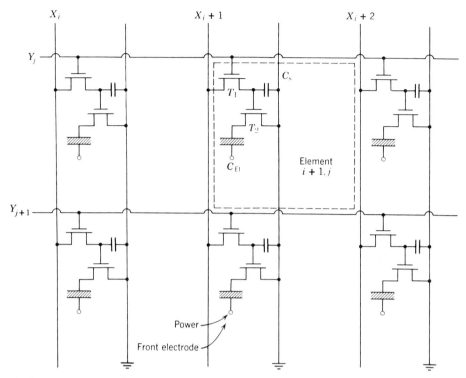

FIGURE 3.79a   Design of elemental matrix circuit for the 15.25 cm × 15.25 cm. 8 lines/cm EL display. After Brody [35a], by permission.

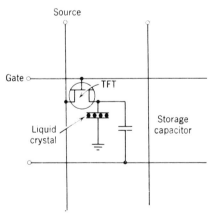

FIGURE 3.79b   Design of elemental circuit for LC display incorporating storage capacitor. After Brody [24], by permission.

structed using this type of assembly, but the majority of attention has been paid to devices using amorphous silicon (a-Si) and polysilicon (p-Si) in both two-terminal and three-terminal forms.

Two-Terminal Devices. These devices operate as nonlinear series elements placed at each X–Y intersection of the display elements matrix and in series with the LC cell as shown in Figure 3.80. The voltage across the cell changes as the two-terminal device is switched from the high- to the low-resistance states, and the equivalent capacitance of the cell is charged in one state and discharged in the other. The requirements imposed on the two-terminal device are:

1. That it be summetrical with respect to the ac drive
2. The current in the low-resistance (select) condition be large enough to charge the LC capacitance to the maximum in the select period
3. The current in the high-resistance (nonselect) condition be low enough not to charge the LC capacitance to threshold
4. The capacitance of the two-terminal device be small compared to the LC cell capacitance

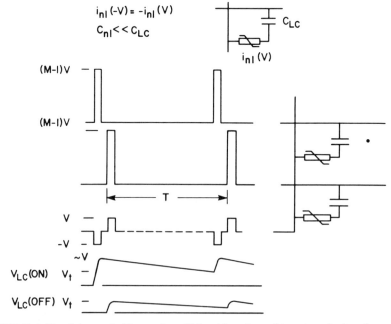

FIGURE 3.80 Schematic illustrating M:1 addressing of two-terminal active matrix with nonlinear resistive element in series with liquid-crystal capacitor. After Howard [35b], by permission.

Mathematically, these requirements are given by

$$i_{n1}(-V) = -i_{ni}(V) \qquad (3.74)$$

This expresses the symmetry requirement:

$$i_{n1}[(M - 1)V] > \frac{2C_{LC}V_tN}{T} \qquad (3.75)$$

This states that the resistance of the nonlinear element is low enough during the charging period for twice the threshold voltage to be reached in the charging period (T), assuming a 2:1 addressing scheme, and an $M \times N$ matrix, with the rows driven sequentially by pulses of magnitude $(M - 1)V$, and the columns by data signals of magnitude $\pm V$;

$$i_{n1}[(M - 2)V] < \frac{C_{LC}V_tN}{2T} \qquad (3.76)$$

This ensures that half selected cells are charged to less than half the threshold voltage;

$$i_{n1}(2V) < \frac{C_{LC}V_t}{2T} \qquad (3.77)$$

This ensures that C_{LC} will not be discharged by more than half V_t in time T.

The major types of nonlinear devices that have been used for two-terminal AM addressing are the varistor, metal–insulator–metal (MIM), back-to-back a-Si diodes, and ring a-Si diodes. They are shown schematically in Figure 3.81, with representative current–voltage variations in Figure 3.82. These drive configurations result in improved contrast ratio over conventional multiplexed matrix drive. However, they require uniformities that are difficult to achieve for high values of N, and the high photoconductivity of a-Si has a negative effect, although samples have been built of all which achieved multiplexing between 500 and 1000 lines. In addition, another approach using $n–i–n$ diodes has been reported on by Yaniv, for which high contrast ratios have been claimed for 256 lines. Therefore, the AM nonlinear diode approaches are not to be forgotten. In addition, there are three-terminal diode arrangements first proposed by Lechner and discussed in the next section, along with the three-terminal transistor devices, which are more popular.

Three-Terminal Devices. The Lechner three-terminal diode circuit was first proposed in the early 1970s and has recently seen some renewal of interest. The basic circuit, shown in Figure 3.83a, consists of two thin-film *p-i-n* a-Si diodes in series with the LC cell between the diode connection point and the scan input line. The plus and minus data lines make up the other two terminals,

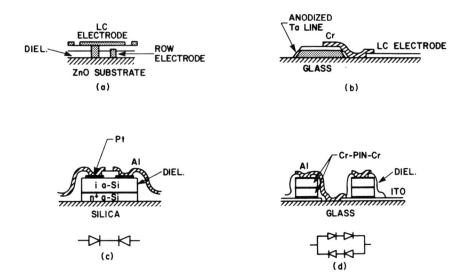

FIGURE 3.81   Structural schematics of nonlinear elements used in addressing liquid crystals: (*a*) ZnO varistor; (*b*) edge junction MIM device; (*c*) back-to-back amorphous silicon diodes; (*d*) amorphous silicon *p-i-n* diode rings. After Howard [35b], by permission.

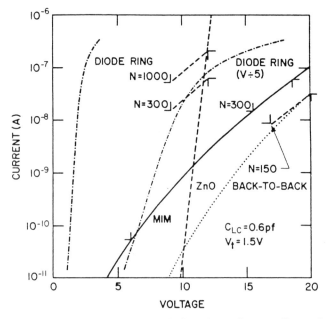

FIGURE 3.82   Sample current–voltage variations for various nonlinear elements with windows representing addressing requirements for different values of N. After Howard [35b], by permission.

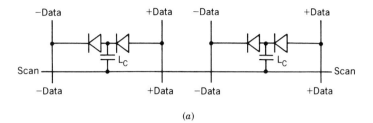

(a)

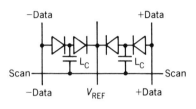

Advantages:
- Charge storage
- Diodes are small
- Redundancy, series/parallel
- On/off ~ 10^8

Disadvantages:
- 2X row interconnect lines
- Poor storage capacitors
- Complicated color plate back plane
  Column lines and ITO on top of filters
- Uniformity of diode threshold

(b)

FIGURE 3.83   Three-terminal diodes. (a) Lechner circuit; (b) D2R (fewer connections). After Bruce [36], by permission.

and applying the scan select pulse across the cell causes the data input to be activated at the selected matrix intersection. The circuit shown in Figure 3.83b allows the number of data connections to be reduced but is still $2M + N$, which is larger than any of the other AM approaches.

The three-terminal AM devices are primarily those using *thin-film transistors* (TFTs) of the type initially developed by Brody, and using CdS, but a-Si has become the most popular material. This is not to say that CdS types of TFTs using other material, such as poycrystalline silicon, are completely forgotten, and typical structures for devices made out of all of these materials are shown in Figure 3.84. The TFT consists of a source, gate, and drain, with a sample layout of the inverted staggered structure for a single cell shown in Figure 3.85. However, CdS and polycrystalline TFTs may require the addition of a capacitor to each cell to mask excessive leakage, as shown schematically for a single cell in Figure 3.86, where it serves to increase the storage time. It is necessary for the LC material to respond in a time shorter than the time constant of the total capacitive resistive network, and that there be sufficient current to drive the element as expressed by

$$I\tau_1 > C_E R_{\text{off}} V_E R_E \tag{3.78}$$

where I = drive current
τ_1 = line dwell time
C_E = capacity in parallel with element
V_E = voltage required to drive element
R_E = element resistance

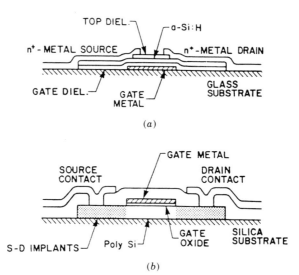

(a)

(b)

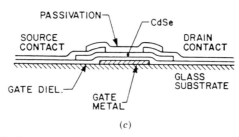

(c)

FIGURE 3.84 Typical structures for most common types of thin-film transistor: (a) hydrogenated amorphous silicon TFT; (b) polysilicon TFT with ion-implanted contacts, on fused silica; (c) CdSe TFT; inverted-staggered structure on glass. After Howard [35b], by permission.

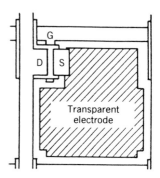

FIGURE 3.85 Sample layout of "generic" LV/TFT cell incorporating inverted-staggered a-Si:H TFT. After Howard [35], by permission.

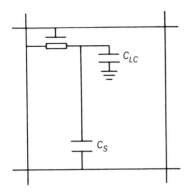

FIGURE 3.86 Schematic of LC/TFT cell with thin-film storage capacitor in parallel with liquid crystal, for increased storage time. After Howard [35], by permission.

In addition, there is the leakage time constant referred to, related to the optical response time of the liquid-crystal material by

$$\tau_r = C_E R_{\text{off}} \tag{3.79}$$

where R_{off} is the TFT off resistance. Similarly, if we wish a 100% duty cycle at each element, the time constant should be larger than the frame time, or

$$\frac{R_{\text{off}}}{R_{\text{on}}} \gg \frac{\tau_f}{\rho_1} \tag{3.80}$$

where τ_f is the frame time.

A number of different TFT–LCD assemblies have been built by various manufacturers, and they are being used to a rapidly increasing extent by vendors of laptop computers and portable television sets, particularly when color is desired. Table 3.12 is a list of representative TFT arrays produced by different manufacturers and illustrates the variety available. It may be anticipated that development will continue and further improvements will occur. In any event, it appears to be certain that AM addressing using TFTs will be the preferred form of matrix addressing for LCD panels. This list is

TABLE 3.12   TFT Arrays

Area (mm)	Matrix Size	Material	Color
152 × 203	480 × 640 × 3	a-Si	4096
150 × 214	1120 × 780 × 3	a-Si	512
67 × 120	1024 × 1440 × 1	a-Si	1[a]
66 × 88	480 × 720	a-Si	NTSC[a]
202 × 323	800 × 1280 × 3	a-Si	4096
229 × 305	480 × 640 × 3	a-Si	4096
180 × 270	750 × 1120 × 3	a-Si	4096

[a]Light valve.

representative of what has been achieved, and larger sizes may be anticipated. Of special interest are the light valve units used in projectors and applicable to HDTV. It should be noted that all of these units use a-Si.

Electrochromic, Ferroelectric, and Electrophoretic Panels. As is the case for the alphanumeric devices using these technologies, there are not many examples of successful matrix displays based on any of these three approaches. Unfortunately, as our previous discussions have pointed out, they all suffer from one or more of the limitations that militate against the use of conventional, or in some cases even special, approaches to matrix addressing. Thus electrochromic and ferroelectric devices have poorly defined break points, and electrochromic and electrophoretic arrays are limited by their slow response times as well. Thus although there is at least one example of an 184 × 32 dot matrix electrophoretic panel, it requires 40 s to write the entire panel, which is a significant deterrent to its use, although the inherent memory does make it possible to address this panel in a matrix fashion. The situation is even worse for electrochromic arrays, since a reverse voltage is required to erasure, and there is no well-defined threshold, so that this material offers very little possibility of ever being used in matrix assemblies. Finally, direct matrix addressing of ferroelectric arrays, although possibly feasible, has not been demonstrated, and an entirely different approach has been used to make it possible to write a large number of points without individually driving each point. This is to add a photoconductor layer as is shown in Figure 3.46 and to address the panel by a combination of a fixed light beam and a set of matrix connections. The absence of a well-defined transition point makes this combination difficult to implement successfully, and a scanning light beam has been used without any electrical matrix connections. An example of this type of addressing is shown in Figure 3.46, but, whereas it is possible to conceive of a large-area, directly viewed panel constructed in this fashion, the actual application has been as a light valve in a projection system, so that it does not qualify as a true matrix panel. Unfortunately, therefore, none of these technologies can be considered as a fully viable candidate for matrix-addressed arrays at present. However, before dismissing them entirely, we should mention a few developments that indicate the directions that matrix-addressed displays using electrochromics and electrophoretics are taking.

First, in the case of the electrochromic display, certain special drive waveforms have been used to overcome crosstalk, and 20 × 144 element matrix panel capable of displaying up to 48 5 × 7 characters in two rows of 24 characters has been reported [37] and may lead to a useful, if limited, matrix display. Next, the addition of a third electrode into an electrophoretic matrix display, as shown in Figure 3.87 causes the equivalent of a threshold to exist, so that matrix addressing is feasible [38]. Although it still may not be the poor-man's panel television, it does show some promise and may become a useful technique.

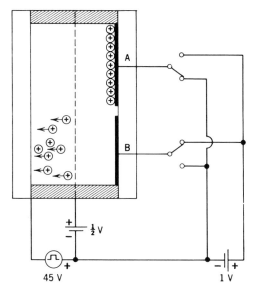

FIGURE 3.87   Schematic of control-grid EPID device. After Dalisa [39], by permission.

Older Technologies. One of the earliest forms of dot matrix displays to achieve some use has been the animated advertising displays made up of a multiplicity of incandescent light bulbs, and there is extensive use of incandescent sources in message and score boards such as those used in sporting arenas. However, they are essentially assemblies of alphanumerics of the type previously described and do not qualify as matrix addressed displays, so we do not consider them further.

Multiplexing. Finally, we come to that aspect of matrix addressing, to which the cognomen of multiplexing is applied. We may define multiplexing as any repetitive scanning sequence whereby all elements of a matrix display are sequentially addressed. It may be one element at a time, as in a standard television format, or it may be a line at a time, as in the scans described for the various matrix displays previously discussed, but its major use has been to describe methods for addressing and driving arrays of multiple alphanumerics. We limit the use of the term to such arrays and use scanning for multielement matrix displays. Of course, each character can be driven individually, just as each element in a matrix display may be separately activated, and whereas this approach is completely impractical for a matrix array of any size, it is sometimes preferable for small groups of characters, especially when, as for liquid crystal displays, multiplexing may introduce more problems than it solves. Thus although it is ridiculous to think of making individual connections to each element of 100-point matrix, requiring 101 leads instead of

20, it is not unreasonable to connect to each element of a four-digit numeric display, requiring only 29 leads, when a multiplexed display would still require 11 leads. However, there are significant savings possible in multiplexing such arrays, and it is the question of the total effect on cost and complexity of the display that determines whether multiplexing is to be used.

An example of the interconnections for an N-digit multiplexed display is shown in Figure 3.88. This is essentially an $N \times 8$ matrix, and each digit is addressed by selecting its common electrode in sequence. At the same time that the common is addressed, the appropriate segments of the digit pattern are also addressed, so that the selected digit exhibits the proper pattern. Then, if the multiplexing occurs at a refresh rate sufficiently high that each individual digit is refreshed at above the CFF, the digits do not flicker, and the display appears constant. The duty-cycle factor is $1/N$, which means that each digit is on for 16.6/N ms at a refresh rate of 60 Hz. This is perfectly acceptable for LEDs, and LED digits are usually multiplexed when four or more digits are involved. However, for liquid-crystal units, with decay times of over 100 ms, this is clearly not as acceptable since if the decay time is long enough for the integrating effect to occur, the rms condition exists, and the contrast ratio cannot be larger than that obtained with a continuous drive signal whose rms value is the same as that of the multiplexing signal. This leads to an expression for voltage ratio, which may be derived from equation 3.68

$$\frac{V_{\text{on}}}{V_{\text{off}}} = \left(\frac{8}{N} + 1\right)^{1/2} (3:1) \tag{3.81}$$

so that the contrast ratio for eight digits will be 47% of the maximum contrast ratio. If we add the angle dependence for twisted nematic displays, the results are usually quite unsatisfactory. Nothing daunted by this unpromising situation, various techniques have been investigated for speeding up response

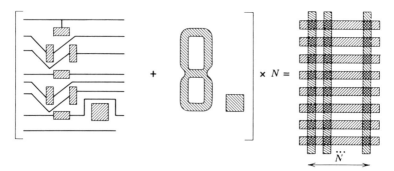

FIGURE 3.88 Example of interconnection pattern for front and rear electrodes of multidigit, multiplexed seven-segment numeric display. After Kmetz [40], by permission of Plenum Press.

time by material and cell structural improvements, and at least four-digit multiplexed assemblies appear within reach, if not completely demonstrated, as is covered in Section 3.4.

3.4 DEVICE CHARACTERISTICS

3.4.1 Introduction

We have examined what seems to be the infinite promise of matrix displays, and we may now ask what has been or appears to be the fulfillment. A number of technologies are involved and have achieved a varying amount of success in providing devices to be used in the real world rather than in the laboratory. We must of necessity limit ourselves to those devices and combinations that have resulted in products available to the prospective user or sufficiently advanced in their development that we can predict and anticipate the characteristics of the resultant device. To do otherwise would require us to traverse the endless path of abortive and only partially successful attempts to find the golden matrix display, be it a multielement panel, or a four-digit numeric. Therefore, in the interest of some economy of space and time, we restrict the ensuing descriptions and discussions in the main, to such unquestionably effective displays as the LED and liquid-crystal numerics and alphanumerics, with some attention to gas-discharge digits and older types such as incandescent and vacuum fluorescent for completeness, and to gas-discharge matrix displays with only incidental mention of some apparently promising results in EL, liquid crystal, and LEDs, in the area of matrix displays with a large number of elements. In addition, although we are primarily interested in nonmechanical displays, there are several magnetically activated devices that warrant some attention. Thus although we have none of the wealth of selection available as among cathode-ray devices, there is still enough to occupy us for a reasonable number of pages ending with a short section on solid-state imagers. As was done for the cathode-ray devices, we include separate sections on application considerations for each general category where appropriate, as well as discussion of the significance of the various performance parameters used to designate the operational capabilities of each class of device. By this means we may arrive at an understanding of what alphanumeric and matrix displays can and cannot do, and avoid using them in inappropriate ways and places.

3.4.2 Alphanumeric Devices

Electroluminescent Devices

Light-Emitting Diodes. As previously mentioned, probably the most successful example of the use of the matrix structure in displays is to be found in the many examples of numeric and alphanumeric displays using assemblies of LEDs as the display medium. Of course, since LEDs have been used as simple indicators, replacing incandescent and neon bulbs in many applications, but since they introduce no special requirements or problems, we do not include them in the discussion, and concentrate on the use of LEDs as light-emitting elements arranged so as to permit the generation of a large variety of characters, not necessarily restricted to alphanumerics alone.

The basic patterns used in these displays are the 5×7 or the 7×9 matrix, and the 7-, 14-, and 16-segment patterns shown in Figures 1.25, 1.26, 1.28, and 1.29. The method of connection to a 5×7 matrix is illustrated in Figure 3.89. This is one specific form of the basic matrix shown in Figure 3.54, and is subject to the same requirements and constraints that exist for any matrix assembly. It may be scanned on a row-at-a-time or a column-at-a-time basis, or even an element at a time, but a row at a time is most common, since that leads to the smallest number of individually addressed elements per scan, and somewhat simplifies the circuitry, as described in Chapter 5. In any event, the form of the character generator determines the scan sequence and the font of the display, and the arrangement pictured in Figure 3.89 is compatible with any of the common dot matrix character generators. Assuming the row-at-a-time scan, the waveforms shown in Figure 3.89 lead to the letter "A" in the format shown.

The manner in which the "A" is generated may be understood by examining the timing sequence for the waveforms applied to the matrix. First, row 1 is set at the most negative potential by waveform R_1, whereas only column 3 is high, so that, assuming 2:1 addressing, only the LED at the intersection of row 1 and column 3 will be on. Similarly, when row 2 goes low, columns 2 and 4 go high, and so on through the entire sequence. The row-scan and column-selection patterns repeat at a rate compatible with having the frame rate exceed the CFF and thus avoid flicker. Since any selected element is on for $\frac{1}{7}$ of the frame time, this is the duty factor of the display, and the peak luminances from the individual LEDs is reduced by the duty factor, according to equation 3.49 or 3.50. Since values of C_p over 100 are quite common for LEDs, the resultant C_s of 15 or more is acceptable.

We may extend the scanning process further by multiplexing a group of LED digits, using the technique illustrated by the waveforms in Figure 3.90. The enabling waveforms for each digit allow the matrix-scanning signals shown in Figure 3.89 to be applied to each digit in sequence, but this reduces the value of C_s by an additional factor of 5, so that values of C_p above 350 are required for an effective contrast ratio above 10. Although this is not too difficult to achieve, since it is possible to operate LEDs under pulse excitation at luminances above 3000 nits, it is sometimes not too clear from the specifications just what the expected contrast ratio will be. There are two problems in interpreting the specifications. First, the light output may be given in millicandelas rather than nits, so a knowledge of the area of the emitting portion and also whether the luminous intensity given refers to only the illuminated portion or the entire area of the display is necessary. Next, even

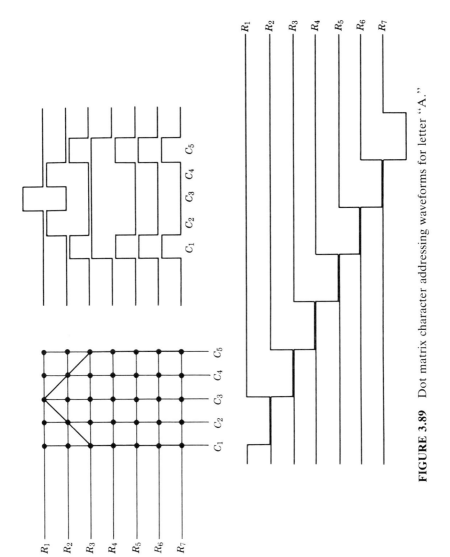

FIGURE 3.89 Dot matrix character addressing waveforms for letter "A."

319

320

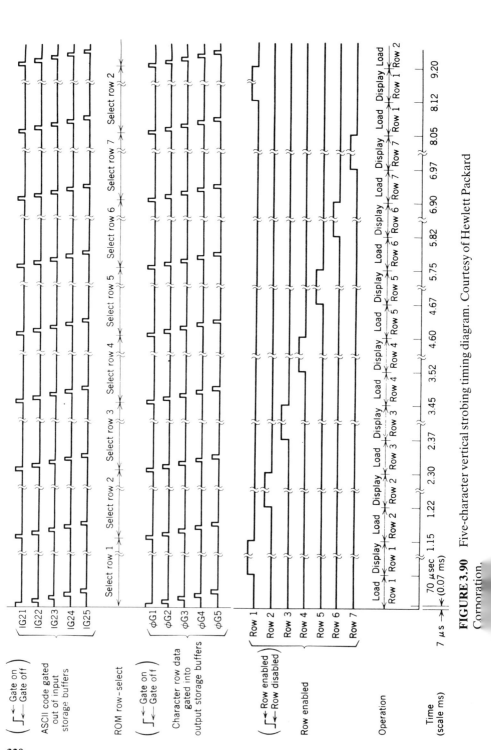

FIGURE 3.90 Five-character vertical strobing timing diagram. Courtesy of Hewlett Packard Corporation.

assuming that the device emits no light when it is not excited, information about its reflective characteristics is needed so as to arrive at the actual contrast ratio under operational ambient-light conditions. Unfortunately, these data are too frequently missing, as is also been the case for CRTs, so that the user must either make measurements of the parameters or contact the manufacturer for more complete data. Tables 3.13 and 3.14 list a range of parameters for single- and multidigit LED alphanumeric displays, giving the values as found in the usual specification sheets, and it is apparent that one must probe further to convert them into useful data. This, unfortunately, remains an exercise for the student, since it is not possible to list all the many types of such displays available, including converted data for each one. However, we may outline a procedure for obtaining the necessary information and performing the conversion, in the event the specification sheet is inadequate. This is done later in this section under "application considerations."

Another type of LED display in common use is the numeric array configured in the double-hung window pattern. It has the advantage over the dot matrix format in that each element may be addressed in parallel, so that no scanning is required for the individual digit. This means that a larger number of digits may be multiplexed before the duty factor effect on the contrast ratio becomes excessive. It is in this form that the majority of the numeric arrays used in watches and calculators, as well as readouts for a number of instruments, may be found. The manner of addressing and multiplexing a multidigit assembly of this type is shown in Figure 3.88 and has been described in the preceding section. The selected segments remain on only during the multiplexing interval, and as a result, the peak contrast ratio is reduced by the multiplexing duty cycle alone, with the consequent improvement in average contrast ratio. The simplicity of this form of digit display and the advantages accruing to the ability to multiplex the eight or more digits found in calculators has led to a wide use of LED digit arrays in this type of application, although it is being somewhat superseded by liquid-crystal displays because of their lower power requirements, as is described later. However, until faster liquid-crystal displays are developed, allowing multiplexing of multidigit arrays, we may expect LED digits to hold a place, despite their higher power requirements.

One interesting and rather unique feature of LED displays is their ability to produce several different colors, although not usually in the same unit. They are available in red, green, yellow, and amber, with red capable of the highest luminances and overall efficiency, and the others at lower but acceptable levels of output. Representative power requirement versus luminance are, for 1.5 cm² of emitting surface, about 2 mW per nit, with a range of 1 to 5 mW per nit. Digit sizes from 2.5 mm to 2.5 cm are easily achieved, but for sizes larger than 2.5 cm it is necessary to go to assemblies of discrete LEDs, arranged in either the dot matrix or double-hung window format, which tends to increase the cost and power consumption to levels that may be unacceptable. In addition, these may be special designs so that the cost

TABLE 3.13 Single-Character LED Display

Parameter	Symbol	Test Conditions	Min.	Typ.	Max.	Unit
Luminance	L		600	900		nit
Wavelength at peak emission	λ_{peak}		6300	6500	6700	Å
Spectral bandwidth between half-power points	BW_λ	$I_F = 10$ mA		200		Å
Static forward voltage	V_F		1.5	1.6	1.75	V
Average temperature coefficient of static forward voltage	αV_F	$I_F = 10$ mA, $T_A = 0\text{–}70°C$		−1.4		mV/°C
Static reverse current	I_R	$V_R = 3$ V			100	μA
Anode-to-cathode capacitance	C	$V_R = 0$, $f = 1$ MHz		80		pF
Luminous intensity/segment		5 mA dc	90	200		μcd
(Digit average)	I	20 mA dc		1200		μcd
		60-mA peak: 1 of 6 duty factor		740		μcd
Peak wavelength	λ_{peak}			583		nm
Dominant wavelength	λ_d			585		nm
Forward voltage/segment or DP	V_F	$I_F = 5$ mA		1.8		
		$I_F = 20$ mA		2.2	2.5	V
		$I_F = 60$ mA		3.1		
Reverse current/segment or DP	I_R	$V_R = 6$ V		10.0		μA
Response time	t_r, t_t			90.0		NS
Temperature coefficient of V_F/segment or DP	V_F/°C			−2.0		mV/°C

Source: Courtesy of Dialight.

TABLE 3.14   Four-Character Multiplexed LED Display

Parameter	Symbol	Min.	Typ.	Max.	Unit
Peak luminous intensity per LED (character average at pulse current of 100 mA/LED	$I_{v(\text{peak})}$	1.0	2.2		mcd
Reverse current per LED at $V_R = 4$ V	I_R		10		μA
Peak forward voltage at pulse current of 50 mA/LED	V_F		1.7	2.0	V
Peak wavelength	λ_{peak}		655		nm
Spectral line half-width	$\Delta\lambda_{1/2}$		30		nm
Rise and fall times[a]	t_r, t_f		10		ns

Source: Courtesy of Hewlett Packard.

[a]Time for a 10 to 90% change of light intensity for step change in current.

advantage of large quantity production is lost, even though the cost of the individual LEDs may be quite low. Maximum average luminances of more than 100 nits per digit are easily obtained, and 30 nits is quite common. Therefore, from the point of view of the various perceptual factors, LEDs constitute an excellent answer to most requirements. Their main lack is in the area of power consumption and size, as indicated, but in every other respect they remain one of the best devices for direct numeric and alphanumeric readouts.

Thin-Film EL Devices. Although it is possible to fabricate A/N arrays using TFEL technology, it has not turned out to be a practical approach, and there are no examples of such displays available. Therefore, this technology may be ignored when examining the various types of A/N devices offered. However, the problem is an economic one, and if techniques for fabricating small A/N arrays at low cost using TFEL are developed, the situation may change. At present, the other technologies, particularly LEDs, dc plasma, VFDs, and LCDs are far in the lead, and there is no sign that TFEL will offer any competition. However, TFEL matrix panels may be considered for larger A/N arrays.

Gas-Discharge Displays

Planar Displays. Alphanumeric gas-discharge displays are primarily of the dc type, although it is possible to use the ac types previously described as an A/N display. However, for relatively small groups of characters it is impractical to throw away much of the capacity of the ac panel and it is not considered an A/N display of the type discussed in this section. This discussion, therefore, is restricted to the dc versions, in both segmented and dot matrix configurations. These are available in several physical formats, generally referred to as the planar gas discharge (PGD), one of which is similar to that developed by Burroughs and illustrated in Figure 3.91. Burroughs is no longer in existence as a separate company, and its display products have been taken over or improved by several other companies. However, their products are sufficiently similar to the original Burroughs design for it to serve as the basis for a description of a segmented A/N display.

Figure 3.91 is an exploded view of this PGD type, and the several sections are combined in a sandwich form to create the complete assembly. There are nine cathode segments, one for each of the digit segments in a variant of the double-hung window, and the cathode segments are continuous through each digit position. The decimal cathodes require one for each position in this construction, and the anode screens are placed so that each one covers all the cathode segments in its position. The common-cathode segments reduce the number of connections required from 11-per-digit position to 9, plus 2 times the number of digit positions, and the reduction is characteristic of what may be achieved in a multiplexed display, as this one is. Multiplexing is achieved by scanning each anode in sequence, from left to right, while the appropriate segments are driven negative as the selected anode is driven positive. The anode supply voltage is about 200 V, and the current is 1 to

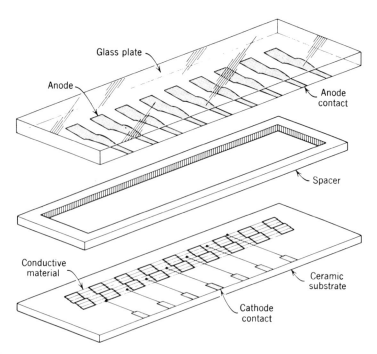

FIGURE 3.91 Exploded view of PGO display. Courtesy of Burroughs Corporation.

2.5 mA per segment. The cathodes are returned to about 100 V, which is high enough so that there is no glow when the anode is pulsed, but not so high that the cathodes act as anodes.

If a potential higher than the ionization potential occurs between adjacent electrodes, then the one at the lower potential glows. Therefore, the off anodes must be biased at 90 to 100 V, since if an off anode drops below this value it may act as a cathode. As a result, an anode adjacent to an on digit position may have a glow discharge around it if it drops below the recommended bias voltage. Similarly, the cathode must be biased at 90 to 120 V to avoid glow when its anode is turned on while still remaining low enough to avoid acting as an anode.

One important factor controlling the operation of this form of dc gas-discharge display is the reionization time as it is scanned. This time is reduced for intermediate digits because charged particles leak through from the previously ionized digit. However, this is not true for the first digit of a scanned group, and its ionization time is reduced by returning the anode to 200 V. At least 125 μs are required to fully ionize a digit, and this sets a limit on the number of digits that can be scanned at rates high enough to avoid flicker. In addition, each digit must be completely turned off for some period of time before the next digit is energized, so that the off digit is truly off, and not in the sustaining mode, which requires a much lower voltage to maintain, as given by equation 3.31. This period of time is 25 μs if both anode and cathode are turned off, and 100 μs if only the anode is turned off. The number of digits that may be scanned is then given by

$$N_d = \frac{T_s}{T_i + T_o} \tag{3.82}$$

where T_s = scanning time
 T_i = ionization time
 T_o = off time

Using these values and a scan rate of 60 Hz or 16.6 ms leads to a maximum number of 100 digits, but it is more usual to maintain each digit on for 1 ms because of the duty-cycle effect, so that 16 digits constitute a realistic maximum. This allows luminances above 150 nits at a voltage of 200 V and a current of 0.5 mA or less than 1 mW per nit, which compares favorably with LEDs. The trade-off is voltage for current, and now that high-voltage multiple drivers are readily available, achieving the required higher voltage is no great problem. Various sizes, numbers of digits, and formats are available, but the only color possible is the usual neon orange. The characteristics are given later in Tables 3.16, 3.17 and 5.6.

Raised Cathode Displays. The raised cathode display is based on a design originated by Sperry and taken over by Beckman. However, Beckman has

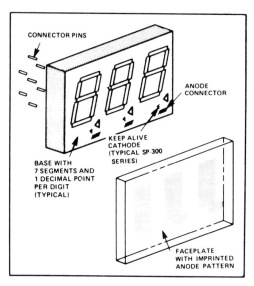

FIGURE 3.92   Beckman planar display mechanical construction. Courtesy of Beckman Corporation.

also left the display field, and its designs have been taken over by the same companies that now offer the Burroughs designs. The structure used is shown in Figure 3.92 and differs from the previously described unit in that each segment in a package is brought out to a separate pin on the connector, and at least one keep-alive cathode is contained in the envelope so as to provide an internal source of ions and reduce ionization time. This cathode is continuously on, even when multiplexing, and should be at least 160 V below the anode off voltage for best results. As shown in Figure 3.92, there is a different anode for each digit position, and they are brought out through separate connector pins. Multiplexing is accomplished by connecting the equivalent digit segments together and applying waveforms of the type and magnitude shown in Figure 3.93 to the anodes and keep-alive cathodes in sequence. The same requirements for maintaining the proper voltage difference between off anodes and on segments to avoid anode glow holds as for the other planar unit, which is to be expected, as the units are essentially the same in their operating principles. The Beckman unit is termed the *planar gas-discharge* display or PGD and has the possible advantages of more continuous segments and the option of special patterns at very nominal extra cost. It also offers higher luminances, going up to over 600 nits, and larger sizes, with a maximum of 1 in. However, the power is still in the range of 1 mW per nit, and the color is orange, so that the visual results for the two units are very similar. The number of external connections is larger for the PGD than for the other planar unit, because of the unique construction of the latter, but conversely, the PGD may be operated in a nonscanning mode, which may be desirable for a small number of digits. These units are compared

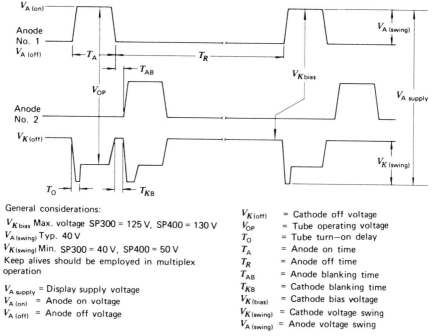

General considerations:

$V_{K\,bias}$ Max. voltage SP300 = 125 V, SP400 = 130 V
$V_{A\,(swing)}$ Typ. 40 V
$V_{K\,(swing)}$ Min. SP300 = 40 V, SP400 = 50 V
Keep alives should be employed in multiplex
operation

$V_{A\,supply}$ = Display supply voltage
$V_{A\,(on)}$ = Anode on voltage
$V_{A\,(off)}$ = Anode off voltage

$V_{K\,(off)}$	= Cathode off voltage
V_{OP}	= Tube operating voltage
T_{O}	= Tube turn–on delay
T_{A}	= Anode on time
T_{R}	= Anode off time
T_{AB}	= Anode blanking time
T_{KB}	= Cathode blanking time
$V_{K\,(bias)}$	= Cathode bias voltage
$V_{K\,(swing)}$	= Cathode voltage swing
$V_{A\,(swing)}$	= Anode voltage swing

FIGURE 3.93   Multiplex circuit waveforms sequential scan for Beckman planar multidigit display. Courtesy of Beckman Corporation.

further in the "applications" section, and some circuitry is given in Chapter 5. We may note that the increased luminance is possible because the dwell time on each digit is over 200 μs, whereas the off time between digits is 80 to 150 μs, so that no more than 20 digits can be multiplexed while retaining the higher luminance. Thus the keep-alive cathode does not contribute to scanning rate, but does have the feature that interlaced scanning is possible because firing is not dependent on charged particles from the previously scanned digit. In this case the blanking may occur while the interlaced digit is scanned and the blanking time saved.

Self-Scan.   The Self-Scan technique described previously was initially intended for A/N displays of up to 80 characters and was expanded to 2000 characters in later versions. However, although the larger-capacity panels have been superseded by the new designs, those with up to 12 lines of 40 dot matrix characters in a 5 × 7 matrix, or up to 96 × 240 fully addressable dot matrix assemblies remain on the market. Another use of the Self-Scan technique is in the bar graph displays described in Chapter 5.

Vacuum Fluorescent Displays.   The basic principles of operation for VFDs are described in Section 3.3.6, and the mode of addressing and driving for matrix units is covered in Section 3.3.15. However, VFDs have achieved the greatest

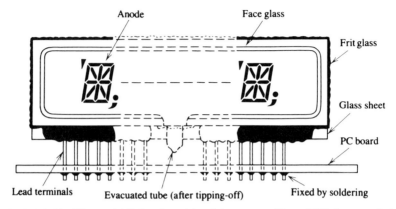

FIGURE 3.94   Flat multidigit tube. After Matsumoto [5, p. 220], by permission.

acceptance as A/N units, and further information on these types is given next. The preferred form is the flat multidigit tube shown in Figure 3.94, where the display consists of an array of multisegment numeric or A/N characters. Examples of these arrays are pictured in Figure 3.95 and are similar to the equivalent plasma displays. Bar graph and dot matrix displays are also available for use in a variety of limited character presentations. They may use the static drive illustrated in Figure 3.96*a*, where each anode segment is connected to a separate terminal, with the cathodes and grids for all characters connected in common. The desired A/N is selected by driving the independent anodes, leading to the requirement for separate anode segment selection circuits.

This drive technique is only suitable for a small number of characters, as the number of drive circuits increase rapidly when the number of characters increases. The alternative is the dynamic drive circuit shown in Figure 3.96*b*, where the anode segments in the same position are connected within the tube and to common external terminals. The grids are separated, and character selection is achieved by scanning through the grids, with the anode selected at the appropriate time, as shown in Figure 3.97. The dot matrix display may also be used as a limited character display, in which case the matrix drive technique is used.

Liquid-Crystal Displays.   There is a plethora of A/N LCDs, and it is the favored technology for all applications where power is of significance or battery operation is the customary mode. The format is varied, including segmented

FIGURE 3.95   Examples of segmented VFD arrays. Courtesy of Babcock.

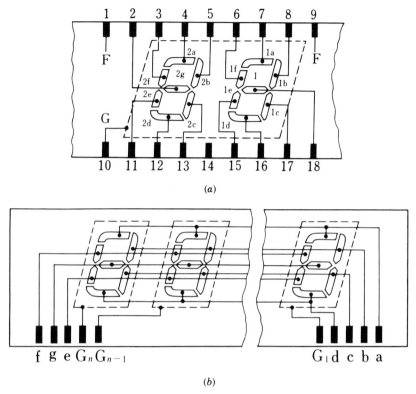

FIGURE 3.96 (*a*) Electrode connections of (a) static- and (*b*) dynamic-drive VFD. After Matsumoto [5], by permission.

and dot matrix types, and multiplexed drive is most common, with some examples of static drive. Dynamic scattering is the forgotten technology, and the field-effect units are the only ones offered. These have been largely of the twisted nematic type, with supertwist units rapidly taking over. The basic cell is constructed as shown in Figure 3.27, and consists of a bottom plane with the common electrode and a top plane with the segmented array made of a transparent conductor. The liquid crystal material is contained between the two planes, sealed at the edges so as to contain the liquid and avoid the introduction of air or other contaminents. The polarizer–analyzer pair are placed in either the parallel or orthogonal mode, depending on whether light-on-dark or dark-on-light characters are desired, according to the principles described previously. The twist in the molecules is built into the cell by the manufacturing process, and the cell may be constructed for use in the transmissive mode, as shown in Figure 3.30, or in the reflective mode by adding a reflective surface behind the common electrode, which is also transparent. Individual connections must be made to each of the elements, and, although there are some multiplexed units, in general each digit in an array has its own set of connections that are driven in parallel.

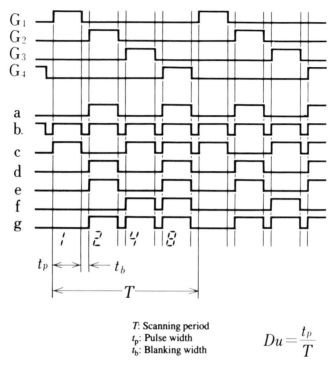

T: Scanning period
t_p: Pulse width
t_b: Blanking width

$$Du = \frac{t_p}{T}$$

FIGURE 3.97 Timing chart of grid and anode segment signals, displaying the digits "1248." After Matsumoto [5], by permission.

The outstanding feature of this type of twisted nematic display is the extremely low power consumed. Typically, the power dissipation is between 1 μW/cm^2 and 1 mW/cm^2 at voltages of 3 to 15 V ac, which lead to total power for a seven-segment, 10-mm digit of about 150 μW in a representative unit. We cannot arrive at a number for nits per mW since no light is emitted, so that the comparison with light-emitting displays must be made on a contrast-ratio basis. However, different liquid crystal displays may be compared as to their power requirements per digit or segment, and powers an order of magnitude lower than that presented have been attained in a number of units. Again, the contrast ratio must be considered since low power without adequate contrast ratio is of no value. However, contrast ratios of 20:1 are quite common, although this is the on axis value, and it drops off rapidly past the $\pm 45°$ points, as previously noted. Various sizes, ranging from the 5 mm for watches to 2.5 cm for the high alphanumeric are available, and arrays contain one to six characters. The alphanumeric uses the 16-stroke starburst shown in Figure 1.29, since dot matrix arrays are not practical because of the scanning problem.

Reference to the scanning problem makes this an appropriate point to examine those characteristics of liquid-crystal displays that are less than ideal.

The first, of course, is the very long response times encountered, ranging from 100 to 500 ms or more at the lowest temperature of operation, usually 0°C. The top temperature is similarly limited to 60 to 70°C, not by response time, which may improve by an order of magnitude at the top temperature, but by the liquid going out of the nematic mode, so that we are left with a clear liquid. Fortunately, the liquid will return to the nematic mode when the temperature is lowered below the transition point, although exposure to temperatures above the transition temperature for long periods of time may cause irreversible damage, and recommended storage temperatures are usually only 10°C above the maximum operating temperature. The low-temperature storage limit is not quite as severe, with 15 to 20°C below the minimum temperature considered acceptable. However, the combination of limited operating temperature range and slow response is a serious limitation of these twisted nematic, field-effect displays.

The displays are activated by applying the appropriate level of ac, usually 5 to 15 V rms between the selected segments and the back plane, and the untwisting of the molecules occurs only in those areas with the field across them. Thus the different alphanumerics may be achieved, with good contrast ratio and legibility. It is important to note that ony a very limited amount of dc component is acceptable, usually well under 50 mV, or the display will not achieve its expected life of over 30,000 h. The mechanism of degradation due to the dc is not well understood, but the result is either a gradual deterioration of the contrast ratio, which might be acceptable, or a sudden failure, which is not. However, the early plague of failures was due to poor seals and contamination that have been eliminated so that a long life expectancy appears warranted. Table 3.7 contains a representative group of parametes for presently available units and may be used as a basis for determining the applicability of this type of display to particular requirements.

Finally, one attempt to produce a simple LCD bar graph is that which combines the full "on" drive and "off" selection technique described previously in the section on multilevel addressing but using only a two-level cell. The basic structure of this display is shown in Figure 3.98, and it operates by driving all the major sectors in the bottom layer to saturation with the exception of the one containing the fine segments to be selected. In this sector the back plane is ground and the selected fine segments are driven to saturation with a voltage 180° out of phase with that driving the back planes. Thus either the saturation voltage or twice the saturation voltage drives all selected sectors and fine segments. The top cell has only those sectors driven that cover the visible bar graph areas. Since the cells are of the twisted nematic type, with parallel polarizer–analyzer pairs, the undriven areas block the light and only the driven areas in both cells are transmissive, as illustrated in Figure 3.99. This approach does not require any special switching or storage elements and is quite effective for small-scale, static arrays.

The full "on" drive technique may also be used on a single-cell matrix-addressed bar graph, with all sectors driven except that selected to be shown.

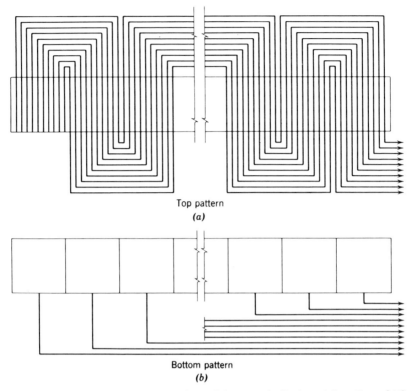

Top pattern
(a)

Bottom pattern
(b)

FIGURE 3.98   Bottom-cell patterns for LC bar graph display. After Sherr [41], by permission.

Either a light-on-dark or a dark-on-light display may be achieved by proper orientation of the analyzer–polarizer pair, and breakpoint uncertainties are avoided by this approach. However, the supertwist units in conjunction with conventional 3:1 matrix selection techniques have proved quite effective, and the full "on" technique has only limited value.

Electrochromic, Ferroelectric, and Electrophoretic Displays.   These three technologies are lumped together because they have not as yet produced any

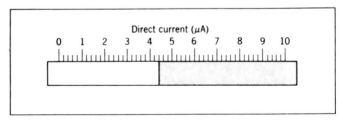

FIGURE 3.99   Appearance of LC bar graph meter display. After Sherr [41], by permission.

significant group of devices for general use. However, it is advisable to know what may be expected of them, and they should not be ignored because they have not reached the state of development of the other technologies. A list of performance characteristics that have been attained in experimental and prototype units is given in Tables 3.10 and 3.15, and we may use this to determine whether they offer any possibility of being useful in certain applications. The structures used are shown in Figures 3.41 and 3.46 to 3.48 and are not repeated here. Except for the ferroelectric types, which have also been used as light valves in large-area projection displays, and are discussed further detail in Chapter 5, they are all of the standard numeric type and use the same kind of format as the ones already described. The expected or realized characteristics of displays using these technologies that are listed in Tables 3.10 and 3.15 may be used for evaluation of these devices, and the technical descriptions given earlier will aid in separating what may truly be anticipated from what is essentially a proponents dream.

In general, we may say that ferroelectrics and electrophoretics suffer from the relatively high voltages required, and they all tend to be rather slow, although ferroelectrics do have the definite possibility of speeds in the microsecond range. Both electrochromics and electrophoretics have been used to make displays with excellent appearance, and all three have the advantage of a memory mode. The material and fabrication problems remain formidable, but given enough effort they may be solved. Until then, we can only wait and see.

TABLE 3.15   Comparison of Nonemissive Displays

	EC	EP	FELC	DSLC
Contrast ratio	10	40	10	10
Viewing angle	Wide	Wide	Narrow	Narrow
Optical mode[a]	T.R.P	R	T.R.P	T.R.P
Color	2	2	B/W or dye	B/W
Resolution	Mostly electrode limited			
Operating mode	Dc pulse	Dc pulse	Ac	Ac
Voltages (V)	0.25–20	30–80	2–10	10–30
Power (μW/cm^2)		15	<0.1	1–10
Energy (mJ/cm^2)	10–100	6×10^{-4}		
Memory	Yes	Yes	No/yes	No/yes
Threshold	Poor	No	Poor	Poor
Write time (ms)	100–1000	60	20	20
Erase time (ms)	100–500	30	1500	100
Operating life (10^4 h)	?	?	>2	>1

Source: After Chang [42], by permission of Plenum Press.
[a]T, transmission; R, reflection; P, projection.

Older Technologies. In the interest of completeness, we conclude this section on alphanumeric devices with short descriptions of several other types of displays that have been around for some time but still offer some advantages that warrant their consideration, even though they are not all electronic in nature. These are the incandescent, vacuum-fluorescent, and electromagnetic units. They are all products of well-developed technologies and have been in use in some form for a long time. However, recent improvements in performance entitle them to be included among this group of devices.

The characteristics of these devices are given in Table 3.16 and are compared there with other technologies. The incandescent units come in both vacuum tube and specially designed vacuum-chamber arrangements, with the second permitting the filaments to be brought closer to the viewing surface. They feature extremely high luminances, of over 15,000 nits, and lifetimes of more than 100,000 h, in which respect they are superior to any of the ones previously considered, but they do generate considerable heat, dissipating as much as 950 mW per digit. However, this is only about 70 μW/nit, so that for very high luminance they appear to be the best solution. Color is obtained by means of filters, and with such large luminances the light loss in the color filters is trivial. They may be obtained in various configurations, such as the double-hung window, the 16-segment starburst, and the dot matrix formats. It should be pointed out that possible operating ratings are 5 V at 18 mA per segment for a luminance of 15,000 nits, an impressive figure for a 12.5-mm digit. Maximum sizes are in the order of 30 mm, with the power correspondingly larger. Altogether a very impressive set of characteristics if the high luminance is required and the power consumed is not a drawback.

There are numerous variations of light-bulb alphanumerics, where the bulbs are used as elements in a matrix, or to illuminate colored segments, but these are mainly used in large outdoor displays and suffer from the large amount of heat generated and the considerable amounts of power consumed. They have seen some applications in racetracks and outdoor sports arenas but are not practical for more general use. Of more interest are the electromagnetic types, which rotate a disk or a segment on application of an electrical pulse to a magnetic circuit and thus change the reflectivity or color of the display surface. Of this group, the Ferranti-Packard rotating-disk matrix display is the most versatile type and may be used either as a dot matrix alphanumeric or as a large-scale matrix display board. Since its main application has been in such large displays, we find further discussion in Section 3.4.3 on matrix displays.

Application Considerations. With this plethora of alphanumeric displays to choose from, it is a major problem to decide which one to use for a given application. A first step is to establish the criteria for the choice and then use them as a basis for comparison. To do this, we may examine the data contained in Tables 3.10, 3.15, and 3.16, which contain, in summary form, the range of performance characteristics of the various types we have been discussing.

TABLE 3.16 Comparison of Digit Display Technologies

Parameter	LED	Gas Discharge	Fluorescent	Incandescent	Dynamic Scattering LCD	Field-Effect LCD	Electro-magnetic
Power/digit (mW)	10–140	30–100	100	250–1000	0.1	0.001–0.01	1000 Peak
Voltage (V)	5	180	15–25	5	15–50	3–10	4.2
Temperature range (°C)	−55 to +125	0–55	−55 to +100	−55 to +100	−10 to +60	−10 to +70	−40 to +79
Switching speed	1 μs	1 ms	1 ms	150 μs	100–300 ms	100–300 ms	1–100 ms
Life (h)	100,000	30,000	100,000	10,000–100,000	30,000	30,000	10,000–100,000
Colors	R, O, Y, G	Orange	Blue-green	All with filters	Depends on light	Depends on light	White, orange, green
Luminance (nits)	30–3000	30	30	100–15,000	Na	NA	NA
Contrast ratio	10	20	10	20	20	20	20
Appearance	Good to excellent	Excellent	Excellent	Excellent	Good to excellent	Good to excellent	Excellent
Viewing angle (°)	150	120	150	150	90–150	90–120	150
Font	7-, 14-, 16-segments; dot matrix	7-segment; dot matrix	7-segment; dot matrix	7-, 14-, 16-segment; dot matrix	7-, 14-, 16-segment	7-, 14-, 16-segment	7-segment; dot matrix
Vertical size (mm)	2.5–25 Monolithic: ≤100 discrete	5–18 Standard: ≤200 special	13–19	Up to 25 high intensity; over 200 standard bulbs	5–200	5–25	5–150

336 MATRIX AND ALPHANUMERIC DEVICES

One important factor that is not included is cost, because it is too variable and dependent on circumstances and quantity. However, once the acceptable units have been selected on the basis of the parameteres given, the cost data may be obtained and factored in. We may begin with the same basic parameters that have been used previously, that is, luminance, contrast ratio, and size, and then add the other parameters of power dissipation, angle of view and response time. Finally, temperature dependence and range, reliability, memory capabilities, and color may be considered, as well as any other special features that appear significant, such as compatibility with microcircuits and circuit complexity. Examining Tables 3.10, 3.15, and 3.16, we see that a very wide range of luminances is available, from 30 nits at the low end of the LED group to over 30,000 nits at the top of the EL group. Of course, it is necessary to have the information in the same dimensions for all the types to make this comparison, which is not always the case initially. For example, the LED data may be in microcandelas, and it is necessary to convert this value to nits. Some manufacturers provide the information in both forms, but if this is not the case for the units being considered, the conversion must be made, remembering that nits are given in candelas per square meter. Therefore, the area of the emitting surface must be determined and the value in luminance calculated as the ratio of the luminous intensity and the emitting area. This appears to be simple, but the information required is not always readily available and is confused by the method of measurement, which may give the maximum rather than the average. Table 3.17 contains several examples of LEDs with both luminous intensity and luminance given, as an example.

Of course, the luminance of the nonemitting displays is determined by the amount of light available from some external source, which may be supplied by the manufacturer or may be added by the user. In general, however, we must now consider that the contrast ratio, as the more significant parameter, is also of prime importance for the light-emitting units. Contrast ratio is usually given for the passive displays but may not be readily available for the light-emitting types, and it is necessary to know what the ambient conditions will be and what the reflection characteristics of the device are under operating

TABLE 3.17 Typical Performance Characteristics of LED Numeric Displays

	Monolithic Numeric Red	Reflector Numeric	
		Red	Orange
Character height (mm)	2.5	7.5	7.5	14
Segment area (cm²)	1.6×10^{-3}	27×10^{-3}	27×10^{-3}	93×10^{-3}
Luminous intensity (μcd/10 mA dc)	275	250	750	700
Surface brightness (nits/10 mA dc)	1700	80	255	78

Source: After Craford [43], by permission.

conditions. This, in turn, impacts on the luminance requirement, since high levels of ambient illumination coupled with high reflectivity means that the device luminance must be proportionally high. For example, if the display must be viewed in direct sunlight without special arrangements to reduce the amount of light impinging on the viewing surface, then either the very high luminance or the light-reflecting devices must be used.

Size is the next parameter to be established. As previously discussed, this is a function of the viewing distance, and equation 1.29 is the relevant formula. If the required size is larger than that obtainable with some of the technologies, it is necessary to restrict the choice to those types that offer the larger sizes, so that this may be a limiting parameter. It is also affected by the character font since the dot matrix font is usually more legible than the double-hung window and may permit smaller sizes to be legible at a given viewing distance. The trade-off between the most cost-effective size and the most legible font should be carefully examined before the selection of display type. Angle of view also enters into this aspect of the specification since a size and font combination that may be acceptable within a restricted angle may be completely inadequate at the wider angles.

Power dissipation for a given luminance and contrast ratio, as well as the effect of environmental factors may, in a particular temperature range, further restrict the choice, as may the associated factor as to whether a high voltage or current is acceptable. The limitations imposed by the need for operating from a battery are quite obvious and have led to increasing acceptance of liquid-crystal displays for watch applications, in spite of their visual limitations, and are a prime example of the overriding effect of one parameter. Reliability also enters at this point, with long life at a minimum failure rate the predominant feature.

Finally, we may consider whether color capability is a necessary or merely desirable feature, and whether it can be static or must be dynamic. The advantages of selective color are usually moot, so that insistence on a color capability in the display device should be made only after careful consideration of the actual needs and alternatives. Similarly, response time sets significant limits on the choice, and the very fast response capabilities of certain devices may be wasted in the application unless cost advantages are large enough to be meaningful. Memory as an inherent feature may also reduce the dependence on rapid response time, even though it is not necessary from an operational point of view. Circuit requirements are affected by these two factors, as well as by whether multiplexing is possible and whether high voltages or currents are required. In addition, although we have not considered circuit requirements in any great detail here, deferring that examination to Chapters 4 and 5, the impact of circuit complexity and cost on the choice of device type may be significant.

This completes the list of commonly encountered parameters, to which must be added any special factors too specific to a particular situation to be included in our list. They are summarized in Table 3.18, which is a sample

TABLE 3.18   Alphanumeric Specification Parameter Ranges

Parameter	Value
Character height (cm)	0.25–25
Number of characters	10–128
Format	7-, 14-, 16-segment; 5 × 7, 7 × 9 matrix
Font	Numeric, alphanumeric
Number of character positions	1–36
Luminous intensity (mcd)	0.3–3
Luminance (nits)	
Single character	30–300
Single character multiplexed	30–300
Current for rated luminance or intensity (mA)	3–30
Voltage	
Magnitude	1.5–30 V
Frequency	Dc–1 kHz
Power per character	10 μW–100 mW
Energy (mJ)	10^{-3}–1000
Response time (ms)	
On	0.1–100
Off	0.1–500

specification for an alphanumeric display. It is intended only as a guide, and deviations from this form are to be expected in any specific case. However, it does include the most important parameter considerations and may be used with whatever additions or alterations seem warranted by the special features of any particular application.

REFERENCES

[1] Piper, W. W., and Williams, F. E., "Electroluminescence," in F. Seitz and D. Turnbull, Eds., *Solid State Physics*, Vol. 5, Academic, New York, 1957.

[2] Ivey, H. F., "Electroluminescence and Related Effects," in L. Martin, Ed., *Advances in Electronics and Electronic Physics*, Suppl. I, Academic, New York, 1963.

[3] Goodman, L. A., "The Relative Merits of LEDs and LCDs," *SID Proc.*, **16**/1, 1975, 8–19.

[4] Bhargava, R. N., "Recent Advances in Visible LED's," *SID Proc.*, **16**/2, 1975, 103–112.

[5] Matsumoto, S., Ed., *Electronic Display Devices*, Wiley, New York, 1990.

[6] Karawada, H., and Ohshima, N., "DC EL Materials and Techniques for Flat-Panel TV Display," *Proc. IEEE*, **61**/7, 1973, 907–914.

[7] Vecht, A., "AC and DC Electroluminescent Displays," *SID Sem. Lect. Notes*, 1990, F2.31.

[8] Soxman, E. J., *Electroluminescent Thin Film Research*, JANAIR Report 72093, Office of Naval Reseach, Washington, D.C., July 15, 1972.

[9] Nasser, E., *Fundamentals of Gaseous Ionziation and Plasma Electronics*, Wiley, New York, 1971.

[10] Cola, R., "Gas Discharge Panels with Internal Line Sequencing (Self-Scan® Displays)," in B. Kazan, Ed., *Advances in Image Pickup and Display*, Academic, New York, 1977.

[11] Chodil, G., "Gas Discharge Displays for Flat-Panel," *SID Proc.*, **17**/1, 1976, 14–22.

[12] Jackson, R. N., and Johnson, D. E., "Gas Discharge Displays: A Critical Review," in L. Martin, Ed., *Advances in Electronics and Electronic Physics*, Vol. 35, Academic, New York, 1974.

[13] Morimoto, K., and Pykosz, T. L., "Vacuum Fluorescent Displays," *SID Sem. Lect. Notes*, 1986, 1.2.20.

[14] Soref, R. A., "Liquid Crystal Display Phenomena," *SID Proc.*, **13**/2, 1972, 95–104.

[15] Goodman, L. A., "Passive Liquid Crystals, Electrophoretics, and Electrochromics," *SID Proc.*, **17**/1, 1976, 30–38.

[16] Goodman, L. A., "Liquid Crystal Displays," *RCA Rev.*, **35**/6, Dec. 1974, 613–650.

[17] Scheffer, T. J., et al., "24 × 80 Character LCD Panel Using the Supertwisted Birefringence Effect," *SID 1985 Dig.*, 120–123.

[18] Pyrce, Dave, "Liquid Crystal Displays," *EDN*, Oct. 12, 1989, 104.

[19] Crossland, W. A., et al., "Prospects and Problems of Ferroelectric LCDs," *SID Proc.*, **29**/3, 1988, 238.

[20] Deb, S. K., "Physics of Photochromic and Electrochromic Phenomena in Inorganic Solids," *Conference Record of 1974 Conference on Display Devices and Systems*, IEEE, SID, AGED, 159–163.

[21] Meitzler, A. H., and Maldonado, J. R., "Ferroelectric Display's Big Bonus: Selective Erase/Write Capability," *Electronics*, Feb. 1, 1971, 34–39.

[22] Maldonado, J. R., and Meitzler, A. H., "Strain-Biased Ferroelectric-Photoconductor Image Storage and Display Devices," *Proc. IEEE*, **59**/3, 1971, 368–382.

[23] Land, C. E., and Smith, W. D., "PLZT Ceramic Numeric Display Devices," *1974 IEDM Tech. Dig.*, 356–359.

[24] Dalisa, A. L., "Electrophoretic Display Technology," *IEEE Trans. Electron. Devices*, **ED-24**/7, 1977, 827–834.

[25] Ota, I., "Electrophoretic Image Display (EPID) Panel," *Proc. IEEE*, **61**/7, 1973, 832–836.

[26] Rachner, H., and Morrissy, J. M., *New Results in Display Technology*, SAE Technical Paper Series, 830036, Society of Automotive Engineers, Warrendale, Pa., 1983.

[27] Saxe, R. L., et al., "Suspended Particle Display with Improved Properties," *Proc. 1982 International Display Research Conference*.

[28] Van Raalte, J. A., "Matrix TV Displays: Systems and Circuit Problems," *SID Proc.*, **17**/1, 1976, 8–13.

[29] Frescura, B. L., "Limitations on the Size of Monolithic XY Addressable LED Arrays," *SID 1976 Dig.*, 54–55.

[30] Miller, M. R., "Advances in Thin Film EL Displays," *SID Sem. Lect. Notes*, 1991. M3/8.

[31] Dick, G. W., "Advances in Plasma Display Technology," *SID Sem. Lect. Notes*, 1990, F9.33–F9.35.

[32] Weber, L. F., "Plasma Displays," *SID Sem. Lect. Notes*, 1989, 5.29.

[33] Goodman, L., and Meyerhofer, D., "Liquid Crystal Field-Effect Devices Operating in the Multiplexed Mode," *SID 1975 Dig.*, 76–77.

[34] Alt, P. M., and Pleshko, P., "Scanning Limitations of Liquid Crystal Displays," *IEEE Trans. Electron. Devices*, **ED-21**/7, 1974, 146–154.

[35a] Brody, T. P., "Large Scale Integration for Display Screens," *SID Proc.*, **17**/1, 1976, 39–55.

[35b] Howard, W. E., "Active Matrix Techniques for Displays," *SID Sem. Lect. Notes*, 1986, 7.2.20–7.2.24.

[36] Bruce, R., "Active Matrix Liquid Crystal Displays," *SID Sem. Lect. Notes*, 1991, F3/8.

[37] Arellano, A. G., et al., "A Refreshed Matrix-Addressed Electrochromic Display," *SID 1978 Dig.*, 22–23.

[38] Dalisa, A. L., and Singer, B., "An X-Y Addressable Electrophoretic Display," *SID Proc.*, **18**/3,4 1978, 255–266.

[39] Dalisa, A. L., and Delano, R. A., "Recent Progress in Electrophoretic Displays," *SID 1974 Dig.*, 88–89.

[40] Kmetz, A. R., "Matrix Addresing of Non-emissive Displays," in A. R. Kmetz and F. K. von Willisen, Eds., *Nonemissive Electrooptic Displays*, Plenum, New York, 1976.

[41] Sherr, A., "A Liquid Crystal Bar Graph Meter," *SID 1976 Dig.*, 42–43.

[42] Chang, I. F., Electrochromic and Electrochemichromic Materials and Phenomena," in A. R. Kmetz and F. K. von Willisen, Eds., *Nonemissive Electrooptic Displays*, Plenum, New York, 1976.

[43] Craford, M. G., "Recent Developments in Light-Emitting Diode Technology," *SID Proc.*, **18**/2, 1977, 151–159.

4

CATHODE-RAY-TUBE SYSTEMS AND EQUIPMENT

4.1 INTRODUCTION

In this chapter we are concerned with those systems that use the CRT as the prime display device and the equipment that make up the component parts of these systems. The systems are very varied in nature, ranging from relatively simple consoles to elaborate combinations of minicomputers or microcomputers with special character and vector generators and including a wide variety of monitors with special features such as full color or image storage. These systems remain the workhorses of the industry, used in a wide variety of applications, as is described in Chapter 6 in some detail. However, at this point we are interested only in presenting and discussing the technical aspects of the performance of these systems so that it will be possible to understand the capabilities and limitations of this type. Another important aspect of these systems, which applies to all display systems, is the manner in which data are entered into the system, both manually and from other sources, such as computers or sensors. Although it is not our intention to become involved in any elaborate discussion of the latter two, we must pay considerable attention to the form in which they provide inputs to the display system and how these inputs may be combined with those generated directly at the display system by associated input devices in common use. To this end, we must include some description of the input devices, as well as the specific characteristics of the signals from the other data sources. Thus we are concerned with the total system configuration, and the exact structure of the display system depends on these considerations as well as those unique to the system configuration used. However, to avoid getting bogged down in computer hardware and software, which deserve, and have received, separate treatment in many texts, we restrict our exploration of the large, mainframe computer to the impact that its outputs have on the structure of the display system and its directly connected peripherals. This is less of a restriction than it may appear to be at first glance, since many display systems incorporate their own computers, and some discussion of these dedicated computers is necessary and appropriate.

Having delineated the areas of interest, it is necessary, for clarity, to use some mode of classification to break up the multiplicity of display systems into several general categories with significant elements in common. We may use several taxonomic schemes, such as mode of application, display device technology, data format, or data-writing sequence. Since the applications are manifold and are covered in Chapter 6, we exclude them from consideration here and concentrate on the other three. Display device technology is a convenient way to group display systems, since there are only two basic types, refresh and storage, to be considered, with color as a subgroup of the first. However, the data-writing sequence (i.e., whether raster scan or random deflection is used) imposes significant differences on the systems using one or the other or even combinations of the two. Finally, whether the data are displayed in a fixed alphanumeric format or have the greater flexibility of the random deflection, vector format, determines the form that many of the functional elements of the display system must take, such as the inclusion of vector generators. Thus we are hard put to exclude any of these modes of classification and must use them all, for completeness and clarity. To avoid undue repetition we begin with a generalized system containing all the elements used in each type of system and then concentrate in the ensuing sections on the unique characteristics imposed by the particular classification scheme being used. Therefore, we begin with the display device type to establish the general considerations involved in refresh and storage systems, then go on to raster versus random, which applies to either type of display device, and end up with format, which does not exclude any of the previously established groups but does impact on the form of the total display system. With these rules of procedure established, we may now embark on an examination of CRT display systems.

4.2 GENERALIZED SYSTEM

A generalized display system is one that contains all the basic functional elements to be found in any display system and is sufficiently complete so that any specific configuration includes no elements not found in the generalized system. In its simplest form it may be represented by the diagram shown in Figure 4.1, where the mainframe computer represents all sources of computer-generated data and the input block includes all other input sources such as sensors and manually operated input devices. The display processor may be a computer in its own right, and it sometimes takes on functions

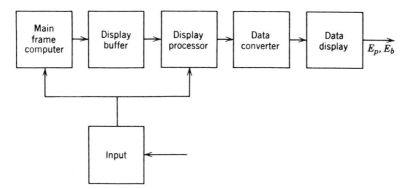

FIGURE 4.1 Generalized display-system block diagram.

normally assigned to the main frame or gives up functions to it, depending on the total information system configuration. This creates some ambiguity, as in the case of the so-called intelligent terminal, or self-contained system with a dedicated computer, and we minimize this uncertainty by assuming that if the computer is essentially restricted to serving the needs of the display system, it becomes the display processor and fits our functional scheme. Similarly, the main frame computer may perform some functions unique to the display system, but in this case we represent the display system as being only partially complete and do not include the computer as part of that partial system. The functions that are normally performed by the display processors, whether they are called *computer* or *controller*, are those of interface buffer, timing, control, and coordinate conversion as a minimum, to which may be added a number of special functions, such as data insertion and deletion, image alteration and rotation, image formation, and various other forms of data manipulation. The minimum functions consist of the housekeeping operations involved in timing, format, and control, with the operation of coordinate conversion of prime importance, since, in order to display the data in any reasonable form, they must be converted into display coordinates and thus establish position, shape, luminance, and color of the visual image. We may truly say that without performing this function we have no display system, but merely a random combination of images.

The display processor may include the refresh memory if it is required for the display device, and the refresh memory contains one or more pages of data, still in digital form, but in coordinates compatible with the display format. The refresh memory performs the function of storing the frames of data in display words and then outputting them at a rate compatible with the visual requirements. It may not be necessary if some other form of storage is available, as in the storage CRT, but it is found in all other types of display systems using a CRT as the display device.

The data-converter function comes next, and this encompasses a wide range of specific operations. It is needed because the CRT is an analog device, and we have assumed the data to be in digital form to this point. The data converter acts on these digital data to produce the various analog signals used to deflect and intensify the electron beam of the CRT. Indeed, the entire display system between the data source and the data display may be considered as essentially a data converter, with all the other functions subsidary to that one. A data converter may be required even when the data are received in analog form, as from a sensor, to put the information into a form compatible with the display, or the data converter may deal directly with a visual image and perform the same conversion function, as is the case with a television camera. All these types of data converters are covered in detail later.

Finally, we come to the *raison d'être* for the whole system, the display device on which the data display is made visible for viewing. In this chapter we are concerned only with the CRT as the display device, but it may take on a multiplicity of forms, as we have seen in Chapter 2, and may be used in a variety of ways, as is discussed later. We include projection systems in that discussion, since they are basically CRT systems when a CRT is the light source, although the inclusion of optics and a screen does expand the concept of what constitutes a CRT display system. We also include other cathode-ray devices, such as the Eidophor, for want of a better place to put them.

4.3 REFRESH SYSTEMS

4.3.1 General Description

The most salient characteristic of a refresh system is that the display device has no built-in memory and retains the image for only a limited period of time. As has been described in Chapter 1, in the section on flicker, the human visual system is adversely affected by luminance variations that occur below the CFF, so it is necessary to provide a means for repeating, or refreshing the image at a rate higher than the minimum required to avoid the sensation of flicker. This is normally in the range 50 to 60 Hz, at the usual luminance levels, and imposes certain requirements on the speed of the memory. The memory need perform no other functions than accepting data from either the digital data source or the display processor and then making these data available in the proper sequence to the data converter. Figure 4.2 shows three possible configurations for a refresh system, with the location of the memory determined by the exact form of the data from the digital source, or the amount of processing required in the display system to convert the data into a form suitable for the data converter. For example, if the computer outputs its data in a format directly acceptable by the display system, then the processing in the display system is minimal, and the refresh memory may be at the input and act as a display buffer as well. However, if much processing is involved, the memory should be between the processor and the converter to avoid having any extensive processing occur on every refresh cycle. Indeed,

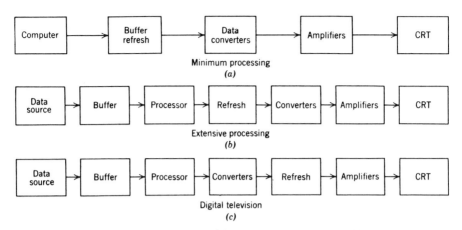

FIGURE 4.2 Refresh CRT systems: (*a*) minimum processing; (*b*) extensive processing; (*c*) digital television.

in certain cases, such as the digital television system described later, the refresh memory may be located after the converter and may interface directly with the display. These three possible arrangements are shown in Figure 4.2*a*, *b*, and *c*, respectively.

Once we have placed the memory in the proper location for the type of system involved, we must arrive at a specification for this memory. The significant parameters are capacity and speed, with the type of memory, that is, core, solid state, or rotating, as a separate consideration. The capacity is determined by the amount of data contained in a frame of visual information and the format of those data. For example, if a frame is to contain a maximum of 2000 characters, and each character requires 30 bits to establish position, luminance level, color, and shape, then clearly the memory capacity must be 60,000 bits. In general, then, the capacity may be expressed by

$$C = N_f n_c \tag{4.1}$$

where N_f is the number of characters in a frame and n_c is the number of bits per character. To this must be added any additional bits needed for control or other special data designations.

The speed of response is influenced by the rate at which the bits can be accepted by the converter and the display unit. If we assume the same 30 bits per character and 2000 characters and a refresh frequency of 50 Hz, then the 30 bits must be outputted in 10 μs for 30 bits in parallel, or 333 ns per bit for serial output. The general formulas are

$$T = \frac{1}{N_f n_c f} \tag{4.2}$$

for serial operation, and

$$T = \frac{1}{N_f f} \qquad (4.3)$$

for parallel operation, where T is the memory access time in seconds and f is the refresh frequency in hertz.

In certain cases, such as digital television described later, the output rate may be considerably higher. To anticipate the more complete discussion, both the memory capacity and the access time may have entirely different requirements than those established by equation 4.2 or 4.3 because the memory contains at least one location for each picture element (pixel). This may lead to memory capacities of 10^6 bits in certain cases and may dictate the choice of the type of memory to be used. This becomes clearer later when the various digital television systems are discussed. Another factor affecting memory size is the number of pages to be stored, even though only one page is to be displayed at a time. The increase is obviously a simple multiplication of the number of pixels times the number of pages.

4.3.2   Random Deflection Vector (System Configuration)

Random deflection refresh display systems were the first type to achieve any large-scale acceptance and usage. Although they are essentially no longer in use, having been supplanted by the many new systems embodying microprocessors, various types of computers, and bit-mapped CRT displays, they do embody many of the functions and principles contained in modern systems and are of more than merely historical interest. Therefore, we begin with a review of these principles and the designs used to implement the functions that is essentially unchanged from that contained in the first edition of this volume. We compare the characteristics of the various approaches later, and confine the discussion here to those aspects of random deflection systems that impose unique requirements on the elements of such systems. For simplicity, we use the term *vector* as applying to all random-deflection systems, even when they do not include a vector drawing capability. This is appropriate since only the data-converter function is affected by the absence of a vector capability, and we may delete it from the total system without significantly affecting the general considerations of interest.

Vector systems, then, are those in which the data for each character come from the digital source without any specific prearrangement as to position, luminance, size, or any other parameters of the visual image, although there may be cases where some partial preformating is used. Figure 4.3 presents the form such a system may take, with the functional elements shown in Figure 4.1 expanded into specific operational units. The details of each unit are discussed later, in turn, and we may examine them from the point of view of their system functions as well. We begin with the data-display unit, as it

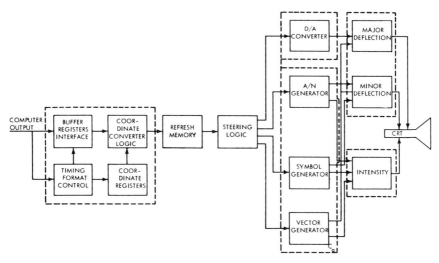

FIGURE 4.3 Digital display-system block diagram. After Sherr [6, p. 211], by permission.

is the most prominent interface between the user and the display system and has the most immediate affect on whether the system is acceptable for the application. We then proceed backward through the data converters, refresh memory, display processor, and buffer to the data source, including manual input devices as one form of data source.

Display Unit. The total display unit, also referred to as the *monitor*, may be represented by the diagrams shown in Figure 4.4 for a magnetic deflection

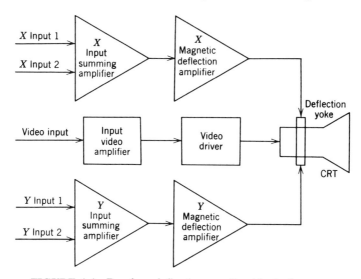

FIGURE 4.4 Random-deflection monitor block diagram.

CRT, with the electrostatic deflection unit discussed later. The relevant equations for both types may be found in Section 2.4.2 for the monochromatic types we discuss here. Beginning with the magnetic deflection CRT as the one most commonly used, if we examine equation 2.57, we see that we can trade off voltage, current, and inductance to arrive at specific deflections. However, we must initially consider the effect of yoke inductance on deflection time, to arrive at a deflection time consistent with the amount of data to be presented. The yoke is part of the deflection amplifier circuit, although it is shown as a separate element in Figure 4.4 for the purposes of this analysis and is included in the transfer function for the small signal response of the amplifier. This is not true for large inputs, which cause the amplifier to saturate, and the deflection time is initially determined by the time taken by the yoke to reach its required current for the particular deflection desired. This is the usual condition for all major deflections, consisting of moving the electron beam from one character position to the next character position, where the two positions are randomly related to each other, and may be a full CRT diameter apart. We may also note that by "character" we mean any designated shape, the start of a vector, or any other pictorial graphic element for which the starting point needs to be established.

The data-display unit contains some form of direct-view CRT, plus the deflection and video amplifiers and the power supplies and special circuits necessary to ensure proper operation of the CRT.

Given a step input of sufficient magnitude to saturate the amplifier, then the yoke time constant prevails, and the time required to reach some value of current (i) through the yoke is expressed by the standard time constant formula.

$$i = \frac{[1 - \exp(-Rt/L)]E}{R} \qquad (4.4)$$

where R = sum of yoke resistance and external series resistance
      L = yoke inductance
      E = B supply voltage

If Rt/L is much smaller than 1, this reduces to

$$i = \frac{Et}{L}$$

or

$$t = \frac{iL}{E} \qquad (4.5)$$

as an approximate formula in common use. The formula is correct to about 1% in calculating the time that it will take for the current in the yoke to reach 99% of its final value but may be error by as much as 25% for the 99.9% point. The latter is frequently used, so that equation 4.5 is only indicative, and equation 4.4 is the proper one to use for best accuracy. The significance of the time it takes the current through the yoke to reach some percentage of its final value, also known as *settling time*, is that the beam is moving during that time and will cause a smeared image unless the CRT is biased to cutoff until the beam is close enough to its final position so that the motion will be too small to be observable. Equation 1.21 indicates that this distance is about 0.1% of the CRT diameter for a viewing distance between two and three times the diameter, which is a usual distance, so that 0.1% settling time is a good value for avoiding smear. It should be understood that the writing of the character or other visual data does not begin until the beam has reached this point, and it is important to keep the deflection time as short as possible if we wish to attain any meaningful data density. This is as a result of the total frame time being limited by the need to have a refresh frequency above the CFF. In a manner parallel to equation 4.2, we may write the expression for the number of characters as

$$N_c = \frac{1}{f(t_d + t_c)} \tag{4.6}$$

where t_d is the character deflection time and t_c is the character writing time.

The character writing time is the time required to move the beam through the required pattern, which may be an alphanumeric or a full diameter vector and hence is variable in length. The character deflection time may also be made variable since it is a function of the amount of beam movement involved in going from one beam position to the next. In a fully random system this may range from a minimum of one character position to a maximum of a full diameter, and if the next deflection length is known, the blanking signal can be similarly varied in length. However, it is customary to use the maximum deflection as the standard and design the system as though each deflection were a full-diameter one, so that equation 4.6 applies. If a variable deflection time is used, the average deflection time will be approximately half the full deflection time, and the number of characters may be doubled for the same values of refresh frequency and deflection time if the character writing time is much smaller than the deflection time. In any event, it is clear that the minimum possible deflection time is a desideratum. Referring to equation 4.5, we see that this requires the highest E and the smallest IL that is compatible with cost and technology. Here we are constrained by the lowest inductance and the highest voltage that can be used while still providing enough current to deflect the beam, as defined by equation 2.57. Unfortunately, the deflection angle is proportional to the square root of the yoke inductance times the current, so that if we decrease the inductance, we must increase the current, although there is the advantage of the square-root factor. Increasing E is usually easier, and fast deflection systems use voltages in the order of 80 to 100 V. This leads to a power-dissipation problem, somewhat minimized by switching to a lower value of E (5 to 10 V) once the initial large deflection has been completed.

Next we come to the deflection amplifier driver stage itself. Of course, there are two of these, one for vertical and the other for horizontal deflection, just as there are two yokes. One basic configuration of a deflection amplifier driver stage is shown in schematic form in Figure 4.5, and the relation of the deflection yoke to the amplifier and the feedback loop is more clearly shown there. As we have noted, it is characteristic of such an amplifier that it will saturate when a step input of sufficient magnitude is applied to the input and thus break the feedback loop. However, for small-amplitude signals the loop is closed, and it is this closed-loop amplifier response that establishes the character writing times, as well as linearity and general fidelity of the image from a spatial sense. Therefore, it is important, in terms of what fidelity may be expected in the visual image, to know the response characteristics of the deflection amplifiers. The two types of inputs most commonly encountered are the small-signal step input and the ramp. The first may be used to move the beam small distances, for example, from one character position to another close by, and, as in the case of the large signal deflection, it is the settling time that signifies, as well as the overshoot, both of which may lead to blurring

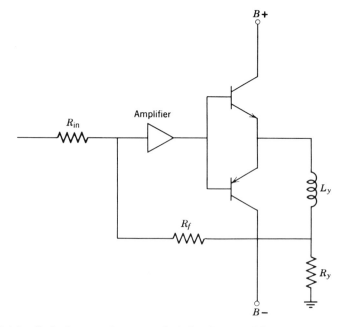

FIGURE 4.5   Cathode-ray-tube magnetic deflection amplifier driver stage schematic.

of the image. We find the time at which the overshoot is down to where the output amplitude is at a specified percentage of the final value by solving the simplified expression

$$a\% = 100 \times \frac{1}{(1 - \delta^2)^{1/2}} \exp(-\delta W_n t) \qquad (4.7)$$

where a = fraction of final value
$\quad\;\; \delta$ = damping factor
$\quad W_n$ = natural frequency

A curve of damping factor versus overshoot is shown in Figure 4.6 and illustrates the influence of this parameter on the final value of the deflection signal.

The response to a ramp input may also be expressed in simplified form as

$$C(t) = \frac{EK}{t_0} \frac{t - 2\delta}{W_n} \qquad (4.8)$$

where E = ramp amplitude
$\quad K$ = constant determined by gain and feedback parameters
$\quad t_0$ = ramp duration
$\quad t$ = time

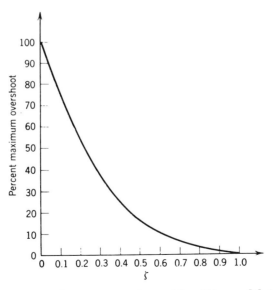

FIGURE 4.6   Damping factor vs. overshoot. After Shinners [2], by permission.

The second term in equation 4.8 indicates a delay that may be minimized by proper choice of the damping factor and the natural frequency. These are design parameters, and a properly designed deflection amplifier will keep this delay to a minimum. The linearity of the ramp response will depend on the gain versus amplitude constancy and is another important parameter of the amplifier. Finally, we are interested in the bandwidth, or step-function time response. This is given bv

$$T_r = \frac{0.45}{f_c} \tag{4.9}$$

where T_r is the time required for output to go from 10% to 90% and f_c is the amplifier 3-dB bandwidth.

The ramp response time may be similarly expressed as

$$T_r' = \frac{0.5}{f_c} \tag{4.10}$$

The ramp response time may also be expressed in terms of microvolts per microsecond or similarly related numbers.

The next part of the data-display unit to be considered is the video amplifier. This amplifier performs the function of intensifying the beam at the proper time, when it has reached the end of its travel and the character or vector writing begins. The usual equation for the bandwidth of this type of amplifier is the simple one derived from the time-constant response to a step, or

$$T_r'' = \frac{0.35}{f_c} \tag{4.11}$$

and either this or equation 4.9 may be used, depending on whether we have a first or a second-order system. As an example, if we require a video pulse width of 0.1 μs, which implies a rise time of less than 0.5 μs, then the bandwidth must be at least 9 MHz. We must also expect a dynamic range in the output of more than 50 V so as to be able to drive the CRT from cutoff to saturation. Typical video bandwidths are 10 to 30 MHz, with the higher value needed when very fast character writing times are used.

Data-Converter Unit. We may now go on to the data converter unit, which performs the all-important function of converting the digital data into the analog form required by the CRT. It consists of a number of different elements, as shown in Figure 4.7. The digital-to-analog converter (D/A converter) converts those bits in the digital word that represent the position information into an analog voltage of the proper amplitude to drive the deflection amplifier to the level needed to generate the necessary current in

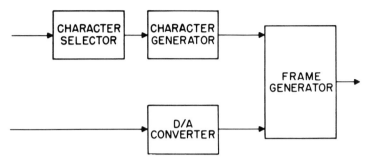

FIGURE 4.7   Block diagram of data converters.

the yoke. Since D/A converters are now available in either microcircuit or hybrid form, it is not important to examine all the detail involved in producing this conversion. Rather, we may limit ourselves to the relevant operating parameters and the general configuration. This configuration, illustrated in Figure 4.8, may all be contained in a single package or may have the reference voltage and the output amplifier as separate elements. The basic formula for the output voltage is

$$E_0 = E_r \sum_{n=1,2,3\dots n}^{n} \frac{R_f}{2^n R} \left[1 - \exp\left(\frac{-t}{\tau}\right) \right] \tag{4.12}$$

where E_r = reference voltage
   n = number of bits in digital input
   R_f = amplifier feedback resistor
   R = ladder network resistor
   τ = D/A time constant

We may deduce from equation 4.12 that the important parameters are the number of bits that can be accepted, the time constant, and the accuracies of the reference voltage and the resistors. A typical D/A specification will contain each of these values in the form of number of bits of resolution, the

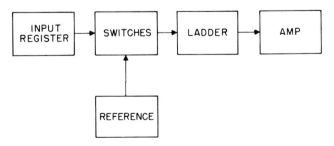

FIGURE 4.8   Digital-to-analog converter block diagram.

settling time to some fraction of the final value, and the absolute accuracy as a percentage of the maximum output voltage. The number of bits of resolution establishes the positional resolution in the displayed image, but it is important to recognize that this may not be the same as the actual visual resolution, which is determined by the spot size. This is frequently a source of misunderstanding, and the two types of resolution should be clearly defined as separate parameters. The positional resolution as defined by the D/A converter capability is usually greater than the visual resolution and is thus given greater prominence in the manufacturer's specification sheet, leading to the potential misunderstanding as to the meaningful resolution capability of the display system.

The next functional element in the data converter is the character generator. This unit performs the very important function of decoding the applicable bits in the data word and generating the deflection and video waveforms necessary to produce the visual image corresponding to the instruction. There are a number of ways to generate these signals, but we restrict ourselves to the two most popular, the dot matrix and the sequential stroke or cursive types. Several other techniques using the extruded beam CRT and the monoscope are described in Chapter 2, at least insofar as the basic process is concerned, and we do not expand on that description here. In addition, we limit character generation to mean alphanumerics and certain symbols, with vector and circle generators as separate functions, to be discussed next. The dot matrix character generator is the most popular type, available in many configurations and used extensively for the dot-matrix alphanumeric assemblies described in Chapter 3. There is some discussion of the dot matrix character generation technique there, and we expand on that discussion here. We have already noted in Chapters 1 and 3 that a full aphanumeric set plus the punctuation marks and some special symbols may be generated from the 5×7 or 7×9 matrices shown in Figures 1.25 and 1.26. Devices that output the proper waveforms (see Figure 3.89), on application of the appropriate number of inputs bits, are available from many sources, and use very similar formats, so that the choice of a source is controlled by factors of cost and reliability we must eschew from our considerations. The basic configuration used is that illustrated in Figure 4.9, which shows one form that a dot matrix character may take. The digital input may be either serial or parallel, and it is stored in a character store register that is long enough to contain all of the bits in the character select portion of the digital word. The character register has n output lines, where each line represents one bit of the character byte. The character decode logic selects one of 2^n lines, which then drives those elements of the character matrix that represent the character to be generated. The X counter steps through each X position, and the Y counter moves down a line at a time at the end of each X count, and each line of bits is transferred successively to a shift register, from which it is transferred out as a video signal by the X counter. This operation is depicted in Figure 4.10, which includes the character matrix for the letter E, where each dot represents a

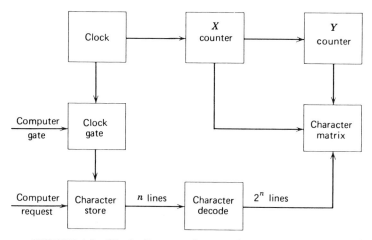

FIGURE 4.9   Block diagram of raster character generator.

gate. All these operations are performed in the character-generator chip, so it is not necessary to examine each step of the generation process, but it is useful to understand how the generator operates because of the impact it has on the video and deflection requirements for the deflection and video amplifiers of the display. For example, if we assume

$$\text{horizontal deflection speed} = 10 \ \mu s/cm$$

$$\text{vertical deflection speed} = 70 \ \mu s/cm$$

$$\text{dot resolution} = 0.02 \ cm$$

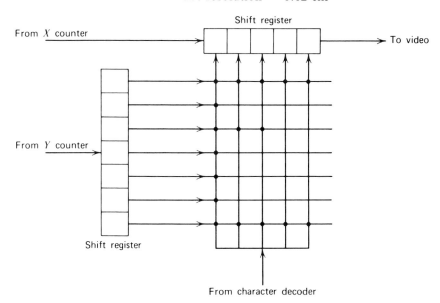

FIGURE 4.10   Video waveform diode matrix.

and for a 5×7 matrix character width and height of

$$W_c = 0.1 \text{ cm}$$

$$H_c = 0.14 \text{ cm}$$

this leads to a character writing time of

$$T_c = 10 \times 0.7 + 70 \times 0.14 = 16.8 \text{ } \mu s$$

assuming that each line is scanned one dot at a time. The time may be reduced to 8.4 μs by making the vertical deflection speed the same as the horizontal deflection speed, and the linear bandwidth of the deflection amplifiers, using equation 4.10, must be at least 625 kHz. However, this necessitates the use of a triangular scanning waveform, and the dots must be scanned first from left to right and next from right to left in sequence as the vertical scan steps down. A ramp waveform for scanning is more convenient but introduces the need for a rapid retrace, which might be 0.1 μs in our example, and the required bandwidth becomes 4.5 mHz, using equation 4.9. In either case, the small signal bandwidth is greater than that determined by the settling time capability in the large signal case and becomes the controlling factor in establishing bandwidth for the deflection amplifiers.

The video bandwidth may be calculated in a similar fashion. Since five dots must be scanned in 1 μs, or 0.2 μs per dot, this indicates a rise-time requirement of about 0.035 μs, resulting in a video bandwidth of 10 MHz, using equation 4.11. The video bandwidth comes from the consideration that individual video pulses may be as short as the video dot time, although some video pulses may be five dots long. An example of the different video pulse durations possible is shown in Figure 4.11, where the X and Y scanning waveforms and the video waveform for the letter "E" are illustrated. As noted, the X waveform may be a series of steps or the Y waveform a ramp, and the unit will still operate properly.

We may now write a complete specification for the character generator and the amplifiers following it. This is given in Table 4.1 and may be used as a prototype for this kind of specification. Higher character rates and/or more dots in the matrix require corresponding increases in these parameters. It can be seen that the dot matrix character generator leads to relatively simple circuits, with the main burden placed on the video portions, although high character rates will increase the difficulty in achieving sufficient small signal bandwidth in the deflection amplifiers. Due to its availability from many manufacturers in microcircuit form and its applicability to raster display systems, this is the most popular type of character generator, although it is somewhat limited by usually not having the capability for lowercase characters, or some special symbols.

The second form of character generator that we are considering is the one known by several names, among which cursive writing and sequential stroke

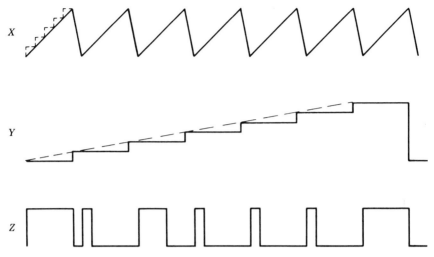

FIGURE 4.11   Raster generator waveforms for letter "E."

are the most common. Its unique feature is that it generates a succession of short strokes in sequence that are combined to form an approximation of written script or cursive writing. An example of such a stroke sequence for the letter "C" is shown in Figure 4.12, and 16 strokes are shown because this example is produced by a 16-stroke generator, with the dashed strokes not intensified. More or less strokes may be used, and in general the more strokes available, the better the appearance of the character. The strokes are produced by combining a repertoire of X and Y deflections, where each deflection may consist of one or more units in either the plus or minus direction. If we select $\pm X$ and $\pm Y$ as the available deflections, then there are two lengths and eight directions possible, whereas if we allow $\pm X$, $\pm Y$, $\pm 2X$, and $\pm 2Y$, then 24 different strokes are possible in the four quadrants, as shown in Figure 4.13. It is clear that there can be a further improvement in quality by going to an even larger repertoire, but unfortunately there is also some increase in complexity, so that it is not always feasible. In the interest of simplicity, we

TABLE 4.1   Character Generator Specifications

Parameter	Value	
	Dot	Stroke
Number of characters	64–128	64–128
Matrix or number of strokes	$5 \times 7, 7 \times 9$	16–24
Video amplifier bandwidth (MHz)	10–15	8–12
Line scanning or stroke time (μs)	0.5–1	0.1–0.2
Character time (μs)	10–20	2–4
Horizontal deflection bandwidth, (MHz)	0.6–5.0	6–10
Vertical deflection bandwidth (MHz)	0.4–3.5	6–10

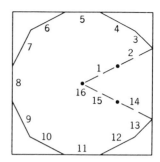

FIGURE 4.12 Stroke sequence for letter "C."

restrict the discussion to a 24-stroke system, which can achieve quite acceptable quality if enough character strokes are used, even though the actual repertoire is limited. The basic form of the sequential stroke character generator is illustrated by the block diagram shown in Figure 4.14 and represents one possible form that this type of generator may assume. Since there are no special chips available, each design may be unique, although it is feasible to create a medium scale integration (MSI) chip to perform the functions. Referring to Figure 4.14, the input character request bits set the states of the "n" bits in the character-store register, with each of the "n" output lines from the register corresponding to the state of the associated bit. The character decode block then decodes the "n" bits into one of the 2^n lines, where each line defines one of the 2^n possible characters. The selected line is routed by its character matrix so as to drive the appropriate stages in the various stroke determining m-bit registers, four of which are shown. The clock then shifts the registers out serially, so that each time slot will produce either a 1 or a

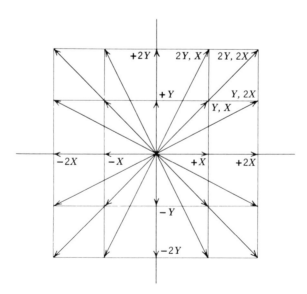

FIGURE 4.13 Twenty-four-stroke repertoire.

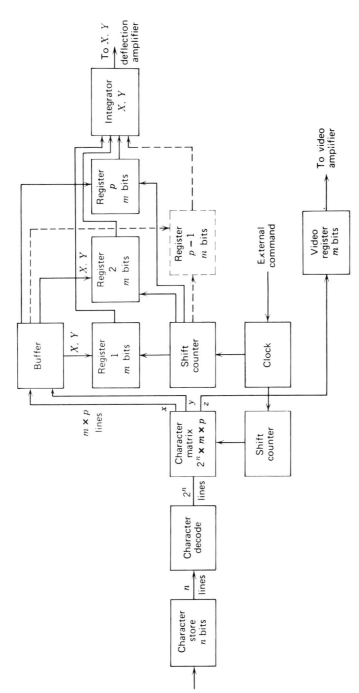

FIGURE 4.14 Block diagram of sequential-stroke character generator.

0, depending on the state of the register. The register outputs drive the X and Y integrators, and there are as many registers as there are X and Y values available. Finally, the video register outputs an intensification pulse at the times corresponding to the deflection strokes, so as to intensify the electron beam. As an example, assume a 64-character, 16-stroke generator with $\pm X$, $\pm 2X$, $\pm Y$, and $\pm 2Y$ as the available slopes. This results in values of 6 for n, 16 for m, and 8 for p, and the lines from the each element are 6, 64, and 128 up to the buffer. The character C (Figure 4.12), given this repertoire, may be traced out by means of the X and Y waveforms shown in Figure 4.15 from t_1 to t_{16} and the video waveform illustrated, with the character itself constructed on an 8×8 matrix. The actual form of the decoding matrix for the same letter is depicted in Figure 4.16, with each dot representing a diode or other type of gate. We can see that at time t_1 the X and Y waveforms are $(-X)$ and unit Y, respectively, whereas at time t_2 they are $(-2X)$ and unit Y, respectively, with a video pulse at each time interval. It should be recognized that time t_1 in Figure 4.16 corresponds to the time t_3 in Figure 4.15, with the first two time intervals used to deflect the beam to the starting point of the character. The other strokes are similarly decoded by the matrix, and each character in the total set has its own matrix. The actual waveforms are

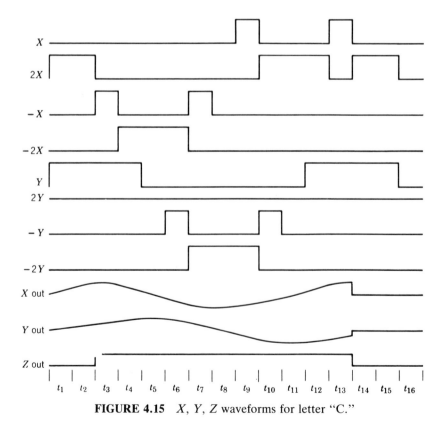

FIGURE 4.15 X, Y, Z waveforms for letter "C."

To all registers-one set per register

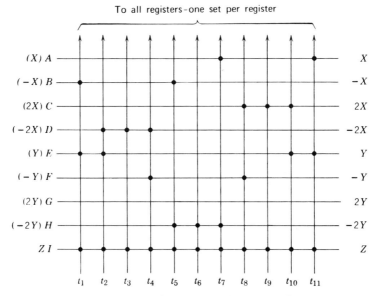

FIGURE 4.16   Diode matrix for letter "C."

generated by the integrators to which the pulses are applied, and the output voltages from the integrators are given by

$$E_o = \frac{E_i t}{RC} \tag{4.13}$$

where E_i is the input pulse amplitude, t the duration, and RC the time constant of the integrator. Thus a succession of ramps is generated that deflect the beam through the prescribed sequence and write the selected character.

One point that must be made about the sequential-stroke character generator is that when different slope ramps are used in the same time interval the speed of deflection, and thus the luminance of the line on the CRT will vary proportionately. In the case where three different levels of X and Y are used this variation may be as large as 5:1 and may create detectable differences in luminance within the character. Although it is possible to adjust for this variation by means of different amplitude video pulses, it is not very convenient, which is one reason for using the single-amplitude X or Y design, when possible. However, the single-amplitude approach will require as much as 50% more strokes, so the choice is not always easy to make.

A specification similar to that for the dot-matrix generator may also be written for the sequential-stroke type. The same considerations of deflection speed and amplifier bandwidth are involved. However, unless the unit X,Y deflection scheme is used, the maximum deflection speed required will be that for the largest deflection, which may be five times as long as the unit deflection. The time interval used for each deflection is determined by the number of strokes per character and the total character time allowed. Thus if we establish a character writing time of 1.6 μs and 16 strokes as the maximum number per character, then the stroke time is 100 ns, and the total bandwidth required is greater than 4 MHz, or 10 times the minimum needed for the dot matrix generator. This indicates a possibly significant advantage to using the dot matrix generator, against which must be balanced the potential improvement in quality of the image by using the sequential-stroke unit, although the data given in Chapter 1 do not indicate any significant improvement in legibility. Therefore, the choice may be made for esthetic reasons rather than to enhance the information transfer, unless special considerations such as the need for lowercase characters, special symbols, or typographical quality is involved, any of which may preclude the use of a dot matrix generator or make it necessary to employ a large matrix, thus negating the bandwidth advantage. Table 4.1 lists the relevant parameters of the two types of generators for comparison.

Although we have shown several other functional elements in the data-converter portion, we need not concern ourselves further with the symbol generator, since it is basically a specialized character generator and may use the same techniques that have been described for the alphanumeric version. Rather, we concentrate on the vector and circle generators as completing the group of data converters. We begin with the vector generator, also termed a *graphics* generator, as the more general form, of which the circle generator, or indeed any specific shape generator may be a special subgroup. The function of the vector generator is to provide X and Y deflection signals of the proper magnitude and direction to deflect the electron beam linearly from one specified location to another. The beam is intensified throughout the deflection period, in contradistinction to the major deflection period used to move the beam rapidly from one location to the next location at which writing begins. We may mention here, in anticipation of a fuller discussion later, that the vector or graphics generator is a basic functional element of the vector graphics systems covered in the equipment section of this chapter.

The basic structure of a vector generator, used for both simple lines and complex graphics images, is given in Figure 4.17. The vector writing operation is initiated by the receipt of the digital words designating the starting and stopping points of the vector in display coordinates. The two points are subtracted from each other to obtain the X and Y values for the vector length and are then converted by means of the D/A converters into the signal levels applied to the integrators, to generate the X and Y deflection ramps. Similarly, the duration of the video pulse may be derived directly from the digital word, as available through programming, or may be of a fixed duration designed into the generator. As in the case of the sequential-stroke character generator, a fixed-duration video pulse results in different speeds of deflection for different length vectors with the consequent variations in luminance, but it is much simpler to compensate by using different amplitude video pulses, since

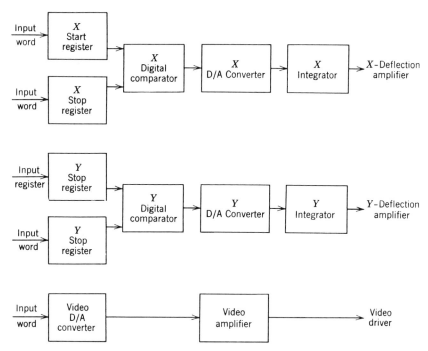

FIGURE 4.17   Block diagram of graphics vector generator.

the periods are much longer than in the previous case. Constant-slope vectors are also used when it is convenient to generate a variable duration video pulse, and this ensures constant luminance as well. The amplitudes and slopes of the deflection ramps must be compatible with the amplifier bandwidths, as previously, with the difference that the dynamic range is much larger, since the character generator outputs need deflect the beam only over small distances, whereas the vector generator must be capable of linearly deflecting the beam over a full diameter of the CRT. Thus the bandwidth requirement may be the same for both, but the linear dynamic range may be as much as 100 times greater.

The method described for determining the length of the video pulse assumes different time durations for different length deflections. As noted, this has the advantage of maintaining constant deflection speed, so that the line luminance is also constant. If a constant time video pulse is used, with variable-slope vectors, video compensation may be achieved with as few as three video levels, and not more than five. The video pulse amplitude may be derived directly from either the larger of the two deflection signals, or more accurately, from the vector sum of the two signals. Given a proper range of lengths and directions, the vector generator may be used to produce a large variety of vectors and other graphic forms, as is basic to any vector graphics system. Simplified versions, with a restricted number of lengths and directions, are also employed in the limited graphics systems described later and are common in many monitoring and control applications. When either variable time or variable amplitude video is used, the results are quite acceptable and cover a wide range of applications.

Other forms of generators that may be included are the circle and conic generators. Although reasonable facsimiles of circles may be achieved by using a vector generator with small enough increments and a sufficient number of slopes to produce a piecewise approximation, this may be very time consuming for large circles, and possibly visually inadequate. To overcome these objections, a separate circle generator is needed, which applies the time-honored and well known *Lissajous* techniques for generating circles and ellipses, so that symmetrical shapes may be formed in reasonable time periods. As is well known, the technique consists of applying equal sine and cosine waveforms to the X and Y deflection amplifiers, respectively, for the circles, and varying one or the other in fixed ratios to generate ellipses. This is usually the preferred method if more than a few circles are anticipated.

Finally, we have the most flexible type of vector generator, usually designated as a conic generator. It differs from the vector generator previously described in that other deflections than the straight lines produced by the standard vector generator may be achieved. In brief, conic curves are produced instead of the straight lines characteristic of vector generators, and smooth curves developed so that the visual image may be improved over that obtainable with a straight-line generator for those cases where a large number of complex curves is needed. In addition, the conic generator may be used for curves and ellipses, so that the circle generator is eliminated. One form of conic generator is illustrated in Figure 4.18, and designs accepting com-

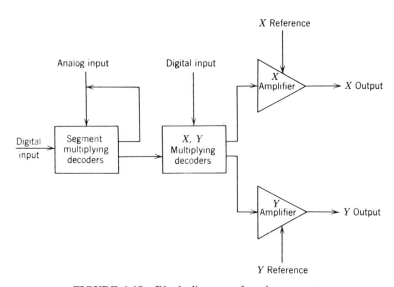

FIGURE 4.18   Block diagram of conic generator.

pletely digital inputs are also available. The system operates by means of special algorithms that convert input points into the curves necessary to represent the visual image. It is claimed that this approach simplifies the input of graphic information in that curved shapes can be represented by digitizing only a few points along the contour, so that data-input reductions greater than 10:1 are possible. This is essentially a curve-fitting software technique, with the resultant curves produced by the conic generator. The generator is available as a separate piece of equipment and may be incorporated in a display system by using it in place of the various generators, or a total system may be obtained with the conic generator as the unique element. If it is desired to use the generator alone, the system must contain a display processor of sufficient speed and capacity to perform the data transformations required. Such a system may be useful when high-quality, complex images are involved, although its advantage for simpler graphics is moot.

Refresh Memory. Leaving the data-converter group, we come next to the logic that selects those bits of the digital word that pertain to the various elements of that group and routes them to the appropriate element. This may be done by placing the entire word in a register and then reading out the bits in parallel, under control of the system clock if the bits are read out from the refresh memory in serial form, or routing them directly from the memory if parallel readout is used. In either case, this routing logic is intimately associated with the refresh memory that we now consider. There fresh memory performs the function of storing at least one full frame of information in digital form and outputting it at a sufficiently high rate to avoid flicker in the visual image. As discussed in Chapter 1, this rate must be higher than 45 Hz at the usual levels of luminance employed, and 60 Hz is a common rate to permit locking on to the line frequency, thus avoiding beats between the line frequency and the refresh frequency. These beats may create unwanted luminance variations that appear like low-frequency flicker and cannot be eliminated by merely raising the refresh frequency a small amount. It is possible to minimize the beats due to electrical interactions by carefully shielding all line-frequency components and filtering the power supply adequately. However, there is another source of beats not as simple to eliminate. This is due to the reflections from the CRT face, coming from fluorescent lighting that has significant components at 60 Hz. These reflections may interact optically with the displayed image and produce visual beats that are as undesirable as those generated electrically. Since fluorescent light has components over the entire visual spectrum, peaking in the green region, it is difficult to filter out these components optically, and, unless the reflections are at a very low level, the visual beat will be quite perceptible. Thus the display-system designer is caught between the desire to use the lowest refresh frequency to allow the largest amount of data to be presented and the need to avoid the beat effects. The latter is easiest to achieve by operating at the line frequency and locking the refresh frequency to the line frequency.

The advantage in operating at the lowest possible refresh frequency is demonstrated by examining the equation for refresh time.

$$T_R = T_C X + T_S Y + T_D(X + Y) \tag{4.14}$$

where T_R = refresh time
T_C = character time
X = number of characters
T_L = average line or vector time
Y = number of lines
T_D = deflection time

It is apparent, that as any one of the terms on the right-hand side of equation 4.14 is increased, the refresh time is increased and thus the refresh frequency is decreased. This sets an upper limit on the number of characters and lines that can be displayed, once the refresh time is set, and makes it desirable to operate at the lowest possible refresh frequency. For example, if we use representative numbers, such as

$$T = 2 \ \mu s$$

$$X = 1000$$

$$T_L = 50 \ \mu s$$

$$Y = 200$$

$$T_D = 10 \ \mu s$$

Then T_R is 15,000 μs and the refresh frequency is 66.66 Hz. Clearly, it is advantageous to operate at the lowest acceptable refresh frequency, and in some cases this frequency is made variable to accommodate increases in data density for short periods of time whole accepting the flicker that may result. The other parameters of the refresh memory of interest are the capacity and access time previously referred to and defined by equations 4.1 and 4.2 or 4.3. Capacities over several hundred thousand bits and access times less than 1 μs are common and are usually adequate for most applications. A nominal frame of information may contain 2000 words of information, with each word made up of 30 bits, or 60,000 bits total, and will require access times of under 10 μs for each group of 30 bits.

The most common form of refresh memory is the solid-state memory. The solid-state memory has the full capacity for at least one frame of information and is the only refresh memory required by the system. This type is usually in the form of an array of metal oxide silicon field-effect transistors (MOS-FETS), arranged in the configuration shown in Figure 4.19, or some similar flip-flop type of connection. Figure 4.19 represents a single cell, and there

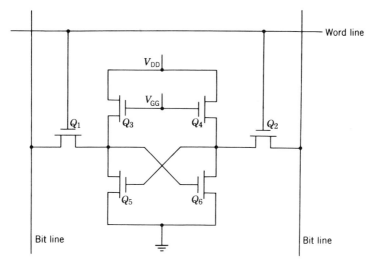

FIGURE 4.19   Six-transistor static MOS cell. After Frankenberg [3], by permission.

are as many cells as there are bits to be stored. The cell is written into by turning the word line on, thus either switching Q_5 and Q_6 off the turning Q_1 and Q_2 on if they are in the alternative condition, representing a "1," or causing no change if they are already in the "0" state. The readout is accomplished by turning the word line on the sensing the polarity of the differential current between the BIT and $\overline{\text{BIT}}$ lines. Other configurations and both p and n MOS types are also used. This form of memory is random access so that data may be written in any sequence and read out in any other sequence. It may also be volatile in some configurations, in which case the contents of the memory must be rewritten periodically if it is desired to retain the information when the memory is not being used to refresh the display. In any event, the information must be rewritten every refresh cycle to insure that no data are lost. Data rates of under 1 µs and capacities of over 2000 words make this type of memory compatible with the requirements of display systems, and their relatively low bit cost results in economic acceptability.

Processing Unit. Finally, we arrive at the last functional element in the chain depicted in Figure 4.3, which is the system logic or processing unit. It may, in its simplest form, consist only of wired logic to perform the minimal required operations of interface, coordinate conversion, timing, format, and control, with all other processing performed in the host computer, but with the advent of the microcomputer it has become more common to have all these functions resident in the local dedicated microprocessor, and the capabilities of the system have been expanded to include a variety of other functions. It is thus necessary to introduce some description of the structure and operation a microcomputer at this point, although we do not become involved in any extensive description since we are interested only in those functions unique to the display system.

A microcomputer is the same in all its basic attributes as any digital computer, differing from its mini- and macroequivalents primarily in the size of the memory and in the number of commands available for programming. Thus it may be represented, in its most rudimentary form, by the block diagram shown in Figure 4.20, arranged to reveal its conventional computer structure. The input, output, and memory units are usually expandable, with the amount of expansion determined by the number of input/output ports available and the manner in which the memory is made accessible. Both random access and read-only memories (RAM and ROM) may be used and are available as peripheral devices. We have not discussed the latter type as yet, but it is essentially of the same general structure as the RAM, except that it contains a fixed arrangement of bits, and data can be transferred out without altering this fixed arrangement. The various solid-state character generators previously described are of the ROM type, and a variety of different programs may be stored in the memory or created by means of the programmable read only memory (PROM), which is a memory that can be made to contain specific configurations unique to the requirements of the display system. A typical microprocessor will have the required memory capacity, either as part of the basic computer central processing unit (CPU) or as specially designed peripherals for use with the CPU. Large amounts of memory, amounting to as much as or more than 640 kilobytes, may be directly addressed, and auxiliary memory may be maintained on disk or tape. Thus a microprocessor is a very powerful machine for display-system purposes, and may be expected to become an integral part of most display systems. The one potential drawback in the use of a microprocessor is the need to write the necessary programs to perform the desired functions. This may involve more effort, when only a few simple functions are involved, than wiring in the functions directly. However, display systems with their logic limited to only the minimum functions are becoming less common, and the increased

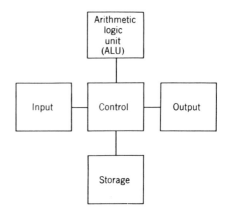

FIGURE 4.20   Microcomputer simplified block diagram.

versatility and flexibility offered by the incorporation of the microcomputer directly into the display system is of great value, particularly in the so-called intelligent terminals, discussed later in the equipment section. It is apparent that a new concept—namely, programming—must be considered when the microcomputer is used, and whereas we have no intention to present any detailed discussion of programming here, as being well beyond the scope of this book, a few comments appear to be in order to enhance the understanding of the use of a microcomputer in a display system. First, it should be understood that the microcomputer is essentially a logic machine, capable of performing the various logical operations under control of a set of instructions stored in the memory. The sequence and form of these instructions constitute the program of the machine, and various languages have been developed to enable programs to be written without knowing anything about the actual structure of the machine. These general-purpose languages, known by various acronyms such as FORTRAN and BASIC, are constructed in such a way that the user, once he has learned the set of instructions and the manner in which the program should be written, may proceed to construct programs independent of the machine to be used.

This completes our traversal of the elements making up a vector graphics display system, with the exception of the input devices. Since those are the same for the raster and storage systems described later, we defer any description of these devices until we have completed the discussion of the other display systems. However, before we embark on the raster system we must return to the data-display unit to provide more detail on the units employing electrostatic deflection CRTs as the display device. The other elements of the system are the same as for the magnetic deflection unit but the use of an electrostatic deflection CRT does introduce different factors into the operation of the data-display unit and thus into the operation of the total system.

Electrostatic Deflection CRT Monitor. The electrostatic deflection CRT monitor is shown in block diagram form in Figure 4.21, and equation 2.47 is the

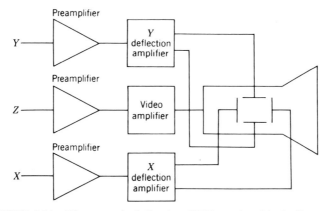

FIGURE 4.21   Electrostatic deflection CRT monitor block diagram.

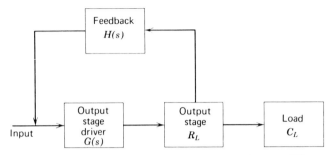

FIGURE 4.22   Block diagram of CRT electrostatic deflection amplifier output driver.

relevant expression for deflection. In this case we are dealing with deflection voltages, rather than deflection currents, and with the characteristics of the deflection plates. These plates are driven by electrostatic deflection amplifiers, and we are primarily concerned with the relationship between the output driver, shown in block diagram form in Figure 4.22, and the load time constant as represented by the RC network depicted in Figure 4.23. This load-time constant consists of the total capacity of the deflection plates and associated wiring, and the resistive component of the output stage. We may then write the expression for the settling time of the output stage as

$$aE_f = E_d \exp\left(-\frac{t}{\tau}\right) \tag{4.15}$$

where a = fraction or percentage of full-scale voltage = $(E_f - E_d)/E_f$
$\quad E_f$ = full-scale voltage
$\quad E_d$ = actual deflection voltage
$\quad\ t$ = time to arrive at desired fraction
$\quad\ \tau$ = time constant $(R_L C_L)$

For example, if

$$t = 10 \ \mu\text{s}$$

$$a = 0.001 \ (0.1\%)$$

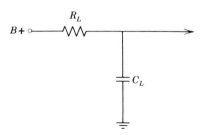

FIGURE 4.23   Load-time constant.

then

$$0.001 = \exp\left(-\frac{t}{\tau}\right)$$

$$\frac{t}{\tau} = 7$$

$$\tau = 1.5 \ \mu s$$

$$R_L C_L = 1.5 \ \mu s$$

Since C_L is usually about 100 pF, R_L must be 15,000 Ω, which is quite reasonable. Indeed, with the high-deflection-sensitivity CRTs available, a value of 1500 Ω for R_L is usable and permits the time t to be reduced to close to 1 μs. This shows that electrostatic-deflection, data-display monitors may be designed to achieve a deflection speed of 1 to 2 μs without any special difficulties and demonstrates the major advantage of this type of unit. This is possible because the time constant is much shorter than that attainable with magnetic deflection units, and the required maximum voltage swing of 1000 V for a 50-cm-diameter CRT requires less than 1 A of current. Of course, some penalty is paid in luminance and resolution, as described in Chapter 2, but not enough to make the speed advantage trivial. Thus it is completely feasible to use an electrostatic unit in a vector graphics system, if speed is required, without changing the rest of the system except that more rapid operation of the other elements is possible. Thus far we have dealt only with the large signal response to a step input, but we are also interested in the small-signal linear response, as we were for the magnetic deflection amplifier. The complete expression for small-signal step response is rather complicated, but a simplified expression that might be used for analysis is

$$C(t) = E_1 m\left[1 - \exp\left(-\frac{tA}{m\tau}\right)\right] \qquad (4.16)$$

where E_1 = pulse amplitude
     m = feedback ratio
     A = amplifier gain

This is the same as the standard time-constant formula, modified by A/m, and the settling time is given by

$$t_s = \frac{7m}{A} \qquad (4.17)$$

for 0.1% settling. The pulse rise time is calculated from equation 4.9 and the ramp response, from equation 4.10, with the substitution of the appropriate small-signal bandwidths. Since bandwidths of 4 mHz are easily obtained, rise times of 0.1 µs and ramp responses of the same order are possible. Thus we may conclude that an electrostatic-deflection-data-display unit offers excellent response under all operating conditions.

4.3.3 Raster (Analog) System

System Configurations. A raster system has as its prototype the standard television configurations and formats that are so common and well known. In general, raster systems may include any preorganized deflection patterns, and these are found in a number of scanning sequences and number of scanning lines. The basic patterns are shown in Figure 4.24, where the noninterlaced pattern has each line scanned in sequence from the top to the bottom with the dashed lines not visible. These lines occur during what is termed the *retrace time*, with the line-to-line retrace called the *line retrace*, and the bottom to top retrace called the *frame* or *field retrace*, depending on whether the noninterlaced or interlaced pattern is used. The interlaced pattern is the same as the standard television scanning format, with the number of lines, the time required for each line, and the retrace times, depending on the scanning standard.

The main television scanning formats are NTSC, PAL, and SECAM, and they differ in frame rate and number of lines per frame. In addition, high-definition television has introduced a number of new formats, with the final choice for the United States still to be determined. In addition, a number of other factors such as horizontal and vertical blanking time, aspect ratio, and video bandwidth are established by the applicable standards. Table 4.2 contains a list of applicable standards.

PAL and SECAM are the European standards and differ only in the color-coding technique. NTSC is the U.S. standard and we use the convention of 525 scanning lines, 30 Hz per frame, and 60 Hz per field, with each field containing half the number of lines, either all odd or all even. The 60-Hz field rate is chosen instead of the exact rate of 59.94 Hz for simplicity, and

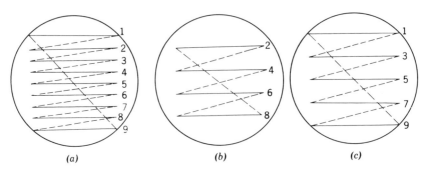

FIGURE 4.24   Raster scan patterns: (*a*) noninterlaced; (*b*) interlaced even lines; (*c*) interlaced odd lines.

TABLE 4.2 Television Standards

Standard	Field Rate (Hz)	Frame (Hz)	Horizontal (kHz)	Lines/Frame	Field
NTSC	59.94	30	15.750	525	262.5
PAL	50	25	15.625	625	312.5
SECAM	50	25	15.625	625	312.5
HDTV (NHK)	60	30	33.750	1125	562.5
HDTV (NBC)	60	60	45.000	750	750.0
HDTV (NBC)	59.94	30	31.500	1050	525.0

it is within the acceptable tolerance. The exact field rate was chosen to be compatible with the line frequency and need not concern us. Further detail on the NTSC system and the manner in which all of the relevant parameters were determined may be found elsewhere, but only those parameters shown in Table 4.2 are significant to the discussion in this section.

A few additional standards of interest that should be mentioned are the Electronics Industry Association (EIA) standards RS-170, RS-330, and RS-343. These are industrial and studio standards, related to NTSC by operating at 60 Hz, with RS-170 essentially equivalent to NTSC, RS-330 slightly different in that some of the horizontal timing relationships are rounded off, and RS-343 adding a number of additional scan rates. Table 4.3 includes some of the relevant parameters added by these standards, and the full standards can be obtained from EIA. Finally, there are the graphics standards used for computer systems. These are the CGA, EGA, VGA, Super VGA, and 8514, which specify the display resolution, and are shown in Table 4.4. CGA and EGA are in limited use and have largely been superseded by the others.

TABLE 4.3 EIA Raster Standards

Scan Rates[a]	Horizontal Line Time (μs)	Horizontal Frequency (MHz)	Horizontal Blank Time (μs)
525	63.5	15.748	11.1
729	45.7	21.881	8.0
875	38.0	26.315	6.7
945	35.2	28.409	6.2
1023	32.6	30.675	5.7
1029	32.4	30.865	5.7
1225	27.2	36.765	4.76
Standards			
RS-170[a]	63.5	15.748	11.1
RS-330[a]	63.5	15.748	11.0
RS-343[a,b]	49.3	20.284	8.6

[a]Vertical scan rates are all 30 Hz, 2:1 interlace.
[b]Horizontal scan rates are from 675 to 1023.

TABLE 4.4 Graphics Display Standards

Standard	Number of Colors	Resolution
CGA (color graphics adapter)	4	320 × 200
CGA	2	640 × 200
EGA (enhanced graphics adapter)	16	640 × 350
VGA (video graphics array)	16	640 × 480
VGA	256	320 × 200
S-VGA (super VGA)	256	800 × 600
S-VGA	16	1024 × 768
8514/A	256	1024 × 768

System Configurations: Analog. Returning to the interlace pattern shown in Figure 4.24*b* and *c*, since the adjacent lines are in different fields, the eye response to the frame as though it were at 60 Hz rather than at 30 Hz, and flicker is avoided while dividing deflection speed and the required video bandwidth in half: Each scanning line takes 58 μs, and the time available to return from the end of one line to the beginning of the next is about 5 μs, which is the retrace time. These numbers are, of course, changed when either the number of scanning lines, the frame rate, or both are different from the 525-line, 30-Hz standard, and the selected combination has impact on the requirements for the deflection and video amplifiers, as well as on the visual characteristics of the display image, as is discussed later.

There are several types of raster display systems, which may be divided into the two general categories of analog and digital. The analog system is one in which all data are obtained in analog form and handled by the system without converting them into digital signals at any point. This approach is represented by the system shown in Figure 4.25. It consists of three main elements, the data-display unit or monitor, the raster generator, and the synchronizer unit equivalent to the timing and control portion of the vector system, and the various image converters, similar in function to the data converters of the vector system. In spite of the similarity in function of the elements in the two types of systems, the raster system elements perform these functions in a unique way and warrant a separate description.

Data-Display Unit. Beginning, as before, with the data-display unit, it consists of the CRT, usually a magnetic deflection, electrostatic focus type, its associated *X* and *Y* deflection yokes, and the amplifiers needed to drive these yokes. To these must be added the video amplifier and, in some cases, an independent raster generator, driven from a common synchronizer unit. The yokes, although basically the same as those used for the vector display unit, are much higher in inductance than those required for the vector unit, because the deflection speed is so much slower—58 μs for the horizontal time, as compared with the 10 μs or less needed for the other system. This speed and

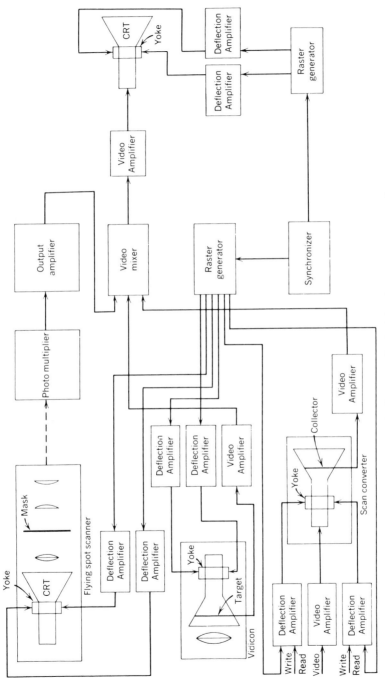

FIGURE 4.25 Block diagram of television image-converter subsystem.

the vertical deflection rate are of prime importance, with the horizontal deflection time of significance in determining horizontal deflection and video amplifier characteristics, whereas the field rate of 60 Hz similarly establishes a vertical deflection time of 15 ms and a retrace time of 1.6 ms and specifies the vertical deflection-amplifier characteristics.

The horizontal deflection amplifier may be either a linear amplifier with a bandwidth adequate to handle a 58-μs ramp or a large signal pulse amplifier with a rise time appropriate for the 58-μs ramp. In the case of the pulse amplifier we may assume that approximately a 48-μs rise time is adequate, and by using equation 4.9 the bandwidth (BW) is obtained as

$$ \text{BW} = \frac{0.45}{0.48} = 1 \text{ MHz} $$

This may be compared with the 4-MHz bandwidth and less than 10-μs pulse rise time required for the random deflection amplifier. Clearly, this type of raster deflection system imposes much less severe requirements than does the usual random-deflection system.

Thus far we have dealt only with the ramp voltage used to provide the horizontal sweep. However, there is the need to handle the retrace of 5 μs, which could impose a 5-μs settling time on the amplifier, and this would be more severe than the random-deflection system. However, there is an expedient that permits the relatively slow system to handle a 5-μs retrace when magnetic deflection is used, as is the case in the majority of television monitors. Known as *resonant flyback*, this operates by using the self-resonant frequency of the deflection yoke to generate a fast reverse voltage when hit by the ramp voltage return. The resonant flyback causes the yoke to ring for one cycle of the resonant frequency and is independent of the amplifier bandwidth. The amplifier is not in the linear mode during flyback, as it is during the forward deflection period, and may not be used for beam positioning to any location other than that caused by the resonant flyback, but it is entirely adequate for returning the beam to the starting point during the horizontal flyback time. Thus a moderate-speed amplifier serves a high-speed function, and a high yoke inductance permits low yoke currents and low power consumption.

The vertical-deflection amplifier has much less rigid specifications since it has to respond to a sweep rate of 60 Hz or 16,666 μs and a retrace time of about 1600 μs, which impose no problems and are readily met by all equipment except only in the case where it is desired to use the retrace period for some purpose such as writing random characters. In this case linear high-speed amplifiers are required and the considerations adduced for random deflection amplifiers apply.

The video amplifier bandwidth requirement is determined by the combination of the frame or field rate, the number of lines per frame of field, and the number of resolution elements per line. An expression for the cutoff frequency is

$$f_c = \frac{4.493}{2\pi} \frac{w}{h} n^2 N \qquad (4.18)$$

where w/h = aspect ratio ($\frac{4}{3}$ for standard television)
$\quad\quad n$ = number of lines
$\quad\quad N$ = frame rate (frames per second)

Another form of equation 4.18 uses the standard video bandwidth expression

$$BW = 0.45n^2N \qquad (4.19)$$

Using standard television numbers of

$$N = 30 \text{ F/s}$$

$$n = 525$$

then

$$BW = 4 \text{ MHz}$$

where equation 4.18 gives the result

$$f_c = 8 \text{ MHz}$$

Since the standard television bandwidth is 4 MHz, equation 4.19 is adequate. However, for good pulse response, equation 4.19 should be used, and for true high resolution about 25% more bandwidth than that indicated by equation 4.18 is required. This leads to 8 MHz and 10 MHz, respectively, and a good monitor for a 525-line system will have at least 10-MHz bandwidth, approximately equal to the bandwidth requirement for the video amplifier used in a random deflection system, and for comparable horizontal resolution there is no advantage for the raster system. However, if we assume a 10-raster-line-high by seven-element-wide-character window, corresponding to a 7 × 5 character matrix, then for 470 lines and 470 horizontal elements there is a maximum character density of over 3000 characters, which appears better than the 2000 possible with the vector system operating at 50 Hz. Unfortunately, the raster system cannot be operated at its full density without possible flicker, since any single horizontal line such as might appear at the top of an "E" would be refreshed at 30 Hz and would flicker at moderate luminance. Thus the raster system is usually arranged so that the same data appear on both fields, resulting in a 60-Hz refresh, which is good, and half the number of lines, which is not so good. In spite of this restriction, 2000-character raster systems are quite common, and the vast majority of alphanumeric and limited graphics terminals are of the raster type. This is discussed further in section 4.7.

Kell Factor.   The analog raster system shown in Figure 4.25 is a quite effective means for producing visual images from several sources but has one significant limitation resulting from the scanning process. Since the input data are stored in locations that have no fixed relationship to the placement of the scanning beams it is possible for the scanning beam to only partially traverse the data poings or possible miss some of them entirely. This is illustrated in Figure 4.26, and the resultant loss in information is know as the *Kell factor*. The resolution of the system is effectively reduced by about 30% from what it would be if all points were scanned, and this loss in resolution may be detrimental to the total system performance.

The effect of the Kell factor on both the horizontal and vertical resolution can be determined by using equations that relate the resolutions to the bandwidth, and then multiplying the result by the Kell factor. The horizontal resolution in TV lines per picture height is given by

$$\text{horizontal resolution (HR)} = 2 \times \text{BW} \times \frac{\text{AST}}{\text{AR}} \qquad (4.20a)$$

where BW = bandwidth = 4.2 MHz for NTSC
    AST = active line scan time = 53.5 μs (NTSC)
      AR = aspect ratio = $\frac{4}{3}$ (NTSC)

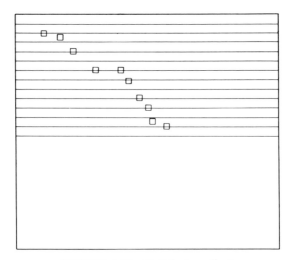

FIGURE 4.26   Kell factor effect.

and using the NTSC values

$$HR \simeq 330 \, \frac{TVL}{PH} \, \frac{(TV \, Lines)}{(Picture \, Height)}$$

The vertical resolution is given by

$$vertical \, resolution \, (VR) = ASL \times Kell \, factor \qquad (4.20b)$$

where ASL = active number of scan lines = 484 (NTSC)
    KF = Kell factor $\simeq 0.7$

or

$$VR \simeq 484 \times 0.7 = 338.8$$

Thus the vertical and horizontal resolutions are approximately the same, which is a desirable condition.

It is of some interest to compare the resolutions resulting from the scanning and video bandwidth values used for the PAL and HDTV systems. These are shown in Table 4.5, as calculated using equation 4.20a and the other parameter values as listed in this table.

Raster Generators and Image Converters. Associated with the data-display unit, either as part of the monitor or as a separate sweep generator unit, are the horizontal and vertical deflection raster generators. These circuits provide the sawtooth signals used for horizontal and vertical deflection that are applied to the X and Y deflection amplifiers that drive the yokes and cause the electron beam to follow the patterns given in Figure 4.24. In the system shown in Figure 4.25 the raster generator associated with the data-display units is synchronized with the one used to scan the several types of image converters

TABLE 4.5   Television Parameters

	System			
Parameter	NTSC	PAL	NHK	Sarnoff/NBC
Aspect ratio	4:3	4:3	5.33:3	5.33:3
Scan lines	525	625	1125	1050
Active scan lines	484	576	1035	966
Scan format	2:1	2:1	2:1	2:1
Rate (Hz)	59.94	50	60	60
Video bandwidth (MHz)	4.2	5.0	27	29
Horizontal resolution (TVL/PH)	330	400	785	580
Vertical resolution (TVL/PH)	338	400	725	508

Source: After Lechner [4].

shown, although, as noted above, it is possible to use a single-raster generator for all units, so that no synchronizer is needed.

However, for the sake of standardization of the monitor, it usually includes it own raster generators, and a separate synchronizer is required. Two of the image converters included in the analog television system are fully described in Chapter 2 and are not discussed further here, except insofar as their operation in this system is concerned. These are the scan converter and Vidicon units, used respectively for electrical and visual inputs. The signals that are stored on the cathode-ray devices are scanned out in synchronism with the scan of the CRT, and the video signals are applied to the grid of the display CRT so that the result is a visual image corresponding to the original information. This illustrates an important feature of the raster system, namely, that electrically and visually produced information may be combined in the final image. The third converter is included merely to illustrate another means for entering information into the system and consists of a high-resolution CRT whose beam is made to scan some type of transparent mask, again in synchronism with the display raster, and the output light passing through the mask is converted by means of a photosensitive device such as a photomultiplier into the video signal that is mixed with the other two signals through the video amplifier. This flying-spot scanner is a device somewhat similar in its operation to the monoscope described in Chapter 2 but uses an external mask with the light beam from the CRT focused on it, instead of the secondary emission mask contained within the vacuum envelope for the monoscope. The light beam performs the same function for the flying-spot scanner as the electron beam does for the monoscope, and the transparent mask is the equivalent of the secondary emission mask. The input to the photomultiplier is determined by the CRT spot luminance and the optical density of the mask, whereas the photomultiplier output is controlled by these factors as well as the photomultiplier sensitivity. Thus we may write

$$i_p = L_f T_m S_p \qquad (4.21)$$

where i_p = photomultiplier output current
L_f = CRT luminance
T_m = mask transmission
S_p = photomultiplier sensitivity factor

The actual structure of a photomultiplier is somewhat complex, and we do not go into it further here, other than to note that it contains a photosensitive cathode followed by a number of secondary multiplication dynodes to increase its sensitivity, as shown in Figure 4.27, in a manner similar to that described for the image orthicon. Thus it functions in some respects like an image-pickup tube and may be thought of as a specialized type of this category of cathode-ray devices. At any rate it converts visible light into electrical signals and thus acts as another form of image converter.

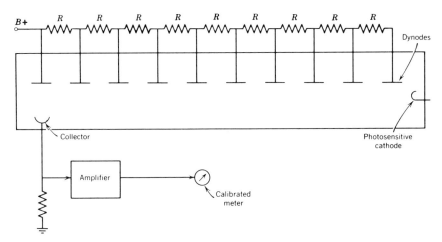

FIGURE 4.27   Photomultiplier schematic diagram.

Bit-Mapped (Digital) System. Bit-mapped raster systems were originally referred to as digital television and subsequently as *digital scan conversion.* At
present, the first term is reserved for TV systems that employ digital transmission of the station signal, and the second exclusively for systems that
convert from one type of signal to another. However, the digital scan conversion process is essentially the same as that used for the bit-mapped system,
and the following discussion applies to both. with the only difference being
the inclusion of an output display unit in the bit-mapped system. In addition,
there is another more important distinction in bit-mapped systems between
a limited-graphics or alphanumeric system and a full-graphics system, and
these two types are described separately, beginning with the full-graphics
system as containing all of the essential elements, and then going to the simpler
and more limited form represented by the other configuration. Alphanumeric
terminals have been leaving the marketplace with the reduced cost and high-
performance capabilities of modern desktop and portable computers, but
there is some return in the growth of X terminals, which have considerable
resemblance to limited-graphics systems and should be covered here. In any
event, each system type accepts data in digital form and then converts them
into raster form for presentation.

The basic structure of a full-graphics system is shown in Figure 4.28 and
represents that portion of the total bit-mapped system between the data
sources and the display monitor. As noted previously, it may also be considered as a digital scan converter. The conversion to raster format and the
generation of the video signal are done by logical elements, and the signal
storage required for such conversion is accomplished by digital rather than
analog memory units. In general terms, the process is analogous to that used
by the television camera or the analog scan converter. Just as these devices
construct an electrical equivalent of the visual scene or of the electrical input
in the same format as the final viewed image, so does the digital converter

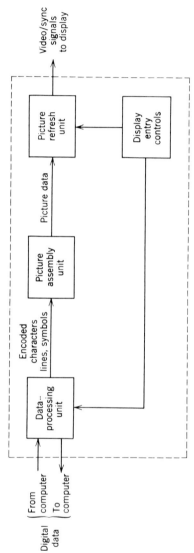

FIGURE 4.28 Simplified bit-mapped television system block diagram. After Sherr [5], by permission.

construct an electrical equivalent in dot raster form of the digital input. Referring to Figure 4.29, which is an expansion in one specific configuration of the basic block diagram shown in Figure 4.28, the data-processing unit receives the computer generated data as digital words, in any sequence, and containing the X and Y coordinate addresses as well as the coded designations of symbols, alphanumerics, lines, or other conics. The digital input may also be the elements of a digitized picture or other visual data. These data are stored in the input buffer memory, still in computer or other digital word format, and then decoded by the program logic to address the generators. The operation of these generators is described later, and at this point we discuss system operation only. The outputs of the generators are directed by means of the write, read, and address logic to the appropriate locations in the memory portion of the picture assembly unit, where the decoded words are stored as a geometric pattern that duplicates the visual image to be displayed in electrical "1s" and "0s." This memory may then be scanned out and used as the refresh memory for the display, or it may have its contents transferred to some type of rotating memory that acts as the refresh memory for its associated display unit, while the picture assembly unit memory is being used to form another picture for a different display unit. By this means a single-picture assembly unit memory may be used for a number of display units, and the cost of multiple large RAMs may be minimized. The reason for the high cost of the RAM is that one memory element is needed for each element in the display, so that for a 1000×1000 element display, 10^6 memory elements are required. However, with the rapidly falling costs of solid-state memories, this may not be excessive, and a separate RAM for each display may be quite reasonable. The other operations shown in the picture refresh unit block are necessary in either case, with the synchronization-generator performing the same function as for the analog system. Similarly, the parallel-to-serial conversion is necessary to go from the slower access time of the memory to the fast access required by the display unit, as has been noted previously, and equations 4.2 and 4.3 are the relevant relationships. Using 60 μs per line and 500 data elements, if the memory time is 1 μs, then eight elements in parallel are sufficient, and that is the required length for the parallel to serial video conversion register, although two registers are necessary, with one filled while the other is emptied. These registers are scanned out in sequence, in synchronization with the scan used in the display monitor, and provide the video signal for the monitor. Only two video levels are possible with this arrangement, and additional bits must be used to define multiple video levels, or gray shades, leading to an expansion of the memory size. Also, some decoding is necessary to convert the bits into levels.

Returning to the manner in which the digital inputs are converted into the memory-plane equivalent of the visual image, this is illustrated in Figure 4.30. For ease of explanation, the picture assembly unit memory is considered to be a single rectangular array, and the purpose of the logic is to selectively place bits in the appropriate areas to form the electrical image of the desired

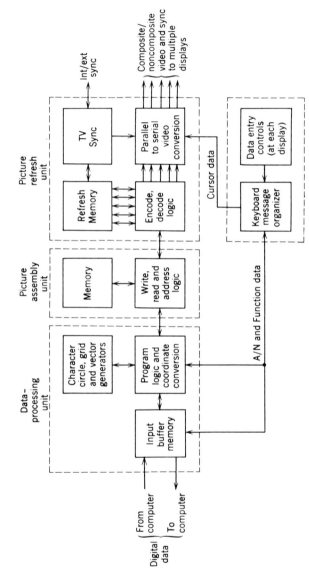

FIGURE 4.29 Expanded bit-mapped television system block diagram. After Sherr [5], by permission.

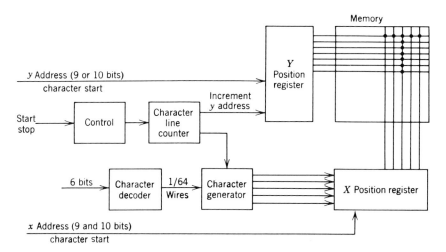

FIGURE 4.30 Character generation and assembly block diagram. After Sherr [5], by permission.

character in the proper location. For example, if the letter "T" is to be displayed at a specific position, the X and Y addresses and the character-selection bits are decoded to energize the lines in the memory-address input block that will cause those bits to be energized, which will produce the image when scanned out. The operation of the character generator portion in Figure 4.29 is the same as previously described for a dot matrix generator, and the character is created with one scanning line at a time. Once the entire frame of data has been placed in the memory, it is ready to be scanned out by the scanning raster and displayed on the monitor, and the memory may now act as a refresh memory. Of course, if an entirely new frame of information is to be displayed, the refresh operation must be stopped while the new frame is being created, and this may cause an undesirable interruption of the displayed image, which is why a separate rotating memory may be necessary. However, in general only a small part of the frame is changed at any one time, so that the change may be made rapidly enough as to be indiscernible to the viewer.

Vectors are generated by a similar technique, except that a vector generator is used that converts the start and stop coordinates into a series of points giving the best fit to a straight line between the two ends. This does lead to some jaggedness in the line, as is shown in Figure 4.31, and the question as to whether this jaggedness is unacceptable can be settled either by viewing the image or by using the eye resolution capability as expressed by equation 1.21 to calculate whether the dots will be visible. If either approach leads to unacceptable results, then the only solution is a higher-resolution system, and 1000-line systems are available in monochrome, as is described in the equipment section. Color is another story, but we leave that for later. In any event, this digital television system achieves its main purpose, which is to eliminate

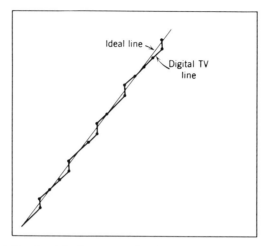

Ideal line

Digital TV line

FIGURE 4.31   Straight-line approximation in digital television system.

the Kell factor while still retaining the many advantages of raster systems. We can understand how this is accomplished by examining how the data are scanned out of the memory. Since there is one memory element for each picture element and the memory readout scan is addressed exactly to each line of memory, no bits are missed, and the loss of resolution due to the analog scanning is completely eliminated. This improvement in resolution is apparent in the photograph of a group of characters on a digital television monitor, shown in Figure 4.32, where the density and clarity is well beyond that achievable with a standard analog system. Of course, this assumes that the input data are digital, and if it is necessary to digitize analog data before entering them into the system, a similar loss will occur due to quantizing, but this is another problem that exists in all digital systems and may be minimized by increasing the number of quantization levels. In addition, analog data may be entered directly into the video channel and mixed with the digital data, without any additional loss of resolution, thus retaining one important feature of television systems.

The bit mapped system just described, while providing excellent results for alphanumeric and graphic systems, does pay the penalty of requiring relatively large memories and sacrificing speed for flexibility in image formation. Another approach, used extensively in alphanumeric systems, with at best a limited graphics capability, is to eliminate the picture assembly unit and convert the input data, a television line at a time, on each refresh cycle. The way this is done is illustrated in Figure 4.33, which is a simplified block diagram of an "on the fly" system, so designated because the conversion is accomplished on each refresh cycle as the data are being shown on the monitor CRT. The process is the same as that pictured in Figure 4.29, except that instead of the full frame being created and stored in the picture assembly unit memory, only one line of characters, a television line at a time, is converted

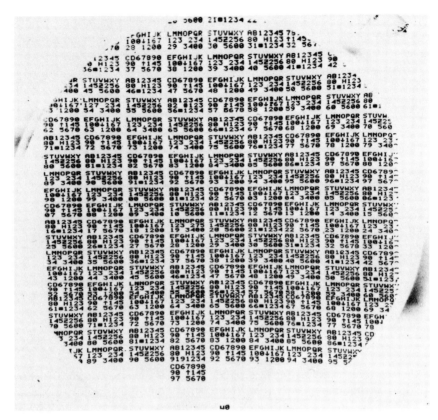

FIGURE 4.32 Four-thousand-character display in high-resolution digital television system. After Sherr [5], by permission.

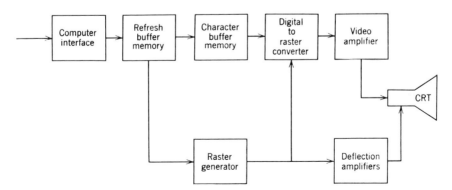

FIGURE 4.33 "On the fly" bit-mapped television block diagram.

and scanned directly into the display without an intervening frame memory. Thus the frame may be stored in computer words, and the memory size is reduced from a quarter of a million bits for a 525-line system, to perhaps 60,000 bits for a frame of 2000 characters. This is possible because in the first case a memory element is required for each picture element, whereas in the second case 30 bits per character may suffice. Of course, we never get something for nothing, and conversion speed must be increased to compensate for the reduction in memory size. This is apparent when we calculate the conversion speed, given by

$$T_c = N_c T_p \tag{4.22}$$

where T_c = conversion time per character
N_c = number of horizontal picture elements per character
T_p = time at each picture element

Using a 5×7 matrix, 500 picture elements per line, and 63 μs per line gives

$$T_c = \frac{5 \times 63}{500} = 630 \text{ ns}$$

for the conversion time, which is rather fast as compared with the leisurely 10 to 100 μs that might be used for the other system. It is possible to increase the conversion time by converting a number of characters in parallel, by this means more circuitry and more cost, so that a proper breakpoint between speed and cost must be found. Fortunately, modern microcircuits can be operated at nanosecond rates and the conversion accomplished without undue increase in complexity. This technique is limited to a fixed format, with each of the characters placed in a specified location, as in a typewritten page, and it is possible to reduce the storage requirement for the full graphics system by using the same format, but this would remove one of the advantages, namely, that data may be accepted in a random sequence while making it impossible to use standard scanning signals for the memory readout. Thus again it is a matter of trade-off between increases in circuit complexity and reduction in memory size to 70,000 bits for a 2000-character frame.

One important limitation in the "on the fly" system has been alluded to, namely, that it is necessary for the data to be presorted into the typewriter format, with each character falling within its own window. This considerably restricts the ability of such a system to render graphics other than those images that may be constructed of the fixed array of dots available, usually referred to as *limited graphics*, which are exemplified in Figure 4.34. It is evident that only horizontal and vertical lines may be drawn, basically by constructing the lines out of individual segments in the character window. It is possible to draw lines at other angles by extending the character set to include segments

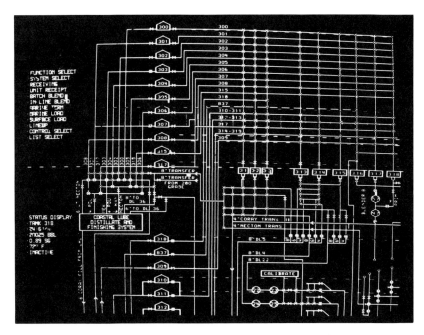

FIGURE 4.34 Example of high-resolution limited graphics display. Courtesy of Hazeltine Corporation.

at various angles, but since the lines must be drawn from endpoint data, it becomes an extremely complex and time-consuming process to covert the endpoint data on each refresh cycle into the proper angle segment for each particular location. In the full-graphics system the same process is involved, but much more time is available, and it is only done once when the picture is being assembled. However, even these limited-graphics capabilities have proved to be very useful in a number of applications, particularly when color monitors are used, as is described later. One other approach used to achieve a somewhat more flexible graphics is to provide a memory location for each of the dots or pixels on the display that are used in the character presentation and to change the input decoding so that each dot can be addressed separately. By this means, various simple dot patterns may be created, although it is still beyond this technique to create any complex patterns. However, if simple patterns such as bar graphs and charts are sufficient, this extension may be added to some available systems at rather low cost. It is important to remember that the resolution is limited to the number of dots used, in the order of 400 horizontal by 170 vertical if a 5 × 7 matrix and a 2000-character frame is used.

A final caveat that has been noted previously but bears repeating has to do with the flicker that will occur if all the available scanning lines are used instead of repeating the same data on each field. Some attempts have been made to write different data on each field and thus double the character capacity of the frame, but the flicker is objectionable unless slow phosphors are used, which leads to unacceptable smear. As a result, the standard appears to be 80 characters per line, and 24 lines of characters, or 1920 characters in the frame. The limitation on the number of character lines may be derived from

$$C_L = \frac{L_f}{L_c + L_s} \qquad (4.23)$$

where C_L = number of lines of characters
$\quad L_f$ = number of scanning lines per field (240 for standard television)
$\quad L_c$ = number of lines per character height (7 for a 7 × 5 matrix)
$\quad L_s$ = number of scanning lines between adjacent character lines (usually 2)

Using the number given above, this leads to

$$C_L = \frac{240}{7 + 2} = 26.66$$

with 24 or 25 lines as the customary limit. More character lines require more scanning lines, which is feasible for monochrome but not always for color because of the resolution limits placed by the standard color CRTs, as is described in Chapter 2. It is for this reason that raster systems were not as effective in achieving the best character fidelity as are the vector systems, particularly in color, when the penetration CRT is used. In addition the character size cannot be less than 1/24 of the total frame size for the standard raster system, whereas for the vector system it is limited only by the spot size, to which should be added the requirement that in the raster systems the input data must be preorganized so that the sequence corresponds to the fixed scanning sequence used for the display monitor. This preorganization may be done in the host computer or in the resident microcomputer, if it has the capacity and speed necessary to accomplish the arrangement.

4.4 STORAGE SYSTEMS

Systems using storage cathode-ray devices are of two types, those using direct-view storage CRTs and those with the electrical storage device separate from the viewing CRT. These two are represented in Figures 4.35 and 4.36 and differ from the refresh systems in that no refresh memory is used between the data sources and the display CRT. They both will accommodate either vector or raster inputs but in general are used primarily with vector inputs,

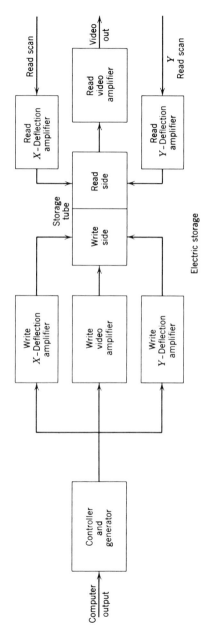

FIGURE 4.35 Block diagram of electrical storage display system.

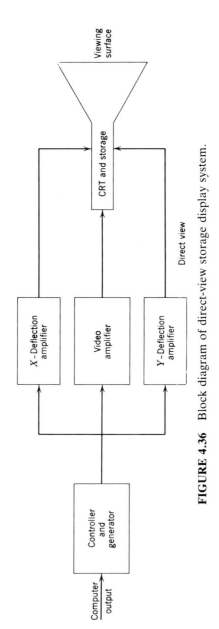

FIGURE 4.36 Block diagram of direct-view storage display system.

either digital or analog, which must be converted by the data converters contained in the controller and generator unit into the proper analog signals to deflect the CRT beam and intensify it to the proper level of luminance. In most respects these functions are performed in the same manner as has been described for the vector system, and it is only in the absence of the magnetic or solid-state memory unit that the difference is significant, except for some of the special characteristics of the storage devices themselves. Since both storage devices have enough capacity to store all the pixels in a full frame, they can present large amounts of data, equal in density to a raster system with the same resolution. The electrical storage device, in particular, is another means for preorganizing data so that they may be presented in raster format on a standard television monitor.

Beginning first with the system using the electrical storage CRT, depicted in Figure 4.35, we see that it is essentially the same as that portion of the analog raster system, shown in Figure 4.25, which uses the scan converter to process the input data and output them in analog raster format. It is repeated here merely to show that it may be considered to be in the same category as the direct-view storage-tube system and is not merely another converter that may be used only to handle television-type input formats. The application of the scan converter to CRT graphic display systems has been alluded to in Chapter 2, with the silicon dioxide type as the one used most successfully for this purpose. The high resolution possible with this scan converter, as well as other features such as selective erase and good gray scale range, make a system built around this device an effective competitor to either digital television or vector display systems. It is still subject to the Kell factor but uses its high-resolution capability of over 2000 television lines to end up with a total resolution as good as that possible with the other systems, with the limit imposed more by the CRT than by the scan conversion unit. It is compatible with either raster or vector inputs, and although it does not have the essentially infinite storage time of a digital system, it can hold images for many minutes under continuous readout and is adequate for numerous uses. One point in its favor is the many gray levels that can be stored, without needing additional storage space, in contrast to a digital system, where additional gray levels mean additional bits of storage.

It can be seen from Figure 4.35 that the display system using an electrical storage device is essentially the same as that using a digital memory, with the electrical storage device replacing the digital memory and performing the dual functions of picture assembly and picture-refresh memory. The other components of the system such as the logic, control, coordinate conversion, data conversion, and image generation are the same as for the digital system and operate in much the same fashion. Thus insofar as the input to a system with an electrical storage device is concerned, no difference may be discerned, and the output is a CRT driven in a raster format, as for the digital television system. In between, however, all digital signals must be converted into the equivalent analog format before they are applied to the storage unit and must remain analog from that point onward. It may also mix direct television signals with the digital data and is a possible alternative to digital television when such combination is desired.

The other form of storage system is the one that embodies the direct-view storage CRT, as shown in Figure 4.36. The CRT has been described in detail in Chapter 2, and we only note here that it combines the function of storage and display in one device, eliminating the refresh memory entirely, and thus all flicker problems associated with refresh systems. This advantage does not apply to the system using the electrical storage CRT, which still ends up with a refreshed CRT as the output device. The complete absence of flicker is one very salient characteristic of this type of display system and should be considered when different approaches are being evaluated. Of course, one must pay for everything, and in this case there is the loss of selective erase and low values of luminance and contrast ratio to detract from the overall performance. Erasure may require more than 200 ms, and the display must be erased every 10 to 15 s to avoid phosphor burn. However, in spite of these drawbacks, the direct-view storage CRT system, employing the bistable tube, created something of a revolution in graphics, primarily due to its low cost, which has forced manufacturers of refresh systems to similarly lower their costs and thus bring graphics within the reach of a much greater number of users than before. Apart from the display monitor and the absence of the refresh memory, the direct-view storage CRT system is very similar to the vector refresh systems described previously, and the controller-generator unit contains the necessary elements to perform the required conversion and generation functions. The resultant display may be of high resolution, with over 800 television lines possible, and CRT sizes up to 62.5 cm are available. The system found many applications, where its low cost and high resolution are desirable and where the detracting factors mentioned were not too limiting. It was available from only one supplier, but this did not restrict its acceptance. The basic features of the two types of storage display systems are listed in Tables 4.6 and 4.7 and may be compared with those given in Tables 4.4 and 4.5 for raster systems, to arrive at an evaluation of the different systems and develop a basis for choice. No hard-and-fast rules can be established for this choice, and it is up to the user to determine which has the most appropriate features and best meets the application. In general, vector systems, whether refresh or storage, provide the highest-quality imagery, whereas refresh systems offer the fastest response, as well as the possibility of color at some additional cost. Luminance and contrast ratio are poorest for the bistable storage type, whereas the others are approximately the same in these characteristics. One is faced with an embarrassment of riches in some respects, especially when only an alphanumeric display is required, and this condition does not make the choice any easier. We defer further discussion to the equipment section of this chapter.

TABLE 4.6   Direct-View Storage Terminal Parameters

Parameter	Value
Display type	25–48 cm DVST
Display size (cm)	5–10 × 16–36
Deflection settling time (μs)	10 (to one spot diameter)
Spot writing time (μs)	5 (max.)
Deflection sensitivity (V)	±5
Resolution (pixels/cm)	28–31
Erase time (s)	1.5
Selective erase time	NA
Viewing time (min)	15 (min.)
Stored vector writing rate (cm/ms)	10

4.5   COLOR SYSTEMS

4.5.1   Introduction

Color systems differ primarily from the monochromatic described previously in that a color monitor replaces the monochromatic monitor, and an associated color card is added to the computer portion of the system. They may also require some expansion of the computer memory, in that multiple bits of storage are needed for each data element in order to encode the color information. In addition, a bit-mapped system will need 3 bits of storage in the refresh memory for each bit of monochromatic memory. This demonstrates one advantage of the nonraster or single-gun analog type of CRT color system, as represented by the penetration CRT, in that the tripling of refresh storage is not required. However, this is a trivial advantage, given the present low

TABLE 4.7   Electrical Storage Terminal Parameters

Parameter	Value
Display type	Any CRT raster monitor
Deflection settling time (μs)	10 (to one beam diameter)
Spot writing time (ns)	10–30
Slew rate (μs per diameter)	3
Deflection sensitivity (V)	0.75
Raster writing time (μs per scan line)	20
Resolution	1400 TV lines (shrinking raster)
Erase time (ms)	250–500 (full target)
Selective erase time (μs)	250–500 (per scan line)
Retention time (min)	30 (active viewing)
Small-signal bandwidth (MHz)	1.5
Video bandwidth (MHz)	30
Video sensitivity (V)	1
Deflection sensitivity (V)	0.75–5 (full screen)

cost of storage, and the other potential advantage in resolution is not very great now that high-resolution vector CRTs are readily available. However, the penetration systems remain of some limited, if mainly historical interest, and are covered in Section 4.5.2 for completeness.

The color card is added to the system at this point because it is an essential component, given the wide variety in resolution and number of colors that can be achieved. However, as it is intimately involved in the performance of the raster color CRT monitors, it is included with them in the discussion found in Section 4.4.3.

4.5.2   Vector Format

In general, color systems using the penetration color CRT have fallen into desuetude, but as noted previously, it should not be completely forgotten. To that end, some information on this type of vector system is included here. Its main use is for the design of a single-gun vector system, and it main approximate the resolution performance of a single-gun monochromatic system in vector format.

As the result of the single-gun design, the performance of a vector color system may approximate that of a monochromatic system in such aspects as resolution and image quality, as well as deflection time, character writing time, and video bandwidth. The number of usable colors is restricted to four, for reasons given in Chapter 2, and the CRT may be as large as 50 cm in diameter. Thus in many respects the vector color system embodying a monitor containing the penetration CRT has all of the desirable features of the monochromatic one, with the sometimes desirable addition of color. It is also possible, of course, to use it for an alphanumeric system of the cursive writing type, but this is done only when alphanumerics of higher quality than that obtainable from the raster units are desired. With all these excellent features, one might ask why vector color systems have not gained wider acceptance. The answer is probably found in the increased cost of a vector color system due to the special nature of the monitor, leading to low-quantity production and high unit cost. The special aspects of the monitor design relate to the need for a switching power supply and the variations in deflection sensitivity and beam focus resulting from the changes in acceleration voltage as expressed by equations 2.48, 2.57, and 2.74. The block diagram of a monitor incorporating these special circuits is shown in Figure 4.37, and the corrections must be made in synchronism with the high-voltage switching so that reasonably constant deflection sensitivities and spot sizes are maintained for the different colors. We see from the relevant equations that both the deflection sensitivity and the spot size vary as the inverse square root of the accelerating voltage, so that it is necessary to introduce a correction in the focus voltage and the deflection amplifier gain corresponding to the change in acceleration voltage that occurs for the different colors. Fortunately, this is not too difficult to accomplish, and the available monitors attain acceptable results. However,

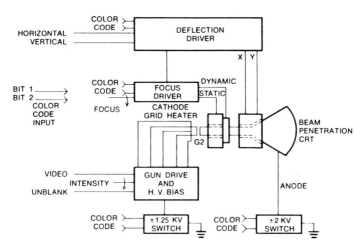

FIGURE 4.37   Penetration color CRT monitor block diagram. Courtesy CPS.

the high-voltage switching is another story and is the main contributor to the high cost of the monitor. The problem arises from the speed at which the voltage change must take place, if any data density is to be achieved without preorganizing the data by color. If we examine equation 4.14, we see that the switching time should not be longer than the deflection time if the same data density is to be maintained as for the monochromatic CRT monitor. This means that switching times below 10 μs are necessary for the 6 kV that may be required. With the input capacity of the CRT in the order of 100 pF, considerable energy is used, the the design of the switching supply becomes quite difficult. Supplies that switch at the requisite speed are available and are used in the monitors, but it has not been possible as yet to lower the cost of this element sufficiently to make the penetration color monitor competitive with the raster types, and the increase in cost may not be compensated for by the improvement in resolution and picture quality. In addition, only four colors may be reliably generated, and the lack of compatibility with standard television further limits the range of applications. Thus it would appear that until the cost can be reduced significantly this type of color system will remain restricted in its acceptance.

4.5.3   Raster Format

The situation is entirely different when the standard television color monitor is used. The systems come in various forms, depending on whether they are used for alphanumerics only, or if graphics and/or standard television are included. The alphanumeric and limited-graphics versions are most common, and such a system is the same as that shown in Figure 4.33, but with the addition of the color decoding circuitry and the color monitor. The most important asset of this system is that it uses the standard color-television monitor so that the advantages of standardization and quantity production may be attained. Thus although a high-quality color monitor may cost several times as much as the monochromatic monitor (black and white), its impact on the cost of the entire system is much less than in the case of the penetration CRT monitor, and the use of color becomes reasonable in many applications. Of course, one is still subject to the various performance limitations of the television type of color CRT, as described in Chapter 2, but these limitations in resolution and luminance appear not to be too detrimental in many applications. By the same token, there may be applications where the addition of color does not sufficiently compensate for the loss of detail, and it is advisable to carefully examine the application requirements before opting for color, even when it is economically feasible.

An "on-the-fly" color display system has the usual features of alphanumeric and vector generation to the extent that it is possible in this type of limited graphics system. The color aspect is controlled by the color-decoding circuitry that is added, which may either take those portions of the digital word that specify the color and decode them to select the appropriate combination of color intensities, or, if a standard television color signal is used, then circuitry for extracting the color information from the signal is also included in the monitor. Thus the color monitor is compatible with either digital or analog inputs of various forms and makes it possible to mix signals from many different sources. It is also feasible to add a color monitor to the full-graphics raster system shown in Figure 4.29, if 3 more bits are added per character to allow selection of up to seven different colors, with the appropriate decoding circuits. A system with this capability is very versatile, and the additional memory size and circuit complexity may be quite acceptable, if color is deemed necessary. Finally, the limitations in resolution imposed by the standard 525-line color-television monitor may be overcome by using the high-resolution versions of the shadow-mask CRT and Trinitron that are available and have been incorporated in some monitors. Systems built around CRTs have these many important advantages, and have reached the stage of quantity manufacture, so that the cost advantage pertaining to the standard versions does apply. The demand will probably approach that for the standard monitors as HDTV becomes more common, and we may anticipate that there will be significant reductions in cost once the demand for high-resolution color television becomes larger. All in all, much can be done with raster color CRT display systems, and they are worthy of serious consideration for many applications. For simple alphanumerics, where the limited resolution possible with low cost raster color is not a detriment, color may be a very practical solution, and this also applies to limited graphics. However, when high-quality graphics are desired, monochromatic vector systems give the best images, although penetration color is not far behind. The last category of high resolution raster color is capable of good-quality images while retaining many of the other features of raster systems, but at a loss of the basic advantage of using standard components and monitors, which have been the main selling point for raster as opposed to vector systems. The choice is very wide, and there is surely something for everyone in this list.

System Descriptions. The basic diagram of the color monitor portion of a video display system is shown in Figure 4.38. The color monitor is of the shadow-mask or Trinitron type, and the range of colors and resolutions available is quite large. The ability to use standard television monitors is an important asset, as it allows the advantages of mass manufacturing and marketing to keep down the cost of the monitor. It has been somewhat limiting, as the majority of such monitors are designed to satisfy the needs of the NTSC system, thus limiting the color resolution to about 300 × 350. However, the advent of HDTV promises to improve this situation considerably, and in the interim the CRT manufacturers have made the higher-resolution color CRTs available at reasonable prices.

Returning to the color capability, in the case of standard television, it will be limited by the television system specifications, but for nontelevision applications the characteristics of the graphics board determine the display capabilities. Table 4.8 lists the relevant characteristics of the existing standards as well as several relevant specifications proposed by IBM and Texas Instruments that have received wide acceptance by vendors of these cards. There are other proprietary cards made by various vendors that offer different combinations of resolution and number of colors that can be viewed simultaneously, but those listed in Table 4.8 are sufficient to demonstrate the types of display color formats that are available. It should be noted that the CGA standard is obsolete for all practical purposes, and EGA is rapidly approaching the same state. In addition, although the standard lists the number of colors that may be viewed simultaneously, the total palette may be as high as 16.7 M colors, with 256 k as another popular number.

With this plethora of choices in performance capability for color systems, it is of some interest to compare the different requirements imposed by the different types of graphics systems. These are shown in Table 4.9, with those for a vector drawing system shown in Table 4.10 for comparison. It is clear that raster color systems can match or exceed the performance of vector color systems for all except the highest-resolution requirements, which is why vector systems are falling into desuetude with no great probability of recovery, especially with flat panel systems as the most logical alternative. However, the information on the vector color CRT systems is included here for historical reasons, and because there is always the possibility of a resurgence as long as CRT vendors continue to offer single-beam vector color systems. This possibility is somewhat supported by the continuing availability of both penetration and Currentron types of single-gun color CRTs.

It is obvious from these data that excellent performance can be achieved with raster color systems so that there appears to be little need for vector color, especially with the extreme limitation in the number of colors. However, it is still possible to obtain higher resolution with single-gun CRTs so

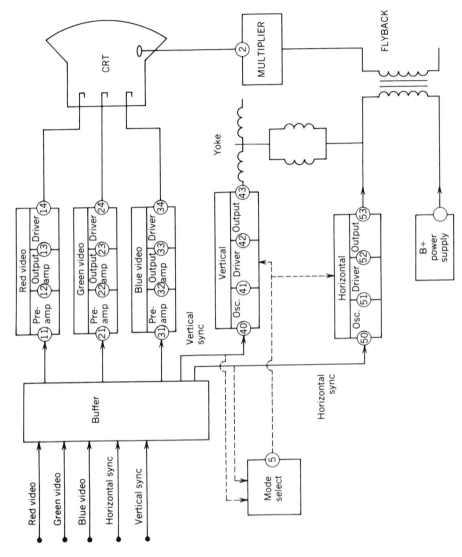

FIGURE 4.38 Computer monitor block diagram (separate horizontal and vertical sync lines). Courtesy Sencore.

TABLE 4.8   Graphics Boards

Standard[a]	Resolution	Number
CGA	320 × 200	4
EGA	640 × 350	16
CGA	320 × 200	4
EGA	640 × 350	16
VGA	320 × 200	256
	640 × 480	16
SVGA	640 × 480	256
	800 × 600	256
	1024 × 768	16
8514a	640 × 480	256
	1024 × 768	256
XGA	1024 × 768	256
	640 × 480	65,536
	4000 × 4000 (proposed)	
TIGA	4000 × 4000	256

[a]CGA, color graphics adapter; EGA, enhanced graphics adapter; VGA, video graphics array; SVGA, super VGA; XGA, IBM EGA; TIGA, Texas Instruments Graphics Architecture.

TABLE 4.9   Graphics Systems Parameters

Parameter	Value	
	Full-Graphics Workstation	X Terminal
Resolution	1280 × 1024	1280 × 1024
Color palette	16.7 M	16.7 M
Color display	4096	256
Active diameter (in.)	19	19
Refresh rate (Hz)	60 (noninterlaced)	72
	30 (interlaced)	
Video interface	0.7 p-p, 75 Ω	RS-232
	RS-170A	

TABLE 4.10   Vector Terminal Parameters

Parameter	Value
Deflection time (μs)	10
Line writing speed (μs/in.)	2.5
Resolution	1000 × 1000
Number of colors	4
Refresh rate	30

that for extremely high resolution with the addition a vector color workstation of at least a few colors may still find a place. In any event, they should not be totally forgotten.

4.6   LARGE-SCREEN SYSTEMS

4.6.1   Projection Systems

There are two major types of large-screen systems that use the CRT or some form of cathode-ray device as the major element of the display portion of the system. The first one is built around the projection CRTs described in Chapter 2, with the CRT acting as the image source for a projection system. The total display system is configured like the raster displays shown in Figures 4.25, 4.29, and 4.33, with the projection CRT replacing the CRT used in the standard monitors. The projection CRT is usually made part of a Schmidt projection system, as shown in Figure 4.39, which is a type of optical projection system that allows higher efficiencies to be achieved than in the normal direct projection found in slide projectors, for example. It is a reflective projection arrangement, consisting of a spherical mirror and a correcting lens. A reflective optical system is used to focus the large field consisting of the CRT faceplate, commonly 13 to 17 cm in diameter on the viewing screen. The relatively low output of the CRT, as noted in Chapter 2, enforces the need for a high-efficiency system, and this type of optics is the one commonly used for CRT projection. The correcting lens is required to compensate for spherical aberrations in the mirror and the CRT faceplate and enters into the

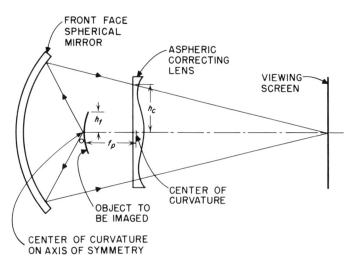

FIGURE 4.39 Schmidt projection system. After Pender and McIlwain [6], by permission.

overall system efficiency according to

$$e_m \cong \left(\frac{h_c}{f_p}\right)^2 \frac{m_p^2}{(h_c/f_p{}^2 + (m_p + 1)^2} \tag{4.24}$$

where h_c = semiaperture of correcting lens
$\quad f_p$ = focal length
$\quad m_p$ = optical system magnification

In addition, a part of the reflecting mirror must be masked to block out the CRT faceplate for contrast improvement, and the masked part of the mirror has the efficiency

$$e_t \cong \left(\frac{h_t}{f_p}\right)^2 \left(\frac{m_p^2}{m_p^2 - 1}\right)^2 \tag{4.25}$$

where h_t is the half-height of CRT faceplate. The efficiency of the total system is then

$$e_p = e_m - e_t \tag{4.26}$$

an efficiency of 25% or better is common, so that with the luminous flux (lumens) now available from projection CRTs it is possible to achieve luminances of over 30 nits, which is better than movie projection but still requires a rather dimly lit room. Thus its applications are limited to those situations where the room illumination can be controlled, but this is compensated for by the relatively low cost of the projection system in monochrome. A color display is achieved by having three monochrome systems with appropriate filters to create the three primary colors. Of course, what we are terming a *monochrome system* must be one that emits white light, so that all the colors are available. Then the three projectors may be treated as though they were the three guns of a standard television color CRT and signals applied to the deflection and video amplifiers in the same manner as for the standard color television system discussed previously. The projection CRT must have its own yokes, deflection amplifiers, video amplifier, and all the other elements that go to make up a monitor, with the difference that the image appearing on the CRT is not directly viewed, but is projected onto a screen. The system has achieved some acceptance for closed-circuit programs, homes that want large-screen television displays, and for bars and other places of public gathering. Within its limitations of luminance and resolution, it is an effective large-screen display, and may also be used for the presentation of digitally derived data, again with the addition of the data converter and other elements used in a digital television system.

Other forms of CRT projection are the direct projection systems illustrated in Figure 4.40 for rear-screen projection and Figure 4.41 for front-screen

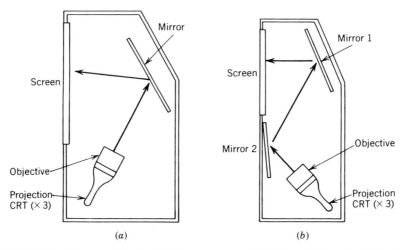

(a)   (b)

FIGURE 4.40   Three projection CRTs are combined with one (a) or two (b) mirrors to reflect image onto screen in rear projection systems. After Gibilini and House [7], by permission.

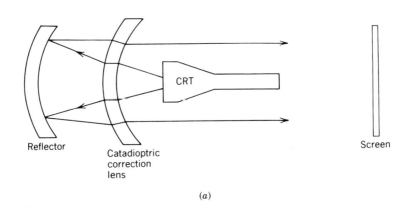

(a)

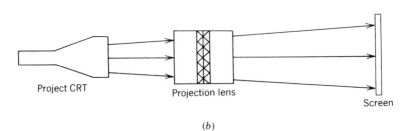

(b)

FIGURE 4.41   Direct projection system: (a) reflective projection CRT system; (b) transmissive projection CRT system. After Gibilini and House [7], by permission.

projection. The systems differ from the Schmidt projection system in that no mirror is part of the lens, although one or more reflecting mirrors may be needed in the rear-screen projection system to permit the CRT to be behind the screen and shorten the space between the CRT and the screen. In this type of projection system, the optical parameter of interest is the total conjugate length (TCL), which is the distance between an object and the image of that object produced by the lens. For the rear projection system it is desirable to minimize the TCL so as to keep the cabinet as small as possible. The relation between the TCL, the system magnification (m), and the focal length of the projection lens (f) is given by

$$f = \frac{m(\text{TCL})}{(m + 1)^2} \tag{4.27}$$

where m is the ratio of the active CRT display area and the selected screen area. Therefore, the shorter the TCL, the shorter the required focal length of the lens.

For front-screen projection, the requirement for a short TCL does not hold and might be undesirable. However, mirrors cannot be used conveniently to make the optical axis of the lens normal to the screen, as can be done in the rear projection system. Therefore, the lens axis is always at an angle with respect to the screen for front projection systems. However, if the lens axis is not normal to the screen, the plane of the CRT phosphor surface must be tilted to keep the image in focus across the screen. This relationship is known as the *Scheimpflug condition*, which requires that the planes of the screen, the phosphor surface, and the normal to the lens axis intersect at one point for the image to be in focus across the screen. The orientation of the three surfaces to fulfill this condition is illustrated in Figure 4.42. However, this leads to variations in TCL across the screen, as illustrated in Figure 4.43, and the result is keystoning in the image, where a rectangle on the CRT face becomes a trapezoid on the screen. This in turn leads to the requirement for a long TCL and a shorter angle between the lens and the screen to minimize keystoning.

For all their effectiveness, relatively low cost, and popularity for home entertainment systems, these CRT projection systems are still limited, as we have noted, to situations where the ambient lighting may be controlled and maintained at levels low enough so that sufficient contrast ratio is attained for good viewing. Alternatively, the screen size must be kept to about 1 m^2 if higher ambient light is anticipated, such as may be found in a well-lit room. Finally, the CRT projection system is completely useless for outdoor viewing, especially under the high light levels used in sporting events, and then what becomes of instant replay. The answer to this dilemma is found in another type of projection system, that uses a special type of cathode-ray device in combination with unique optics to provide a visual result that is eminently satisfactory for all applications not satisfied by the projection CRT system. This projection system goes by the generic name of *light-valve system*, and

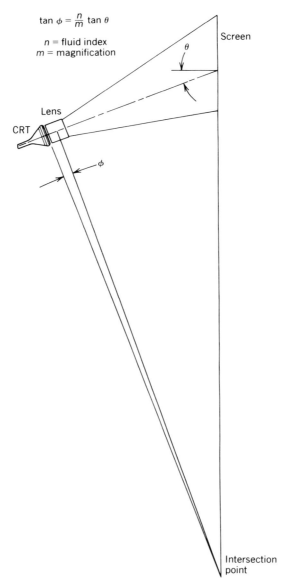

FIGURE 4.42   Orientation of the screen, phosphor, and lens to fulfill the Scheimpflug condition. After Moskovich et al. [8], by permission.

there are several examples of large-screen displays using this basic principle, of which we discuss the two most successful in detail.

4.6.2   Light Valve

A number of techniques have been applied to the development of what are termed *light-valve display systems*, and it might be said that light valves include

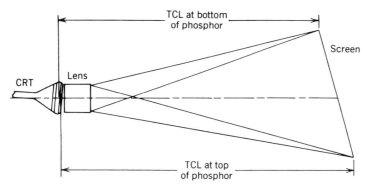

FIGURE 4.43 TCL varation across phosphor after the Scheimpflug condition. After Moskovich et al. [8], by permission.

any device that controls the intensity of the light by varying some optical characteristic of the transmission medium. Since this chapter is concerned with CRTs, we restrict the discussion to those examples that use an electron gun as the control means for changing the optical transmission of the valve. The most successful form of electron beam control has been with an oil film as the transmission medium that is altered, and Figure 4.44 is a simplified schematic arrangement of such a light valve. It contains a light source that illuminates the slits created by the first set of parallel bar gratings (f_1), and the slits are imaged by the Schlieren lens on the second set of bars (f_2), so that when the oil film is smooth no light will pass through to the projection lens. However, if the oil film is deformed by the electron beam placing charges on its surface, a ripple is created that refracts the light at that point, and part of the refracted light passes through the slit in the second set of bars. The amount of light is essentially proportional to the depth of deformation because

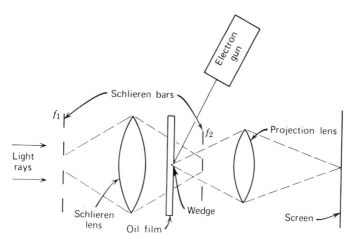

FIGURE 4.44 Refractive oil film light-valve system. After Sherr [1, p. 211], by permission.

the angle of refraction is proportional to this depth, and the depth of deformation, in turn, is proportional to the energy in the electron beam. Thus by either intensity or width modulation, the electron beam can control the amount of light that appears at the screen.

Unfortunately, this simple system is difficult to design with good contrast ratios because it depends on maintaining close tolerances between the sizes and position of the two bar gratings, as well as the Schlieren lens. Also, only small diffraction angles can be practically obtained, so that the ratio between maximum and minimum illumination is small. These difficulties have been overcome by creating a diffraction grating on the oil film, as is shown in Figure 4.45, with the electron beam creating the grating at a location dependent on the amplitude of the deformation. The solution for the light intensity is found in terms of Bessel functions and need not concern us here. Suffice it to say that by this approach it has become possible to achieve contrast ratios over 100, with the maximum light intensity determined primarily by the intensity of the light source, and light levels over 7000 lm have been attained with xenon light sources. It has also been found capable of over 1000 television lines of resolution so that the combination of high luminance at the screen and good resolution is very effective.

The actual form of a commercial system based on these principles is shown in Figure 4.46. It differs from the one pictured in Figure 4.45*b* in that a single set of Schlieren bars is used, and they are imaged back on themselves by means of the spherical mirror on which the oil film is placed. Thus, this is a reflective rather than transmissive system, but the principles of operation are the same for both. Transmissive systems have not been too successful, and the commercially available version, called *Eidophor* from the greek for "image bearer," is the one shown in Figure 4.46.

The electron beam is part of a magnetically deflected and focused electron gun, and it may be considered to act in the same way as the equivalent gun in a CRT. Thus equations 2.9 and 2.57 apply and may be used to establish the deflection and focus requirements for the amplifiers and focusing circuits. Similarly, the input video may be used to intensity modulate the beam, or, as is more common, to focus modulate the beam and achieve the required changes in the oil film. It is completely compatible with raster inputs and

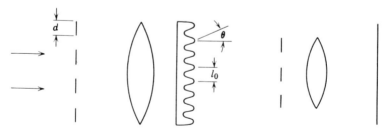

FIGURE 4.45   Diffraction grating oil film light-valve system. After Sherr [1, p. 211], by permission.

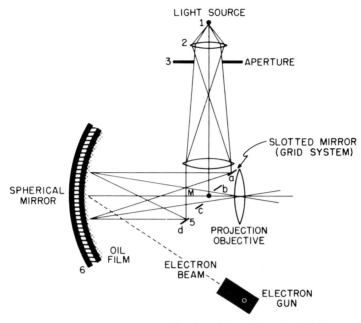

FIGURE 4.46   Eidophor light-valve projection. After Horowitz [9], by permission.

simply replaces the CRT monitor in those types of display systems. Indeed, it can be used effectively only with raster scan, and has seen its greatest application in large-screen displays of television images. Color is produced by using three complete systems, as for the projection CRT system, and the cost does become rather high. However, the results are the best that have been obtained to date in any dynamic large-screen color system, and the ability to produce high luminance levels at high resolution makes it unique in the field.

Before leaving this type of oil-film light valve, certain special problems associated with the system should be noted. These are primarily related to the chemical characteristics of the oil film and the particular burdens placed on the cathode of the electron gun. The oil-film chemistry is probably the most unusual and proprietary aspect of the unit that has achieved successful operation. Since the oil film must have enough viscosity to retain the deformations during a frame time and yet allow them to decay quickly enough to be ready for the next frame, the problem is akin to that encountered in the development of phosphors for CRT displays. In addition, contaminants and residual charges must be removed for effective operation. This is accomplished by constantly replenishing the film from an oil bath and by controlling the chemical composition and the temperature of the film to tight tolerances. Furthermore, the glass envelope containing the electron gun and the oil film is constantly pumped to remove hydrogen resulting from oil-film bombardment and to maintain a high vacuum. The cathode problem is due to the rather high energies in the electron beam, which produce ions that strike the cathode, and also the contamination of the cathode by the oil decomposition products. These difficulties have been minimized by using an extremely rugged structure and by providing a turret arrangement with as many as seven cathodes, which may be individually rotated into position. By these measures it has been possible to reach over 1000 hours of life for the cathode and oil-film combination, and the excellent visual result has made this one of the best choices available for high luminance and resolution on screens as large as 6 m on a side.

With all its fine features, the high cost and difficulties in maintenance, especially for color systems, have made another approach of considerable interest. This is one where the color is produced not by three separate projectors, but rather by placing three separate gratings on one oil film, as is shown in Figure 4.47. The three gratings are able to completely determine color and intensity by the way in which the light from the source is split up at the input and output spatial filters. The diffraction gratings are written simultaneously with the single electron beam, by moving it while it scans out the raster. The first grating results from the raster lines and is controlled by a vertically defocusing carrier, modulated by the video information. This carrier is added to the vertical deflection waveforms, and two differently pitched gratings orthogonal to the raster lines are written by adding other carriers to the horizontal-deflection waveforms. The result is a line array of charges perpendicular to the raster lines, and video modulation of the carrier amplitudes controls the corresponding diffraction gratings on the oil film. The different frequencies of the carriers are such that the grooves have the proper spacing to diffract the proper color through the output slots. A full color projection display is the result, using a single gun and a single oil film, with a corresponding decrease in cost, although both luminance and resolution are also limited, to an output of under 500 lm and 525 television lines. However, this is quite adequate for many indoor applications, and the system has proved an effective substitute when the color Eidophor is too expensive. There is also another advantage in its favor, in that it uses a sealed-off light-valve tube, as shown in Figure 4.47. These sealed tubes have achieved in use life of over 3000 hours without having external oil reservoirs or vacuum pumps, and with a single cathode. Thus the combination of the completely sealed tube and the single gun has led to a much lower cost while still maintaining fairly effective visual performance. The choice of which one to use in any particular application must depend on a combination of all these performance factors and is discussed in Section 4.7.7

There are also a number of other developments of light-valve systems using the same basic principles, but with different kinds of deformable media. Several of them use special material such as liquid crystals to achieve light control, but since they are not, strictly speaking, CRT systems, even though the CRT may be used as the image source, we defer discussion of their characteristics to Chapter 5. As to the many approaches that have used an

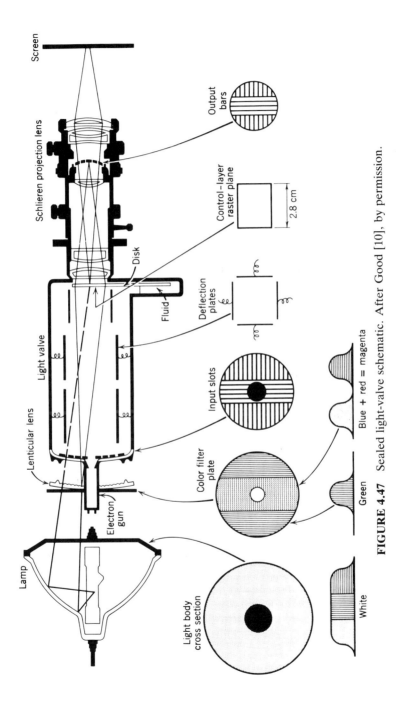

FIGURE 4.47 Sealed light-valve schematic. After Good [10], by permission.

Screen

Schlieren projection lens

Output bars

Control-layer raster plane

2.8 cm

Disk

Fluid

Light valve

Deflection plates

Input slots

Lenticular lens

Color filter plate

Blue + red = magenta

Green

Electron gun

Lamp

Light body cross section

White

411

electron beam but not an oil film, they are too numerous for adequate discussion here, and in any event they have not achieved commercial availability, nor does it appear that they will do so in the foreseeable future. Therefore, we forgo the pleasure and interest of describing them to conserve both space and time. The reader who wants more information may consult reference 10.

4.7 EQUIPMENT

4.7.1 Introduction

At present, and probably for the foreseeable future, the bulk of equipment using the CRT as the display device will feature the wide range of raster monitors, both color and monochrome, that are available. These monitors come in a variety of shapes sizes and formats, and it is frequently difficult to decide which is best for any particular application. It is the purpose of this section to further develop the information presented in the previous sections, and thus establish some basis for making the choices, as well as clarify the meaning of the performance parameters to a greater extent as they apply to system performance. To this end we survey the various types in terms of the technologies employed, so as to establish a relationship between the technical discussion in the previous sections and the performance characteristics described here. We follow the same sequence, beginning with the data-display unit and proceeding backward to the data input, thus allowing us to relate this material to that covered previously. Although we can by no means be completely exhaustive without becoming completely exhausted, we cover at least one example of each type, and we support the descriptions with tables listing relevant performance parameters and range of performance to be anticipated. More detail on specific units may be found in a number of compendia and surveys that unfortunately become incomplete almost as soon as they are issued. However, by applying the same procedures to any new unit, it is possible to arrive at comparisons, without having to wait for the next issue of any particular available compendium. The material from the first edition that covers the random deflection and storage monitors is also included first in a somewhat truncated form for information, but the bulk of the new material is concerned with the raster monitors that have taken over the market.

4.7.2 Data-Display Unit

Direct-View CRTs

Monochromatic-Random Magnetic (Vector) CRTs. Data-display units using random magnetic deflection CRTs may be generally represented by the diagram shown in Figure 4.48, which is an expanded version of the simple

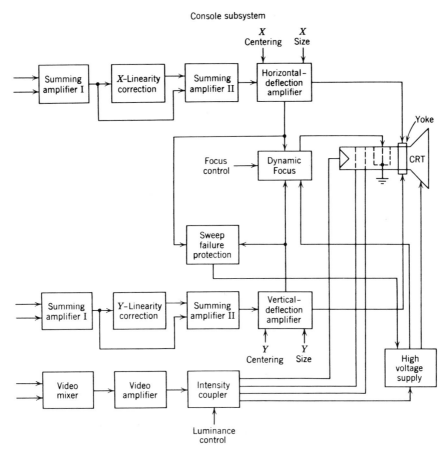

FIGURE 4.48 Random-deflection monitor block diagram. After Sherr [1], by permission.

schematic shown in Figure 4.4 and includes a number of special circuits necessary for proper operation. This type of equipment is not usually offered as an independent component, since each unit is closely tied in its operation to the rest of the vector system and if obtained separately, will not necessarily be compatible with any other vector system than the one for which it is intended. However, there are several manufacturers who do make it available as a separable component, and it should be described independently of the rest of the system, if only for comparison with its equivalents in raster and storage systems. In addition, although at this point we are discussing only the monochromatic version, there are color units offered as separate monitors, described later, that use the monochromatic types as the basic starting point, and any information on the monochromatic units is of relevance for the color ones as well. Therefore, we present information on available equipment of the random vector type.

TABLE 4.11   Magnetic Deflection CRT Monitor Parameters

Parameter	Value
Deflection settling time (μs)	10
Small-signal bandwidth (MHz)	2
Video bandwidth (MHz)	15–30
Linear writing speed (μs/cm)	1
Resolution	>1000 (shrinking raster) TV lines
Luminance (nits)	300
Spot size (mm)	0.25 (53 cm CRT)
Viewing areas (cm)	33 × 33 cm (53 cm CRT)
Accelerator voltage (kV)	10
Phosphor	Various
Refresh data (Hz)	30–60
Power consumption (W)	250

A representative set of specifications for this monochromatic random magnetic deflection vector data-display unit is given in Table 4.11, and, as has been previously pointed out, the most significant parameters are the linear writing speed, the deflection settling time, and the resolution. Admittedly, the luminance and contrast ratio are not to be neglected, but the three parameters just referred to have a prime effect on the number of lines and characters that can be presented without flicker during one refresh cycle. Figure 4.49 shows photographs of displays generated on two representative units and are indicative of the image quality and complexity that may be achieved. If we apply the parameter values given in Table 4.11 to equation 4.14 we have

$$10X + 10Y + 10(X + Y) = 20,000$$

$$X + Y = 1000$$

and if we note further from Figure 4.49b that the average line length is 25% full scale, then 1000 random characters 250 full-scale lines, or combinations of both are possible. This is not very impressive when compared with the 2000 or more characters that can be displayed on television monitors, but the quality of the image may compensate for the limited data density possible. It should also be understood that the limitation is not due to the resolution since the 1000 or more television lines that may be achieved in this type of monitor will allow over 10,000 characters to be displayed, if they could be generated during a refresh cycle. This is possible if we use a 2-μs character time and a 50-Hz refresh but allows no time for deflections, and it is rather pointless to have all the characters in the same location. Realistically, over 4000 characters may be generated on this type of monitor, but only if a fixed format is used and the deflections from one character position to the next are made small, as has been done in at least one alphanumeric system.

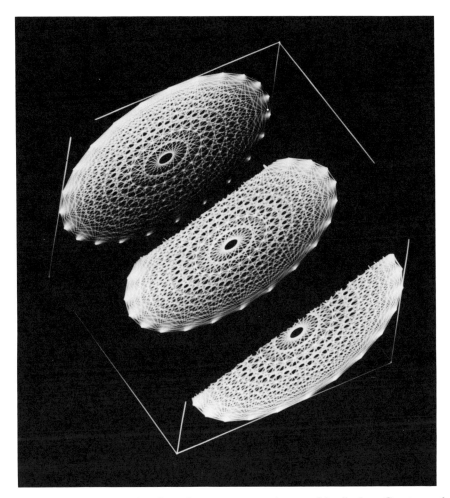

FIGURE 4.49a Example of random vector complex graphic display. Courtesy of Vector General.

One example of this type of monitor is shown in Figure 4.50, with the selection made on a random basis from the various units available from different manufacturers. The units chosen for presentation here and later are not to be considered as better or worse than any other, and no preference is intended, although one cannot say that they bear no resemblance to any unit, alive or dead. This should be enough disclaimer, which applies to any equipment that happens to be shown as representative of its type. The monitors may be included in a complete system and contained in the same console as the rest of the system, as shown in Figure 4.50, but we are considering them here only as separate units, to the extent that they may be available in this form. One important reason for these monitors not being offered as separate units is their relatively high cost, so that it is usually more reasonable to obtain

FIGURE 4.49b   Example of random vector average-line-length display. Courtesy of Lundy Corporation.

them as part of a total system, but as it is sometimes necessary to have more than one monitor, the characteristics of the individual monitor must be considered. Otherwise, it can be treated solely as the output display of the total system, and whereas the parameters given in Table 4.11 still apply, they apply to the full system and are affected by the characteristics of the rest of the total system, as is discussed later.

Random Electrostatic Deflection. Monitors using random electrostatic deflection CRTs have a schematic very similar to that shown in Figure 4.48, except that electrostatic deflection amplifiers are used, there is no yoke, and the CRT contains deflection plates. Of course, the details of the circuits differ, as has been covered in the earlier sections of this chapter, but the basic configuration is what concerns us here, and for this no additional schematic is necessary. One such unit is pictured in Figure 4.51, and performance characteristics are given in Table 4.12. It can be seen from Table 4.12 that faster deflection, line drawing, and character writing speeds are significant advantages found in this monitor when compared with its magnetic deflection equivalent, whereas the lower luminance and resolution are the usual disadvantages. All this might be expected from the previous descriptions of these types of units, as well as the necessity for balancing the deflection voltages required

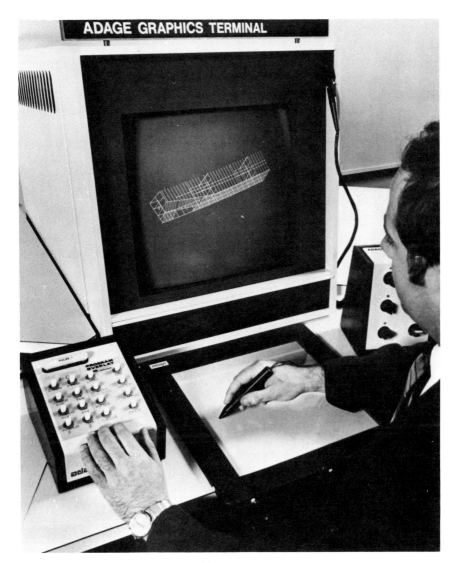

FIGURE 4.50 Example of random vector system monitor. Courtesy of Adage Corporation.

against the currents needed for the magnetic deflection unit. In any event, the fast deflection and character writing times possible with modern electrostatic systems make this approach attractive when high data density is a prime factor and raster systems are not acceptable. For example, using equation 4.14 and the values for the relevant parameters in Table 4.12 lead to

$$X + Y = 4000$$

FIGURE 4.51   Example of electrostatic deflection CRT monitor. Courtesy of Hewlett Packard.

TABLE 4.12   Electrostatic Deflection CRT Monitor Parameters

Parameter	Value
Deflection settling time (μs)	<1 (to one spot diameter)
Small-signal bandwidth (MHz)	5
Video bandwidth (MHz)	25
Linear writing speed (cm/μs)	25
Resolution (lines/cm)	17 (shrinking raster)
Luminance (nits)	150–500
Spot size (mm)	0.25–0.38
Viewing area (cm)	28 (high) × 38 (wide)
Acceleration voltage (kV)	28
Phosphor	P-31
Power consumption (W)	130–140

which is four times the density possible with the representative performance given in Table 4.11. However, luminance levels of over 150 nits cannot readily be attained, and resolutions of more than 1000 television lines are not available, although there are units with luminance of 500 nits and 500 lines so it is necessary to sacrifice one aspect of overall performance to achieve the others. This type of monitor has been incorporated in a few alphanumeric and vector systems.

Storage. Direct-view storage CRT monitors were available essentially from only one manufacturer but are interacting enough to be discussed separately, because of their unique characteristics and since they were incorporated in various storage CRT vector systems. The basic schematic shown in Figure 4.48 applies, with the addition of the flood-gun circuitry, and there is no need for fast deflection to achieve high data density. Of course, no refresh memory is required, but since it is not usually included in a monitor in any case, we defer further discussion of the refresh memory until later. Table 4.13 contains a list of the relevant parameters for this type of monitor, and the latest developments have made units with a 50-cm diagonal possible and a data density of over 10,000 characters. The slow deflection speeds and the low luminance given in Table 4.13 are representative and reflect both the advantages and disadvantages of this type of monitor. The inclusion of a write-through mode has made the use of a cursor or light pen possible, but it is still not too convenient for data entry unless some kind of data tablet is used.

TABLE 4.13   Electrical and Direct-View Storage Monitor Parameters

Parameter	Value	
	Electrical Storage	Direct View
Deflection settling time	10 μs/diameter	3.5 μs/cm + 5 μs to one spot
Dot writing time (storage)	20 ns	5 μs
Deflection sensitivity	1 V for full scale	1 V for full scale
Resolution	1024 cm × 1024 cm— CRT limited	400 lines (shrinking raster)
Size of CRT	Any CRT	50 cm diameter
Viewing area	Depends on CRT	20 cm × 18 cm
Erase time	400 ms full screen, 500 ns for dot	500 ms
Viewing time (min)	30	15
Power consumption (W)	150 + CRT	250
Luminance (nits)	CRT limited up to 150	30
Nonstore mode	Cursor at 150 nits	Available
Phosphor	Any CRT	Similar to P-1

It should be noted that no color versions were available, although they were conceivable.

Data-display units using electronic storage in association with a standard raster monitor are perhaps not legitimately considered as a class of monitors, since it is the raster monitor that constitutes the actual monitor, with the storage unit acting as a combined refresh memory and converter. However, it is possible to combine the storage system with other types of monitors, and the unique properties of the resultant monitor systems warrant their inclusion in this section. Again, as was the case for the direct-view storage CRT monitor, there was effectively only one source, and the characteristics given in Table 4.13 are taken directly from the published data on the unit supplied by this manufacturer. These data are for a combination that uses a raster monitor as the output display, but, as we have noted, it is possible to combine other types of monitor with the electrical storage unit and thus convert any nonstorage monitor into a storage unit with many of the desirable characteristics of the direct-view storage monitor, but without the deficiencies of low luminance and contrast ratio, as well as the difficulties in using light-pen inputs associated with that unit. Thus the combination of electrical storage with a nonstorage display in one system was a potentially useful arrangement, but was not explored to any great extent. Of course, in some cases the substitution of a digital memory may be quite as satisfactory, but for continuous gray scale and the rapid readout needed for scanning systems, the electrical storage system was probably the best. A photograph of the monitor is shown in Figure 4.52 for historical purposes.

FIGURE 4.52   Example of direct-view storage CRT monitor. Courtesy of Tektronix.

Raster Deflection. Although raster deflection may be associated with either magnetic or electrostatic deflection, given sufficiently fast deflection amplifiers to accommodate the retrace, the monitors used for raster displays are now exclusively of the magnetic defection type, and we consider only these units. Since they are designed primarily to be compatible with standard television, the differences among the various available units lie essentially in the extent to which they exceed the requirements of standard television and whether they include special features such as variable line standards and wideband video. In addition, most manufacturers offer high-resolution monitors capable of going to over 1000 scanning lines with equivalent horizontal resolution. Due to the standardization of television monitors, the units are more or less interchangeable, and are low in cost because of the quantity production, although this is not quite as true for the high-resolution versions, of which much smaller numbers are produced. However, in either case, the advantages of standardization apply, and they are much cheaper than the equivalent vector units. We may repeat here that only a few high-resolution units are available with color, although this situation may change if the demand increases. We do not speculate further on this possibility, and the color monitors discussed later are primarily restricted to the 525-line units. The characteristics of both the standard and high-resolution black-and-white units are given in Table 4.14 and represent the most commonly provided performance capabilities. The screen sizes and phosphor types are limited only by what CRTs may be used, with P-4 the most common phosphor and the sizes and screen shapes those found in ordinary television sets. The units are available in a variety of forms, varying from open rack mountings to attractive wood cabinets. One such unit is shown in Figure 4.53, and cabinetry may be a not insignificant contribution to cost if special factors of decor or esthetics are involved. We do not attempt to examine these aspects further since we are not concerned with physical form, except insofar as it is determined by function.

TABLE 4.14   Standard and High-Resolution Monochrome Raster Monitor Parameters

Parameter	Value	
	Standard	High Resolution
Scanning lines	525	768–1280
Refresh rate (Hz)	30, 60	30, 60
Video bandwidth (MHz)	4–10	10–100
Screen size diag (cm)	20–40	30–50
Phosphors	P-2, P-4, P-39, others	P-2, P-4, P-39, others
Luminance (nits)	120–300	120–300
Power (W)	45–65	200
Accelerator voltage (kV)	12–16	18–25
Linearity (%)	2	1

FIGURE 4.53   Example of monochromatic raster monitor. Courtesy of Javelin Electronics.

Color Monitors

Vector Monitor. Vector color monitors are based exclusively on the use of the penetration type of color CRT, for the reasons given previously, although it is perfectly possible to design a vector color monitor with a standard television color CRT. However, if this were done, the advantages of high resolution would be lost unless the special high-resolution CRT were used, in which case the cost advantage might by dissipated. In any event, only penetration CRT units are available, and we restrict the discussion to these types. Theoretically, a three-phosphor color-penetration CRT could be used, but since only two-phosphor CRTs are made, all the monitors available use these types. Red and green are the basic colors, and the monitors are designed to provide up to four distinguishable colors. Table 4.15 presents the operating parameters of such a monitor, and units of this type were available from several manufacturers. The schematic of the unit is similar to that for the monochromatic random deflection monitor, with the addition of a switching power supply and correction circuits to compensate for the changes in deflection sensitivity and focus at the different acceleration voltages. It may also include decoding circuitry for the color selection signal, in the event that this decoding is not done externally. The cost was quite high, primarily due to the low quantity, and the need for fast switching of the high voltage supply, but the costs were coming down and might have reached levels more com-

TABLE 4.15   Vector Color Monitor Parameters

Parameter	Value
Type of CRT	Penetron
Size of CRT	40–53 cm (diameter)
Deflection settling time (μs)	10–15 (to 0.05%)
Small-signal bandwidth (MHz)	2.5
Video bandwidth (MHz)	5–10
Spot size (cm)	0.030–0.038
Color switching time (μs)	10–15
High-voltage range (kV)	6–12
Luminance (nits)	75
Number of colors	4
Deflection speed (μs/cm)	1
Phosphors	P-22 red, green
Refresh rate (Hz)	30
Power (kW)	1.1

petitive with raster color monitors while still retaining the advantage of high resolution. It did not seem probable that more than four colors would be attained unless a three-phosphor CRT were developed, but four colors are sufficient for many applications. This type of color monitor was capable of producing an attractive image, and could be used for graphic displays that could not be satisfactorily achieved with raster systems. The physical appearance of the unit is similar to the monochrome version shown in Figure 4.50, with a few additional controls for the color adjustment. It is also compatible with the display generators used for the monochrome units, if the color-selection signal is added, and may be used in combination with those monitors. However, the advent of lower cost high resolution raster color monitors sounded its death knell.

Raster Deflection. As noted previously for the monochromatic raster units, color CRT monitors that use raster deflection are also essentially of the type used for standard television; that is, they employ magnetic deflection and electrostatic focus. The block diagram for this type of unit is shown in Figure 4.40, and photographs of representative units are shown in Figure 4.54. The block diagram is similar in many respects to that shown in Figure 4.25 for the monitor portions of the image converter subsystem. In addition, the performance characteristics as described for the data-display unit is Section 4.3.3 apply to the raster deflection monitors. However, some additional design features are of sufficient interest to warrant further discussion at this point. These are related to the yoke design, dynamic convergence, and multiscan monitors.

Beginning with some of the yoke design considerations, some information on deflection yoke design is given in Section 2.4.2 and may be used to de-

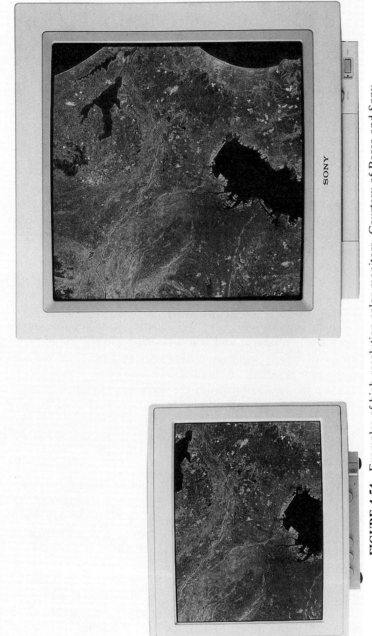

FIGURE 4.54 Examples of high-resolution color monitors. Courtesy of Barco and Sony.

termine the desired yoke characteristics. In addition, a yoke selection procedure has been promulgated by the Electronic Industries Association, and may be obtained from that organization (TEPAK No. 22). The relevant parameters are the CRT deflection angle, neck size, and anode voltage. Then the yoke energy constant may be obtained from the manufacturer, the half-angle deflection time and the maximum allowable induced voltage determined, and the maximum allowable yoke inductance calculated from

$$L_m = \frac{V^2 T^2}{2k} \tag{4.28}$$

where L_m = maximum allowable yoke inductance in μH
 V = maximum allowable induced voltage in volts
 T = half-angle deflection time in μs
 k = yoke energy constant

Similarly, the required current for half-angle deflection may be calculated from

$$I = \left(\frac{2k}{L}\right)^{1/2} \tag{4.29}$$

Misconvergence is a major problem with color CRT monitors, and occurs when the red, blue, and green beams are not properly aligned. Most delta gun yokes contain static convergence assemblies consisting of pole pieces that can be adjusted to obtain best alignment, as well as separate dynamic convergence coils. CRTs with in-line guns are self-converging, but also require some dynamic adjustment. Figure 4.55 is a block diagram for a dynamic convergence circuit that has been developed by Hitachi for use in color monitors with delta or in line-gun CRTs. This circuit allows corrections for dynamic misconvergence to the introduced so as to reduce the misconvergence to acceptable levels. The procedure is for the operator to adjust the convergence, and the EEPROM stores the data so as to simplify the adjustment process.

Finally, there are the multiscan monitors that accept a variety of standard inputs. These monitors provide variable scan rates for both vertical and horizontal scans, and are compatible with all of the fixed scan standards. These monitors scan the range of horizontal scan rates and lock into the scanning frequency provided by the video graphics board in use, as well as a number of special computer platforms offered by IBM and Apple. The vertical frequencies available range from 38 to 150 Hz, and the horizontal frequencies are from 15 to 72 kHz, although the full range is not found in every monitor. Table 4.16 lists the scan rates, resolution, and standards met by several representative monitors of this type.

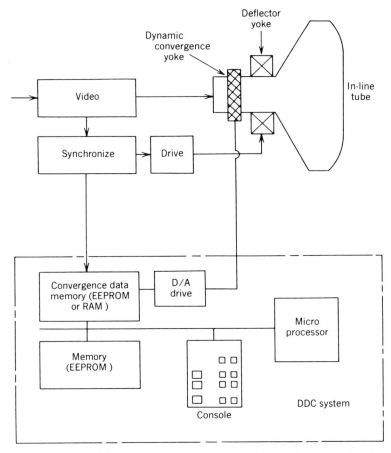

FIGURE 4.55 Digital dynamic convergence system block diagram. After Aldersey-Williams [11], by permission.

TABLE 4.16 Multiscan CRT Monitor Parameters

CRT Size (in.)	Vertical Scan (Hz)	Horizontal Scan (kHz)	Resolution	Standards
20	45–87	15–36	1024 × 768	RGB, CGA, EGA, VGA, 8514A
37	40–120	24–64	1260 × 1024	All
20	50–90	30–67	1280 × 1024	All
27	40–100	15–38	640 × 480	RGB, CGA, EGA
20	50–100	15–36	720 × 480	RGB, CGA, VGA

These are all full-color monitors and can be operated at a noninterlaced scan rate with video amplifiers bandwidths of 100 MHz. It should also be noted that a 3000-line monochrome CRT monitor requires over 10 times the video bandwidth and four times the horizontal sweep rate.

4.7.3 Display Generators and Controller

Vector System. Vector display systems have been replaced to a considerable extent by raster systems, but it is of some interest to present information on the vector types even if they are not in active use. To this end, the material contained in the first edition is included here.

Vector display systems in general do not offer the display generator as a separate element without at least one data-display monitor as part of the purchased system. However, the display generator is frequently completely separate from the monitor and may be used to drive a number of monitors, either in parallel or with each operating as a unique unit. The same consideration applies to the display controller, which may be an independent microprocessor, programmed to provide the control and timing functions, or a special, hardwired unit, designed specifically for the system in which it operates. Therefore, although it is not feasible in most cases to use these units with display units other than the ones for which they are designed, it is still reasonable to examine them as independent functional elements, since the functions will be implemented in any system that may be obtained, to a greater or lesser extent. This situation does not hold for the raster equivalents, which are provided as separate units and are compatible with any of the raster display monitors discussed previously.

Due to the lack of standardization for the vector generators and controller, it is not possible to list one set of specifications that applies to all units. However, the characteristics given in Table 4.17 are reasonably representative and serve as a guide to what may be expected and what should be specified. These parameters can be understood best by referring to the block diagram shown in Figure 4.56, which is a somewhat more specific schematic than that given in Figure 4.3 and contains all the functions that may be included in these units. We have discussed the interface features previously, and we may add to that discussion the information that any controller may have several interface options to make it compatible with various host computers, or it may be designed to operate with one mini- or microcomputer, in which case the interface requirements are delegated to the resident computer. The refresh memory operates at the refresh rate designed into the system, and its capacity determines the number of pages of data that may be stored in the system at any one time. There may also be an auxiliary bulk memory (not shown), for off-line storage of data, but this is usually optional. A refresh rate of 60 Hz is common, and some units have a variable refresh rate, which may be lowered as the data density increases, and the resultant flicker accepted for short periods of time. This feature may be useful when high data density is infre-

TABLE 4.17   Example of Specifications for Generator–Controller Unit of Vector Display System

Function generator:

Vector

Setup time: 3.5 μs

Writing time: 2 μs per cm on-axis projection

Linearity: ±0.5% of full scale

Accuracy: ±0.5% of full scale

Delay: less than 100 ns between x and y and intensity symbol; intensity rise and fall time, >50 ns

Circle

Setup time: 167 μs maximum

Writing time:

167 μs (×1 magnification)

334 μs (×2 magnification)

668 μs (×3 magnification)

668 μs (×4 magnification)

Radius: 512-bit resolution for 15-cm radius, intensity compensation, intensity signal proportional to circle radius, resulting in circles of uniform intensity

Arc

An arc is drawn along the circumference of the circle described by the circle command

Arc begin: 1024 addressable locations

Arc end: 1024 addressable locations

Arc reference: addresses referred to the negative x-axis; a circle is drawn in clockwise direction

Point

Point-positioning time: 1 microsecond plus 1.25 μs of on-axis movement.

Point-intensification time: 500 ns

Other functions

Random positioning: 1 μs plus 1.25 μs of on-axis movement

Intensity levels: 4 levels including blank

Line structure: solid, dot, dash, and dot-dash

Scissoring: analog scissoring limits visible display to the top 30 cm × 30 cm area

Magnification: ×2, ×3, or ×4

Translation: display may be shifted for windowing operations by ±512 addressable locations along the x and y axes while in magnification; translation is also scaled by magnification

Drive capability: 30 m

Independent channels: 4

Multiple drives: 4 CRT monitors

Blink: 0.5 s on: 0.5 s off

Character generator:

Display method: stroke

Character set: 64 uppercase ASCII; 64 special symbols (optional)

Character sizes: 32 mm, 48 mm, 64 mm, 86 mm high

Aspect ratio: 4:3 (height : width)

Writing time: is a function of the CRT used to display the data. When a Model 8013 is used,

48 mm characters—3.5 μs average

80 mm characters—7.0 μs average

Text mode: yes

Character spacing: 1½-character width

Line spacing: 1½-character height

Rotation: 90° counterclockwise

Source: Courtesy of Aydin Controls.

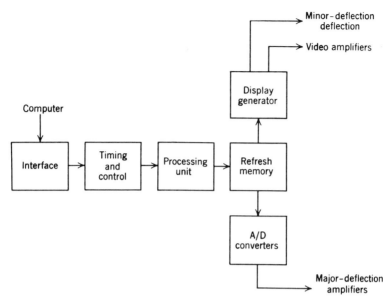

FIGURE 4.56   Vector system generator–controller block diagram.

quent and it is not economical to pay for increased speed required to handle the high data-density condition.

Next we have the display generator, which contains the various generators such as character, vector, circle, and conic, all of which have been discussed in detail previously. The significant parameters are the times required to generate the characters and draw lines, circles, and conics. There may also be some special features such as video compensation to achieve constant luminance when constant-time generators are used and video control to obtain several luminance levels. In color systems, the additional functions of color selection, voltage switching, and the other compensation signals necessitated by the characteristics of the penetration CRT are added, but otherwise these units are the same, and we do not consider color systems separately. Other aspects of the generators are the number of character types, the font, and whether dot matrix or stroke writing is used, as well as the linearity of the line generators, although the deflection amplifiers have the greater effect on this linearity.

Finally, there are the D/A converters that define the number of addressable locations and thereby the positional resolution of the system. Again, we should stress that this is not the same as the visual resolution, controlled by the resolution of the display unit. The positional resolution available is at least 10 bits, with 12 bits not uncommon, and since this is frequently better than the visual resolution, one must not be misled by the positional resolution specification into expecting better visual resolution than the system can provide. The speed of the D/A converters is also important, but this is usually much better than the deflection amplifiers settling time, and speeds of less than 1 μs are common. There are many units available from different manufacturers, with a wide range of performance and features to satisfy most requirements, if one is willing to pay the price. Since each manufacturer has his own approach to assemblying the functional elements, it is essential to carefully examine the complete specification, using Table 4.17 as a guide, to be certain that all functions are performed and meet the application requirements. Again, as a final warning, it is not generally possible to mix portions of units from different sources, so that all desired functions must exist in the selected units or be available as options from the same source.

Display generation and control for storage CRT monitors are basically of the same type as those described for the vector system, with the exception that no refresh memory is used, and the generation rates are much slower, as determined by the characteristics of the monitor. These slower rates are compatible with data transmission over telephone lines, and the controller may be connected directly to the host computer, without the intervention of a resident microcomputer. However, since the controller and generators are usually part of a complete system, including self-contained graphics capabilities there may be no connection to other data sources, and we defer parameter listing until we discuss the complete system.

Raster System. The functions required from the raster–controller generator unit are frequently provided by some form of microcomputer, with software determining how the unit operates. Therefore, there is no special hardware configuration involved when this architecture is used. However, there is one type of raster terminal that does function as a controller–generator unit in addition to its other capabilities. This is the X windows terminal, which has achieved considerable success as an alternative to a fully self-contained workstation. The basic typical architecture of such a terminal is shown in Figure 4.57. The unit accepts inputs through the Ethernet controller and performs all of the graphics and video functions with the graphics processor and video logic under software control. The processors and memory act to some extent as the microcomputer portion of the unit but do not have the full data processing capabilities of a standard desktop or portable computer, and depend on a separate computer to provide those functions. However, the terminal also accepts inputs from devices such as the mouse and a keyboard, and drives both a monitor and some type of hard copy device such as a plotter. The architecture shown in Figure 4.57 is a first-generation type. Later versions use one microprocessor and RISC technology, and the parameters are given in Table 4.18.

4.7.4 Computer

In addition to the X stations and specialized boards that may be used as controller–generators, computers in their various configurations may also be

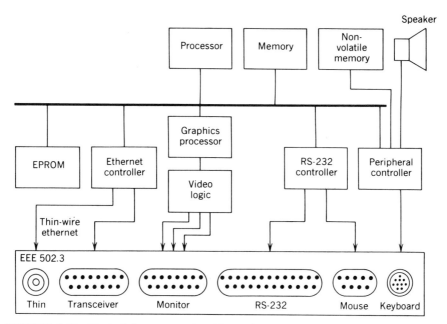

FIGURE 4.57   Typical first-generation X terminal architecture. After Wilson [12], by permission.

incorporated in the display system to play the controller–generator role as well as perform the other functions for which computers are intended. Microcomputers in their various forms are the most common types used for this function, and the performance characteristics of interest are shown in Table 4.19. Of course, the actual microcomputer has a much broader capability than is shown in this table. These units accept a wide range of software, as well as various plug-in cards that enhance the operating capabilities of the total computer. Thus they are well equipped to perform the controller–generator function.

TABLE 4.18   RISC X Windows Specifications

Parameter	Value
Processor speed (MHz)	22.7
User memory (Mbytes)	4–18
Video memory (Mbytes)	2
Monitor type	19-in. color
Resolution	1280 × 1024
Colors	250
Color palette	16.7M
Refresh rate (Hz)	72

Source: Courtesy of Hewlett Packard.

TABLE 4.19   Microcomputer Specifications

Parameter	Value
Word length (bits)	8, 16, 32
Processor speed (MHz)	8, 10, 16, 33
Memory (RAM) (MB)	1–32
Memory (fixed disk) (MB)	20–420
Memory access time (ms)	28–16
Graphics standards	All
Monitors	Various
Input devices	Various
Disk drives (in.)	3.5, 5.25

4.7.5   Terminals

General-Purpose Terminals. Some performance data on X terminals are given in Table 4.9, and additional information on these and other types of terminals are presented in this section. Briefly, X terminals may be described as relating to graphic workstations in the same way as general-purpose terminals relate to multiuser systems. A general-purpose terminal, sometimes referred to as a *dumb* or ASCII terminal, is one that has minimal computing power and is used primarily with a host computer as part of a multiuser system. In its simplest form, it is represented by the block diagram shown in Figure 4.58, and a photograph of a representative terminal is shown in Figure 4.59. The specifications for this type of terminal may cover a range of capabilities, and such a range is shown in the set given in Table 4.20.

X Windows. The X terminal operating in an X window system provides an environment where a number of data processing sources can be accessed over a local area network. It is essentially like a diskless workstation and therefore lacks a number of the hardware facilities found in the workstations, such as large memory management units. As a result, the X terminals are considerably simpler and cheaper than workstations and can perform many of the same functions. Thus an X terminal may be considered to be a workstation that is

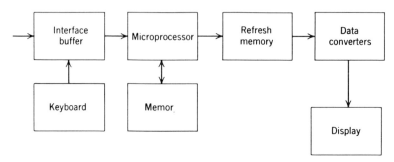

FIGURE 4.58 Block diagram of *dumb* alphanumeric terminal. Courtesy of Wyse.

FIGURE 4.59   Dumb alphanumeric terminal. Courtesy of Wyse.

designed for specific applications and operating under the X windows system protocol. To this end, the typical terminal may have two processors, one for the CPU and the other for graphics, as noted previously and shown in Figure 4.57. The place of the X terminal in a typical window manager environment is shown in Figure 4.60, where the terminal is connected to the host window manager through the network communications. This can be somewhat simplified by using a local window manager so that the burden on network communications can be somewhat reduced. Finally, typical specifications for an X windows terminal are given in Table 4.18, with a representative unit shown in Figure 4.61.

4.7.6   Workstations

Workstations offer the ultimate in performance with both data processing and graphics capabilities available from stand-alone systems. They include

TABLE 4.20   Terminal Specifications

Parameter	Value
Phosphor color	G, A, W
Compatibility	ASCII, ANSI
Refresh rate (Hz)	60–85
Character resolution	10×12 to 16×208
Columns	80/132
Lines	26/44
Keyboard	ASCII, ANSI

Source: Courtesy of Wyse.

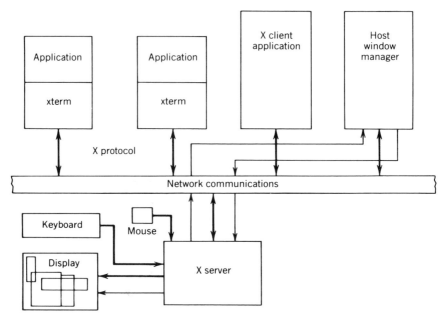

FIGURE 4.60   Typical host window manager environment. Courtesy of NCR.

FIGURE 4.61   Hewlett Packard's Series 700 work stations. These RISC-based work stations provide the ability to access simultaneously and display software residing in different computers.

full graphics, but may also be used for nongraphics applications. However, the trend is toward the use of extensive graphics, and they should be considered as full-graphics systems. The basic block diagram of such a system is shown in Figure 4.62, where the block labeled "operator inputs" includes as many of the input devices as may be required. Similarly, the block labeled "display" connotes all of the monitors that may be part of the system. The host computer subsystem may consist of a single microcomputer, or a group of supercomputers, and may be internal to the workstation cabinet or located at a remote location. In the case where the computer subsystem consists of a single microcomputer, it approaches a desktop computer system, and most of the available desktop and portable computers can be operated as a lower-level workstation or even as a full-graphics workstation. In the latter case there is considerable overlap between the capabilities of the computer and the workstation.

However, the true high-end workstation contains a number of special elements, as shown in Figure 4.63, in particular the special processors and memories. However, these can be emulated by software in general-purpose microcomputers, so that the dividing line between true workstations and desktop or portable computers is increasingly blurred. In any case the performance of either type of unit is limited by the capabilities of the monitor, as well as the input devices, and a wide range of these units are found in conjunction with the processing portions of the workstation. A representative monitor parameter specification is given in Table 4.16 and a more complete workstation specification in Table 4.21.

To this should be added a number of peripherals for input and output and for memory expansion purposes, as well as the monitor.

4.7.7 Large-Screen Displays

As has been pointed out previously, there are only three commercially available types of large-screen display systems using the CRT or some form of cathode-ray device as the display device. These are, to reiterate, the projection CRT and the two forms of light-valve systems described earlier in this chapter. These are all raster systems, although it is possible to operate some projection systems in the vector mode. However, since the large majority of the applications have been for raster systems, we restrict this discussion to that form.

In their simplest form, these large-screen systems have the projection display unit operating in much the same fashion as the monitor of the alphanumeric and graphics systems just covered. Thus the system diagrams for the small-screen systems shown in Figures 4.25, 4.33, 4.36, 4.37, 4.57, 4.58, and 4.60 apply, as well as some of the other diagrams associated with CRT systems. The major use of the large-screen systems has been for display of standard television, with some special applications where other data in raster format have been presented on the large screen. In actuality, any information that can be presented by a CRT monitor can also be presented on these large-

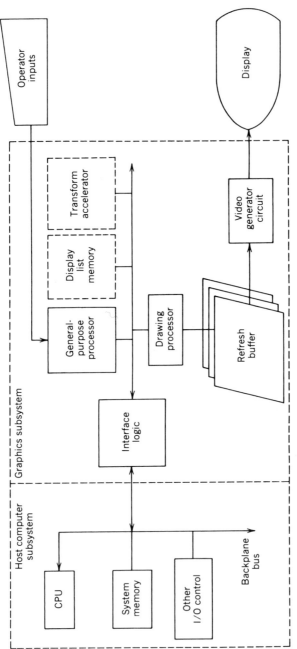

FIGURE 4.62 Representative workstation block diagram. After Breen [13], by permission.

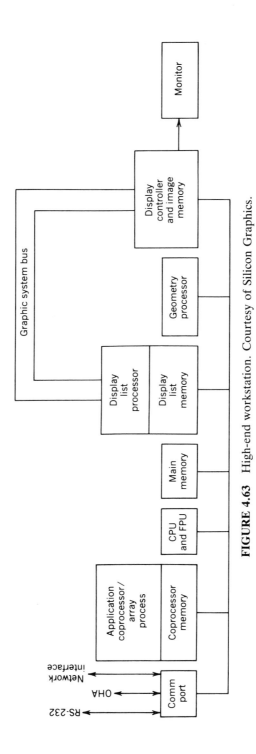

FIGURE 4.63 High-end workstation. Courtesy of Silicon Graphics.

TABLE 4.21   Workstation Specifications

Parameter	Value
Memory capacity (Mb)	8–32
Mb/board	1.2–8 M
Display memory (bit planes)	8–32
Processor speed (MHz)	12–33
MIPS	0.9–40

screen display systems, and the same characteristics of performance are involved, with the additional aspects deriving from the optical portions of the total system. The general forms of such systems including the optics, are represented in Figures 4.39, 4.46, and 4.47, and Tables 4.22 to 4.25 list the relevant performance parameters of the three types of large screen systems we are discussing. All are available in color versions, with three separate systems required for the projection and Eidophor units, with the resultant increase in complexity and cost. The best resolution, luminance, and contrast ratios are obtained with the Eidophor system, although the latest GE Talaria units, which use three projectors, have come closer to the Eidophor, with a maximum output of 32,000 lm against 56,000 lm for the Eidophor, and there are numerous other models that offer performance capabilities that may be sufficient for most purposes and at a lower price than the highest-performance Eidophors. As to direct CRT projection systems, they provide reduced but usually adequate performance for most applications at a considerably lower price than either the Eidophor or the Talaria, and are the preferred type for home use.

The characteristics of the projection screen also affect the performance of the large-screen projection system. Briefly, for a Lambertian screen, that reflects light in all directions and follows Lambert's law, that is,

$$I = I_0 \cos \theta \tag{4.30}$$

where I = light reflected from screen
I_0 = light impinging on screen
θ = angle between plane of screen and light beam

The display luminance normal to the screen is given by

$$L_s = L_c \times \frac{T}{4f^2} \times \frac{1}{(1 + m)^2} \tag{4.31}$$

where L_s = display luminance
L_c = CRT luminance
T = optics transmission
f = lens aperture number
m = magnification

TABLE 4.22   Eidophor Performance Specifications

Parameter	Value
Maximum image size (diag. in.)	630, 750
Minimum image size	120, 222
Maximum projection distance (ft)	500, 1508
Minimum projection distance	16, 48H
Output (lm)	28,800, 56,000, 30,000
H/V scan frequency (Hz)	15.75K–36K, 40–1204
Video bandwidth (MHz)	50
Inputs	Composite, RGB
Front, rear projection (F, R)	F, R

Source: Adapted from *AV Video*, October 1990, pp. 96–98. Courtesy of Gretay.

TABLE 4.23   Talaria Performance Specifications

Parameter	Value
Maximum image size (diag. in.)	180–720
Minimum image size	60, 70, 100, 120
Maximum projection distance (ft)	9–280
Minimum projection distance	4.5–15
Output (lm)	475–32,000
H/V scan frequency (Hz)	15.75K–36K, 38–100
Video bandwidth (MHz)	30, 40, 70
Inputs	Composite, RGB, TTL
Front rear projection (F, R)	F, R

TABLE 4.24   CRT Projection Performance Specifications

Parameter	Value
Maximum image size (diag. in.)	40–434
Minimum image size	40–150
Maximum projection distance (ft)	10–408
Minimum projection distance	5–15
Output (lm)	350–1000
H/V scan frequency (Hz)	14K–72K, 38–120
Video bandwidth (MHz)	9–120
Inputs	Composite, RGB, TTL

Source: AV Video.

TABLE 4.25 Specifications for CRT Schmidt Projection System

Projection head
  Size and type: 35 cm Schmidt Optics
  Throw distance, 2.7–5.4 m
  Display area: 120 cm $\times$ 120 cm
  Linearity: $\pm 1\%$
  Light output: 30 nits at 32 m
  Writing speed: 2.5×10^6 cm/s
  Line width: 2.5 mm
Z-axis
  Input sensitivity: $+3$ V for full intensity
  Input impedance: 75-Ω termination is standard
  Rise time: 50 ns
  γ Correction: Light output is linear with respect to
    input voltage
  Delay time: zero differential delay of z-axis with
    respect to X and Y signals
Major deflection
  Input sensitivity: 5 V p-p for 120 cm deflection
  Input impedance: 75-Ω termination is standard
  Large signal response: 20 kHz
  Small signal response: 500 kHz at 3 dB
  $X-Y$ phase shift: less than 1 line separation at 15
    kHz
  Settling time: 25 μs for full-screen deflection to
    settle to within 0.25%; 3 μs for 2.5 cm to settle
    to within 0.25%
Minor deflection
  Input sensitivity: 5 V p-p for 5 cm deflection
  Input impedance: 75 Ω (termination)
  Frequency response: 1 MHz at 3 dB
  $X-Y$ differential phase shift: less than 1 line
    separation at 1 MHz
Inputs (BNC connectors, rear)
  X-input major deflection
  X-input major deflection
  Y-input major deflection
  Y-input major deflection
  Z-input
Operator controls
  On/off
  Focus
  Intensity
Service adjustments (internal)
  X-input deflection sensitivity
  X-input dc level
  Y-input deflection sensitivity
  Y-input dc level
  Z-input dc level
Power requirements: 115 V $\pm$ 10% 60 Hz, 300 W

Source: Courtesy of Aydin Controls.

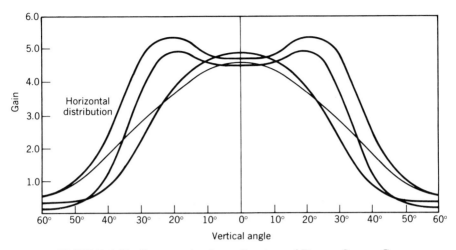

FIGURE 4.64   Screen gain chart. Courtesy of Draper Screen Co.

TABLE 4.26   Optical Characteristics of Projection Screens

Parameter	Cine 25	Cine 15	Cine 50	Cine 10
Gain	2.5	1.5	5.0	1.2
Transmission (%)	62	50	65	47
Reflectance (%)	3	3	3	3
Resolution (lines/mm)	70	60	75	55

Source: Courtesy of Draper Screen.

Directive screens used in CRT projection systems reflect light within a limited solid angle directed toward the observer and are usually characterized by a gain within that angle in relation to a Lambertian screen. Gain curves for different types of screen from one representative source are shown in Figure 4.64, and Table 4.26 presents further information on the optical characteristics of these screens.

The combination of screen gain and light output from the source, be it a CRT or a light valve, can result in fairly high luminance values, even on a very large screen. However, the use of a screen with gain limits the area within which the viewing conditions are uniform, as shown in Figure 4.64. Thus the choice is between improved performance in a limited area and relatively uniform performance over a larger area. In general, the former is preferred in order to achieve the highest screen output.

REFERENCES

[1] Sherr, S., *Fundamentals of Display System Design*, Wiley, New York, 1970.

[2] Shinners, S., *Control System Design*, Wiley, New York, 1965.

[3] Frankenberg, R. J., "Designer's Guide to: Semiconductor Memories—Part 2," *EDN,* Aug. 20, 1975, 58.

[4] Lechner, B. J., "HDTV Systems," *SID Sem. Lec. Notes* 1990, M3.27.

[5] Sherr, S., "Applications of Digital Television Displays to Command and Control," *SID Proc.*, **11**/2, 1970, 61–70.

[6] Pender, H., and McIlwain, K., Eds., *Electrical Engineers' Handbook*, 4th ed., Wiley, New York, 1950.

[7] Gibilini, D., and House, W. R., "CRTs Project High-Definition Television Pictures," *Laser Focus World*, Sept. 1990, 125.

[8] Moskovich, J., et al., "CRT Projection Optics," *SID Sem. Lect. Notes*, 1991, M7/17–M7/18.

[9] Horowitz, P., "Concept for Design and Implementation of Mobile Computer-Generated Display System," *Inform. Display*, **3**/4, 1966, 27.

[10] Good, W. E., "Projection Television," *SID Proc.*, **17**/1, 1976, 3–7.

[11] Aldersey-Williams, H., "Raster Monitors: Limits to Resolution," *Electron. Image.*, Jan. 1985, 37.

[12] Wilson, D., "X Windows Terminals Search for a Single Processor Solution," *Comput. Design*, Aug. 1991, 78.

[13] Breen, P. T., "Review of Workstation Technology," *SID Sem. Lect. Notes*, 1991, M9/11.

5

ALPHANUMERIC AND MATRIX PANEL SYSTEMS AND EQUIPMENT

5.1 INTRODUCTION

Alphanumeric (A/N) and *matrix panel systems* may be grouped under the basic rubric of *flat-panel displays* (FPDs), but they do differ from the equipment and system point of view to a sufficient extent that a separate treatment is justified for each group. The main characteristics they have in common one that all use the same basic technologies, and their mechanical configurations are such as to produce units whose displays have depths that are small compared to the other dimensions. In the latter respect they differ notably from the majority of the CRT-based systems described in Chapter 4, although there are a few such systems that could also be classified as FPDs. However, the bulk of FPDs are those based on the technologies used for matrix and A/N devices, and the cognomen of FDPs is largely limited to the types using the technologies covered in Chapter 3 and those included in this chapter.

Before beginning this discussion, it should be noted that not all of the technologies covered in Chapter 3 are given equal treatment here. In particular, the most important technologies for A/N systems and equipment are LEDs, dc plasma, VFDs, and LCDs, whereas for matrix panels the main technologies are ac/dc EL, ac/dc plasma, VFDs, and LCDs. Therefore, only equipment and systems that use one or more of these technologies are covered in this chapter. These include those listed previously, and most specifically, of the various possible types of LCDs, only the supertwist and double-supertwist versions of the LCD equipment, with the addition of active matrix for the systems, are given extended treatment.

This is an acceptable approach for several reasons. First, although the TN types retain some portion of the market because of their lower costs, the ST versions predominate particularly for A/N equipment and systems, and do not introduce any significantly different considerations from those points of view than do the older TN types. Similarly, the ST and super-ST are preferred for equipment, and active matrix systems are becoming important, whereas ferroelectric types still have a way to go before they are in common use. Therefore, this limitation does not neglect any significant aspects, while simplifying the discussion considerably. With these provisos and limitations, we now proceed to the technical discussions, beginning with A/N and panel equipment, proceeding to the system configurations for these categories of equipment, and ending up with large-screen projection systems as a separate group of panel systems given special importance because of their application to HDTV and related applications. The projection panels in themselves may have much in common with panels intended for other purposes.

5.2   ALPHANUMERIC EQUIPMENT AND SYSTEMS

5.2.1   Light-Emitting Diodes

A major application for light-emitting diodes (LEDs) is as the display device for A/N equipment and systems. Indeed, this technology was preeminent for many years as the display for watches, calculators, and a wide variety of readouts for instruments and other types of measuring and indicating equipment. This preeminence has been considerably eroded with the development of LCDs and VFDs for these purposes, but LEDS are not completely superseded and retain a place in the market.

The readouts exist in two major forms, that is, as 7-, 14-, or 16-segment numerics (see Figures 1.28–30) and as dot matrix units in either 5×7 or 7×9 formats (see Figures 1.25 and 1.26). The numeric units may be found with as few as one digit up to as many as eight in the simplest configurations, and up to 32 in 16-segment digits in single-line assemblies. Another format is the bar graph, for which 10-element units may be obtained in the simplest form. Some of the single- and double-digit units may be obtained without any multiplexing or drive electronics, but the vast majority of LED readout displays are found in either direct-drive units with or without storage, as shown in Figure 5.1, or in multiplexed systems as shown in Figure 5.2a. The bar graph array may be similarly multiplexed, as shown in Figure 5.2b. The input to the decoding section is usually in the form of BCD parallel signals, and the outputs are the driving signals to the selected segments, so that they will be lit and the proper number shown. Multiplexing is achieved by driving the column elements sequentially while the proper segments are energized for each digit position. The combination of the voltage on the common element and that on the selected segments results in only the segments of the selected digit being lit. This is the standard 2:1 matrix arrangement described in Chapter 3 and is quite effective for LED displays since the breakpoints are sharp and well defined, and the saturation levels are easily reached with

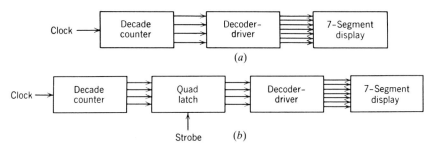

FIGURE 5.1   Seven-segment digit display systems:(*a*) direct drive; (*b*) direct drive with storage.

twice the breakpoint voltage. Since the digits are being scanned, the usual considerations of flicker and the effect of duty cycle on the contrast ratio apply and establish limits on the number of digits that may be scanned. Flicker is not too great a problem since the speed of response of the LED is in the microsecond range, and even at 60 Hz well over several thousand digits could be scanned without difficulty. However, the duty-cycle effect is another mat-

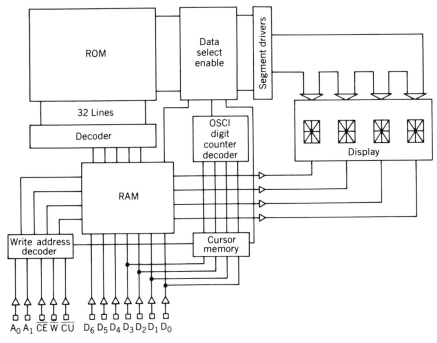

Internal schematic

(*a*)

FIGURE 5.2   (*a*) Sixteen-segment four-digit multiplexed LED display; (*b*) LED bar graph display. Courtesy of Siemens.

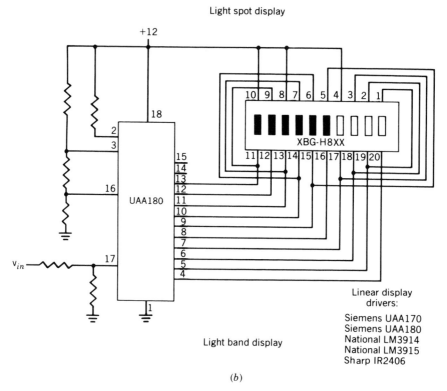

(b)

FIGURE 5.2   (*Continued*)

ter, since if we assume a 0.1% duty factor, then, using equation 3.50, repeated here as

$$C_s = 0.001C_p \qquad (5.1)$$

if we wish C_s to be a minimum of 10, C_p must be 10,000, which is not attainable with available LED displays. In addition, the actual luminous output is reduced by the same factor, and the resultant luminance is equally affected. Peak luminances in the order of 3000 nits are possible, but not more than 100 digits can be scanned while still achieving acceptable levels of luminance/contrast ratio. Fortunately, this is no limitation in the majority of applications, with 12 to 16 digits as usually adequate, and the scanning can be accomplished while retaining sufficiently high luminances and contrast ratios for acceptable visual presentations.

This ability to easily scan numbers of digits is an important feature of LED displays and accounts for their widespread use in those applications where multiplexing achieves significant reductions in complexity and cost while still retaining an acceptable visual image. Another important advantage of multiplexing, referred to in Chapter 3, is that it reduces the number of connections required between the drivers and the digits. The expression for the number of leads required in a multiplexed, seven-segment numeric display is

$$T_m = 7 + n \tag{5.2}$$

where T_m is the number of leads and n is the number of digits, whereas that for a nonmultiplexed display is

$$T = 7n + 1 \tag{5.3}$$

It is clear that for 10 digits multiplexing reduces the number of connections required from 71 to 17, and that is a very significant reduction. Further reduction in the number of connections is made by including the decoder-driver in the same package with the display, so that only the four BCD input leads and the multiplexing signals are involved, resulting in $(n + 2)$ less leads if internal multiplexing signals are provided in the package, and only a clock input is needed to generate those signals. This approach is being used in some commercially available products and achieves an attractive simplicity for the user when connected to the rest of the system. The resultant savings are also obtained in the dot matrix arrays, as is described later, and the use of internal multiplexing is found in both types to an equal extent. Numeric display systems may be driven directly from any source of either ASCII or BCD signals, and, of course, it is also possible to obtain the display alone and add the decoder and drivers to make up a system of this type. However, it may be most convenient to obtain the complete package and not have to worry about the rest of the circuit. Calculators and watches are exceptions in that the chip has outputs for driving the segments directly, usually with multiplexing signals, so that it is only necessary to connect the display to the chip to have a complete package, and the manufacturer of the chip frequently has a display module to mate with the chip. The characteristics of one of these display modules are given in Table 5.1, and it accepts seven-segment decoder outputs, with the light output given in nits.

The second form in which LED display systems are found is that using a matrix array of diodes, usually 7×5 or 9×7 and the appropriate dot-matrix character generator, although other combinations are also used. In these cases row or column multiplexing must be used, as well as the digit multiplexing found in the numeric systems. The structure of such a one-character system is shown in Figure 5.3 and the multiplexing waveforms are essentially those shown in Figure 3.89, applied here through a specific system configuration. The matrix advantage in lead reduction may be expressed by

$$T_m = P_r + P_c \tag{5.4}$$

TABLE 5.1 Operating Characteristics of Single-Digit LED Display at 25°C Ambient-Air Temperature

Parameter	Symbol	Test Conditions	Min.	Typ.	Max.	Unit
Luminance (photometric brightness)	L	$V_{CC} = 5$ V	700	1000		nits
Wavelength at peak emission	λ_{peak}	$V_{CC} = 5$ V	6300	6500	6700	Å
Spectral bandwidth between half-power points	BW_λ	$V_{CC} = 5$ V		200		Å
High-level input voltage	V_{IH}		2			V
Low-level input voltage	V_{IL}				0.8	V
Input clamp voltage	V_I	$V_{CC} = 4.75$ V, $I_I = -12$ mA			-1.5	V
High-level output voltage	V_{OH}	$V_{CC} = 4.75$ V, $I_{OH} = $ max	2.4			V
Low-level output voltage	V_{OL}	$V_{CC} = 4.75$ V, $I_{OL} = $ max			0.4	V
Input current at maximum input voltage	I_I	$V_{CC} = 5.25$ V, $V_I = 5.5$ V			1	mA
Serial carry					40	μA
High-level input current, RBI/RBO node	I_{IH}	$V_{CC} = 5.25$ V, $V_I = 2.4$ V		-0.5		mA
Other inputs					20	μA
Serial carry					-1.6	μA
Low-level input current, RBI/RBO node	I_{IL}	$V_{CC} = 5.25$ V, $V_I = 0.4$ V			-2.4	mA
Other inputs					-0.8	mA
Short-circuit output current, O_A, O_B, O_C, O_D	I_{OS}	$V_{CC} = 5.25$ V	-9		-27.5	mA
Maximum count			-15		-55	mA
Supply current	I_{CC}	$V_{CC} = 5.25$ V		165	250	mA

Source: Courtesy of Dialco.

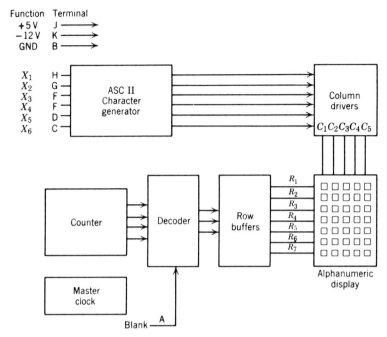

FIGURE 5.3   Block diagram of matrix alphanumeric LED display system. Courtesy of Dialco.

where T_m = total number of leads
P_r = number of row elements
P_c = number of column elements

and by

$$P_t = P_r P_c \tag{5.5}$$

where P_t is the total number of elements.

It is clear the number of leads is reduced from the 35 required in a 5 × 7 matrix, if every element is individually addressed and driven, to 12 in the matrix format. Further reduction is achieved by multiplexing several characters as in the case of the numeric unit, and the final result is given by

$$T_{tm} = T_m + n \tag{5.6}$$

where T_{tm} is the total number of leads for multiplexed assembly and n is the number of alphanumeric positions, instead of

$$T_t = nT_m + 1 \tag{5.7}$$

where T_t = total number of leads for a nonmultiplexed assembly. For a 10-position 5×7 matrix unit the lead reduction is from 121 to 22, which is quite significant. Thus matrix units are invariably multiplexed, although frequently seven elements at a time may be addressed to keep the duty factor effect as low as possible. A 10-position, 5×7 assembly would have a duty factor of 2% in this arrangement and 0.287% without parallel element addressing, so the trade-offs between the number of positions and contrast ratio or luminance are apparent.

Alphanumeric matrices of this type are usually sold as complete assemblies that may be connected directly to a source of ASCII signals and decode and multiplex without additional external circuitry. They may be obtained in packages containing 1 to 10 character positions, with even larger assemblies possible on special order. It should be noted that only seven input leads are required, so that the connections are reduced to a bare minimum if the complete package is used. As we have noted, the savings are almost as substantial here as for the numeric unit, with the leads reduced from 22 to 7, against the reduction from 17 to 4 in the numeric case. Although more than 10 positions in a single assembly is not readily available, it is possible to use a number of smaller groups side by side so as to achieve a display of any reasonable length. Table 5.2 lists the characteristics of a representative four-position display assembly with built-in decoder–drivers and multiplexing, and although there may be variations in character size and luminous intensity, the data shown are a fair indication of what may be obtained. They are generally the display portion of a larger piece of equipment such as a multimeter or as the indicator unit of a data collection system, to name only a few of the many possible applications for LED display equipment and systems.

All of the LED displays discussed to this point have been generally limited in size for multidigit assemblies to under 1 in. However, some special individual dot matrix units can be obtained as large as 4.5 in., and larger displays can be constructed from discrete diodes. There are also multiline and stackable displays that permit large board units to be assembled containing up to eight lines of up to 80 dot matrix characters per line and sizes as large as 6 in. A characteristic unit of this type is shown in Figure 5.4, and a representative set of sizes and matrix format is given in Table 5.3. Of course, it is not possible to get all of the maximum values simultaneously, but the data in Table 5.3 do indicate some of the possibilities. These large board message displays using LEDs are found in numerous locations.

5.2.2   Gas Discharge (DC Plasma)

There are essentially no A/N FPDs that use the ac plasma technology, although Fujitsu did offer some units for a while. However, the panel units are the only ones that have achieved any measure of success, so any discussion of ac plasma equipment and systems is deferred to Section 5.3.2 on matrix panel displays using ac plasma technology. In this section the concentration is on dc plasma units.

TABLE 5.2 LED Digit Displays

Description	Symbol	Test Conditions	Min.	Typ.	Unit
Yellow HCMS-2701/-2711/-2721					
Peak luminous intensity per LED (digit average)[a,b]	I_v	$V_{DD} = 5.0$ V, $V_{COL} = 3.5$ V $V_B = 2.4$ V, $T_i = 25°C$[c]	400	750	µcd
Dominant wavelength[d,e]	λ_d			585	nm
Peak wavelength	λ_{PEAK}			583	nm
High-Efficiency Red HCMS-2702/-2712/-2722					
Peak luminous intensity per LED (digit average)[a,b]	I_v	$V_{DD} = 5.0$ V, $V_{COL} = 3.5$ V $V_B = 2.4$ V, $T_i = 25°C$[c]	400	1430	µcd
Dominant wavelength[e]	λ_d			626	nm
Peak wavelength	λ_{PEAK}			635	nm
High-Performance Green HCMS-2703/-2713/-2723					
Peak luminous intensity per LED (digit average)[a,b]	I_v	$V_{DD} = 5.0$ V, $V_{COL} = 3.5$ V $V_B = 2.4$ V, $T_i = 25°C$[c]	400	1550	µcd
Dominant wavelength[d,e]	λ_d			574	nm
Peak wavelength	λ_{PEAK}			568	nm
Orange HCMS-2704/-2714/-2724					
Peak luminous intensity per LED (digit average)[a,b]	I_v	$V_{DD} = 5.0$ V, $V_{COL} = 3.5$ V $V_B = 2.4$ V, $T_i = 25°C$[c]	400	1400	µcd
Dominant wavelength[e]	λ_d			602	nm
Peak wavelength	λ_{PEAK}			600	nm

Source: Hewlett Packard.

451

FIGURE 5.4 LED panel display. Courtesy of Uticor.

Most of the A/N displays using the dc plasma technologies are based on the early developments by Burroughs leading to what is termed *Self-Scan*, and the ones designated *Planar*, begun by Sperry and carried to product forms by Beckman. All of these companies have long left the display market, and Sperry and Burroughs do not exist as separate entities. However, the technology has been acquired and new products developed by a number of companies, so that A/N displays in the Self-Scan and Planar formats are available.

Self-Scan. Beginning with Self-Scan, the basic technology is described in Chapter 3, and a representative display is shown in Figure 5.5, with the block diagram of the system shown in Figure 5.6. Various formats are available, and representative specifications are given in Table 5.4.

The bar graph versions use the same technology, but the layout of the emitting elements is different, as shown in Figure 5.7. The basic drive circuitry is shown in Figure 5.8, with the dual bar graphs requiring two anode drivers. The unit operates more like a graphics display containing two columns of 100 elements each, but it is included in the A/N section because of the fixed format.

TABLE 5.3 Large-Size Digit Discrete LED Display Parameters

Parameter	Value
LED size (in.)	0.2 diameter
Character form	2 in. = 5 × 7 dot matrix
	4 in. = 10 × 14 dot matrix
	6 in. = 15 × 21 dot matrix
Display field (in.)	9.2 × 30.8 to 98 × 242
Characters per line	6–80
Number of lines	1–40
Matrix (H × W)	24 × 96 to 192 × 480

FIGURE 5.5   Self-Scan panel display. Courtesy of Burroughs Corporation.

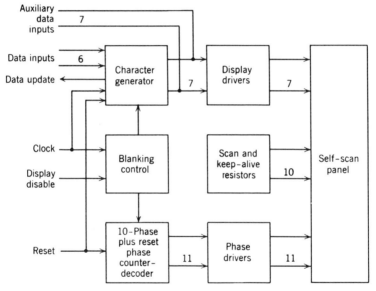

FIGURE 5.6   Block diagram of Self-Scan alphanumeric panel display system. Courtesy of Burroughs Corporation.

TABLE 5.4   Self-Scan A/N Display Module

Parameter	Value
Viewing area (in.)	0.4×6.7 to 2.3×8.4
Number of characters	16–480
Character height (in.)	0.14–0.33
Luminance (fL)	30–80
Scan rate (Hz)	60–75

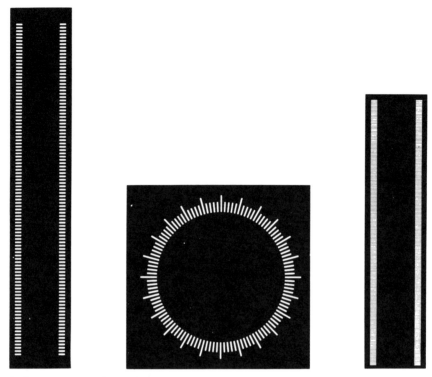

FIGURE 5.7 Self-Scan bar graph displays. Courtesy of Burroughs Corporation.

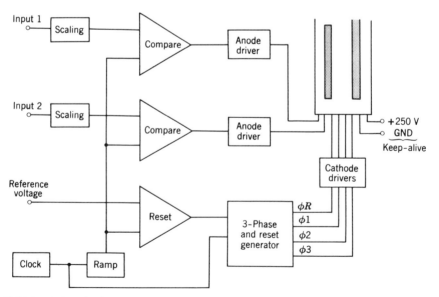

FIGURE 5.8 Block schematic of dual Self-Scan bar graph system. Courtesy of Burroughs Corporation.

TABLE 5.5   Self-Scan Bar Graph Display Module Parameters

Parameter	Value
Number of elements	101, 201
Resolution (%)	0.5, 1
Segment length (in.)	0.1–0.25
Segment height (in.)	0.01–0.025
Luminance (fL)	30–70
Refresh rate (Hz)	70

The basic operating parameters for these units are given in Table 5.5, and this type of display has found numerous applications in various different types of measuring equipment. It has also been used for automotive display of speed, fuel, and other similar readouts. They have been relatively unsuccessful in the latter applications because of the high voltages required, and the unacceptable levels of electrical noise generated by the gas discharge. However, for other applications, such as meters and the display of dynamic operating parameters, it has been found acceptable in a number of locations where the bar graph format is desired, and the drawbacks are not significant.

Planar. The other form of dc plasma technology used primarily for A/N displays is that probably best known as *planar*, although *raised cathode* and *screened image* are terms that are used for specific types. Planar construction is covered to some extent in Chapter 3, and the screened image construction is another version that uses a thick-film screen printing process that allows custom designs to be created at low cost. These are all segmented displays that may be constructed in many formats, such as numerics, A/N, bar graphs, and dot matrix, and the construction stages for one type are shown in Figure 5.9, with typical anode and cathode waveforms shown in Figure 5.10 and one possible block schematic in Figure 5.11. It can be seen that this is the up-to-date version of the Beckman unit shown in Figure 3.92 and Table 5.6 lists performance parameters for these multidigit units, which are available in a multiplicity of forms from several manufacturers that have taken over and improved the original designs.

5.2.3   Vacuum Fluorescent Displays

Vacuum fluorescent displays have achieved considerable success as small numeric, A/N, and bar graph displays. The units are expansions of the structures shown in Figure 3.24, and they are shown in Figure 5.12 for the segmented, and Figure 5.13 for the dot matrix versions of numeric and A/N displays. They may be obtained as displays without electronics, or as complete modules with full character generation, multiplexing, and control capabilities, as shown in the block diagram presented in Figure 5.14. In addition to spe-

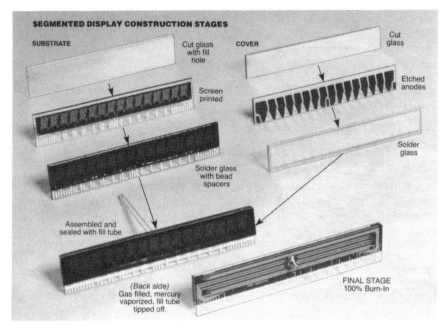

FIGURE 5.9 Dc plasma panel construction stages. Courtesy of Dale.

cialized seven-segment numeric displays for many applications, there are the single- and multiline A/N displays in 14/16 segments and 5 × 7 dot matrix configurations. Finally, there are a number of small bar graphs and various one- and two-column 101 segment units. A basic static driving circuit for the seven-segment units is shown in Figure 5.15 and can be extended to cover the larger number of segments. Similarly, the block diagram shown in Figure

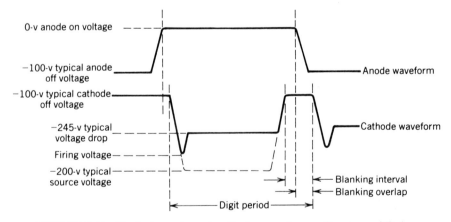

FIGURE 5.10 Typical anode and cathode waveforms. Courtesy of Dale.

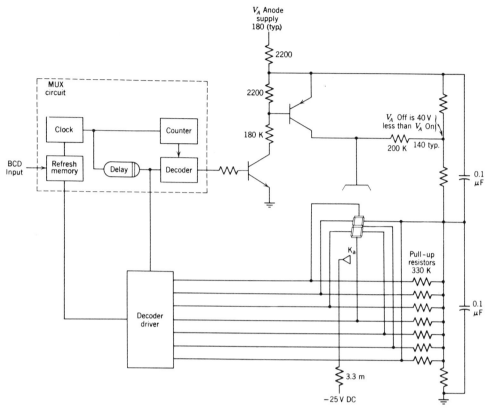

FIGURE 5.11   Block schematic of planar dc gas-discharge digit display system. Courtesy of Beckman Instruments.

5.14 can be applied to 14/16 segments as well as 5×7 dot matrix units. All of these A/N types cover a range of parameter values, as shown in Table 5.7.

The specialized numeric units have similar characteristics but are designed primarily to meet the special requirements of the applications. Electrically, the VFDs are notable in that they operate at voltages in the 25 V/dc range, but the modules generally accept 5 V/dc and step it up to the proper level for the display tube. It should be remembered that a filament voltage is also needed, as these are basically flat CRTs.

TABLE 5.6   Planar DC Plasma Display Parameters

Parameter	Value
Number of characters	4–32
Character height (in.)	0.25–2
Luminance (fL)	60–150

FIGURE 5.12 Segmented VFD panels. Courtesy of Babcock.

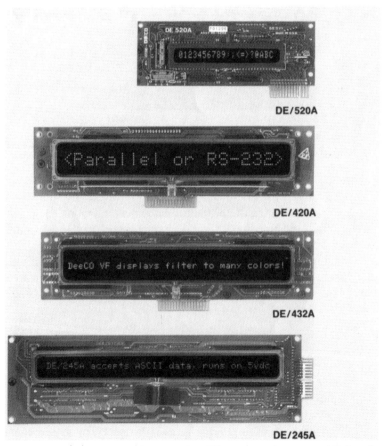

FIGURE 5.13 Dot matrix VFD panels. Courtesy of Babcock.

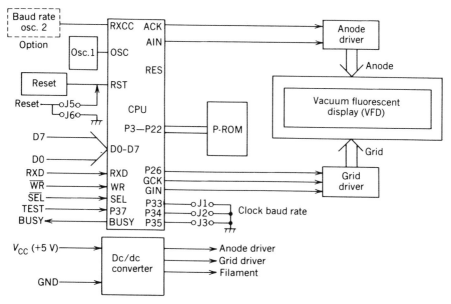

FIGURE 5.14 Block diagram of VFD module. Courtesy of Futaba.

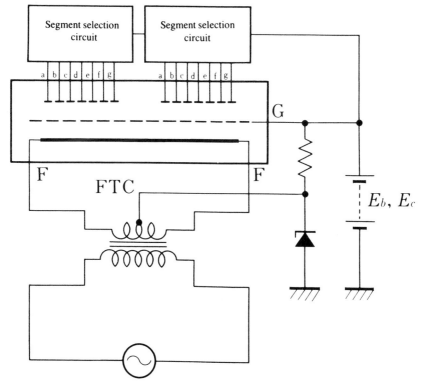

FIGURE 5.15 Static drive circuit for 7-segment VFD limits. After Matsumoto [1, p. 241], by permission.

TABLE 5.7   Vacuum Fluorescent A/N Display Parameters

Parameter	Value
Lines × characters	
14/16 segments	1 × 2 to 2 × 20
5 × 7 dots	1 × 6 to 2 × 40
Bars	1 × 51 to 2 × 101
Character size	
H × W mm, segments	5 × 3 to 13 × 7.8
H × W mm, dot	5.0 × 3.0 to 15.1 × 8.2
Bar size (mm) (H × W)	5 × 50.4 to 8 × 100
Luminance (ft·L)	60–200

5.2.4 Liquid-Crystal Displays

There are as many types of numeric and A/N displays using liquid-crystal technologies as there are dc plasma and VF, so that the three technologies compete on a fairly equal basis for the relevant applications. However, the low power requirements of the LCDs tend to give those units a significant advantage over the others, and LCDs have essentially taken over the battery-operated units. This is particularly true for clocks, watches, calculators, and multimeters, but can be extended to other types, with automotive displays as a special case.

The usual complement of numerics, A/Ns, and bar graphs are available to which should be added special displays for automotive use. These are offered using both twisted nematic and the different types of supertwist technologies, with different colors achieved by using colored polarizers or guest–host formulations. An additional feature is the use of back or side lighting in many of the units to improve contrast ratios. The drive techniques are similarly varied with direct drive used for the numeric or A/N units with a small number of characters, or bar graphs with a small number of bars, and multiplexing for the A/N displays with larger numbers of characters.

A typical direct-drive circuit for a seven-segment numeric is shown in Figure 5.16a, with the accompanying waveforms shown in Figure 5.16b. The symmetrical waveform with less than 50 mV of dc offset is essential for all TN units to avoid degradation. The same circuit may be duplicated for a larger number of digits and expanded for a larger number of segments with Figure 5.16a, showing only one possible block diagram. These arrangements make it possible to handle various combinations of digits and characters up to the maximum reasonable numbers for direct-drive displays. A set of parameter values for these types of segmented units are given in Table 5.8, and may be considered as representative for these types of units. These types may be obtained with or without backlighting and in the transmissive, reflective, and transflective configurations.

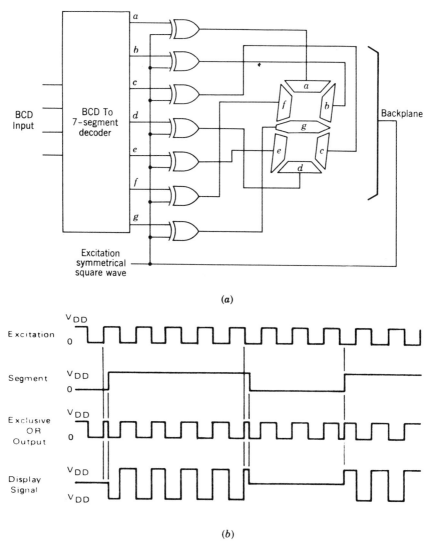

(a)

(b)

FIGURE 5.16 (a) Block schematic and (b) waveforms of liquid-crystal digit display.

TABLE 5.8 Liquid-Crystal Segmented Display Parameters

Parameter	Value
Number of digits (7 segments)	1–8
Number of characters (16 segments)	1–4
Digit height (in.)	0.16–1
Contrast ratio	10/1–20/1
Temperature range (°C)	−40–104
Response times, rise/fall (25°C)	30–50/50–100
Viewing angle (deg)	150–165

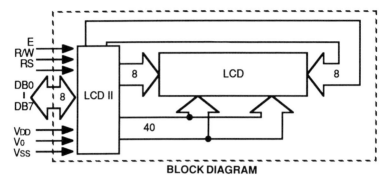

FIGURE 5.17   Block diagram of 16 character by one line, 5 × 7 dot matrix LCD module. Courtesy of Standish.

The dot matrix units in general contain enough characters to warrant the use of multiplexing. There are a variety of multiplexing circuits possible, and that shown in Figure 5.17 is a block diagram for a simple configuration of one line at 16 characters in 5 × 7 matrices. The 8 rows by 80 columns allow the 16 characters to be addressed on a multiplexed basis at one character at a time. Similarly, the much larger assembly of two lines at 40 characters a line can be addressed by the block diagram shown in Figure 5.18. Here there are 16 rows and 200 columns, which allows the 80 characters to be multiplexed. Table 5.9 contains the list of parameter values for these types of dot matrix A/N displays. These units may be obtained in TN and STN technologies, with a variety of transmission, color, and backlighting.

5.2.5   Other Technologies

There are no commercially available examples of electrochromic or electrophoretic numeric or A/N systems. Therefore, although these technologies have not been completely forgotten, they do not warrant more than a cursory

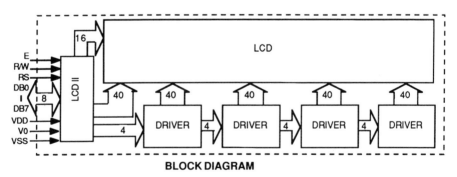

FIGURE 5.18   Block diagram of 5 × 7 dot matrix LCD module, 40 characters by two lines. Courtesy of Standish.

TABLE 5.9   Dot Matrix Liquid-Crystal A/N Display Parameters

Parameter	Value
Characters × lines	16 × 1 to 40 × 2
Character height (mm)	3.3–12.7
Viewing area (mm)	35 × 15 to 245 × 68
Response time, rise/fall (ms)	100–400
Contrast ratio	3/1–10/1
Temperature range (°C)	−20–70
Viewing angle (deg)	40–75

discussion. The same might be said about incandescent displays, but the electromagnetic segmented and dot matrix character displays remain in use, especially for outdoor and message displays. Some drive circuits for electrochromic systems are shown in Figure 5.19, and data on electrophoretic systems in Table 5.10. Block diagrams for seven-segment incandescent digit display systems are shown in Figure 5.20, and further information about the characteristics of the latter are given in Tables 5.11 and 5.12.

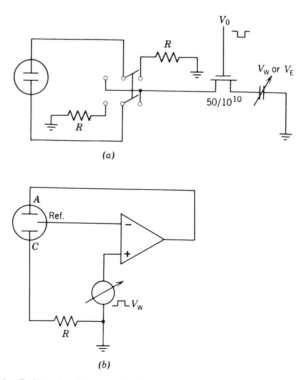

FIGURE 5.19   Drive circuits for electrochromic systems: (*a*) two-terminal drive; (*b*) three-terminal potentiostatic drive. After Chang and Howard [2a] by permission.

TABLE 5.10 Characteristics of Electrochromic and Electrophoretic Displays

Parameter	EC	EP
Contrast ratio	10	40
Viewing angle	Wide	Wide
Color	2	2
Resolution	Electrode limited	
Operating mode	Dc pulse	Dc pulse
Voltage (V)	0.25–20	30–80
Power (μW/cm^2)		15
Energy (mJ/cm^2)	10–100	6×10^{-4}
Memory	Yes	Yes
Threshold	Poor	No
Write time (ms)	100–1000	60
Erase time (ms)	100–500	30
Operating life (10^4 h)	?	?

Source: After Chang [2b, p. 185], by permission.

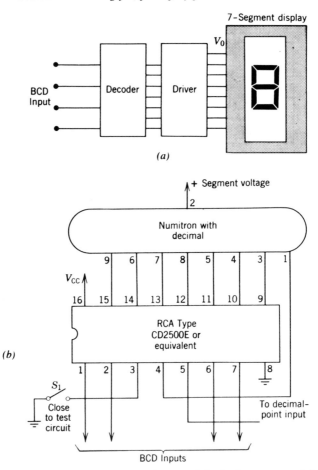

FIGURE 5.20 Block diagrams for incandescent digit display systems: (*a*) open, courtesy of Alco Electronic Products; (*b*) closed, courtesy of RCA Corporation.

TABLE 5.11   Characteristics of Open-Type Incandescent Digit Displays

Character Height (mm)	Voltage (V)	Current (mA/segment)	Life (hours/segment)	Luminance (nits/segment)
6	3	8	100,000	3,500
8	3	8	100,000	3,500
8	4	16.5	100,000	17,500

Source: Courtesyof Pinlites.

Of more significance are those interlopers in this volume on electronic displays: namely, the electromagnetic display systems. They come in both seven-segment and dot matrix varieties, and one system diagram is shown in Figure 5.21. In each case it is possible to use the standard decoders for the type involved, but special drivers are needed to supply the high peak currents to pulse the electromagnets. Although they cannot be multiplexed because of the slow response times, it is possible to drive them sequentially at a rapid rate and to allow the self-latching feature to place and hold each digit in its proper format. Thus some of the advantages of multiplexing are achieved in reducing the number of decoders, but it may still be necessary to have a separate driver for each segment, which negates some of the advantage of multiplexing. The dot matrix unit allows standard matrixing techniques to be used on the individual matrices, and this is covered in further detail in the section on matrix display systems. Table 5.13 lists the characteristics of some of these systems, and the unique features are that they have internal memory and are not light-emitting. In the latter respect they are matched only by the liquid-crystal systems but have the visual advantage that the background may be made completely nonreflective, with the digits coated with phosphorescent paint for best contrast ratio. The results are visually excellent from the point of view of contrast ratio, and, if the electromechanical nature of the display is no obstacle, these systems may be quite acceptable, particularly for large-sized displays in arenas, terminals, and outdoor areas.

5.2.6   Comparison of Technologies

It is really quite difficult to make a reasoned choice among the various systems that have been described since each has some advantages and disadvantages. In an attempt to somewhat simplify, or at least aid the selection process, a list of relevant performance features is given in Table 5.14, with some comments on the manner in which each of the technologies meets or fails to meet the desired performance level. The comments in Table 5.14 summarize what may be found in the previous tables in this chapter and in Chapter 3, and it is hoped that this codification and description will act as a guide in determining which factors are significant. The numerical values may then be consulted in the other tables.

The major features that should be examined in making a choice are power consumption, luminance and/or contrast ratio, size, color, the number of digits

TABLE 5.12 Characteristics of Closed-Type Incandescent Digit Displays

Operating Voltage Range (dc V)	Segment Voltage (dc V)	Segment Current (dc mA)	Life (h)	Viewing Angle (deg)	Segment Luminance (nits)	Response Time (ms)	Contrast Ratio
3.5–5	4.5	24	100k	140	25,000	15	30:1
3.5–5	4.5	24	100k	120	25,000	15	30:1
1.5–3	2.5	14	100k	120	14,000	8	20:1

Source: Courtesy of RCA.

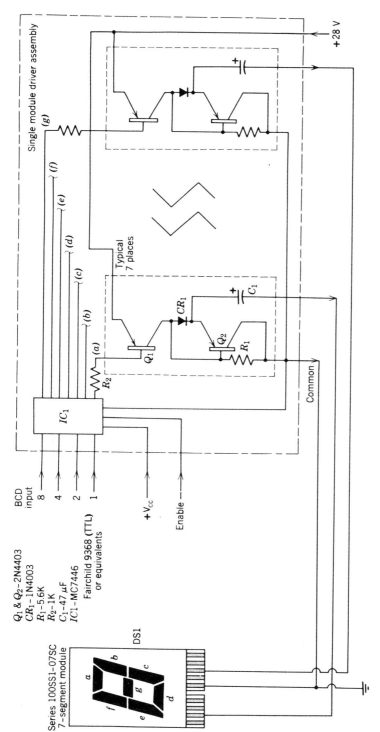

FIGURE 5.21 Decoder–driver for single-coil electromagnetic digit display. Courtesy of Ferranti-Packard.

467

TABLE 5.13 Specifications for Electromechanical Digit Displays

	Series 840	Series 1200	Series 1800
Overall size			
With frame	Model 841XY2-35: 312 mm high, 215 mm wide, 71 mm thick	Model 1201XY2-35: 457 mm high, 317 mm wide: 74 mm thick	Model 1801XY2-35: 660 mm high, 457 mm wide, 76 mm thick
Without frame	NA	Model 1200XY2-35: 335 mm high, 244 mm wide, 87 mm thick	Model 1800XY2-35: 457 mm high, 333 mm wide, 95 mm thick
Character size	215 mm high, 150 mm wide	328 mm high, 231 mm wide	452 mm high, 320 mm wide
Module weight			
With frame	850 g	2635 g	3910 g
Without frame	NA	595 g	822 g

Viewing characteristics typical	Viewing angle (degrees from normal)	Distance (m)	Viewing angle (degrees from normal)	Distance (m)	Viewing angle (degrees from normal)	Distance (m)
	0.0	120	0.0	180	0.0	270
	45.0	110	45.0	160	45.0	240
	60.0	90	60.0	120	60.0	180
	75.0	40	75.0	60	75.0	90
	82.5	20	82.5	30	82.5	40

Common to all series

Character format: 5 × 7 —dot matrix. Other formats available on special order.

Operating voltages (at 25°C ambient to achieve required operating current (3.4 A) from a current-limited source)

Volts	Minimum pulse duration (per coil) (ms)
16	1
21	400
30	250
46	150
90	80

Operating current: 3.4 A minimum at recommended pulse width; maximum pulse width at 4 A at 40°C—1 s; maximum coil current at recommended pulse width—5 A

Coil resistance: 4 Ω ± 10% at 25°C; resistance temperature coefficient + 1.2%/°C

Maximum power dissipation: 2.5 W/coil (at 25°C, ambient)

Coil temperature coefficient: 25°C per watt to maximum coil temperature of 90°C

Temperature range: −40°C to + 75°C ambient

Relative humidity: ≤95% provided no condensation

Power to maintain displayed: Zero

Source: Courtesy of Ferranti-Packard.

TABLE 5.14 Advantages and Disadvantages of Different Technologies

LED	Gas Discharge	LCD	Fluorescent	Incandescent	ElectroMag
		Advantages			
Wide temperature range	Attractive color	Very low power	Moderate voltage	Low voltage	Low voltage
Very reliable	Good appearance	Low ac voltage	Low power	Very high L	Reflective
Long life	Long life	Read in sun	Good color	All colors	Memory
Very fast response	Fast response	High CR	Multiplex	Large size	Large size
Multiplex	Large size	Large size	Matrix	Matrix	Matrix
Matrix	Multiplex	Reflective			
Color	Matrix				
		Disadvantages			
Limited number of characters	High voltage	Light needed	Glass	Slow	Slow
Mono A/Ns	Moderate L	Limited view	Filament	High power	High current
High power	Moderate CR	Slow	Fragile	Fragile	Mech
Limited size	Special drivers	Limit temperature			
		Limit multiplex			

that can be multiplexed and compatibility with standard decoding and driving microcircuits. Of course, price is always a factor, but this is so variable and subject to change that it cannot be included in Table 5.14 in any meaningful way. At best, we can say that digit prices appear to be fairly uniform once the technology is sufficiently established for large-scale production to exist, but system costs, which are more significant, may vary widely and are ultimately the overwhelming factor. In addition, long-term costs must include maintenance and replacement expenditures, so that reliability is very important as well. Also, there are hidden aspects, such as the need for a light source in some liquid-crystal systems. This adds to the power requirements and affects both cost and life. In addition, the possibility of noise being generated by the display, leads to potential interference with the operation of other parts of the system. Finally, we cannot neglect environmental factors, such as temperature range of operation and susceptibility to shock or vibration. The weight that is assigned to any of these parameters will vary with each different application, so no general statements as to the overall advantages of one technology over another may be made. Certain applications have tended to use certain technologies, as indicated by Table 5.14.

5.3 GRAPHICS MATRIX PANEL SYSTEMS

5.3.1 Light-Emitting Diodes

Although LEDs could be classified as electroluminescent devices, they differ significantly in their physical characteristics and modes of operation from the types of devices that are usually listed under the EL technology. Therefore, LEDs are treated under their own rubric in Section 5.2.1, and the same procedure is followed here.

As noted previously, the main application for LEDs in FPDs is as the numeric and A/N displays covered in the earlier section. However, there are a few examples of graphics LED panels that have some unique characteristics and warrant further discussion. The first example is the panels using discrete diodes that can be individually addressed, which are also used as message displays containing only characters. These can be turned into graphics displays by properly addressing the LEDs so that relatively simple graphics images can be generated such as those shown in Figure 5.22. The parameter values for these displays are essentially the same as those given in Table 5.3 and demonstrate a fair graphics capability.

The other form that LED graphics displays take is a basic 16 × 16 module, assembled in a multimodule panel with four different color types of LEDs in the different modules. A typical circuit block diagram for the assembly is shown in Figure 5.23. An example of a display is illustrated in Figure 5.24 and some module parameters in Table 5.15.

A wide range of module combinations is possible, and the equivalent of a 640 × 400 CRT display is considered reasonable with a LED dot for each

(a)

(b)

FIGURE 5.22 LED graphic displays. Courtesy of Display Tech.

element. Of course, to achieve a full color display, three LEDs per matrix element are required and blue remains a problem, although blue LEDs have become available, albeit not yet incorporated into these modules.

5.3.2 Electroluminescent Technologies

There are five EL technologies listed in Table 3.3, and for the reasons given in Section 3.3.4 we concentrate on the ac-driven thin-film and dc-driven powder types here. These technologies have achieved considerable success in producing FPDs with extensive graphics capabilities in their matrix panel form, and are covered in detail beginning with the ac-driven thin-film versions, usually termed TFEL.

The TFEL matrix panels were originally developed by Sharp, which had a virtual monopoly for a number of years. However, a U.S. company—Planar—has broken the usual pattern and taken the lead away from Sharp

Dual power type

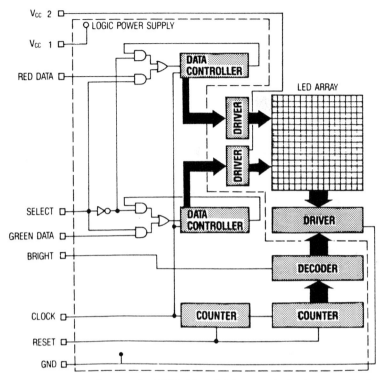

FIGURE 5.23 Block diagram for LED 16 × 16 dot matrix dual-power-display module. Courtesy of Toshiba.

as well as acquiring the third company in this field—the Finnish company Lohja, whose U.S. outlet was Finlux. In addition, several other U.S. companies obtain the panels from one of these sources and incorporate them into display systems of varying complexity so that there is a sufficiency of sources for total systems, although there are few manufacturers of the actual panels.

Planar has made many advances in the technology, particularly in adding multicolor capabilities to the products. However, the major products remain the monochromatic matrix FPDs, of which the one shown in Figure 5.25 is representative. This is a 512 × 256 matrix panel, which consists of the EL glass panel containing the active material and addressing lines, and a circuit board with the control electronics. These are assembled into a single thin package, and the combination can replace an equivalent CRT monitor. The assembly of the EL monitor is illustrated in Figure 5.26 and the circuit block diagram in Figure 5.27. The specific addressing technique is shown in Figure 5.28, where there are 512 column and 256 row drivers. The panel is addressed one row at a time with the active row placed at a voltage below the threshold and the data shifted to the "on" columns, while the "off" columns are grounded

FIGURE 5.24 Display on screen of LED matrix display panel. Courtesy of Toshiba.

and the nonactive rows float. The sequence is repeated for every row until the whole frame is written, after which the columns are grounded and all of the rows are raised to a positive value sufficient to supply the reverse voltage pulse need to prepare the panel for the next frame. Some of the parameter values for this and similar monitors are given in Table 5.16. A multicolor version has also been announced by Planar, and its parameter values are given in Table 5.17. These values are indicative of what may be achieved, and further growth may be anticipated. For example, a 640 × 400 unit with six colors has been developed, and an experimental 8 × 8 matrix of a white-light-emitting unit with red, green, and blue phosphors has been developed.

The dc powder versions of EL matrix panel displays are of more recent vintage, at least in the United States, having been developed in England at Phosphor Products and taken over by Cherry, which has developed several

TABLE 5.15 Graphics LED Module Parameters

Parameter	Value
Luminance/dot (nits)	50–190
Color	R, G, A, HR
Module matrix	4 × 4 to 16 × 16
Current/LEDs (A)	1.3–2.4
Module size (mm²)	63.7–95.7

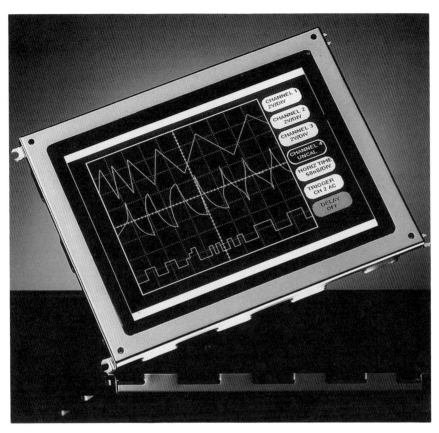

FIGURE 5.25 Matrix TFEL display panel. Courtesy of Planar.

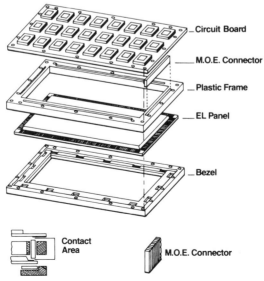

FIGURE 5.26 Exploded view of TFEL panel. Courtesy of Planar.

475

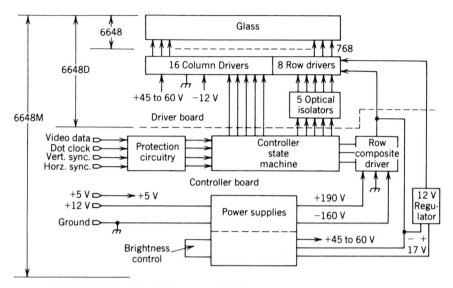

FIGURE 5.27 Block diagram of TFEL monitor. Courtesy of Planar.

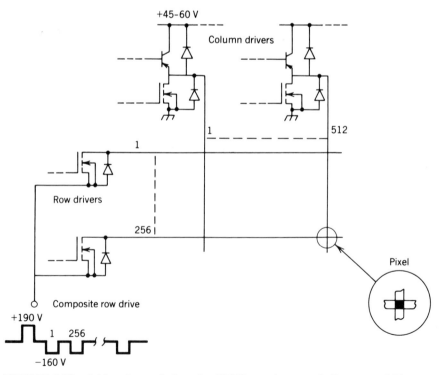

FIGURE 5.28 Addressing technique for TFEL monitor panel. Courtesy of Planar.

TABLE 5.16   TFEL Monitor Parameter

Parameter	Value
Matrix	276 × 128 to 1024 × 864
Active area (in.) (W × H)	5.7 × 2.7 to 13.6 × 11.5
Pixel size (in.)	0.009 × 0.009 to 0.305 × 0.305
Luminance (fL)	16–46
Color	Yellow-orange
Contrast ratio	50–150

products using this technology. Specifically, these products are matrix panel displays that use dc EL technology to achieve equivalent or better performance that can be attained with ac TFEL. The dc approach uses thick-film technology because it was anticipated to result in high luminance and long life, in addition to low manufacturing cost and selling price. The accuracy of these predictions has not yet been fully established, but some of the performance parameters may be compared with those for TFEL given in Table 5.16.

Before proceeding to examine DCEL parameter values, it is instructive to investigate how these devices are manufactured and what electronics is used to drive them. The similarities between TFEL and DCEL are apparent when the structure shown in Figure 5.29*a* for a DCEL panel is compared with that for a TFEL panel shown in Figure 5.29*b*. First, and foremost, the DCEL panel must have both sides of the phosphor layers connected directly to the signal source, whereas the ac-driven TFEL has a dielectric layer on both sides of the phosphor layer, and between it and the row and column electrodes. However, it the phosphor panel unit is treated as a separable assembly, the mode of assembly of the total DCEL display is quite similar to that for the TFEL display, as can be seen by comparing Figure 5.29*b* with Figure 5.26, where the basic construction is the same for both.

The drive circuitry does differ in the need for a dc constant drive to the columns after the precharge pulse, as shown in Figure 5.30. The block diagram of a complete DCEL drive system is shown in Figure 5.31 and includes a level shifter to convert the 5-V dc logic levels to the 12 V dc required by the column drivers. A single chip has been designed to perform most of the functions, and parameter values are given in Table 5.18. It is not apparent

TABLE 5.17   TFEL Color Monitor Parameters

Parameter	Value
Number of color pixels	640 × 200
Number of colors displayed	4 per pixel
Active area (in.) (W × H)	7.6 × 4.8
Luminance (fL)	7.5
Colors	Red, green, yellow

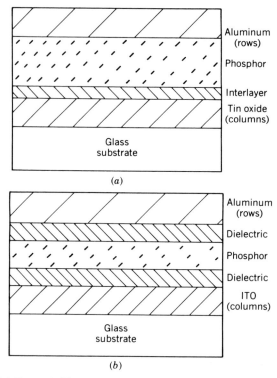

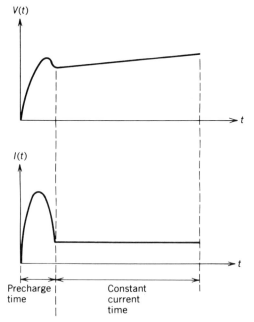

FIGURE 5.29 (*a*) Dc and (*b*) ac EL panel construction. After Channing et al. [3], by permission.

FIGURE 5.30 Voltage and current waveforms during precharge and constant current time. After Channing et al. [4] by permission.

SYSTEM BLOCK DIAGRAM

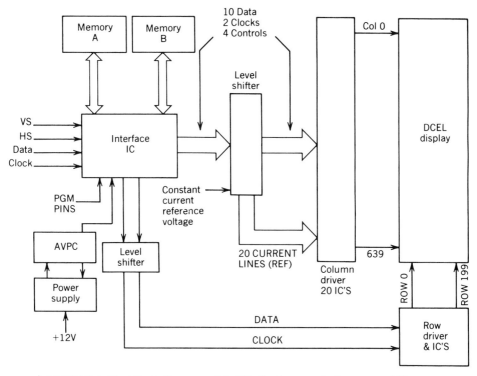

FIGURE 5.31 Block diagram of dc EL display panel. Courtesy of Cherry.

from these numbers that DCEL is necessarily better than TFEL, but the claims of lower cost and longer life for the former remain to be fully established and may make a difference in the final acceptance.

5.3.3   Plasma Panels

As noted previously, ac-driven plasma panels are essentially available only in graphics form, whereas the dc-driven types can be found in both A/N and graphics displays. Beginning with the dc types, these are similar to some of the A/N dot matrix units, with the difference that a full matrix assembly is

TABLE 5.18   DCEL Panel Parameters

Parameter	Value
Luminance (fL)	25–30
Active area (in.)	3.68 × 2.94 to 8.64 × 6.48
Matrix	320 × 256 to 640 × 480
Color	Amber
Contrast ratio	15–20

provided and each panel is individually addressable and can be multiplexed. This differs from the Self-Scan approach in that the internal scan is missing and the full complements of anodes and cathodes must be addressed directly. This allows a fully populated matrix to be addressed, but requires the addition of scanning and drive circuitry. The early version of the refreshed dc plasma dot matrix type developed by Matsushita, shown in Figure 3.65, consists of anode strips printed above a black layer to partially shield the viewer from the priming glow. Then a dielectric barrier strip is printed above the cathode, thus defining a priming area beneath the anode.

In operation, the cathode selection is achieved by switching a cathode at a time in sequence from a drive source, for each anode position, rather than from the multiphased Self-Scan. The anode line capacitance is used to provide priming energy by allowing each anode to remain connected for a short period between cathode selection and become fully charged. This sequence of events is illustrated in Figure 3.66, and when the cathode switch is closed all of the cell in the selected row see a high enough discharge voltage to create a priming voltage. Then, to remain on, the anode pixels are left connected so that the priming charge can spread. A set of parameter values for this type of dc-driven dot matrix plasma panel is given in Table 5.19. A representative block diagram for these panels is shown in Figure 5.32 and differs primarily in the pulse generator for the various versions, depending only on the number of gray scales provided.

Another approach to the dc plasma matrix panel is that originated by Dixy and taken over by Mitsubishi. This technique uses capacitively coupled inner electrodes to achieve ac triggering, as shown in Figure 3.67. The trigger electrode is buried under the dielectric layer and the panel is scanned from top to bottom as for the Matsushita structure. The combination of multiplexed cathodes and the trigger electrode allow rapid row at a time selection. This technique has been adopted by Matsushita in its Panasonic-produced units because of the higher contrast ratios and wider gray scale that can be achieved. A block diagram for this type of unit is shown in Figure 5.33, with the trigger driver the main unique feature and the parameter values do not differ significantly from those given in Table 5.19.

The final aspect of dc plasma displays that should be mentioned is the effort to achieve color displays. This effort has been largely driven by possible

TABLE 5.19   Refreshed DC Dot Matrix Panel Parameters

Parameter	Value
Viewing area (mm)	89×195 to 160×256
Matrix	88×192 to 480×640
Luminance (nits)	50–250
Contrast	10–150
Color	Neon orange
Number of gray scales	2–16

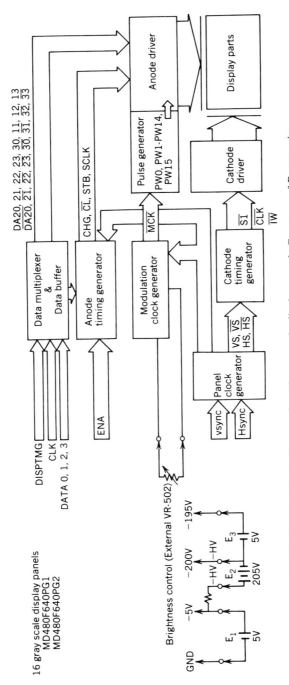

FIGURE 5.32 Block diagram for 16-gray-scale display panel. Courtesy of Panasonic.

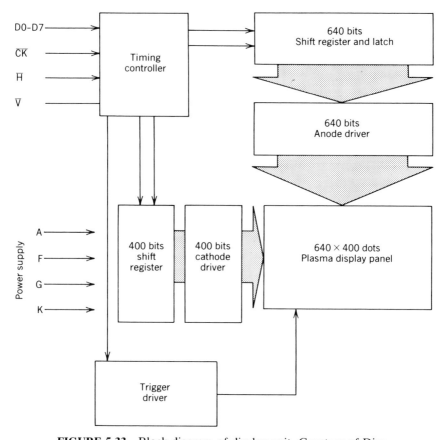

FIGURE 5.33   Block diagram of display unit. Courtesy of Dixy.

TV applications over the last 15 years without much success, but has been given a new lease on life with the advent of HDTV. Matsushita has produced 17-in.-diagonal demonstration models of units for which the parameter values shown in Table 5.20 appear suitable for desktop computers, although both luminance and luminous efficiency are still too low. The basic structure used is compared with that for a monochromatic display in Figure 5.34, where the R, G, and B phosphors are deposited on the ITO anode, and activated by the UV plasma output.

TABLE 5.20   Color DC Plasma Panel Parameters

Parameter	Value
Active area (mm)	259×346
Number of colors	4096
Number of pixels	$480 \times 640 \ (\times 3)$

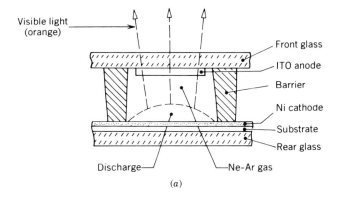

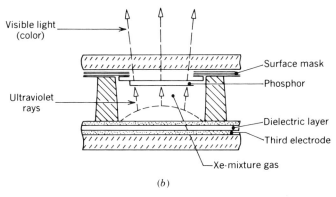

FIGURE 5.34 Comparison of electrode structure between (*a*) monochrome and (*b*) Matsushita color plasma display. After Uchiike [5], by permission.

More successful has been the NHK effort, which has succeeded in demonstrating a high-definition TV picture on a 33-in.-diagonal dc color plasma display. The electrode structure of this design is shown in Figure 5.35 and the panel consists of a front and rear glass, each 3 mm thick, with each color pixel consisting of four discharge cells made up of one red, one blue, and two green cells. The parameter values for this unit are given in Table 5.21.

Despite the considerable success achieved by dc plasma matrix panels as computer displays and the rather dismal record of IBM in marketing the ac plasma panels it designed and manufactured, ac plasma panels have continued to show a certain amount of life. This has been largely generated by circuit improvements found in the products offered by Plasmaco, the company that took over from IBM, and the interest in large panels for HDTV, supported by DARPA. The major source for large panel and color development in the United States has been Photonics Systems, but several other companies, in particular Thomson Tubes in France and Fujitsu in Japan, have devoted some effort to attaining these goals with notable success, although Photonics re-

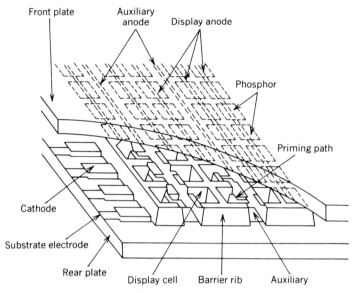

FIGURE 5.35 Electrode structure of NHK's dc plasma display. After Uchiike [5], by permission.

mains the leader in size. The results are intriguing and are covered later, but the first discussion is limited to monochromatic ac plasma panels, suitable for computer and other data displays.

These panels were originally developed by Bitzer and Slottow at the University of Illinois, and early product development was carried out by Owens Illinois. Activity by these two organization has more or less ceased, as has that by IBM, but a number of U.S. and Japanese companies and at least one in France have continued to develop and manufacture ac-driven matrix plasma panels. The basic structure used in the original Owens Illinois panel is shown in Figure 3.20, with the drive waveforms given in Figure 3.22. To these should be added the nonmemory mode shown in Figure 3.65, for which the block diagram is given in Figure 3.59. In this structure, the rows are scanned a line at a time with a high-frequency sustain signal (V_y), while the columns are driven with a low-amplitude sustain signal (V_x) that adds to or subtracts from

TABLE 5.21 HDTV DC Color Plasma Panel Parameters

Parameter	Value
Size (mm)	520 × 665
Number of cells	800 × 1024
Luminance (nits)	85
Luminous efficacy (1m/W)	0.15
Contrast ratio (no ambient light)	820

the row select signal. This approach has the advantage of being able to use pure neon and not having any memory margin requirement, but loses out in optical efficiency with respect to the standard approach.

An additional feature of ac plasma panels is the possibility of reducing the number of drivers by using in-panel decoding techniques. One approach used by Fujitsu is to have each row conductor coupled to two drive lines so that an "and" function can be performed. As illustrated in Figure 3.60, this can reduce the number of drivers by means of a 2×3 selection matrix. In a larger panel, a 20×20 matrix can be used to drive a 400×400 panel at the cost of requiring increased addressing power.

The other panel decoding scheme is that introduced by Plasmaco and termed ISA (independent sustain and address). This technique separates the addressing and sustain operations by having independent electrodes for each operation. This is illustrated by the 5×5 matrix shown in Figure 3.61, and the configuration reduces the number of drivers required by a factor of 2. Selection is achieved by time-division multiplexing, and the timing of input pulses on the X_{ai} inputs establishes the state of the four display pixels around each address cell. The addressing operations for erase and write use electron charge spreading along the anode dielectric as the physical mechanism, and the drivers are both fewer in number than for other techniques and have lower current requirements than other drive and erase techniques. It is used in the panels offered by Plasmaco, which offer the same performance as do those from several other vendors, but with reductions in the driver costs.

Finally, for monochromatic panels, there are the large panels developed by Photonics Technology, which are probably the largest FPD made to date. These units have an active diagonal of 1.5 m and a resolution of 2048×2048, so they are of particular interest in light of the effort that is being expended on large-size FPDs for HDTV. A display architecture for this type of display applied to video inputs is shown in Figure 5.36, and a block diagram for smaller displays, in Figure 5.37. A comparison of power requirements for ac plasma vs. CRTs and TFT-LCDs may be found in reference 6. Finally, Table 5.22 lists parameter values for monochromatic ac plasma panels.

Insofar as color ac plasma panels are concerned, there has been considerable effort expended by several manufacturers to achieve multicolor displays. Several electrode structures have been employed, with Figure 5.38a representing that used by Fujitsu, Figure 5.38b that of the Thomson CSF unit, both surface discharge types, whereas Photonics uses the two-substrate approach. The two types of electrode structures are compared in Figure 5.39, and the latter is considered to have the disadvantages of low luminance and luminous efficiency. However, the advantage of this technique for a large area display is that it can be the same as is used by Photonics for its largest units. In any event, both approaches have resulted in workable units, and their performance characteristics are compared in Table 5.23. It should be remembered, however, that these are somewhat preliminary values, and improvements should be anticipated before too long. These values are quite

486

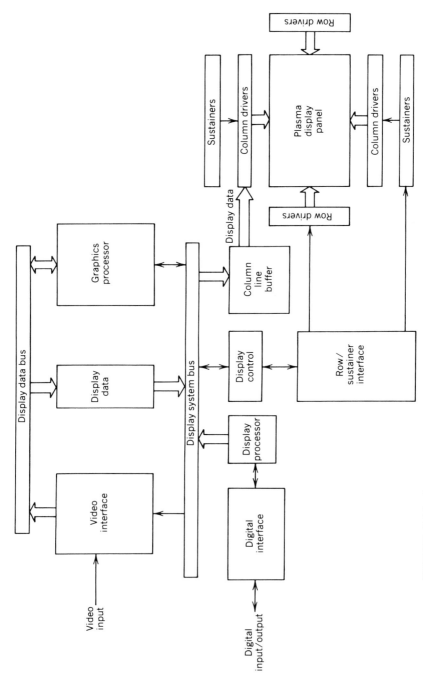

FIGURE 5.36 Large-screen ac plasma panel display architecture. After Friedman et al. [6], by permission.

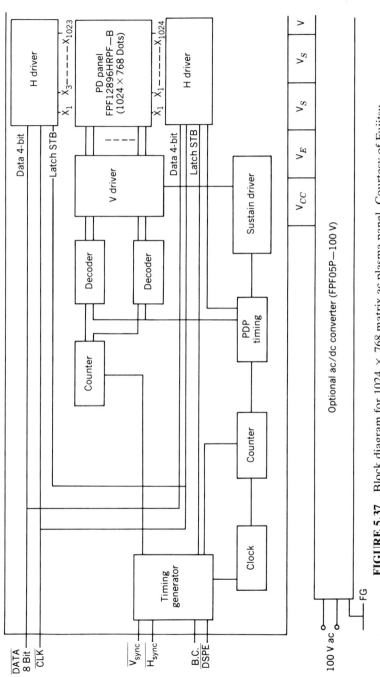

FIGURE 5.37 Block diagram for 1024 × 768 matrix ac plasma panel. Courtesy of Fujitsu.

487

TABLE 5.22 AC Plasma Panel Parameters

Parameter	Value
Viewing area (in.)	4 × 4 to 31.4 × 23.8
Pixel matrix	240 × 80 to 2048 × 2048
Pixel size (in.)	0.008–0.2
Resolution (lines/in.)	60–85
Luminance (fL)	6–85
Contrast ratio	10–20
Display color	Neon orange

similar, and it remains to be seen whether the experience in making large-screen displays will carry over successfully to the color displays. In any event, there is enough effort being expended and successful results to make color ac plasma technology worth conderation for HDTV and other applications.

5.3.4 Vacuum Fluorescent Displays

As noted previously, the major applications for VFDs are for the various numeric, A/N, and bar graph units that have achieved such wide acceptance for many applications. However, there is also a group of graphics panel displays using this technology that should be included in this review, as they are feasible displays for certain applications.

The main limitation for VFDs is size, as the maximum panel dimensions are 7.1 × 6.3 in., although a resolution of 640 × 400 is attained within these dimensions. Various colors can be achieved with filters, but only one at a time. To compensate for this limitation, luminances as high as 400 fL are possible in certain configurations, mainly those with fairly small matrices. There are also a few unique construction and drive techniques used for graphics displays besides the simplest single-matrix approach—dual-wire grid scanning and triple-matrix anode—which reduce the production cost and improve the display appearance.

The basic electrode structure of the dual-wire technique designed for use on a single-matrix system is illustrated in Figure 5.40a, and the timing chart for the grid and anode is shown in Figure 5.40b. In this structure the anodes are formed as stripes and the grid wires are placed orthogonal to the anodes. Two neighboring grid wires are shifted sequentially and turned on while synchronized "on" and "off" signals are applied to the anode. Then, as shown in the timing chart, the anode between the two neighboring grids is turned on. The main advantages of this approach are that the anode construction allows lower tolerances, thus reducing cost; and the vertical, horizontal, and oblique lines all appear continuous, thus improving appearance.

The electrode structure of the triple anode VFD is somewhat more complicated, as shown in Figure 5.40c, where the anode connections are made in three matrices, connecting anodes 1, 4, 7, . . . 3; 6, 9, . . .; and so on. The

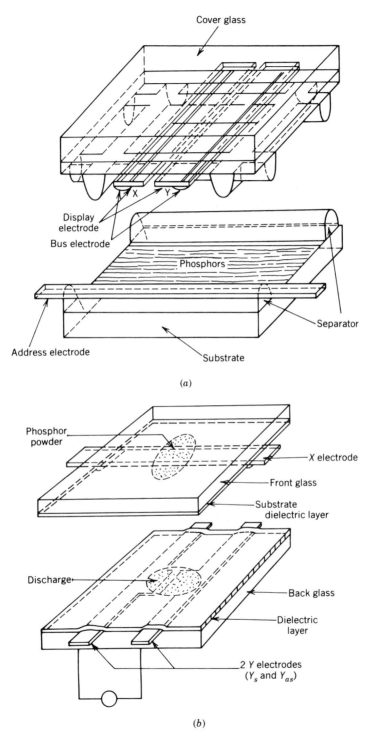

Cover glass

Display
electrode

Bus electrode

Phosphors

Address electrode

Separator

Substrate

X Y

(a)

Phosphor
powder

X electrode

Front glass

Substrate
dielectric layer

Discharge

Back glass

Dielectric
layer

2 Y electrodes
(Y_s and Y_{as})

(b)

FIGURE 5.38 Electrode structure of color ac plasma displays of (a) Fujitsu and (b) Thomson CSF. After Uchiike [5], by permission.

489

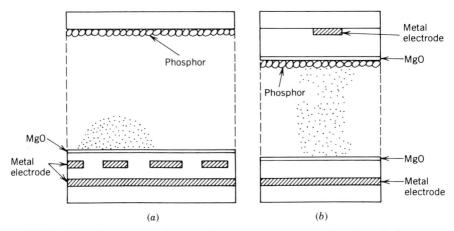

FIGURE 5.39   Comparison of electrode structures between (*a*) surface-discharge and (*b*) two-substrate ac plasma displays. After Uchiike [5], by permission.

grids are arranged to cover two anodes, as shown in Figure 5.40*d*, so that whereas the number of anode connections is three times the number of dots in a vertical line, the number of grid connections is half that in a horizontal line. Then, according to the timing chart shown in Figure 5.40*e* and the scanning sequence given in Table 5.24, the effect of neighboring grids is eliminated; higher luminance can be achieved by repeating the duty cycle, as two dots are covered by one grid; and the drive voltage can be lowered. These improvements compensate for the increase in connections.

There is one version that accepts RGB signals, and combining any two provides a halftone display, whereas the use of an LCD color shutter allows three colors to be displayed. In addition, there have been some attempts to use active matrix drive for VFDs, where each pixel consists of a phosphor layer on the drain electrode of a MOSFET, but these have not achieved much success and are not yet incorporated into any products. However, they may be in the future and should not be forgotten as a possible way to improve

TABLE 5.23   Surface Discharge and Two-Substrate Color Plasma Display Parameters

Parameter	Value	
	Two-Substrate	Surface-Discharge
Display area (in.)	12.3 × 12.3	13.3 × 10
Diagonal (in.)	17.4	16.6
Pixel matrix (RGB)	384 × 384	341 × 256
Number of colors	8 per RGB pixel	262,144
Luminance, white (fL)	25	30
Contrast ratio	20	100

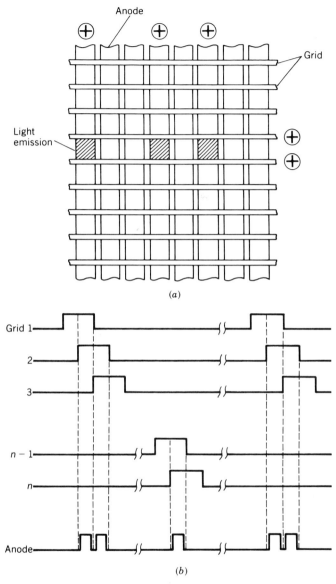

FIGURE 5.40 (*a*) Electrode structure of dual-wire scanning VFD; (*b*) timing chart of grid and anode for dual-wire scanning VFD; (*c*) electrode structure of triple anode VFD; (*d*) operational principle of triple-anode VFD; (*e*) timing chart of grid and anode for triple-anode VFD; (*f*) structure of front luminous VFD (FLVFD). Courtesy of Futaba.

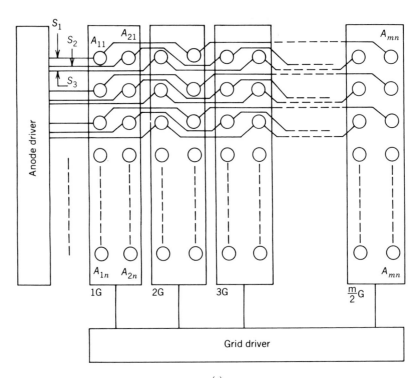

(c)

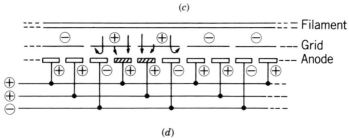

(d)

FIGURE 5.40   (*Continued*)

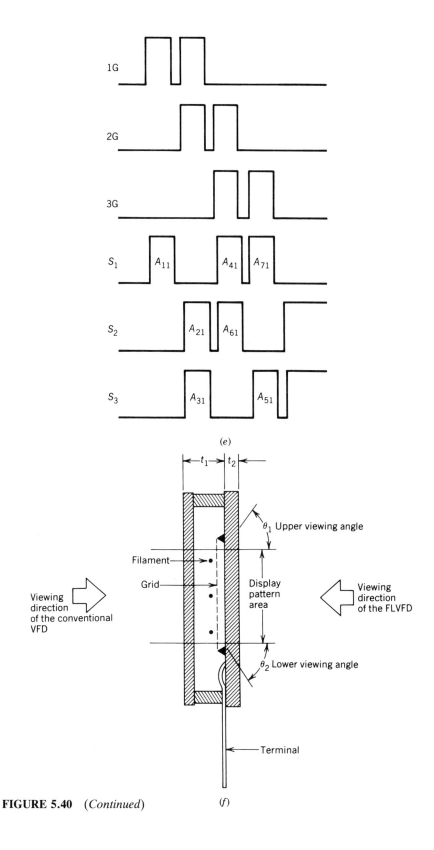

FIGURE 5.40   (*Continued*)

TABLE 5.24   Relationship Between Grid Scan and Anode Data

Scan Sequence	Anode Wiring			Selected Grid	
	S_1	S_2	S_3		
0	A_{1n}	0	0		1 G
1	0	A_{2n}	A_{3n}	1 G	2 G
2	A_{4n}	A_{5n}	0	2 G	3 G
3	A_{7n}	0	A_{6n}	3 G	4 G
4	0	A_{8n}	A_{9n}	4 G	5 G
5	A_{10n}	A_{11n}	0	5 G	6 G
6	A_{13n}	0	A_{12n}	6 G	7 G
.	.	.	.	.	.
.	.	.	.	.	.
.	.	.	.	.	.

VFDs still further. In any event, the parameter values for representative graphics VFDs are given in Table 5.25.

One other characteristic of some of the graphic panels is that they are constructed so that they may be viewed from the front instead of the viewing direction of the conventional VFD. This is illustrated in Figure 5.40*f* and allows both a wider viewing angle and better space factor than the conventional units. This is another example of how attempts are being made to improve the visual performance of VFDs.

5.3.5   Liquid Crystals

Liquid crystals constitute what is probably the most varied and investigated technology for FPDs. Indeed, they were the first of the technologies to show some potential for matrix displays but were held back by poor response time. Other deficiencies in contrast ratio and multiplexing capabilities led to a temporary rejection of LCDs, but significant improvements have been achieved with new materials and designs, so that LCDs are now leading all technologies, particularly for battery-operated equipment. This preeminence also exists for FPDs used for computer displays, and successful development of multicolor, active matrix units has placed LCDs far ahead of panels using the other technologies for use as both computer and video displays. The HDTV ap-

TABLE 5.25   Vacuum Fluorescent Display Parameters

Parameter	Value
Display area (mm)	48×25 to 179×112
Matrix	64×34 to 640×400
Luminance (nits)	50–690
Dot size (mm)	0.22–0.65

plication is somewhat special in that it concentrates on projection systems and is covered in Section 5.4, but it should be noted that video displays fall within the capabilities of some LCDs, and they should play a significant role in the general TV market in the future.

LCD matrix panels come in a variety of forms and technologies, of which the one shown in Figure 5.41 is a representative example. This is a high-

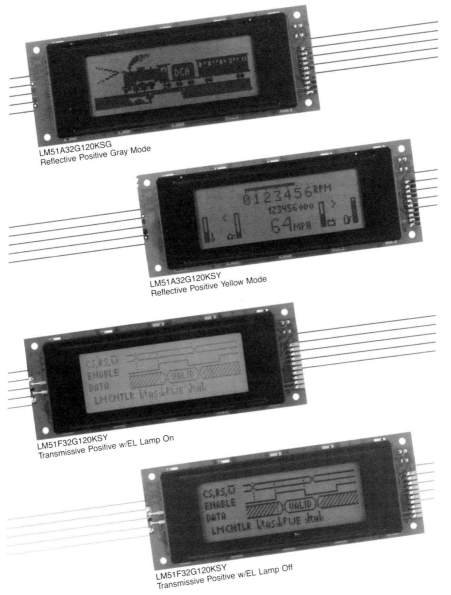

LM51A32G120KSG
Reflective Positive Gray Mode

LM51A32G120KSY
Reflective Positive Yellow Mode

LM51F32G120KSY
Transmissive Positive w/EL Lamp On

LM51F32G120KSY
Transmissive Positive w/EL Lamp Off

FIGURE 5.41   LCD panel. Courtesy of Densitron.

contrast-ratio monochromatic unit which uses a polymer film and ST technology to achieve a black-and-white display at a resolution of 640 × 480 on a viewing surface of 206 × 156 mm. The actual structure is that shown in Figure 3.34a, for the double supertwist, with one cell repeated in a more detailed form in Figure 5.42 to show the compensating film. This is expanded to include the full complement of rows and columns, and is backlit with either an electroluminescent or fluorescent bulb. Equivalent panels are available in the ST technology with purple-on-gray or blue-on-white colors. The three types are similar in all parameter values from at least one source, except for contrast, where the compensated ST shows the best results at 12, versus 6 for the blue and 3.5 for the purple. The list of parameter values for ST panels

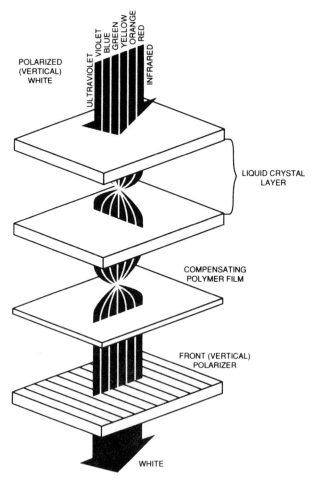

FIGURE 5.42 Structure of compensated supertwist LCD using polymer film. After Lieberman [7], by permission.

TABLE 5.26   STN LCD Parameters

Parameter	Value
Viewing area (mm)	46 × 18 to 220 × 166
Number of pixels	32 × 80 to 480 × 640
Dot size (mm)	0.24–0.5
Response time (ms)	200–300
Contrast ratio	3–12
Duty cycle	1/32–1/240

is given in Table 5.26. A block diagram for a large pixel array is shown in Figure 5.43.

There is an interesting variant on the basic STN panel, which claims to overcome the limitations of such LCDs in achieving a high number of multiplexed lines. An approach that has been used is to divide the column electrodes in half and driving the upper and lower halves separately in what is known as the double-matrix structure. The alternative approach that has been proposed is to construct pairs of cells with large inactive regions between the rows and the rows arranged so that when the cells are placed one on the other, the active regions of one will cover the inactive regions of the other, as shown in Figure 5.44. In this arrangement the inactive regions of one compensate the active regions of the other, as shown in Figure 5.45. A high-resolution black-and-white display has been built using this technique, consisting of two 1280 × 512 panels, each operated at a 256:1 duty ratio.

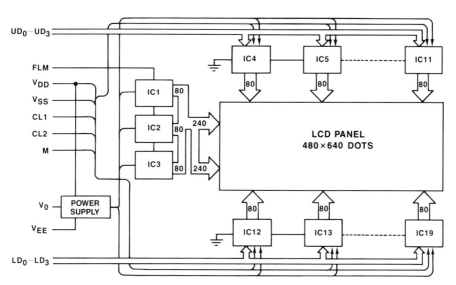

FIGURE 5.43   Block diagram of 480 × 640 supertwist LCD panel. Courtesy of Densitron.

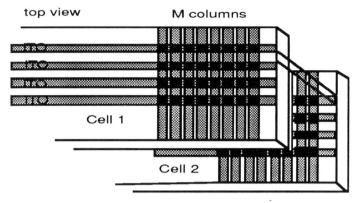

FIGURE 5.44   Illustration of stacked STN layers to achieve high resolution. After Conner and Gulick [8], by permission.

Another significant problem that exists in STN LCDs is the prevalence of two types of crosstalk, termed vertical and horizontal. The first is due to changes in the display patterns along the data lines, and the second by changes in the rates of the active and inactive pixels on successive scanning lines. The result is a darkening of certain patterns that are affected by the crosstalk. The solution has been to control the number of polarity transitions by inverting the polarity every two lines using the polarity controller, as illustrated by the block diagram shown in Figure 5.46. This is essentially a basic schematic for driving a panel modified to introduce the crosstalk reduction circuitry.

Insofar as color displays are concerned, there are a few sources for panels that use the compensated supertwist configuration that provides a black-and-white display in its monochromatic version. To this is added an RGB color mosaic filter, which is placed over the panel, and the number of column

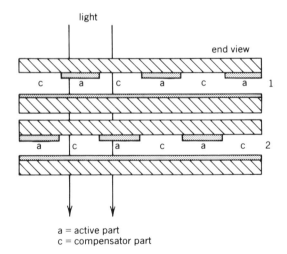

FIGURE 5.45   Principle of mutual compensation. a, Active part; c, compensator part. After Conner and Gulick [8], by permission.

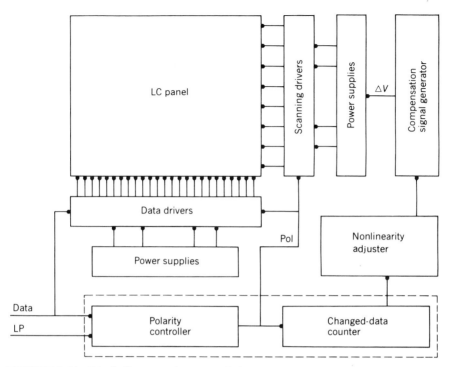

FIGURE 5.46   Block diagram of a crosstalk-free STN-LCD. After Kaneko et al. [9], by permission.

electrodes is tripled converting the individual pixels into the three colors represented by the mosaic. The performance parameters of one example of this type are given in Table 5.27. These types are in limited supply and will probably be supplanted by the active matrix color units that are described in Section 5.3.6.

Another approach is that used for the stacked layer system described above. A limited number of colors can be achieved with this configuration by using two colored polarizers on the outside of a four-LCD-layer assembly with a neutral polarizer in the middle as shown in Figure 5.47. With this arrangement and the colors shown, it is possible to attain a red, white, cyan, and black

TABLE 5.27   Color STN Display Parameters

Parameter	Value
Display area (mm)	182×140 to 250×187
Number of pixels	1920×400 to 1920×480
Number of colors	8–16
Contrast ratio	15–20
Response time (ms)	100–200
Luminance (nits)	Depends on light source

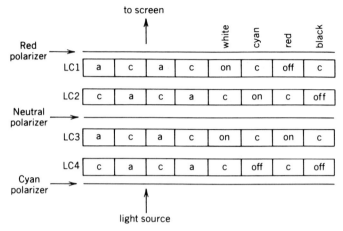

FIGURE 5.47 Multicolor high-resolution display schematic. After Conner and Gulick [8], by permission.

display. This type of panel has been applied to LCD projection systems with some success and is discussed further in Section 5.3.7.

5.3.6 Active Matrix

Although active matrix addressing was first developed to drive EL panels and has been tried with VFDs, its major success has been with LCDs, and the discussions in this section are limited to those types. In particular, this approach has been most successful in producing color LCDs and is the accepted way to provide those FPDs for use in television sets and computers. A list of TFT arrays in use for color displays is given in Table 3.12 and may be referred to for further information on this technology.

The actual construction format of a TFT active matrix array together with a liquid-crystal cell and color filter is pictured in a somewhat schematic form in Figure 5.48a, with the color filter pixel layout shown in Figure 5.48b. This is only one representative structure, and other structures may be used to achieve a full-color unit. For example, Figure 5.49 shows a more detailed cross-sectional view of another layout, where a storage capacitor (C_s) is constructed under the pixel to allow operation at high temperatures (85°C), and black stripes are applied on the color filter to improve contrast ratio. This unit has a contrast ratio above 45:1 and a pixel resolution of 1024 × 1024 on a 6.8 in. × 6.8 in. viewing surface, with a full-color capability. Another full-color structure is the one shown in Figure 5.50, which is built around a MIM rather than a TFT active matrix but otherwise is quite similar to the others. Therefore, it may be concluded that there are a variety of approaches to producing active matrix, full-color LCDs, and they are increasingly available for computer and television display panels. However, it should be noted that essentially all of the color units use some type of backlighting, usually flu-

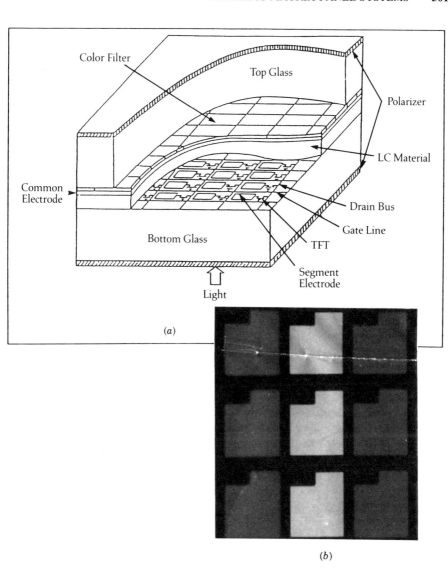

FIGURE 5.48 Active matrix TFT LCD. After Lessin [10], by permission.

orescent, and the choice of the type of lighting affects some of the parameter values. A range of parameter values is given in Table 5.28.

5.3.7 Other Technologies

Despite early promise for matrix systems using electrochomic or electrophoretic technologies, no products have been produced and these technologies remain to be developed in the future, if ever. However, for historical reasons, the characteristics of early EPID systems are given in Table 5.29 and a basic drive circuit in Figure 5.51.

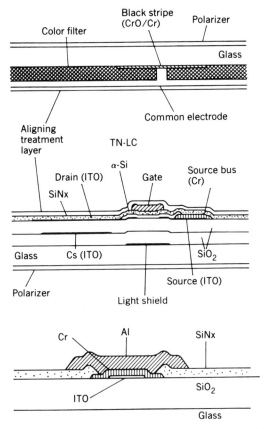

FIGURE 5.49 Cross-sectional view of source bus line in TFTs. After Nakagawa et al. [11], by permission.

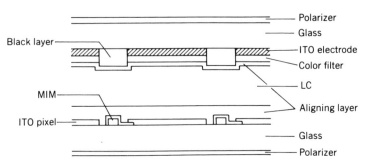

FIGURE 5.50 Cross-sectional view of MIM-LCD. After Aruga et al. [12], by permission.

TABLE 5.28   Active Matrix Color LCD Panel Parameters

Parameter	Value
Display area (mm)	62×62 to 278×221
Number of pixels	388×394 to 1920×480
Number of colors	8–4096
Contrast ratio	30–100
Response time (ms)	14–40
Luminance (nits)	Depends on light source

TABLE 5.29   Characteristics of EPID Displays

Appearance	Excellent contrast over very wide viewing angles
Color capability	Many color combinations, including black/white
Speed	Approximately 20 ms at 50 V
Lifetime	$> 10^8$ switches or 8500 h
Voltage (V)	15–50
Power consumption (μW/cm^2)	< 5
Memory (hr)	≈ 100
Matrix addressing	Control grid technique under development; TTL or CMOS compatible and addressing at 1 ms/ line
Resolution (lines/mm)	With above addressing scheme: ≈ 5
Temperature (°C)	Operation: 10–70; storage: -40–100
Size	Very flexible (< 2.5 cm^3 to > 30 m^2)
Cost	Expected to be low cost; low materials cost and simple fabrication

Source: From Dalisa [13], by permission.

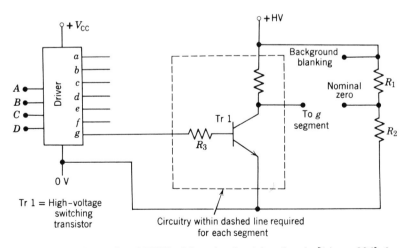

FIGURE 5.51   Schematic of EPID drive circuit. After Lewis [14, p. 236], by permission.

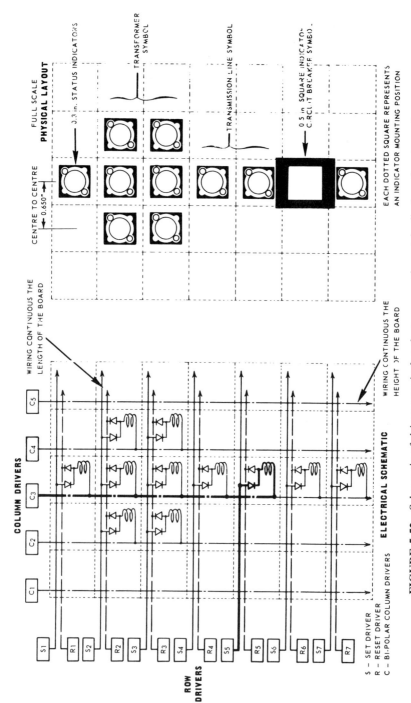

FIGURE 5.52 Schematic of driver matrix for electromagnetic matrix display. Courtesy of Ferranti-Packard.

However, some of the older technologies have been used for matrix displays, in particular the electromechanical and incandescent. The latter has been used primarily for large outdoor displays made up with standard light bulbs as signs and message displays and are fairly conventional in structure and limited in applications. However, the electromechanical (EM) displays have been more successful and are found in a variety of locations, principally airports and other transportation stations. The principles of operation are the same as for the A/N versions but are expanded to cover a much larger matrix of elements. The arrangement of column and row drivers for a rotating disk display is shown in Figure 5.52 and a photograph of a representative display board in Figure 5.53. These boards are built up of assemblies of individual disks for which driver–decoder boards are available. They are intended primarily for A/N messages, but they can also be used to create limited graphics, depending on how may elements are included. The operating characteristics of some of these dot matrix elements are given in Table 5.30.

Finally, there is one other matrix display that uses a form of EM technology, and that is the one termed *Rapidot* by its vender, Densitron. The basic technique is illustrated in Figure 5.54 and consists of colored vanes that move in and out of the viewing area, activated by miniature solenoids. Six different colors are available for each pixel by mixing three primary colors in two positions, and more colors can be achieved by mixing adjacent pixels. Some relevant parameters are given in Table 5.31. These displays can be constructed

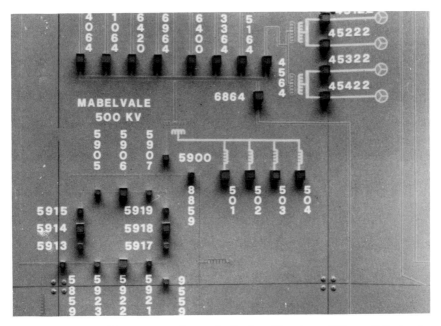

FIGURE 5.53 Electromagnetic matrix display. Courtesy of Ferranti-Packard.

TABLE 5.30   Electromagnetic Matrix Display Element Parameters

Parameter	Value
Temperature range (°C)	−40–92
Minimum pulse current (mA)	53–350
Minimum pulse duration (ms)	1–1.5
Minimum pulse amplitude (V)	3.3–25
Coil resistance (Ω)	12–430

in a wide variety of sizes, and the system can include a computer and modem so as to address a number of signs from a single control center.

5.3.8   Comparisons of Technologies

In general, the same performance factors are involved in the matrix systems as examined for the A/N systems, so that most of the material contained in Table 5.14 is equally applicable here. However, there are some unique factors, such as display resolution and size, and system interfaces, so that additional data are necessary and are given in Tables 5.15 to 5.31. It is apparent that whereas there are many ways to produce matrix FPDs, there are relatively few technologies for truly large-screen matrix displays other than discrete LEDs, light bulbs, and the two EM approaches. It is true that ac plasma has provided some fairly large units, and the development efforts supported by DARPA and HDTV in general may lead to other examples using this and some of the other technologies. However, at present, the main hope for full-color large-screen systems using FPDs seems to rest most with active matrix-addressed LCD projection systems, discussed next. This is not to belittle the successes achieved by Photonics in making moderately large color panels, but for full-sized color displays, projection LCDs appear to be best.

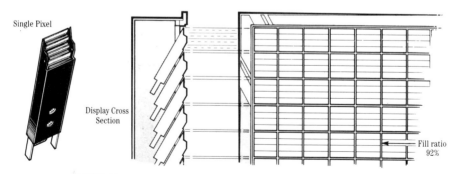

FIGURE 5.54   Display cross section. Courtesy of Densitron.

TABLE 5.31   Rapidot Display Parameters

Parameter	Value
Dot size (mm)	24×24
Module pixel format	8×8
Pixel switching speed (ms)	10–70
Switching power (W)	5–10
Operating voltage	10
Number of colors	6

5.4   LARGE-SCREEN PROJECTION SYSTEMS

5.4.1   Light Valves

CRT Addressed. The large-screen projection systems discussed in this section are not, strictly speaking, matrix systems. However, since they use several of the technologies covered in this chapter they may, without too much violation of pedagogical logic, be included in this chapter. Specifically, they are systems in which the light-control element is a cell whose transmission characteristic for light is modified by the application of both optical and electrical signals. The first one we cover is that having a liquid crystal panel as the light-control element, to which a photoconductive layer is added in the manner shown in Figure 5.55, with one electrode on the photoconductive layer, and the other on the liquid-crystal cell. Thus if a voltage is applied to the entire structure, it is across both the photoconductive layer and the liquid-crystal cell. By this means the areas of the liquid crystal that are activated can be controlled by the light impinging on the photoconductive layer. The light valve operates because the photoconductive resistance is high enough in the absence of light inpinging on it that insufficient voltage appears across the liquid-crystal portion for the liquid crystal to be activated. However, when the writing light hits the photoconductor, it will drop in resistance in those areas where the light hits, and the voltage across the liquid-crystal layer will be large enough to activate it in those areas, so that the cell can be rendered transparent to the projection light only in those areas. This light valve is incorporated in the system shown in Figure 5.56 and the dielectric mirror reflects the light from the projection light source so that it may be modulated by the light valve. If a CRT is used as the writing light source, the image generated on the CRT is transferred to the liquid crystal light valve and projected onto the projection screen, thus achieving a large-screen display. Color may be produced by operating the liquid-crystal cell in the tunable birefringent mode, described in Chapter 3 as the DAP effect and defined by equation 3.37, and it has been found possible by careful control of the pretilt angle in the liquid crystal to construct a cell that successfully produced a multicolor display. However, a more successful version uses three CRTs as sources for the red, green, and blue signals. Thus three light valves are shown

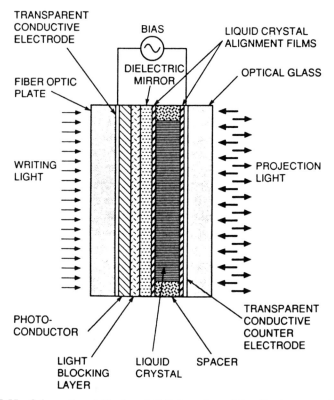

TRANSPARENT
CONDUCTIVE
ELECTRODE

BIAS

LIQUID CRYSTAL
ALIGNMENT FILMS

DIELECTRIC
MIRROR

OPTICAL GLASS

FIBER OPTIC
PLATE

WRITING
LIGHT

PROJECTION
LIGHT

PHOTO-
CONDUCTOR

TRANSPARENT
CONDUCTIVE
COUNTER
ELECTRODE

LIGHT
BLOCKING
LAYER

LIQUID
CRYSTAL

SPACER

FIGURE 5.55   Schematic of Hughes LC light valve. After Lackner et al. [15], by permission.

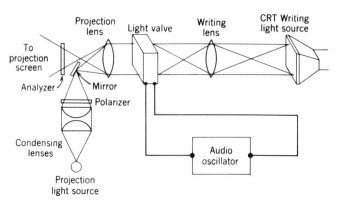

Projection
lens

Light valve

Writing
lens

CRT Writing
light source

To
projection
screen

Analyzer

Mirror

Polarizer

Condensing
lenses

Audio
oscillator

Projection
light source

FIGURE 5.56   Schematic of typical light-valve system. After Jacobson [16], by permission.

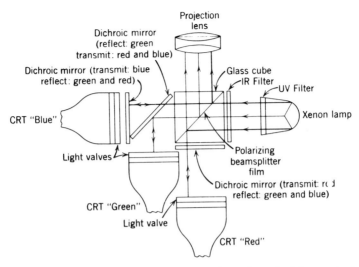

FIGURE 5.57   Schematic of hybrid effect light-valve color-television projector. After Jacobson [17], by permission.

in Figure 5.57, and the monochromatic and multicolor modes are given in Table 5.32. This system has reached an advanced state of manufacture, so it may be considered as a way to achieving a multicolor large-screen display.

A perspective view of a full-color projector built by Hughes Aircraft is shown in Figure 5.58. In this projector, the images from three CdS-photosensor hybrid field-effect (HFE) liquid-crystal light valves (LCLVs) are used to generate a full-color image and project the image using a single lens. The hybrid field effect uses positive dielectric anisotropy LCs in an off-state twist, typically 45°, of tilted parallel surface alignment. Alternatively, a new tilted perpendicular alignment (TPA) has been developed that allows a contrast ratio over 300:1 to be achieved in this type of projector. Some other parameter values for this full-color projector are given in Table 5.33.

Laser Addressed. Another large-screen system using liquid-crystal technology is that given the imaginative cognomen *Paperless Plotter* by one manufacturer, although it is basically only another approach to the liquid-crystal light valve, of which the Hughes system is one of the earliest. The major differences between the two are that this one uses smectic A liquid-crystal material for the light valve and heat to change the transmission characteristics of the LCLV. The recognition by Sasaki, Kahn, and others that thermoelectric effects in smectic material could be used for controlling a light valve dates back to the early 1970s, but it has taken many years for this effect to be incorporated in actual equipment.

In the products that have emerged, the actual heat source is a single beam combined from two IR lasers, and the associated deflection system and one system configuration are shown in Figure 5.59. The beam deflector is a servo-

TABLE 5.32a   Characteristics of Liquid Crystal Light-Valve Projection Display Systems: Monochrome

Input light sensitivity (full contrast):	100 μW/cm^2
Resolution (50% MTF):	60 lines/mm at 515 nm
Contrast:	>30: 1
Response time:	30 fps
Gray scale rendition:	9 gray shades
Voltage:	16 V_{RMS} at 10 kHz
Aperture size:	2.5 cm × 2.5 cm

Source: After Jacobson [16], by permission.

TABLE 5.32b   Characteristics of Liquid Crystal Light-Valve Projection Display Systems: Color

Characteristic	Performance
Color content	Full color
Resolution (limiting)	600 lines
Contrast	10: 1
Light output	600 lm
Lens	f/2.8
Power	
Lamp	2 kW
(1.6-kW xenon arc)	
Electronics	2 kW
CRT Voltage	12 kV
Convergence scheme	Open loop: linear deflection with common power supplies
Light-valve aperture	5 cm, circular
Light-valve voltage	8 V at 10 kHz

Source: After Jacobson [17], by permission.

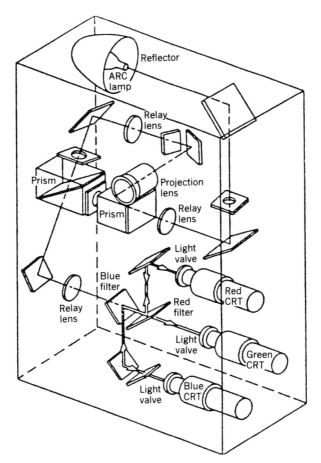

FIGURE 5.58 Perspective view of optical cabinet. After Lackner et al. [15], by permission.

TABLE 5.33 Hughes Color Projector Parameters

Parameter	Value
Light output (lm)	650–1000
Contrast ratio	30–100
Screen size (m)	1–5 square
Throw distance (m)	1–5
Vertical resolution (scan lines)	>1024
Horizontal resolution (TV lines)	>1400

Source: After Lackner et al. [15].

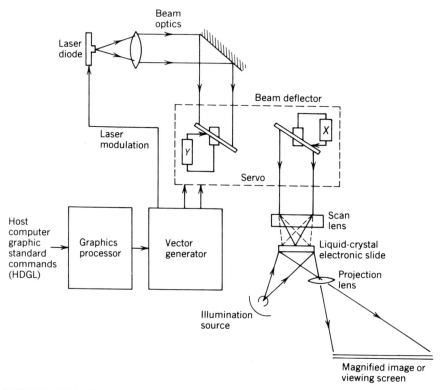

FIGURE 5.59 Schematic showing operating principles. After Kahn [18], by permission.

driven $x-y$ galvonometer scan system, and the optical projection path is shown in Figure 5.60. The structure of the electronic slide, shown in Figure 5.61, constitutes a laser-addressed smectic A LCLV. The actual operation consists of driving the laser beam to the desired location and using the heat from the beam to darken the selected area in the absence of voltage across the LCLV. Total erasure is achieved by applying a high voltage without heating, and partial erasure by a combination of low voltage and laser heating. Multicolor is achieved by devoting specific areas of the cell to specific primaries and obtaining the colors from the light source by means of a dichroic beam splitter. Operating parameters for this type of system are given in Table 5.34.

Another approach to the use of smectic LCLV is that pictured in Figure 5.62, which provides a larger projected screen image. It also differs from the system described previously in that three cells are used corresponding to the three primary colors. However, it uses the same type of laser diodes and deflection systems to provide the heat source and therefore falls into the same projection system group. Its parameters are given in Table 5.35.

LCD Projection Panels. Probably the most significant developments in flat-panel projection systems are the LCD projection panels that have proliferated

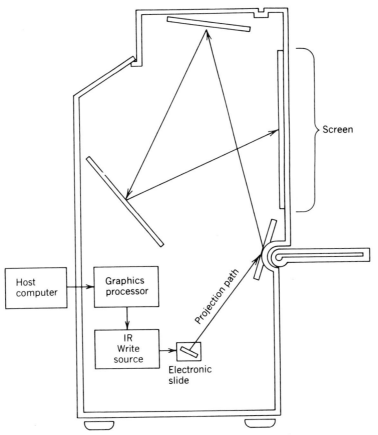

FIGURE 5.60 Optical projection path. After Kahn [18], by permission.

in a variety of forms and with various capabilities. They were introduced in 1986 with only monochrome capabilities, then were extended to eight colors in 1989 and to full color by 1991. The panels are available from a number of vendors and are designed generally to operate with overhead projectors as dynamic slides. The panel shown in Figure 5.63 is intended for use with an overhead projector and is representative of this type. In general, these panels can be connected to a computer and generate large-screen projected displays of dynamic output from the computer.

The panels are technically equivalent to those designed for direct computer output using both passive and active matrix techniques, and the operational characteristics in general correspond to those found in the LCDs described in Section 5.3.5. The parameter values for the projection panels are given in Table 5.36.

In addition, whereas the projection panels to be used with overhead projectors are most prevalent, there are several manufacturers that sell complete

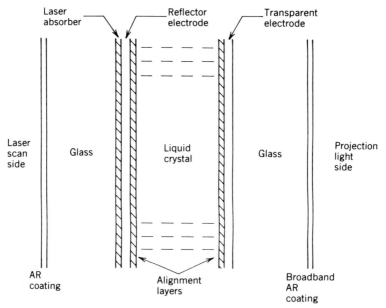

FIGURE 5.61   Cross section of electronic slide. After Kahn [18], by permission.

TABLE 5.34   Smectic LCLV Color Projector Parameters

Parameter	Value
Screen size (in.)	22 × 34
Addressability (dpi)	400
Pixel resolution	2200 × 3400
Contrast ratio	16:1
Colors	4096
Writing speed (ips)	2000

Source: After Kahn [18].

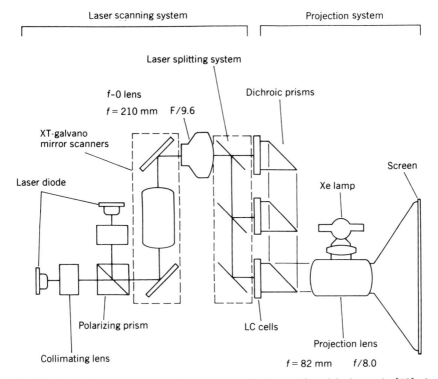

FIGURE 5.62 Optical system of prototype display. After Mori et al. [19], by permission.

TABLE 5.35 Three-Cell LCLV Projector Parameters

Parameter	Value
Screen size (M)	2×2
Pixel resolution	2000×2000
Writing speed (mps)	30
Luminous flux (lumens)	1000

Source: After Mari et al. [19].

FIGURE 5.63 LCD projection panel. Courtesy of Dukane.

projectors that incorporate one or more LCD panels to allow monochromatic or color displays to be projected. An optical schematic for one such projector is shown in Figure 5.64 and it uses dichroic mirrors to create the three primary colors from a single light source, in conjunction with three active matrix LCD panels, one for each color. This unit can accept composite video or S-video and provide large-screen projection images. Parameter values for these types are given in Table 5.37.

TABLE 5.36 LCD Projection Panel Parameters

Parameter	Value
Display area (in.)	7.9×5.3 to 13×13
Resolution (pixels)	320×200 to 1250×1024
Colors	Monochrome to 24,389
Technologies	STN, DSTN, AM
Contrast ratio	15:1–200:1

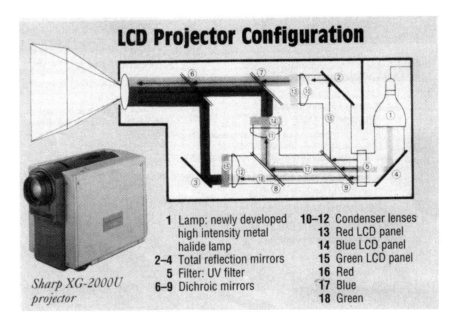

LCD Projector Configuration

Sharp XG-2000U projector

1 Lamp: newly developed high intensity metal halide lamp	**10–12** Condenser lenses
	13 Red LCD panel
	14 Blue LCD panel
2–4 Total reflection mirrors	**15** Green LCD panel
5 Filter: UV filter	**16** Red
6–9 Dichroic mirrors	**17** Blue
	18 Green

FIGURE 5.64   LCD projector configuration. Courtesy of Sharp.

Ferroelectric LCLV. The last type of LCLV projection panel is the one that uses ferroelectric LC technology. This is the most recent development, and a few examples are included here as representative of what is being developed. A schematic drawing of a video rate LCLV with gray-scale capabilities is shown in Figure 5.65. This is a photoactivated unit that has been operated in the system shown in Figure 5.66 and has demonstrated the performance capabilities given in Table 5.38.

This is a preliminary version intended as a possible replacement for the smectic A LCLV described previously. A somewhat more advanced unit is the surface-stabilized high-resolution ferroelectric LCLV (SSFLCLV). This LCLV has been incorporated in the projection system shown schematically

TABLE 5.37   LCD Color Projector Parameters

Parameter	Value
Technology	Active matrix
Number of LCD panels	3
Panel size (in.)	3.1×3.1 to 3.5×3.5
Pixel resolution (H $\times$ V)	160×239 to 450×245
Contrast ratio	60:1–100:1
Throw distance (ft.)	3–20

Source: Courtesy of Sharp.

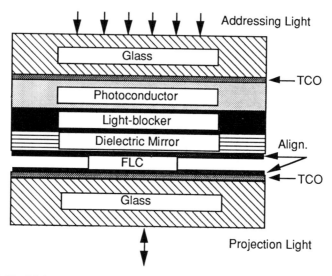

FIGURE 5.65   Light-valve schematic drawing. After Bone et al. [20], by permission.

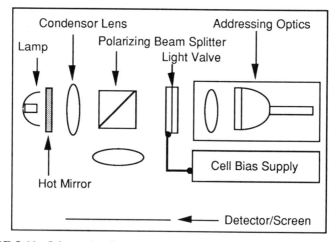

FIGURE 5.66   Schematic of test system. After Bone et al. [20], by permission.

TABLE 5.38   Ferroelectric LCLV Parameters

Parameter	Value
Contrast ratio	>30:1
Switching speed (ms)	<0.6
Resolution (lp/mm)	>20
Gray scale	Analog

Source: After Bone et al. [20].

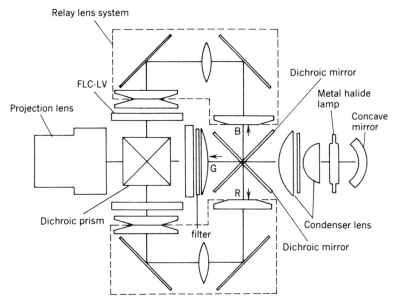

FIGURE 5.67   Basic structure of projector. After Iwai et al. [21], by permission.

TABLE 5.39   SSFLCLV Parameters

Parameter	Value
Display area (mm)	60×60
Pixel size (μm)	26×26
Address time (μs/line)	140

Source: After Iwai et al. [21].

TABLE 5.40   Projection Display Parameters

Parameter	Value
Display area (mm)	66.7×66.7
Color	8
Luminance (fL)	40
Contrast ratio	>20:1
Renewal time (seconds/screen)	0.5

Source: After Iwai et al. [21].

in Figure 5.67, with parameter values given in Table 5.39 for the LCLV and in Table 5.40 for the combination of the optical system and the LCLV. A two-slot driving scheme is used, with the black matrix achieved by controlling the field with black matrix (BM) pulses.

These are fairly impressive results and indicate what may be achieved in the future. These developments are still rather new and are presented here for information about what some of the most advanced developments are in LCLV projectors. It may be anticipated that further improvements will occur and marketable products result.

REFERENCES

[1] Chang, I. F., and Howard, W. E., "Performance Characteristics of Electro-chromic Displays," *IEEE Trans. Electron. Devices*, **ED-22**/9, 1975, 751.

[2] Chang, I. F., "Electrochromic Materials and Phenomena," in A. R. Kmetz and F. K. von Willisen, Eds., *Nonemissive Electrooptic Displays*, Plenum, New York, 1976.

[3] Channing, D., Theroux, T., and Wolf, A., *EL Addressing Technology*, Cherry Electrical Products, Waukegan, IL.

[4] Channing, D., et al., *Drive System for a 640 × 200 DC EL Display*, Cherry Products, Waukegan, IL.

[5] Uchiike, H., "Color Plasma Displays," *SID Sem. Lect. Notes*, 1991, M8/11–M8/19.

[6] Friedman, P. S., et al., "1.5-m-Diagonal AC Gas Discharge Display." *SID Proc.*, **28**/4, 1987, 367.

[7] Lieberman, D., "New Twist in LCD Designs Makes Them Thin, Light Power-Savers," *Comput. Design*, Apr. 1, 1989, 37.

[8] Conner, A. R., and Gulick, P. E., "High Resolution Display System Based on Stacked Mutually Compensated STN-LCD Layers," *SID 1991 Dig.*, 755.

[9] Kaneko, Y., et al., "Crosstalk-Free Driving Methods for STN-LCDs," *SID Proc.*, **31**/4, 1990, 333–336.

[10] Lessin, J., "TFT Acting Up a Storm Onscreen," *Comput. Technol. Rev.*, Apr. 1992, 30.

[11] Nakagawa, T., et al., "A 6.85 × 6.85 High-Resolution Active-Matrix Full-Color LCD," *Proc. Jap. Dis. '89*, 1989, Post deadline Paper 5.

[12] Aruga, H., et al., "A 10-in.-Diagonal Full Color MIM Active Matrix LCD," *Proc. Jap. Dis. '89*, 171.

[13] Dalisa, A. L., "Electrophoretic Display Technology," *SID Proc.*, **18**/1, 1977, 49.

[14] Lewis, J. C., "Electrophoretic Displays," in A. R. Kmetz and F. K. Von Willisen, Eds., *Nonemissive Electrooptic Displays*, Plenum, New York, 1976.

[15] Lackner, A. M., et al., "Photostable Tilted-Perpendicular Alignment of Liquid Crystals for Light Valves," *SID Proc.*, **31**/4, 1990, 321–326.

[16] Jacobson, A. D., "A New Television Projection Light Valve," *SID 1975 Dig.*, p. 27.

[17] Jacobson, A. D., "A New Color-TV Projector," *SID 1977 Dig.*, 106.

[18] Kahn, F. J., "A Paperless Plotter Display System," *SID Symp. Dig.*, 1987, 255.

[19] Mori, Y., et al., "Multi-color Laser Addressed Liquid Crystal Projection Display," *Proc. Jap. Dis. '86*, 420.

[20] Bone, M., et al., "Video-Rate Photoaddressed Ferroelectric LC Light Valve with Gray Scale," *SID 1991 Dig.*, 254–256.

[21] Iwai, Y., et al., "Multi-color, High Resolution Projection Display," *Proc. Jap. Dis. '89*, 182.

6

INPUT AND OUTPUT DEVICES AND SYSTEMS

6.1 INPUT DEVICES

6.1.1 Introduction

An essential component of any information display system is some means for entering commands and data into the system. Thus input devices form a category common to all display systems, and they are treated here as a separate equipment group, independent of the display system configuration. However, the place of input devices in a representative display system may be clarified by reference to Figures 4.1, 4.29, and 4.30, which show the location of the main input device categories in relation to the portions of the generalized display system that accept the inputs. These categories and the devices are listed in Table 6.1.

6.1.2 Keyboards

Keyboards are essentially electromechanical devices and fall somewhat out of the purview of this text. However, they are still so ubiquitous, despite the inroads of other input devices, that they deserve at least limited treatment. The primary form for the keyboard as an input device for electronic display systems is the alphanumeric form, so well known in its typewriter application but with additions and expansions in the form of numeric, special, and function keys. This basic keyboard is pictured in Figure 6.2, which shows the A/N portion, a separate numeric set to the right, and a group of function keys at the top. It is apparent that at least the A/N format corresponds to the standard QWERTY layout and can be used by experienced typists. An alternative

TABLE 6.1   Input Devices

Category	Designation	Operation Mode
Keyboard	Alphanumeric	Electromechanical
	Function	Electromechanical
Pointing	Light pen	Screen pointing
	Touchscreen	Screen pointing
	Pen tablet	Tablet pointing
Coordinates	Digitizer	X–Y conversion
	Data tablet	X–Y location
Curser	Mouse	Movement
	Trackball	Movement
	Joystick	Movement
Image	Scanner	Conversion
Verbal	Voice	Conversion

layout is the Dvorak, one that has been proposed and accepted by ANSI but has not received much use despite its advantages in increased efficiency. At present, the overwhelming majority of display system keyboards still use the QWERTY layout, and it is the only one considered here.

As can be seen from Figure 6.1, and as should be anticipated from its name, the keyboard consists of a number of keyswitches, and the exact structure of these switches is the most important aspect of keyboard design. The relevant aspect of keyswitch operation are life, actuation force, travel dis-

FIGURE 6.1   Alphanumeric keyboard. Courtesy of IBM.

TABLE 6.2 Keyboard Parameter Values

Parameter	Value		
	Snap Switch	Elastomer	Foam Pad
Key travel (mm)	3.8	3.2	3.8
Force (g)	>60	>50	>30
Life (cycles)	10M	10M	10M
Feedback	Audio mechanical	Audio electronic	Tactile

tance, and feedback. Accepted values are shown in Table 6.2 for different types of keyswitch designs.

The elastomer type is preferred to a limited extent over the other two when the electronic audio feedback is included. This indicates that some type of audio feedback is desirable. The life requirement is estimated on the basis of workstation users operating at approximately half the accepted rate of 20M actuations per key used for electronic typewriters. The actual layout and content of the keyboard may vary greatly, ranging from the standard typewriter arrangement, through different combinations of alphanumerics and symbols, to the special-function keyboards that contain legends and symbols specific to the particular application. However, the outputs of each type are the same in that they must contain coded signals that relate the action to be performed by the display system to that defined by the key being operated, in terms of the input code of the display system. Thus many of the keyboards output the ASCII code, and the display system is usually designed so that it can accept this type of standard code. Incidentally, ASCII (the American Standard Code for Information Interchange) is the standard means for encoding alphanumerics and a group of selected symbols for transmission to a display system, among others. It is the standard code used in the United States and most other English-speaking countries and corresponds to the ISO 7-bit code. The 7-bit ASCII is usually used, and it should be noted that for serial data transmission an eighth bit is added for parity. Various keyboard arrangements are possible, and many variants are found in particular applications. The means for coding the key operation may be through magnetic reed relays, solid-state circuits, or more exotic devices such as Hall effect sensors. However, we do not pursue these means any further to avoid getting bogged down in an entire new class of device characteristics that are only incidental to the display system operation. Similarly, we do not discuss the human-factors aspects of keyboard design, not because they are not important, but because apart from the visual considerations, the other factors have to do with tactile and physical features best left to others.

6.1.3 Light Pen

The light pen initially was a very popular means for accomplishing manual input to the random deflection information display systems, but fell out of favor when raster systems became more popular due to its being somewhat difficult to use with raster systems. This device goes by a misleading cognomen, as despite its name it does not emit light and is not a pen, other than being somewhat similar to one in its physical appearance, as shown in Figure 6.2. However, when we consider its functional characteristics, the validity of the term becomes apparent since it is used to cause the electron beam to "write" patterns on the CRT that are defined by the motion of the light pen on the CRT faceplate. Leaving semantics aside, the light pen operates by sensing the existence of light output at the particular location to which it is directed and then sending information as to the existence or nonexistence of light output back into the display system, thus closing the loop around the human operator in a dynamic fashion. The exact means by which this is achieved is rather simple in terms of operator actions, a feature that probably accounts for the popularity of the light pen as an input device for CRT systems, despite some limitations in speed of response and accuracy of location. All that the operator need do is point the light pen to the location of interest on the CRT faceplate, usually by placing its end directly on the surface or very close to the surface and then letting the computer do the rest. Figure 6.3 contains a schematic of a light-pen unit in sufficient detail to serve as the basis for a functional description of its operation. First, the light from the CRT surface is collected by the optical elements consisting of a lens and a fiber-optics transmission bundle, and then this light is focused directly on the light-sensitive portion of a photodetector, such as a phototransistor. The electrical output of the photodetector is amplified to a level sufficient to operate some type of triggering circuit that produces a pulse at the time the

FIGURE 6.2   Light pen. Courtesy of FTG Data Systems.

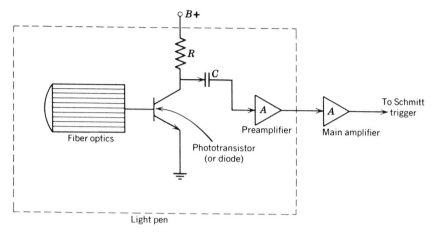

FIGURE 6.3   Light-pen schematic.

light emission occurs, plus any incidental delays in the triggering operation. This pulse may then be sent to the display system input and used to time the operation of other elements of that system. The manner in which this may be accomplished is illustrated by Figure 6.4 where a complete, closed-loop system is shown. Since the light pen signal occurs at a time corresponding to when the light pulse is emitted by the CRT phosphor, the computer is signaled at this time and may perform operations on the data represented by the light output, such as deletion, intensification, or alteration, as commanded by programmed or other instructions. The position of the light beam at this time is known because the beam deflection has been commanded by the data input from the computer and may be retained until the operation has been accomplished. Light-pen programs have been written to achieve all these operations, as well as the more complex ones such as graphic drawing and inquiry list sequencing among others.

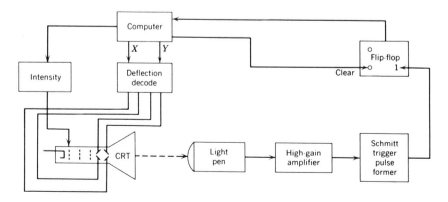

FIGURE 6.4   Block diagram of light-pen/computer system.

There are two characteristics of light-pen operation that should be noted and understood since they do set bounds on the capabilities of this input device. The first is the sensitivity of the light pen to the light emitted, which establishes the minimum amount of light output that can be sensed by the light pen. This sensitivity is given by

$$S = E_L \eta_p A_p A_m \eta_s \eta_f t_L \tag{6.1}$$

where E_L = illuminance at photodetector
η_p = photodetector sensitivity
A_p = preamplifier gain
A_m = main amplifier gain
η_s = Schmitt trigger sensitivity
η_f = flip-flop sensitivity
t_L = optical loss

Equation 6.1 includes all the parameters specific to the light-pen system and may be used to calculate the light output required from the CRT to ensure reliable operation. The phosphor of the CRT is involved in this calculation, and the phosphor parameters given in Chapter 2 and elsewhere may be used to arrive at a final determination. The phosphor also contributes to the overall delay between the application of a signal to the CRT and the response of the light pen to that signal. The phosphor has a buildup delay represented by

$$N = \frac{\eta J M}{\eta J + \alpha} \{1 - \exp[-(\eta J + \alpha)]t\} \tag{6.2}$$

where N = number of excited electrons in phosphor
M = number of excitable electrons
J = beam current density
α = reciprocal of mean excited lifetime
η = excitation quantum efficiency constant

and the total delay of the light-pen system, including the delays in the photodetector, the amplifers, and triggering elements, is given approximately by

$$E_{out} = E_{in} \left[1 - \exp\left(-\frac{t}{\tau} \right) \right] \tag{6.3}$$

with all the delays included in τ. This is the standard delay formula for any low-pass filter and is sufficiently accurate for most calculations. The delay is important because it sets limits on the accuracy with which a location may be designated on the CRT, since the computer will relate the triggering signal to the time it arrives at the computer, and will designate the location that the electron beam is occupying at that time. This difference between the time the light output occurs and that at which the computer sends back the location coordinates may not be significant when the beam is moving slowly or when corrective actions are possible, but in other cases, such as in raster displays, the response time may be too slow to pick up the desired spot location, and a radius of uncertainty exists. The uncertainty is further compounded by the physical dimensions of the light pen, enabling it to detect an area that may be considerably larger than a spot size, with the consequent broadening of the detection circle. These limitations in light-pen accuracy are covered further in the equipment section, and it suffices to note at this point that they have not appreciably limited the use of the light pen as an input device in many applications. One reason for the wide acceptance is probably the apparent ease of use, requiring the operator to merely point at the location, and not adding the complications of learning to typewrite or to use a complicated function keyboard. However, it should also be stated that this ease is sometimes more apparent than real, with fatigue setting in after prolonged use and errors resulting. In addition, the light pen is not as rugged as some of the other input devices and is more subject to misuse than, for example, the track ball discussed later. It should be noted, however, that the light pen is coming back into favor as improvements in accuracy, ease of operation, and reliability occur, and it is once more a valid input device.

6.1.4 Data Tablet (Graphics, Digitizer)

A very convenient means for data entry, retaining some of the ease of operation of the light pen but with much better accuracy, are the various forms of data tablets available. These tablets differ from the light pen in another significant way in that they do not require a moving spot of light to detect the location of the beam or direct it to a new location. This need for a moving light spot made the light pen difficult to use in the direct-view storage tube systems, and the tablets were initially designed to overcome this limitation and still use a device with a penlike input. The first successful example was the Rand tablet, shown schematically in Figure 6.5. It is a digital device in that each resolvable point is selected by having the wand pick up pulses from the X and Y pulse generators. By determining the number of pulses on the X and Y lines, the exact location of the wand is established in terms of the number of pulses during the time period. This location is converted into display coordinates and used to position a cursor on the CRT screen. The cursor may then be used as a visual feedback element so that the operator can correct the position of the wand until the cursor is properly placed. At this time the information from the tablet may also be transferred to either the host computer or the resident desktop or portable computer, as desired. Since the cursor is not used to signal its position to a pickup device, as is the case with the light pen, it may be used with any type of display system, including the non-light-emitting FPDs. Another advantage of the tablet is

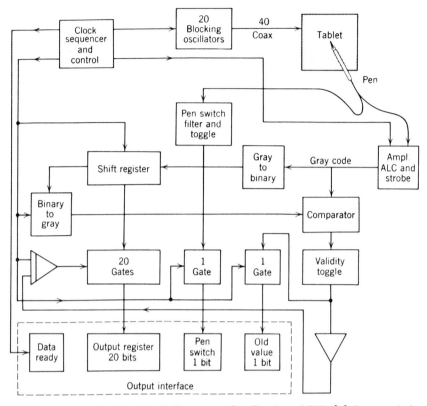

FIGURE 6.5   Rand tablet block diagram. After Davis and Ellis [1], by permission.

that it may be used to position cursors in the blank areas of the display, where no light pulses are available unless they are specially generated by the light pen system.

Subsequent to the development of the first data tablet as exemplified by the Rand tablet, there have been numerous improvements and new developments using a variety of technologies. These technologies include magnetostrictive, electromagnetic, electrostatic or capacitive, scanned $X-Y$ grid, resistive, and sonic. Of these, electromagnetic tablets dominate the digitizer market, but magnetostrictive is still of some interest as a technology because of its innovative aspects and initial success. One example of how this technique was implemented is shown in Figure 6.6, which illustrates how a pulse may be propagated along a line and the distance between the start and finish determined from the time it takes to propagate. The speed of the strain wave along the magnetostrictive element is nominally 5000 m/s, which is 200 ns/mm. The resolution is then given by

$$R = \frac{S}{F} \tag{6.4}$$

where R = resolution
$\quad S$ = speed of travel
$\quad F$ = propagating frequency

If we wish a resolution of 40 lines/nm, then, using the propagation time given above, we obtain

$$F = 20 \text{ MHz}$$

The resolution is also affected by the size of the pickup head since it can only sense wavelengths smaller than its size, and this is overcome by making the pickup head out of a multiturn coil. One possible configuration for a tablet using this technique is shown in Figure 6.6, and a single head may be used to pick up both X and Y components. Other configurations have been used to achieve high-resolution data tablets with fast response time. Once the location of the pen has been calculated from the time data, the coordinates of the pen location on the tablet may be sent to the display system and used to either position the CRT beam or select the FPD matrix coordinates.

As noted previously, electromagnetic is the most popular technology for high-performance digitizer tablets. Operation is based on transformer principles, whereby a conductor carrying ac creates a magnetic field around it that induces a current in a second conductor. The digitizer tablet uses the amplitude and phase of the induced current to determine digitizing data. The tablet contains an $X-Y$ pattern of conductors beneath its surface, in a manner similar to the Rand tablet, but instead of counting pulses in a time period, a circular conductor is used as the pickup element for the induced current. This coil is placed on the tablet surface, and its position is determined by measuring the phase and amplitude of the current in the coil. Its center is interpolated by sweeping through the $X-Y$ grid lines and demodulating the signal in the coil to determine the phase reversal point or by calculating this point using digitized data fed into a microprocessor. The $X-Y$ coordinates may be re-

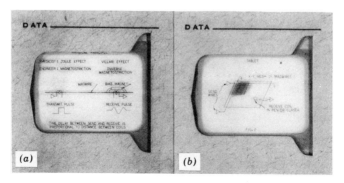

FIGURE 6.6 Magnetostrictive tablet operation: (*a*) matrix arrangement; (*b*) illustration of transmit and receive pulse. Courtesy of Summagraphics.

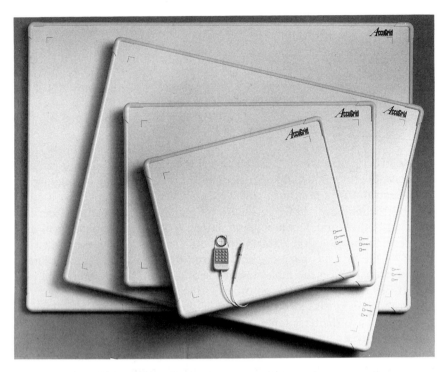

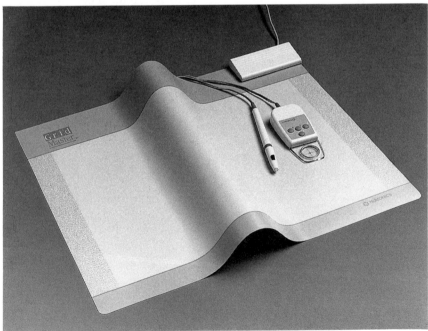

FIGURE 6.7   Data tablets. Courtesy of Summagraphics.

solved to better than 0.025 mm using either of these two techniques. Figure 6.7 is a photograph of a representative digitizer tablet.

Another digitizer technology that should be noted is that using the measurement of the time required for sound waves to travel from a source to movable microphone pickups. This sonic technology has the advantage that no special digitizing board is required, and either a stylus or a cursor can be used as the digitizer. Two sonic sources are contained in an L frame so that both X and Y coordinates can be determined by calculating the time it takes for the sound wave to reach the microphones contained in the pickup device. This calculation is made on the basis of sound traveling at 345 m/s at 20°, and the accuracy is dependent on stable ambient conditions. This tends to limit the resolution to about 300 lpi, and the accuracy to ±0.1%.

Digitizers are used primarily for inputting accurate coordinate data from maps and engineering drawings. Their high accuracy requirements have led to relatively high prices. Alternative means for inputting data are the data and graphics tablets, which meet most input requirements at a lower cost and accuracy. The main technology is still electromagnetic, and the units are essentially the same as the digitizers but with lower accuracies. However, several of the other technologies have also been used to achieve lower costs. Most successful among them are the capacitive and resistive versions, which may also be used as digitizers. The capacitive units, also termed *electrostatice*, use capacitive coupling where the coupling between the tablet and the cursor or stylus is determined by the capacitance made up of the tablet surface as one plate and the pickup element as the other. In this case, the capacitance is given by

$$C = f \frac{eA}{d} \tag{6.5}$$

where C = capacitance
$\quad\quad F$ = proportionality factor
$\quad\quad e$ = permittivity of dielectric
$\quad\quad A$ = relative area of two plates
$\quad\quad d$ = distance between plates

A scanned grid approach is used to determine the location of the cursor. As in the electromagnetic tablet, an $X-Y$ grid of conductors is embedded in the tablet, with semiconductor switches on each line providing contact on a scanned basis. The charge flowing from each capacitance is summed through a summing amplifier as shown in Figure 6.8. The resultant voltage peaks twice, once for the X and once for the Y lines, as they are scanned. The peak positions are digitized by means of a counter that starts at the beginning of the scan and runs at some multiple of the scan rate. The digital values represent the coordinates of the cursor location.

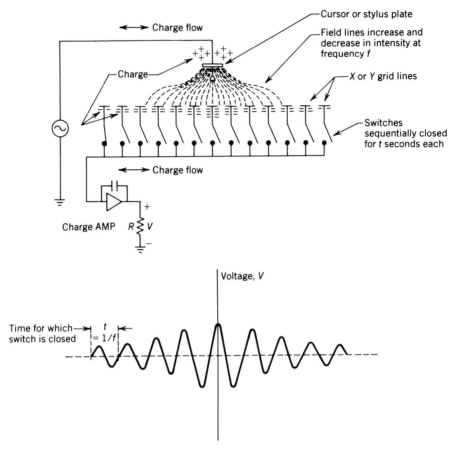

FIGURE 6.8   Capacitive technology. After Davies et al. [2, p. 186], by permission.

6.1.5   Mouse

The mouse has gone a long way from its original invention by Engelbart in 1965, through its redesign at Xerox and introduction by Apple as a main input device, and its general acceptance by computer users as an important addition to the group of input devices. It should be noted, in passing, that the mouse is essentially an upside-down trackball, although the latter is now being referred to as an upside-down mouse. However, the trackball has priority, as described further in Section 6.1.6.

Mice contain motion-sensing elements and are operated by moving mechanical or optical elements. One form uses wheels and shafts to drive the sensing elements, as shown schematically in Figure 6.9. The angular velocity (ω) of the wheel and shaft is given by

$$\omega = \frac{V_r}{R} \quad \text{rad/s} \tag{6.6}$$

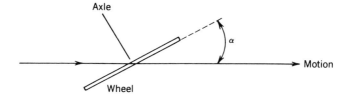

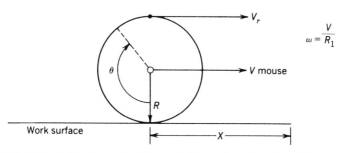

FIGURE 6.9 Wheel showing velocities and slip angle. After Goy [3], by permission.

where V_r is the velocity of wheel and R is the wheel radius. The rotation angle (θ) is given by

$$\theta = \frac{X}{R} \qquad \text{rad} \tag{6.7}$$

where X is the distance moved. This type of mouse has two sets of wheels and shafts, one for horizontal and the other for vertical motion.

A more popular type of mechanical mouse is the one that uses a ball for the motion-sensing device, as shown in Figure 6.10. Again, the velocity of the ball circumference equals the velocity of the mouse, and the angular velocity is given by

$$\omega = \frac{V}{R_1} \qquad \text{rad/s} \tag{6.8}$$

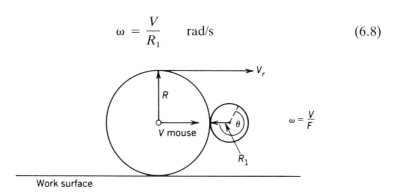

FIGURE 6.10 Ball and shaft. After Goy [3], by permission.

where R_1 is the shaft radius. The smaller the shaft, the more rapid its rotation for a given mouse velocity.

Another form of the ball and shaft mouse is the one that uses an optical interrupter, as shown in Figure 6.11. In this form, the light from the LEDs is interrupted by the coded disks that are rotated by the shafts and is then picked up by the phototransistors and converted into the digital signal that represents the disk rotation. An optical interrupter is also used for the optomechanical mouse, and its form is shown in Figure 6.12. Here the interrupter contains a set of slots, and as the interrupter rotates, quadrature signals are created that correspond to the shaft rotation.

In addition to the shaft and optomechanical mice, an early form of mouse used multiturn potentiometers connected to the wheels, and the output voltage that represented the motion varied in direct proportion to the mouse

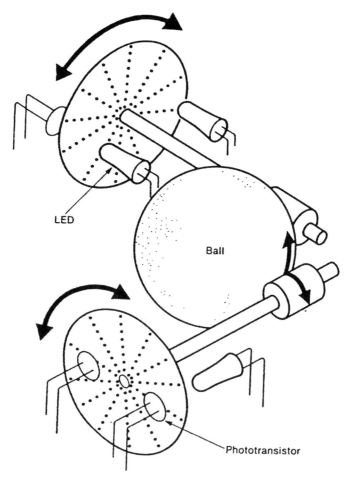

LED

Ball

Phototransistor

FIGURE 6.11   Ball and shafts with optical interrupter. After Goy [3], by permission.

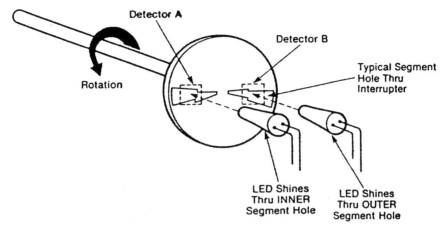

FIGURE 6.12 Optical interrupter. After Goy [3], by permission.

motion. The voltage was then converted by means of a A/D converter into digital form for input to the computer.

Finally, there are the true optical mice that use a special surface that is printed with a set of geometric shapes, usually a grid of lines or dots, that are illuminated and focused on a light detector. The most common form uses a grid made up of orthogonal lines, with the vertical and horizontal lines printed in different colors. These colors absorb light at different frequencies so that the optical detectors can differentiate between horizontal and vertical movement of the mouse. If a structure such as that shown in Figure 6.13 is used as the mouse, the photodetector will pick up a series of light–dark impulses consisting of the reflections from the mirror surface and the grid lines and convert them into square waves. A second LED and photodetector that is mounted orthogonally to the first is used to detect motion in the orthogonal direction, and the combination of the two inks avoids confusion between the two directions of motion. The system then counts the number

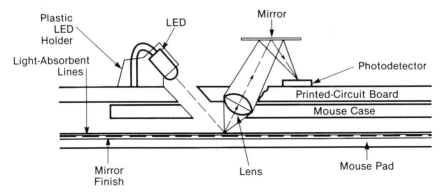

FIGURE 6.13 Optical mouse system. After Goy [3], by permission.

of impulses created by the mouse motion and converts the result into motion information for the cursor. This type of mouse has the advantage that no mechanical elements are required.

6.1.6   Trackball

As noted previously, the trackball uses technology similar to the mouse, but preceded it as an input device. Thus the comment that it is an upside-down mouse should be reversed. The movable element is housed in an assembly as shown in Figure 6.14, and the assembly remains stationary so that much less desk space is required than for the mouse. In addition, the trackball may be mounted on a keyboard so that very little additional desk space is needed. The movable element can be the same as used in the mouse, and the output can be a set of bits corresponding to the coordinates to which the cursor should be driven, or where the command should be carried out. The output format is essentially equivalent to that used for the mouse, and the same protocols are used.

The typical trackball has an $X-Y$ optical encoder that generates a pulse for each incremental 0.76 mm of incremental motion of the ball. This means that the pulse train may range from 10 to 2500 pps, depending on how fast the ball is rotated. This is much more rapid than required for satisfactory updates, which need not be greater than about 100 times per second. This

FIGURE 6.14   Three-inch trackball.

can easily be accommodated by the RS-232 protocol using an 8-bit word. Thus the trackball is an excellent alternative for the mouse and is rapidly returning to a preferred position as an input device.

6.1.7 Joystick

The joystick has not achieved much acceptance as an input device for electronic display systems, except for video games, although it has been the preferred control for many types of aircraft. However, it can be used to some extent in display system other than those used in video games and therefore warrants inclusion in this section.

There are two basic types of joysticks, one of which is termed "displacement" and the other, "force-operated." A typical displacement joystick is shown in Figure 6.15, and may have two or three degrees of freedom. In addition, the handle shown in Figure 6.15 may vary in size from that which might be operated with a few fingertips to one that accommodates a full hand. The activating means may vary from as few as four switches mounted 90° apart, to full potentiometers for analog output, and optical encoders for digital output. A third axis may be added by allowing the handle to rotate and drive

FIGURE 6.15   Three-axis grip-type displacement joystick. Courtesy of Measurement Systems.

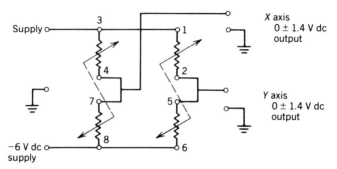

FIGURE 6.16 Typical schematic of strain gauge connections in a force joystick. After Doran [4], by permission.

a third potentiometer. Spring forces of 5 to 10 lb are usual for the other two axes, and displacements go from 6 to 30°.

The force joystick operates by responding to pressure on the handle to generate the $X-Y$ coordinates. It may be either a two- or three-dimensional version, with the same types of handles as for the displacement joysticks. However, it is difficult to use a rotating handle for the third dimension because some force is usually transmitted to the other dimensions, causing crosstalk. Therefore, a separate lever is preferred. The force is detected by means of piezoelectric sensors that are bonded to a handle rod, and a voltage source is applied across the network, as shown in Figure 6.16. The output is taken from the strain gage and the analog voltage will be proportional to the amount of force. The same type of protocol and output circuitry may be used as for the displacement unit, and both can generate either position or rate data. An exponential curve with a dead zone threshold is preferred for pulse rates to avoid starting pulse rate uncertainties, with the first pulse starting as soon as the threshold is exceeded.

6.1.8 Touch Input

Touch input devices come in two basic forms, either placed directly on the display surface or as a separate panel attached to the computer system. In its second form it is essentially a data tablet and differs mainly in that it acts as another display unit with some form of a touch-sensitive surface. In this implementation it is essentially the same as the *touchscreen* input device, and this discussion concentrates on the technologies used for touchscreens.

There are five different technologies used for touch input devices, which are capacitive or resistive overlays, piezoelectric, light-beam interruption, and surface acoustic wave. The system may be divided into the sensor unit, which senses the location of the painting element, and the controller, which interfaces with the sensor and communicates the location information to the system computer. Since the controller is an electronic device that does not use technology different from the computer, it is not covered here. The major differences among the different touch input devices are due to the choice of sensor technology, and the discussion concentrates on these technologies.

Capacitive Overlay Technology. Capacitive overlay technology is illustrated in Figure 6.17, where a transparent metallic coating is placed over the display screen and the finger or stylus capacitance is sensed to determine the touch location. The overlay may consist of a group of separate sections etched into the surface with each separate section connected to the controller, or a continuous surface connected at the four corners. The first form is termed *discrete capacitive*, and touch location is determined by having each section sequentially connected to an oscillator circuit, where the frequency of oscillations is affected by the pointing device. The oscillation frequency is measured and compared to a stored reference frequency. If the frequency difference is large enough, it is recognized as a touch at that location. It is a simple system but suffers from low resolution and slow response, so that it is only practical for menu selection.

The analog capacitive system uses the same metallic overlay, but the metallic surface is continuous rather than etched. The connections at the four ends are each connected to a separate oscillator, and the frequency of each is measured and stored. Then when the overlay is touched, the change in capacitance will have a different effect on the frequency of each oscillator. These are measured and the differences are used to determine the coordinates of the touch by means of an algorithm. This technique is capable of much higher resolution (250 × 250) than the digital approach and is preferred for graphics or other high-density displays.

Resistive Overlay Technology. Resistive overlay technology requires a more complex assembly consisting of two layers, as illustrated in Figure 6.18. The layers both contain transparent metallic surfaces and are separated by spacers,

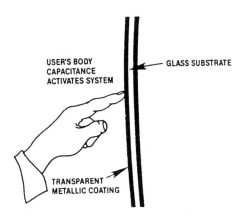

FIGURE 6.17 Capacitive overlay technology. After Carroll and Carstedt [5], by permission.

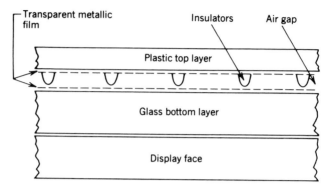

FIGURE 6.18   Resistive overlay technology. After Carroll and Carstedt [5], by permission.

so that an air gap exists between the layers in the absence of any pressure on the touch panel. The metallic layers face each other, and when the outer panel is pressed, the metallic layers make contact and form a conductive path at the point of contact. When a voltage is applied between the top of the outer layer and the bottom of the inner layer, the two layers act as a voltage divider, and the voltage at the point of contact may be measured in the X and Y directions by applying the voltage in first one and then the other direction. The measured voltages are then transmitted to the controller, where they are converted into coordinates which are then sent to the computer.

The panel may be discrete, in which the conductive coating on the top layer is etched in one direction and that on the bottom layer in the other direction, or analog, where the conductive coatings in both layers are continuous. In the discrete case, the panel then acts as an $X–Y$ matrix, and the resolution is determined by the number of etched lines. The analog configuration requires the addition of linearization networks on each edge of the panel as shown in Figure 6.19, so that a large-area resister is created with a voltage drop in one direction. Other linearization techniques are also possible, but only the four-element system shown in Figure 6.19 is described here. In this arrangement, one of the layers acts as the large-area resistor and the other as a voltage probe where either can function in either role. For the Y-coordinate value the top layer is the voltage probe, and the voltage is applied by the controller to the bottom layer. Similarly, the X coordinate is found by connecting the voltage to the top layer and making the bottom layer into the voltage probe. In either type of system, the resolution can be very high, but the transmissivity is reduced to under 80%.

Piezoelectric Technology.   The piezoelectric technology uses pressure-sensitive transducers as the means for determining the location of the touch, as shown in Figure 6.20. The sensor is a glass plate with transducers connected to the four corners. Pressure on the plate causes readings to occur at each of the transducers, which depend on the location of the pressure. Thus the controller

Linearization networks

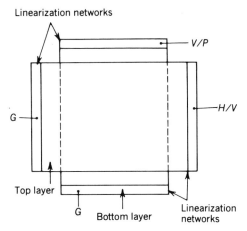

FIGURE 6.19 Four-wire analog resistive. After Carroll and Carstedt [5], by permission.

can measure the readings and obtain the coordinates by means of a proper algorithm. This technique allows a high-transmissivity plate to be used that can be curved to follow the CRT faceplate curvature, but it allows only a limited number of touch points to be used.

Light-Beam Interruption. This is a fairly straightforward technology that requires a matrix of light sources and detectors facing each other in the X and Y directions. When the beams from the X and Y light sources are interrupted, this is sensed by the facing light detectors, and the signals are sent to the controller. The light beams are turned on sequentially by pulsing the LEDs and thus create a full matrix of light beams without requiring each of them to be on continuously. This system does not reduce the screen transmissivity, as there is no obstruction of the screen output, but it is limited in resolution

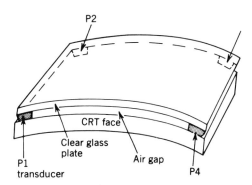

FIGURE 6.20 Piezoelectric technology. After Carroll and Carstedt [5], by permission.

to the number of LED detector pairs that can be placed on the periphery of the screen.

Another approach to light interruption is to use a rotating beam of light, which has the advantage that only one light source–detector pair is required. This technology, depicted in Figure 6.21, consists of a LED and a light detector plate inside a rotating drum which has a slit that allows light to be transmitted outside the drum. The light is swept across the surface and strikes the retro-reflectors, which send it back directly to the detector. The beam scan is sampled 256 times on each scan, and Figure 6.21 shows how two angles of interruption are created, angle B by direct interruption and angle C by mirror reflection interruption. The result is that the location of the interruption can be calculated by comparing the two angles. Again, there is no obstruction of the screen, but a moving element must be added and parallax errors may occur.

Pen-Based Computing. This is an application of touch input devices that is growing at a rapid rate. The input device comes in several forms, each of which can recognize hand printing, or act as an input switch, with the special operating system and software recognizing this type of input. The pen-based input device comes in several forms, of which *Touchpen* is one type that can function both as a digitizer with a touch tablet, and as the touch input device with a touch input pen-based computer system. A second one is that developed

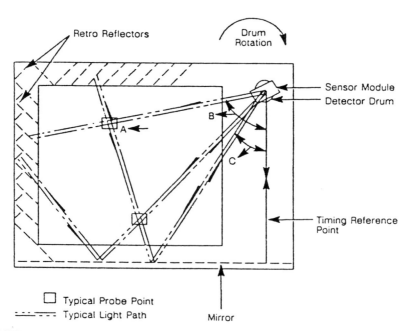

FIGURE 6.21   Rotating infrared beam technology. After Carroll and Carstedt [5], by permission.

by Wacom Inc. primarily for the GO Systems computer, but used by other pen-based systems as well. Finally, a third unit is that made by Sciptel Corp. and used by Wang Laboratories in its system.

TouchPen was developed by Microtouch Systems, Inc., initially for use in GridPad, made by the Grid Systems Corp. It is essentially a high-resolution digitizer consisting of an all-glass tablet that can be used with a number of stylus input operating systems to digitize handwriting. It is basically a touch input device using resistive techniques to digitize the handwriting appearing on the display surface of pen-based computer systems. The glass tablet is placed on the display surface, and the system pen is used to transmit the digitized data to the computer. As noted previously, the tablet may also be used as a standard touch input device.

The second form of pen-based input device is one that uses electromagnetic technology and consists of a grid of wires that transmit radio waves, which are picked up by a tuned circuit in the stylus. This circuit resonates at its own frequency and transmits that signal back to the wires at the grid location it is touching. The pen also transmits its signal to the computer, which turns off the grid transmission and locates the position of the pen by determining which of the grid wires pick up the pen signal. The pen does not actually need to touch the display surface and does not require any power, which is an advantage somewhat counteracted by the higher cost.

Finally, the Scriptel unit is similar to that made by Microtouch, but differs in that it uses electrostatic technology and is also similar to the capacitive touch panel.

Surface Acoustic Wave (SAW) Technology.   This technology is more recent than others and has not yet received wide acceptance. It is based on the transmission of surface acoustic waves generated by transducers mounted on the glass overlay through the glass. These waves are detected by receivers also mounted on the glass, and the time of arrival of the waves at the receivers is known because the wave velocity is known. The placing of a finger on the glass weakens the signal and the location of the finger can be determined by the difference in its effect on the SAW.

There are two types of SAW systems in use, which are those using reflective techniques and those using attenuation as the source of position information. The reflective systems are similar to sonar, and the time from the source to the pointing finger and then from the finger to the receiver is measured to arrive at finger location. The attentuation technology is illustrated in Figure 6.22 and consists of two transducers, two receivers, and four reflector strips, all mounted on a glass substrate. One transducer–receiver pair is used for X and the other for Y location. Figure 6.22 shows the X-axis pair, and the transducer transmits a burst of acoustic energy in a horizontal wave. The wave is partially reflected by the top reflector strips and travels down to the bottom strip, where the reflectors are at an angle that it is reflected to the lower left corner receiver. The wave now has a long rectangular shape, and

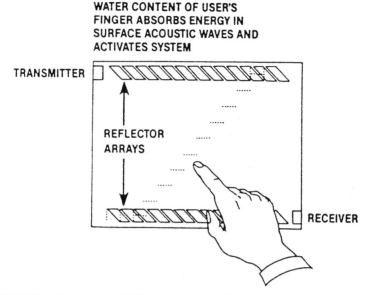

FIGURE 6.22   Attenuation SAW technology. After Carroll and Carstedt [5], by permission.

each point in time corresponds to a specific vertical path across the substrate. The Y axis is scanned in the same fashion after the X wave dies out. Then, when the finger touches the substrate, its water content absorbs some of the energy in the wave, and the wave is attenuated. The dip in the wave amplitude corresponds to the amount of absorbed energy, and the time of the lowest point can be determined, allowing the location of the finger to be calculated. Finally, in addition to the X and Y coordinates, a Z coordinate can be determined, depending on how hard the user presses. This depends on surface contact, which affects the amount of attentuation. The advantages of this system are high resolution and speed of transmission, and the availability of a Z-axis component. Its main disadvantage is the variation in moisture content in fingers and sensitivity to local moisture on the substrate. However, it is being used in developmental units and should be considered as another input device technology.

6.1.9   Scanners

Scanners are a means of inputting text and/or images directly into the computer system, thus avoiding the need for retyping and redrawing information contained in other sources. It is a relatively convenient way to avoid repetition if the data to be entered already exist in readable form. This is done by special image recognition software that accompanies the scanning hardware and can transfer an entire image containing both text and illustrations, but without the capability to modify the image. However, the addition of *optical character recognition* (OCR) software allows the entered text to be modified as if it were entered by typewriter. This can greatly simplify entering and editing text from some preexistent source and has resulted in a proliferation of devices that can perform this function.

These devices come in two main forms, *hand-held* and *page scanners*, with or without OCR software, in addition to the standard image recognition software. A typical hand-held scanner shown in Figure 6.23 consists of a light source, a light-sensitive device such as a charge-coupled device (CCD) array, and the electronics to actuate the elements of the array sequentially under software control. The scanner window is placed over the page and is moved down or across the page so that the window covers as much of the page as falls within the capability of the software. The light source is reflected from the page to the CCD and the charge in the CCD is modified by the reflectivity of the printed material. (See Section 2.6.8 for further information on the operation of CCDs.)

The window area ranges from 4 to 5 in. in width by 0.5 in. in height, and may be moved through 14 to 20 in., so that a fairly large area may be covered in a single manual scan. Images wider than the maximum window may be scanned in two passes, and the OCR software can stitch the two scans together into a single image, although this procedure requires considerable care in scanning so that the scans line up properly. Therefore, when images wider than the window of the hand-held scanner are to be scanned, it is advisable

FIGURE 6.23   Hand-held scanner. Courtesy of Logitech.

(a)

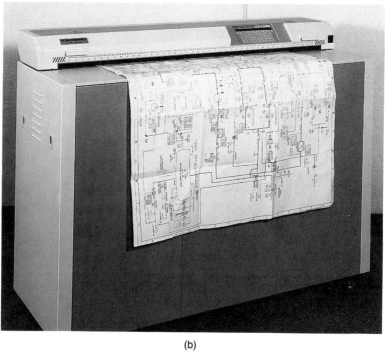

(b)

FIGURE 6.24 Page scanners. (*a*) Courtesy of Agfa; (*b*) courtesy of Scan-Graphics.

to use a *flatbed scanner* of the type shown in Figure 6.24, which can handle a full 8.5-in. by 11-in. page, or some of the larger scanners that can accept large drawings and input them into the computer system. Resolutions of 400 dpi and higher are available with up to 250 levels of gray and 24 bits of color resolution available. Thus scanners offer a wide variety of choice and performance capabilities and are powerful input devices when prepared data in visual form are to be entered into the computer system.

6.1.10 Voice Input

Voice input is an intriguing approach to data input, with particular attractiveness to upper-level managers who want a simple and direct means for inputting data and commands. For many years this technology tended to promise more than it could achieve, but recent developments have brought it to the point where it can be considered as a feasible input means. This has been due primarily to new developments in software that have made it possible to minimize the amount of training required and increased the success rate to close to 100%.

One basic approach to speech recognition is represented by the block diagram shown in Figure 6.25. This is a system that is built around a special chip developed by Texas Instruments. This system uses templates and special algorithms for recognizing the input speech patterns. The system is speaker dependent, with the capability of storing up to 32 word templates and user-defined phrases. The output portion may be superfluous when the system is used only for inputting data and commands, but can be a useful adjunct to the visual response. Other chips are available from other manufacturers, and other techniques, such as speaker independent and phoneme recognition systems, are also available. Vocabularies range from 50 to 5000 active words, and both isolated and connected words can be recognized, although the larger numbers tend to be associated with isolated word systems. In general, it seems

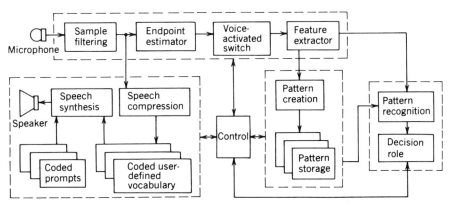

FIGURE 6.25 Block diagram of speech recognition and synthesis chip. After Leonard [6], by permission.

TABLE 6.3   Input Device Functional Evaluation[a]

Input Device	Function			
	Control	Data/Text	Data/Graphics	Total
Keyboard	E	E	P	9
Light pen	G	G	E	10
Tablet	E	G	E	11
Mouse	E	G	E	11
Trackball	E	G	E	11
Joystick	F	F	G	5
Touchscreen	G	F	G	8
Scanner	F	E	G	9
Voice	G	F	P	6
Total	29	23	28	80

[a]E, excellent = 4; G, good = 3; F, fair = 3; P, poor = 2.

feasible that a combination of speech input and pen-based computing may find a viable market.

6.1.11   Summary

The multiplicity of input devices that are available make it difficult to determine which is most suitable for any specific set of requirements. However, the limited functional comparison of the input devices covered in this section shown in Table 6.3 may be of some use and, in any event, is a starting point in this evaluation. It should be noted that what appears best at one time may become unpopular or obsolete at a later time, as occurred for light pens and trackballs, both of which have come back into favor.

In addition to the generalized evaluation shown in Table 6.3, it is also of interest to examine representative performance parameters. These are shown in Table 6.4 and, while representative, do not necessarily cover the range of performance parameters offered. More data may be obtained from the vendors of these devices.

6.1.12   Advantages and Disadvantages

Input devices make up one of the functional groups of the display systems, and their technical characteristics are covered in some detail in Section 6.1, with performance information provided in Section 6.1.10, by means of a number of tables containing characteristic parameter values for each type, as available. The following material expands somewhat on that information by placing these devices in the context of a full-graphics display system, and evaluating the functions that the various types of input devices perform in that type of system in terms of their advantages and disadvantages.

TABLE 6.4   Input Device Parameters

Type	Parameter	Value
Light pen	Response time (ns)	150–500
	Spectral response (A)	4200–9500
	Luminous sensitivity (nits)	0.03–0.7
	Field of view (in.)	0.02–0.1
	Ambient rejection (nits)	350
Data tablet (digitizers)	Resolution (lines/in.)	100–2000
	Accuracy (in.)	0.0005–0.02
	Active area (in.)	12 × 12 to 60 × 120
	Active height (in.)	0.02–2.5
	Digitizing rate (pps)	100–350
	Transducers	Stylus, puck, cursor
Mouse	Resolution (dpi)	10–1000
	Speed (in./s)	1–20
	Accuracy (dpi)	25–1000
Trackball	Resolution (cpi)	100–1000
	Speed (bps)	1200–9600
	Accuracy (dpi)	100–1000
	Ball diameter (in.)	1.5–2.5
Joystick	Travel (°)	25–30
	Accuracy (%)	5–10
	Repeatability (%)	1
Touchscreen	Resolution	256 × 256 to 4096 × 4096
	Transmissivity (%)	60–100
	Viewing area (in.)	3 × 4.5 to 15 × 20
	Speed (touch points/second)	80–200
Scanner	Resolution (dpi)	75–1600
	Scan rate (in./s)	0.5–2.0
	Scanning width (in.)	4.1–36
	Gray shades	32–256
	Scan time (s/page)	1–30
Voice	Active vocabulary (words)	13–5000

One specific relationship between the input devices and the operating display system is illustrated in Figure 1.40 and it is of some interest to compare the advantages and disadvantages of each type at this point, as listed in Table 6.5.

This is an imposing list and may be used to aid in choosing the best input devices for the specific applications to be considered.

6.2   HARD-COPY OUTPUT DEVICES

6.2.1   Introduction

In addition to the CRT displays, there are the various forms of hard-copy units that provide another form of output display that is usually part of a

TABLE 6.5   Input Devices: Advantages and Disadvantages

Device	Advantages	Disadvantages
Keyboard	Simple operation	Requires many keys
	Well known	Requires training
	Standard interface	No graphics
Light pen	Eye–hand coordination	Arm fatigue
	Low-cost models	Limited resolution
	No desk space required	May block display
Graphic tablet	Natural hand movements	Eye–hand conflict
	Screen not blocked	Requires desk space
	No parallax	Breakable stylus
	Good for graphics	Poor for A/N entry
Mouse	Small space needed	Some space needed
	Low cost	Slow transmission
	Screen viewing	Low resolution
	Any surface may be used	Grid for optical
	Optical noiseless	Mechanical noise
Trackball	High resolution	Poor for A/N input
	Fixed desk space	Slow transmission
	Screen viewing	Mechanical noise
	Tactile feedback	Three dimensions difficult
Joystick	Fixed desk space	Low accuracy
	Low fatigue	Low resolution
	Low cost	No A/N input
Touch screen	Eye–hand coordination	Arm fatigue
	Minimal training	May block display
	Minimum input errors	Varied resolution
	User acceptance	Parallax
	No special commands	Slow data entry
Scanner	Full A/N page input	Hand scanner width
	Color scan input	High cost for color
	High resolution	Slow input
	OCR software	Compatibility
Voice	Ease of use	Limited words
	Minimal training	Machine training
	No special devices	Graphics difficult

CRT system. These output displays are also part of most flat-panel display systems and could be covered in association with them. However, since they were first associated with CRT systems and continue to be an integral part of these systems, they are discussed here with the implicit assumption that the material presented here is equally applicable to flat-panel display systems.

Although a single term is used to define all hard-copy systems, they exist in a number of forms that are quite different from each other. However, there is one characteristic that ties all of them together: that they present the same information in static form that is shown in dynamic form on the CRT display. Thus the term *output* is used to define both types, but the term *hard copy* is added to differentiate these types from the CRT displays. In general, they are designated as plotters, printers, and printer/plotters, with camera outputs or slides as another category of hard-copy outputs. Table 6.6 contains a list of the major types, grouped by categories, technologies, and whether the mode of operation is impact or nonimpact. It should be noted that the film-based category includes equipment that produces hard-copy outputs that require separate viewing devices, whereas all of the others produce images on paper that can be viewed directly.

The use of impact and nonimpact to describe the modes of operation is not, strictly speaking, accurate, although it is commonly accepted as one means to differentiate the types. For example, ink jet and thermal among the technologies are classified as nonimpact, but in actual fact, the ink impacts on the paper for the ink jet, and the ribbon or wax contact the paper for the thermal types. It would be more accurate to use noiseless versus noisy to differentiate the units, but we will adhere to the standard modes. Several of the devices appear in both the printer and printer/plotter categories. This is because they are offered both in forms that stress the printer function and as units that are capable of being used only as printers or for both the printing and plotting functions. Basically, there are only two types that are limited to printing only, and these are the units that use the ball or daisy wheel printheads, which are also found on typewriters. All the other printer types are also available as printer/plotters, with those designated as printers alone intended for high-speed multiple-page printers.

TABLE 6.6   Hard-Copy Output Devices

Category	Mode	Technology
Plotter	Impact	Pen
	Nonimpact	Electrostatic
	Impact	Flatbed
	Impact	Drum
Printer	Impact	Ball
	Impact	Daisy wheel
	Nonimpact	Ink jet
	Nonimpact	Laser
	Nonimpact	Thermal
	Impact	Wire matrix
Printer/plotter	Nonimpact	Ink jet
	Nonimpact	Laser
	Nonimpact	Thermal
Printer/plotter	Impact	Wire matrix
Film-based	Nonimpact	Microfilm
	Nonimpact	Overheads
	Nonimpact	Slides

6.2.2   Technologies

Pen Plotters. Pen plotters are best defined by the means used to convert the data input into a visual image on some form of hard-copy media. The word pen describes the source of the visual image, and either solid or fluid material may be used. In addition, there may be one or more pens, and the media may be placed on a flat surface or on a rotating drum. Figure 6.26 shows examples of flat surface types, commonly termed a *flatbed*, whereas Figure 6.27 illustrates the rotating surface or drum type. These two operate in significantly different ways and need to be described separately.

Beginning with the flatbed type, it consists of a surface where the medium, usually paper, is placed, with from one to eight pens located at the bottom of the unit. The pens produce different colors, as determined by the color of the inks with which they are filled, or the pencils that are inserted, and are selected by the writing in accordance with commands from the data source. The pen or pencil is then made to contact the paper and moved across the paper in both the vertical and horizontal directions, thus writing an image on the paper in from one to eight colors or combinations thereof. Figure 6.28*a* illustrates one type of drawing that is produced by these means, and it is clearly a vector drawing, as differentiated from a raster or dot matrix drawing. A set of parameter values is given in Table 6.7.

Drum plotters come in a variety of sizes and shapes, with the ones shown in Figure 6.27 representative of the more popular types and drawing examples shown in Figures 6.28*b* and *c*. Drum plotters differ from flatbed plotters in that the pens move in only one direction, and the paper is moved by one of several techniques to provide the orthogonal direction. The devices employed are termed *rollerbed*, *grit wheel*, and *drumfeed*, and most drum plotters use a combination of grit wheel and pinch roller, as shown in Figure 6.29. This friction-feed approach was introduced by Hewlett Packard in 1981 and replaced the traction-fed technique for moving paper, with teeth on sprockets placed at opposite ends of the drum driving holes perforated along the end of the paper. The grit wheel consists of a drum coated with tiny particles of some material, such as aluminum oxide, and a rubber pinch roller that presses the paper against the drum. The grit surface is embossed on the media surface at the first pass, which ensures good registration on all future passes. The much lower cost of the grit wheel has led to its wide acceptance, with both cut sheet and roller versions available. A set of parameters is given in Table 6.7.

Electrostatic Plotters. Electrostatic plotters have long been the only nonimpact type of plotter that could match the pen plotters in quality and versatility while exceeding them in speed. Again, "nonimpact" is a matter of terminology, as the medium is impacted by electrical charges and toner in order to product the image, and "silent" is more accurate as a cognomen that "nonimpact." The technology is based on using a printhead consisting of a matrix of pins under which the medium passes, as shown in Figure 6.30. The

DPX-4600
ANSI-E/ISO-AO SIZE

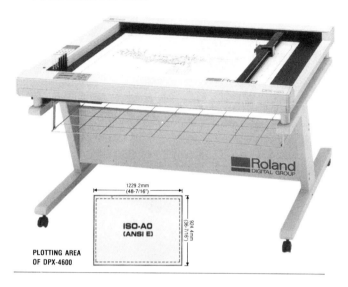

PLOTTING AREA
OF DPX-4600

DPX-3500
ANSI-D/ISO-A1 SIZE

PLOTTING AREA
OF DPX-3500

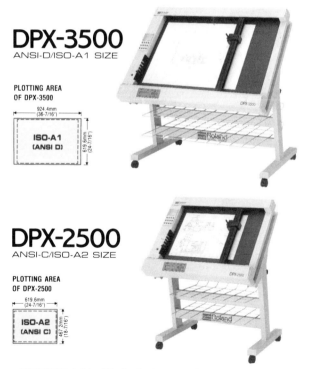

DPX-2500
ANSI-C/ISO-A2 SIZE

PLOTTING AREA
OF DPX-2500

FIGURE 6.26   Flatbed plotters. Courtesy of Roland.

MODEL	OVERVIEW

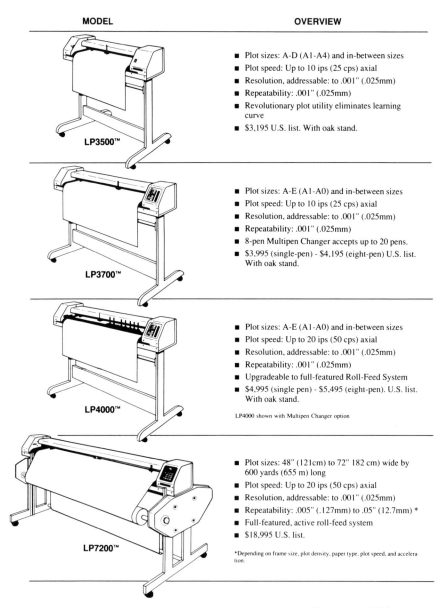

LP3500™

- Plot sizes: A-D (A1-A4) and in-between sizes
- Plot speed: Up to 10 ips (25 cps) axial
- Resolution, addressable: to .001" (.025mm)
- Repeatability: .001" (.025mm)
- Revolutionary plot utility eliminates learning curve
- $3,195 U.S. list. With oak stand.

LP3700™

- Plot sizes: A-E (A1-A0) and in-between sizes
- Plot speed: Up to 10 ips (25 cps) axial
- Resolution, addressable: to .001" (.025mm)
- Repeatability: .001" (.025mm)
- 8-pen Multipen Changer accepts up to 20 pens.
- $3,995 (single-pen) - $4,195 (eight-pen) U.S. list. With oak stand.

LP4000™

- Plot sizes: A-E (A1-A0) and in-between sizes
- Plot speed: Up to 20 ips (50 cps) axial
- Resolution, addressable: to .001" (.025mm)
- Repeatability: .001" (.025mm)
- Upgradeable to full-featured Roll-Feed System
- $4,995 (single pen) - $5,495 (eight-pen). U.S. list. With oak stand.

LP4000 shown with Multipen Changer option

LP7200™

- Plot sizes: 48" (121cm) to 72" 182 cm) wide by 600 yards (655 m) long
- Plot speed: Up to 20 ips (50 cps) axial
- Resolution, addressable: to .001" (.025mm)
- Repeatability: .005" (.127mm) to .05" (12.7mm) *
- Full-featured, active roll-feed system
- $18,995 U.S. list.

*Depending on frame size, plot density, paper type, plot speed, and acceleration.

FIGURE 6.27   Schematic drawings of drum plotters. Courtesy of Iolene.

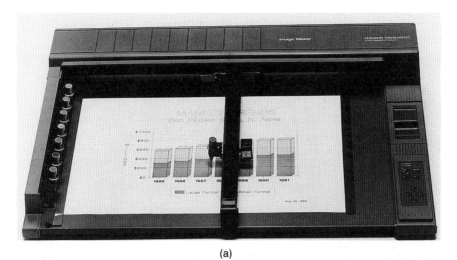

(a)

(b)

FIGURE 6.28 Drum drawing examples. Courtesy of CalComp.

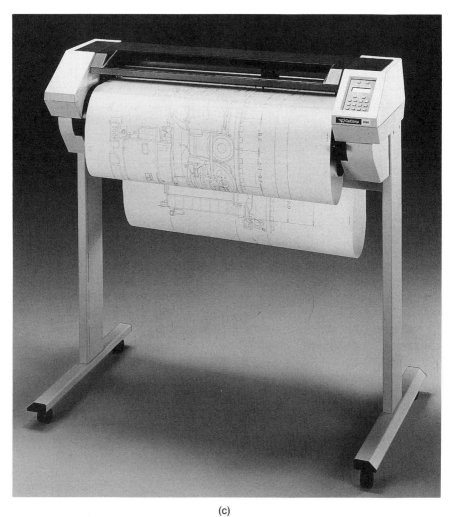

(c)

FIGURE 6.28   (Continued)

TABLE 6.7   Plotter Performance Parameters

Parameter	Value	
	Flatbed Plotter	Drum Plotter
Media size (in.)	8 × 11 to 36 × 48	11 × 17 to 36 × 48
Pens, colors (no.)	1–8, 1–109	1–14, 1–10
Speed (ips)	10–30	3–47
Resolution	0.0002–0.0035	0.00006–0.005
Accuracy (% of move)	0.1–0.3	0.01–0.5
Repeatability (in.)	0.001–0.005	0.0004–0.005

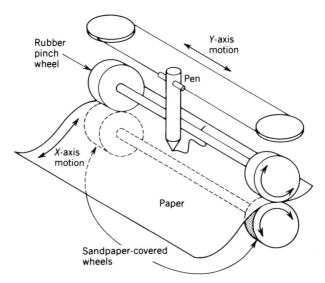

FIGURE 6.29 Drawing of grit wheel paper drive mechanism. After Patterson and Lynch [7], by permission.

resolution capability of the unit is determined by the pin spacing, and the pins charge the paper in accordance with the image to be produced. Finally, the paper is passed through a succession of liquid toner modules as shown in Figure 6.31, each containing a different color toner in order to produce multicolor images. In general, the number of toners is limited to four, consisting

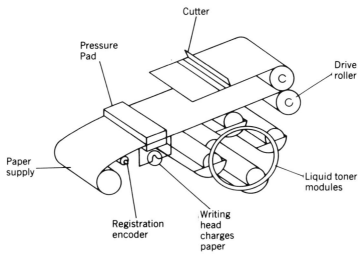

FIGURE 6.30 Schematic drawing of electrostatic plotter. After Meyer [8], by permission.

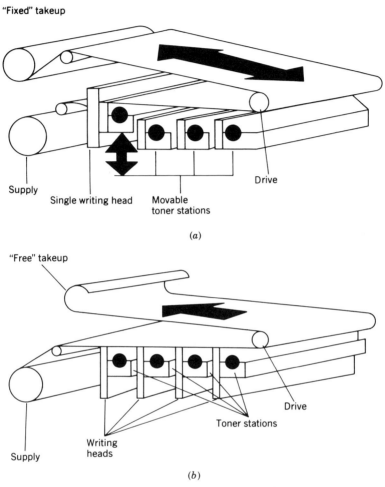

FIGURE 6.31   Electrostatic color plotter (*a*) with four toner stations and single head and (*b*) using four heads and toner baths for single-pass operation. After Wright [9], by permission.

of cyan, magenta, yellow, and black, and four passes by the plotting medium are required to produce the color image unless four heads are used.

There are also monochrome plotters, which was the only type available for a number of years that require only one pass and are much faster than the multicolor units as a result. The electrostatic plotters are much faster than the pen plotters and are usually equipped with roll-fed paper and automatic cutters. A color plotter is shown in Figure 6.32, and a representative group of performance specifications are given in Table 6.8 for both monochromatic and color versions.

Ink Jet Printer/Plotters.   Although the ink jet printer is listed in both the printer and printer/plotter sections of Table 6.6, its operational attributes and pa-

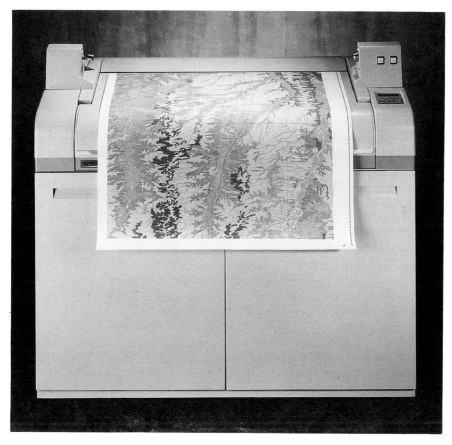

FIGURE 6.32   Electrostatic color plotter. Courtesy of Versatec.

rameter values are essentially the same whether it is used as a printer or a printer/plotter. Therefore, the more inclusive terminology is used for this discussion, as well as for the other jointly designated types, that is, the *laser*, *thermal*, and *wire matrix* hard-copy output devices. It is listed as a noncontact type, again because the actual printhead does not touch the medium, although

TABLE 6.8   Electrostatic Plotter Performance Specifications

Parameter	Value	
	Monochrome	Color
Media width (in.)	11–46	24–48
Resolution (dpi)	200, 406	200, 406
Accuracy (% of line)	0.1–0.2	0.1–0.2
Speed (ips)	0.3–2	0.3–2.5

the ink that produces the image must strike the surface, albeit in a noiseless fashion.

The basic principle used in ink jet printers is the emission and deflection of ink drops, so that they impinge on some type of printing medium and leave a permanent image, in much the same manner in which a CRT produces its dynamic image. There are two main techniques for producing the ink: the continuous and the drop-on-demand approaches. One form of the continuous-stream ink jet technique is illustrated in Figure 6.33. Here the ink is driven from the ink cylinder by pressure on a constant basis to the control valve. This valve ensures that the proper pressure is supplied to drive the ink to the printing medium and cause it to print on that medium.

Next, the ink enters the ink nozzle where the ceramic crystals convert the continuous stream into drops by piezoelectric action engendered by electrical pulses from the control circuitry. The pulses generate a wave action in the ink that causes it to break up into drops after leaving the nozzle opening. A jet is formed by hydrostatic pressure driving the ink through a small opening in the nozzle, where the ink velocity (V_j) is given by

$$V_j = \left(\frac{2P}{p}\right)^{1/2} \tag{6.9}$$

where P is the pressure and p is the fluid density, and the jet will normally break up into nonuniform dots. Uniform dot formation is accomplished by the pulses applied to the piezoelectric crystals, with the frequency given by

$$F = \frac{V_j}{4.5D_j} \tag{6.10}$$

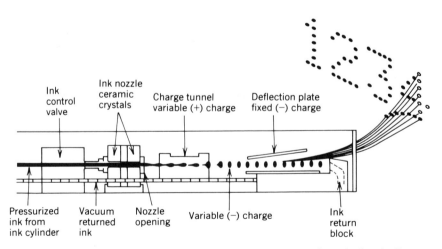

FIGURE 6.33 Schematic drawing of continuous-stream ink jet printhead. Courtesy of Videojet Systems.

where D_j is the jet diameter. Printers are designed to operate at frequencies close to where the instability growth is greatest, and a characteristic frequency is in the order of 60 kHz. This results in over 60-kHz drops and allows rapid printing speeds.

The actual printing occurs when the ink drops are charged and then deflected by electrostatic deflection plates as shown in Figure 6.34. The magnitude of the electrical charge on each drop is determined by the desired deflection of the dots as illustrated in Figure 6.34, where the voltage on the deflection plates changes as the paper moves under the printhead. The uncharged ink dots are returned to the reservoir and the deflection (D) is given by

$$D = \frac{qeL}{2mV^2L\ (Z - L)} \tag{6.11}$$

where q = charge on drop
$\quad\ \ e$ = deflection field
$\quad\ \ L$ = deflection length
$\quad\ m$ = mass of drop
$\quad\ V$ = drop velocity
$\quad\ Z$ = distance from deflection plates entrance to medium

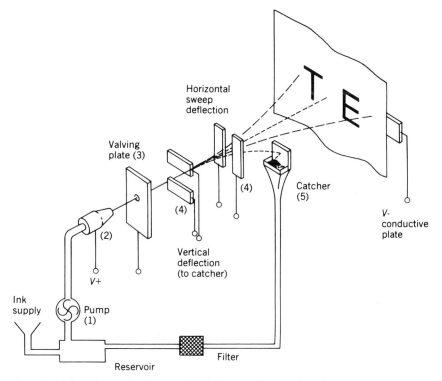

FIGURE 6.34   Schematic diagram of ink jet printhead using piezoelectric transducer to energize jet to eject drops of ink. After Poa [10], by permission.

The similarity to electrostatic deflection in the CRT is apparent except for the velocity and mass terms not found in equation 2.47.

Another version of this technology that claims to achieve better resolution is the one that uses the uncharged drops for printing and is termed Hertz, after C. Helmuth Hertz, who was its developer. The basic structure of this printhead is shown in Figure 6.35, and is similar to that shown in Figure 6.33, except that the charged drops are deflected down to the gutter and the uncharged drops hit the paper. An off pulse to the charge control will permit uncharged dots to pass through the deflection plates and strike the medium, which is contained on a drum as shown in the system diagram part of Figure 6.36. The combination of controlled drum and printhead motion allows color images to be written by filling a small area containing a 4×4 matrix of dots with the four colors of ink, using a technique called *dithering*. This technique uses the ability of the eye to average subtractive color dots that are closely spaced and thus perceive a color shade, allowing many different color shades to be perceived.

The other basic approach to ink jet printers in the one termed *drop-on-demand* (DOD), which, as the phrase indicates, differs from the continuous types in that ink drops are produced only when printing takes place. One way whereby the DOD units produce ink drops is by decreasing the volume of the ink chamber at a rapid-enough rate to start a pressure wave that forces a single drop through the nozzle. Modern units use a piezoelectric crystal to create the pressure wave and eject the drop through the nozzle in the fashion illustrated in Figure 6.37. Thus the units operate at ambient pressure, and the ink chamber is refilled by capillary action. The charging and deflection of the dots occurs in the same fashion as for the continuous types.

A second approach of producing dots for DOD units is the bubble or thermal technique introduced by Canon and Hewlett Packard, respectively. In this approach, heat energy is used to vaporize a small amount of ink and eject drops through very small orifices. It had been first termed *ThinkJet* and most recently *PaintJet* by HP, which has achieved a leading position in the market for ink jet printers. The principles of operation of the printhead for the latter are the same as for the former, and are illustrated in Figure 6.38. The printhead is a disposable unit which contains the ink supply and multiple nozzles with associated thin-film resistors for heating the ink. The ink is sent to the selected chambers and is vaporized by the heated resistor so that a bubble is formed and momentum is transferred to the ink above the bubble. This causes the ink to be ejected through the orifice onto the paper, and the image is created by programming the multiple orifices to produce the appropriate combinations. The printhead is moved by means of a servosystem to the proper locations that in combination with the printhead programming generate the desired output hard copy in monochromatic or color form.

Other approaches to the DOD ink jet printer are the SparkJet, which uses a high-voltage discharge to sputter particles off a solid ink rod or vaporize ionic liquid ink and expel a spray of droplets, and the solid ink jet that uses

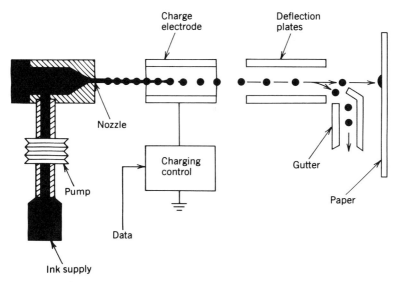

FIGURE 6.35   Operation of binary continuous jet Hertz printhead. After Thompson [11], by permission.

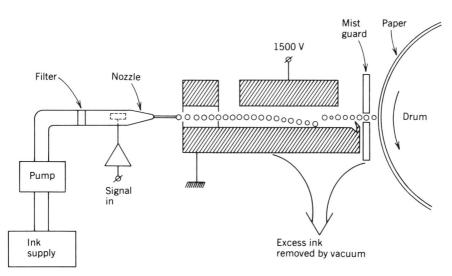

FIGURE 6.36   Schematic diagram of Hertz continuous jet printhead with media on drum. After Mills [12], by permission.

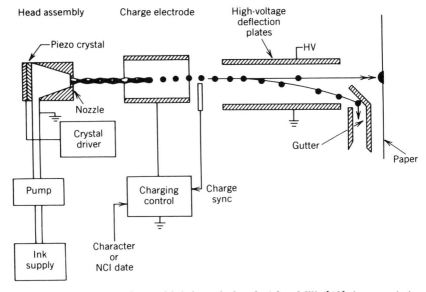

FIGURE 6.37 Drop-on-demand ink jet printhead. After Mills [12], by permission.

hot melt inks. Table 6.9 lists the performance parameter values for representative units that are available.

Although these printers are rated on a page per minute (ppm) speed in the monochromatic mode, they all have excellent graphics capabilities and color is available in a number of units. In addition, the thermal types seem to predominate, using some version of the Canon engine.

Laser Printer/Plotters (Electrophotography). Laser printer/plotters uses the electrophotographic printing process, first invented by Carlson and embodied

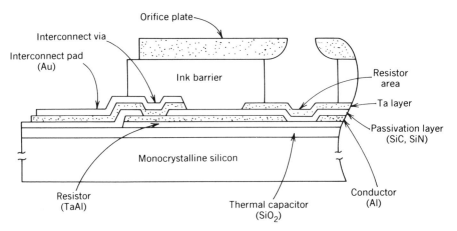

FIGURE 6.38 Cross-sectional view of the PaintJet printhead. After Askeland et al. [13], by permission.

TABLE 6.9   Ink Jet Printer/Plotter Parameters

Type	Parameter	Value
Thermal DOD	Resolution (dpi)	180–360
	Speed (cps)	167
	Number of jets	12–64
Continuous	Resolution (dpi)	1200×1800
	Speed (min)	A-size, 3.5
	Number of jets	64
Liquid ink DOD	Resolution (dpi)	300
	Speed (ppm)	$\frac{1}{2}$–4
	Number of jets	64
Solid ink DOD	Resolution (dpi)	300
	Speed (ppm)	$\frac{1}{2}$
	Number of jets	64

in the well-known Xerox copiers. They provide the closest approximation to the letter-quality printing that keeps the daisy wheel and ball printers still in use. Indeed, some of the most advanced laser printers match this quality with the important advantage that they also have extensive graphics capabilities. When to this advantage is added high speed and color, the only thing that keeps laser units from taking over completely is the relatively high cost.

The basic technology in part is similar to that used for the electrostatic plotter in that an electrostatic charge is used to deposit toner on the print media. The purpose of the laser is to discharge areas selectively on a photoconductive sheet usually laid on a drum. A representative sequence of events is illustrated in Figure 6.39, including the transfer of toner to paper by charging

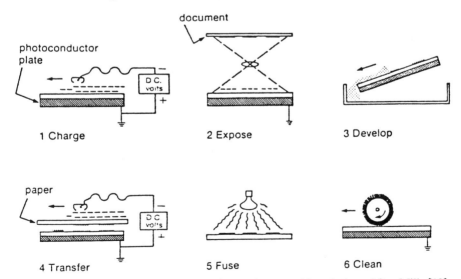

FIGURE 6.39   Sequence of steps for electrophotographic printing. After Mills [12], by permission.

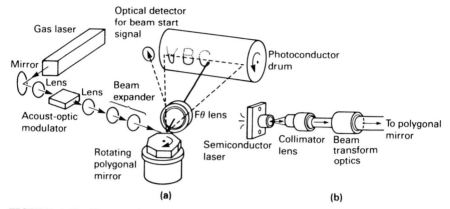

FIGURE 6.40   Two versions of a laser printhead: (*a*) a typical gas laser printhead; (*b*) a typical diode laser printhead. After Jaffe and Burland [14, p. 235], by permission.

the back of the paper with charges opposite to the toner charges, using a corona charge. Finally, the image is fused to the paper by melting the toner and the photoconductor is cleaned of excess toner so that the process can be repeated. The laser portion of the system is shown in Figure 6.40, including the scanning mirror that deflects the light across the drum. Diode lasers are popular for lower-priced units, but gas lasers provide the best quality at a proportionately higher price. Color is achieved by repeating the sequence of events once for each basic color, leading to three or four passes. There are color units available, and Table 6.10 lists the parameter values for both monochromatic and color types.

It should be noted that some electrophotographic printers use LEDs and LCD shutters as light sources, particularly for the lower-cost units. These are also called laser printers, and appear identical from the outside.

Thermal Printer/Plotters.   Thermal printing is a relatively old approach, dating back to the 1960s. The earliest method was direct printing on heat-sensitive paper, using an array of heater pins in a printhead as shown in Figure 6.41. The heat-sensitive paper contains a heat-sensitive coating of die-forming chemicals that are colorless at room temperature and take on a color when heated. This technique has seen something of a comeback for plotters due primarily to its low cost and relative simplicity. This plotter is a raster plotter and is somewhat similar to the electrostatic plotter in that respect. Its main

TABLE 6.10   Laser Printer/Plotter Parameters

Parameter	Value
Resolution (dpi)	240, 300, 400, 600
Text speed (ppm)	4–120; 5 (color)
Graphics speed (gppm)	0.5–5

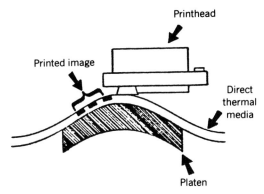

FIGURE 6.41 Schematic drawing illustrating direct thermal technology. After Chevallier [15], by permission.

drawbacks are that the quality may not be as good as for electrostatic and laser plotters, and the paper cost is higher. The performance parameters can be seen in Table 6.11, which contains the characteristic values for this type of thermal plotter.

However, the more popular technology is that which uses thermal transfer printing on plain paper. The basic technique is illustrated in Figure 6.42, where the ribbon has a low melting point, waxlike ink coated on a thin-paper or polyester-film carrier layer. Heat on the order of several joules is needed in the printhead to melt the solid ink sufficiently so that it will flow onto the paper. Alternatively, a resistive ribbon may be user, as shown in Figure 6.43, where the ribbon is heated by current flowing through it from the printhead to the aluminum film. Table 6.12 lists the parameter values for this type of printer.

A third type of thermal printer is the dye sublimation thermal transfer. This is derived from the thermal transfer technology, except that the dye is refined before being transferred to the media, thus allowing the dye to be diffused directly into the receiver layer of the media. The color density can be controlled by varying the heating characteristics, and the color reproduction is continuous tone, whereas the thermal transfer is bimodal.

Dot Matrix Printer. Last, but by no means least, come the many different types of dot matrix printers, most of which can also do graphics plotting. These are among the oldest types that include graphics printing capabilities

TABLE 6.11 Thermal Plotter Parameters

Parameter	Value
Speed (ips)	0.5–3
Resolution (dpi)	100–400
Output width (in.)	11, 24, 34, 46

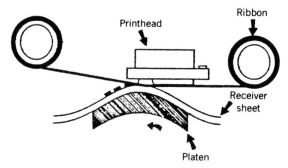

FIGURE 6.42   Thermal transfer technology. After Chevallier [15], by permission.

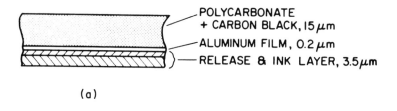

(a)

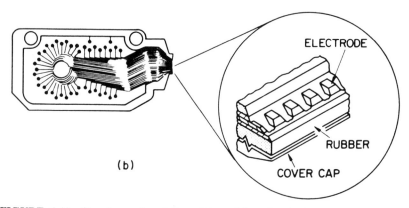

(b)

FIGURE 6.43   Structure of resistive ribbon (*a*) and printhead arrangement (*b*) of IBM Quietwriter thermal printer. After Dove and Sahni [16, p. 286], by permission.

TABLE 6.12   Thermal Transfer Printer/Plotter Parameters

Parameter	Value
Resolution (dpi)	200–300
Speed (ppm)	1–3
Number of passes for color	3, 4
Size (in.)	8.5 × 11 to 11 × 17

along with adequate quality, now approaching or equaling daisy wheel and ball printing for characters, and competing to some extent with some of the high-quality nonimpact printer/plotters. Of course, dot matrix printers are impact printers, with the basic mechanism consisting of a printhead made up of a matrix of wires, each of which can be individually activated so as to strike the ribbon. A representative wire matrix printhead is shown in Figure 6.44a,

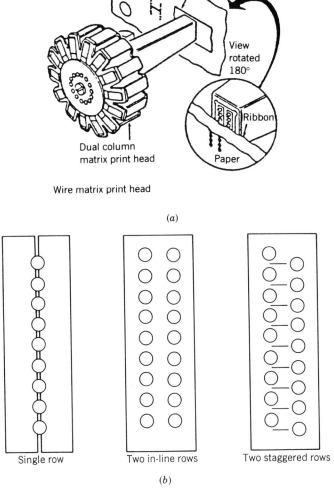

FIGURE 6.44   (a) Schematic drawing of wire matrix printhead. After Mills [12], by permission. (b) Types of print guides used for wire matrix printing. After Williams [17, p. 178], by permission.

where the individual wires are actuated by solenoids while the printhead is moved across the paper, guided by what are termed print wire jewels, as shown in Figure 6.44*b*. The number of wires are either 9 or 24, leading to the 9-pin and 24-pin wire matrix printer/plotters. The printer may operate in draft quality on a 7×9 matrix, through near letter quality, where the number of dots is doubled, to full letter quality, and where the 24-pin unit can operate with matrices as high as 35×48. In addition, graphics resolution can be as high as 360×360, and color is available on many units by using multicolored ribbons. The high printing speeds and the low cost of most of these units more than compensate for the noise and somewhat lower quality than found in the best nonimpact printers, so that dot matrix units remain a workable type for many applications. Table 6.13 presents a list of characteristic parameters for both the 9-pin and 24-pin units. The speeds shown are the highest attainable for the specific units, and apply to the draft mode. The other modes range from one-fourth to one-third of these speeds.

Film-Based Devices. Film-based hard-copy output devices encompass all those that generate the image on some type of film material and then transfer it to some permanent or semipermanent form, such as slides of prints. The basic process is fully nonimpact, except in the case of when the overheads are made by plotting or printing directly on the medium, in which case they fall into the category represented by the hard-copy device. Here we concentrate only on the means that use actual photographic materials and techniques.

The CRTs used for hard-copy output are basically of the same type as used for direct view, but some of them differ in a few significant details. First, although it is possible to photograph the screen of a standard CRT directly by placing an appropriately designed camera directly in front of the screen, those CRTs used for professional slide making have special fiber-optics faceplates so that the image generated at the phosphor may be coupled directly to the film without spreading and at high efficiency. The difference between the transmission from a conventional faceplate and a fiber-optical faceplate is illustrated in Figure 6.45, and the improvement to be obtained is quite apparent. If this type of CRT is then coupled to some type of film transport system and driven by appropriate deflection amplifiers, as shown in block diagram form in Figure 6.46, the output can be either slides or prints of the visual material.

TABLE 6.13 Dot Matrix Printer/Plotter Parameters

Parameter	Value	
	9-Pin	24-Pin
Speed (cps)	120–250	200–360
Resolution	60×240 to 240×240	180×180 to 360×360
Character cell	9×9 to 18×20	12×24 to 24×48

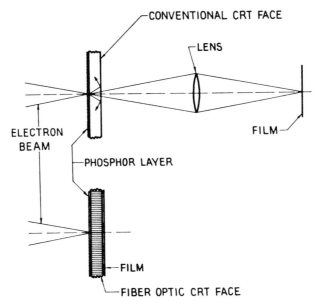

FIGURE 6.45 Comparison of lens and fiber-optic coupling. After Wurtz [18], by permission.

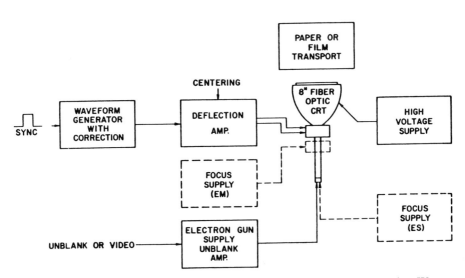

FIGURE 6.46 Simplified block diagram for CRT recorder or scanner. After Wurtz [18], by permission.

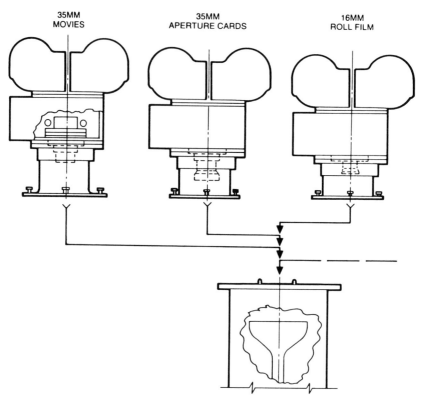

FIGURE 6.47 Interchangeable recorders with film transport and optics integrated into a single unit. After Gaw [19], by permission.

In addition to the special CRTs with fiber-optic faceplates that can record a full-screen image, there are special recording tubes that generate a single line at a time, and use fiber optics for visual and direct wires for electrostatic writing. However, these are used primarily for electronic typesetting and fall somewhat out of the scope of this volume. Therefore, they are only mentioned in passing, and we concentrate on the full-screen units. The CRT may be part of the recording unit and contain interchangeable optic units as well as universal film transports, as shown in Figure 6.47, in which case the same unit can produce roll film, microfilm, and slides.

A final requirement for a film-based system is the lensing system that focuses the CRT image on the film. This system consists of a combination of thin, finite-conjugate lenses, for which the basic parameters and design equations are shown in Figure 6.48. The application of these equations to the design of the optical portion of the film-based system is beyond the scope of this volume, but a representative approach may be found in Durbeck and Sherr [19, p. 103]. The performance characteristics of slide-making systems

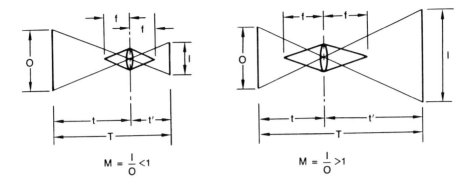

$$M = \frac{I}{O} < 1 \qquad\qquad M = \frac{I}{O} > 1$$

Back Conjugate $\quad t' = (1 + M) \times f$

Front Conjugate $\quad t = \dfrac{(1 + M) \times f}{M}$

Total Track $\qquad T = \quad t' + t$

Focal Length $\qquad f = \dfrac{M \times T}{(1 + M)^2}$

Magnification $\quad M = 1 - \dfrac{T}{2f} \pm \dfrac{1}{2} \sqrt{(\dfrac{T}{f} - 2)^2 - 4}$

Effective Aperture at a Given Magnification

$$f_e = f_\infty \times (1 + M)$$

Range of Magnification

$$\frac{1}{M_{designed}} - \frac{1}{M_{desired}} < \pm\, 0.025$$

FIGURE 6.48 Some useful equations for evaluating thin, finite-conjugate lenses. After Gaw [19], by permission.

are given in Table 6.14. These systems range from the simplest type that is placed directly on the CRT and uses instant film, to highly complex units that incorporate high-resolution monitors that can generate very high quality images that can be transformed into slides, overheads, or prints in full color. These complete the groups of hard-copy devices that can be used with either CRT or flat-panel systems.

TABLE 6.14 Slide Making Systems

Parameter	Value
Resolution (TV lines)	800–8000
Colors	RBG, 16–16.7 M
Camera backs, film (in.)	35 mm, $3\frac{1}{4} \times 4\frac{1}{4}$, 4×5, 8×10
Speed	30 s–5 min

REFERENCES

[1] Davis, M. R., and Ellis, T. V., "The Rand Tablet, a Man–Machine Graphical Communication Device," *AFIPS Conf. Proc*, 27, Part 1, 1966, 847–854.

[2] Davies, T. E., Mathews, H. G., and Smith, P. D., "Digitizers and Input Tablets," in S. Sherr, Ed., *Input Devices*, Academic, New York, 1988.

[3] Goy, C., "Mice," in S. Sherr, Ed., *Input Devices*, Academic, New York, 1988.

[4] Doran, D., "Trackballs and Joysticks," in S. Sherr, Ed., *Input Devices*, Academic, New York, 1988.

[5] Carroll, A. B., and Carstedt, J., "Touch Input Technology," *SID Sem. Lect. Notes*, 1987, 15.30–15.35.

[6] Leonard, M., "Speech Poised to Join Man–Machine Interface," *Elec, Design*, Sept. 26, 1991, 43–48.

[7] Patterson, M. L., and Lynch, G. L., "Development of a Large Drafting Plotter," *Hewlett-Packard J.*, Nov. 1981, 3.

[8] Meyer, A. M., "Color Output Technologies," *Microcad News*, Oct. 1990, 23.

[9] Wright, M., "Fast Plotters Produce Color and Monochrome," *EDN*, June 21, 1990, 94.

[10] Poa, H. C., "High-Voltage ICs for Higher-Quality Color Printer/Plotters," *ECN*, Apr. 1991, 13.

[11] Thompson, T., "Hertz Ink-Jet Technology," *Comput. Graphics World*, Jan. 1986; reprint Iris Graphics.

[12] Mills, R. N., "Color Hard Copy," *SID SEM. Lect. Notes*, 1989, 7.28–7.39.

[13] Askeland, R. A., et al., "The Second-Generation Thermal InkJet," *Hewlett-Packard J.*, Aug. 1988, 28.

[14] Jaffe, A. B., and Burland, D. M., "Electrophotographic Printing," in R. C. Durbeck and S. Sherr, Eds., *Output Hardcopy Devices*, Academic, New York, 1988.

[15] Chevallier, F., "Thermal Color," *Plan Print*, Sept. 1991, 13.

[16] Dove, D. B., and Sahni, O., "Thermal Printing," in R. C. Durbeck and S. Sherr, Eds., *Output Hardcopy Devices*, Academic, New York, 1988.

[17] Williams, R. A., "Wire Matrix Printing," in R. C. Durbeck and S. Sherr, Eds., *Output Hardcopy Devices*, Academic, New York, 1988.

[18] Wurtz, J., "CRTs for Hard Copy," in R. C. Durbeck and S. Sherr, Eds., *Output Hardcopy Devices*, Academic, New York, 1988.

[19] Gaw, J., "Camera Hardcopy," in R. C. Durbeck and S. Sherr, Eds., *Output Hardcopy Devices*, Academic, New York, 1988.

7

PERFORMANCE EVALUATION

7.1 INTRODUCTION

After a display system has been assembled according to the various criteria given in the previous chapters, it is necessary to subject it to a rigorous series of tests and measurements to determine whether it meets its objective performance requirements, and, most importantly, whether it will perform the functions for which it is intended in the operational situation. This leads to two types of tests, those made with instruments, and those made with humans in either a real or simulated operational condition. Of course, the instrument tests also need the human observer to read and interpret the results, and in some cases such as the shrinking raster resolution test, the human observer is an important part of the measurement system. However, the function of the observer is much different in the instrumented tests, even when acting as a direct intermediary, than in those tests where the response of the observer to the visual data is the only measure of performance. Therefore, we may clearly distinguish between the two categories, and they are discussed separately in this chapter, although there is also included material to relate the results of the instrument tests to what may be expected from the operational tests. Some of this material is also presented in Chapter 1, in the section on legibility, and is repeated here for convenience and from an expanded view of the significance of the relationship. Thus the present chapter is concerned with the ultimate purpose of the discussions of the technology, requirements, and applications of electronic display systems as covered in the previous chapters, to ensure that the visual presentation meets the requirements of the applications and that the best technological approach is selected for implementing the system. To this end, we begin with the basic photometric parameters, proceed to the specialized measurements of CRT characteristics and the unique features of the various types of matrix displays, and conclude with some psychometric techniques for determining the ultimate quality of the system performance.

There have been some indications of a trend to specify display-system performance only on the basis of the response of the human observer to the displayed data, and this is an attractive approach to anyone who writes the performance specification. Tests can be made of legibility, accuracy of identification, or specific work-oriented tasks, and the system can be accepted or rejected on the basis of these tests. Unfortunately, simulation of the total system is expensive, especially when the operational environment is considered, and these final acceptance tests offer no objective guide to the design of all the elements of the system so that some level of acceptable performance can be assumed prior to the selection of the system. Therefore, we must remain with the tried, if not necessarily true, measures of system performance described in Chapter 1 and use whatever data are available to relate these measurements to the performance that may be anticipated from the total system. This does not exclude the observer from the testing process, especially since certain measurements, as noted, must include an observer as a direct part of the measurement, and not merely as a recorder of the data value. However, our wish is to free as many measurements as possible from being influenced by the psychophysical characteristics of the observer. This is particularly difficult when the system performance is directly affected by those characteristics. Our goal is to come up with a reasonably objective, if not necessarily optimum, group of tests and measurements that may be made on the system at various points in its development in terms of a set of specifications based on parameters that can be tested by these methods.

7.2   PHOTOMETRY

Photometry is the measurement of the photometric parameters described in Chapter 1. Since these parameters may be encountered in any display system, photometric measurements are basic to the evaluation of almost all display system performance characteristics. A list of the relevant photometric parameters is given in Table 7.1 for convenience, and we discuss methods of measurement for each one.

Luminous intensity is expressed in candelas and may be measured by means of an instrument known as a *visual photometer*, which operates by matching the brightness from a known source to that from an unknown. This technique is possible because the human observer, although not capable of determining absolute values of brightness, can match two sources of the same spectral composition to a very high degree of accuracy. Note that we are using bright-

TABLE 7.1   Partial List of Photometric Parameters

Name	Symbol	Unit MKS
Luminous intensity	I	Lumen/ω (candela)
Luminance	B	Lumen/$\omega \times m^2$ (cd/m²)
Illuminance	E	Lumen/m² (lux)

ness in its correct sense, and not as an equivalent for luminance, and eliminate the physiological effects by using a source of the same color composition as the unknown. The matching is accomplished by moving the known source until its brightness matches that of the unknown and then calculating the illuminance of the unknown by means of the formula for illuminance

$$E = \frac{I_0 \cos \theta}{d^2} \tag{7.1}$$

with the parameters as defined by Figure 7.1. If θ is equal to zero, equation 7.1 reduces to

$$E \frac{I_0}{d^2} \tag{7.2}$$

which is the same as equation 1.2.

For a point source, equation 7.2 is accurate to better than 5% when d is more than five times the largest dimension (r) of the source. This may be readily established by using the geometry shown in Figure 7.2. If we assume

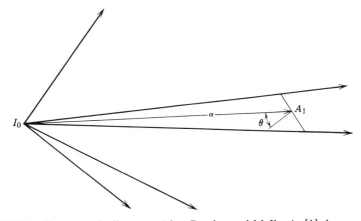

FIGURE 7.1   Photometric diagram. After Pender and McIlwain [1], by permission.

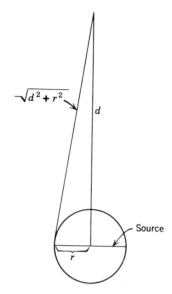

FIGURE 7.2   Photometric geometry. After
Sherr [2], by permission.

that

$$d = 10r \tag{7.3}$$

then

$$\frac{d}{(d^2 + r^2)^{1/2}} = \frac{10r}{(10^2 + r^2)^{1/2}}$$

$$= \frac{1}{1.049}$$

and hence the error in assuming a point source is less than 5%. If this amount
of error is unacceptable, or if the source is larger than this limit, equation
7.2 becomes

$$E_0 = \frac{I_0}{d^2 + r^2} \tag{7.4}$$

where r is the radius of the circular disk shown in Figure 7.2, and equation
7.4 may be applied to rectangular sources by using a disk that covers the
rectangular area. Equation 7.2 is obtained from Equation 7.4 by multiplying
the latter by $(d^2 + r^2)/d^2$, which is the correction made to obtain the true
luminous intensity at infinite distances from a measurement at a finite distance. The basic form of the configuration used in a visual photometer is that
shown in Figure 7.3 and is known as the *Lummer–Brodhun photometer*.

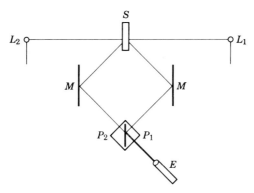

FIGURE 7.3 Lummer–Brodhum photometer. After Kingslake [3], by permission of Academic Press.

Referring to Figure 7.3, the illumination from the two sources of the two sides of the opaque screen (with white diffusers as the reflecting surfaces) is seen side by side as a result of the prism (P) and the mirror (M) arrangement. The known source is moved until the two brightnesses are matched, and the value of the unknown is read off from a calibrated dial linked to the moving element. Another common form of visual photometer of this type is the *Macbeth illuminometer*, where both sources are combined by means of a prism, so that the unknown is seen as a central circle surrounded by an outer circle representing the known. The known source is moved and the result read off from a calibrated dial.

In addition to the eye, there are various photosensitive devices that generate a voltage or current when irradiated with light, and these have been incorporated in instruments that measure the different photometric parameters and provide a calibrated scale so that the values may be read directly. A list of the most commonly used devices is given in Table 7.2, and it is clear that the entire visible spectrum is covered by one or more of these devices. The response characteristics of several materials found in light meters are

TABLE 7.2 Photosensitive Devices

Type	Relative Sensitivity	Spectral Characteristics (nm)	Response Time
Cadmium sulfide	Good	400–800	Milliseconds
Cadmium sulfide	Very good	500–900	Milliseconds
Lead sulfide	Good to excellent	500–3000	Milliseconds
Photodiode	Good	400–1100	100 ns to microseconds
Phototransistor	Fair	400–1100	Microseconds
Silicon voltaic	Poor	380–800	Milliseconds
Selenium voltaic	Poor	350–800	100 μs to 1 ms
Photomultiplier	Excellent	240–1100	10–100 ns

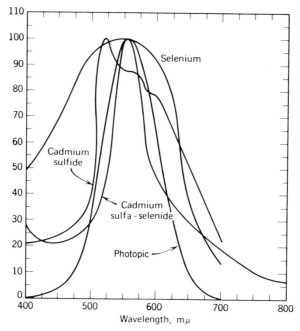

FIGURE 7.4 Response characteristics of photoelectric cells. After Sherr [2], by permission.

compared with the photopic curve in Figure 7.4, and the match is fairly good for all of them, although correction filters are usually necessary to calibrate the cell and ensure that the proper photometric values are read. The photosensitive material is generally used directly with a high-sensitivity, low-resistance meter, or with a bridge-type circuit, as shown in Figure 7.5. With r_3 constant and r_2 adjusted for balance in the meter, the current in r_3 and

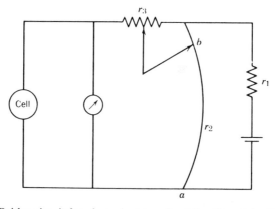

FIGURE 7.5 Bridge circuit for photoelectric cells. After Kingslake [3], by permission of Academic Press.

that from the photoelectric cell are equal and proportional to the voltage between the sliding contact and ground, which in turn is nearly proportional to the resistance between these two points. Thus the slider may be calibrated to read light output at accuracies of better than 0.5%, as compared to the 2% or 3% possible with direct reading current meters. However, the direct reading meters are adequate for many purposes and are very simple to use so that they are frequently the best choice for this measurement in spite of their rather low accuracy. A photograph of one such meter is shown in Figure 7.6, and it is used by pointing the probe (at a proper distance as defined by equation 7.2) at the source and by reading the photometric value directly on the meter. The meter may be calibrated in any of the various terms used to describe illuminance and luminance, although for luminance the area of the surface must be controlled since luminance is given in candelas per unit area. For a perfect diffuser or any surface that follows Lambert's law, that is,

$$I = I_0 \cos \theta \qquad (7.5)$$

FIGURE 7.6 Direct-reading paddle-type illuminance or luminance meter. Courtesy of Weston Corporation.

FIGURE 7.7   Construction of baffle for luminance meter. After Stimson [4, p. 173], by permission.

with the terms as shown in Figure 7.1, then

$$L = \frac{I_0}{A} \tag{7.6}$$

where L is the luminance. There are several sources of error due to the effect of the angular field since luminance is directional. These may be overcome by using a well-baffled tube of sufficient length to meet the criteria, with the sensor at the end. This permits the field to be well defined and eliminates errors due to stray light as well. The construction of one such meter is shown in Figure 7.7, and accuracies of better than 0.2% may be achieved by this means, as compared with the errors of 25% or more found with standard meters. The only problem may be with sensitivity, and this is overcome by employing a meter using a photomultiplier as the light-sensitive device. The photomultiplier is the vacuum-tube device described in Chapter 4 that achieves high sensitivity by means of a photosensitive cathode, followed by as many as 10 stages of secondary-emission multiplication using separate plates called *dynodes*. Figure 2.15 shows the response of several materials used in photomultipliers, with the S-4 response closest to the photopic curve and hence best for photometric measurements since the least amount of correction is required.

The photomultiplier circuit is more elaborate than that shown in Figure 7.5 since it is a multiplier vacuum tube, similar to the image orthicon described in Chapter 2. One such circuit is shown in Figure 4.27 for a unit with 10 dynodes and achieving the maximum possible sensitivity, limited only by noise or dark current due to thermionic emission. This sensitivity may be expressed by

$$S_n^2 = \frac{i_p}{2eB} \tag{7.7}$$

where S_n = signal to noise
    i_p = photocathode current (equation 4.21)
    e = electron charge
    B = bandwidth

and the minimum levels measured may be as slow as 1 nit.

One type of instrument that is frequently used in the measurement of luminance is the spot photometer shown in Figure 7.8. This is a photometer in which the area being measured is determined by a combination of lenses that control the size of the area and ensure that it is focused directly on the photosensor. These types of units are extremely useful in the measurement

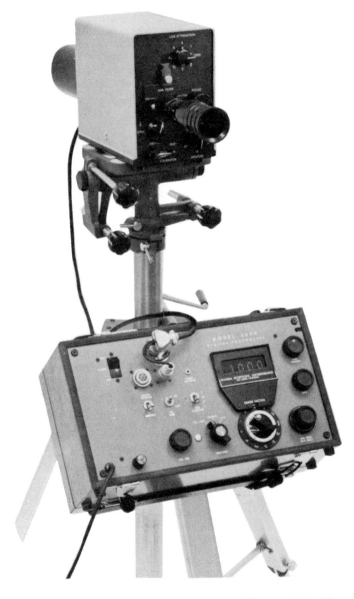

FIGURE 7.8   Digital telephotometer. Courtesy of Gamma Scientific.

of CRT spots and matrix elements, since the size of the aperture may be made smaller than that of the spot or element being measured. They may be directly calibrated by a standard light source of proper dimensions and usually contain their own standard for such calibration. They, as well as the other instruments discussed, may also contain various filters for adjusting the spectral response of the photosensor to match the photopic curve, and other filters to change the sensitivity of the instrument. Calibration sources also exist in several forms, and should be used to calibrate the photometer when it does not contain its own standard source. Accurate measurements of the photometric parameters are not always easy to make, and the only saving feature for display systems is that very accurate measurements are infrequently required since there is usually considerable margin in the performance of the equipment.

7.3 CATHODE-RAY-TUBE MEASUREMENTS

7.3.1 Luminance

Luminance is one of the most important parameters in determining the performance characteristics of a CRT display system, as should be evident from the many references to it in Chapters 2 and 4. Luminance may be measured with any of the photoelectric instruments described, provided the instrument is fitted with a probe of the type shown in Figure 7.7, or a proper lens systems, and is calibrated in luminance values. Modern instruments usually have both the international nit and the foot lambert on the scale. There are three luminance measurements that might be of interest, that is, spot, line, and raster luminance, with the procedure to be used somewhat different for each one. The spot luminance is easiest to measure because it only requires that the CRT beam be activated by means of a dc video signal of the proper value to produce maximum luminance, which may be done by merely turning up the luminance control, usually labeled *brightness*, and turning off all the sweep signals if a television monitor with internally generated sweeps is being used. For complete accuracy, the acceleration voltage and the beam-current density should be known, but for practical measurements they are probably limited by the monitor in which the CRT is placed, and only the luminance control is accessible. Spot luminance is best measured with a spot photometer of the type pictured in Figure 7.8, with an aperture somewhat larger than the size of the spot to be measured. The aperture is then focused on the spot after the meter is calibrated for that aperture, and the luminance reading is taken directly from the scale of the meter. The advantage of this method of measurement is that it makes it possible to determine what the peak spot luminance is, and the average luminance can be calculated once the duty factor is known from

$$L_{av} = L_p\tau \tag{7.8}$$

where L_{av} = average luminance
L_p = peak luminance
τ = duty factor

Therefore, this peak spot luminance measurement should give all the necessary information for determining the average luminance under any refresh and duty factor conditions. The major drawback to this method of establishing the operating luminance is that peak or highlight luminance is rarely given for the CRT, so the measurement must be made to obtain the information. A more common method of measurement uses a raster of a specified size and either a spot photometer with an aperture large enough to encircle the raster or a photometer with an attachment of the type shown in Figure 7.7, again with an aperture large enough to accommodate the raster. In this case, a setup of the kind shown in Figure 7.9 is necessary, so that the raster size may be adjusted to be somewhat larger than the photometer field of view. The raster size should be carefully measured, once it has been adjusted, and the area in square centimeters determined. The sweep generators should be capable of producing a raster of at least 100 lines, at a refresh rate of 60 Hz, and the generated raster should have linearity of better than 5% in each axis. Again, the accelerating potential and the beam current should be monitored or adjusted if possible to some selected value, with the luminance control at maximum. In this case the incident illumination on the face of the CRT also should be known, since it might contribute significant reflections and affect the reading. This is not as important for the spot measurement, because the spot area is so small and its luminance so large that the incident illumination has little effect on the reading. Once these adjustments and measurements are made, the raster luminance may be read directly from a calibrated photometer, and the result holds for any size raster in which the beam is traveling at the same speed as the test raster and the other conditions are the same as

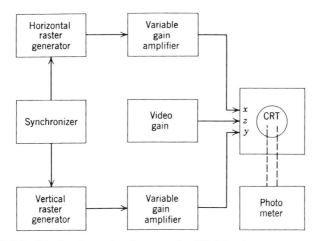

FIGURE 7.9   Block schematic of system for CRT luminance measurement.

the test conditions. In the event that the operating conditions are different from the test conditions, it is interesting to note the approximate proportionality

$$L \alpha I_b f_r V_a \tag{7.9}$$

where I_b = beam current
f_r = refresh rate
V_a = accelerating voltage

from which it may be possible to approximate the actual luminance under operating conditions that differ from the test conditions. This approximation is good over only limited ranges of voltage and current, and a more exact expression has been developed empirically for a moving spot, which is

$$L_m = Kft_w \left(\frac{I_b}{25}\right)^\alpha \left(\frac{V_a}{14}\right)^\beta \tag{7.10}$$

where β is 1.3 to 2, t_w is the dwell time, and some values for α and K are given in Table 7.3. With equations 7.9 and 7.10 it is possible to arrive at a probable value for luminance for any condition, once the value for one specific condition is known.

The luminance of a single line may be important in nonraster systems where only a small number of single lines or vectors are to be displayed. This measurement may be made by generating one scan line and moving the photometer across the scan line so that the maximum luminance may be measured. Alternatively, the luminance may be measured at specified locations with a fixed photometer position. The actual line luminance may then be calculated as the average of the various readings with fair accuracy.

TABLE 7.3   **Phosphor Constants**

Phosphor	K	α
P-1	0.069	0.945
P-2	0.162	0.780
P-4	0.094	0.888
P-7	0.094	0.888
P-11	0.022	0.883
P-19	0.054	0.856
P-20	0.164	0.915
P-28	0.094	0.888
P-31	0.215	0.917

Source: After Sherr [2], by permission.

7.3.2   Contrast Ratio

The measurement of contrast ratio is subject to the same conditions as the measurement of luminance, since the value of luminance obtained in the previously described measurement is one term in the numerator of equation 1.7. The other term is the background luminance, which is also the term in the denominator. There are several ways to obtain the value of the background luminance, of which one is illustrated in Figure 7.10. In this case the first measurement is of the point on the screen that is under observation without any display, and the second is made with the visual data at the expected level of luminance, and with all other conditions the same as for the first measurement. The contrast ratio is then the ratio of the second: first measurement value for data luminance greater than the background luminance, and the inverse for the opposite situation. Another method is to maintain the data luminance for both measurements and move the photometer until its measurement point is outside that data luminance area. This method is somewhat more meaningful than the other since it simulates the actual viewing conditions and includes stray light that may emanate from the CRT screen because of internal reflections. The internal reflections are due to light from the CRT phosphor striking the faceplate at such an angle that it is partially or totally reflected back to the phosphor, after which it will continue to be reflected back and forth until it finally escapes to the outside at some distance from the original source of the light, and at some luminance level depending on the losses from the multiple reflections. This stray light is usually kept to a very low level by matching the index of refraction of the glass in the faceplate

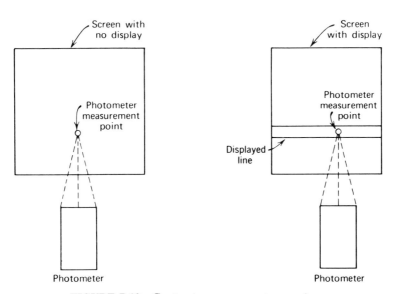

FIGURE 7.10   Contrast-measurement procedure.

to that of the safety plate and the air, but enough may be reflected so that it will contribute significant amounts at small contrast ratios. In any event, it is an effect to be remembered and considered when careful contrast ratio measurements are made. Apart from this difference, the two methods of measurement are equally acceptable. Of course, the same restrictions apply in these measurements of the two luminances as have been described previously, and if for some reason the other equation for contrast ratio is desired, then the transformation given by equation 1.8 may be used.

7.3.3 Resolution

Resolution in CRT units is particularly difficult to measure, not so much because the techniques are so involved as because there are so many different methods, each resulting in different numbers for what is effectively the same parameter, so that if the method used is not known, the results may be misleading. We cover several of the most commonly used methods and provide in Table 7.4 the means for converting the numbers found from using one method to the equivalent numbers if any of the other techniques listed is used. The techniques discussed are television limiting, shrinking raster, 50% amplitude, and modulation-transfer function, although the television-limiting method is more appropriate to total television systems, and is expanded when we cover television systems later.

Television Limiting. This method is a convenient way to measure resolution since it is well defined and has an established set of standards and procedures for its use. The procedure consists of beginning with a standard television-resolution chart of the types shown in Figures 1.4 and 7.11, placing the chart in a light box, and viewing the light box with a television camera, the output of which is sent to the monitor under test. The system used in performing this test is shown in Figure 7.12 and is similar to part of the analog television system shown in Figure 4.25, in particular that containing the television camera as the image converter. Since this test system is a raster system, the only

TABLE 7.4 Multiplication Factors for Converting Among Various Resolution Criteria

	To:				
To convert from:	TV Limiting	10% MTF	Shrinking Raster	50% Amplitude	50% MTF
TV limiting (1.185)	1	0.80	0.59	0.50	0.44
10% MTF (1.470)	1.25	1	0.74	0.62	0.55
Shrinking raster (2.000)	1.7	1.36	1	0.85	0.75
50% amplitude (2.350)	1.0	1.6	1.17	1	0.88
50% MTF (2.670)	2.26	1.82	1.33	1.14	1

Source: After Slocum [6], by permission.

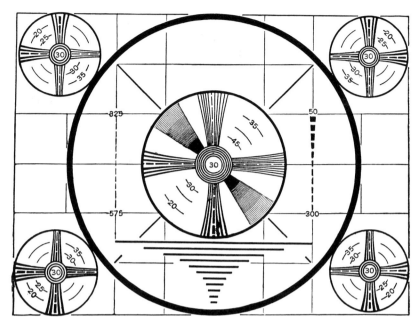

FIGURE 7.11   Resolution chart. After Pender and McIlwain [1], by permission.

CRTs that can be tested are those contained in a raster monitor, which limits using this method when CRTs in general are to be tested. The image of the resolution chart appears on the face of the CRT, and it is possible by determining visually the point at which the black-and-white lines merge to read of the resolution of the total system, expressed in television lines, where each black-and-white line is counted. The problem in using this approach to measure CRT resolution alone is that the resolutions of the camera and the video amplifier chain are also included in the measured resolution. Hence unless these are much better than that of the CRT, the actual CRT resolution can be found only by calculation if the resolutions of the other elements are known. Another drawback is that it is a subjective test, in that the observer

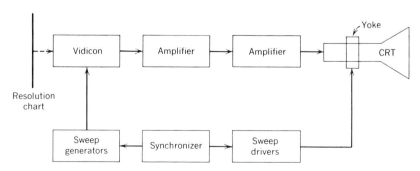

FIGURE 7.12   Block diagram of test setup for system resolution measurement.

must decide at which point the black-and-white lines merge, and this decision is subject to observer error and may differ from observer to observer. Thus it is a method of limited utility for general purpose measurements of CRT performance and has as its main attractions its simplicity and widespread usage for television systems. We should reiterate here that the line number found differs from the line-pair designation sometimes used in that a line pair counts a black-and-white line as one line pair rather than counting each line, whether black or white, as a separate entity.

Shrinking Raster. The next most popular method is the shrinking-raster technique, where a raster containing a specific number of lines is generated on the face of the CRT, using a system similar to that shown in Figure 7.9 for luminance measurements. The raster contains a known number of lines, and the spacing between lines is reduced until the lines appear to merge for the observer, as shown in Figure 1.5. The height of the raster is then measured, and the resolution is given by

$$R_r = \frac{L_r}{H_r} \tag{7.11}$$

where R_r = resolution in lines per raster height
$\quad\ L_r$ = number of raster lines
$\quad\ H_r$ = raster height

This may be related to the television-limiting lines by converting from the raster height to the CRT viewing dimension and then using the conversion factor given in Table 7.4. It should be noted that these conversion factors assume that the luminance profile of the CRT spot is given by the Gaussian distribution. This is valid for the majority of CRTs since the current distribution in the spot may be expressed to a good approximation by

$$I_b = 2\pi\rho_0\sigma^2 \tag{7.12}$$

where I_b = current
$\quad\ \rho_0 = J(r)$ = current density radius r
$\quad\ \sigma$ = standard deviation (the radius at which the current density is $1/e \times I_{max}$)

or

$$\rho_\sigma = \frac{\rho_0}{e} \tag{7.13}$$

and

$$r_\sigma = 2^{1/2}\sigma \tag{7.14}$$

Similarly, the width at half luminance is given by

$$w_{1/2} = 2.35\sigma \tag{7.15}$$

which is significant when we wish to compare the other measurement values with those obtained by measuring spot width.

Spot Width. There are a number of ways to measure or estimate spot width, but we restrict our discussion to the two most commonly used. The first is quite direct, and consists of moving a spot photometer across the CRT spot and recording the values of luminance indicated on the meter for a number of carefully calibrated points on a traveling microscope bed. The resultant luminance curve may be plotted as shown in Figure 7.13, and the width of the spot at various amplitudes may be obtained directly from this curve. Of course, any magnification in the optical system must be included for accurate results, but this method may be used for comparative measurements without calibration.

It is also possible to perform the same measurement visually by estimating the point at which the spot luminance drops to some specified value, but this is subject to the usual subjective uncertainties, although perhaps not much worse than for television-limiting and shrinking-raster techniques. A second and more accurate way to determine spot width is to use a device known as a *single-* or *double-slit analyzer*, in which the spot is caused to travel across the slit or slits and the luminance change is picked up by a photomultiplier. The electrical signal from the photomultiplier is fed to an oscilloscope as vertical deflection while the horizontal deflection is synchronized with the deflection of the CRT spot. The total system is pictured in Figure 7.14, as well as the appearance of the oscilloscope trace. If the time base of the oscilloscope sweep is set to correspond to the distance between the slits in terms of the spot velocity, then the oscilloscope may be calibrated by means of the two response waveforms, as shown in Figure 7.14, and the spot width

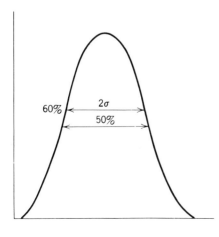

FIGURE 7.13 Luminance profile of CRT spot showing 2σ and 50% widths.

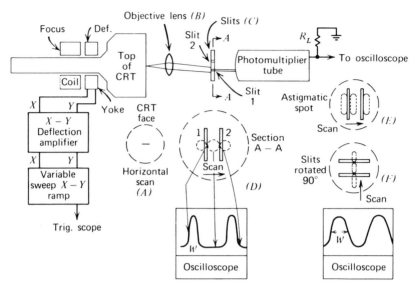

FIGURE 7.14   Block diagram of slit analyzer system. After Constantine [5], by permission.

read off directly from the trace on the oscilloscope. The measurements made by this technique can be extremely accurate, if the instrument is well designed, and can minimize any observer error. Therefore, it is preferred when accurate, repeatable measurements of spot width are desired, whether half-luminance width as shown in Table 7.4, or any other width. Unfortunately, the equipment for performing this test is much more expensive than that needed to perform the other resolution tests described to this point, and CRT manufacturers do not relish undertaking the expense and time required to perform this test on every unit. Thus if the test is used at all by a CRT manufacturer, it is probably only for design verification or limited sampling tests, although the manufacturer of a terminal using a CRT may decide to conduct more extensive test by this method on the total unit. In any event, the method is available for either user or supplier and is both accurate and reliable.

Modulation-Transfer Function (MTF). The last method for measuring resolution that we discuss is known as the modulation transfer function (MTF) measurement. The MTF is a measure of the sine-wave response of a display component, or an entire system, and is particularly useful in that it can be applied to each component separately and does not require the intervention of human estimates, as is necessary for television limiting and shrinking raster. In this respect it is as reliable as the slit-scan technique and more general in its application than that approach. It should be noted also that the television-limiting resolution chart effectively uses square waves generated by the black-and-white lines to achieve its results, and the comparative results given in

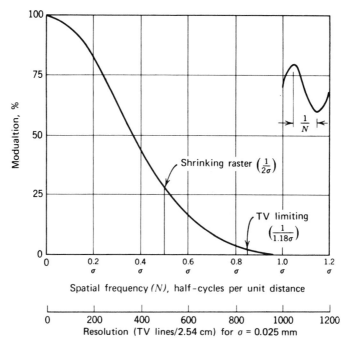

FIGURE 7.15   Form of MTF plots. After Slocum [6], by permission.

Table 7.4 relate this square-wave measurement to the MTF sine-wave measurement. These relationships are shown graphically in Figure 7.15, which demonstrates the general form of MTF plots and the points at which the television-limiting and shrinking-raster numbers fall on the plot of luminance modulation percentage versus σ and the spatial frequency along a line, where the spatial frequency is that number of half cycles of the modulating frequency. The meaning of the MTF may be further clarified by examining one method for producing this plot as shown in Figure 7.16, where the relationship between the field frequency and the modulating frequency is an integer and a continuous vertical displacement is added by introducing a drift frequency so that the spatial frequency variations on the CRT are converted into one frequency of luminance variation at the point seen by the photomultiplier. The low-pass filter allows only this frequency to pass, and by changing the field frequency different amplitudes of the drift are obtained, and the MTF is traced out. In the curve shown in Figure 7.15, these amplitudes are normalized into percent modulation, and the spatial frequency is given in terms of the standard deviation.

Another technique for obtaining the MTF uses a form of slit analyzer in conjunction with a grating of black-and-white bars, as shown in Figure 7.17. A single horizontal scan line is generated and is focused on the slit, which is at right angles to the scan line. The grating consists of equal-width black-and-white bars that are moved past the slit at a constant velocity, thus causing

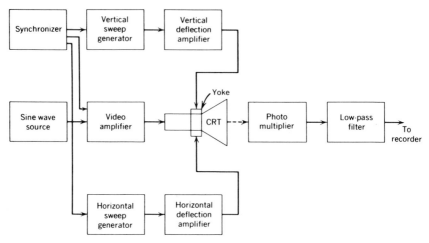

FIGURE 7.16   Block diagram of system for MTF measurements. After Sherr [2], by permission.

the light to be chopped at a frequency depending on the number of bars and the rate of movement. The line must be written at a rate greater than twice this chopping frequency according to the sampling theorem, to avoid sampling errors, and the photomultiplier picks up this chopped light signal, converting it into an electrical signal. The spatial frequency in the output is varied by rotating the slit in relation to the grating, and since this is a square-wave measurement due to the structure of the grating, a narrow band filter is used to obtain the sine-wave fundamental, the amplitude of which is equal to the MTF for different spatial frequencies. Modulation-transfer functions for a number of different CRTs plotted by this method are given in Figure 7.18,

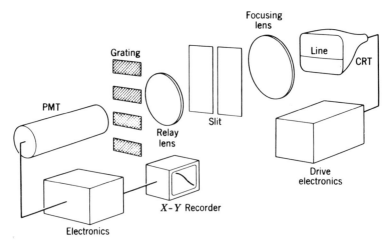

FIGURE 7.17   MTF measurement system. After Bedell [7], by permission.

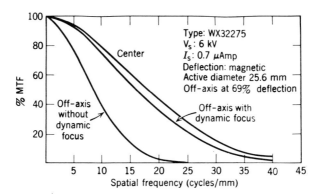

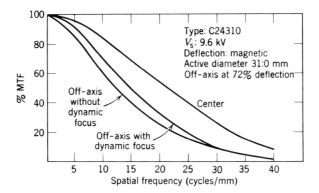

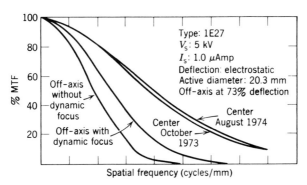

FIGURE 7.18 Modulation-transfer-function curves for different CRTs. After Bedell [7], by permission.

and the similarity to Figure 7.15 is evident. It should be noted that these curves take into account differences that occur for changes in beam current, focus, and off-axis conditions of the CRT, all of which affect the MTF to varying degrees.

The advantage of the MTF, apart from its not being dependent on observer estimates, is that for a Gaussian distribution the combined resolution of several elements of a display system may be calculated by adding the square roots of the sum of the squares of the different elements. The mathematical reason is that when a sine-wave pattern is scanned across a Gaussian aperture such as a CRT spot, the result is a convolution function, and the Fourier transform of the convolution integral is the product of the Fourier transforms of the individual elements. Therefore,

$$f_t(x) = \frac{1}{2\pi(\sigma_1^2 + \sigma_2^2 + \sigma_3^2 + \cdots + \sigma_n^2)} \exp\left[\frac{-x^2}{2(\sigma_1^2 + \sigma_2^2 + \cdots + \sigma_n^2)}\right]$$

(7.16)

and the total system resolution may be found by determining the MTFs for the different elements, getting the different values of σ from the plots, and then solving for the result. The relationships among the various methods for measuring the resolution given in Table 7.4 may be used for computing the standard deviation if MTFs are not available for all the elements, and the total resolution may be calculated from these results. It can be seen that the total process of measuring the MTF and computing the final system resolution is considerably more complicated than the television-limiting and shrinking-raster approaches, so that it is not in as common use, but it has the important advantage previously mentioned of being accurate and reliable. Therefore, even though the information may not be fully available from the manufacturers, it may still be desirable to obtain it by measurements to fully determine the display-system performance.

7.3.4 Deflection Settling Time

Deflection settling time has been covered in Chapter 4 and is defined by equations 4.4, 4.5, and 4.15 for the electromagnetic and electrostatic deflection systems. It may also be expressed as the time required for a deflected beam of energy to arrive within some percentage of its final location, usually specified in terms of some percentage of full-scale deflection. Visual considerations usually set this percentage at 0.1% to avoid spot broadening or jitter. The measurement may be made on the electrical signal that drives the beam, but it is better to make it directly on the CRT spot, to avoid errors due to yoke residual magnetism and other lags in actual beam motion. This measurement may be made by means of the system shown in Figure 7.19. The

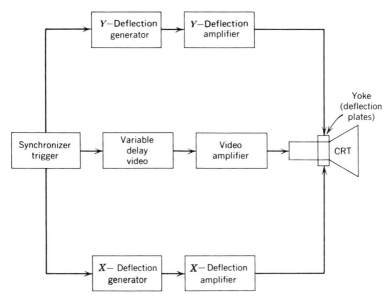

FIGURE 7.19   Block diagram of settling-time measurement system. After Sherr [2], by permission.

full-scale deflection signals are applied to the deflection amplifiers, and a variable delay video signal is applied to the video amplifier. The video pulse should be at least two spot sizes wide and is moved in time until the minimum spot is displayed. It is then backed off until the spot is increased by an amount corresponding to the settling time accuracy; that is, for a 0.1% settling time accuracy on a 50-cm CRT and a 0.05-cm spot, two spots sizes should be displayed. The waveforms employed and the appearance of the spots are shown in Figure 7.20.

7.3.5   Dynamic Focus

As discussed in Chapters 2 and 4, the focus of an electron beam changes with the position of the beam. To minimize this change, dynamic focusing is used, and it is important to be able to evaluate the effectiveness of the dynamic focus circuitry. This may be done by means of the system shown in Figure 7.21 and the waveforms shown in Figure 7.22. The spots that appear on the CRT screen may then be examined with a traveling microscope to establish whether any changes in spot size occur at the different spot positions. Another method is to generate a ramp for deflection and turn the beam on for the full deflection period. If this is done, a slit analyzer may be moved along the line that is generated and the width measured at several points along the line. Either technique is feasible and provides important information as to the constancy in spot size maintained by the dynamic focus circuitry.

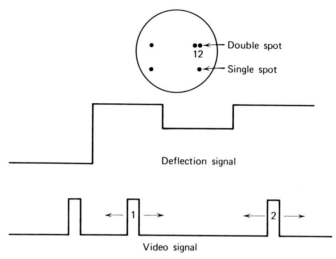

FIGURE 7.20 Single-pulse settling-time measurement technique. After Sherr [2], by permission.

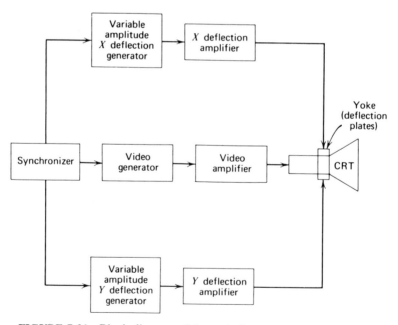

FIGURE 7.21 Block diagram of dynamic focus measurement system.

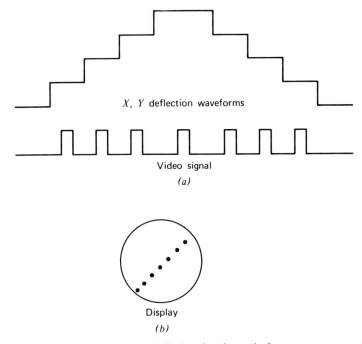

FIGURE 7.22   Waveforms and display for dynamic focus measurement.

7.3.6   Positional Accuracy, Pattern Distortion, and Linearity

Positional accuracy defines the deviation of the actual spot position from that set by the input signal level. It may be tested on both a static and dynamic basis, using the systems shown in Figures 7.23 and 7.24, with the grid over the face of the CRT accurately calibrated as to position. If the inputs to the D/A converter are set statically by means of the switch box, or dynamically by means of a word generator, the locations of the spots may then be compared with the expected location indicated on the grid, and the deviation may be computed from

$$A_a(\%) = \frac{P_a - P_p}{P_t} \times 100 \qquad (7.17)$$

where A_a = accuracy
  P_a = actual spot position
  P_p = overlay position
  P_t = full-scale deflection distance

Relative accuracy may be found by using the relative distance rather than the full-scale deflection for P_f.

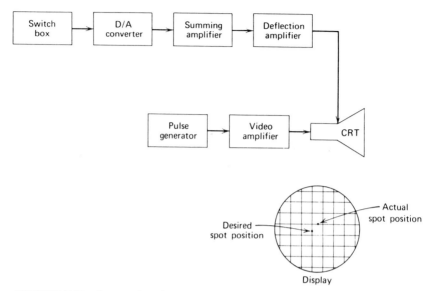

FIGURE 7.23   System for visual measurement of static settling-time accuracy.

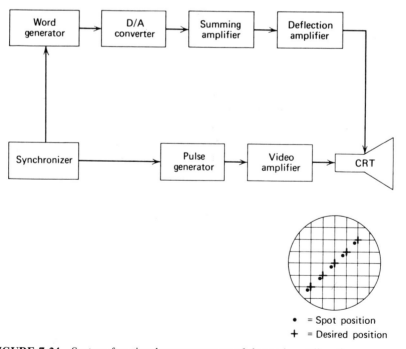

FIGURE 7.24   System for visual measurement of dynamic settling-time accuracy.

Pattern distortion may also be measured by means of an overlay consisting of two concentric rectangles and two cross lines bisecting the rectangles and mutually perpendicular to their sides, as shown in Figure 7.25. The dimensions of the rectangles to be used may be computed by multiplying the dimension of the minimum useful scan of each axis by the percentage of scan on which the pattern distortion test is to be made, thus arriving at the dimensions of the inner rectangle. The outer rectangle will be displaced from the edge of the inner rectangle by an amount equal to the dimensions of the inner rectangle multiplied by the maximum allowable percentage of pattern distortion. A line of the selected dimension will be generated and lined up with one of the cross hairs of the overlay, with the overlay positioned so that the center of the rectangles is at the center of the CRT face. Then, at some given line position the entire length of the line will fall within the boundaries of the rectangles. The other axis may be measured by generating a line in the other axis of the proper length by following the same test procedure. Of course, the accuracy will be only as good as the overlay accuracy, which holds as well for the positional accuracy test. This pattern-distortion test measures all sources of pattern distortion, such as keystone, pincushion, and barrel effects at the same time. Linearity is measured by using an overlay of the type shown in Figure 7.26. The reference straight line is drawn of the requisite length to cover a full diameter, and the allowed limits are used to calculate the maximum deviation. This deviation is then the maximum excursion of the limit curves from the straight line, and any straight line generated by the system must not fall outside of the limit curves. When combined with pattern distortion and positional accuracy, the positional characteristics of the display system are fully specified.

7.3.7 Television Systems

There are several tests developed specifically for determining characteristics of television systems, and these may be used for raster systems in general.

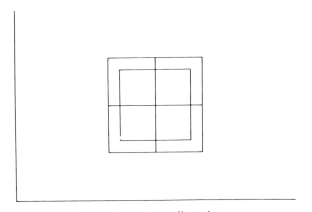

FIGURE 7.25 Overlay for pattern-distortion test measurement.

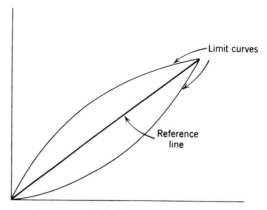

FIGURE 7.26   Linearity test diagram.

The first is the resolution test using the EIA-type resolution chart shown in Figure 1.4 or the one in Figure 7.11, and following the procedure described in Section 7.3.3. Since this method is intended primarily for the measurement of television-system resolution, it should be used circumspectly when non-television raster systems are involved, but is fully standardized for use in television-system measurements. Another test that may be made with the same charts, using gray shade bars that may be on the charts, is the measurement of gray shades in the television system. We have noted previously that the exact definition of gray shades is a succession of luminance levels, each differing from the previous level by $2\frac{1}{2}$, and the gray scales used on the charts are set at this levels. The gray-scale range of the display may then be determined by counting the number of different levels that can be distinguished on the display, much as the resolution number is found by selecting the number at which the resolution lines merge. This test may be extended to nontelevision raster systems by reproducing the gray-scale levels on the display and proceeding as before.

A third test to be made on TV systems is linearity, using the chart shown in Figure 7.27, which is used in place of the resolution chart in the same kind of total system shown in Figure 7.12. When the chart is adjusted so as to fill up the screen with a 4:3 aspect ratio, the inner circles represent 1% nonlinearity, and the outer circles set the 2% nonlinearity boundary. If two marker signals are injected at the video input, one at 315 kHz and the other at 900 Hz, the resultant markers will fall directly within the inner circles if the system has 1% linearity, and within the outer circles for 2%. The appearance of the displayed image will be a crosshatch of lines, some falling within and some falling outside the circles if the 2% linearity error is exceeded, and the linearity of the total display may be established by visual inspection. This method is reasonably adequate for measuring the 2 to 3% nonlinearity characteristic of most commercial television systems but is not recommended when more accurate measurement of system nonlinearly is desired.

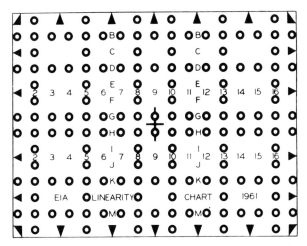

FIGURE 7.27 Chart for measurement of television system linearity. Courtesy of Electronics Industries Association.

7.3.8 Automatic Test and Alignment Systems

An interesting development in CRT measurements is the increasing availability of automatic systems that perform the desired measurements on some or all of the CRT parameter discussed previously under computer control. These systems permit the relevant tests to be made in an expeditious fashion and save significant amounts of time. They are of great value when many units need to be tested and/or aligned, although they may be somewhat too expensive for small quantities. In any event, they are available if desired and permit many of the tests to be performed in an expeditious fashion. They are primarily CRT test systems and can be used with displays that have CRTs as the dynamic output device. However, some of them can be used for non-CRT FPDs as well when the parameter ranges are compatible.

These test units do not necessarily supersede those that perform measurements of individual parameters on a manual basis, as they have designed primarily with production quantities in view. However, there are also units that concentrate on development needs and are useful to expedite meeting these requirements. Table 7.5 lists some of the automatic test units and the parameters they can test. These systems are available from various sources, some of which also provide the manual measurement units.

7.3.9 Standards Organizations

Other sources of useful information on test procedures and standard requirements are the standards groups set up by several organizations. Most active in the United States are the Society for Information Display (SID), the Human Factors Society, the Institute of Electrical and Electronic Engineers (IEEE), the Illumination Engineering Society, (IES), the American National Stand-

TABLE 7.5 Automatic CRT Test Systems

Type	Parameters
Inspection and alignment	Luminance
	Focus
	Centering
	Active area
	Distortion
	Linearity
	Color
Response time	Rise, fall, decay
	Turn on/off
Spectral	Luminous intensity
	Luminance
	Illuminance
	Color, dominant wavelength
Analysis	Line, spot width
	MTF
	Luminance
	Convergence
	Color

ards Institute (ANSI), and the Electronic Industries Association (EIA), all of which produce or participate in producing standards for test and measurement to which adherence is optional. In addition, the David Sarnoff Research Center has recently formed under government support a National Information Display Laboratory, which has as one of its goals the development of test procedures for CRT display monitors and various FPDs. This should centralize much government display activity and provide another source for display standards and procedures.

Among international societies, most relevant to the measurements discussed here are the Commission Internationale de Eclairage (CIE), the International Standards Organization (ISO), and the International Electrotechnical Commission (IEC). In addition, a number of countries, such as France, Germany, Great Britain, Italy, Sweden, and Japan, have their own standards groups, which produce a variety of display measurement standards, some of which have achieved international acceptance. A complete list of these and other groups can be found in the reference 8, and they provide much useful test information.

7.4 FLAT-PANEL DISPLAYS

7.4.1 Introduction

Flat-panel displays might be considered to include those that use CRT technology, but for our purposes we consider that these are covered in the CRT section, so only the non-CRT types are included here. Of course, the same parameters are involved in measuring non-CRT FPD performance, and in general, the same procedures are used as for the CRT types. However, there are several parameters, such as resolution, character format, matrix size, and viewing area, that require some special consideration in order to arrive at the best results. Therefore, each technology is treated separately in terms of the relevant parameters in the sections that follow.

7.4.2 Light-Emitting Diodes

Luminous Intensity/Luminance. Light-emitting diode numeric and alphanumeric displays are usually characterized in terms of luminance intensity in candelas rather than luminance. This creates some problems when it is desired to compare their performance with CRTs or other light-emitting devices whose light output is given in luminance terms. The argument for using luminous intensity is that LEDs appear as point sources and the eye responds to radiant flux density expressed in photometric terms such as candelas. However, although this has much merit for LEDs and other fixed-point source types of light-emitting devices, it is also useful to know what the actual luminance is, for comparison purposes. This luminance may be measured directly, using the same equipment and techniques used for CRTs, or it may be calculated if the dimensions of the emitting area are known, using the formula for luminance given by equation 7.6. It had initially been the practice to give the LED data in luminance terms, but this has been largely replaced by luminous intensity of the dot or line segment, which is desirable from the point of view of standardization and ease of measurement but does leave the user somewhat in limbo unless it is possible to relate this quantity to that used for the other devices. It may obscure the comparative performance when different technologies are involved, but is is possible to arrive at some comparisons by calculating the luminance after the candela measurement has been made, and element size determined, using equation 1.6 or its equivalent in international terms.

Since the luminous intensity may be from the low microcandela through the millicandela range, it is necessary to use a sensitive wide-range photometer to make the measurement. There are several types of photometers available from different manufacturers that have adequate sensitivity for this measurement, and it is necessary to specify the current through the LED at which the measurement is made, since the luminous intensity is dependent on the value of current used. In the case of the multisegment or multidot array, it is also desirable to measure each element separately so that the uniformity of the digit light output may be determined. It is customary for the manufacturer to specify what the maximum variation is, and variations greater then 20% are readily perceived, although as much as 50% variation may be acceptable under some viewing conditions. Another point of interest is the spatial distribution of the LED output, which may not follow Lambert's law, so that a measurement of the peak value does not represent the actual off-axis performance. This affects the angle of view and is especially important when lenses are used to gather the light or increase the apparent size of the digit, as is frequently the case in available devices.

Contrast Ratio. As a corollary of the measurement of luminous intensity, we are also interested in the contrast ratio of the display under operating conditions, and this cannot be determined from knowledge of the luminous intensity alone. Therefore, a measurement of luminance in the presence of the expected ambient illumination is unavoidable to fully characterize the performance of the display. Thus whereas some problems in measurement have been avoided by standardizing on luminous intensity for light output, they return once it is desired to fully specify the complete performance characteristics of the device. Thus the problem is shifted from the manufacturer to the user, and it behooves the latter to obtain the necessary information by some means. Contrast ratio measurements may be made on the individual elements and/or the entire panel. The same procedures may be used as described in Section 7.3.2 for CRTs, and the same considerations apply.

Resolution. The one performance parameter that is easily determined for LEDs and other matrix displays is resolution, as it is defined by the number of elements involved with some possible effect from the light profile for the displays that use discrete LEDs. However, for all practical purposes the number of light-emitting elements and the resolution are equivalent.

Character Matrix. It is frequently of interest to know what the format of the numeric or A/N is in terms of the number of strokes or the dot matrix used. This might also be termed the character matrix and defines the resolution of the characters. As a corollary, once the character matrix is known and the overall resolution, it is possible to calculate the total number of characters in terms of characters per line and number of lines.

Color. Color is of special interest for LEDs because they are available in at least five different colors as well as IR. Thus to a limited extent they are the equivalent of phosphors. LED color can be measured with spectrophotometers, and scanning systems that cover the range 390 to 1070 nm are available for rapid determination of color. Therefore, this measurement may be performed without difficulty, although for most practical purposes the physics of the device control the color and the manufacturer's specifications may be accepted.

Other Parameters. Other parameters of interest include element and character size, and viewing area. The size measurements are simple physical operations and require no special procedures. Finally, when positional accuracy, linearity, and pattern distortion are considered, one of the important advantages of matrix and other types of FPDs becomes apparent. These displays differ drastically from CRTs in that they are made up of assemblies of fixed elements or locations and are not subject to the variability found in CRTs. Therefore, these parameters need not be measured except to determine whether they fully meet the manufacturer's physical specifications. This is true for all FPDs.

7.4.3 Electroluminescence (TFEL, DCEL)

Luminance. From the point of view of luminance measurements, all EL panels may be treated as though they were CRTs. Therefore, the same procedures may be followed as for CRTs, and the same considerations apply as to equipment. This is particularly true when full-panel measurements are involved and even more so for color displays, where CRT-type phosphors are used to create the colors. The measurements are made with the same equipment as is used for CRTs, and the same luminance parameters may be used.

Contrast Ratio. Again the equivalence between CRTs and EL panels holds, and the same procedures may be followed.

Color. Color is becoming a significant parameter for EL displays now that multicolor panels are becoming available. The measurements are fully equivalent to those made on CRTs, as the same types of phosphors are used to create the colors.

Resolution. Resolution for EL panels is a function of the number of $X-Y$ crossovers, where the intersections correspond to the individual LED elements. This is because the EL panel is made up of microscopic emitting molecules that are much smaller than the resolution pitch of the panel. Therefore, it is only necessary to count the number of intersections to determine the resolution, which may be given in terms of number of pixels in both dimensions or addressable lines per inch (cm).

Other Parameters. These are primarily the linearity and accuracy measurements and are subject to the same conditions as the LED displays.

7.4.4 Gas-Discharge (Plasma) Displays

Luminance. Although there was some confusion initially as to how to designate the light output from plasma displays, with some types using luminous intensity and others, luminance, there is now general agreement on luminance, with the same parameters as for CRTs and EL panels in use. Thus, as for EL panels, the measurements may be made using the same equipment and following the same procedure as given for the equivalent CRT or LED measurements. In the dc plasma case, the dot or segment correspond to the

CRT spot, and the entire panel to the CRT faceplate, whereas for ac plasma only the dot formed at the crossover points apply.

Contrast Ratio. Again, CRT procedures may be followed, although the existence of the memory state for ac plasma makes this type of device closer to the storage CRTs, which are no longer in use, However, the measurement technique remains the same for both the dc and ac plasma devices, with the duty-factor effect eliminated for the ac types.

Color. The same considerations apply for plasma displays as for EL displays where color is concerned. The same phosphors are used and the result is a display that is fairly equivalent to a CRT color display.

Resolution. This measurement is performed exactly as for the EL panels, with either the number of crossovers or lines per inch (cm) the relevant values. However, there may be some overlap due to the luminance profile of an individual pixel. Therefore, it is desirable to make direct measurements of that profile for high numbers of lines per inch.

Character Matrix. For character displays the character matrix must be considered in order to arrive at the character resolution. In general, these will be readily ascertainable.

Other Parameters. Linearity and accuracy are determined completely by the geometry of the panel.

7.4.5   Vacuum Fluorescent Displays

Luminance. Vacuum fluorescent displays are essentially CRTs, and their luminance measurements may be made in the same manner and using the same instruments as for CRTs. However, it should be remembered that VFDs are matrix or character devices and the luminance measurements are of discrete fixed rather than moving spots. Thus the luminance profiles are somewhat different than for CRTs, and this fact should be borne in mind when determining the luminance.

Contrast Ratio. Again, the similarity to CRT measurements is obvious and no new considerations apply.

Color. VFDs are somewhat similar to LEDs insofar as color is concerned in that a number of different colors can be generated, but only one at a time. There have been some attempts to produce multicolor units but with only very limited success. Therefore, individual color measurements may be made using spectrophotometers.

Resolution. The matrix types of VFDs have the same measurement characteristics as the EL and plasma types.

Character Matrix. The character matrices are the same as for the other FPDs.

Other Parameters. Linearity and accuracy are subject to the same factors as apply to the other matrix FPDs.

7.4.6 Liquid-Crystal Displays

Luminance. Luminance measurements of LCDs introduce some special problems because they are not light-emitting devices and require some external light source to produce a visual display. Therefore, the LCD luminance is first a function of the light source that is available, and then of the LCD itself. As a result, the luminance parameter value is frequently not given, especially if there is no built-in light source. However, it would be useful to know transmission loss through the cell, as this will have a significant effect on the luminance regardless of the light source. In addition, now that many LCD panels are provided with internal light sources, luminance measurements can be made with the panel activated so that the equivalent of the luminance from a light-emitting FPD can be determined. In general, this will be full-panel luminance, although spot luminance can also be measured by operating the panel in a discrete spot mode.

Contrast Ratio. Contrast ratio is the most significant parameter for LCDs in that it remains the prime determinant of legibility. To establish contrast ratio it is, of course, necessary to have a light source, which could be the expected ambient for those units that do not include a built-in light source. In cases where the light source is part of the unit under test, the light source converts it into a light-emitting device, so that the contrast ratio may be determined by measuring the luminance with the light source on and the unit in the active and passive states. The luminance ratio is then the contrast ratio for the LCD in the transmissive state. The contrast ratio for the reflective type is determined in a similar manner, except that they are nonemissive, so that the luminance is dependent on what the ambient at the surface of the LCD happens to be. Therefore, it is best to perform the measurements under expected ambient conditions.

Response Time. Response time is of particular importance for LCDs because it is relatively slow compared to the other technologies and may set limits on the number of elements that can be multiplexed. It may vary over a wide range from one type to another, and be equivalent to that of the switching element when active matrix drive is used. The measurement of response time is best performed by switching the LCD on and off at some specified rate and examining the shape of the response curve by means of an oscilloscope which shows the light output as converted by a photoconductor into an electrical signal. The rise and dwell times of the actuating pulse must be long enough to permit the light output to reach its steady-state value, and the fall time should be short enough so as not to contribute significantly to the decay time of the light output. Figure 7.28 shows these parameters where

$$K_v = \text{pulse amplitude}$$

$$t_o = \text{time to } 10\% \ K_v$$

$$t_e = \text{rise time—from } 10\% \text{ to } 90\% \ K_v$$

$$t_a = \text{fall time—from } 100\% \text{ to } 33.3\% \ K_v$$

These definitions apply to any measurements of response time and may be used for all of the other technologies.

Color. Modern LCDs are a far cry from what they were in the not-too-distant past, in that they are now capable of providing a multiplicity of colors and can emulate CRT displays to a convincing extent. Therefore, color measurements can and should be made over the full gamut, using the same equipment as is available for CRT measurements. This will enable the LCDs to be compared directly with their CRT equivalents and permit objective judgments to be made as to their comparative performance. Of course, these may differ from subjective judgments made from direct visual viewings, but this does not detract from the value of the objective measurements.

Other Parameters. The same considerations apply to linearity and accuracy as have been adduced for the other technologies.

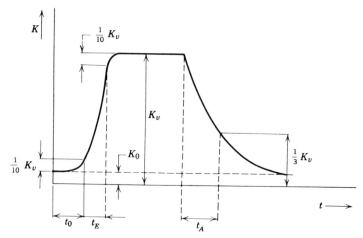

FIGURE 7.28   Definition of response times of liquid crystal cells. Courtesy of E. Merck.

7.4.7 Other Technologies

The other technologies that are of some, if minimal, interest are electromagnetic, incandescent, electrochemical, and electrophoretic, with other particle displays still not established as a meaningful technology. It is interesting to note that only incandescent of these is a light-emitting technology, so that the LCD considerations apply, in particular those applying to contrast ratio and response time. They do not introduce any new requirements and are not discussed further.

7.5 LEGIBILITY

Legibility is the convenient catchall for all of the parameters used to specify the performance of a display system and has become increasingly significant to the designer and user of display systems because of the trend toward specifying performance in operational rather than parametric terms. We have defined legibility in Chapter 1 as the number of correct identifications that a viewer may make in an operational situation, and whereas this may be adequate as a definition, it by no means delineates the manner in which legibility tests should be performed, nor does it fully indicate the task orientation that must be included if such tests are to be meaningful. As an illustration, a test setup may be used where a set of symbols is flashed in front of an observer, and the viewer must identify these symbols to some level of accuracy within a given time limit. However, even if all the test parameters are carefully established and controlled, the results may not apply to the actual task for which the displayed system is intended, where other attention-distracting elements may exist, or where word groups rather than symbols are involved. Thus the difficulty in setting up a meaningful legibility test is very great, and there still must be a large number of measurements made at different values of the parameters such as luminance and resolution before the legibility results can be translated into useful specifications for the manufacturer and user of the display system. Figure 7.29 is an example of one such set of curves, and if this is to be done for all the relevant parameters under each set of task conditions, the number of measurements required becomes very large, and the entire process, though probably best for ensuring proper performance, is impractical for any reasonable test program. Therefore, it is probably best to use legibility for the criterion of performance only when the other methods are difficult or inadequate or when the operational conditions can be so well defined that a single set of parameter measurements is sufficient, which is surely the millenium. On this hopeful note we conclude, and trust that a feasible method may be found for most if not all conditions. These measurements may be considered to include all of the human factors parameters covered in Chapter 1 not covered by the tests discussed in previous sections of this chapter.

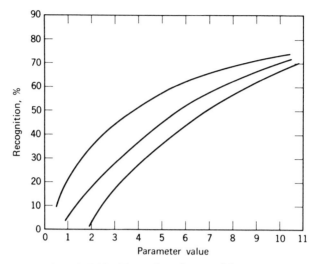

FIGURE 7.29   Examples of recognition curves.

REFERENCES

[1] Pender, H., and McIlwain, K., Eds., *Electrical Engineers' Handbook*, 4th ed., Wiley, New York, 1950.

[2] Sherr, S., *Fundamentals of Display System Design*, Wiley, New York, 1970.

[3] Kingslake, R., Ed., *Applied Optics and Optical Engineering*, Vol. 1, Academic, New York, 1965.

[4] Stimson, A., *Photometry and Radiometry for Engineers*, Wiley, New York, 1974.

[5] Constantine, J. M., "Two Slit Spot Analyzer," *Proceedings 7th National Symposium, SID,* Oct. 1966, 96–97.

[6] Slocum, G. K., "Airborne Sensor Display Requirements and Approaches," *Inform. Display,* **4**/6, 1968, 45–46.

[7] Bedell, R. J., "Modulation Transfer Function of Very High Resolution Miniature Cathode Ray Tubes," *SID Proc.,* **16**/3, 1975, 212–215.

[8] Greeson, J. C., "Display Standards," *Information Display,* **6**/12, 26–28.

INDEX